Nelson

PRINCIPLES of MATHEMATICS 9

Series Author and Senior Consultant
Marian Small

Senior Consultants
Chris Kirkpatrick • David Zimmer

Authors
Crystal Chilvers • Santo D'Agostino • Doug Duff
Kristina Farentino • Ian Macpherson • Joyce Tonner
James Williamson • T. Anne Yeager

THOMSON

NELSON

Australia   Canada   Mexico   Singapore   Spain   United Kingdom   United States

THOMSON

NELSON

Principles of Mathematics 9

Series Author and Senior Consultant
Marian Small

Senior Consultants
Chris Kirkpatrick, David Zimmer

Authors
Crystal Chilvers, Santo D'Agostino, Doug Duff, Kristina Farentino, Ian Macpherson, Joyce Tonner, James Williamson, T. Anne Yeager

Contributing Authors
Kathleen Kacuiba, Krista Zupan

Math Consultant
Kaye Appleby

Literacy Consultant
Joanne Simmons

General Manager, Mathematics, Science, and Technology
Lenore Brooks

Publisher, Mathematics
Colin Garnham

Associate Publisher, Mathematics
Sandra McTavish

Managing Editor, Mathematics
David Spiegel

Product Manager
Linda Krepinsky

Program Manager
Erynn Marcus

Developmental Editors
Alasdair Graham, First Folio Resource Group, Inc.; Theresa Gross; Tom Shields; Bob Templeton, First Folio Resource Group, Inc.; Carmen Yu

Contributing Editors
Amanda Allan; Jenna Dunlop; Linda Watson, First Folio Resource Group, Inc.; Caroline Winter

Editorial Assistant
Caroline Winter

Executive Director, Content and Media Production
Renate McCloy

Director, Content and Media Production
Linh Vu

Senior Content Production Editor
Susan Aihoshi

Junior Content Production Editor
Natalie Russell

Proofreader
Christine Hobberlin

Production Manager
Cathy Deak

Senior Production Coordinator
Sharon Latta Paterson

Design Director
Ken Phipps

Interior Design
Peter Papayanakis

Cover Design
Eugene Lo

Cover Image
The Blue Water Bridges spanning the St. Clair River between Port Huron, Michigan and Point Edward, Ontario. © Mark Scheuern / Alamy.

Production Services
GEX Publishing Services

Director, Asset Management Services
Vicki Gould

Photo/Permissions Researcher
Karen Becker

Photo Shoot Coordinator
Lynn McLeod

Set-up Photos
Dave Starrett

Printer
Transcontinental Printing Ltd.

Reviewers and Advisory Panel

Table of Contents

0.34%
-0.13%
0.47%
-0.29%
-0.84%
-1.59%
0.64%
1.09%
-1.55%
-0.47%
-1.86%

+0.36

-0.47

-0.10

-0.68

Rational Numbers

▸ GOALS

You will be able to

- Relate rational numbers to decimals, fractions, and integers
- Evaluate expressions involving rational numbers

? What might the negative values in the photo represent?

WORDS YOU NEED to Know

1. Match each term with the example that most closely represents it.

a) opposite integers   d) lowest common denominator   g) power
b) numerator   e) mixed number   h) base of a power
c) denominator   f) improper fraction   i) exponent

i) $\dfrac{34}{9}$

iv) $+5$ and -5

vii) $\dfrac{2}{3} = \dfrac{10}{15}$
$\dfrac{1}{5} = \dfrac{3}{15}$

ii) $1\dfrac{2}{3}$

v) 7^3

viii) 7^3

iii) 7^3

vi) $\dfrac{5}{7}$

ix) $\dfrac{5}{7}$

Study | Aid

- For more help and practice, see Appendix A-6 and A-7.

SKILLS AND CONCEPTS You Need

Addition of Fractions

You can add two fractions using fraction strips, number lines, or by using a common denominator.

EXAMPLE

$\dfrac{1}{3} + \dfrac{2}{5}$

Solution: fraction strips

Solution: common denominator

$= \dfrac{1 \times 5}{3 \times 5} + \dfrac{2 \times 3}{5 \times 3}$

$= \dfrac{5}{15} + \dfrac{6}{15}$

$= \dfrac{11}{15}$

Solution: number line

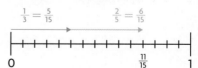

2. Determine each sum.

a) $\dfrac{1}{2} + \dfrac{1}{3}$ c) $\dfrac{3}{10} + \dfrac{3}{5}$

b) $\dfrac{3}{4} + \dfrac{1}{8}$ d) $\dfrac{2}{5} + \dfrac{2}{3}$

Subtraction of Fractions

You can subtract two fractions using fraction strips, number lines, or by using a common denominator.

$$\frac{2}{3} - \frac{1}{5}$$

Solution: common denominator

$$= \frac{2 \times 5}{3 \times 5} - \frac{1 \times 3}{5 \times 3}$$

$$= \frac{10}{15} - \frac{3}{15}$$

$$= \frac{7}{15}$$

Solution: fraction strips

$\frac{2}{3} = \frac{10}{15}$

$\frac{1}{5} = \frac{3}{15}$

$\frac{10}{15} - \frac{3}{15} = \frac{7}{15}$

Solution: number line

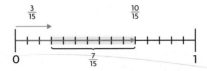

3. Determine each difference.

a) $\dfrac{1}{2} - \dfrac{1}{3}$ b) $\dfrac{3}{4} - \dfrac{1}{8}$ c) $\dfrac{3}{5} - \dfrac{3}{10}$ d) $\dfrac{6}{7} - \dfrac{1}{2}$

Multiplication of Fractions

You can use an area model to help you visualize the product of two fractions.

$$\frac{5}{8} \times \frac{2}{3}$$

Solution: multiplying

$$= \frac{5 \times 2}{8 \times 3}$$

$$= \frac{10}{24}$$

$$= \frac{5}{12}$$

Solution: area model

4. Determine each product.

a) $\dfrac{1}{2} \times \dfrac{1}{4}$ c) $\dfrac{2}{5} \times \dfrac{3}{10}$

b) $\dfrac{2}{3} \times \dfrac{3}{4}$ d) $\dfrac{1}{6} \times \dfrac{4}{5}$

PRACTICE

Study | **Aid**

- For help, see the Review of Essential Skills and Knowledge Appendix.

Question	Appendix
6 and 7	A-6
8	A-7
9 and 10	A-3
11	A-4
12	A-9
13	A-1
14	A-2

5. Complete the equation. Use a diagram to show how you got the answer.

$$5\frac{7}{4} = 6\frac{\blacksquare}{4}$$

6. The number line represents the sum of two numbers. Write an equation to show the numbers being added and their sum.

7. a) Use a number line to determine how much greater $4\frac{1}{3}$ is than $1\frac{2}{3}$.

   b) Write the subtraction equation that gives the same result as in part a).

8. Evaluate.

   a) $\dfrac{2}{5} \times \dfrac{9}{8}$

   b) $\dfrac{3}{4} \div \dfrac{9}{10}$

9. Evaluate.

   a) $(-3) + 7$
   b) $(-5) + (-2)$
   c) $11 - (-4)$
   d) $-3 - (-8)$

10. Tiger Woods finished a golf tournament with a score of five under par. Another player finished with a score of two over par. How many shots behind Tiger Woods was the other player?

11. Evaluate.

   a) -4×6
   b) $(-5) \times (-3)$
   c) $20 \div (-1)$
   d) $(-12) \div (-6)$

12. Evaluate.

   a) $0.32 + 3.9$
   b) $15.4 - 3.91$
   c) 0.6×1.1
   d) $24 \div 1.2$

13. Express each power as repeated multiplication, and then, evaluate.
   a) 8^2
   b) 5.2^3

14. Follow the order of operations to determine the value of each expression.

   a) $\dfrac{-12 + 3}{4 + 5}$

   b) $7^2 - (-6 + 2) \times 4$

15. Copy and complete the chart to show what you know about mixed numbers.

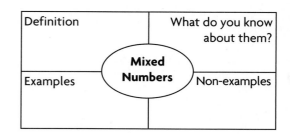

APPLYING *What You Know*

Fraction Patterns

Andrew and Kim are exploring a sequence of fractions.

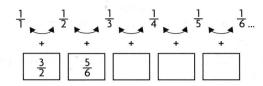

? How can you use patterns to predict the 20th sum, difference, product, and quotient using these fractions?

A. Describe the pattern in Andrew and Kim's original sequence of fractions.

B. Add consecutive terms (pairs of neighbouring fractions) until five sums have been calculated. For example: $\dfrac{1}{1} + \dfrac{1}{2} = \dfrac{3}{2}$, $\dfrac{1}{2} + \dfrac{1}{3} = \dfrac{5}{6}$, etc.

C. Describe the pattern and use it to predict the 20th sum.

D. Copy Andrew and Kim's original fraction sequence. Subtract consecutive terms instead of adding them.

E. Describe the pattern and use it to predict the 20th difference.

F. Repeat parts D and E using multiplication.

G. Repeat parts D and E using division.

H. Explain why the values in the pattern decrease for each operation.

I. Which patterns do you think were the easiest to predict? Why?

Addition and Subtraction of Mixed Numbers

YOU WILL NEED
- fraction strips

> **GOAL**
>
> Add and subtract mixed numbers using a variety of methods.

LEARN ABOUT the Math

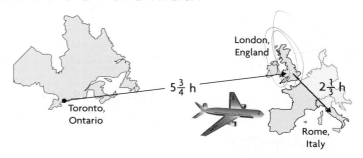

Alisa and Greg plan to travel from Canada to Italy for March break. Dawn is driving to her aunt's in Ottawa for March break. According to a travel website, Dawn's trip should take 4 h 36 min.

? How many hours longer is Alisa and Greg's trip than Dawn's trip?

| **EXAMPLE 1** | **Selecting a strategy to add mixed numbers** |

Calculate the time to travel from Toronto to Rome by plane.

Alisa's Solution: Using a strategy involving equivalent fractions

$5\frac{3}{4} + 2\frac{1}{3}$ ⟵

> I estimated the answer to be between 8 h and 9 h because $5 + 2 = 7$ and $\frac{3}{4} + \frac{1}{3}$ is greater than 1 but less than 2.

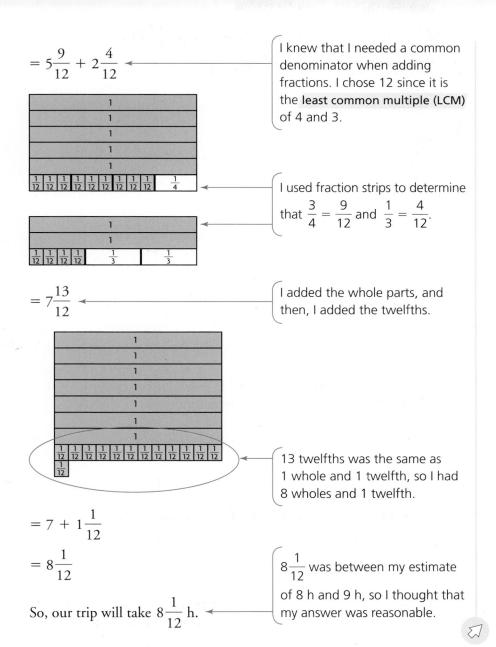

$$= 5\frac{9}{12} + 2\frac{4}{12}$$

I knew that I needed a common denominator when adding fractions. I chose 12 since it is the **least common multiple (LCM)** of 4 and 3.

least common multiple (LCM)

the least **whole number** that has all given numbers as factors (e.g., 12 is the least common multiple of 4 and 6)

I used fraction strips to determine that $\frac{3}{4} = \frac{9}{12}$ and $\frac{1}{3} = \frac{4}{12}$.

$$= 7\frac{13}{12}$$

I added the whole parts, and then, I added the twelfths.

13 twelfths was the same as 1 whole and 1 twelfth, so I had 8 wholes and 1 twelfth.

$$= 7 + 1\frac{1}{12}$$

$$= 8\frac{1}{12}$$

$8\frac{1}{12}$ was between my estimate of 8 h and 9 h, so I thought that my answer was reasonable.

So, our trip will take $8\frac{1}{12}$ h.

Greg used a different strategy from Alisa. He changed the mixed numbers into improper fractions in order to add them.

Greg's Solution: Using a strategy involving improper fractions

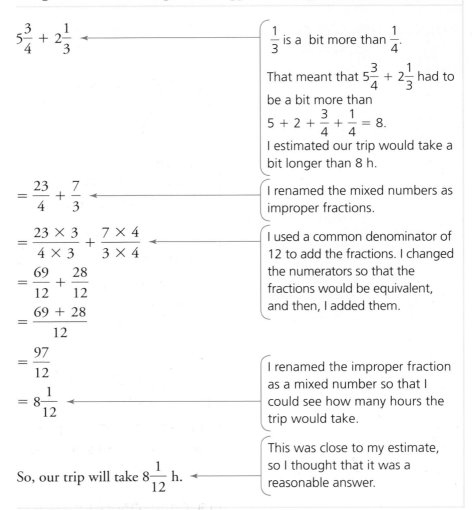

$$5\frac{3}{4} + 2\frac{1}{3}$$

$\frac{1}{3}$ is a bit more than $\frac{1}{4}$.

That meant that $5\frac{3}{4} + 2\frac{1}{3}$ had to be a bit more than
$5 + 2 + \frac{3}{4} + \frac{1}{4} = 8$.
I estimated our trip would take a bit longer than 8 h.

$$= \frac{23}{4} + \frac{7}{3}$$

I renamed the mixed numbers as improper fractions.

$$= \frac{23 \times 3}{4 \times 3} + \frac{7 \times 4}{3 \times 4}$$

$$= \frac{69}{12} + \frac{28}{12}$$

$$= \frac{69 + 28}{12}$$

I used a common denominator of 12 to add the fractions. I changed the numerators so that the fractions would be equivalent, and then, I added them.

$$= \frac{97}{12}$$

$$= 8\frac{1}{12}$$

I renamed the improper fraction as a mixed number so that I could see how many hours the trip would take.

So, our trip will take $8\frac{1}{12}$ h.

This was close to my estimate, so I thought that it was a reasonable answer.

Both Greg and Alisa have determined the time it will take to fly from Toronto to Rome. Now, they must calculate how much longer this is than Dawn's trip to Ottawa.

EXAMPLE 2   Selecting a strategy to subtract mixed numbers

Calculate the difference in time between the trip to Rome and the trip to Ottawa.

Alisa's Solution: Using a strategy involving equivalent fractions

Dawn's travel time:

4 h 36 min

$= 4\dfrac{36}{60}$ h

$= 4\dfrac{3}{5}$ h

Since there are 60 min in an hour,

$36 \text{ min} = \dfrac{36}{60}$ h.

$8\dfrac{1}{12} - 4\dfrac{3}{5}$

I subtracted to determine the difference in travel times.

$8 - 4 = 4$, and $\dfrac{3}{5}$ is more than $\dfrac{1}{2}$, so I estimated the difference to be between 3 h and 4 h.

$= 8\dfrac{1 \times 5}{12 \times 5} - 4\dfrac{3 \times 12}{5 \times 12}$

I chose 60 as the common denominator since it is the LCM of 12 and 5.

$= 8\dfrac{5}{60} - 4\dfrac{36}{60}$

$= 7\dfrac{60 + 5}{60} - 4\dfrac{36}{60}$

$= 7\dfrac{65}{60} - 4\dfrac{36}{60}$

I noticed that if I subtracted $\dfrac{5}{60} - \dfrac{36}{60}$, the numerator would be negative. I renamed $8\dfrac{5}{60}$ to make the first numerator greater than the second.

$= (7 - 4) + \left(\dfrac{65}{60} - \dfrac{36}{60} \right)$

$= 3\dfrac{(65 - 36)}{60}$

I subtracted the whole numbers, and then, the fractions.

$= 3\dfrac{29}{60}$

$3\dfrac{29}{60}$ h was within my estimate of between 3 h and 4 h, so I thought that my answer was reasonable.

So, we will take $3\dfrac{29}{60}$ h longer than Dawn will to arrive at our destination.

> **Communication** | *Tip*
>
> LCM is an abbreviation for Least Common Multiple.

Greg used a different strategy from Alisa. He changed the travel times for each trip into improper fractions in order to subtract them.

Greg's Solution: Using a strategy involving improper fractions

Dawn's travel time:

4 h 36 min

$$= 4\frac{36}{60} \text{ h}$$

$$= 4\frac{3}{5} \text{ h}$$

$$8\frac{1}{12} - 4\frac{3}{5}$$

$$= \frac{97}{12} - \frac{23}{5}$$

$$= \frac{97 \times 5}{12 \times 5} - \frac{23 \times 12}{5 \times 12}$$

$$= \frac{485}{60} - \frac{276}{60}$$

$$= \frac{485 - 276}{60}$$

$$= \frac{209}{60}$$

$$= 3\frac{29}{60}$$

So, we will take $3\frac{29}{60}$ h longer than Dawn will to arrive at our destination.

I decided to express Dawn's travel time as a mixed number measured in hours.

$8 - 4 = 4$

I knew that $\frac{1}{12}$ was close to zero and $\frac{3}{5}$ was close to $\frac{1}{2}$, so $4 - \frac{1}{2} = 3\frac{1}{2}$. I estimated the answer to be around $3\frac{1}{2}$ h.

I renamed the mixed numbers as improper fractions, and created equivalent fractions using a common denominator of 60.

Then, I subtracted the numerators.

I renamed the improper fraction as a mixed number so that I would know the number of hours.

$3\frac{29}{60}$ h was really close to my estimate of $3\frac{1}{2}$ h, since $3\frac{1}{2} = 3\frac{30}{60}$, so my answer seemed reasonable.

Reflecting

A. Which of Alisa's or Greg's addition strategies would you choose? Why?

B. Which of Alisa's or Greg's subtraction strategies would you choose? Why?

C. How else might you calculate the difference in trip times?

APPLY the Math

| EXAMPLE 3 | Using a number line to represent addition and subtraction |

Evaluate.

a) $1\dfrac{2}{3} + 3\dfrac{1}{2}$

b) $4\dfrac{1}{8} - 1\dfrac{3}{4}$

Olecia's Solution

a) $1\dfrac{2}{3} + 3\dfrac{1}{2} = 1\dfrac{4}{6} + 3\dfrac{3}{6}$ ⟵ I created equivalent fractions for the mixed numbers because it used smaller numbers than renaming the mixed numbers as improper fractions.

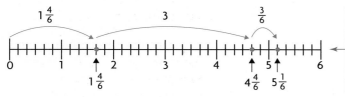

⟵ I used a number line to help me visualize the sum.

I used intervals of $\dfrac{1}{6}$ on the number line to match the **lowest common denominator (LCD)** of the fractions.

$1\dfrac{4}{6} + 3\dfrac{3}{6} = 5\dfrac{1}{6}$ ⟵ I determined that the answer was $5\dfrac{1}{6}$.

b) $4\dfrac{1}{8} - 1\dfrac{3}{4} = 4\dfrac{1}{8} - 1\dfrac{6}{8}$ ⟵ I created equivalent fraction parts for the mixed numbers, using the LCD of 8.

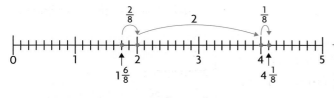

⟵ I used a number line with intervals of $\dfrac{1}{8}$ to help me visualize the difference.

The sum of the "jumps" between $1\dfrac{6}{8}$ and $4\dfrac{1}{8}$ on my number line was $2\dfrac{3}{8}$.

$4\dfrac{1}{8} - 1\dfrac{6}{8} = 2\dfrac{3}{8}$ ⟵

Measurements of length made by carpenters, plumbers, and electricians still use the imperial system: yards, feet, and inches. Construction materials are also sold in imperial units. This leads to calculations involving mixed numbers.

EXAMPLE 4 Solving a problem involving mixed numbers

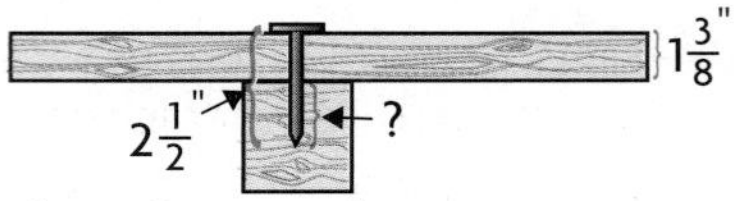

If a $2\frac{1}{2}$ in. nail is hammered through a board $1\frac{3}{8}$ in. thick and into a support beam, how far into the support beam does the nail extend?

Communication *Tip*

In the imperial number system, the symbol " represents inches while the symbol ' represents feet.

Stefan's Solution: Using equivalent fractions

$2\frac{1}{2} - 1\frac{3}{8}$

To determine the length of the nail in the support beam, I subtracted the thickness of the board from the nail's length.

$= 2\frac{4}{8} - 1\frac{3}{8}$

$= 1\frac{1}{8}$

I created equivalent fraction parts.
$2 - 1 = 1$ and $\frac{4}{8} - \frac{3}{8} = \frac{1}{8}$

The nail will extend $1\frac{1}{8}$ in. into the support beam.

Doug used a calculator that can perform fractional operations.

Doug's Solution: Using technology

$2\frac{1}{2} - 1\frac{3}{8}$

I estimate the answer to be between 1 and 2.

$2 - 1 = 1$ and $\frac{1}{2}$ is a little bit greater than $\frac{3}{8}$.

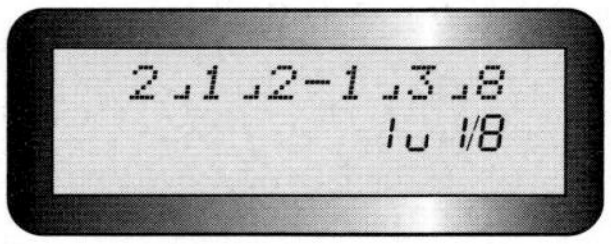

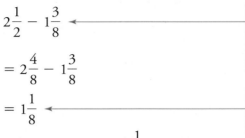

I used a calculator with a fraction key: [A b/c]

I used this sequence of keystrokes:
[2] [A b/c] [1] [A b/c] [2] [−]
[1] [A b/c] [3] [A b/c] [8] [ENTER]

Tech *Support*

Not all calculators with fraction operations use this exact set of keystrokes. Check your user manual to see how to enter fractions in your calculator.

Therefore, the nail will extend $1\frac{1}{8}$ in. into the support beam.

$1\frac{1}{8}$ was within my estimate of between 1 and 2, so I thought that my answer was reasonable.

In Summary

Key Idea

- You can add or subtract mixed numbers by dealing with the whole number and fraction parts separately, or by renaming them first as improper fractions.

Need to Know

- Sometimes, the sum of the fraction parts of two mixed numbers is an improper fraction. You can rename the fraction part as a mixed number and add once more.

$$\text{For example: } 1\frac{2}{3} + 5\frac{2}{3} = 6\frac{4}{3}$$
$$= 6 + 1\frac{1}{3}$$
$$= 7\frac{1}{3}$$

- Sometimes, a mixed number has a lesser fraction part than the number being subtracted. You can rename the mixed number with its whole number part reduced by one and its fraction part increased accordingly.

$$\text{For example: } 3\frac{1}{3} - 1\frac{2}{3} = 2\frac{4}{3} - 1\frac{2}{3}$$
$$= 1\frac{2}{3}$$

- You may use a number line to visualize the sum or difference of two mixed numbers.
  - Rename each fraction using the lowest common denominator (LCD). Draw a number line with intervals that correspond to the LCD of the fractions.
  - For addition, begin at the location on the number line of one of the fractions. Use the number line to "add on" an amount equal to the second fraction.
  - For subtraction, mark the location of each fraction on the number line and count the intervals between the numbers.
- Most strategies used to add or subtract two mixed numbers with different denominators require you to use equivalent fractions with a common denominator.

CHECK Your Understanding

1. Use the diagrams to help you evaluate each expression.

   a) $2\frac{1}{3} + \frac{5}{3}$

   b) $5 - \frac{2}{3}$

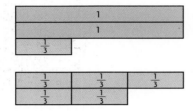 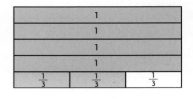

2. Use fraction strips to explain how to evaluate each expression. What is the value of each expression?

   a) $3\frac{5}{6} + 7\frac{1}{2}$

   b) $9\frac{1}{8} - 6\frac{3}{4}$

PRACTISING

3. Use number lines to evaluate the following expressions.

   a) $7\frac{3}{8} + 4\frac{1}{8}$

   b) $7\frac{3}{8} - 4\frac{1}{8}$

   c) $6\frac{2}{3} + 5\frac{2}{3}$

   d) $3\frac{2}{5} - 1\frac{4}{5}$

4. Between which two whole numbers will each sum lie?

   a) $4\frac{1}{2} + 8\frac{1}{6}$

   b) $3\frac{3}{4} + 6\frac{1}{5}$

   c) $4\frac{1}{3} + 12\frac{5}{8}$

   d) $1\frac{4}{5} + 6\frac{2}{3}$

   e) $34\frac{7}{10} + 16\frac{3}{4}$

   f) $11\frac{1}{2} + 41\frac{3}{5}$

5. Evaluate the expressions in question 4.

6. Estimate.

   a) $3\frac{1}{2} - 1\frac{1}{5}$

   b) $7\frac{3}{4} - 6\frac{1}{3}$

   c) $8\frac{1}{4} - 2\frac{1}{2}$

   d) $4\frac{7}{8} - 3\frac{8}{9}$

   e) $29\frac{5}{8} - 23\frac{7}{16}$

   f) $42\frac{1}{2} - 16\frac{2}{3}$

7. Evaluate the expressions in question 6.

8. Zofia spent $4\frac{1}{3}$ h weeding her garden on Monday and $1\frac{4}{5}$ h on Tuesday. How many hours did she spend weeding her garden altogether?

9. Alexis left her house at 7:45 p.m. to go shopping for clothes. She returned at 10:30 p.m.
   a) Express the time in hours that Alexis spent away from home.
   b) If Alexis spent $1\frac{1}{2}$ h shopping for clothes, then how much time did she spend doing other things?

10. A recipe for cookies calls for $1\frac{1}{2}$ c chopped dates, $\frac{3}{4}$ c water, $1\frac{1}{2}$ c sugar, $\frac{1}{2}$ c chopped nuts, $\frac{2}{3}$ c butter, and 3 c flour to be mixed together in a bowl. When these ingredients are combined, how many cups will there be altogether?

11. Determine two mixed numbers, with different denominators, that
T have the following properties.

   a) a sum of $3\frac{4}{5}$

   b) a difference of $3\frac{4}{5}$

   Explain how you chose your numbers.

12. Explain each of the following. You may use diagrams to show your
C explanations.

   a) Why is $3\frac{2}{5} - 1\frac{4}{7}$ the same as $\frac{3}{7} + 1\frac{2}{5}$?

   b) Why is $3\frac{2}{3} - 1\frac{5}{6}$ the same as $3\frac{5}{6} - 2$?

log of practice session

- ran $5\frac{1}{4}$ laps
- walked $1\frac{3}{4}$ laps
- ran $4\frac{2}{3}$ laps
- walked $1\frac{1}{3}$ laps
- ran $3\frac{4}{5}$ laps

13. John trains by running on the school track. When he gets tired, he
A walks until he is able to run again. His log for one training day is shown to the left.

    a) Determine how many laps around the track John ran.

    b) Determine how many laps he walked around the track.

    c) Determine how many more laps John ran than he walked.

    d) If one lap around the school track is 400 m, determine the total distance John travelled.

14. Jane is putting wood trim around a doorway like the one shown to the right. How many linear feet of wood will Jane need altogether? (Hint: 1 ft = 12 in.)

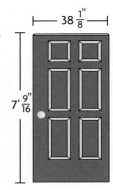

$38\frac{1}{8}"$

$7'\frac{9}{16}"$

15. a) Create an addition or subtraction question involving mixed numbers.

    b) How do you think most people would choose to solve your question: by creating equivalent fractions for the fraction parts, or by renaming the mixed numbers as equivalent improper fractions? Explain.

Extending

16. a) Determine the value of $3\frac{1}{4} - 1\frac{1}{2}$.

    b) Recalculate $3\frac{1}{4} - 1\frac{1}{2}$ by following the steps below.

      i) Find the difference between the whole parts.

      ii) Subtract the fraction in the first mixed number from the fraction in the second mixed number.

      iii) Subtract the answer in part ii) from the answer in part i).

    c) Repeat parts a) and b) for $5\frac{1}{3} - 1\frac{3}{4}$.

    d) Repeat parts a) and b) for $4\frac{2}{5} - 2\frac{2}{3}$.

    e) Explain why the process in part b) gives the same answer as in part a).

17. The sum of two mixed numbers is $2\frac{1}{2}$ more than the difference. What are the two numbers?

Curious | Math

Inches

In Canada, the metric system is the official system of measurement. Before 1970, the imperial system was used, and it is still widely used in construction. Because of this, most measuring tapes found in hardware stores are marked in both inches and centimetres.

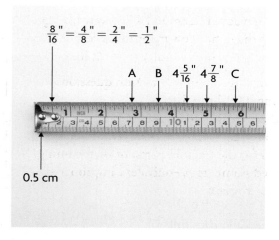

Recall that between 0 and 1 cm there are nine markings to create ten equal parts. The distance between adjacent markings represents 1 mm or 0.1 cm. The marking halfway between 0 and 1 cm is a little longer than the other markings. It represents 5 mm or 0.5 cm.

Similarly, between 0 and 1 inch there are 15 markings to create 16 equal parts. The distance between adjacent markings represents $\frac{1}{16}$ of an inch. There are different lengths for the markings to represent measurements of $\frac{1}{2}, \frac{1}{4}, \frac{1}{8}$, and $\frac{1}{16}$ of an inch.

1. What measurement, in inches, is indicated by the arrows A, B, and C?

2. Calculate the total length in inches of A, B, and C.

3. Use the photo of the measuring tape to estimate the number of centimetres in one inch.

4. Most people know their height in feet and inches, but not in centimetres.
   a) Determine your height in inches.
   b) Use your estimate in question 3 to calculate your height in centimetres.

Multiplication and Division of Mixed Numbers

Multiply and divide mixed numbers.

LEARN ABOUT the Math

Mario is using small boxes to transfer cans of soup from $2\frac{2}{3}$ large boxes in the kitchen of the food shelter to the basement.

A large box holds $1\frac{1}{2}$ times as many cans as a small box.

Once the transfer is complete, there are a total of $7\frac{3}{4}$ small boxes full of cans in the basement.

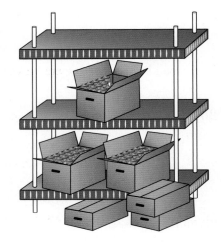

> **?** How many small boxes of cans were moved to the basement? How many large boxes would hold all the cans that are now in the basement?

EXAMPLE 1　　Selecting a strategy to multiply mixed numbers

Determine how many small boxes the cans in the kitchen of the food shelter will fill.

Carly's Solution: Representing the product as partial areas

$2\frac{2}{3} \times 1\frac{1}{2}$ ◄———————————

A large box holds $1\frac{1}{2}$ times as much as a small one, so $2\frac{2}{3}$ large boxes fill $2\frac{2}{3} \times 1\frac{1}{2}$ small boxes.

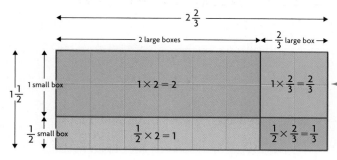

To multiply, I drew a rectangle $2\frac{2}{3}$ by $1\frac{1}{2}$. The area told me how many small boxes Mario would fill with soup cans.

$$2\frac{2}{3} \times 1\frac{1}{2} = 2 + \frac{2}{3} + 1 + \frac{1}{3}$$

I added the partial areas to get the total area.

$$= 4$$

Four small boxes of cans were moved to the basement.

The cans in the kitchen of the food shelter will completely fill 4 small boxes.

Bobby changed the mixed numbers to improper fractions before he multiplied.

Bobby's Solution: Using a strategy involving improper fractions

I estimate $2\frac{2}{3} \times 1\frac{1}{2}$ to be less than $4\frac{1}{2}$.

$2\frac{2}{3} \times 1\frac{1}{2}$ is less than $3 \times 1\frac{1}{2}$.

$3 \times 1\frac{1}{2} = 3 + \frac{1}{2}$ of 3.

So, the number of small boxes is less than $3 + 1\frac{1}{2}$.

$$2\frac{2}{3} \times 1\frac{1}{2} = \frac{8}{3} \times \frac{3}{2}$$

I decided to rename the mixed numbers as improper fractions because I knew how to multiply entire fractions.

$$= \frac{8 \times 3}{3 \times 2}$$

$$= \frac{24}{6}$$

I multiplied the numerators, and then, multiplied the denominators. I simplified by dividing.

$$= 4$$

4 was less than $4\frac{1}{2}$, so I thought that my answer was correct.

Four small boxes were moved to the basement.

The cans in the kitchen of the food shelter will fill 4 whole small boxes.

EXAMPLE 2 Selecting a strategy to divide mixed numbers

Determine how many large boxes all the cans in the basement will fill.

Tony's Solution: Using a number line model

$7\frac{3}{4} \div 1\frac{1}{2}$ ⟵——————————— Since there were $7\frac{3}{4}$ small boxes and it took $1\frac{1}{2}$ small boxes to fill a large box, I had to divide to determine how many $1\frac{1}{2}$s were in $7\frac{3}{4}$.

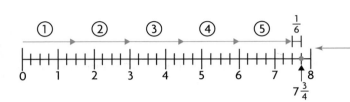

I created a number line divided into intervals of fourths, since 4 was the lowest common denominator of the fraction parts.
I marked off the number of times I could fit the **divisor** $1\frac{1}{2}$ into the **dividend** $7\frac{3}{4}$.

Therefore, the cans in the basement will fill $5\frac{1}{6}$ large boxes. ⟵

One fourth was left on the number line when I needed a jump of $1\frac{1}{2}$ or 6 fourths, so the fraction was $\frac{1}{6}$.

Darla and Enid both used division algorithms they had learned before.

Darla's Solution: Using a strategy involving common denominators

$7\frac{3}{4} \div 1\frac{1}{2} = \frac{31}{4} \div \frac{3}{2}$

$\quad = \frac{31}{4} \div \frac{6}{4}$ ⟵ I renamed the fractions as improper fractions with a common denominator.

$\quad = \frac{31}{6}$ ⟵ I divided the numerators to determine how many groups of 6 there were in 31.

$\quad = 5\frac{1}{6}$ ⟵ I renamed the improper fraction as a mixed number so that I could get a better sense of the number of boxes.

I checked my answer using multiplication.

$5\frac{1}{6} \times 1\frac{1}{2} = \frac{31}{\overset{}{6}} \times \frac{\overset{1}{3}}{2} = \frac{31}{4} = 7\frac{3}{4}$

Therefore, the cans in the basement will fill $5\frac{1}{6}$ large boxes. ⟵

Since I got $7\frac{3}{4}$, I knew that my work was correct.

Enid's Solution: Using a strategy involving the reciprocal

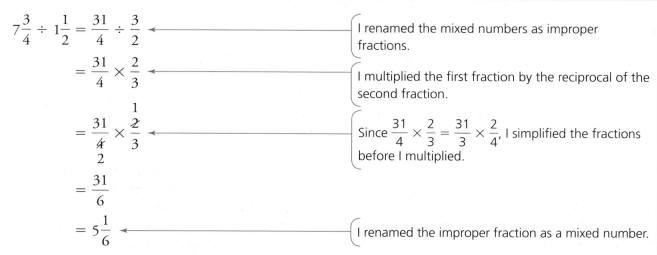

$$7\frac{3}{4} \div 1\frac{1}{2} = \frac{31}{4} \div \frac{3}{2}$$ ← I renamed the mixed numbers as improper fractions.

$$= \frac{31}{4} \times \frac{2}{3}$$ ← I multiplied the first fraction by the reciprocal of the second fraction.

$$= \frac{31}{\overset{2}{4}} \times \frac{\overset{1}{2}}{3}$$ ← Since $\frac{31}{4} \times \frac{2}{3} = \frac{31}{3} \times \frac{2}{4}$, I simplified the fractions before I multiplied.

$$= \frac{31}{6}$$

$$= 5\frac{1}{6}$$ ← I renamed the improper fraction as a mixed number.

Therefore, the cans in the basement will fill $5\frac{1}{6}$ large boxes.

Reflecting

A. How could Carly determine the partial areas without drawing all the squares?

B. How did Bobby's and Enid's rearrangement of the numerators and denominators make the multiplication calculations easier?

APPLY the Math

EXAMPLE 3	Selecting a strategy to determine a product

Calculate $2\frac{3}{4} \times 5\frac{1}{3}$.

Tina's solution: Using an area model

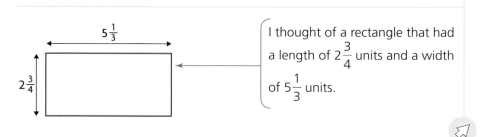

I thought of a rectangle that had a length of $2\frac{3}{4}$ units and a width of $5\frac{1}{3}$ units.

Instead of using the multiplication sign to express a product, brackets may be used around the second factor.

For example: $2 \times 3 = 2(3)$.

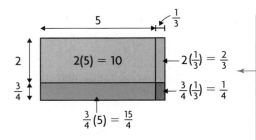

I visualized the large rectangle as 4 sections. The dimensions of each of these smaller rectangles were the whole number or fraction part of each mixed number in the product. I multiplied the dimensions of each rectangle to find their areas.

$$= 10 + \frac{15}{4} + \frac{2}{3} + \frac{1}{4}$$

I added the partial areas to find the total area.

$$= 10 + 3\frac{3}{4} + \frac{2}{3} + \frac{1}{4}$$

$$= 10 + 3 + \frac{3}{4} + \frac{1}{4} + \frac{2}{3}$$

$$= 13 + 1 + \frac{2}{3}$$

$$= 14\frac{2}{3}$$

Todd's Solution: using improper fractions

$$2\frac{3}{4} \times 5\frac{1}{3}$$

I expressed each mixed number as an improper fraction.

$$= \frac{11}{4} \times \frac{16}{3}$$

$$= \frac{11}{\overset{}{\underset{1}{\cancel{4}}}} \times \frac{\overset{4}{\cancel{16}}}{3}$$

I simplified by dividing 4 into 4 in the denominator and 4 into 16 in the numerator. Then, I multiplied the numerators and the denominators.

$$= \frac{44}{3}$$

$$= 14\frac{2}{3}$$

I simplified by dividing the numerator by the denominator.

EXAMPLE 4 Connecting products to powers of mixed numbers

Determine the volume of this cube.

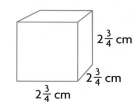

$2\frac{3}{4}$ cm

$2\frac{3}{4}$ cm

$2\frac{3}{4}$ cm

Paul's Solution

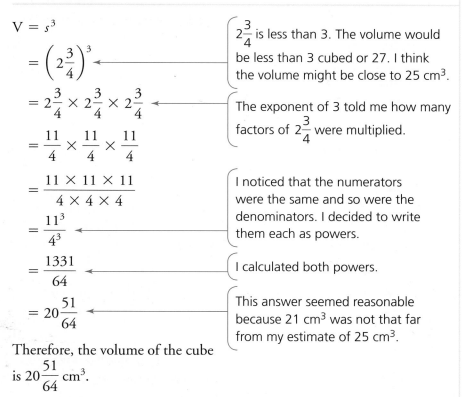

$V = s^3$

$= \left(2\frac{3}{4}\right)^3$ ← $2\frac{3}{4}$ is less than 3. The volume would be less than 3 cubed or 27. I think the volume might be close to 25 cm³.

$= 2\frac{3}{4} \times 2\frac{3}{4} \times 2\frac{3}{4}$ ← The exponent of 3 told me how many factors of $2\frac{3}{4}$ were multiplied.

$= \frac{11}{4} \times \frac{11}{4} \times \frac{11}{4}$

$= \frac{11 \times 11 \times 11}{4 \times 4 \times 4}$ I noticed that the numerators were the same and so were the denominators. I decided to write them each as powers.

$= \frac{11^3}{4^3}$ ←

$= \frac{1331}{64}$ ← I calculated both powers.

$= 20\frac{51}{64}$ ← This answer seemed reasonable because 21 cm³ was not that far from my estimate of 25 cm³.

Therefore, the volume of the cube is $20\frac{51}{64}$ cm³.

EXAMPLE 5   Problem solving using mixed numbers

Devon's father is installing new wood flooring. He bought boards that are 10 ft long, $\frac{3}{4}$ in. thick, and $\frac{11}{24}$ in. wide. Determine the number of boards Devon's father will need for a 10 ft by $16\frac{1}{2}$ ft room.

Devon's Solution

I estimate the answer to be a little more than 32.

$$16\frac{1}{2} \div \frac{11}{24}$$

$$= \frac{33}{2} \div \frac{11}{24}$$

The boards are as long as the room, so I only had to worry about the width. If the boards were $\frac{1}{2}$ ft wide, I would need 2 boards for every foot of width. For 16 ft, I would need 32 boards.

$$= \frac{33}{2} \times \frac{24}{11}$$

Instead of dividing, I wrote the equivalent multiplication by multiplying by the reciprocal of $\frac{11}{24}$.

$$= \frac{\overset{3}{\cancel{33}}}{\underset{1}{\cancel{2}}} \times \frac{\overset{12}{\cancel{24}}}{\underset{1}{\cancel{11}}}$$

I simplified by dividing both 2 and 24 by 2, and both 11 and 33 by 11.

$$= 36$$

36 was close to my estimate, so I thought that I was correct.

Therefore, my father will need 36 boards for the room.

In Summary

Key Idea

- The strategies you use for multiplying and dividing proper and improper fractions can be used to multiply and divide mixed numbers.

Need to Know

- The most efficient strategy to multiply or divide two mixed numbers is to perform the operations on their equivalent improper fractions.
- You can model the product of two mixed numbers as the area of a rectangle in which the numbers are the length and width. You can then determine the area of each section of the rectangle. The product of the mixed fractions is the sum of these partial areas.

  For example, $8\frac{3}{4} \times 2\frac{2}{3}$ can be calculated as follows:

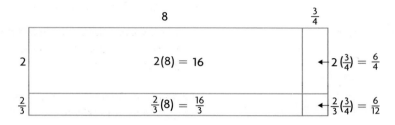

  Then, the partial areas are added together.

$$8\frac{3}{4} \times 2\frac{2}{3} = 16 + \frac{6}{4} + \frac{16}{3} + \frac{6}{12}$$
$$= 16 + \frac{3}{2} + \frac{16}{3} + \frac{1}{2}$$
$$= 16 + 2 + 5\frac{1}{3}$$
$$= 23\frac{1}{3}$$

- One way you can divide one fraction by another is by multiplying the first fraction by the reciprocal of the second fraction.
- Another way you can divide one fraction by another is by renaming the fractions as equivalent fractions with the same denominator, and then, dividing the numerators.

CHECK Your Understanding

1. a) State the multiplication problem represented by the following area model.
   b) Use the model to determine the product.

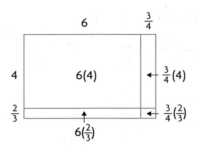

2. Use improper fractions to calculate $7\frac{1}{2} \times 2\frac{2}{5}$.

3. State the division problem and its answer shown by the number line.

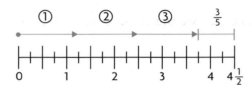

4. Calculate $1\frac{7}{15} \div 1\frac{11}{25}$ by multiplying by the reciprocal.

PRACTISING

5. a) State the multiplication problem represented by each area model.
   b) Use the model to determine each product.

   i)
   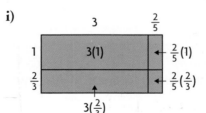
   ii)
   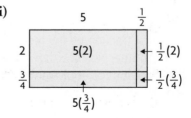

6. Estimate.

   a) $2\frac{1}{5} \times 2\frac{5}{6}$

   b) $5\frac{7}{8} \times 6\frac{3}{4}$

   c) $5\frac{1}{2} \div \frac{9}{10}$

   d) $8\frac{5}{6} \div 1\frac{5}{8}$

7. Calculate each product.

a) $2\dfrac{1}{6} \times 4\dfrac{2}{3}$ **c)** $\dfrac{3}{4} \times 6\dfrac{11}{12}$ **e)** $4\dfrac{1}{8} \times 5\dfrac{1}{3}$

b) $1\dfrac{3}{4} \times 2\dfrac{2}{3}$ **d)** $5\dfrac{1}{9} \times 3\dfrac{3}{4}$ **f)** $2\dfrac{2}{7} \times 2\dfrac{7}{8}$

8. Determine the value that makes each equation true.

a) $\left(\dfrac{2}{3}\right)^7 = \dfrac{2^{\blacksquare}}{3^7}$ **b)** $\left(2\dfrac{1}{2}\right)^{\blacksquare} = \dfrac{5^4}{2^4}$ **c)** $\left(6\dfrac{1}{3}\right)^2 = \dfrac{\blacksquare^2}{3^2}$

9. Calculate each power.

a) $\left(\dfrac{3}{4}\right)^3$ **b)** $\left(\dfrac{5}{2}\right)^3$ **c)** $\left(3\dfrac{1}{5}\right)^3$

10. Calculate each quotient.

a) $2\dfrac{2}{5} \div \dfrac{4}{5}$ **c)** $9\dfrac{2}{3} \div 2\dfrac{2}{3}$ **e)** $8\dfrac{2}{3} \div 10\dfrac{1}{2}$

b) $1\dfrac{1}{4} \div 3\dfrac{4}{5}$ **d)** $2\dfrac{7}{8} \div 3\dfrac{5}{6}$ **f)** $8\dfrac{3}{4} \div 5\dfrac{2}{5}$

11. a) Show that the two calculations are equivalent in each set below.

i) $\dfrac{4}{9} \div \dfrac{2}{3}$ and $\dfrac{4 \div 2}{9 \div 3}$

ii) $\dfrac{28}{15} \div \dfrac{4}{5}$ and $\dfrac{28 \div 4}{15 \div 5}$

iii) $\dfrac{35}{48} \div \dfrac{5}{12}$ and $\dfrac{35 \div 5}{48 \div 12}$

b) Show how you could rewrite $\dfrac{2}{3}$ as $\dfrac{8}{12}$, and then, use the strategy in part a) to evaluate $\dfrac{2}{3} \div \dfrac{1}{4}$.

12. Calculate.

K

a) $7\dfrac{3}{5} \times 3\dfrac{3}{4}$ **b)** $1\dfrac{2}{3} \div 5\dfrac{5}{6}$

13. A farmer made a square chicken coop with a length of $6\dfrac{1}{2}$ m.

A

a) Determine the perimeter of the chicken coop.
b) Determine the area of the chicken coop.

14. Gavin made a patio area out of square blocks that are $1\dfrac{1}{2}$ ft by $1\dfrac{1}{2}$ ft.

The area of his patio is $175\dfrac{1}{2}$ sq ft and the length is $19\dfrac{1}{2}$ ft.

a) Determine the width of his patio.
b) Determine the number of blocks Gavin used to make his patio.

15. Show that dividing a number by $5\frac{1}{2}$ gives the same answer as

C multiplying the number by $\frac{2}{11}$.

16. Which whole numbers can replace the box to make the product of $3\frac{1}{5}$

and $\blacksquare\frac{3}{4}$ greater than 25?

17. a) In each case, determine the numbers represented by the rectangle

T and the triangle.

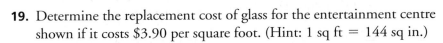

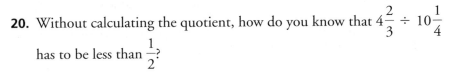

b) Describe the connection between the number represented by the rectangle and the number represented by the triangle.

c) Create a question of your own that shows this connection.

18. A large bottle holds $1\frac{3}{4}$ times the amount of liquid of a small bottle. Determine the number of large bottles that would hold the same amount as $10\frac{1}{2}$ small bottles.

19. Determine the replacement cost of glass for the entertainment centre shown if it costs \$3.90 per square foot. (Hint: 1 sq ft = 144 sq in.)

20. Without calculating the quotient, how do you know that $4\frac{2}{3} \div 10\frac{1}{4}$

has to be less than $\frac{1}{2}$?

21. Some people multiply fractions by first renaming them as equivalent fractions with a common denominator. They get the correct answer, but why is this not always an efficient method?

Extending

22. Sherri divided a mixed number by $2\frac{3}{4}$. The quotient was a whole number larger than 10. What are two possibilities for the mixed number?

23. A rectangle measuring $8\frac{1}{4}$ units by $3\frac{3}{4}$ units is to be completely covered by squares that are all the same size. What are the largest possible dimensions of the squares?

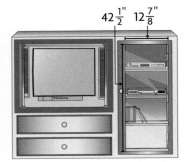

$42\frac{1}{2}"$ $12\frac{7}{8}"$

1.3 Integer Operations with Powers

GOAL

Evaluate integer expressions involving order of operations and powers.

LEARN ABOUT the Math

Many contests make you answer a skill-testing question before you can claim your prize. Suppose you won a contest and you had to answer this question:

$$-2^4 + (-1 - 1)^3 + 5(-2)^4.$$

? What is the answer to the skill-testing question?

EXAMPLE 1 | Using the order of operations to evaluate an expression

Determine the correct answer to $-2^4 + (-1 - 1)^3 + 5(-2)^4$.

Michelle's Solution

$-2^4 + (-1 - 1)^3 + 5(-2)^4$

$= -2^4 + (-2)^3 + 5(-2)^4$

$= -16 + (-2)^3 + 5(-2)^4$

$= -16 + (-8) + 5(-2)^4$

$= -16 + (-8) + 5(16)$

$= -16 + (-8) + 80$

$= 56$

> I applied the **order of operations** to calculate the answer.

> I did the subtraction first because it was in the brackets.

> For the first power, since there were no brackets, the base of the power was 2, not −2. So, I treated it as $-(2^4)$.
> I calculated $2^4 = 16$, and then, I multiplied it by −1.

> I calculated $(-2)^3 = (-2)(-2)(-2)$ or −8.

> I calculated $(-2)^4 = (-2)(-2)(-2)(-2) = 16$.

> I multiplied before adding.

Reflecting

A. If m is 1, 2, 3, 4, and so on, how can you predict the sign of $(-2)^m$?

B. Why is the value of -2^m never positive for any value of m?

C. How is the use of the order of operations to evaluate an integer expression similar to evaluating a whole number expression? How is it different?

APPLY the Math

EXAMPLE 2	**Selecting a strategy to calculate an expression with powers**

Calculate $-3^4 + [-2 - (-4)^3] + \sqrt{16}$.

Anthony's Solution: Applying the order of operations

$-3^4 + [-2 - (-4)^3] + \sqrt{16}$ ◄——— In the square brackets, there was a subtraction and a power.

$= -3^4 + [-2 - (-64)] + \sqrt{16}$ ◄——— I calculated the power before the subtraction because I followed the order of operations.
I knew that when the base is negative and the exponent is odd, the answer is negative.

$= -3^4 + (-2 + 64) + \sqrt{16}$ ◄——— I did the subtraction in the brackets. To subtract -64, I added its opposite.
$= -3^4 + 62 + \sqrt{16}$

$= -81 + 62 + \sqrt{16}$ ◄——— I calculated the power.

$= -81 + 62 + 4$ ◄——— I calculated the square root before adding.

$= -15$

- You can use the memory aid BEDMAS to remember the rules for order of operations.
  Perform the operations in Brackets first.
  Calculate Exponents and square roots next.
  Divide and Multiply from left to right.
  Add and Subtract from left to right.

- When there are multiple brackets, complete the operations in the inner brackets first. For example:
  $$[(2 + 3) \times 3]^2$$
  $$= [5 \times 3]^2$$
  $$= 15^2$$
  $$= 225$$

- When a square root sign covers an expression, it contains the expression just like brackets.

Many scientific and graphing calculators are programmed to follow the order of operations. Peng used her graphing calculator to calculate the answer.

Peng's Solution: Using a calculator with brackets keys

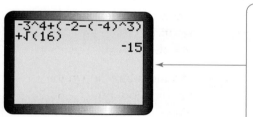

My calculator only had round brackets so I had to be careful to make sure that the brackets matched the order in the original expression.

I also had to make sure that I used the negative sign key to enter negative numbers instead of the subtraction key.

To evaluate an algebraic expression for given values of the variables, substitute these given values into the expression. This results in a numerical expression that can be calculated following the order of operations.

EXAMPLE 3   Evaluating an expression in fraction form

Evaluate the expression $\dfrac{3x^3 + 16}{-y^3}$ when $x = -4$ and $y = 2$.

Talia's Solution

$\dfrac{3x^3 + 16}{-y^3}$	I knew that a fraction represents a division and that the numerator and denominator have to be evaluated before the division can be done.
$= \dfrac{3(-4)^3 + 16}{-(2)^3}$	I used brackets to show where I substituted the values for the variables.
$= \dfrac{3(-64) + 16}{-8}$	I used the order of operations to evaluate the expressions in the numerator and the denominator separately.
$= \dfrac{-192 + 16}{-8}$	
$= \dfrac{-176}{-8}$	I knew that dividing integers with the same sign gave a positive result.
$= 22$	

In Summary

Key Idea

- You can use the same order of operations (BEDMAS) for integer expressions as you used for whole number expressions.

Need to Know

- For exponent $n = 1, 2, 3, 4$, and so on:
  - $(-a)^n = \underbrace{(-a)(-a)(-a) \dots (-a)}_{[n \text{ factors}]}$

    For example: $(-2)^3 = (-2)(-2)(-2)$
  - $-a^n = -(a^n)$

    For example: $-2^4 = -(2^4)$
  - If $a < 0$, then $(a)^n$ is positive if n is even and negative if n is odd.

    For example: $(-2)^4 = 16$ and $(-2)^3 = -8$
- You can evaluate an expression for given values for the variable(s) by replacing each variable with its numeric value in brackets. Then, follow the order of operations.

CHECK Your Understanding

1. Without calculating, state whether the answer will be positive or negative.
   a) -2^3
   b) $(-2)^3$
   c) $-(-2)^3$
   d) -2^4
   e) $-(-2)^4$
   f) $-(-2^4)$

2. Without using a calculator, determine the answers in question 1.

3. Show the steps required to evaluate the following expressions.
   a) $-7^2 - 2(-3)^3$
   b) $-4^2 - (-4)^2 - 4^2$

PRACTISING

4. Calculate.
   a) $\dfrac{-4(15)}{-10}$
   b) $\dfrac{20}{2(-5)}$
   c) $\dfrac{-10(6)}{-3(-2)}$

5. Determine the value that makes each equation true.
   a) $\blacksquare^3 = 27$
   b) $(-3)^\blacksquare = -27$
   c) $-\blacksquare^2 = -25$
   d) $-4^\blacksquare = -64$
   e) $\blacksquare^5 = 32$
   f) $\blacksquare^5 = -32$

6. Evaluate.
   a) -5^3
   b) $(-6)^2$
   c) -4^3
   d) $(-4)^3$
   e) $+(-3)^4$
   f) $+(-3)^3$

7. Solving the equation $\blacksquare^2 = 64$ gives two possible integer values. Determine the values.

8. Evaluate each expression without using a calculator.
   a) $5(-2)^3$
   b) $-4(-5) - (-3^3)$
   c) $[-2(-1)^3]^6$
   d) $-2^3 - (-10 + 5^2)$
   e) $\dfrac{(-2)^2 - 22}{-3^2}$
   f) $\dfrac{3^3 + 3(7)}{-2^4} + \dfrac{3(-5)^2}{-15}$

9. Find the error in each solution. Explain what was done incorrectly.
   A Redo the solution, making the necessary corrections.
   a) $-4[5 - 2(-3)]$
      $= -4[3(-3)]$
      $= -4(-9)$
      $= 36$

   b) $-2(3)^2$
      $= (-6)^2$
      $= 36$

10. Both Claire and Robin calculated $5(-2) - 3(-2)$.

C Claire's calculations   Robin's calculations

$5(-2) - 3(-2)$ $5(-2) - 3(-2)$

$= -10 + 6$ $= 2(-2)$

$= -4$ $= -4$

Both students are correct. Explain Robin's reasoning.

11. Evaluate each expression when $x = -2$ and $y = -1$.

a) $x^2 + y^3$ **c)** $2y^5 - (3 + x)^2$ **e)** $\dfrac{8(x + y^2)}{x^2}$

b) $5y^3(-x^4)$ **d)** $x^2 + [5x - 2(y - x)]$ **f)** $\dfrac{y^5 + y^3 + y}{y^6 + y^4 + y^2}$

12. Evaluate the expression $-y^2 - 4x^3$ when $x = -2$ and $y = 3$.

K

13. Assume b and n are positive integers. For each situation below, decide
T whether $-b^n + (-b)^n$ is positive, negative, or zero. Explain your
reasoning.
a) The exponent is an odd number.
b) The exponent is an even number.

Extending

14. a) Use a calculator to calculate the following.

     i) $(-2)^3(-2)^4$ **ii)** $(-2)^2(-2)^6$ **iii)** $(-2)(-2)^5$

b) Express each answer in part a) as a power with a base of (-2).

c) Look for patterns. How could you get the power in part b) just by
looking at the question in part a)?

15. a) Use a calculator to calculate the following.

     i) $\dfrac{(-3)^9}{(-3)^7}$ **ii)** $\dfrac{(-3)^8}{(-3)^4}$ **iii)** $\dfrac{(-3)^5}{(-3)}$

b) Express each answer in part a) as a power with a base of (-3).

c) Look for patterns. How could you get the power in part b) just by
looking at the question in part a)?

16. Evaluate $3(2^n) - 2^n$ and 2^{n+1} for various values of n.
a) What pattern do you notice?
b) Why does the pattern work?

FREQUENTLY ASKED Questions

Q: What strategies can you use to add or subtract mixed numbers?

A: The most efficient method is to create equivalent fractions with the same denominator for the fraction parts of the mixed numbers. You can add or subtract the whole number parts and the fraction parts separately. Rename mixed numbers when necessary.

You can also rename the mixed numbers as improper fractions with a common denominator, but this often results in having to work with large numerators.

Study | **Aid**

• See Lesson 1.1, Examples 1 and 2.
• Try Mid-Chapter Review Questions 1 to 4.

EXAMPLE

$$4\frac{6}{7} + 5\frac{2}{3}$$

$$= 4\frac{18}{21} + 5\frac{14}{21}$$

$$= 9\frac{32}{21}$$

$$= 10\frac{11}{21}$$

$$7\frac{1}{3} - 2\frac{3}{4}$$

$$= 7\frac{4}{12} - 2\frac{9}{12}$$

$$= 6\frac{16}{12} - 2\frac{9}{12}$$

$$= 4\frac{7}{12}$$

Q: What strategies can you use to multiply mixed numbers?

A1: The most efficient method is to write each mixed number as an improper fraction. Then, multiply as if they were ordinary fractions. You may be able to simplify parts of the fractions prior to multiplying.

Study | **Aid**

• See Lesson 1.2, Examples 1 and 3.
• Try Mid-Chapter Review Questions 5 and 7.

EXAMPLE

$$4\frac{1}{2} \times 3\frac{2}{3}$$

$$= \frac{9}{2} \times \frac{11}{3}$$

$$= \frac{\overset{3}{\cancel{9}}}{2} \times \frac{11}{\underset{1}{\cancel{3}}}$$

$$= \frac{33}{2}$$

$$= 16\frac{1}{2}$$

A2: You can use a rectangular area model to represent the product of two mixed numbers. Use the model to determine the partial areas and add them to calculate the final product.

EXAMPLE

$$3\frac{2}{3} \times 4\frac{1}{2}$$

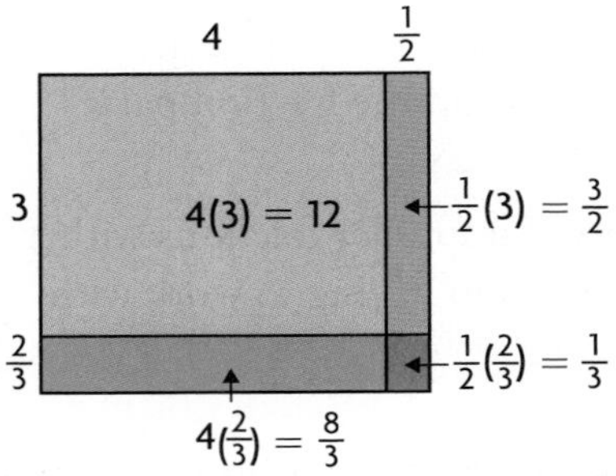

$$= 12 + \frac{8}{3} + \frac{3}{2} + \frac{1}{3}$$

$$= 12 + \frac{3}{2} + \frac{8}{3} + \frac{1}{3}$$

$$= 12 + \frac{3}{2} + \frac{9}{3}$$

$$= 12 + 1\frac{1}{2} + 3$$

$$= 16\frac{1}{2}$$

Study | **Aid**

• See Lesson 1.2, Example 2.
• Try Mid-Chapter Review Questions 6 and 7.

Q: What strategies can you use to divide mixed numbers?

A1: The most efficient method is to rename the mixed numbers as improper fractions, and then, multiply the dividend by the reciprocal of the divisor. You may be able to simplify parts of the fractions prior to multiplying to get the final result.

EXAMPLE

$$5\frac{1}{2} \div 3\frac{2}{3} = \frac{11}{2} \div \frac{11}{3}$$

$$= \frac{\overset{1}{\cancel{11}}}{2} \times \frac{3}{\underset{1}{\cancel{11}}}$$

$$= \frac{3}{2}$$

$$= 1\frac{1}{2}$$

A2: You can first rename the mixed numbers as equivalent improper fractions with the same denominator. Then, divide the numerators.

EXAMPLE

$$5\frac{1}{2} \div 3\frac{2}{3} = \frac{11}{2} \div \frac{11}{3}$$

$$= \frac{33}{6} \div \frac{22}{6}$$

$$= 33 \div 22$$

$$= 1\frac{11}{22}$$

$$= 1\frac{1}{2}$$

Q: What strategies can you use to evaluate integer expressions with powers?

A: When you evaluate an expression for given values for the variable(s), replace each variable with its numeric value in brackets, and then, follow the order of operations.

> **Study** | *Aid*
> - See Lesson 1.3, Examples 1, 2, and 3.
> - Try Mid-Chapter Review Questions 12 and 13.

EXAMPLE

Evaluate $(x - y)^2 + (x + y)^3$ when $x = -3$ and $y = 2$.

Solution

$(x - y)^2 + (x + y)^3$

$= [(-3) - (2)]^2 + [(-3) + (2)]^3$

$= (-5)^2 + (-1)^3$

$= 25 + (-1)$

$= 24$

PRACTICE Questions

Lesson 1.1

1. Calculate.

a) $7\dfrac{1}{3} + 2\dfrac{1}{2}$ c) $6\dfrac{3}{4} - 6\dfrac{2}{3}$

b) $4\dfrac{2}{5} + 1\dfrac{3}{4}$ d) $9\dfrac{1}{7} - 4\dfrac{4}{5}$

2. Explain how you can use estimation to tell that your answers in question 1 are reasonable.

3. John works part-time at a restaurant. On Friday he worked $3\dfrac{1}{4}$ h and on Saturday he worked $6\dfrac{1}{2}$ h. How many hours did he work altogether?

4. Why does it make sense that $3\dfrac{1}{5} - 2\dfrac{1}{4}$ has the same answer as $\dfrac{3}{4} + \dfrac{1}{5}$?

Lesson 1.2

5. Calculate each product without using a calculator.

a) $2\dfrac{5}{8} \times \dfrac{4}{11}$ c) $2\dfrac{3}{5} \times 3\dfrac{1}{3}$

b) $1\dfrac{3}{5} \times 1\dfrac{2}{7}$ d) $7\dfrac{1}{5} \times 4\dfrac{5}{6}$

6. Calculate each quotient without using a calculator.

a) $5\dfrac{3}{4} \div \dfrac{1}{2}$ c) $6\dfrac{2}{3} \div 2\dfrac{1}{6}$

b) $\dfrac{1}{2} \div 5\dfrac{3}{4}$ d) $10\dfrac{5}{8} \div 5\dfrac{1}{3}$

7. Determine the value that makes each equation true.

a) $6\dfrac{3}{4} \times \blacksquare = 19\dfrac{1}{8}$ c) $\blacksquare \div 5\dfrac{1}{3} = 4\dfrac{2}{3}$

b) $\blacksquare \times 1\dfrac{1}{4} = \dfrac{5}{8}$ d) $7\dfrac{3}{4} \div \blacksquare = 5\dfrac{1}{6}$

8. Melissa is adjusting the two removable shelves in her cupboard. The shelves are to be equally spaced in the cupboard. How much space is above or below each shelf?

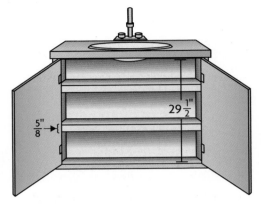

9. Suppose the onscreen cursor represents any numeric character. Determine the number of numeric characters that can fit on the calculator screen.

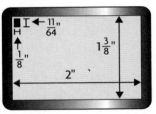

Lesson 1.3

10. Calculate.

a) $(-11)^2$ c) -7^2

b) $(-4)^3$ d) -6^3

11. Determine at least four other powers that have the same value as 8^2.

12. Answer the following skill-testing question.

$-[(5)(-1)]^3 - 2(-4)^3$

13. Evaluate when $x = 2$, $y = -3$, and $z = -1$. Do not use a calculator.

a) $x^2 + y^2 + z^2$ c) $\dfrac{2y + 4z}{-x}$

b) $2[x - (y - z)^4]$ d) $\dfrac{x - y^2}{2z - x + y}$

GOAL

Connect rational numbers to other number systems.

LEARN ABOUT the Math

Shahreen looked at the thermometer outside. The temperature was a **rational number** between $-18\ °C$ and $-19\ °C$. It was closer to $-19\ °C$.

❓ What might the temperature be?

EXAMPLE 1	Using a number line to represent rational numbers

Determine a possible temperature value that is between $-18\ °C$ and $-19\ °C$, but is closer to $-19\ °C$.

Mark's Solution: Using fractions and a number line

I marked the approximate position of the temperature value on a number line. Then, I marked the **opposite** of the value because I can read fractions more easily if they are positive. I estimated the positive value to be about $18\frac{3}{4}$.

A possible temperature value between $-18\ °C$ and $-19\ °C$ is $-18\frac{3}{4}\ °C$.

I knew that the opposite of $18\frac{3}{4}$ was $-18\frac{3}{4}$. This meant $-18\frac{3}{4}$ was just as far from zero as $18\frac{3}{4}$ but in the negative direction.

So, $-18\frac{3}{4}$ must be the same as $-18-\frac{3}{4}$ because it was farther to the left of 0 than -18.

$-18\frac{3}{4}$ is a rational number because it can also be expressed as $-\frac{75}{4}$.

$18\frac{3}{4}$ is $\frac{75}{4}$. Its opposite is $-\frac{75}{4}$.
So, $-18\frac{3}{4} = -\frac{75}{4}$.

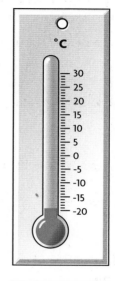

rational number

a number that can be expressed as the quotient of two integers where the divisor is not 0

opposites

two numbers with opposite signs that are the same distance from zero (e.g., $+6$ and -6 are opposites)

George's Solution: Using decimals and a number line

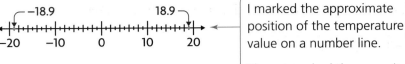

−18.9   18.9

−20   −10   0   10   20

I marked the approximate position of the temperature value on a number line.

Then, I marked the opposite of the value because I can read decimals more easily if they are positive. I estimated the positive value to be about 18.9.

A possible temperature value is −18.9 °C.

I knew that the opposite of 18.9 was −18.9. This meant −18.9 was as far from zero as 18.9 but in the negative direction.

So, −18.9 must be the same as −18 − 0.9 because it was farther to the left of 0 than −18.

−18.9 is a rational number because it can also be expressed as $-\dfrac{189}{10}$.

As a mixed number, $18.9 = 18\dfrac{9}{10}$ or $\dfrac{189}{10}$. Its opposite is $-\dfrac{189}{10}$. So, $-18.9 = -\dfrac{189}{10}$.

Reflecting

A. How would you describe how to place a "negative fraction" like $-\dfrac{2}{5}$ on a number line?

B. Why is −20 less than −18.9 even though 20 is greater than 18.9?

C. How are rational numbers similar to fractions and integers? How are they different?

APPLY the Math

EXAMPLE 2	Representing rational numbers as decimals

Which of the following represent the same rational number?

$$\frac{-2}{3}, \frac{2}{-3}, -\frac{2}{3}, \frac{3}{-2}, \frac{-3}{-2}, \frac{3}{2}$$

Abby's Solution

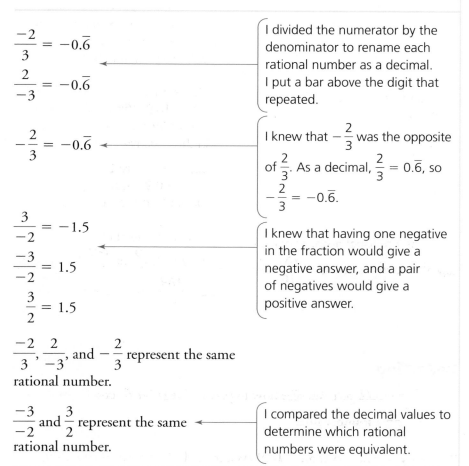

$$\frac{-2}{3} = -0.\overline{6}$$

$$\frac{2}{-3} = -0.\overline{6}$$

I divided the numerator by the denominator to rename each rational number as a decimal. I put a bar above the digit that repeated.

$$-\frac{2}{3} = -0.\overline{6}$$

I knew that $-\frac{2}{3}$ was the opposite of $\frac{2}{3}$. As a decimal, $\frac{2}{3} = 0.\overline{6}$, so $-\frac{2}{3} = -0.\overline{6}$.

$$\frac{3}{-2} = -1.5$$

$$\frac{-3}{-2} = 1.5$$

$$\frac{3}{2} = 1.5$$

I knew that having one negative in the fraction would give a negative answer, and a pair of negatives would give a positive answer.

$\dfrac{-2}{3}, \dfrac{2}{-3}$, and $-\dfrac{2}{3}$ represent the same rational number.

$\dfrac{-3}{-2}$ and $\dfrac{3}{2}$ represent the same rational number.

I compared the decimal values to determine which rational numbers were equivalent.

When it is necessary to compare the size of two or more rational numbers, a number line is a useful tool to use.

EXAMPLE 3 | Representing rational numbers using a number line

Determine which number is greater: $-1\frac{3}{10}$ or $-1\frac{2}{5}$.

Andrew's Solution

$$-1\frac{2}{5} = -1\frac{4}{10}$$

I knew that I could compare these numbers if they had equivalent fraction parts. I renamed the fraction part for $-1\frac{2}{5}$.

$-1\frac{3}{10}$ is the opposite of $1\frac{3}{10}$. Since $1\frac{4}{10}$ is farther from zero than $1\frac{3}{10}$, $-1\frac{4}{10}$ is farther from zero than $-1\frac{3}{10}$.

Therefore, $-1\frac{3}{10} > -1\frac{2}{5}$.

Since $-1\frac{3}{10}$ is to the right of $-1\frac{4}{10}$ on the number line, $-1\frac{3}{10}$ is greater than $-1\frac{4}{10}$.

Communication | *Tip*

Traditionally, sets of numbers have been represented by letters. The symbol Q is used for rational numbers because they are a *quotient* of two integers.

Set	Definition	Examples	Symbol
Natural Numbers	the counting numbers	1, 2, 3, ...	N
Whole Numbers	the counting numbers and zero	0, 1, 2, 3, ...	W
Integers	positive and negative whole numbers	..., -3, -2, -1, 0, 1, 2, 3, ...	I
Rational Numbers	numbers of the form $\frac{a}{b}$ where a and b are integers and $b \neq 0$	$\frac{3}{4}$, $-\frac{2}{3}$, $-3\frac{5}{8}$, 2.35, -3.921, $-8.\overline{234}$	Q

In Summary

Key Idea

- Rational numbers include integers, fractions, their decimal equivalents, and their opposites.

Need to Know

- Rational numbers can be positive, negative, or zero.
- Every integer is a rational number because it can be written as a quotient of two integers: itself as the numerator and 1 as the denominator.

    For example, zero can be expressed as $\dfrac{0}{1}$.

- To compare rational numbers, it helps to rename them to a common form, either as decimals or as fractions.
- The rules for renaming rational numbers are the same as the rules for positive fractions and decimals.
- When comparing rational numbers, one number is greater than another if it is farther to the right on a number line.
- A negative mixed number is a subtraction of its parts.

    For example: $-7\dfrac{1}{4} = -7 + \left(-\dfrac{1}{4}\right)$

    $$= -7 - \dfrac{1}{4}$$

    Similarly, for decimals: $-7.25 = -7 + (-0.25)$
    $$= -7 - 0.25$$

CHECK *Your Understanding*

1. Rename the following rational numbers as quotients of two integers.

    a) $-2\dfrac{1}{4}$ b) $-5\dfrac{6}{7}$

2. Rename the following rational numbers as decimals.

    a) $\dfrac{1}{5}$ c) $\dfrac{3}{-4}$

    b) $\dfrac{-4}{7}$ d) $-7\dfrac{5}{6}$

3. Rename the following rational numbers as quotients of integers.

    a) -0.35 b) 4.625 c) -11.46

PRACTISING

4. Identify the values represented by a, b, c, d, and e, in decimal form.

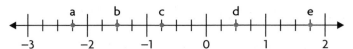

5. Identify the values represented by a, b, c, d, and e, as quotients of two integers.

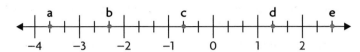

6. Two students renamed the mixed number $-2\frac{1}{2}$ to its corresponding improper fraction. Who did it correctly, Tammy or Jasmine? Identify the error made in the incorrect solution.

Tammy

$$-2\frac{1}{2} = -\left(2\frac{1}{2}\right)$$

$$= -\left(\frac{(2 \times 2 + 1)}{2}\right)$$

$$= -\left(\frac{(4 + 1)}{2}\right)$$

$$= -\frac{5}{2}$$

Jasmine

$$-2\frac{1}{2} = \frac{(-2 \times 2 + 1)}{2}$$

$$= \frac{(-4 + 1)}{2}$$

$$= -\frac{3}{2}$$

Communication | **Tip**

When reading from left to right:
> is the symbol for "greater than"
< is the symbol for "less than."

7. Use $>$, $<$, or $=$ to make true statements. Explain how you know each statement is true.

a) $0 \blacksquare -0.5$

c) $-1\frac{2}{5} \blacksquare 1\frac{2}{5}$

e) $5.6 \blacksquare 5\frac{3}{5}$

b) $-4.3 \blacksquare -3.4$

d) $-4\frac{1}{2} \blacksquare -\frac{9}{2}$

f) $-2\frac{3}{10} \blacksquare -2.\overline{3}$

8. Explain why $-3\frac{1}{4}$ can be renamed as $-3 - \frac{1}{4}$ and not as $-3 + \frac{1}{4}$.

9. **a)** Name three fractions between $\dfrac{2}{8}$ and $\dfrac{3}{8}$.

C
   b) How would your answers to part a) help you name three rational numbers between $-\dfrac{2}{8}$ and $-\dfrac{3}{8}$?

   c) Are your answers in part a) rational numbers? Explain.

10. True or false? Justify your answer.

T
   a) All mixed numbers can be renamed as decimals.
   b) A rational number can be expressed as any integer divided by any other integer.
   c) Two rational numbers are opposites if they have different signs.
   d) $1 > -1\ 000\ 000$

11. To write $0.833\ 333\ldots$ as a fraction, Rhys thought of this as:

A
   $0.8 + \dfrac{1}{10}$ of $0.333\ 333\ldots$

   This is the same as:

   $$\dfrac{8}{10} + \dfrac{1}{10} \times \dfrac{1}{3}$$

   $$= \dfrac{8}{10} + \dfrac{1}{30}$$

   $$= \dfrac{24}{30} + \dfrac{1}{30}$$

   $$= \dfrac{25}{30}$$

   $$= \dfrac{5}{6}$$

   Use Rhys's approach to write each of the following as fractions.

   a) $0.4333\ldots$ **b)** $0.1\overline{6}$ **c)** $0.25\overline{3}$

12. Draw a diagram to show the relationship between these sets of numbers: Integers, Whole Numbers, Natural Numbers, and Rational Numbers. Use one circle for each set of numbers.

Extending

13. If a and b are positive numbers and $a < b$, how do $-a$ and $-b$ compare? Explain why.

1.5 Rational Number Operations

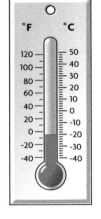

C temperature
$= \frac{5}{9}$ **(F temperature − 32)**

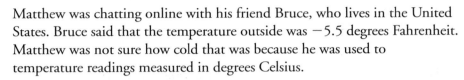

Evaluate expressions involving rational numbers.

LEARN ABOUT the Math

Matthew was chatting online with his friend Bruce, who lives in the United States. Bruce said that the temperature outside was −5.5 degrees Fahrenheit. Matthew was not sure how cold that was because he was used to temperature readings measured in degrees Celsius.

He found the following conversion formula from a weather website:

$$C = \frac{5}{9}[F - 32]$$

where C is the temperature in degrees Celsius and F is the temperature in degrees Farenheit.

? **What is the Celsius temperature equivalent to −5.5 °F?**

EXAMPLE 1   **Evaluating a rational number expression**

Determine the Celsius temperature equivalent to −5.5 °F.

Ishtar's Solution: Connecting to integer and fraction operations

I estimate −5.5 °F to be about ← | I estimated by looking at the thermometer.
−21 °C.

$$C = \frac{5}{9}[(-5.5) - 32]$$ ← | I substituted the Fahrenheit temperature value into the formula.

$$= \frac{5}{9}\left[\left(-5\frac{1}{2}\right) - 32\right]$$ ← | I decided to rename all the numbers as fractions because $\frac{5}{9}$ would become a repeating decimal. This would give me a rounding error in my final answer.

$$= \frac{5}{9}\left[-\left(5 + \frac{1}{2}\right) - 32\right]$$

I followed the order of operations and did the subtraction within the brackets first.

$$= \frac{5}{9}\left(-5 - \frac{1}{2} - 32\right)$$

$$= \frac{5}{9}\left(-5 - 32 - \frac{1}{2}\right)$$

$$= \frac{5}{9}\left(-37 - \frac{1}{2}\right)$$

$$= \frac{5}{9}\left(-37\frac{1}{2}\right)$$

$$= \frac{5}{9}\left(\frac{-75}{2}\right)$$

I decided to multiply using improper fractions.

$$= \frac{5}{\overset{}{\underset{3}{9}}}\left(\frac{\overset{-25}{\cancel{-75}}}{2}\right)$$

I used what I knew about integers to determine the sign.

$$= -\frac{125}{6}$$

$$= -20\frac{5}{6}$$

I renamed the answer as a negative mixed number, so that I could get a better sense of the number of degrees.

$$= -20.8\overline{3}$$

Since the Fahrenheit temperature was expressed in decimal form, I decided to rename my answer as a decimal.

Therefore, $-5.5\ °F$ is equivalent to about $-20.8\ °C$.

I thought my answer was reasonable because it was close to my estimate.

Calculations involving rational numbers can also be performed using scientific and graphing calculators.

Sherry's Solution: Using a calculator

$$C = \frac{5}{9}(F - 32)$$

$$= \frac{5}{9}[(-5.5) - 32]$$ ← I substituted -5.5 into the conversion formula and entered it into my calculator.

My calculator follows the order of operations, so I assumed it would give the correct answer.

Therefore, $-5.5\ ^\circ$F is equivalent to $-20.8\overline{3}\ ^\circ$C or about $-20.8\ ^\circ$C.

Reflecting

A. How did Ishtar use what he knew about integer operations to complete the calculation?

B. How did Ishtar use what he knew about fraction operations to complete the calculation?

APPLY the Math

EXAMPLE 2	Connecting the addition of rational numbers to adding fractions and integers

Calculate $-\dfrac{4}{5} + \dfrac{2}{-3}$.

Thai's Solution

I estimate the answer to be between -1 and -2. ←

I knew that $\frac{4}{5}$ and $\frac{2}{3}$ were each greater than $\frac{1}{2}$, and that $\frac{4}{5} + \frac{2}{3}$ must be between 1 and 2. So, $-\frac{4}{5} + \frac{2}{-3}$ must be between -1 and -2.

$$-\frac{4}{5} + \frac{2}{-3}$$

$$= \frac{-4}{5} + \frac{-2}{3}$$

I am used to adding fractions when both denominators are positive. I knew that $\frac{2}{-3}$ was the same as $\frac{-2}{3}$ because the quotient of a positive and a negative is negative.

$$= \frac{-12}{15} + \frac{-10}{15}$$

I created equivalent fractions using a common denominator of 15.

$$= \frac{-12 + (-10)}{15}$$

I added the numerators.

$$= -\frac{22}{15}$$

$$= -1\frac{7}{15}$$

Since $-1\frac{7}{15}$ was within my estimate, I thought that my answer was reasonable.

To evaluate an algebraic expression whose given values for the variables are rational number, substitute the given values, and then, follow the order of operations.

EXAMPLE 3	Using the order of operations to evaluate a rational number expression

Evaluate $-2\frac{1}{2}x \div y$ when $x = 5\frac{1}{3}$ and $y = -1\frac{7}{9}$.

Uma's Solution

$$-2\frac{1}{2}x \div y$$

I substituted the given values for the variables.

$$= -2\frac{1}{2}\left(5\frac{1}{3}\right) \div \left(-1\frac{7}{9}\right)$$

I estimated the answer by rounding each mixed number to its nearest integer value and got $-3(5) \div (-2) = 7\frac{1}{2}$.

$$= -\frac{5}{2}\left(\frac{\overset{8}{\cancel{16}}}{3}\right) \div \left(-1\frac{7}{9}\right)$$

I followed the order of operations the same way I would if the numbers were all integers or fractions.

$$= -\frac{40}{3} \div \left(-1\frac{7}{9}\right)$$

$$= \frac{-40}{3} \div \frac{-16}{9}$$

Rational Numbers **51**

$$= \frac{-\overset{-5}{\cancel{40}}}{\underset{1}{\cancel{8}}} \times \frac{-\overset{-3}{\cancel{9}}}{\underset{2}{\cancel{16}}}$$

I divided by multiplying by the reciprocal. I simplified before I multiplied.

$$= \frac{15}{2}$$

$$= 7\frac{1}{2}$$

$7\frac{1}{2}$ was the same as my estimate, so I was confident that my answer was correct.

EXAMPLE 4 | **Solving a problem involving rational numbers**

These temperatures were recorded at noon on January 1 from 1998 to 2006 at Ottawa MacDonald-Cartier International Airport. Determine the average noon temperature on January 1 for the years given.

Year	Temperature (°C)
1998	−20.9
1999	−22.7
2000	−5.4
2001	−11.4
2002	−10.9
2003	−5.0
2004	−4.7
2005	−2.8
2006	−9.6

Mark's Solution

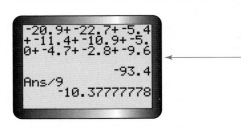

```
-20.9+-22.7+-5.4
+-11.4+-10.9+-5.
0+-4.7+-2.8+-9.6
              -93.4
Ans/9
        -10.37777778
```

I divided the sum of the temperatures by 9, the number of temperature readings, to determine the average noon temperature.

Therefore, the average noon temperature at the Ottawa airport on January 1 is $-10.3\overline{7}$ °C or about -10.4 °C.

I decided to round my answer to one decimal place because all the numbers in the table were given to one decimal place.

In Summary

Key Idea

- The strategies and order of operations you used for calculations with integers, fractions, and decimals can be extended to all rational numbers.

Need to Know

- Calculations with rational number operations may be simpler to perform if you rename mixed numbers as improper fractions, and rewrite negative fractions with the negative sign in the numerator.

CHECK *Your Understanding*

1. Evaluate without using a calculator.

a) $2.5 - 7.5$

b) $-2(9.5)$

c) $-4.2 + (-2.8)$

d) $\dfrac{8}{-0.5}$

2. Evaluate without using a calculator.

a) $-\dfrac{4}{3} + \dfrac{1}{3}$

b) $\dfrac{3}{4} - \dfrac{5}{4}$

c) $\dfrac{-4}{7} \times \dfrac{6}{-5}$

d) $\dfrac{2}{5} \div \left(-\dfrac{5}{8}\right)$

3. Without evaluating, determine which expressions have the same answer as $\dfrac{3}{4}\left(\dfrac{5}{8}\right)$.

a) $-\dfrac{3}{4}\left(-\dfrac{5}{8}\right)$

b) $\dfrac{-3}{4}\left(\dfrac{5}{-8}\right)$

c) $\dfrac{-3}{4}\left(\dfrac{-5}{8}\right)$

d) $\dfrac{3}{-4}\left(-\dfrac{5}{8}\right)$

PRACTISING

4. Estimate the two consecutive integers between which each answer will lie.

a) $3.64 + 72.9$

b) $-6.5(-10.1)$

c) $-9.37 - 5.93$

d) $-\dfrac{3.046}{10}$

5. Determine the answers in question 4 without using a calculator.

6. The daily changes in selling price for a particular stock during a week were $-\$2.78$, $-\$5.45$, $\$0.38$, $\$1.38$, and $\$2.12$.
   a) If the selling price of the stock was $\$58.22$ at the start of the week, then what was the selling price at the end of the week?
   b) What was the average daily change in selling price for the stock during this week?

7. The temperature at Moosonee, Ontario on December 25 at 5:00 a.m. **A** from 2000 to 2005 is shown in the table. Determine the average temperature on December 25 at 5:00 a.m. for the given years.

Year	Temperature (°C)
2000	-23.9
2001	-10.0
2002	-7.5
2003	-22.3
2004	-35.7
2005	-14.4

8. Calculate. Show your work.
   a) $-\dfrac{3}{8} + 1\dfrac{3}{4}$
   c) $-7\dfrac{3}{5} + \left(-8\dfrac{1}{4}\right)$
   e) $-3\dfrac{1}{3} - 5\dfrac{4}{5}$
   b) $-5\dfrac{1}{2} + 2\dfrac{2}{3}$
   d) $\dfrac{6}{5} - \dfrac{3}{2}$
   f) $-9\dfrac{1}{2} - \left(-10\dfrac{3}{4}\right)$

9. Calculate. Show your work.
   a) $\left(\dfrac{5}{-12}\right)\left(-\dfrac{8}{15}\right)$
   c) $3\dfrac{6}{7}\left(-8\dfrac{1}{3}\right)$
   e) $-4\dfrac{2}{3} \div \dfrac{7}{12}$
   b) $-2\dfrac{1}{2}\left(-1\dfrac{3}{5}\right)$
   d) $\dfrac{15}{16} \div \left(-1\dfrac{1}{24}\right)$
   f) $-2\dfrac{5}{6} \div \left(-1\dfrac{1}{12}\right)$

10. Yaroslav takes $\dfrac{3}{4}$ h to cut his family's front lawn and $1\dfrac{1}{3}$ h to cut the back lawn. How much longer does it take Yaroslav to cut the back lawn?

11. Determine the value that makes each equation true.
   a) $-1\dfrac{3}{4} + \blacksquare = 1$
   c) $-1\dfrac{3}{4} \times \blacksquare = 1$
   b) $-1\dfrac{3}{4} - \blacksquare = 1$
   d) $-1\dfrac{3}{4} \div \blacksquare = 1$

12. a) In each case, determine the numbers represented by the rectangle and the triangle.
   i) $-3\dfrac{1}{2} + 5\dfrac{2}{3} = \square$
   $\square - 5\dfrac{2}{3} = \triangle$
   ii) $-6\dfrac{4}{5} \times \left(-2\dfrac{1}{4}\right) = \square$
   $\square \div \left(-2\dfrac{1}{4}\right) = \triangle$

   b) Describe the connection between the number represented by the rectangle and the number represented by the triangle.
   c) Create a similar question that demonstrates this connection.

13. Without calculating, determine the sign for each answer. Then, use a
K calculator to complete the calculation.

    a) $-3.2(4.2 - 10)$ **d)** $6.2(-3.1)(7.3 - 0.9)$

    b) $-0.7 - 5.8(12)$ **e)** $\dfrac{3.2}{-1.2} + \dfrac{-4.5}{-6}$

    c) $-3.4(-2.3) + 5.7(-9.1)$ **f)** $\dfrac{8.5 - (-2.3)}{2(-1.2)}$

14. Evaluate each expression.

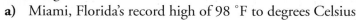

    a) $-\dfrac{2}{5} + \dfrac{3}{-4} - 2\dfrac{2}{3}$ **c)** $-2\dfrac{1}{3} + \left(\dfrac{3}{-4}\right) \times \left(-1\dfrac{5}{6}\right)$

    b) $-\dfrac{15}{16} \times 3\dfrac{1}{5} \div \left(-1\dfrac{2}{3}\right)$ **d)** $-2\dfrac{1}{4} \times \left(1\dfrac{3}{4} - 5\dfrac{1}{2}\right)$

15. The formula to convert temperatures between degrees Fahrenheit and
degrees Celsius is $C = \dfrac{5}{9}(F - 32)$. Apply the formula to convert the
following.

    a) Miami, Florida's record high of 98 °F to degrees Celsius
    b) Anchorage, Alaska's record low of -38 °F to degrees Celsius
    c) 0 °C to degrees Fahrenheit

16. The formula to convert Celsius temperatures to Fahrenheit
temperatures is $F = \dfrac{9}{5}C + 32$. Use this formula to convert the
following.
    a) The boiling point of water, 100 °C, to degrees Fahrenheit
    b) Normal body temperature, 37.0 °C, to degrees Fahrenheit

17. Evaluate each expression for the given values.
    a) $x - 2y$ when $x = -9.78$ and $y = 3.2$
    b) $(x + y)(x - y)$ when $x = 2.5$ and $y = -7.8$
    c) $x(x + y)$ when $x = -2\dfrac{1}{2}$ and $y = 3\dfrac{3}{4}$
    d) $\dfrac{x}{y} + \dfrac{y}{x}$ when $x = -1\dfrac{1}{2}$ and $y = 2\dfrac{1}{4}$

18. Calculate.
    a) $-3.4 + 2\dfrac{1}{2} - 0.68\left(2\dfrac{16}{17}\right)$
    b) $5.25\left(-2\dfrac{7}{8}\right) - 8.5\left(-3\dfrac{3}{4}\right)$

19. James finished a full marathon in a time of 3:57:53.3 (hours:minutes:seconds). The winner of the marathon finished in a time of 2:25:55.6. Determine how much longer James took to complete the marathon than the winner did.

20. a) Calculate $-2\frac{3}{5} + 1\frac{1}{4}$ without using a calculator.

b) Calculate $-2\frac{4}{7} + 1\frac{1}{6}$ without using a calculator.

c) Use the decimal equivalents for the fractions in parts a) and b) and evaluate each expression.

d) Would you prefer to do similar calculations using decimal form or fraction form? Explain.

Extending

21. Calculate.

a) $-\left(2\frac{1}{4}\right)^2 + 1.5^3$

b) $-5\frac{2}{3} + 3.\overline{6}(0.\overline{3})^2$

22. $1 + \cfrac{1}{1 + \cfrac{1}{1 + \cfrac{1}{2}}}$ is an example of a continued fraction.

a) Verify that the value of the continued fraction is $1\frac{3}{5}$.

b) Determine the continued fraction representation for $1\frac{4}{5}$.

Hint: $\dfrac{4}{5} = \cfrac{1}{\dfrac{5}{4}}$

23. The width of a rectangle is $\frac{1}{4}$ of the length. If you increase the width by 12 m and double the length, you obtain a perimeter of 120 m. Determine the dimensions of the original rectangle.

Evaluate rational number expressions involving powers.

LEARN ABOUT the Math

Taylor walks one lap around a track. Then, she turns and walks half as far in the other direction. She changes direction again and walks half as far as her previous distance. She changes direction one last time and again walks only half as far as her last distance.

❓ What fraction around the track is Taylor's final position?

EXAMPLE 1   Solving a problem involving powers of rational numbers

Determine Taylor's final position on the track.

Haley's Solution: Representing the problem using a number line

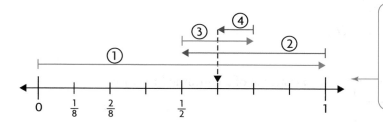

I used a number line to model the problem.

I used red arrows to show Taylor's initial direction around the track and blue arrows to show when she walked in the opposite direction.

Therefore, Taylor ended at $\dfrac{5}{8}$ of the way around the track from where she started.

Keely's Solution: Connecting to powers of integers and fractions

$$1 + \left(-\frac{1}{2}\right) + \left(-\frac{1}{2}\right)^2 + \left(-\frac{1}{2}\right)^3$$

After Taylor's first lap, I expressed each distance as a power of $-\frac{1}{2}$. I used the negative to represent the change in direction. I used powers with base $-\frac{1}{2}$ since she walked half as far each time.

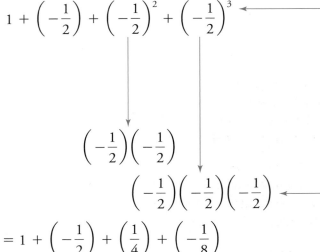

$$\left(-\frac{1}{2}\right)\left(-\frac{1}{2}\right)$$

$$\left(-\frac{1}{2}\right)\left(-\frac{1}{2}\right)\left(-\frac{1}{2}\right)$$

I expanded the powers using what I had learned about calculating powers with integer and fraction bases.

$$= 1 + \left(-\frac{1}{2}\right) + \left(\frac{1}{4}\right) + \left(-\frac{1}{8}\right)$$

$$= 1 + \left(-\frac{4}{8}\right) + \left(\frac{2}{8}\right) + \left(-\frac{1}{8}\right)$$

I renamed the fractions using a common denominator of 8 and added them.

$$= 1 + \left(-\frac{3}{8}\right)$$

$$= \frac{5}{8}$$

Therefore, Taylor ended at $\frac{5}{8}$ of the way around the track from where she started.

Because Taylor always walked half of her previous distance, she would end up somewhere in the third quarter of the track. Since $\frac{5}{8}$ was between $\frac{1}{2}$ and $\frac{3}{4}$, my answer seemed reasonable.

Reflecting

A. How is calculating a power with a negative fraction base similar to calculating a power with an integer base?

B. Why did Keely evaluate the powers before she added the rational numbers?

APPLY the Math

EXAMPLE 2	Evaluating an expression with negative decimal bases

Calculate $(-3.2)^2 - 2(-6.5)^3$.

Ahmed's Solution: Using the order of operations

$(-3.2)^2 - 2(-6.5)^3$

$= 10.24 - 2(-6.5)^3$ ← I followed the order of operations. First I calculated the powers. I knew that multiplying pairs of negatives gave a positive answer.

$= 10.24 - 2(-274.625)$ ← I knew that, for negative integer bases, if the exponent was odd, the answer would be negative. Also, $6.5^3 = 274.625$.

$= 10.24 - (-549.25)$ ← I multiplied by 2, and then, subtracted by adding the opposite.

$= 10.24 + 549.25$

$= 559.49$

When rational numbers are expressed as decimals in an expression, an efficient calculation strategy is to use a calculator.

Faith's Solution: Using a calculator with brackets keys

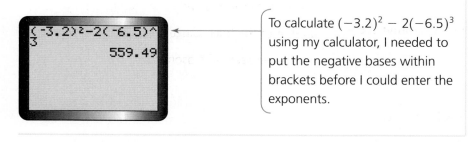

To calculate $(-3.2)^2 - 2(-6.5)^3$ using my calculator, I needed to put the negative bases within brackets before I could enter the exponents.

Communication | *Tip*

If rational numbers are expressed as fractions in an expression, then express your final answer this way as well. Changing fractions into decimal equivalents prior to making calculations can often result in incorrect answers due to rounding errors.

EXAMPLE 3 Evaluating an expression with negative fraction bases

Calculate $-2\frac{2}{3} + \left(-1\frac{3}{4} - \frac{5}{6}\right)^2$.

Ivan's Solution

$$-2\frac{2}{3} + \left(-1\frac{3}{4} - \frac{5}{6}\right)^2$$

To calculate this expression, I needed to follow the order of operations.

$$= -2\frac{2}{3} + \left(-\frac{7}{4} - \frac{5}{6}\right)^2$$

$$= -2\frac{2}{3} + \left(-\frac{21}{12} - \frac{10}{12}\right)^2$$

$$= -2\frac{2}{3} + \left(-\frac{31}{12}\right)^2$$

I performed the subtraction within the brackets first.

$$= -2\frac{2}{3} + \frac{961}{144}$$

I calculated the power.

$$= -2\frac{2}{3} + 6\frac{97}{144}$$

I expressed the second fraction as a mixed number.

$$= -2\frac{96}{144} + 6\frac{97}{144}$$

I made sure that the fraction parts had a common denominator before adding.

$$= 4\frac{1}{144}$$

I had to remember that the 96 in the numerator of the first mixed number was also negative.

EXAMPLE 4	Solving a problem involving powers of rational numbers

Josée worked at the mall this summer to help pay for her future university education. She invested $3000 in an account earning interest at a rate of 3.5% per year. How much money will her investment be worth in 4 years?

Invest to Earn

The Magic of Compounding

$$A = P(1 + i)^n$$

A = future value of investment
P = amount of money invested
i = decimal value of the interest rate used each time interest is earned
n = number of times interest is earned while money is invested

Josée's Solution

$A = P(1 + i)^n$
$= 3000(1 + 0.035)^4$

```
3000(1+0.035)^4
      3442.569002
```

I substituted values for the variables.
$P = 3000$ because that is the amount of money that I invested.
$i = 0.035$ because I had to change the interest rate given as a percentage to decimal form.
$n = 4$ because I receive interest once a year for 4 years.

Therefore, my investment will be worth $3442.57 in four years.

I rounded my answer to the nearest penny because the problem is about money.

In Summary

Key Idea

- Powers with rational bases are calculated in the same way as powers with integer bases.

Need to Know

For exponent $n = 1, 2, 3$, and so on:	Example
$\left(\dfrac{a}{b}\right)^n = \underbrace{\left(\dfrac{a}{b}\right)\left(\dfrac{a}{b}\right)\cdots\left(\dfrac{a}{b}\right)}_{[n \text{ factors}]}$	$\left(\dfrac{2}{3}\right)^3 = \left(\dfrac{2}{3}\right)\left(\dfrac{2}{3}\right)\left(\dfrac{2}{3}\right)$ $= \dfrac{8}{27}$
$\left(\dfrac{a}{b}\right)^n = \dfrac{a^n}{b^n}$	$\left(\dfrac{2}{3}\right)^3 = \dfrac{2^3}{3^3}$ $= \dfrac{8}{27}$
$-\left(\dfrac{a}{b}\right)^n = -\underbrace{\left(\dfrac{a}{b}\right)\left(\dfrac{a}{b}\right)\cdots\left(\dfrac{a}{b}\right)}_{[n \text{ factors}]}$	$-\left(\dfrac{2}{3}\right)^3 = -\left(\dfrac{2}{3}\right)\left(\dfrac{2}{3}\right)\left(\dfrac{2}{3}\right)$ $= -\dfrac{8}{27}$
$\left(\dfrac{-a}{b}\right)^n = \underbrace{\left(\dfrac{-a}{b}\right)\left(\dfrac{-a}{b}\right)\cdots\left(\dfrac{-a}{b}\right)}_{[n \text{ factors}]}$	$\left(\dfrac{-2}{3}\right)^3 = \left(\dfrac{-2}{3}\right)\left(\dfrac{-2}{3}\right)\left(\dfrac{-2}{3}\right)$ $= \dfrac{-8}{27}$
If $\dfrac{a}{b} < 0$, then $\left(\dfrac{a}{b}\right)^n$ is positive if n is even, and negative if n is odd.	$\left(-\dfrac{2}{3}\right)^2 = \dfrac{4}{9}$; $\left(-\dfrac{2}{3}\right)^3 = -\dfrac{8}{27}$

CHECK Your Understanding

1. Use $4.5^2 = 20.25$ and $4.5^3 = 91.125$ to evaluate the powers.

   a) $(-4.5)^2$ **b)** -4.5^2 **c)** $(-4.5)^3$ **d)** -4.5^3

2. Without evaluating, state if the answer is positive or negative.

   a) $\left(-\dfrac{2}{3}\right)^2$ **c)** $-\left(-\dfrac{2}{3}\right)^2$ **e)** $-\left(\dfrac{2}{3}\right)^3$

   b) $-\left(\dfrac{2}{3}\right)^2$ **d)** $-\left(-\dfrac{2}{3}\right)^3$ **f)** $\left(\dfrac{-2}{-3}\right)^5$

3. Evaluate the powers in question 2.

4. Use the expression $-4.5 + 2(3.1 - 9.8)^2$ to answer the following.
   a) Describe the order of operations required to calculate the answer.
   b) Calculate the answer.

PRACTISING

5. Calculate.
   K a) $8.9 - 3.2^2$

   b) $-2(-3.1)^3$

   c) $-7.1^2 + 7.1^2$

   d) $0.6^2 - 2(3.4 - 5.2)$

   e) $-6.02 - 2(-6.71) + 2.3^3$

   f) $\dfrac{2.3^3 - 5.4}{-3^2}$

6. Calculate.
   a) $2\left(-\dfrac{1}{3}\right)^2$

   b) $-2\dfrac{1}{3} - \left(-\dfrac{2}{3}\right)^3$

   c) $-\left(\dfrac{4}{5}\right)^2 + \left(\dfrac{5}{4}\right)^2$

   d) $\left(-4\dfrac{1}{5}\right)^2\left(\dfrac{25}{4}\right)^2$

   e) $\dfrac{-\dfrac{1}{3} + \left(\dfrac{1}{4}\right)^2}{-1\dfrac{1}{6}}$

   f) $\left(-\left(2\dfrac{1}{2}\right)^2\right)^2$

7. Determine the value that makes each equation true. Explain how you got your answers.
   a) $2.4^{\blacksquare} = 5.76$

   b) $-2.4^{\blacksquare} = -5.76$

   c) $(3.5)^{\blacksquare} = 42.875$

   d) $\blacksquare^3 = -42.875$

8. Rob invests $100 in an account earning interest at a rate of 5% per year for 10 years. Sharon invests the same amount of money as Rob but she earns interest at a rate of 10% per year for 5 years.
   a) Predict whose investment would be worth more in the end and explain why.
   b) Calculate the value of both investments.

Invest your money!

$A = P(1 + i)^n$

9. Diego invested $2000. The amount of money in his account is shown over 5 years.
   a) Explain why the exponent in the expression at the end of 5 years is 10.
   b) Determine the amount in his account at the end of 5 years.

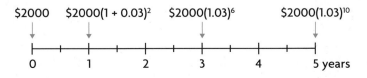

$2000 \quad \$2000(1 + 0.03)^2 \quad \$2000(1.03)^6 \qquad \$2000(1.03)^{10}$

0   1   2   3   4   5 years

Rational Numbers **63**

10. Tanjay invests $100 and earns interest at a rate of 4% per year for 10 years. Eda invests $100 and earns interest at a rate of 2% every 6 months for 10 years.
    a) Calculate the value of both investments.
    b) Explain why Eda's investment is worth more at the end of 10 years.

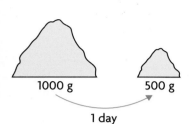

1000 g   500 g

1 day

11. A radioactive material has a half-life of 1 day. The material decays

    A according to the equation $M = 1000\left(\dfrac{1}{2}\right)^t$. Mass M is measured in grams and time t is measured in days.
    a) What is the mass of the sample after 1 day? 2 days? 10 days?
    b) Use a calculator with an exponent key to compute the mass of the sample after 1 year. Explain what the answer means.

12. Evaluate the following expressions.
    a) $x^2 - 4x + 3$ when $x = -2.5$
    c) $x^3 - 5x$ when $x = 0.5$
    b) $3x^2 + 5x - 12$ when $x = -1.5$
    d) $4x^3 + 4x^2$ when $x = -4.2$

13. Evaluate the following expressions.
    a) $x^2 + x - 5$ when $x = 1\dfrac{3}{4}$
    c) $5x^2 - 3x + 9$ when $x = -\dfrac{11}{5}$
    b) $x^3 + 6x^2$ when $x = -\dfrac{1}{3}$
    d) $x^2 - 3x + 6$ when $x = -2\dfrac{1}{2}$

14. Explain why $-\left(1\dfrac{1}{2}\right)^3 = \left(-1\dfrac{1}{2}\right)^3$, but $-\left(1\dfrac{1}{2}\right)^4 \neq \left(-1\dfrac{1}{2}\right)^4$.

15. What must you consider when applying the order of operations to
    C evaluate rational number expressions, that you don't need to consider when evaluating whole number expressions?

Extending

16. A small office buys a computer for $4575. Each year, its value is
    T expected to be 65% of its value the previous year. Find the value of the computer after five years.

17. Determine two values for x that will make the following equation true.
    $$5\left(\dfrac{x}{3}\right)^2 - 3\dfrac{1}{9} = -\dfrac{8}{9}$$

FREQUENTLY ASKED *Questions*

Q: **What strategies can you use to evaluate an expression involving rational numbers?**

A: You can extend the same strategies and order of operations (BEDMAS) used for calculations with integers, fractions, and decimals to all rational numbers.

Study | *Aid*

- See Lesson 1.6, Examples 1 and 3.
- Try Chapter Review Question 14.

EXAMPLE

$$\frac{2\left(-1\frac{3}{4} + 1\frac{3}{5}\right)^2}{\left(-\frac{1}{10}\right)^3} = \frac{2\left(-1\frac{15}{20} + 1\frac{12}{20}\right)^2}{\left(-\frac{1}{10}\right)^3}$$

$$= \frac{2\left(-\frac{3}{20}\right)^2}{\left(-\frac{1}{10}\right)^3}$$

$$= \frac{2\left(\frac{9}{400}\right)}{-\frac{1}{1000}}$$

$$= \frac{\frac{9}{200}}{-\frac{1}{1000}}$$

$$= \frac{9}{\overset{1}{\cancel{200}}} \times \frac{\overset{-5}{\cancel{-1000}}}{1}$$

$$= -45$$

PRACTICE Questions

Lesson 1.1

1. Calculate without using a calculator.

   a) $1\frac{2}{3} + 9\frac{1}{2}$ **c)** $4\frac{3}{8} + 2\frac{1}{4}$

   b) $8\frac{1}{6} - 7\frac{2}{3}$ **d)** $5\frac{5}{6} - 3\frac{3}{4}$

2. A piece of wood $8\frac{7}{8}$ in. long is cut from a piece $45\frac{1}{2}$ in. long. If $\frac{1}{16}$ in. is wasted for the cut, how much wood is left?

3. Stock shares of Champs Sporting Equipment opened at $12\frac{1}{8}$ and closed at the end of the day at $9\frac{1}{2}$. Calculate the change in the stock on this day.

Lesson 1.2

4. Calculate without using a calculator.

   a) $1\frac{3}{4} \times 3\frac{1}{2}$ **c)** $1\frac{2}{3} \div 4\frac{5}{6}$

   b) $5\frac{7}{9} \times 6\frac{3}{4}$ **d)** $4\frac{3}{4} \div 9\frac{1}{2}$

5. Calculate $\left(2\frac{2}{5}\right)^2$.

6. Determine the volume of a cube that has a side length of $1\frac{3}{4}$ m.

7. For the rectangle shown calculate:
   a) the perimeter
   b) the area

   $2\frac{2}{3}$ in.

   $4\frac{3}{4}$ in.

Lesson 1.3

8. Use words to explain the different steps you would take to evaluate -8^2 and $(-8)^2$.

9. Evaluate.

   a) $(-8 + 2)^2 \div (-4 + 2)^2$

   b) $\dfrac{(-16 + 4) \div 2}{8 \div (-8) + 4}$

   c) $16 - [3(6 - 3) - 12]$

   d) $\dfrac{20 + (-12) \div (-3)}{(-4 - 12) \div (-2)}$

10. Evaluate.

    a) $x^2 - 4x$ for $x = -3$

    b) $yx^2 + xy$ for $x = -4$ and $y = 5$

    c) $\dfrac{-x^4 - 5x}{x + (-1)^3}$ for $x = -2$

    d) $\dfrac{-x^2 - y^2}{x^2 + y^2}$ for $x = 2$ and $y = 3$

Lesson 1.4

11. Explain where each value is located on a number line.

    a) -2.6 **b)** $-\dfrac{24}{5}$

12. Which is a negative rational number between -10 and -9? How do you know?

    a) $-\dfrac{29}{3}$ **b)** $-\dfrac{31}{3}$

13. The temperature in Powassan was $-4.8\ ^\circ$C. The temperature in Callander was $-4\frac{5}{6}\ ^\circ$C. In which town was the temperature colder? Explain.

14. Write these rational numbers in order from least to greatest.

    a) $\dfrac{-3}{5}, \dfrac{1}{-3}, -1\frac{1}{3}$

    b) $-\dfrac{2}{5}, -2\frac{1}{5}, \dfrac{4}{5}$

    c) $0.7, -0.3, -0.\overline{3}$

    d) $0, -1.5, -2$

15. Use $>$, $<$, or $=$ to make true statements. Explain how you know each statement is true.

a) $\dfrac{-2}{3}$ ■ $-\dfrac{5}{6}$

b) $\dfrac{2}{3}$ ■ $\dfrac{5}{8}$

c) $-2\dfrac{1}{4}$ ■ $-\dfrac{9}{4}$

d) $\dfrac{2}{-5}$ ■ $\dfrac{3}{10}$

Lesson 1.5

16. The daily changes in selling price for a particular stock during a week were: $-\$4.50$, $-\$0.95$, $\$0.25$, $-\$2.36$, and $-\$3.72$. What was the average daily change in selling price for the stock during this week?

17. Calculate. Show your work.

a) $2\dfrac{1}{4} - 5\dfrac{1}{3}$

b) $-5\dfrac{2}{5} + 2\dfrac{3}{4}$

c) $-6\dfrac{3}{4}\left(5\dfrac{1}{9}\right)$

d) $1\dfrac{3}{4} \div \left(-\dfrac{30}{49}\right)$

18. Create two other expressions that give the same answer as $-1\dfrac{3}{4}\left(5\dfrac{1}{3}\right)$.

19. Calculate.

a) $6.4 - 4.2 \times 1.5$

b) $-12.4 + (-16.8) \div (-4.2)$

c) $\dfrac{15.3 + 2.7 \div 3}{-2 \times 8.1}$

d) $\dfrac{16 - 4.8 \times 2.1}{6 + 6 \div (-6)}$

20. Calculate.

a) $\dfrac{2}{5} \div \left(\dfrac{-2}{5} + \dfrac{1}{10}\right)$

b) $\dfrac{-5}{6} + \dfrac{-2}{3} \times \dfrac{3}{4}$

c) $\left[\dfrac{1}{8} + \left(\dfrac{-2}{3}\right)\right] \times \dfrac{12}{13}$

d) $-1\dfrac{1}{2} + \dfrac{-1}{-2} - \dfrac{-3}{5}$

Lesson 1.6

21. Calculate.

a) $[5.12 - 3(4.1)]^3$

b) $9.1^3 - 6.7^2$

c) $-2\dfrac{1}{10} + \left(2\dfrac{3}{5} - 3\dfrac{1}{4}\right)^3$

d) $-\dfrac{1}{4} \div \dfrac{5}{4} - 2\dfrac{1}{3} \div \left(-\dfrac{2}{3}\right)^3$

22. Mikka invests $100 in an account earning interest at a rate of 4% every 6 months. Calculate the value of his investment at the end of 4 years.

23. Use $>$, $<$, or $=$ to make true statements. Explain how you know each statement is true.

a) $\left(\dfrac{1}{-2}\right)^3$ ■ $\left(\dfrac{1}{2}\right)^2$

b) $\left(\dfrac{3}{4}\right)^2$ ■ $\left(-\dfrac{1}{4}\right)^3$

c) $(-0.5)^2$ ■ $\left(\dfrac{1}{2}\right)^2$

d) $\left(\dfrac{3}{2}\right)^3$ ■ $\left(\dfrac{3}{-2}\right)^4$

24. The area of a circle can be calculated using the formula $A = \pi r^2$, where $\pi \doteq 3.14$.

Calculate the area of each circle for each of the given radii. Round to the nearest tenth of a square unit.

a) $r = 5.2$ cm

b) $r = 2\dfrac{5}{8}$ in.

c) $r = 8.9$ m

d) $r = 4\dfrac{2}{3}$ in.

25. Evaluate each expression for the given values.

a) $4a^2b^2$; $a = \dfrac{-2}{3}$, $b = -\dfrac{1}{2}$

b) $(2ab)^2$; $a = -0.5$, $b = 1.2$

c) $\left(\dfrac{2a}{5b}\right)^2$; $a = 1\dfrac{1}{2}$, $b = -\dfrac{2}{5}$

d) $(3a - 2b)^3$; $a = -1.1$, $b = 2.2$

1. Which value is equivalent to $\dfrac{-4}{-5}$?

   A. $\dfrac{-4}{5}$　　　**B.** $-\dfrac{4}{5}$　　　**C.** $\dfrac{4}{-5}$　　　**D.** $\dfrac{4}{5}$

2. What does $-3^2 - (-1)^2$ equal?

   A. -8　　　**B.** 8　　　**C.** -10　　　**D.** 10

3. Which set of numbers is arranged in ascending order (least to greatest)?

   A. $-\dfrac{11}{5}, \dfrac{-11}{-5}, -2\dfrac{2}{5}$　　　**C.** $-2\dfrac{2}{5}, -\dfrac{11}{5}, \dfrac{-11}{-5}$

   B. $\dfrac{-11}{-5}, -\dfrac{11}{5}, -2\dfrac{2}{5}$　　　**D.** $-2\dfrac{2}{5}, \dfrac{-11}{-5}, -\dfrac{11}{5}$

4. Calculate without using a calculator.

   a) $5\dfrac{1}{2} + 4\dfrac{2}{7}$　　　　　　**b)** $4\dfrac{7}{12} \times 1\dfrac{4}{11}$

5. A piece of wood trim is $51\dfrac{3}{8}$ in. long. A piece $31\dfrac{5}{6}$ in. long is cut from it. How long is the remaining piece of wood if the cut removes $\dfrac{1}{8}$ in. of wood?

6. Explain how to calculate $(-2)^2$ and -2^4. Then, calculate each expression.

7. Evaluate the expression $-3x^2 + y^3$ for each situation below.

   a) when $x = -4$ and $y = -2$　　**b)** when $x = 0.4$ and $y = -1.1$

8. Which value is farther from zero: $-4\dfrac{1}{3}$ or 4.3? Explain.

9. Calculate.

   a) $\left(\dfrac{-4}{7}\right) - \left(-2\dfrac{1}{2}\right)$　　　**b)** $-2\dfrac{2}{3} \div \dfrac{3}{4}$

10. The high temperatures for a city during a five-day period were $4.5\ ^\circ\text{C}$, $2.3\ ^\circ\text{C}$, $-3.2\ ^\circ\text{C}$, $-11.7\ ^\circ\text{C}$, and $-9.8\ ^\circ\text{C}$. Determine the average temperature during the five-day period.

11. Evaluate $\left[-\dfrac{2}{3}\left(1\dfrac{4}{5}\right)\right]^2 + 2\left(-1\dfrac{1}{2}\right)^3$. Show your work.

Be Rational and Concentrate!

Mariel is creating a rational number concentration game. She is making "condition cards" for players to use to create numerical expressions that equal various numbers. She decides to test her cards using the number $-2\frac{3}{4}$. She finds a card whose condition can't be met to create an expression that equals this number. She places an "x" through this card.

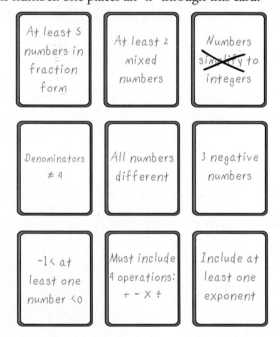

At least 5 numbers in fraction form

At least 2 mixed numbers

Numbers ~~simplify to~~ integers

Denominators $\neq$ 4

All numbers different

3 negative numbers

$-1 <$ at least one number < 0

Must include 4 operations: $+ - \times \div$

Include at least one exponent

❓ Which of Mariel's condition cards could you use to create an expression that equals $-2\frac{3}{4}$?

A. Create an expression that will equal $-2\frac{3}{4}$ when calculated, using as many of the condition cards above as possible. You get bonus points for using **all** of the condition cards!

B. Evaluate your expressions. Show your work.

C. Using only decimals, create an expression that evaluates to -5.6. Provide a minimum of five of your own "condition cards" that would describe the numbers and operations used in your expression.

D. Explain the process you used to create your expression.

Task | *Checklist*

✔ Did you check to make sure that all of the conditions are satisfied?

✔ Did you show all of the steps in your calculations?

✔ Did you check to make sure that your calculations are correct?

✔ Did you explain your thinking clearly?

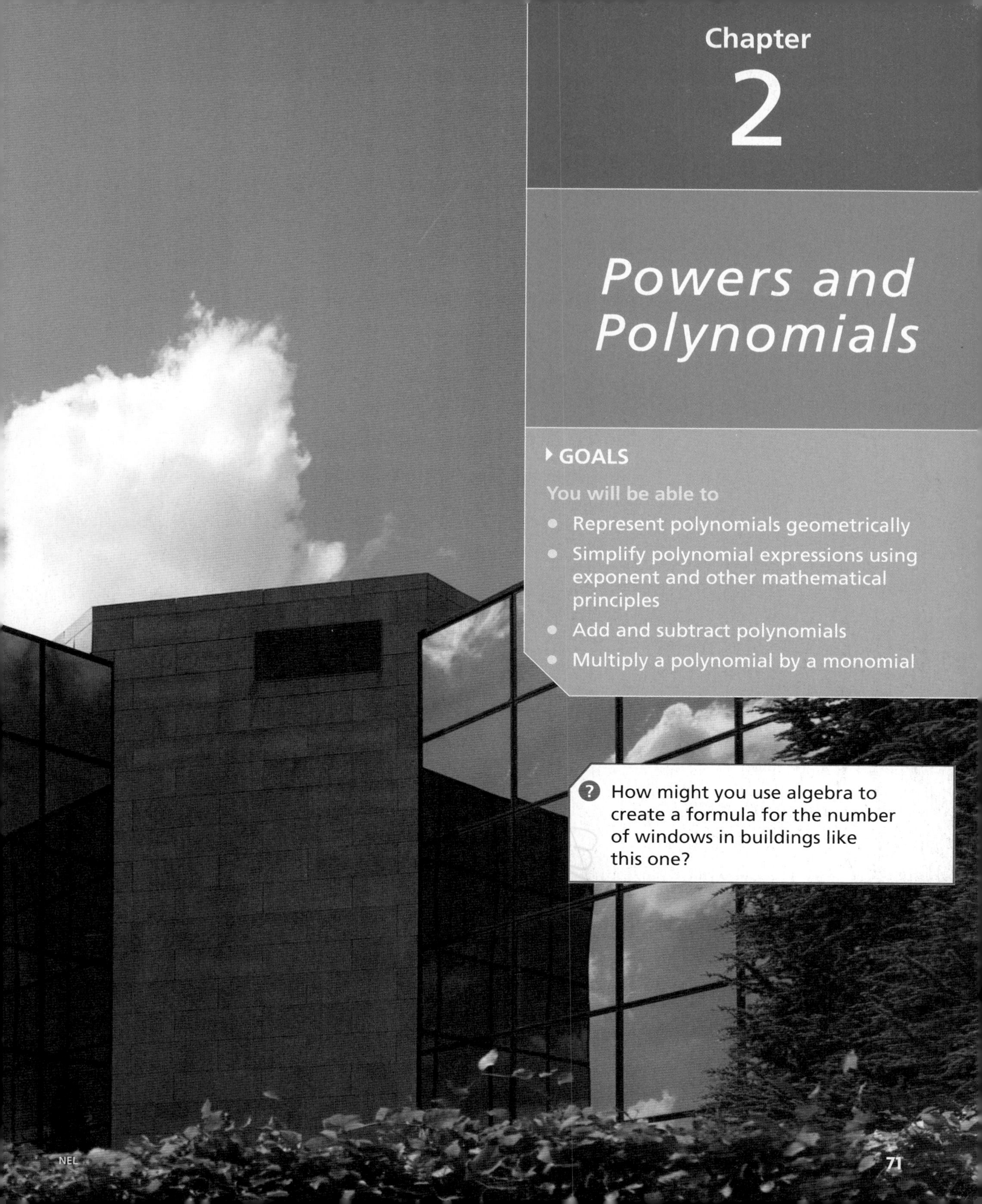

Chapter 7

Powers and Polynomials

▸ **GOALS**

You will be able to

- Represent polynomials geometrically
- Simplify polynomial expressions using exponent and other mathematical principles
- Add and subtract polynomials
- Multiply a polynomial by a monomial

? How might you use algebra to create a formula for the number of windows in buildings like this one?

WORDS YOU NEED to Know

1. Match each mathematical term to the highlighted example it most closely describes.

<table>
<tr><td>a) variable</td><td>c) power</td><td>e) exponent</td></tr>
<tr><td>b) constant</td><td>d) base</td><td>f) algebraic expression</td></tr>
</table>

    i) $5x^2 - 3x + 2$ **iii)** 2^3 **v)** $5x^2 - 3x + 2$

    ii) $5x^2 - 3x + 2$ **iv)** 3^4 **vi)** $5x^2 - 3x + 2$

SKILLS AND CONCEPTS You Need

Using an Area Model to Calculate a Product

You can use an area model to multiply multi-digit numbers. You can visualize how this works by representing the product of two numbers as the area of a rectangle. The final product is the sum of the areas of the smaller rectangles that make up the larger one.

EXAMPLE

To multiply 35×47, visualize this area model.

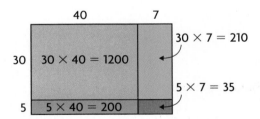

So, $35 \times 47 = (30 + 5) \times (40 + 7)$
$$= 30 \times 40 + 30 \times 7 + 5 \times 40 + 5 \times 7$$
$$= 1200 + 210 + 200 + 35$$
$$= 1645$$

2. Use an area model to evaluate each product.

    a) 24×52 **c)** $2\frac{1}{2} \times 3\frac{3}{4}$

    b) 12×46 **d)** $24 \times 1\frac{1}{4}$

Evaluating Algebraic Expressions

It's a good idea to place the values you substitute for the variables in brackets before you begin evaluating an expression. Then, follow the order of operations represented by the memory aid BEDMAS.

EXAMPLE

Determine the volume of the cylinder.

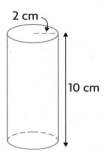

2 cm

10 cm

Solution

The formula for the volume of a cylinder is $V = \pi r^2 h$, where h is the height of the cylinder and r is the radius of its base.

$V = \pi r^2 h$

$\quad = \pi (2)^2 (10)$

$\quad = \pi (4)(10)$

$\quad = \pi (40)$

$\quad \doteq 125.6 \text{ cm}^3$

3. Evaluate these algebraic expressions if $a = 0$, $b = 1$, $c = -1$, and $d = 2$.

a) $b + 3c$

b) $3b + 2c - d$

c) $2a^2 + b - d$

d) $3(2b - 3c)$

e) $-4(a + b + c)$

f) $(5c - 6b)^2$

4. Use each formula and the given values to calculate the value of the indicated variable.

a) $P = 2(l + w)$; determine P when $l = 3$ cm and $w = 5$ cm

b) $A = \dfrac{b \times h}{2}$; determine A when $b = 5.5$ m and $h = 4$ m

c) $V = s^3$; determine V when $s = 12$ cm

d) $c = \sqrt{a^2 + b^2}$; determine c when $a = 5$ m and $b = 12$ m

Study | **Aid**

- For help, see the Review of Essential Skills and Knowledge Appendix.

Question	Appendix
5 and 6	A-1
7 and 8	A-10
10 and 11	A-11

SKATING TODAY

Adults: $5.00
Children: $2.50

PRACTICE

5. Represent each repeated multiplication as a power.
  a) $13 \times 13 \times 13 \times 13$
  b) $(-8)(-8)(-8)(-8)(-8)(-8)$
  c) $7 \times 6 \times 7 \times 6$

6. Represent each power using repeated multiplication.
  a) 7^4 **b)** $(-7)^4$ **c)** -7^4

7. Why does the expanded form $2 \times 10^3 + 6 \times 10^2 + 7 \times 10^1 + 3$ describe 2673?

8. Represent 1254 in expanded form.

9. Which of the following numbers are perfect squares: 16, 35, 100, 25, 1? Explain how you know.

10. Create an algebraic expression to describe the total cost for a group to go skating. Use A to represent the number of adults and C the number of children in the group.

11. Use variables and numbers to represent the total area of the congruent squares and congruent triangles.

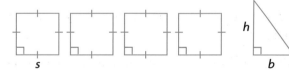

12. A word association chart is shown for the mathematical term "perfect square." Make another chart for one of these terms: base of a power, algebraic expression, or variable.

Math term	Drawing or description
perfect square	 5 ⬜ 5
My definition	**Reminds me of**
A perfect square is a number that is found by multiplying an integer by itself; 25 is a perfect square.	

APPLYING *What You Know*

Paper Folding

YOU WILL NEED
- sheet of paper

Toni folds a piece of paper in half. She does this many times. When she unfolds the paper, there are a lot of sections created by the fold lines.

? If Toni could fold the paper in half 12 times, how many sections would be created?

A. Fold the paper in half. Now open it up. How many sections does the fold create? Refold the paper.

B. Fold the paper in half again. How many sections are there now when you open it up? Refold the paper.

C. Continue to repeat part B for as long as you can. After each new fold, open the paper up and record the total number of sections in a table like this one before refolding.

Number of Folds	Number of Sections
0	1
1	
2	
3	

D. Write an algebraic expression to describe the pattern that relates the number of folds to the number of sections.

E. Use this expression to predict the number of sections if the paper could be folded 12 times.

Representing Powers Up to Degree 3

YOU WILL NEED

- straws
- scissors
- modelling clay

GOAL

Create geometric representations for powers and square roots.

LEARN ABOUT the Math

Anne's landscaping company sells large and small rectangular trim tiles, interior square tiles, and cube planters. She usually fills orders on an order form like the one below. But this time, Anne's supplier wants a one-line order from her.

	Trim Tiles	**Interior Tiles**	**Planters**
Large	60 cm 	60 cm  60 cm	60 cm 60 cm 60 cm 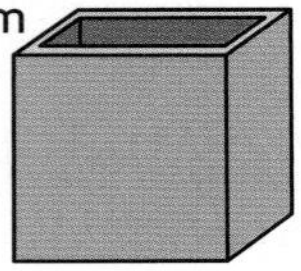
Small	30 cm 	30 cm  30 cm	30 cm 30 cm 30 cm 

Order Form						
Order Number	**Trim Tiles**		**Interior Tiles**		**Planters**	
	Small	**Large**	**Small**	**Large**	**Small**	**Large**
1		20		25		4
2	16		30		2	
3		15		50		1
4	40		100		6	
Total	56	35	130	75	8	5

❓ How can Anne represent the total numbers of each type of tile and planter on a one-line order?

EXAMPLE **1** Representing variables with models

Anne's Solution

I used straw lengths and **algebraic terms** of **degree** 1 to represent the lengths of the trim tiles.

I used straws to model the trim tiles. I used the variables *l* and *s* to represent the lengths of the large and small trim tiles.

I used algebraic terms of degree 2 to represent the areas of the square tiles.

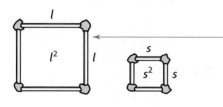

The side lengths of the interior tiles and planters are the same as the trim lengths. I used modelling clay and straws to build models of the square tiles.

I labelled the sides of the tiles and used their areas to name the tiles. The larger tile's area is l^2. The smaller tile's area is s^2.

I used algebraic terms of degree 3 to represent the volumes of the cubes.

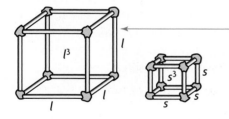

I built models of the planters and labelled their sides.

I used the volume of each of the cubes to name the planters. The larger planter's volume is l^3. The smaller planter's volume is s^3.

The order will ask for $56s$, $35l$, $130s^2$, $75l^2$, $8s^3$, and $5l^3$.

I wrote an algebraic expression to represent the number of each type of tile and planter. The **coefficient** of each term told how many of each I needed to order.

algebraic term

part of an algebraic expression; often separated from the rest of the expression by an addition or subtraction symbol (e.g., the expression $2x^2 + 3x + 4$ has three terms: $2x^2$, $3x$, and 4)

degree of a term

for a power with one variable, the degree is the variable's exponent; when there is more than one variable, the degree is the sum of the exponents of the powers of the variables (e.g., x^4, x^3y, and x^2y^2 all have degree 4)

coefficient

the factor by which a variable is multiplied (e.g., in the term $5x$, the coefficient is 5)

coefficient   variable

Reflecting

A. Why did Anne need only two variables to describe all of the items in her order?

B. How did Anne relate each algebraic expression to the shape it described?

APPLY the Math

EXAMPLE 2   Representing algebraic terms geometrically

Joe is having difficulty understanding the difference between $4t$, $(4t)^2$, and $(4t)^3$. How might his friend Caleb model these expressions to help him see the difference?

Caleb's Solution

I used 4 toothpicks in a row to model $4t$.

$\overline{\quad t \quad t \quad t \quad t \quad}$

I thought that if each toothpick represented a length of t, 4 in a row would represent a length of $4t$.

I used a square with side lengths of $4t$ to model $(4t)^2$.

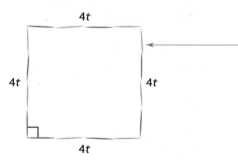

I know that the area of a square is the square of its side length. I represented that square using toothpicks. A square has 2 dimensions, so the exponent of 2 makes sense.

I used a cube with side lengths of $4t$ to model $(4t)^3$.

I know that the volume of a cube is the cube of its side length. A cube has 3 dimensions, so the exponent of 3 makes sense.

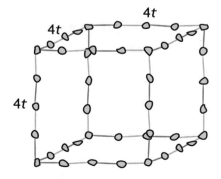

| EXAMPLE 3 | Connecting squares and square roots |

A square wall tile has an area of 116 cm². Determine the length of its side to two decimal places.

Jesselina's Solution

$Area = 116$ cm²
$l^2 = 116$ ◄——————

I knew that the area of a square is calculated by multiplying its side length *l* by itself.

$10^2 = 10 \times 10$
$= 100$
$11^2 = 11 \times 11$
$= 121$ ◄——

I knew that 10 squared is 100 and 11 squared is 121. So, I knew that the length was between 10 and 11.

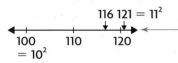

116 is quite a bit closer to 121 than to 100, so I thought that the answer was between 10.5 and 11.

To find the side length, I used my calculator to determine the square root of 116, since this is the inverse operation of squaring.

$\sqrt{116} \doteq 10.77$ ◄——

I rounded the result to two decimal places.

The side length of the tile is about 10.77 cm.

Powers and Polynomials **79**

Key Idea

- You can represent single variable terms with powers of 1, 2, or 3 using concrete materials or drawings. The degree of each term corresponds to the number of dimensions in the model.

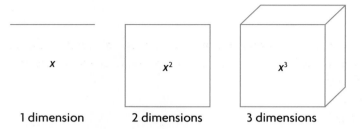

x	x^2	x^3
1 dimension	2 dimensions	3 dimensions

Need to Know

- You can think of $\sqrt{x^2} = x$ as the length of the side of a square with area x^2.
- Expressions involving terms of degree 1, 2, or 3 can be represented using combinations of the models shown above.

CHECK Your Understanding

1. Copy and label each object, then represent it with one of the following algebraic expressions: c, d, c^2, d^2, d^3 c^3.

a)

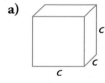

b)

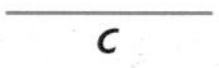

c)

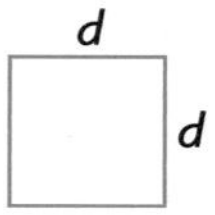

$$d$$
$$d$$

d)

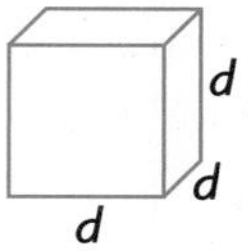

2. a) Calculate the side length of a square with an area of 49 cm².
   b) A square has an area of 110 cm². Without using a calculator, state the two whole numbers between which its side length is located.

PRACTISING

3. Sketch models to represent each of the following algebraic expressions.
The variables x and y do not represent the same number.

a) x^2

b) x^3

c) y

d) $(2y)^2$

4. The areas of some squares are shown. Determine or estimate the length of the sides of each square. Use a calculator to check your answers.

a) 144 km^2

b) 75 cm^2

c) 0.01 m^2

5. Choose the expression that represents the indicated quantity:
$\sqrt{(2x^2)}$, $2x$, $(2x)^2$, $(3x)^3$, $3y$, $(3y)^2$, $(3y)^3$.

a) the volume of the cube

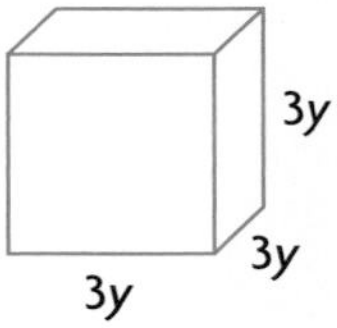

c) the side length

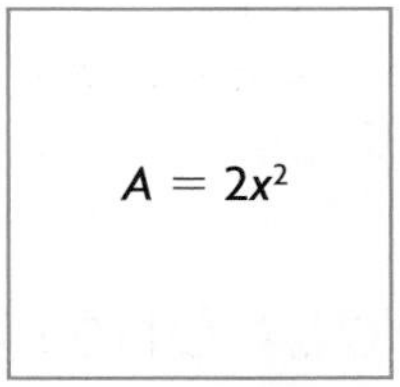

b) the length of the line

d) the area of the square face

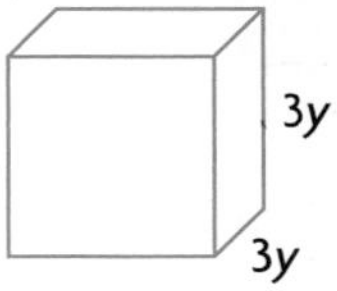

6. If the footprint of a square building has an area of 50 m^2, which is a better estimate for the length of the front of the building: 7.2 m or 7.7 m? Explain how you can answer this without using a calculator.

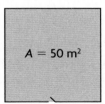

7. If the length of the side of a square game board is $\sqrt{1000}$ cm, what is the area of the game board? How can you check your answer?

8. A mosaic design is created to form a square from nine 2 cm × 2 cm red ceramic tiles and twelve 3 cm × 3 cm blue ceramic tiles.
   a) Sketch how this would look.
   b) What is the length of the side of the completed design?
   c) Explain how you know.

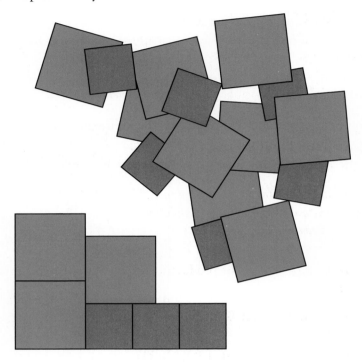

9. We read 4^2 as "4 squared" and 4^3 as "4 cubed." Sketch or build models that show why this makes sense.

Extending

10. Draw or build a model of the algebraic expression ab where a is not equal to b. Explain how this model is the same as and how it is different from a model of the algebraic expression a^2.

11. Draw or build a model of the algebraic expression abc where a, b, and c are not equal to each other. Compare this to a model of the algebraic expression ab^2.

12. The symbol $\sqrt[3]{}$ represents the cube root. For example, $4 \times 4 \times 4 = 64$, $\sqrt[3]{64} = 4$. Create a geometric model to represent $\sqrt[3]{64}$. Explain why the model makes sense.

2.2 Multiplying and Dividing Powers

GOAL

Develop and apply exponent principles to multiply and divide powers.

INVESTIGATE *the Math*

Amir thought there was a way to simplify $\dfrac{(3^6)(3^9)}{3^{12}}$ without using a calculator.

? How could Amir simplify this expression without a calculator?

A. Draw a table like the one shown. Use it to record the products of powers that have the same base but different exponents.

Extend the table until you see a pattern. Use the pattern to determine how to quickly multiply powers with the same base.

Multiplication	Expanded Form	Product Expressed as a Single Power
$(3^1)(3^2)$	$(3)(3 \times 3)$	3^3
$(3^2)(3^2)$	$(3 \times 3)(3 \times 3)$	3^4
$(3^3)(3^2)$		

B. How is the exponent of the product related to the exponents of the factors?

C. Test your answer to part B using these expressions. Check using a calculator.

    a) $(5^2)(5^4)$ **b)** $(2^2)(2^3)(2^4)$

D. Draw a new table like the one shown. Use it to record quotients with the same base and different positive integers for exponents.

Continue to add rows to the table until you see a pattern. Use the pattern to determine how to quickly divide powers with the same base.

Division	Expanded Form	Quotient Simplified and Expressed as a Single Power
$3^2 \div 3^1$	$\dfrac{(3 \times 3)}{3}$	$\dfrac{(3 \times 3)}{3} = 3^1$
$3^4 \div 3^2$	$\dfrac{(3 \times 3 \times 3 \times 3)}{(3 \times 3)}$	$\dfrac{(3 \times 3 \times 3 \times 3)}{(3 \times 3)} = 3^2$

E. How is the exponent of the quotient related to the exponents of the terms in the division statement?

NEL

Powers and Polynomials   **83**

F. Use your results in parts B and E to simplify $\dfrac{(3^6)(3^9)}{3^{12}}$ as a single power with base 3. Check your answer by calculating the value of the original and simplified expressions.

Reflecting

G. How can you determine the exponent of the product of powers with the same base?

H. How can you determine the exponent of the quotient of powers with the same base?

I. Why do the **principles** in parts G and H only apply to products and quotients of powers with the same base?

principle

a basic truth or rule about the way something works

APPLY the Math

EXAMPLE **1**	Representing an expression involving powers

Simplify $\dfrac{(x^7)(x^3)}{x^6}$.

Tony's Solution: Making a conjecture based on numeric examples

$\dfrac{(2^7)(2^3)}{(2^6)}$ I substituted 2 for *x* and calculated the value of the expression.

$= \dfrac{(128)(8)}{(64)}$

$= \dfrac{1024}{64}$

$= 16$

$= 2^4$ 16 is 2 × 2 × 2 × 2, which equals 2^4.

$\dfrac{(3^7)(3^3)}{(3^6)}$ Then, I substituted 3 for *x* and calculated the value of the expression.

$= \dfrac{2187 \times 27}{729}$

$= \dfrac{59049}{729}$

$= 81$

$= 3^4$ 81 is 3 × 3 × 3 × 3, which equals 3^4.

I think that $\dfrac{(x^7)(x^3)}{x^6} = x^4$ ← In both cases, the final power had an exponent of 4.
I thought the same pattern would work for any base.

Danny's Solution: Reasoning using the definition of a power

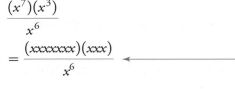

$$\dfrac{(x^7)(x^3)}{x^6}$$

$$= \dfrac{(xxxxxxx)(xxx)}{x^6}$$ ← I looked at the numerator and wrote out the powers in expanded form. This showed me that the numerator was x^{10}.

$$\dfrac{\overset{1}{(\cancel{xxxxxx}x)}(xxxx)}{\underset{1}{\cancel{xxxxxx}x}}$$ ← I wrote out the denominator in expanded form. I simplified the fraction by dividing 6 of the xs in the numerator and denominator.

$xxxx = x^4$ ← This left 4 xs multiplied together, which I wrote as x^4.

So, $\dfrac{(x^7)(x^3)}{x^6} = x^4$.

Patty's Solution: Reasoning using exponent principles

$$\left(\dfrac{x^7}{x^6}\right)x^3$$

$$= (x)(x^3)$$ ← I divided x^7 by x^6 using the exponent principle for division. Subtracting 6 from 7, I got 1. I didn't need to write the exponent because x^1 is the same as x.

$(x)(x^3) = x^4$ ← I used the exponent principle for multiplication. Since $1 + 3$ is 4, my final answer was x^4.

$$\dfrac{(x^7)(x^3)}{x^6}$$

$$= x^{7+3-6}$$

$$= x^4$$ ← I saw that I could have reached the same answer in one step by just adding the exponents in the numerator and subtracting the exponent in the denominator.

> Communication | **Tip**
>
> Any variable without a visible exponent is understood to have an exponent of 1. For example, $x = x^1$, $2y = 2y^1$, and $-4c = -4c^1$.

EXAMPLE **2**

Selecting a strategy to evaluate an expression with two variables

Simplify $\dfrac{(x^4y^3)(x^3y^5)}{x^5y^5}$ and evaluate when $x = 3$ and $y = -2$.

Kathryn's Solution: Using an algebraic strategy to first simplify the expression

$$\dfrac{(x^4y^3)(x^3y^5)}{x^5y^5}$$

$$= \dfrac{(x^4x^3)(y^3y^5)}{x^5y^5}$$

$$= \dfrac{x^7y^8}{x^5y^5}$$

Everything in the numerator was multiplied together. I rewrote it so that powers of the same base were side by side. Then, I simplified by adding the exponents of the powers having the same base.

$$= x^{7-5}y^{8-5}$$

$$= x^2y^3$$

I divided powers having the same base. I did this by subtracting the exponent of the denominator from the exponent of the numerator.

$$= 3^2(-2)^3$$

$$= 9(-8)$$

$$= -72$$

I substituted 3 for x and -2 for y, and evaluated. The result was -72.

Jeremy's Solution: Using a substitution strategy

$$\dfrac{(x^4y^3)(x^3y^5)}{x^5y^5}$$

$$= \dfrac{[3^4(-2)^3][3^3(-2)^5]}{3^5(-2)^5}$$

I substituted 3 for x and -2 for y into the question.

$$\dfrac{[81(-8)][27(-32)]}{243(-32)}$$

I calculated the expressions inside each set of brackets.

$$= \dfrac{[-648][-864]}{-7776}$$

$$= \dfrac{559\,872}{-7776}$$

I did the final multiplication and division.

$$= -72$$

EXAMPLE **3**	Applying exponent principles to simplify expressions where the base has multiple factors

Simplify $\dfrac{\left(-\dfrac{2}{5}xy\right)^5}{\left(-\dfrac{2}{5}\right)^3 xy}$.

Miranda's Solution: Connecting exponent principles to fraction operations

$$\dfrac{\left(-\dfrac{2}{5}xy\right)^5}{\left(-\dfrac{2}{5}\right)^3 xy}$$

$$= \dfrac{\left(-\dfrac{2}{5}\right)^5 x^5 y^5}{\left(-\dfrac{2}{5}\right)^3 xy}$$

I expressed the numerator as three separate powers because I knew that the exponent 5 outside of the brackets referred to each of the factors inside.

$$= \left(-\dfrac{2}{5}\right)^{(5-3)} x^{(5-1)} y^{(5-1)}$$

Then, I divided powers having the same base by subtracting their exponents. I knew that x and y in the denominator each had an exponent of 1.

$$= \left(-\dfrac{2}{5}\right)^2 x^4 y^4$$

$$= \dfrac{4}{25} x^4 y^4$$

I evaluated $\left(-\dfrac{2}{5}\right)^2$ by multiplying.

$$\left(-\dfrac{2}{5}\right)\left(-\dfrac{2}{5}\right) = \dfrac{4}{25}.$$

> **Communication** | *Tip*
>
> You can rewrite a product or quotient raised to an exponent by applying the exponent to each of the terms. For example,
>
> $(xy)^2 = x^2 y^2$ and $\left(\dfrac{x}{y}\right)^3 = \dfrac{x^3}{y^3}$.

If each rational number in an algebraic expression can be expressed as a terminating decimal, you can write each number as such and then simplify the equivalent expression.

Lee's Solution: Connecting exponent principles to decimal operations

$$\frac{(-0.4xy)^5}{(-0.4)^3xy}$$

$$= \frac{(-0.4)^5x^5y^5}{(-0.4)^3xy}$$

I converted each fraction to its decimal equivalent. Then, I expressed the numerator as three separate powers because I knew that the exponent 5 outside the brackets referred to each of the factors inside.

$$= (-0.4)^{(5-3)}x^{(5-1)}y^{(5-1)}$$

I divided powers having the same base by subtracting their exponents. The x and y in the denominator each had an exponent of 1.

$$= (-0.4)^2x^4y^4$$
$$= 0.16x^4y^4$$

I evaluated $(-0.4)^2$. The final result was $0.16x^4y^4$.

EXAMPLE 4   **Using exponent principles to solve a problem involving large numbers**

The M31 galaxy in the constellation of Andromeda is about 2.4×10^{19} km away. Light travels at about 9.5×10^{12} km/year. Estimate how long it would take light to reach Earth from M31.

Kyle's Solution

I used the formula $t = \dfrac{d}{s}$.

I needed to divide the distance to the M31 galaxy by the speed of light to find the time in years.

$d = 2.4 \times 10^{19}$ km
$s = 9.5 \times 10^{12}$ km/year
$$t = \frac{2.4 \times 10^{19}}{9.5 \times 10^{12}}$$

I estimated this to be about
$$\frac{2 \times 10^{19}}{10 \times 10^{12}}.$$

2.4×10^{19} is close to 2×10^{19}, 9.5×10^{12} is close to 10×10^{12}, and 10×10^{12} is 10^{13}.

$$= \frac{2 \times 10^{19}}{10^{13}}$$

I used the exponent principle for quotients to simplify the expression.

$$= 2 \times 10^{19-13}$$
$$= 2 \times 10^6$$

$$\frac{2.4 \times 10^{19}}{9.5 \times 10^{12}} \doteq 2\ 000\ 000 \longleftarrow$$

$10^6 = 1\ 000\ 000$, so 2×10^6
$= 2\ 000\ 000$.

The light from M31 takes about
2 000 000 years to reach Earth!

In Summary

Key Idea

- When two powers have the same base, these principles can be used to simplify their product or quotient:

Exponent Principle for Products	Exponent Principle for Quotients
$(a^m)(a^n) = a^{m+n}$	$(a^m) \div (a^n) = a^{m-n}\ (a \neq 0)$

For example, $(2^2)(2^3) = 2^{2+3} = 2^5$ and $3^4 \div 3^2 = 3^{4-2} = 3^2$.

Need to Know

- These exponent principles only work when the powers involved have the same base.
- It is more efficient to simplify an algebraic expression involving powers before substituting to evaluate it.
- An exponent applied to a product or quotient can be written by applying the exponent to each of its terms. In general $(ab)^m = a^m b^m$ and $\left(\dfrac{a}{b}\right)^m = \dfrac{a^m}{b^m}\ (b \neq 0)$.

CHECK Your Understanding

1. Simplify.
   a) $(2^2)(2^3)$
   b) $(x^4)(x^3)$

2. Simplify.
   a) $\dfrac{2^5}{2^2}$
   b) $\dfrac{y^6}{y^3}$

3. Simplify if possible, and then evaluate.
   a) $\dfrac{(2^7)}{(2^5)}$
   b) $\dfrac{(5^5)(3)(3^4)}{(3^3)(5^4)}$

4. Simplify, and then evaluate for $x = 2$ and $y = 5$.
   a) $\dfrac{(x^4)(x^3)}{x^6}$
   b) $\dfrac{y^6 x^4}{x^3 y^3}$ $y^3 * x$

PRACTISING

5. Simplify.

   a) $(5^2)(5^8)$

   b) $(m^4)(m^2)$

   c) $(7^3)(7)(x^4)(x^2)$

   d) $\left(\dfrac{2}{5}\right)^3\left(\dfrac{2}{5}\right)^2\left(\dfrac{2}{5}\right)^4$

6. Simplify.

   a) $(n^5)(w^6)(n^3)(w^7)$

   b) $(m^3)(m^4)(r^8)(m^2)(r^2)$

   c) $2^5(p^3)2^2(p^2)(p^8)$

   d) $(b^5)3^4(b^3)3^2(b^7)$

   e) $(x^4)(-2)(x^5)(-2)^3$

   f) $(a^5)(3^2)(a^4)(a)(3)$

7. Why do you get the same result for each of these expressions?

   a) $(5^7)(5^4)$ $5''$

   b) $(5^6)(5^5)$ $5'$

   c) $(5^4)(5^2)(5^5)$ $5''$

   d) $(5^3)(5)(5^5)(5^2)$ $5''$

8. Simplify.

   a) $\dfrac{5^7}{5^2}$

   b) $\dfrac{m^4}{m^2}$

   c) $\dfrac{(2^5)(x^3)}{(2^4)(x^2)}$

   d) $\dfrac{(-5)^3 y^{10}}{(-5)(y^6)(y^3)}$

9. Simplify.

   a) $\dfrac{(7^6)(a^3)(7^2)}{(7^3)a}$

   b) $\dfrac{(10^{10})x^4 y^5}{(10^8)xy}$

   c) $\dfrac{(xy)^5}{x^4 y^3}$

   d) $\dfrac{x^2 y^4}{x^3 y}$

10. Create four different expressions involving exponents that simplify to 7^8.

11. Simplify if possible, and then evaluate.

K

   a) $\dfrac{2^8}{2^5}$

   b) $\dfrac{(4^5)(4^6)}{4^7}$

   c) $\dfrac{(7^3)(3^2)(3^4)(7)}{(3^3)(7^2)}$

   d) $\dfrac{(4.2^3)(4.2^5)}{4.2^7}$

   e) $\dfrac{\left(\dfrac{2}{7}\right)^4}{\left(\dfrac{2}{7}\right)^2}$

   f) $\dfrac{\left(\dfrac{4}{5}\right)^5\left(\dfrac{4}{5}\right)^4}{\left(\dfrac{4}{5}\right)^6}$

12. Simplify, and then evaluate for $x = 2$ and $y = 5$.

   a) $\dfrac{(x^5)(x^4)}{x^8}$

   b) $\dfrac{(y^6)(y^4)}{(y^8)(y)}$

   c) $\dfrac{(y^6)(x^4)}{(x^3)(y^3)}$

   d) $\dfrac{250y^6}{125y^3}$

   e) $\dfrac{6(x^4)(y^6)}{3(x^3)y^3}$

   f) $\dfrac{\left(\dfrac{3}{4}xy\right)^3}{\left(\dfrac{3}{4}\right)^2 xy^2}$

13. If you know that the product of two powers is 7^{10} and that the
Ⓐ quotient is 7^2, what could the two powers be? How could you verify
your answer?

14. Scientists estimate that there are 50×10^{12} cells in the average human.
Ⓣ There are approximately 6×10^9 humans in the world. Approximately
how many cells do all the humans on Earth have? Write your answer
using a power with base 10.

15. Explain why it is necessary for the bases to be the same in order to
Ⓒ apply the multiplication and division principles for exponents.

Extending

16. a) Complete the table to show the relationship between the metric
units of length. Express each relationship as a power with base 10.

	Millimetres	Centimetres	Metres	Kilometres
Millimetres				
Centimetres				
Metres				
Kilometres				

   b) Determine the number of centimetres in 5 km.
   c) Determine the number of millimetres in 4 m.

17. A piece of steel plate is used to make a railway car. The plate is 2.5 m
wide, 3.2 m long, and 0.5 cm thick. Determine the volume of steel in
cubic centimetres.

18. The annual worldwide production of all grains is about 9×10^{12} kg.
How much grain is produced per person if there are approximately
6×10^9 people in the world?

19. a) Evaluate $\dfrac{3^5}{3^5}$.

   b) Simplify $\dfrac{3^5}{3^5}$ using the exponent principle for quotients.

   c) Use the meaning of the powers in $\dfrac{3^5}{3^5}$ to simplify the expression.

   d) Discuss what 3^0 might mean.

   e) Discuss whether a^0 would have a similar meaning for any
value of a.

Power of a Power

Simplify expressions involving a power of a power.

LEARN ABOUT *the Math*

Sue and Joe want to spread the news about school picture day. Sue suggests that she call 2 people and ask each person called to call 2 more people, and so on. Joe suggests that he call 4 people and ask each person called to call 4 more people, and so on.

Joe says that with his plan, the same number of people would be called on the 4th round of calls as on the 8th round of calls with Sue's plan.

? Is Joe right?

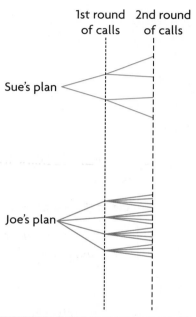

1st round of calls   2nd round of calls

Sue's plan

Joe's plan

EXAMPLE 1   Representing a power as an equivalent power

Determine and compare the number of people called on the 8th round of calls using Sue's plan and on the 4th round of calls using Joe's plan.

Jaan's Solution: Representing 2^8 as a power with base 4

$2^8 = 2 \times 2 \times 2 \times 2 \times 2 \times 2 \times 2 \times 2$

> I started by looking at 2^8, since that is the number of people who would be called in the 8th round with Sue's plan.

$2^8 = (2 \times 2) \times (2 \times 2) \times (2 \times 2) \times (2 \times 2)$
$\quad = (2^2)(2^2)(2^2)(2^2)$
$\quad = (2^2)^4$
$\quad = 4^4$

> I grouped the 2s in pairs. Each pair could be written as 2^2 and was equal to 4. I now had four 4s multiplied together.

4^4 is how many people would be called after the 4th round with Joe's plan.

2^8 is the same as 4^4. So, Joe is right.

> I used my calculator to evaluate the powers.
> $2^8 = 256$ and $4^4 = 256$, so I knew Joe was right.

Marie's Solution: Representing 4^4 as a power with base 2

$4^4 = 4 \times 4 \times 4 \times 4$ ← I started by looking at 4^4 because that is the number called in round 4 of Joe's plan.

$4 \times 4 \times 4 \times 4$
$= (2^2)(2^2)(2^2)(2^2)$ ← I wrote each 4 as 2^2.
$= (2^2)^4$
$= 2 \times 2 \times 2 \times 2 \times 2 \times 2 \times 2 \times 2$
$= 2^8$

4^4 is the same as 2^8. So, Joe is right. ← I used my calculator to evaluate the powers. $2^8 = 256$ and $4^4 = 256$, so I knew Joe was right.

Reflecting

A. How did Jaan and Marie use different representations to show that Joe was correct?

B. Why could 2^8 also have been written as $(2^4)^2$?

C. How could you use Jaan's approach to write 8^4 as a single power of 2? How does this strategy demonstrate a principle for calculating a power of a power?

> **Communication | Tip**
>
> When expressing a power of a power, use brackets to indicate the base to which the outermost exponent applies. For example, $(2^3)^4$ means $(2^3)(2^3)(2^3)(2^3)$.

APPLY the Math

EXAMPLE 2	Selecting a strategy to simplify a power of a power

Simplify $(x^5)^3$.

Jordi's Solution: Reasoning using products of powers with the same base

$(x^5)^3$
$= (x^5)(x^5)(x^5)$
$= x^{5+5+5}$ ← I used the principle for multiplying powers with the same base.
$= x^{15}$

$(x^5)^3$ ← So, x to the power of 5 all to the power of 3 is the same as x to the power of 15.
$= x^{15}$

Parm's Solution: Reasoning using the power-of-a-power principle

$(x^5)^3$
$= x^{5 \times 3}$
$= x^{15}$

> When I use numbers I can multiply or divide exponents if the bases are the same, so I assumed that this would also be true with variables.
>
> I applied the power-of-a-power principle by multiplying the exponents 5 and 3 together.

$(x^5)^3$
$= x^{15}$

> So, x to the power of 5 all to the power of 3 is x to the power of 15.

EXAMPLE 3 | **Simplifying an expression when the base is a term with more than one variable**

Simplify $\dfrac{(2x^2y^3)^3}{(2xy^2)^2}$.

Teresa's Solution: Reasoning using the exponent principle for products

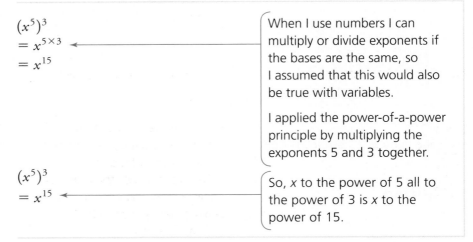

$\dfrac{(2x^2y^3)^3}{(2xy^2)^2}$

$= \dfrac{(2x^2y^3)(2x^2y^3)(2x^2y^3)}{(2xy^2)(2xy^2)}$

$= \dfrac{(2)(2)(2)(x^2)(x^2)(x^2)(y^3)(y^3)(y^3)}{(2)(2)(x)(x)(y^2)(y^2)}$

$= \dfrac{(2^3)(x^6)(y^9)}{(2^2)(x^2)(y^4)}$

> I started by writing the numerator and denominator using repeated multiplication.
>
> Then I rearranged the numerator and denominator by putting the factors with the same base side-by-side.
>
> I rewrote each expression by using the exponent principle for multiplication, adding the exponents where the base was the same.

$$= (2x^4 y^5)$$ ← I simplified the expression by using the exponent principle for division, subtracting the exponents where the base was the same.

Marty's Solution: Reasoning using the power-of-a-power principle

$$\frac{(2x^2y^3)^3}{(2xy^2)^2}$$

$$= \frac{(2)^3(x^2)^3(y^3)^3}{(2)^2(x)^2(y^2)^2}$$ ← The exponents outside the brackets in the numerator and the denominator apply to all of the factors inside the brackets. This means that I could write the expression as a product of separate factors.

$$= \frac{(2^3)(x^6)(y^9)}{(2^2)(x^2)(y^4)}$$ ← To simplify a power of a power, I multiplied the exponents.

$$= 2x^4y^5$$ ← To divide when the bases are the same, I subtracted the exponent in the denominator from the exponent in the numerator.

In Summary

Key Idea

- When a power is raised to another exponent the following principle can be used to simplify the power.

Exponent Principle for Power of a Power
$(a^m)^n = a^{mn}$

For example, $(a^4)^3 = a^{4 \times 3} = a^{12}$.

Need to Know

- If you have the power of a product, the outer exponent refers to each factor inside the brackets. For example:
  $(a^m b^n)^p = (a^m)^p \times (b^n)^p = a^{mp} b^{np}$.
- If you have the power of a quotient, the outer exponent refers to each term inside the brackets. For example:
  $\left(\dfrac{a^m}{b^n}\right)^p = \dfrac{a^{mp}}{b^{np}} \ (b \neq 0)$.

CHECK Your Understanding

1. Express each of the following as a power with a single exponent.

   a) $(7^3)^5$ b) $(x^4)^6$ c) $(c^3)^2$

2. Express each of the following as a power with a different base.

   a) 16   b) 4^3 c) 9^4

PRACTISING

3. Express each of the following as a power with a single exponent.

   a) $(3^4)^2$ c) $(2^5)^3$ e) $(x^2)^3$

   b) $(9^4)^3$ d) $(10^6)^6$ f) $(5^2)^4$

4. Express each of the following as a power with the base indicated.

   a) 16^2 with a base of 4
   b) 16^2 with a base of 2
   c) 25^3 with a base of 5
   d) 27^3 with a base of 3

5. Explain each principle, and then give a numerical example.

   C   a) $(a^m)^n = a^{mn}$

        b) $(a^m b^n)^p = a^{mp} b^{np}$

        c) $\left(\dfrac{a^m}{b^n}\right)^p = \dfrac{a^{mp}}{b^{np}}$

6. Simplify.

   K

   a) $(3^4)^2(3^5)$ c) $\dfrac{(2^3)^3}{2^4}$ e) $\dfrac{(5^5 \times 5^2)^2}{(5^4 \times 5)^2}$

   b) $(5^4)^3(5^4)^3$ d) $\dfrac{(10^4)^2}{(10^2)^3}$ f) $\left(\dfrac{3^5}{3^3}\right)^2$

7. Simplify.

   a) $(y^3)^4$ b) $(m^2)^3$ c) $(c^3)^3$ d) $(n^3)^4$

8. Simplify.

   a) $(v^2)^2(v)$ c) $\dfrac{(k^5)^3}{k^2}$ e) $\dfrac{(x^2 x^3)^4}{(x^5 x)^3}$

   b) $(n^4)^3(n^2)^3$ d) $\dfrac{(j^8)^2}{(j^5)^2}$ f) $\left(\dfrac{y^6}{y^4}\right)^3$

9. Simplify.

   a) $(3a^2)^3$ c) $(-2m^2)^4$ e) $(5a^2 \times 2b^3)^2$

   b) $(5x^5)^2$ d) $(4^3 p^4)^2$ f) $(3x^4 y^2)^3$

10. Simplify.

a) $(4^3 \times 3^2)^2(4^5 \times 3^2)^3$

c) $\dfrac{(2^5 \times 5^2)^2}{(2^4 \times 5)^2}$

b) $(2x^3)^4(2x^2)^5$

d) $\dfrac{(5a^3)^5}{(5a^5b^2)^2}$

11. Simplify.

a) $(2y^3)^4$

c) $(3a^3)^2(3^3a^5b^2)^2$

b) $(3x^5)^2$

d) $\dfrac{(5^3a^4)^5}{(5^4a^3)^2}$

12. Without actually computing the values, explain how you know that
T each expression below is equal to 0.

a) $(3^2)^6 - (3^3)^4$ **b)** $(10^2)^8 - (10^4)^4$ **c)** $(-2^3)^2 - (-2^2)^3$

13. The length of the side of a cube is 3^5. Express its surface area (SA) and
A volume (V) using powers and simplify.

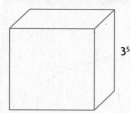

3^5

14. Determine an expression for the area of the square drawn on the
hypotenuse.

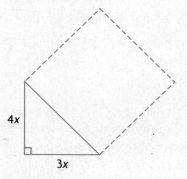

$4x$

$3x$

15. Evaluate.

a) $\dfrac{(2^3)^4}{(2^2)^5}$

c) $\dfrac{(6)(2^3)^3}{(2^2)^4}$

e) $\dfrac{(5^2)(6^6)}{(5^1)^4(6^2)^3}$

b) $\dfrac{(5^3)^6}{(5^3)^5}$

d) $\dfrac{(5^2)^3(7^3)^4}{(7^{11})(5^5)}$

f) $\dfrac{[(2^4)^2]^3}{[(2^2)^3]^2}$

16. Simplify and evaluate each. Use $a = 2$, $b = -1$, and $c = 4$.

a) $\dfrac{a^5}{a^2}$

b) $(b^3)^2$

c) $\dfrac{(c^2)^3}{c^5}$

d) $\dfrac{a^3 b^3}{ab}$

17. Show that 3^{10} is the same as 9^5 using your understanding of exponents.

18. Simplify and evaluate each.

a) $\dfrac{(x^5)^2(x^7)^3}{(x^4)^6}$ when $x = 2$

b) $\dfrac{(m)^{11}}{(m^5)^2} + \dfrac{n^7}{(n^2)^3}$ when $m = 3$ and $n = 4$

c) Explain how using exponent principles helped you to solve these problems.

19. Determine the value of the exponent that makes each statement true.

a) $4^3 = 2^\blacksquare$

b) $6^9 = 216^\blacksquare$

c) $625^2 = 25^\blacksquare$

d) $27^4 = 3^\blacksquare$

20. Write each power in simplified form.

a) 4^5 as a power of 2   c) 27^4 as a power of 3

b) 9^6 as a power of 3   d) $(-125)^7$ as a power of (-5)

21. Knowing that 2^3 is 8 and 3^2 is 9, how do you know that $2^{30} < 3^{20}$?

22. Describe the relationship between the power-of-a-power principle and the other exponent principles you know.

Extending

23. Jody's calculator will only input one-digit numbers. The exponent key and the display are working fine. Explain how she can use her calculator to evaluate each of the following.

a) 25^4 b) 16^2

24. Explain why you can write 2^8 as a power having a base of 4 and an integer as an exponent, but cannot do this for 2^7.

Curious | Math

Google This!

In 1920, mathematician Edward Kassner asked his nine-year-old nephew Milton Sirotta what name he should give to the number 10^{100}. "A googol," came the boy's reply, and the name stuck. How large do you think a googol is?

1. What does 10^{100} mean?

2. If you were to write 10^{100} out in long hand, how many zeros would there be after the 1?

3. The number 10^{googol} is called a googolplex. Describe what the number 10^{googol} would look like.

4. Express 10^{googol} another way.

5. How long might it take you to write all the digits of one million (10^6)? What about one billion (10^9)?

6. Suppose you could keep writing zeros without taking a break. About how long would it take you to write out the whole number equivalent of a googol? What about a googolplex?

7. Can you think of a number greater than a googolplex?

8. Explain why the founders of Google™ might have chosen this name as the name of their search engine.

FREQUENTLY ASKED Questions

Study Aid

- See Lesson 2.1,
  Examples 1 and 2.
- Try Mid-Chapter Review
  Question 1.

Q: How can you use models to represent powers and square roots?

A1: You can draw a line segment to represent the variable x, for example. You can then use it to represent x^2 and x^3.

EXAMPLE

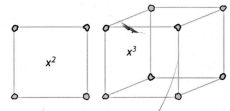

Study Aid

- See Lesson 2.1,
  Example 3.
- Try Mid-Chapter Review
  Question 2.

A2: If x^2 represents the area of a square, then $\sqrt{x^2}$ represents the side length of the square. They are inverse operations of each other.

EXAMPLE

$13^2 = 169$; $\sqrt{169} = 13$.

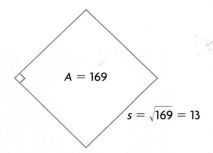

Study Aid

- See Lesson 2.2,
  Example 1 and Lesson 2.3,
  Examples 2 and 3.
- Try Mid-Chapter Review
  Questions 3, 4, 5, and 6.

Q: How can you simplify an expression involving powers?

A: You can apply one or all of the following principles.

	Product Principle for Powers with the Same Base	Quotient Principle for Powers with the Same Base	Power-of-a-Power Principle
Statement of Principle	$(a^m)(a^n) = a^{m+n}$	$(a^m) \div (a^n) = a^{m-n}$ if $a \neq 0$	$(a^m)^n = a^{mn}$
Example	$3^2 \times 3^3 = 3^{2+3}$ $= 3^5$	$5^{10} \div 5^6 = 5^{10-6}$ $= 5^4$	$(4^3)^5 = 4^{3\times5}$ $= 4^{15}$

PRACTICE Questions

Lesson 2.1

1. Suppose you created models of a, b, a^2, b^2, a^3, and b^3 and that a and b are different. How would the models of each pair be alike and how would they be different?
   a) a and b
   b) a^2 and b^2
   c) a^3 and b^3
   d) a^2 and a^3

2. Draw a diagram or make a model to represent each of the following:
   a) $(3y)^2$
   b) $3y$
   c) y^3

3. The area of this square is 72 m^2.
   a) Estimate the length of the side of the square.
   b) Represent the exact side length using the square root sign.
   c) Use a calculator to determine the square's side length to two decimal places.

   $A = 72 \text{ m}^2$

Lesson 2.2

4. Simplify.
   a) $(5^3)(5^6)$
   b) $(-2)^3(-2^7)$
   c) $\dfrac{(5^6)}{(5^2)}$
   d) $\dfrac{(7^3)(7^6)}{7}$
   e) $(7^3)(2^6)(7^2)(2^5)$
   f) $\dfrac{(7^3)(2^6)}{(7^2)(2^5)}$

5. Simplify.
   a) $\left(\dfrac{5}{7}\right)^3\left(\dfrac{5}{7}\right)^6$
   b) $\dfrac{\left(\dfrac{-2}{5}\right)^{13}}{\left(\dfrac{-2}{5}\right)^7}$
   c) $(3.1)^8(3.1)^2$
   d) $\dfrac{(0.012)^3}{(0.012)}$

6. Simplify.
   a) $(x^2)(x^6)$
   b) $(y^3)(y^6)$
   c) $\dfrac{(m^6)}{(m^5)}$
   d) $\dfrac{(n^3)(n^2)}{n}$
   e) $(ab^7)(a^3)(b^4)$
   f) $\dfrac{(x^5)(y^6)}{(x^3)(y)}$

7. Simplify.
   a) $(2^3)(x^2)(2^2)(x^5)$
   b) $(5^3)(y^3)(5^3)(y^6)$
   c) $\dfrac{(4^4)(m^6)}{(4m)}$
   d) $\dfrac{(6^3)(q^5)(q^2)}{6q^4}$

8. Explain why the bases must be the same to apply the exponent principle when multiplying powers.

9. The diameter of the Earth is about 1.3×10^4 km. The diameter of the Sun is about 1.4×10^6 km. About how many "Earths" could you line up along the Sun's diameter?

Lesson 2.3

10. Simplify:
    a) $(5^3)^5$
    b) $(x^3)^4$
    c) $(2x^3)^7$
    d) $\left[\left(\dfrac{8}{5}\right)^3\right]^4$

11. Express each of the following numbers with the base indicated:
    a) 32^3 with a base of 2
    b) 81^2 with a base of 9
    c) 81^2 with a base of 3
    d) 100^{15} with a base of 10

12. Simplify.
    a) $(5^3)^5(5^4)^4$
    b) $(x^3)^4(x^5)^4$
    c) $(m^3)^4(2x^3)^7(m^3)^4(x^3)^7$
    d) $\dfrac{(m^3)^4(2x^2)^7}{2^5(m^3)^3(x^3)^2}$

13. Explain why each of the following simplifies to x^{36}:
    a) $(x^2)^{18}$
    b) $(x^6)^6$
    c) $(x^3)^{12}$
    d) $(x^9)^4$

14. Determine a simplified expression for the surface area and volume of this cube. The length of each side is 2^5 cm.

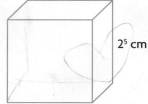

2^5 cm

Adding and Subtracting Polynomials

YOU WILL NEED

- algebra tiles

GOAL

Add and subtract like terms.

LEARN ABOUT *the Math*

A class is playing a game with algebra tiles. The game has the following rules:

- A player gets two pouches. Each contains six randomly selected algebra tiles.
- A player can use the **zero principle** to add the tiles in the two pouches or subtract the tiles in the second pouch from those in the first.
- The goal is to end up with the fewest tiles.

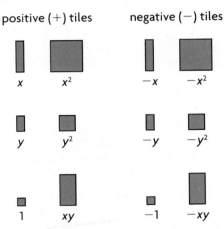

positive (+) tiles   negative (−) tiles

x x^2 $-x$ $-x^2$

y y^2 $-y$ $-y^2$

1 xy -1 $-xy$

? How can you decide if you should add or subtract?

EXAMPLE 1 | **Using a concrete model to represent an operation**

Farell and Peter received the following tiles in their pouches.

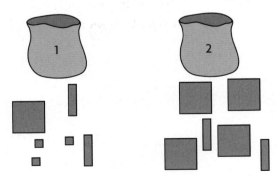

Should they add or subtract to get a result that uses the fewest number of tiles?

Farell's Solution: Representing and simplifying a sum using algebra tiles

x^2 x x 1 1 1

Add (+) ◄──────────

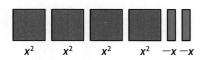

x^2 x^2 x^2 x^2 $-x$ $-x$

I arranged the algebra tiles from the two pouches and decided to add them by combining **like terms**.

like terms

algebraic terms that have the same variables and exponents apart from their numerical coefficients (e.g., $2x^2$ and $-3x$)

I need to calculate
$(x^2 + 2x + 3) + (4x^2 - 2x)$

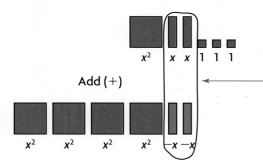

x^2 x x 1 1 1

Add (+)

x^2 x^2 x^2 x^2 $-x$ $-x$

I figured positive- and negative-x tiles could be combined to makes zeros using the zero principle, just as with opposite integers. So, I paired the two positive-x tiles with the two negative-x tiles and removed them.

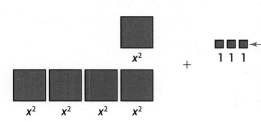

x^2 +   1 1 1

x^2 x^2 x^2 x^2

There were 5 x^2 tiles and 3 unit tiles left. I couldn't combine the x^2 tiles and the unit tiles since they were different things.

The expression I get by adding the two polynomials is $5x^2 + 3$ and that uses 8 tiles.

Peter's Solution: Representing and simplifying a difference using algebra tiles

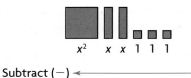

x^2 x x 1   1   1

Subtract (−) ←

> I decided to subtract the tiles of the second pouch from those in the first pouch.

x^2 x^2 x^2 x^2 $-x$ $-x$

> I needed to figure out the difference and how many tiles it would take to represent that difference.

I need to calculate
$(x^2 + 2x + 3) - (4x^2 - 2x)$.

x^2 x x 1   1   1

Add (+)

$-x^2$ $-x^2$ $-x^2$ $-x^2$ x x

> To subtract, I added the opposite of each tile in the second pouch, just like I would do with integers. I replaced red tiles with blue tiles and blue tiles with red tiles, and then added.
>
> The opposite of $4x^2$ is $-4x^2$. The opposite of $(-2x)$ is $2x$.

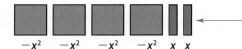

x^2 x x 1   1   1

Add (+)

$-x^2$ $-x^2$ $-x^2$ $-x^2$ x x

> I saw that I could eliminate an x^2 tile and a negative-x^2 tile using the zero principle, just as with opposite integers. Then, I gathered together congruent tiles of the same colour.

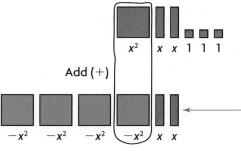

Since $1 + (-4) = (-3)$,
$x^2 + (-4x^2) = -3x^2$.
Since $2 + 2 = 4$,
$2x + 2x = 4x$.

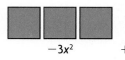

$-3x^2$ + $4x$ +   3

> I saw and counted 3 negative-x^2 tiles, 4 x tiles and 3 unit tiles.

The expression I get by subtracting is
$-3x^2 + 4x + 3$ and that uses 10 tiles.
Subtraction resulted in more tiles than addition, so I should use addition.

EXAMPLE 2   Reasoning about expressions algebraically

Jay and Sierra got two new pouches of tiles. The first pouch contained 1 x^2 tile, 2 y tiles, and 3 unit tiles. The second pouch had 4 x^2 tiles and 2 $-y$ tiles. They represented their contents using algebraic expressions. Jay added and Sierra subtracted the expressions. Which expression results in the fewest tiles?

Jay's Solution: Representing and simplifying a sum algebraically

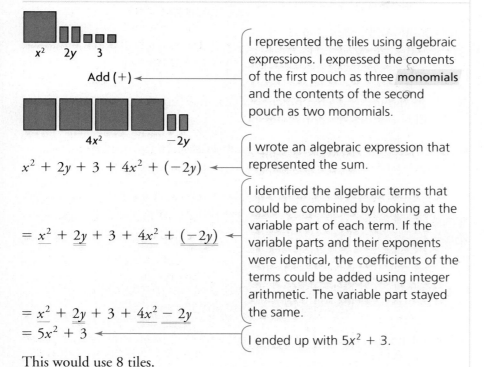

I represented the tiles using algebraic expressions. I expressed the contents of the first pouch as three **monomials** and the contents of the second pouch as two monomials.	**monomial** an algebraic expression with one term; for example, $5x^2$, $4xy$

I wrote an algebraic expression that represented the sum.

I identified the algebraic terms that could be combined by looking at the variable part of each term. If the variable parts and their exponents were identical, the coefficients of the terms could be added using integer arithmetic. The variable part stayed the same.

$$x^2 + 2y + 3 + 4x^2 + (-2y)$$

$$= \underline{x^2} + \underline{\underline{2y}} + 3 + \underline{4x^2} + \underline{\underline{(-2y)}}$$

$$= \underline{x^2} + \underline{\underline{2y}} + 3 + \underline{4x^2} - \underline{\underline{2y}}$$

$$= 5x^2 + 3$$

I ended up with $5x^2 + 3$.

This would use 8 tiles.

Sierra's Solution: Representing and simplifying a difference algebraically

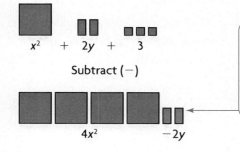

I represented the tiles using algebraic expressions. I represented the contents of the first pouch as a **trinomial** and the contents of the second pouch as a **binomial**.	**trinomial** an algebraic expression containing three terms; for example, $2x^2 - 6xy + 7$ **binomial** an algebraic expression containing two terms; for example, $3x + 2$

$(x^2 + 2y + 3) - (4x^2 - 2y)$ ← I wrote this as a difference of two **polynomials**.

$= x^2 + 2y + 3 + (-4x^2) + 2y$ ← To subtract the second polynomial I added the opposite of each term.

$= \underline{x^2} + \underline{2y} + 3 \underline{- 4x^2} + \underline{2y}$ ← I simplified my expression by combining like terms.

$= -3x^2 + 4y + 3$ ← The result was $-3x^2 + 4y + 3$.

This would use 10 tiles.

Reflecting

A. How did using algebra tiles help Farell and Peter know which terms could be added or subtracted?

B. How did the appearance of algebraic terms help Jay and Sierra know which terms could be added or subtracted?

C. How did an understanding of integer operations and the zero principle help each student simplify his or her polynomials?

APPLY the Math

EXAMPLE 3	**Reasoning about like terms to determine missing terms in a polynomial**

What polynomial must be added to $3x^2 + xy - 2$ to give the result $5x^2 - 3xy - 2$?

Barry's Solution

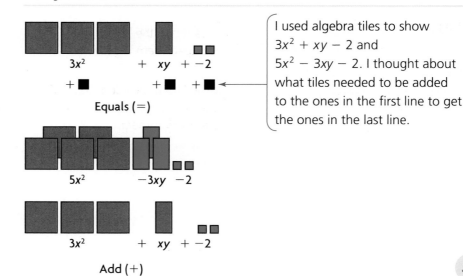

I used algebra tiles to show $3x^2 + xy - 2$ and $5x^2 - 3xy - 2$. I thought about what tiles needed to be added to the ones in the first line to get the ones in the last line.

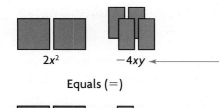

2x²   **−4xy**

I used algebra tiles and integer arithmetic to determine how many and what colour of tiles were needed. I saw that I needed 2 x^2 tiles, 4 negative-xy tiles, and no unit tiles.

Equals (=)

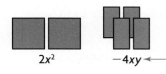

5x²   **−3xy** **−2**

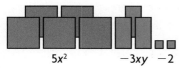

2x²   **−4xy**

When I decided on the algebra tiles I needed, I wrote the algebraic representation.

$$\underline{3x^2} + \underline{1xy} - 2 + \underline{2x^2} - \underline{4xy}$$
$$= 5x^2 - 3xy - 2$$

I checked my work by writing my new expression algebraically and combining like terms.

I have to add $2x^2 - 4xy$.

| **EXAMPLE 4** | **Using algebraic reasoning to simplify a difference of polynomials** |

Simplify $(5x^2y + 4xy) - (2x^2y - xy)$.

Raman's Solution

$$(5x^2y + 4xy) - (2x^2y - xy)$$
$$= 5x^2y + 4xy + (-2x^2y + 1xy)$$

I knew that subtracting a polynomial is the same as adding its opposite terms.

$$= \underline{5x^2y} + \underline{4xy} - \underline{2x^2y} + \underline{1xy}$$
$$= \underline{5x^2y} - \underline{2x^2y} + \underline{4xy} + \underline{1xy}$$

I identified the like terms and grouped them together.

$$= (5 - 2)x^2y + (4 + 1)xy$$
$$= 3x^2y + 5xy$$

I combined the coefficients of the like terms by adding or subtracting them.

| EXAMPLE 5 | Using polynomials to represent and solve a problem |

Joan and Chris both have jobs. They both work the same number of hours per week. Their pay rates and expenses are shown.

	Pay Rate	Weekly Expenses
Joan	$15.50/h	$40 uniform rental
Chris	$14/h	$35 cafeteria charge

Write an algebraic expression in simplest form to describe Joan and Chris's combined take-home pay each week.

Use this polynomial to determine their combined income if they both work 38 hours in a week.

Susie's Solution

Joan and Chris each work h hours in a week.

> I used h for the number of hours per week that Joan and Chris each worked.

Joan's income for a week: $15.5h - 40$
Chris's income for a week: $14h - 35$

> To represent Joan's weekly income, I multiplied her hourly rate by h and subtracted $40 for her uniform.

> To represent Chris's weekly income, I multiplied her hourly rate by h and subtracted $35 for her meals.

combined income

$$= (15.5h - 40) + (14h - 35)$$
$$= 15.5h + 14h - 40 - 35$$
$$= 29.5h - 75$$

> I added the two expressions by combining like terms.

combined income for 38 hours

$$= 29.5(38) - 75$$
$$= 1121 - 75$$
$$= 1046$$

> To determine their combined weekly income, I substituted 38 for h and evaluated.

For 38 hours, their combined income was $1046.

In Summary

Key Idea

- You can simplify a sum or a difference of polynomials by adding or subtracting the coefficients of like terms.

    For example: $(2y + 3x^2) + (8y - 5x^2)$
    $$= (3x^2 - 5x^2) + (2y + 8y)$$
    $$= -2x^2 + 10y$$

Need to Know

- Like terms can be combined by adding or subtracting their numerical coefficients.
- The sum or difference of the coefficients of like terms can be calculated using the principles for adding and subtracting rational numbers.
- It often is easier to subtract two polynomials by using the same strategy you use with integers: adding the opposite.

    For example: $(2y - 2x^2) - (3y + 4x^2)$
    $$= 2y - 2x^2 + (-3y - 4x^2)$$
    $$= 2y - 2x^2 - 3y - 4x^2$$
    $$= -6x^2 - 1y$$

CHECK *Your Understanding*

1. Draw an algebra tile representation of each polynomial.
    a) $2x^2 - x$ b) $x^2 + 3$ c) $2y - 2x + 2$

2. Copy each question. Identify the like terms in each and circle their coefficients.
    a) $3x, 4y, -2x$ b) $6m, -1.5m, 4n, 3m^2$

3. Write an algebraic expression for each algebra tile representation.
    a)    b)

4. Simplify the following algebra tile representation. State your result as a polynomial.

5. Simplify the following.
    a) $2x + 3x$ d) $(2x + 3) + (5x - 4)$
    b) $3y^2 - 2y^2 + 4y^2$ e) $(3x - 5) + (-2x + 6)$
    c) $3x - 2y + 4x$ f) $(3x + 2) - (5x + 2)$

PRACTISING

6. Draw an algebra tile representation of each polynomial.

    a) $x^2 + 3x$ **c)** $xy + 4x$

    b) $2x^2 - y^2$ **d)** $2x^2 - 3x - 4$

7. Copy each question. Identify the like terms in each and circle their coefficients.

    a) $-2g, 3f, -5g$ **c)** $5x, -2.1y^3, -0.8y^3, 2y$

    b) $-\dfrac{1}{2}y, -4x, 2\dfrac{1}{2}y, 6x^2$ **d)** $-3.75rs, 3.3r, -5.1s, 4.25rs$

8. Write a simplified algebraic expression for each algebra tile representation.

    a)

    b)

    c)

    d)

    e)

9. Simplify the following.

    a) $3h + 1 + 2h + 5$ **c)** $\dfrac{3}{4}w^2 - \dfrac{2}{3}w^2 + \dfrac{1}{4}w^2 - \dfrac{4}{3}w^2$

    b) $7y - 3y - x^2 + 4x^2$ **d)** $\dfrac{3}{4}a - \dfrac{1}{5}b - \dfrac{1}{4}a + \dfrac{2}{5}b$

10. Simplify the following.

    a) $(2x - 3y) + (3x + y)$

    b) $(2y^2 - 3y + 4) + (-5y^2 + 5y - 3)$

    c) $(3x^2 - 4xy + 6y^2) + (6x^2 - 8xy - 3y^2)$

11. Simplify the following.

    a) $(5x - 4y) - (3x + 2y)$

    b) $(3y^2 - 2y + 1) - (-5y^2 + 2y + 3)$

    c) $(3x^2 - 4xy + 6y^2) - (6x^2 - 8xy - 3y^2)$

12. Simplify each of the following. Check your answer using a different tool or strategy.

    a) $2y - 3y - x^2 + 3x^2$ **b)** $(y^2 - 2y + 2) - (3y^2 - 2y + 3)$

13. Determine the polynomials that need to be added to each row of the table.

	Initial Polynomial	Polynomial To Be Added	Final Polynomial
a)	$x^2 + 3x$		$-x^2 + 5x$
b)	$2x^2y^2 - 4y^2$		$5x^2y^2 - 3y^2$
c)	$-7xy + 4x$		$-7xy + 3x - 2$
d)	$2x^2 - 3x - 4$		$-2x^2 + 3x - 6$

14. A pool table is always twice as long as it is wide. The Cue Ball
A Company makes pool tables in many different sizes. Each table top must have rubber bumpers around the outside edge and a felt top. The rubber bumpers cost $2.25/m and the felt material for the top costs $28/m². Determine an algebraic expression that represents the total cost for felt and rubber for the table top. Use this to determine the cost of the materials for a top that has a width of 1.5 m.

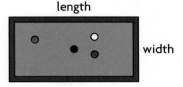
length

width

15. Jan is a plumber. She charges $35 to visit a job site. Her hourly rate is $43.50. Fred repairs furnaces. He charges $41 for a service call plus $38.75/h. Let x represent the number of hours they work.
    a) Represent Jan's bill as a polynomial.
    b) Represent Fred's bill as a polynomial.
    c) Write a new polynomial that represents Jan's and Fred's combined charge, assuming that they both work x hours at a site.
    d) Calculate their combined charge if they both work 8 h at the same complex.

16. Elizabeth and Dragan serve food at different restaurants on a cruise ship. Their earnings are based on tips, as shown, from which they have to pay for room and board.

	Elizabeth	Dragan
Average Weekly Tips	$220/table	$160/table
Room and Board	$160/week	$125/week

   a) Write a polynomial to represent Elizabeth's weekly earnings after she pays for room and board.
   b) Write a polynomial to represent Dragan's weekly earnings after he pays for room and board.
   c) Dragan and Elizabeth work the same number of tables. Write a single polynomial that combines Dragan's and Elizabeth's earnings.

d) Evaluate the earnings for five tables.

e) Suppose Dragan works seven tables and Elizabeth works five tables. Can the single polynomial in part c) be used to calculate their joint earnings? Explain.

17. In a TV game show, each player begins with $1000. For each question answered correctly, a player receives $125. For each one answered incorrectly, a player must pay $250.

a) Express the total winnings for a player using an algebraic expression.

b) Use the expression from part a) to find the total winnings for the three players if:
- player 1 answered 12 questions correctly and 8 incorrectly
- player 2 answered 10 questions correctly and 2 incorrectly, and
- player 3 answered 15 questions correctly and 5 incorrectly.

18. Create two 3-term polynomials such that:

a) When the polynomials are combined there are 5 terms.

b) When the polynomials are combined there are 3 terms.

c) When the polynomials are combined there is 1 term.

19. Describe how your knowledge of the zero principle and of adding and subtracting rational numbers helps simplify a sum or difference of polynomials.

Extending

20. Simplify.

a) $2x + 3y + 4z - 4x + 3y - z$

b) $-4abc - 3ab - 6abc - 4ab$

c) $3xy + 5yz - 2xyz + 6xy - xyz$

21. Simplify.

a) $(2x + 3y) + (5x - 4y) + (2x - y)$

b) $-(4ab - 3a) - (6ab + 4a) + (2ab + 6a)$

c) $(3xy + 5y^2) - (3xy + 5y^2) + (3xy + 5y^2)$

22. Two polynomials are added and the sum is $3x^2 - y + 4$. For each statement, state whether it is always true, sometimes true, or never true. Explain or provide a counter-example to justify your answer.

a) Both are monomials.

b) Both include a y-term.

c) If there is an x-term in one polynomial then there must be an x-term in the other.

d) Both are binomials.

Multiplying a Polynomial by a Monomial

YOU WILL NEED
- algebra tiles
- algebra tile frame

GOAL

Apply the distributive property to polynomials.

LEARN ABOUT the Math

Judy has been asked to determine the product $3(2x + 4)$.

❓ How might Judy think about this operation in order to determine the product?

EXAMPLE 1   **Multiplying a monomial by a polynomial**

Determine the product $3(2x + 4)$.

Judy's Solution: Representing the product using algebra tiles

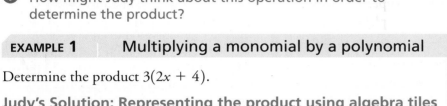

I knew that multiplying a number by 3 is the same as adding 3 copies of that number. I decided to show the same repeated addition strategy using algebra tiles.

I gathered enough algebra tiles to show 3 sets of $2x + 4$.

There were 3 sets of 2 x tiles and 3 sets of 4 unit tiles. That meant altogether there were 6 x tiles and 12 unit tiles.

$3(2x + 4) = 6x + 12$

Tamara's Solution: Representing the product using an area model

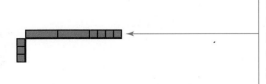

I knew that the area of a rectangle is the product of its length and width. I used algebra tiles to represent the length $2x + 4$ and the width of the rectangle.

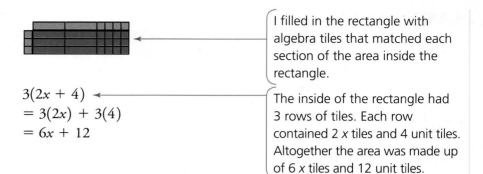

I filled in the rectangle with algebra tiles that matched each section of the area inside the rectangle.

$3(2x + 4)$
$= 3(2x) + 3(4)$
$= 6x + 12$

The inside of the rectangle had 3 rows of tiles. Each row contained 2 x tiles and 4 unit tiles. Altogether the area was made up of 6 x tiles and 12 unit tiles.

Sue's Solution: Representing the product using a diagram

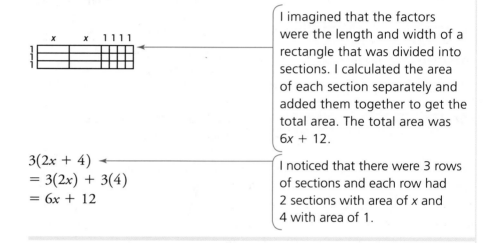

I imagined that the factors were the length and width of a rectangle that was divided into sections. I calculated the area of each section separately and added them together to get the total area. The total area was $6x + 12$.

$3(2x + 4)$
$= 3(2x) + 3(4)$
$= 6x + 12$

I noticed that there were 3 rows of sections and each row had 2 sections with area of x and 4 with area of 1.

Shania's Solution: Comparing the product to a product of numbers

$$20 \times 23 = 20 \times (20 + 3)$$
$$= 20 \times 20 + 20 \times 3$$
$$= 400 + 60$$
$$= 460$$

$$3(2x + 4) = 3(2x) + 3(4)$$
$$= 6x + 12$$

Sometimes, when I have to calculate a product, I split one of the factors into parts and use the **distributive property**.

I decided to use the same strategy to multiply with a polynomial.

distributive property or law

the property that states that when a sum is multiplied by a number, each value in the sum is multiplied by the number separately and the products are then added; for example, $4 \times (7 + 8) = (4 \times 7) + (4 \times 8)$

Reflecting

A. Which student's approach would you use? Why?

B. How does each student's way of thinking about the problem involve an application of the distributive property?

APPLY *the Math*

EXAMPLE **2**	Connecting the distributive property to products of polynomials of degrees greater than 1

Multiply $(2x^3 + 4x - 5)3x^2$.

Peng Bo's Solution

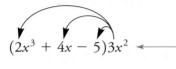

$(2x^3 + 4x - 5)3x^2$ ←

> I used the distributive property to multiply each term in the trinomial factor by the factor $3x^2$.

$$= (2x^3)3x^2 + (4x)3x^2 - (5)3x^2$$
$$= 6x^5 + 12x^3 - 15x^2$$ ←

> I multiplied the coefficients of the terms to get the coefficients of the product. I added the exponents to determine the exponents of the variable terms.

EXAMPLE **3**	Using reasoning and the distributive property to expand a product

Parm is an artist who works in metal and ceramics. He is building a sculpture in the shape of a large trapezoid. The sculpture's proportions are shown on the diagram. To order materials, he needs to determine the trapezoid's area.

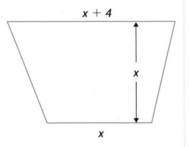

Barry's Solution

$$A = \frac{1}{2}h(a + b)$$

$$= \frac{1}{2}x[x + (x + 4)]$$ ←

> I remembered the formula for the area of a trapezoid. I used x for the height, x for the length of one parallel side, and $x + 4$ for the length of the other side.

$$= \frac{1}{2}x(2x + 4)$$

$$A = \frac{1}{2}x(2x + 4)$$ ←

$$= \frac{1}{2}x(2x) + \frac{1}{2}x(4)$$

$$= x^2 + 2x$$

> I knew that with numbers, I could use the distributive property to multiply each number inside the brackets by the number outside the brackets. I decided to simplify the formula further by multiplying each term inside the brackets by the factor $\frac{1}{2}x$.

Communication | *Tip*

The words "expand," "use the distributive property," and "remove brackets" all mean to multiply a polynomial by a factor.

EXAMPLE **4**

| | **Using reasoning and the distributive property to determine a missing factor** |

Complete and verify this equation: $\blacksquare(2x^2 - 5) = 8x^3 - 20x$.

Mohab's Solution

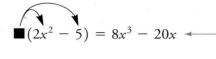

$\blacksquare(2x^2 - 5) = 8x^3 - 20x$ ← Using the distributive property, I knew that whatever factor was represented by the blank box would be multiplied by $2x^2$ and result in $8x^3$.

$4x(2x^2) = 8x^3$ ← $4x$ multiplied by $2x^2$ gives me $8x^3$.

$4x(2x^2 - 5) = 8x^3 - 20x$ ← To check, I replaced the box with the factor $4x$ and multiplied to make sure that the other term was $-20x$.

In Summary

Key Idea

- You can determine the product of a monomial and a polynomial by using the distributive property to expand it.

  For example: $2x(3x^2 + 5) = 2x(3x^2) + 2x(5)$
  $$= 6x^3 + 10x$$

Need to Know

- You can sometimes determine the product of a monomial and a polynomial using the area model. This can be represented with concrete materials or diagrams.

CHECK Your Understanding

1. State the factors and product represented in each model as an algebraic equation.

   a)
   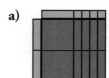
   b)
   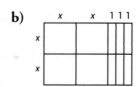

2. Expand.
   a) $2a^3(4a^2 - a)$ **b)** $-2(y^2 - y - 1)$

3. Expand using the tool or strategy of your choice. Verify your answer using a different tool or strategy.
   a) $2(3x + 4)$ **b)** $3x(x + 2)$

PRACTISING

4. Expand using a different tool or strategy for each.

K a) $x(2x + 1)$

b) $4(5 + x)$

c) $(3x + 5)(2x)$

5. What multiplication equation does each model represent?

a)

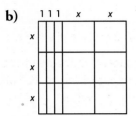

b)

c)

6. Expand.

a) $2(-y^2 - y - 1)$

b) $b^2(2b^3 - 4b + 1)$

c) $3m^3(5m^2 + 6m - 4)$

d) $-(x^2 - 3x + 7)$

e) $-4x(x^2 - 3x)$

f) $-2n^2(3n - 5 + 4n^3)$

7. Determine the missing factor and verify.

a) $\blacksquare(2x - 10) = 6x - 30$

b) $\blacksquare(x^3 - 5x - 4) = 2x^5 - 10x^3 - 8x^2$

c) $-4a^3(\blacksquare + \blacksquare + \blacksquare) = -12a^7 + 4a^4 - 8a^3$

8. Evaluate each statement for $p = 5$ once before you expand it and once

T after you expand it.

a) $4(3p + 2)$

b) $3p(6 - p)$

c) $2p^2(4p + 3)$

d) $p(3p^2 - 4p + 4)$

e) Explain how you know that you should get the same result both before you expand each statement and after you expand it.

f) Was it always easier to evaluate after you expanded? Explain.

9. Write simplified algebraic expressions for the perimeter, P, and area, A,
A of the following figures.

a)

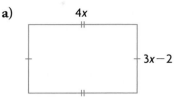

4x

3x−2

b)

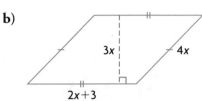

3x   4x

2x+3

c)

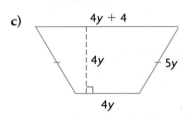

4y + 4

4y   5y

4y

d) Evaluate the perimeter and the area of the rectangle in part a) if
$x = 4$ cm.

10. You could evaluate 20×47 by doing the calculation
C $20 \times 40 + 20 \times 7$. How is this like using the distributive property to
simplify $x(2x + 7)$?

Extending

11. Expand.
   a) $2x(y - 3z)$
   b) $-3x(xy + yz)$

12. Fill in the missing information to make the statements true.
   a) $20x + 15 = 5(\blacksquare + \blacksquare)$
   b) $5x^2 + 25x = 5\blacksquare(\blacksquare + \blacksquare)$
   c) $4x^5 + 8x^3 - 2x^2 = \blacksquare x^2(\blacksquare + \blacksquare + \blacksquare)$
   d) How could you check your answers for parts a), b), and c) to see if
   they are correct?

13. These polynomials were expanded using the distributive principle.
   Restate them as a product of two factors.
   a) $12x^2 - 6x$
   b) $21y^3 + 7y^2 - 14y$
   c) $5x^2 - 10xy + 30x$

Simplifying Polynomial Expressions

GOAL

Expand and simplify polynomial expressions in one variable.

LEARN ABOUT *the Math*

Todd has a landscaping business. He employs 4 truck drivers, 3 assistants, and 15 student labourers. The pay structure for the business is shown below.

Employees	Number	Hourly and Weekly Payment per Employee
Owner	1	$800/week
Truck drivers	4	$17/h plus $150 for gas
Assistants	3	$12/h plus $50 for expenses
Student labourers	15	$10/h

Todd wants to use a spreadsheet to determine his weekly payroll. He assumes that in any one week all of the employees will work the same number of hours, but also that the number of hours they work from week to week will vary.

❓ What formula can Todd use to represent his total weekly payroll in terms of number of hours worked?

Todd's Solution

Let h represent the number of hours each employee works in a week. ← | Employees work the same number of hours each week, so I can use the same variable to represent hours worked.

Truck drivers are paid $17h + 150$. ←
Assistants are paid $12h + 50$.
Student labourers are paid $10h$.

| I wrote an algebraic expression to represent each type of worker's weekly pay.

Pay for truck drivers: $4(17h + 150)$ ←
Pay for assistants: $3(12h + 50)$
Pay for labourers: $15(10h)$
Pay for owner, Todd: 800/week

| I multiplied the representation for each position's weekly pay by the number of people employed in that position.

Total weekly payroll ←
$$P = 800 + 4(17h + 150)$$
$$+ 3(12h + 50) + 15(10h)$$

| I added the weekly payrolls for all of the positions to describe the total weekly payroll.

$$P = 800 + 4(17h + 150)$$

$$+ 3(12h + 50) + 15(10h)$$
$$= 800 + 68h + 600 + 36h$$
$$+ 150 + 150h$$
$$P = 254h + 1550$$

| I simplified this using the distributive property, and then collected like terms.

I can use the formula $P = 254h + 1550$ to represent the total payroll per week.

Reflecting

A. What mathematical principles did Todd use to simplify his formula?

B. What did the only variable in Todd's polynomial expression represent? How did using only one variable help him to expand and simplify the expression to determine the simplified payroll formula?

APPLY the Math

EXAMPLE 2	Simplifying a sum of products of polynomials

Simplify $2(3x + 1) + 3(x - 4)$.

Jaspal's Solution: Reasoning from an algebra tile representation

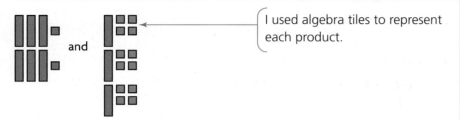

I used algebra tiles to represent each product.

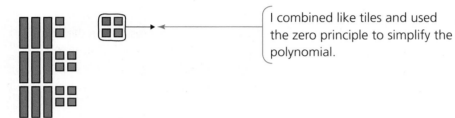

I combined like tiles and used the zero principle to simplify the polynomial.

$2(3x + 1) + 3(x - 4) = 9x - 10$ ◄ I wrote a summary statement by counting the remaining tiles in my representation.

Katerina's Solution: Reasoning using the distributive property

$2(3x + 1) + 3(x - 4)$ ◄ I used the distributive property to expand each product.

$= 6x + 2 + 3x - 12$

$= 9x - 10$ ◄ I collected like terms.

$2(3x + 1) + 3(x - 4)$

$= 9x - 10$

EXAMPLE 3 | Simplifying polynomial expressions

Determine the missing factor:

$(4x^2 - 3x + 2) - (x^2 - 9x - 1) = \blacksquare(x^2 + 2x + 1)$

Jordan's Solution: Reasoning using the distributive property

$(4x^2 - 3x + 2) - (x^2 - 9x - 1)$

$(4x^2 - 3x + 2) + (-1)(x^2 - 9x - 1)$

I simplified the polynomials on the left side of the equal sign. The negative sign in front of the second bracket represents (-1), so I used the distributive property to expand, and then collected like terms.

$= 4x^2 - 3x + 2 - x^2 + 9x + 1$
$= 3x^2 + 6x + 3$

$\blacksquare(x^2 + 2x + 1) = 3x^2 + 6x + 3$

Then, I looked at the original expression on the right side of the equal sign. I thought about what factor outside the brackets would give me $3x^2 + 6x + 3$ when I used the distributive property.

$\blacksquare x^2 = 3x^2$
$\blacksquare = 3$

I started with the first term, $3x^2$. To get this, I would have to multiply x^2 by 3, so I chose the number 3 to fill the box.

$3(x^2 + 2x + 1) = 3x^2 + 6x + 3$

I checked by using the distributive property, and it worked.

$(4x^2 - 3x + 2) - (x^2 - 9x - 1)$
$= 3(x^2 + 2x + 1)$

Danika's Solution: Connecting to adding opposites

$(4x^2 - 3x + 2) - (x^2 - 9x - 1)$

$= 4x^2 - 3x + 2 + (-x^2) + 9x + 1$

$= 3x^2 + 6x + 3$

I simplified the polynomials on the left side of the equal sign. The negative sign in front of the second bracket meant I had to add the opposite of each term inside the bracket. I rewrote the problem and collected like terms.

$3x^2 + 6x + 3 = \blacksquare(x^2 + 2x + 1)$

$\dfrac{3x^2}{3} = x^2,$

$\dfrac{6x}{3} = 2x,$ and

$\dfrac{3}{3} = 1$

$\blacksquare = 3$

I looked at the simplified expression. I thought about what factor was common to each of the terms.

Each term had a factor of 3. When I divided each term by 3, the results were the terms of the trinomial on the right hand side.

$(4x^2 - 3x + 2) - (x^2 - 9x - 1)$
$\qquad = 3(x^2 + 2x + 1)$

EXAMPLE 4 **Connecting exponent principles to simplifying a polynomial expression**

Expand and simplify $3x^2(4x^3 - 2x^2 + 6x) - (x^5 + 5x^4 - 4x^3) + 7x^5$.

George's Solution

$3x^2(4x^3 - 2x^2 + 6x) - (x^5 + 5x^4 - 4x^3) + 7x^5$

$= 12x^5 - 6x^4 + 18x^3 - x^5 - 5x^4 + 4x^3 + 7x^5$

I used the distributive property to expand the product for each bracketed expression. To simplify the first set of brackets, I had to apply the exponent principles for multiplying powers. To simplify the second set of brackets, I multiplied each term by the factor (-1). The last term wasn't multiplied by anything.

$= 12x^5 - x^5 + 7x^5 - 6x^4 - 5x^4 + 18x^3 + 4x^3$

$= 18x^5 - 11x^4 + 22x^3$

I simplified the expression by grouping then collecting like terms.

EXAMPLE 5 | Solving a problem by simplifying a polynomial expression

A sporting goods company provides skis and snowboards to instructors at ski resorts.

	Number Provided	Original Value	Yearly Drop in Value
Skis	200	$600	$50
Snowboards	300	$800	$60

Determine an expression that represents the combined value of the equipment after y years of use. Use this value to determine the combined value of all the equipment after 2 years of use.

Mark's Solution

After y years, the values of the skis and snowboards will be:
- skis: $600 - 50y$
- snowboards: $800 - 60y$

> I wrote algebraic expressions to represent the future value of each item.

> I multiplied each expression by the number of skis or snowboards. This gave me an equation for the combined value V after y years.

$V = 200(600 - 50y) + 300(800 - 60y)$

> I used the distributive property, and then simplified the expressions.

$= 120\ 000 - 10\ 000y + 240\ 000 - 18\ 000y$

$= 360\ 000 - 28\ 000y$

$V = 360\ 000 - 28\ 000(2)$

> I substituted 2 for y to determine their combined value after 2 years.

$= 360\ 000 - 56\ 000$

$= 304\ 000$

After 2 years, the combined value will be $304 000.

In Summary

Key Idea

- You can use the distributive property and collect like terms to simplify a sum or difference of products of polynomials.

Need to Know

- Use the order of operations to determine the sequence in which operations must be performed.

CHECK *Your Understanding*

1. Simplify using the tool or strategy of your choice. Verify using a different tool or strategy.
   a) $3(x - 1) + 2(2x + 2)$
   b) $2(y^2 - 3) - 2(y^2 - 1)$

2. Simplify.
   a) $3x^2(x^3 - 1) + 2x^3(2x^2 + 2)$
   b) $2(y^2 - 3y^5) - 3(y^2 - y^5)$

3. On average, the following numbers of adults and children pay to enter the fall fair.

	Adults	Children
At 9 a.m.	20	25
Each Hour After 9 a.m. Until Closing	95	120

FALL FAIR
9 a.m.–10 p.m.
Children: $8.00
Adults: $12.00

Determine an expression for the total entrance fees collected h hours after opening.

PRACTISING

4. Write an algebraic representation that corresponds to the algebra tile
   C models shown. Simplify the expression using the strategy of your choice.

   a)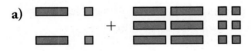

   b)

   c)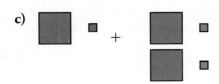

5. Simplify the following expressions using the tool or strategy of your choice. Verify using a different tool or strategy.

   a) $6(8 + 3c) + 4(10 + 2c)$

   b) $5(2x - 3) - 4(3x + 6)$

   c) $2(x^2 - 3x + 6) - 3(2x^2 - 4x - 1)$

   d) $-y(y^2 + 5y + 4) + 3y(2y^2 - y + 6)$

   e) $2(3y^2 + 4y) - 3(2y^2 - y)$

   f) $2(4x^3 - 3x + 6) + 3(2x^5 + x^3 - 4x)$

6. Simplify each expression, and then evaluate for $a = 3$.

   a) $6(2a + 4) - 3a$ **c)** $-10a - 2(a^2 + 7)$

   b) $15 - 2(a - 5)$ **d)** $-(2a - a^3) - a^2$

7. Simplify the following polynomial expressions.

   a) $3(2x^2 - 1) + 6(2x - 3) - (2x^2 - 5x)$

   b) $6(x + 5) - 2(x + 4) + 3(x - 5)$

   c) $3(2y^2 - 1) + 6(2y - 3) - (2y^2 - 5y)$

   d) $3(4p^2 - 2p + 6) + 6(4p - 2) - (7p^2 + 5p + 1)$

8. Simplify.

   a) $4x^2(x^3 - 2x^2) + 2x^3(2x^2 + 2x)$

   b) $2y^2(y^3 - 3y^5) - 3(y^2 - y^5)$

   c) $3m^3(2m^2 - 5m + 3) - 4m(m^4 + 2m^3 - m^2)$

   d) $-5x(x^3 - 2x^2) + 2x^2(3x^2 - 5x) - 4x^3(x - 2)$

9. Expand and simplify.

   a) $\dfrac{3}{5}\left(2\dfrac{1}{3}a - 2\dfrac{1}{2}\right) - \dfrac{1}{2}\left(2\dfrac{1}{5}a + 3\dfrac{2}{3}\right)$

   b) $\dfrac{1}{6}\left(3\dfrac{1}{5}a + \dfrac{2}{3}b\right) + \dfrac{1}{3}\left(\dfrac{1}{2}a - \dfrac{1}{2}\right)$

   c) $-1.25(3.1m + 2.2) - 2.15(1.2m - 3.2)$

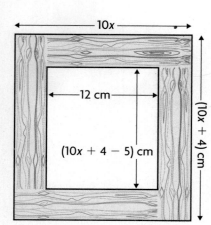

10. Mary is making rectangular picture frames to the proportions shown.

   a) Determine a simplified expression for the outside perimeter of the frame.

   b) Determine the outside perimeter when $x = 5$ cm.

   c) Determine a simplified expression for the area of one picture frame.

   d) Determine the area of one frame when $x = 5$ cm.

   e) Determine a simplified expression for the number of square centimetres of wood needed to make 20 frames the same size. Assume there is no waste.

11. A company purchased two kinds of cars for its sales force. The
A following expressions give the value of each vehicle after it has lost
value for x years.
- sedans: $V = -2400x + 19\ 600$
- sport utility vehicles (SUVs): $V = -3100x + 24\ 500$
  a) The company has 12 sales representatives who drive sedans and
  3 executives who drive SUVs. Write an expression that represents
  the combined value of the company's automobile fleet after x years.
  b) Create a spreadsheet that will determine the cost of each vehicle type
  and the combined value of all the cars each year for 0 to 6 years.
  c) What did the company pay for the SUVs? the sedans?
  d) Which vehicle type is losing value at a faster rate?

12. Simplify.
  a) $15 - 10(x - 4) - (3x + 3)$
  b) In part a), explain why the 10 is not subtracted from the 15 before
  you expand.

13. a) Is the following statement always true, sometimes true, or never
  T true? "Algebra tiles can be used to represent and simplify algebraic
  expressions that require the distributive property."
  b) If you chose "always true" or "never true," explain how you know. If
  you chose "sometimes true," provide an example that shows when
  it is true, and another that shows when it isn't true.

Extending

14. Simplify the following.
  a) $5(2x - 3y) - 4(3x + 6y)$
  b) $x(x + y) + 2x(x - y)$
  c) $2(x^2 - 3xy + 6y) - 3(2x^2 - 4xy - y)$

15. Apply the distributive property to simplify the following.
  a) $(x + 3)(2x + 4)$
  b) $(y + 2)(y + 1)$
  c) $(2x + y)(x + y)$

16. Simplify.
  a) $(x - 3)(x + 4) + 3(x^2 - x + 2)$
  b) $(2x + y)(x - y) - (x^2 + y^2)$
  c) $(3x + 5)(2x - 4) + (x + 1)(2x + 5)$

FREQUENTLY ASKED Questions

Study | **Aid**

• See Lesson 2.4,
  Example 3.
• Try Chapter Review
  Questions 11 and 12.

Q: **What tools and strategies can you use to simplify an algebraic expression?**

A: Sometimes you can recognize like terms by using an algebra tile model to represent the expression. You can always use the variables and the degree to identify like terms. You use rational number arithmetic to add or subtract the coefficients of like terms.

EXAMPLE

Expression	Algebra Tile Model	Identifying Like Terms
$2x^2 - 3x + x^2 + 2x$ $= 3x^2 - x$	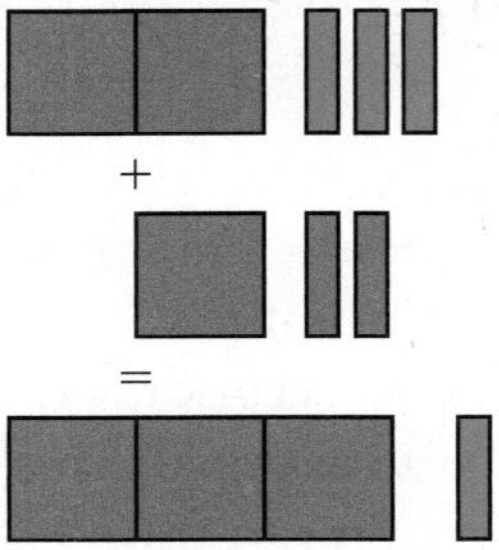	$\underline{2x^2} - \underline{\underline{3x}} + \underline{x^2} + \underline{\underline{2x}}$ $= 3x^2 - x$
$x^2 + 2y^2 - 3xy - 2x^2 + y^2 + 4xy$ $= -x^2 + 3y^2 + xy$	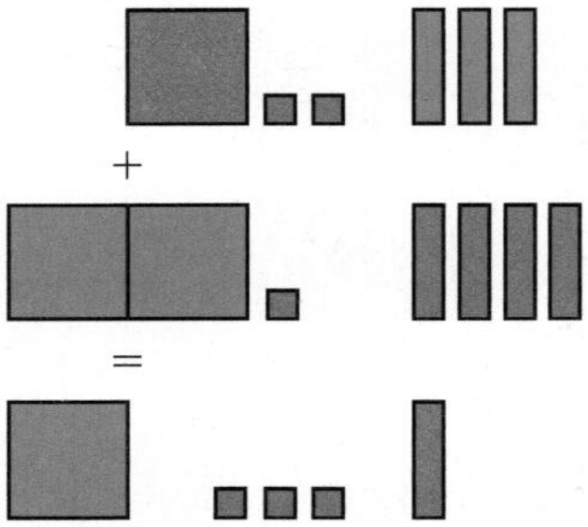	$\underline{x^2} + \underline{\underline{2y^2}} - \underline{\underline{\underline{3xy}}} - \underline{2x^2} + \underline{\underline{y^2}} + \underline{\underline{\underline{4xy}}}$ $= -x^2 + 3y^2 + xy$
$2x^4y - 3xy - 5x^4y - 4xy$ $= -3x^4y - 7xy$	This cannot be modelled with algebra tiles.	$\underline{2x^4y} - \underline{\underline{3xy}} - \underline{5x^4y} - \underline{\underline{4xy}}$ $= -3x^4y - 7xy$

Q: **What strategies can you use to multiply a polynomial by a monomial?**

A: You can use the distributive property to multiply a polynomial by a monomial. Sometimes you can use algebra tiles and an understanding of multiplication as repeated addition. Sometimes you can use an area model.

Study | *Aid*

- See Lesson 2.5, Example 2.
- Try Chapter Review Questions 14 and 15.

EXAMPLE

Expression	Algebra Tile Model	Area Model	Distributive Property
$3(2x + 1)$ $= 6x + 3$	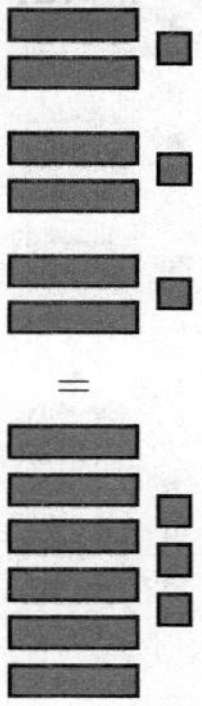	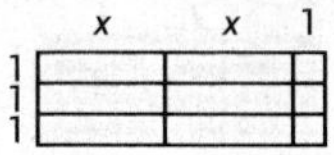 The area is $6x + 3$.	$3(2x + 1)$ $= 6x + 3$
$3x(x + 2)$ $= 3x^2 + 6x$	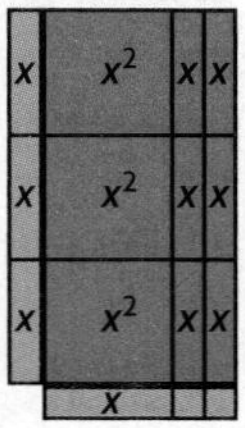	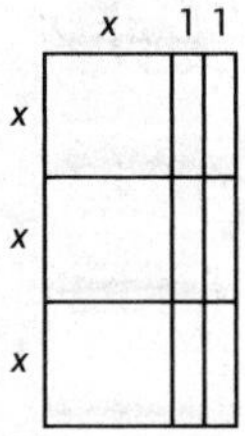 The area is $3x^2 + 6x$	$3x(x + 2)$ $= 3x^2 + 6x$

Study | *Aid*

- See Lesson 2.6,
  Example 2.
- Try Chapter Review
  Questions 17 and 19.

Q: How can you simplify a sum or difference involving products of polynomials?

A: You can multiply any products using the distributive property to expand, and then combine like terms. Sometimes you can use algebra tiles to model and simplify the expression.

EXAMPLE

Expression	Algebra Tile Model	Distributive Property and Algebraic Skills
$2(2x^2 - x) + 3(x^2 - 2x)$ $= 7x^2 - 8x$		$2(2x^2 - x) + 3(x^2 - 2x)$ $= 4x^2 - 2x + 3x^2 - 6x$ $= 7x^2 - 8x$
$2x^2(2x^2 - 3x) + x^2(2x - 1)$ $= 4x^4 - 4x^3 - x^2$	This cannot be modelled with algebra tiles.	$2x^2(2x^2 - 3x) + x^2(2x - 1)$ $= 4x^4 - 6x^3 + 2x^3 - x^2$ $= 4x^4 - 4x^3 - x^2$

PRACTICE Questions

Lesson 2.1

1. Sketch models to represent each of the following algebraic expressions. The variables x and y are not equal.
   a) y^2
   c) $2x$
   b) y^3
   d) $(2x)^2$

2. Rob is finishing a floor with square tiles. Each tile has an area of 412 cm^2. Estimate the length of the side of each tile. Use a calculator to check your answer.

Lesson 2.2

3. Why do you get the same result for each of the following expressions?
   a) $\dfrac{(5^7)}{(5^4)}$
   c) $\dfrac{(5^4)(5^5)}{(5^6)}$
   b) $\dfrac{(5^6)}{(5^3)}$
   d) $\dfrac{(5^4)(5)}{(5)(5)}$

4. Simplify, and then evaluate for $x = -2$ and $y = 3$.
   a) $\dfrac{(x^3)(x^4)}{x^6}$
   b) $\dfrac{(y^6)(x^4)}{(x^2)(y^4)}$
   c) $\dfrac{-32x^6}{16x^3}$

5. If you know that the product of two numbers is 9^6 and the quotient is 9^2, what could the two numbers be? How do you know?

6. About how long does it take for light to travel from one end of our galaxy to the other?
   - It is about 9.5×10^{16} km from one end of our galaxy to the other.
   - Light travels at about 1.1×10^9 km/h.

Lesson 2.3

7. Simplify.
   a) $(a^3)^2$
   b) $(4x^3)^4$
   c) $\dfrac{(2^3y^4)^3}{(2^4y^3)^2}$

8. Without doing the calculations, how do you know that each result will be zero?
   a) $(10^3)^5 - (10^5)^3$
   b) $(9^2)^2 - (3^4)^2$

9. Express each of the following as a power with a lesser base.
   a) 8^3
   b) 25^4
   c) 9^3

10. The length of the side of a cube is 5^3. Express its surface area (SA) and volume (V) using powers and simplify each expression.

Lesson 2.4

11. Simplify.
    a) $5y - 4y$
    c) $2x^2 - 5x + 5x^2 - x$
    b) $3xy^2 + 3xy^2$
    d) $y^2 + 5xy + y^2 - xy$

12. Simplify.
    a) $\dfrac{4}{5}a - \dfrac{1}{5}a$
    b) $2\dfrac{1}{2}a + \dfrac{2}{3}b + \dfrac{1}{2}a - \dfrac{1}{3}b$
    c) $-1.75m + 2.7 - 2.25m + 2.3$

13. Manuel and Kim have a picture framing business. Manuel cuts the wooden frames. He charges $25 for each one plus $10/h for his labour. Kim cuts the picture mats and assembles the product. She charges $8 for each mat plus $9/h for her labour.
    a) Represent Manuel's bill as a polynomial.
    b) Represent Kim's bill as a polynomial.
    c) Write a new polynomial that represents their total charges to frame a picture. Assume that they both work h hours on the frame.
    d) Calculate the cost for a frame if they both work 5 h on it.

14. Expand. Check one of your answers using a different tool or strategy.
   a) $3(y - 2)$ **d)** $-3x(x^2 - x)$
   b) $x(2x + 4)$ **e)** $2y^3(y^3 + 3y^2 - y)$
   c) $5m(3m^3 + 2n)$ **f)** $-a^2(2a - 5a^2 + 4a^3)$

15. Expand.
   a) $\frac{1}{3}(3x + 12)$

   b) $\frac{2}{5}\left(\frac{5}{8}a + 10b\right)$

   c) $-1.5m(2.8m + 2.2)$

16. Rick runs a pet store and is building rectangular pens for the animals. The length of the pens is always 20 cm longer than the width.

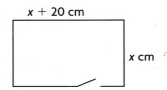

x + 20 cm

x cm

   a) One way of determining the perimeter is to use $P = 2(l + w)$. Use this formula to create an expression for the perimeter in terms of x.
   b) Simplify your formula in part a).
   c) Find the perimeter of a pen with a width of 45 cm.
   d) Suppose you use the formula $P = 2l + 2w$ instead. Use this formula to create another expression for the perimeter in terms of x.
   e) Why should the expressions in parts a) and d) be equivalent?

17. Expand and simplify. Check one of your answers using a different tool or strategy.
   a) $2(x - 3) + 3(x + 2)$
   b) $3(y^2 + y - 2) - (y^2 + 2y + 4)$
   c) $2x(3x - 2) + x^2 + 2(x^2 + 3)$
   d) $3x(4x^2 - 5x) + x^3 - x^2$

18. Ms. Smith needs fabric pieces for an art project for her students. The pieces will be cut to two rectangular sizes, as shown.

x cm

(x + 5) cm

x cm

(x + 10) cm

   a) Determine a simplified expression for the area of fabric needed if 14 students choose the larger size and 12 choose the smaller size.
   b) The class decides that the width of each piece of fabric will be 20 cm. Use your answer from part a) to determine how much material will be needed.

19. Expand and simplify.
   a) $\frac{1}{4}(8x - 12) - \frac{1}{2}(6 - 14x)$

   b) $\frac{5}{6}(6x - 18y) + \frac{2}{3}(21x - 6y)$

   c) $-5.2x(2.5x + 6.6) - 0.25x(1.6x - 2.4)$

20. Mickey has a baseball card collection. He is wondering about the future value of his rookie and big star cards.

Card Type	Number of Cards	Value Today	Increase in Value per Year
Rookie cards	22	$15	$3
Big star cards	18	$12	$2

   a) Write an expression that represents the combined value of these cards in y years.
   b) Use your answer from part a) to determine the combined value of the cards in 6 years.

1. Sketch and label a representation for each of the following algebraic terms. Explain how your sketches are both alike and different.

   a) y^2 b) m c) m^3

2. Jacqueline is making a quilt using finished squares like the one shown. Each square has an area of 310 cm².

   a) Write an expression that represents the length of the side of the square in terms of its area.

   b) Estimate the length. Describe the process you used.

   c) Use a calculator to determine the correct length to two decimal places.

   $A = 310 \text{ cm}^2$

3. Determine the approximate length of the roadway bordering the adjacent square properties.

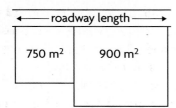

roadway length

750 m²   900 m²

4. Simplify.

   a) $(3^4)(3^6)$

   b) $\dfrac{\left(\frac{4}{5}\right)^6}{\left(\frac{4}{5}\right)^5}$

   c) $\dfrac{(x^3)(x^6)}{x}$

   d) $(6.1)(6.1^6)(6.1^5)(5^2)$

5. Which expression below is equivalent to $(-7)^4(-7^6)$?

   A. -49^{10}

   B. 49^{10}

   C. $(-7)^{10}$

   D. $(-7)^{24}$

   E. none of the above

6. Use an example to explain how you know that, to simplify a power of a power, you multiply the exponents.

7. Simplify.

   a) $(6^3)^2$

   b) $(x^2)^5$

   c) $(5x^4)^5$

   d) $\left[\left(\frac{2}{5}\right)^4\right]^5$

   e) $(y^3)^2(y^5)^2$

   f) $\left(\dfrac{5}{x^2}\right)^2$

8. What is meant by "like terms"? Explain how algebra tiles or diagrams can help you to identify like terms.

9. Simplify. Check one of your answers using a different tool or strategy.
   a) $5x - 2x$
   b) $7xy + 2xy$
   c) $(3x^2 - 5a) + (4x^2 - a)$

10. Which expression below is equivalent to $(y^2 + 5y) - (3y^2 - y)$?
    A. $-2y^2 + 6y$
    B. $4y^2 + 4y$
    C. $2y^2 + 6y$
    D. $-2y^2 + 4y$
    E. none of the above

11. Expand. Check one of your answers using a different tool or strategy.
    a) $2(x - 3)$
    b) $3x(4x^2 - 5x)$
    c) $y^5(5y^4 + 3y^3 - y^2)$

12. Expand and simplify. Check one of your answers using a different tool or strategy.
    a) $2(x - 3) + 3(x + 2)$
    b) $3(y^2 + y - 2) - (y^2 + 2y + 4)$
    c) $2x(3x - 2) + x^2 + 0.2(x^2 + 3)$

13. Mary and Bill are setting up a summer concession stand at the park. They need these jobs filled:

Position	Number of Positions	Hourly Pay Rate and Weekly Bonus
Manager	3	$14/h plus $50 bonus per week for working at least 30 h per week
Server	8	$9/h plus $35 bonus per week for working at least 30 h per week

    a) Determine a simplified algebraic expression to represent the weekly payroll for all 11 employees. Assume that they will always work at least 30 h per week.
    b) Use your expression to determine the weekly payroll if each employee works 32 h per week.

14. Determine an expression that simplifies to $3x^2$ if the expression contains:
    • exactly two binomials
    • the distributive property used once

Candle Fundraiser to Brighten Lives

Your class is going to raise money for charity by ordering and selling candle sets. Each set will contain three different-sized candles. The candles are rectangular prisms with congruent square bases. The other specifications for the candles are as follows:

- The length of the side of the base for each set is between 6 cm and 10 cm.
- The smallest candle's height is equal to the length of the side of the base.
- The middle candle's height is double the length of the side of the base.
- The tallest candle's height is triple the length of the side of the base.
- The wick extends 2 cm past the top of the candle for easy lighting.

The cost of the wick is \$0.004/cm. The candle wax costs \$0.02/cm³. Your class sets the price of each candle as the cost of the materials plus a 40% profit.

❓ What expression can you use to calculate the selling price of any candle set?

A. Determine an expression to represent the volume of a candle set.

B. Determine an expression to represent the wick length needed for a candle set.

C. Determine an expression to represent the purchase price of a candle set.

D. Use your expressions to calculate the purchase price for a candle set when the area of the base is 55 cm².

Task | Checklist

- ✔ Did you choose an appropriate variable to represent the length of the side of the base of the candles?

- ✔ Did you draw and label a diagram accurately?

- ✔ Did you show all of your steps?

- ✔ Did you explain your reasoning clearly?

- ✔ Did you consider all of the information provided?

Distance vs. Time

Linear Relations

▸ **GOALS**

You will be able to

- Recognize direct and partial variation from a graph, a table of values, and an algebraic expression

- Describe properties of linear relations

- Recognize whether a relation is linear or nonlinear from a table of values, a graph, an algebraic expression, or a written description

- Create different representations of linear and nonlinear relations

❓ Which of these relationships between distance and time best describes the distance the sled covers in 4 s?

WORDS YOU NEED to Know

1. Match each term with the most appropriate item.

a) scatter plot   c) pattern rule   e) variable
b) table of values   d) geometric pattern   f) data point

i)

figure 1   figure 2   figure 3

ii)

Figure Number (term number)	Number of Tiles (term value)
1	7
2	11
3	15
4	19
iii) n	iv) $4n + 3$

v)

Number of Tiles vs. Figure Number

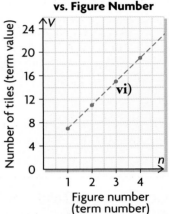

vi)

Number of tiles (term value)

Figure number (term number)

SKILLS AND CONCEPTS You Need

Using the Cartesian Coordinate System

The Cartesian coordinate system describes the location of a point in relation to a horizontal number line (the x-axis) and a vertical number line (the y-axis). The intersection of the axes creates four quadrants.

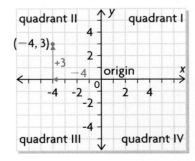

EXAMPLE

State the coordinates of each point.

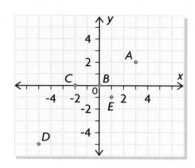

Solution

$A(3, 2)$

$B(0, 0)$

$C(-2, 0)$

$D(-5, -5)$

$E(1, -1)$

2. Plot the following points.

a) $A(4, 6)$ b) $B(0, 2)$ c) $C(-2, -5)$

Construct a Table of Values and a Scatter Plot to Represent a Relation

Study | Aid

• For more help and practice, see Appendix A-13.

EXAMPLE

The cost of a banquet at Juan's Banquet Hall is $450 for the room rental, plus $15 for each person served. Create a table of values and a scatter plot to represent the relation between the number of people and the cost.

Solution

People	Cost ($)
0	450 + 15(0) = 450
10	450 + 15(10) = 600
20	450 + 15(20) = 750
30	450 + 15(30) = 900
40	450 + 15(40) = 1050
50	450 + 15(50) = 1200
60	450 + 15(60) = 1350

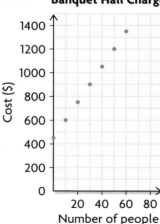

3. Plumbing Elite charges $100 plus an hourly rate of $80/h for a home service call. Construct a table of values and a scatter plot to represent the relation between the time required for a service call and the cost.

Study **Aid**

- For help, see the Review of Essential Skills and Knowledge Appendix.

Question	Appendix
4	A-5 and A-8
6	A-11

4. Evaluate.
   a) $4a + 5$, for $a = 3$
   b) $5 - 2b$, for $b = -1$
   c) $5p + q$, for $p = \dfrac{2}{5}$ and $q = \dfrac{1}{4}$

5. Simplify.
   a) $3(x - 2)$ b) $0.5(2x - 6)$ c) $\dfrac{1}{4}(16 - 9x)$

6. Consider this pattern.

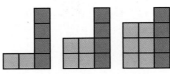

figure 1   figure 2   figure 3

   a) Use an algebraic expression to describe the number of tiles in terms of the figure number.
   b) How do the colours in the diagram relate to the parts of the algebraic expression?
   c) Use the algebraic expression to determine the number of tiles in figure 17.
   d) Make a table of values and draw a scatterplot comparing the figure number to the number of tiles in each figure.

7. State how each term is related to each other term. The relation between scatter plot and ordered pair is done for you.

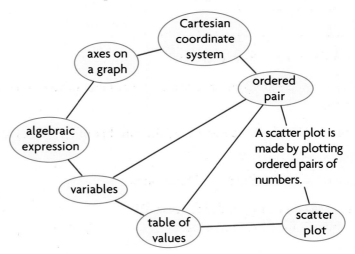

APPLYING *What You Know*

YOU WILL NEED
- grid paper
- square tiles

Patterning Squares

Marco and Renée are placing red stones in a pattern at the entrance to the skate park. They need to order more red stones to finish the job.

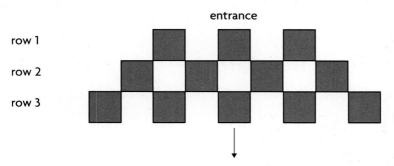

entrance

row 1

row 2

row 3

❓ How many red stones are in the 25th row of this pattern?

A. Determine the number of red stones in row 4, then draw row 5.

B. Copy and complete the table of values.

Row	Number of Red Stones
1	3
2	4
3	
4	
5	

C. Use your table to draw the scatter plot.

D. Write the algebraic expression that relates the number of red stones to the row number.

E. Use the relation in part D to determine the number of red stones in row 20.

F. Determine which row will have 18 red stones.

G. How many red stones are needed for row 25?
Explain how you used the pattern rule.

YOU WILL NEED

- grid paper

GOAL

Represent a relation using a table of values, a graph, or an equation.

LEARN ABOUT *the Math*

Chris runs a window-washing service. She charges a flat rate of $5, plus $3 per window.

? How can Chris's customers calculate the cost to wash their windows?

| EXAMPLE **1** | **Representing a relation in different ways** |

Represent the **relation** between the number of windows washed and the cost to wash them.

Geri's Solution: Representing the relation with a table of values

Number of Windows	Cost ($)
0	5
1	3 × 1 + 5 = 8
2	3 × 2 + 5 = 11
3	3 × 3 + 5 = 14

I created a table of values.

The customer chooses the number of windows to wash, so this is the **independent variable**.

The cost depends on how many windows are washed, so cost is the **dependent variable**.

relation

a description of how two variables are connected

independent variable

in a relation, the variable whose values you choose; usually placed in the right column in a table of values and on the horizontal axis in a graph

dependent variable

in a relation, the variable whose values you calculate; usually placed in the left column in a table of values and on the vertical axis in a graph

Brian's Solution: Representing the relation with a picture

cost to wash 1 window

cost to wash 2 windows

cost to wash 3 windows

I created a series of pictures.

$5 is constant, so it is the same in each picture.

I circled the part that increases with each additional window washed.

The picture represents the relation between cost and windows washed.

Marlene's Solution: Representing the relation with a graph

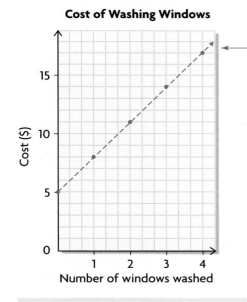

Cost of Washing Windows

I used Geri's table to graph the relation.

The number of windows washed is the independent variable, so I plotted that on the horizontal axis.

Cost is the dependent variable, so I plotted it on the vertical axis.

I connected the points with a dotted line because this set of data is **discrete**. Washing part of a window does not make sense.

discrete
a set of data that cannot be broken into smaller parts

Theo's Solution: Representing the relation with an algebraic expression

Let *W* represent the number of windows washed.
Let *C* represent the cost in dollars.

I represented the variables.

Chris charges a flat rate of $5, plus $3 per window.

I wrote the relation in words.

cost = (3 × number of windows washed) + 5

Constants go at the end of an equation.

$C = 3W + 5$

I replaced the words with variables to create an equation.

Reflecting

A. How do the students' representations all describe the same relation?

B. Which representation would you use? Why?

APPLY the Math

EXAMPLE 2 **Solving a problem involving a relation**

Determine the volume of a cube with a side length of 2.5 cm.

Andrea's Solution: Using a graph to estimate a value

Side Length of Cube (cm)	Volume of Cube (cm³)
1.0	$1 \times 1 \times 1 = 1^3 = 1$
2.0	$2 \times 2 \times 2 = 2^3 = 8$
3.0	$3 \times 3 \times 3 = 3^3 = 27$

I made a table of side lengths and volumes. I used the side length to calculate volume.

continuous

a set of data that can be broken down into smaller and smaller parts and still have meaning

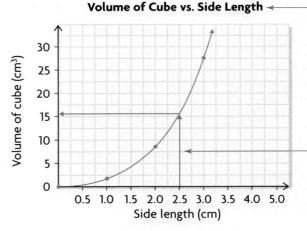

Volume of Cube vs. Side Length

I graphed the relation. This set of data is **continuous**, so I connected the points with a solid line.

interpolate

to estimate a value between two known values

I **interpolated**. I drew a line from 2.5 cm on the horizontal axis to the graph.

I drew a line from that point to the vertical axis.

The volume is about 15 cm³.

My estimate seems reasonable since multiplying $2.5 \times 2.5 \times 2.5$ gives me an exact volume of 15.625 cm³.

Andrea was able to estimate the volume from the graph. Pilar wanted a more exact answer, so she represented the relation using an equation.

Pilar's Solution: Using an equation to determine an exact value

Let x represent the side length of the cube.
Let y represent the volume of the cube.

> The volume depends on the side length.

$y = x^3$

> I described the relation using an equation and calculated the volume for $x = 2.5$.

$y = 2.5^3$
$y \doteq 15.6$

The volume is 15.6 cm³.

> I answered to the nearest tenth, because that is how the side length is given.

You can use a graphing calculator to graph a relation, if you know its equation. You can use this graph to make accurate estimates.

EXAMPLE 3   Using technology to estimate a value

The equation $V = 25\ 000 - 1500\,T$ represents a car's value after T years. When will the car be worth $0?

Otto's Solution

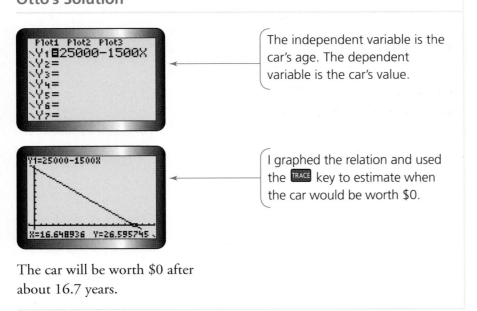

> The independent variable is the car's age. The dependent variable is the car's value.

> I graphed the relation and used the TRACE key to estimate when the car would be worth $0.

The car will be worth $0 after about 16.7 years.

Tech | **Support**
- See Appendix B-5 for information on how to set a calculator window so that a graph is visible.
- For help using the TRACE key, see Appendix B-4.

In Summary

Key Idea

- A relation can be described by a table of values, a graph, an equation, a picture, and words.

Need to Know

- You can use a table of values or a graph to estimate values of a relation.
- You can use an equation to determine exact values of a relation.
- You can graph a relation by entering an equation into a graphing calculator or graphing software.

CHECK *Your Understanding*

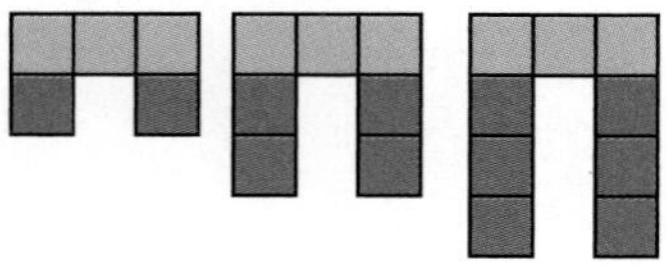

figure 1   figure 2   figure 3

1. Describe a relation between the figure number and the total number of squares using a table of values, a graph, and an equation.

2. Describe each relation using two of the following: a graph, a table of values, a picture, or an equation. Justify your choice.
   a) the perimeter of an equilateral triangle in terms of its side length
   b) the amount John pays for a taxi ride, if the fare is $0.50/km plus a flat rate of $2.50

PRACTISING

3. Graph each relation.

a)

Time (min)	Distance (km)
0	15
5	18
10	21
15	24

b)

Side Length (cm)	Area (cm²)
1	1
2	4
3	9
4	16

c)

x	y
−2	−4
−1	−2
0	0
1	2

4. Describe each relation in the previous question using an equation.

5. Elinor is training for a race. The table shows her times and distances.

Time (min)	Distance (km)
0	0
10	2
20	4
30	6

  a) Which variable is independent and which is dependent?
  b) Estimate the distance Elinor has run after 22 min.
  c) Describe the relation using a graph.
  d) Verify your estimate in part b).

6. Describe each relation with either a table of values or an equation.

a)

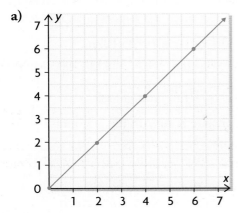

b)

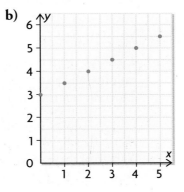

7. This pattern is made of equilateral triangles with sides of 1 cm.
  a) Graph the relation between a figure and its perimeter.
  b) Determine the perimeter of figure 10. Explain your reasoning.
  c) Graph the relation between the figure number and the number of white triangles in the figure.
  d) Determine the number of white triangles in figure 10. Explain.

figure 1   figure 2   figure 3   figure 4

8. The relation between Celsius and Fahrenheit is $C = \dfrac{5}{9}(F - 32)$.
  a) Which variable is independent in this equation? Justify your choice.
  b) Describe the relation using a table of values.
  c) Graph the relation.
  d) Are the data continuous or discrete?
  e) Estimate the Celsius temperature when $F = 100$ using your graph.
  f) Calculate the Celsius temperature when $F = 100$ using the equation.
  g) Why might you predict a value using an equation, instead of a graph or a table?

9. These ordered pairs show the relation between the amount of cell phone use in minutes and the cost, in dollars: (0, 25), (10, 26), (20, 27)

  a) Explain why cost is the dependent variable and what the ordered pair (0, 25) means.

  b) Graph the relation.

  c) Are the data continuous or discrete?

  d) Describe the relation using an equation.

  e) Would you predict the cost of 100 min using a graph, or using an equation? Explain.

  f) Predict the cost of 100 min.

10. Antwan charges \$5/h, plus a flat fee of \$8, in his lawn-mowing business.

  a) Describe the relation between earnings and hours using an equation.

  b) Justify your choice for independent and dependent variables.

11. A van's gas tank holds 75 L. The van uses 0.125 L/km.

  A **a)** Describe the relation between the distance the van travels and the volume of gas in its tank.

  b) How far can the van travel on a full tank of gas?

12. **a)** Which of these ordered pairs are points on the graph of $y = 5x$?
   A. (0, 0) **B.** (2, 10) **C.** (4, 15) **D.** (−2, −10)

  b) Which of these ordered pairs are points on the graph of $y = 3x − 6$?
   A. (2, 0) **B.** (5, 9) **C.** (−1, −9) **D.** (6, 10)

13. Represent each relation using a table of values and a graph.

  a) $y = x$ **c)** $y = -x + 1$ **e)** $y = -\dfrac{1}{2}x$

  b) $y = 2x + 3$ **d)** $y = 0.25x - 3.5$ **f)** $y = -\dfrac{2}{3}x + \dfrac{1}{6}$

14. Match each table to its graph and equation. Explain your reasoning.

a)

x	y
2	6
3	9
4	12

b)

x	y
2	4
3	7
4	10

c)

x	y
2	−4
3	−6
4	−8

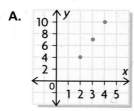

i) $y = -2x$ **ii)** $y = 3x$ **iii)** $y = 3x - 2$

15. Clarise has $50 in her piggy bank. She takes $2.50 from it each week to buy a hot chocolate and a banana from the cafeteria. Create a table of values, a graph, and an equation to describe the amount of money in the piggy bank each week.

16. Jacques surveyed people about their part-time jobs.

Group 1
Abe: $7 per hour
   (waiting tables)
Beth: $20 per lawn
   (mowing lawns)
Carl: 10% commission
   (selling furniture)

Group 2
Anne: $7.50 per hour plus tips
   of $25.00
Boris: $12 per lawn plus a flat
   rate of $5
Carol: 7% commission, plus a
   flat rate of $50

Suppose Abe and Anne each work for 10 h, Beth and Boris each mow 5 lawns, and Carl and Carol each sell $1000 worth of goods. Which group earns more?

17. Describe each relation in words.

   C a) $I = 2.54c$, where I is inches and c is centimetres

   b) $F = \dfrac{9}{5}C + 32$, where F is degrees Fahrenheit and C is degrees Celsius

   c) $k = \dfrac{p}{2.2}$, where p is pounds and k is kilograms

   d) $K = C + 273$, where K is degrees Kelvin and C is degrees Celsius

Extending

18. a) Graph $y = 2x$, $y = 2x + 2$, $y = 3x$, and $y = 3x - 1$ on the same axes.
   b) How do the equations tell you whether the graph will pass through the origin?

19. The table to the right shows several different heights and areas for triangles with a base of 10 cm.
   a) Graph the relation between height and area.
   b) Write an equation to relate the area of the triangle to its height.

Height (cm)	Area (cm²)
2	10
5	25
10	50
20	100

20. A rocket's height in metres, h, at time t, in seconds, is given by $h = -5t^2 + 3t + 2$. Describe the relation between height and time with a table of values and a graph.

3.2 Exploring Linear Relations

YOU WILL NEED

- grid paper

y-intercept

the value of the dependent variable when the independent variable is zero; sometimes called the initial value

direct variation

a relation in which one variable is a multiple of the other

partial variation

a relation in which one variable is a multiple of the other plus a constant amount

linear relation

a relation in which the graph forms a straight line

GOAL

Identify direct and partial variations.

EXPLORE the Math

Rana's Computer Repair Service charges \$45/h. Bill's Computer Repair Service charges a flat fee of \$25 plus \$18/h. Each company charges for parts of hours.

? How are the plans alike and how are they different?

A. Make a table of values that shows solutions for each company's cost for 0, 1, 2, and 3 hours of service.

B. Graph the relation between cost and hours of service for each company.
How are the graphs alike and how are they different?

C. Use an equation to describe the cost in terms of hours of service, for each company.
How are the equations alike and how are they different?

D. Identify the **y-intercept** of each relation. What does it mean in each case?

E. How are the hourly rate and initial value connected to the table of values, graph, and equation for each relation?

F. Identify each relation as a **direct variation** or a **partial variation**. Justify your answer.

Reflecting

G. Why might you have predicted that each graph would be a **linear relation**?

H. If the service time triples, Rana's charge will triple but Bill's won't. Why is that so?

I. How are direct and partial variations alike and how are they different? Refer to graphs, tables, and equations.

In Summary

Key Idea

- You can determine whether a linear relation is a partial or a direct variation by examining its table of values, its graph, or its equation.

Direct Variation	Partial Variation
(0, 0) is an ordered pair in the table of values.	(0, 0) is not an ordered pair in the table of values.
The initial value is 0, so the graph passes through (0, 0).	The initial value is some number, b, so the graph passes through (0, b).
The equation looks like $y = mx$.	The equation looks like $y = mx + b$.

Need to Know

- A solution to a linear relation is an ordered pair that appears in the table of values, lies on the line representing the linear relation, or makes a true statement in the equation of the relation.
- An initial value has a corresponding x-value of zero.

FURTHER Your Understanding

1. Identify each relation as a direct or a partial variation. Support your answer using a table, a graph, and form of the equation.

   a) $y = 2x$

   b) $y = 2x + 3$

   c) $y = 1 - x$

   d) $y = 0.25x - 3.5$

   e) $y = -\dfrac{1}{2}x$

   f) $y = -\dfrac{2}{3}x + \dfrac{1}{6}$

2. A small rocket is launched from a hill 1500 m above sea level. It rises at 35 m/s.
   a) Write an equation for the relation between the height of the rocket and time.
   b) Use a table of values to graph this relation.
   c) Identify this relation as a direct or a partial variation. Explain.

3. Students can choose from two different cafeteria milk plans.
   Plan A: Pay $0.75 per glass of milk
   Plan B: Pay $10, plus $0.25 per glass of milk
   a) Write an equation for each plan.
   b) Determine the cost of 20 glasses for each plan.
   c) Determine the cost of 30 glasses for each plan.
   d) Which plan would you choose? Why?
   e) Identify each plan as a direct or a partial variation.
   f) How does the type of variation affect the cost?

Investigating Properties of Linear Relations

YOU WILL NEED

- grid paper

GOAL

Identify properties of linear relations.

INVESTIGATE the Math

Cole bought a new car for $25 000. This graph shows its value over the first three years.

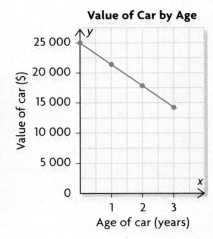

Value of Car by Age

? When will Cole's car be worth $0?

A. Calculate the amount by which Cole's car decreased in value between years 1 and 2.

B. Calculate the **rate of change** in the car's value between years 1 and 3.

C. Calculate the **slope** of the graph between years 1 and 3.

How does the slope compare to your answer in part A?

D. Copy the following table. Complete the **first difference** column. How do the first differences compare to the slope in part C?

rate of change

the change in one variable relative to the change in another

slope

a measure, often represented by m, of the steepness of a line; the ratio comparing the vertical and horizontal distances (called the rise and run) between two points;

$$m = \frac{rise}{run} = \frac{\Delta y}{\Delta x}$$

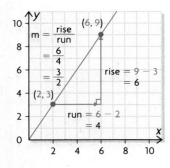

first difference

the difference between two consecutive y-values in a table in which the difference between the x-values is constant

Age of Car, x	Value of Car, y	First Difference, Δy
0	25 000	
1	22 675	22 675 − 25 000 = ■
2	17 850	17 850 − 22 675 = ■
3	13 025	

E. Copy and complete the following table.
Why are the first differences different than in part D?

Age of Car, x	Value of Car, y	First Difference, Δy
0	25 000	
		17 850 − 25 500 = ■
2	17 850	
		■ − 17 850 = ■
4	■	
		■ − ■ = ■
6	■	

Communication | Tip
- The Greek letter "Δ" (delta) represents change, so Δy represent the difference between two y-values.

F. Write an equation for the relation between the car's value and its age. Which parts represent the first differences, the slope, and the y-intercept?

G. Determine the **x-intercept** of the graph. Use it to tell when Cole's car will be worth $0. How do you know?

x-intercept
the value at which a graph meets the x-axis; the value of y is 0 for all x-intercepts

Reflecting

H. What is the connection between the first differences and the slope?

I. When you calculated the slope, did it matter which points you chose? Explain.

J. Use the graph to explain why the first differences were constant.

APPLY the Math

EXAMPLE 1 Applying the connection between slope and rate of change

Andrea and Dana had cycled 30 km after two hours and 60 km after four hours. At what rate were they cycling?

Dana's Solution: Using a table of values

Time in Hours, x	Distance in Kilometres, y	First Difference, Δy
0	0	
		30 − 0 = 30
2	30	
		60 − 30 = 30
4	60	

I made a table of values and calculated the first differences.

The x-values increased by 2, so $\Delta x = 2$.

$$\text{rate of change} = \frac{\Delta y}{\Delta x}$$

> I calculated the rate of change.

$$= \frac{30 \text{ km}}{2 \text{ h}}$$

$$= 15 \text{ km/h}$$

We were cycling at a rate of 15 km/h.

Andrea's Solution: Using a graph

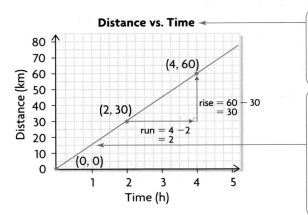

> The distance depended on time, so I chose time as the independent variable.

> I plotted the points and drew a line through them. I assumed they were cycling at a constant rate. I used a solid line because the data are continuous.

$$\text{slope} = \frac{\text{rise}}{\text{run}}$$

> I calculated the slope of the line.

$$= \frac{30 \text{ km}}{2 \text{ h}}$$

$$= 15 \text{ km/h}$$

We were cycling at a rate of 15 km/h.

> The slope gives the speed or rate they were cycling.

Communication | Tip

- We call the horizontal distance between two points the run. The run is positive when it goes to the right and negative when it goes to the left. We call the vertical distance between two points the rise, even if the line goes downward. The rise is positive when it goes upward and negative when it goes downward.

When the data for the independent variable in a table of values do not increase by an equal amount, graphing the data can help you determine if the relationship is linear. If it is, calculating the slope of the line will give you the rate of change of the dependent variable.

EXAMPLE 2 | **Using a graphing strategy to estimate rate of change**

A weather balloon recorded the temperature at these altitudes. Estimate the rate of change of the temperature.

Altitude (km)	6.0	7.0	7.6	8.1	8.7	9.0	9.5
Temperature (°C)	28.0	11.0	2.5	−7.7	−17.9	−23.0	−32.5

Martha's Solution

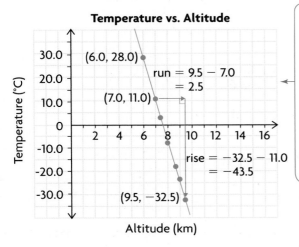

Temperature vs. Altitude

(6.0, 28.0)

run = 9.5 − 7.0
= 2.5

(7.0, 11.0)

rise = −32.5 − 11.0
= −43.5

(9.5, −32.5)

Altitude (km)

I didn't use first differences because the altitude was recorded at irregular times.

I graphed the points and connected them with a solid line.

The graph is straight, so this relation is linear.

$$\text{slope} = \frac{\text{rise}}{\text{run}}$$

$$= \frac{-43.5\ °C}{2.5\ km}$$

$$= -17.4\ °C/km$$

The rate of change is $-17.4\ °C/km$.

I calculated the slope, because it has the same value as the rate of change.

When the altitude increases by 1 km, the temperature decreases by 17.4 °C.

In Summary

Key Idea

- To determine the rate of change of a linear relation, you can do the following:
  - Calculate the first differences in a table in which the x-values increase or decrease by 1.
  - Calculate the slope, $\frac{\text{rise}}{\text{run}}$, using any two points on a graph of the relation. The rate of change has the same value as the slope.

Need to Know

- If the independent values in a table change by a constant amount other than 1, the ratio of the first differences to the change in x, $\frac{\Delta y}{\Delta x}$, is the slope, or the rate of change.

- Δy is the change in y and is equivalent to the rise.
  Δx is the change in x and is equivalent to the run.

CHECK Your Understanding

1. Which of these relations are linear? How do you know?

a)

x	y
1	3
2	6
3	9
4	12

c)

x	y
1	1
2	4
3	9
4	16

b)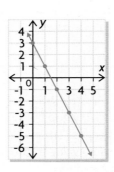

d)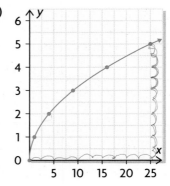

2. Determine the rate of change for each linear relation in question 1.

PRACTISING

3. Determine the rate of change in each linear relation.

a)

x	y
2	11
4	17
6	23
8	29
10	35

b)

x	y
5	0
4	2
3	4
2	6
1	8

c)

x	y
0	0
0.25	2
0.5	4
0.75	6
1	8

d)

x	y
1	−2
4	−8
5	−10
3	−6
2	−4

4. a) Why might this table mislead you about whether the relation is linear?

Age of Car in Years, x	0	3	1	2
Value of Car in Dollars, y	15 000	6 000	12 000	9 000

b) Graph the data.
c) What is the slope and what does it mean?
d) What is the x-intercept? Does this seem realistic? Explain.

5. What is the slope of this roof?

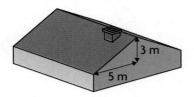

6. There are three steps from the ground to
a front porch 72 cm above the ground,
as shown.
  a) What is the rise of each step?
  b) The horizontal distance across
       each step is 25 cm. Determine the
       length of *AB*.
  c) Determine the slope of the handrail.

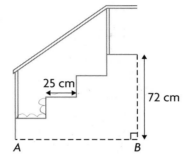

7. Determine the slope of the line that passes through each pair of points.
a) (3, 5) and (0, 2)   **d)** (4, 0) and (6, 18)
b) (3, 3) and (−2, 2)   **e)** (1, −1) and (2, 2)
c) (21, −10) and (20, 24)   **f)** (−3, −8) and (−5, −6)

8. Use the title and axis labels of each graph to tell what the *y*-intercept
and slope mean in each case.

a)

**Cost of a Luncheon at
Vince's Banquet Hall**

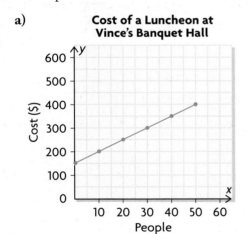

b)

**Depreciation
of a Copier**

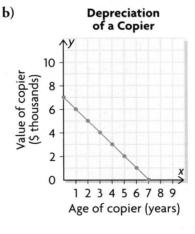

9. Determine two more ordered pairs for each relation. Explain your
reasoning.
  a) rise is 2, run is 3; (2, 5) lies on the line
  b) rise is −3, run is 4; (0, −2) lies on the line
  c) rise is 5, run is 1; (1, −6) lies on the line
  d) rise is −2, run is 1; (−2, −3) lies on the line

Altitude (km)	Air Pressure (Pa)
1	80 000
3	60 000
6	40 000
16	20 000
22	10 000
30	5 000

10. a) Graph the data in the table to the left.
  b) How does the graph show the rate of change?
  c) Estimate the air pressure at an altitude of 20 km.

11. Graph each relation and state the slope.

  a) $y = 3x$
  c) $y = \dfrac{3}{4}x + 1$
  e) $y = -x$

  b) $y = -2x$
  d) $y = -\dfrac{1}{5}x + 1$
  f) $y = \dfrac{2}{3}x - 4$

12. An equation for a house's value is $y = 7500x + 125\,000$, where y is the value in dollars and x is the time in years, starting now.

  a) What is the current value of the house?
  b) What is the value of the house 2 years from now?
  c) Determine the value of the house in 7 years.
  d) At what rate is the house value changing from year to year?

13. The amount of money in Alexander's account is $y = 4000 - 70x$, where y is the amount in dollars and x is the time in weeks.
  a) Which variable is independent and which is dependent?
  b) How do you know the relation is linear?
  c) Determine the rate of change of the money in Alexander's account.
  d) What does the rate of change mean?
  e) How does the rate of change relate to the equation?
  f) When will Alexander's account be empty?

14. This graph shows the maximum heart rate a person should try to achieve while exercising.
  a) What does the y-intercept mean?
  b) What does the slope represent?
  c) Write an equation for the line.
  d) Estimate the maximum heart rate for a 58-year-old.

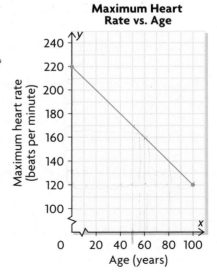

Maximum Heart Rate vs. Age

15. Jae-Ho works at a clothing store. He earns a weekly salary of $300 and
T 5% commission on his total weekly sales. He thinks that if his
commission doubles, so will his earnings. Is he right? Justify your answer.

16. Marie earns $1 for every 4 papers she delivers.
C

a) Show that the relation between papers delivered and money earned
is linear, using a graph and a table of values.
b) What do the first differences mean?
c) What is the rate of change of Marie's earnings?
d) Predict Marie's earnings for delivering 275 papers using an equation.

Extending

17. Write a linear equation for each line.

a) a line with a y-intercept of 2 and a slope of $\dfrac{3}{5}$

b) a line with a y-intercept of 0 and a slope of -4
c) a line that passes through $(0, 5)$ and $(3, 6)$
d) a line with a slope of 2 that passes through $(4, 1)$

e) a line with a slope of $-\dfrac{1}{2}$ that passes through $(3, 0)$

f) a line with a slope of $\dfrac{4}{7}$ that passes through $(7, 2)$

18. a) Make a table of values and a graph for each relation.
C **b)** Copy and complete the table using your results from part a).
c) What connections do you see between each equation and the
values in the table?

Equation	Slope	y-intercept	x-intercept
$2x + 5y = 10$			
$4x - 2y = 7$			
$x + y = -2$			

Linear Relations **159**

FREQUENTLY ASKED Questions

Study | **Aid**

• See Lesson 3.1, Examples 1, 2, and 3.
• Try Mid-Chapter Review Question 1.

Q: How can you describe a relation between two variables?

A: You can use a picture, a table of values, a graph, or an algebraic equation.

EXAMPLE

Tickets to an amusement park cost $6, plus $2 per ride. Describe the relation between the number of rides and the cost.

Solution

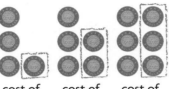

cost of   cost of   cost of
1 ride   2 rides   3 rides

$6 is constant, so it is the same in each picture.
The picture shows the cost increases by $2 with each additional ride.

Solution

Number of Rides	Cost
0	6
1	8
2	10
3	12

The table shows the cost increases by $2 with each additional ride.

Solution

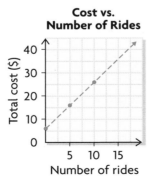

Calculate the cost for 0 rides, 5 rides, and 10 rides. Use the number of rides as the independent variable and the cost as the dependent variable. Only whole numbers of rides make sense, so the data are discrete. Connect the points with a dotted line.

Solution

Let R represent the number of rides, the independent variable.
Let C represent the cost in dollars, the dependent variable.
Cost = 2 × number of rides + 6
$$C = 2R + 6$$

Q: **How do you know whether a linear relation is a direct variation or a partial variation?**

A: You can use a table of values or a graph.

Study | *Aid*

• See Lesson 3.2, Examples, 1, 2, and 3.
• Try Mid-Chapter Review Question 2.

EXAMPLE

Mark delivers groceries to senior citizens for a flat fee of $10 plus $5 per hour and he charges for part hours. Identify the relation between cost and time as a direct or partial variation.

Solution

Time (h)	Cost ($)
0	10
1	15
2	20
3	25
4	30

Each cost is calculated as $5 \times h + 10$. That means it is a partial variation.

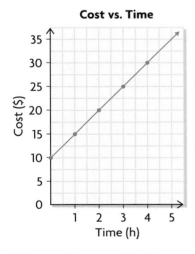

Cost vs. Time

The graph is a straight line, so the relation is linear. The graph passes through (0, 10), so it is a partial variation.

Study | **Aid**

- See Lesson 3.3, Examples 1 and 2.
- Try Mid-Chapter Review Questions 3, 4, and 5.

Q: **How can you determine the rate of change of a linear relation?**

A: You can use a table of values or a graph to calculate slope.

EXAMPLE

Janelle did 5 sit-ups on day 1, 10 sit-ups on day 2, and 15 sit-ups on day 3. Determine the rate of change between sit-ups and days.

Solution

Day, x	Sit-Ups, y	First Difference, Δy
0	0	
		$5 - 0 = 5$
1	5	
		$10 - 5 = 5$
2	10	
		$15 - 10 = 5$
3	15	

The x-variables increase by 1, so the first differences give the rate of change. The rate of change is 5 sit-ups per day.

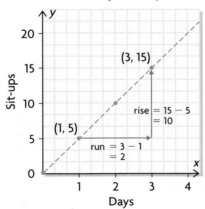

The set of data is discrete, so connect the points with a dotted line. Choose two points and calculate the slope.

$$\text{slope} = \frac{\text{rise}}{\text{run}}$$

$$= \frac{10 \text{ sit-ups}}{2 \text{ days}}$$

$$= 5 \text{ sit-ups/day}$$

The rate of change is 5 sit-ups per day.

PRACTICE Questions

Lesson 3.1

1. **a)** Use a table of values, a graph, and an algebraic expression to describe the relation between the number of circles in each figure and the number of stars in the figure.

figure 1   figure 2   figure 3

   b) How many circles would be in figure 75?
   c) How many stars would be in figure 75?

Lesson 3.2

2. Identify each relation as a partial or a direct variation. Justify your answer.
   a) A hockey player is paid $2 million per year, plus a signing bonus of $500 000.
   b) Cheryl has $800 in her bank account. She adds $25 to the account each week.
   c) Anthony bicycles at 5 m/s.

Lesson 3.3

3. Determine the rate of change in each relation.

   a)

x	y
3	1
6	11
9	21

   b) The number of words Ming can type is related to time. He can type 200 words in 5 min.
   c) $y = 3x$

4. Is each relation linear? Explain your reasoning.

   a)

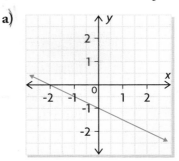

   b) $y = 0.25x - 3$

   c)

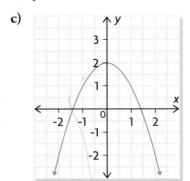

   d)

x	−3	4	−1
y	−6	8	−2

5. Marie withdraws the same amount from her account each week, as shown.

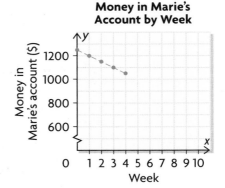

Money in Marie's Account by Week

   a) What is the slope and what does it mean?
   b) What is the y-intercept and what does it mean?
   c) When will Marie's account be empty?

Equivalent Linear Relations

Represent a linear relation in a different form.

LEARN ABOUT *the Math*

A health food store is making a mix of nuts and raisins. Nuts are $30/kg and raisins are $10/kg. The total mix should cost $150. $30n + 10r = 150$ describes the relation between the mass of nuts, *n*, and the mass of raisins, *r*, that cost $150.

? What combinations of nuts and raisins cost $150?

EXAMPLE 1	Connecting the equation and the graph

Determine the combinations of nuts and raisins that will cost $150.

Chelsea's Solution: Using a graphing strategy to determine values of a relation

Mass of Nuts (kg)	Mass of Raisins (kg)
1	$30(1) + 10r = 150$ $30 + 10r = 150$ $30 + 10r - 30 = 150 - 30$ $10r = 120$ $\dfrac{10r}{10} = \dfrac{120}{10}$ $r = 12$
2	$30(2) + 10r = 150$ $60 + 10r = 150$ $60 + 10r - 60 = 150 - 60$ $10r = 90$ $\dfrac{10r}{10} = \dfrac{90}{10}$ $r = 9$
3	$30(3) + 10r = 150$ $90 + 10r = 150$ $90 + 10r - 90 = 150 - 90$ $10r = 60$ $\dfrac{10r}{10} = \dfrac{60}{10}$ $r = 6$

I calculated the mass of raisins needed for 1 kg, 2 kg, and 3 kg of nuts.

Mass of Nuts (kg)	Mass of Raisins (kg)	First Differences
1	12	
		−3
2	9	
		−3
3	6	

The first differences were the same, so the relation is linear.

Mix of Nuts and Raisins

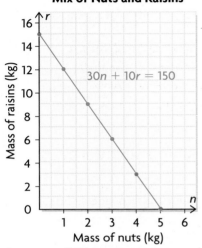

$30n + 10r = 150$

I used nuts as the independent variable.

I drew a solid line, since the data are continuous.

I determined other combinations by identifying other points on the line.

I only used positive numbers for the masses, since it doesn't make sense to talk about a negative mass.

Some possibilities are no nuts and 15 kg of raisins, 4 kg of nuts and 3 kg of raisins, and 5 kg of nuts and no raisins.

Bob used the intercepts to graph the relation quickly.

Bob's Solution: Using the intercepts as a strategy to graph the relation

$30n + 10r = 150$
$30y + 10x = 150$

The equation is of degree 1, so the relation is linear. I chose raisins as the independent variable. I replaced r with x and n with y.

x-intercept	y-intercept
$y = 0$	$x = 0$
$30(0) + 10x = 150$	$30y + 10(0) = 150$
$10x = 150$	$30y = 150$
$\dfrac{10x}{10} = \dfrac{150}{10}$	$\dfrac{30y}{30} = \dfrac{150}{30}$
$x = 15$	$y = 5$

I used the x- and y-intercepts to draw the graph.

Two mixes that cost $150 are 15 kg of raisins and no nuts and 5 kg of nuts and no raisins.

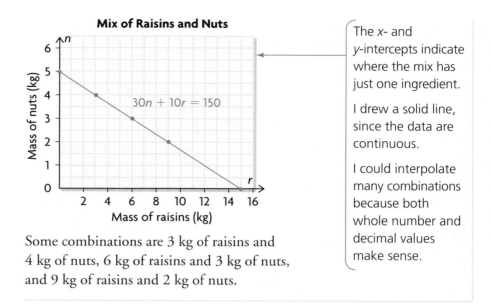

Mix of Raisins and Nuts

$30n + 10r = 150$

The x- and y-intercepts indicate where the mix has just one ingredient.

I drew a solid line, since the data are continuous.

I could interpolate many combinations because both whole number and decimal values make sense.

Some combinations are 3 kg of raisins and 4 kg of nuts, 6 kg of raisins and 3 kg of nuts, and 9 kg of raisins and 2 kg of nuts.

Reflecting

A. Chelsea and Bob chose different independent and dependent variables. How are their tables of values and graphs alike and how are they different?

B. Why did it not matter which variable was independent?

C. How did both Chelsea and Bob show that the relation is linear?

D. Why did Chelsea and Bob create graphs using only the first quadrant?

APPLY the Math

EXAMPLE 2	**Using intercepts as a strategy to graph a line**

Graph the line $2x + \dfrac{3}{4}y = 21$.

Greg's Solution

$$2x + \frac{3}{4}y = 21$$

$$2(0) + \frac{3}{4}y = 21$$

I set $x = 0$ to determine the y-intercept.

$$0 + \frac{3}{4}y = 21$$

$$y = 21 \div \frac{3}{4}$$

$$y = 21 \times \frac{4}{3}$$

$$y = 28$$

I solved the equation.

The y-intercept is 28.

$$2x + \frac{3}{4}(0) = 21$$

I set $y = 0$ to determine the x-intercept.

$$2x = 21$$
$$x = 10.5$$

I solved the equation.

The x-intercept is 10.5.

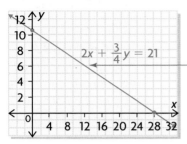

The equation is of degree 1, so the relation was linear. I drew a line through $(0, 28)$ and $(10.5, 0)$.

Since the variables x and y can be any number, I put arrows on the end of the line to show this relationship continues in both directions.

This is the graph of $2x + \frac{3}{4}y = 21$.

EXAMPLE 3   Using a table of values to draw a graph

Complete the table of values for $3x + 2y - 12 = 0$ and then graph the line.

x	0	1	2
y			

Claire's Solution

x	y
0	$3(0) + 2y - 12 = 0$ $2y - 12 = 0$ $y = 6$
1	$3(1) + 2y - 12 = 0$ $2y = 0 - 3 + 12$ $2y \div 2 = 9 \div 2$ $y = 4.5$
2	$3(2) + 2y - 12 = 0$ $6 + 2y - 12 = 0$ $2y = 0 - 6 + 12$ $y = 3$

I solved for y for each value of x.

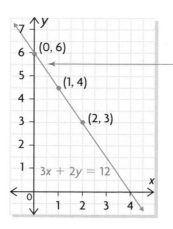

I plotted (0, 6), (1, 4.5), and (2, 3) and drew a solid line through them. I knew the graph was linear because the equation of degree 1.

Since the variables x and y can be any number, I put arrows on the end of the line to show this relationship continues in both directions.

This is the graph of $3x + 2y = 12$.

A graph of a relation can often be a useful tool to help you solve problems.

EXAMPLE 4   Using intercepts to solve a problem

Mia is travelling to a campsite 52 km away. She plans to bike part of the way and canoe the rest of the way. She can bike at 13 km/h and paddle her canoe downstream at 8 km/h. Determine three combinations of biking and canoeing distances Mia can use.

Mia's Solution

If x represents the time in hours I bike, then $13x$ is the distance I can bike.

If y represents the time in hours I canoe, then $8y$ is the distance I can canoe.

The total distance is the distance biking plus the distance paddling.

It doesn't matter which variable is independent.

$$\text{Total distance} = 13x + 8y$$
$$52 = 13x + 8y$$

The equation is of degree 1, so the relation is linear.

$$52 = 13(0) + 8y$$
$$52 = 8y$$
$$52 \div 8 = 8y \div 8$$
$$6.5 = y$$

I calculated the y-intercept by setting $x = 0$.

I can canoe for 6.5 h and bike for 0 h.

$$52 = 13x + 8(0)$$
$$\frac{52}{13} = \frac{13x}{13}$$
$$4 = x$$

I calculated the x-intercept by setting $y = 0$.

I can bike for 4 h and canoe for 0 h.

By Bike and Canoe

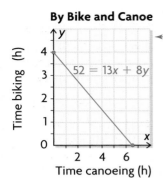

I graphed the relation using the x- and y-intercepts. I identified points on the line and how far I can bike and canoe to reach my campsite.

I drew the graph only in the first quadrant since the time canoeing or biking must be 0 or greater.

I can bike for 1 h and canoe for just under 5 h or any other (x, y) combination on the line.

In Summary

Key Ideas

- You can write a linear relation in the forms $Ax + By = C$ or $Ax + By + C = 0$, or in the form $y = mx + b$.
- You can use the form $Ax + By = C$ to determine the x- and y-intercepts and use them to graph a linear relation.

Need to Know

- The x-intercept is the point at which the line meets or crosses the x-axis. The coordinates of the x-intercept are $(x, 0)$. To determine the x-intercept, set $y = 0$ and solve for x.
- When you write a linear relation in the form $Ax + By = C$, usually it does not matter which variable is independent.

CHECK Your Understanding

1. Graph each relation using the x- and y-intercepts.

   a) $-3x + 2y = 6$ b) $\dfrac{1}{2}x + \dfrac{2}{3}y = \dfrac{1}{6}$ c) $y = 2x - 1$

2. Marie works at a boutique and at a travel agency. In all, she works for 38 h per week.

   a) Write a linear relation to model this case. Use x for the number of hours she works at the boutique, and y for the number of hours she works at the travel agency.

   b) What do the x- and y-intercepts mean?

PRACTISING

3. Locate three points on the line $6x - y = 18$, where x and y are both integers, and draw the line.

4. Graph each relation using the x- and y-intercepts.
   a) $2x - 5y = 10$ **c)** $x + y = 0$
   b) $4x + 5y = 20$ **d)** $2x + 3y = 0$

5. Nicolas has $14.50 in quarters and dimes.
   a) Explain why $0.10x + 0.25y = 14.50$ models this case.
   b) Is this relation linear? Explain.
   c) Determine the x- and y-intercepts. What do they mean?
   d) Are the data continuous or discrete? Explain.

6. Amir earns $9/h working in a coffee shop and $11.25/h working in a grocery store. Last week he earned $288.
   a) Explain why $9x + 11.25y = 288$ models this case.
   b) Is this relation a straight line? Explain.
   c) Determine the x- and y-intercepts. What do they mean?
   d) For how many hours might Amir have worked in each place?

7. A boat travels down the St. Lawrence River at 30 km/h and moors at a
   K spot where the passengers can watch whales. After a while, it travels back up the river to its starting point at 20 km/h. The boat travels 60 km in all.
   a) Explain why $30x + 20y = 60$ models this problem. Explain what x and y represent.
   b) Determine the x- and y-intercepts. What do they mean?
   c) Graph the relation.

8. Graph each relation using the x- and y-intercepts.

   a) $2x + \dfrac{4}{5}y = 11$ **c)** $-\dfrac{5}{6}x + y = -\dfrac{1}{3}$

   b) $\dfrac{1}{4}x - \dfrac{2}{3}y = 1$ **d)** $-\dfrac{1}{8}x + \dfrac{2}{5}y = \dfrac{2}{25}$

9. Two airplanes appear on the same radar screen with a coordinate grid.
   T The path of one plane is $y = \dfrac{2}{5}x - 2$ and the path of the other is $2x - 5y - 7 = 0$. Do the paths cross?

10. Henri charges $3 to sharpen a pair of figure skates and $2.50 to
   A sharpen a pair of hockey skates. Last Sunday, he earned $240.
   a) Determine two possible numbers of pairs of figure skates and hockey skates that Henri could have sharpened.
   b) Henri sharpened 94 pairs of skates. How many of each type did he sharpen to earn $240?

11. Julia is preparing a mix of raisins and nuts for her brother's party. Chocolate raisins are \$0.88/100 g and peanuts are \$1.00/100 g. She plans to spend \$3.00 on the mix.
   a) Explain why $0.88x + 1y = 3$ models this case.
   b) Determine the x- and y-intercepts. What do they mean?
   c) Graph the relation.

12. Jennifer decides to invest \$1200 in mutual funds. One stock is \$3.50/share and the other is \$5.75/share. How many shares of each stock can she buy? Give two possible answers.

13. Copy and complete the table.

Relation	x-intercept	y-intercept	Slope
a) $2x + 3y = 6$			
b) $x + 4y = 9$			
c) $-2x + 5y = -10$			
d) $4x - 6y = 8$			

Extending

14. Look at your answer to question 13. What patterns can help you to determine the slope of any line in the form $Ax + By = C$?

15. Write each equation in $y = mx + b$ form.
   a) $4x + 2y = 8$
   b) $x + y = 2$
   c) $3x - 4y + 1 = 0$

16. Write the equation of each line in the form $Ax + By = C$.
   a) x-intercept 4, y-intercept -2 **c)** x-intercept 1, y-intercept -3
   b) x-intercept $\dfrac{1}{2}$, y-intercept $\dfrac{3}{4}$ **d)** x-intercept $\dfrac{2}{3}$, y-intercept 3

17. The relation $y = 2x^2 - 8$ is not linear. It has two x-intercepts and one y-intercept.
   a) What is the y-coordinate for both x-intercepts?
   b) Calculate the x-intercepts.
   c) Calculate the y-intercept.
   d) Create a table of values and graph $y = 2x^2 - 8$ to verify your answers to parts b) and c).

Linear Relations in the Human Body

Archaeologists use linear relations to determine an adult human's height. The relations they use differ depending on the subject's ethnicity. Also, the relations used are more reliable for predicting the heights of adults than they are for children since an adult's height does not change as much as a child's height does.

For example, the height of an adult female is $H = 2.50t + 74.70$, where H is the female's height and t is the length of the tibia (largest lower leg bone, from knee to ankle), both in centimetres.

The height of an adult male is $H = 2.38t + 78.8$.

1. Test the formulas on yourself and your classmates.

2. Graph the relation between height and tibia length for females and for males.

3. Leonardo da Vinci discovered similar linear relations. For example, the average adult human figure is 7 heads high.

   Write this relation and use it to predict your height and that of your classmates.

4. Measure the height and width of your head.

   Predict the relation between head width and shoulder width.

   Test your prediction on yourself and your classmates.

5. Measure the distance from the end of your wrist to the end of your fingers. Predict the relation between head height and hand length.

   Test your prediction on yourself and your classmates.

6. Can you find other linear relations in the human body?

   Investigate and test your hypotheses.

Linear and Nonlinear Relations

GOAL

Recognize whether a relation is linear or nonlinear.

LEARN ABOUT the Math

Mario is playing a video game in which you gain extra lives by capturing pots of gold. Mario can choose one of two options. He thinks he can capture at least six pots of gold.

Option 1	
Pots of Gold	**Lives Gained**
1	5
2	10
3	15
4	20

Option 2	
Pots of Gold	**Lives Gained**
1	1
2	4
3	9
4	16

? Which option should Mario choose?

EXAMPLE 1 | **Applying properties of linear and nonlinear relations**

Determine which option Mario should choose to gain the most extra lives.

Mario's Solution: Thinking about graphs

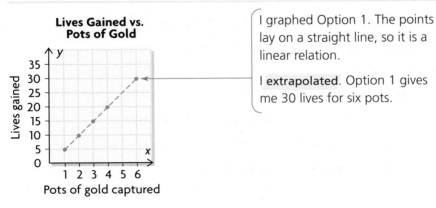

Lives Gained vs. Pots of Gold

I graphed Option 1. The points lay on a straight line, so it is a linear relation.

I **extrapolated**. Option 1 gives me 30 lives for six pots.

extrapolate
to predict a value by following a pattern beyond known values

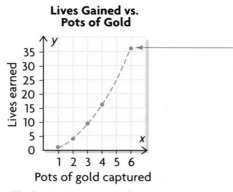

Lives Gained vs. Pots of Gold

Lives earned / Pots of gold captured

nonlinear relation

a relation whose graph is not a straight line

I graphed Option 2. The points did not lie on a straight line, so it is a **nonlinear relation**. I extrapolated. Option 2 gives about 35 or 36 lives for six pots.

I'll choose Option 2 because it gives me more lives.

You can also determine whether a relation is linear or nonlinear from a table of values.

Mika's Solution: Thinking about tables of values

Option 1		
Pots of Gold	**Lives Gained**	**Δy**
1	5	
		5
2	10	
		5
3	15	
		5
4	20	

The first differences in Option 1 are constant, so this relation is linear.

Option 2		
Pots of Gold	**Lives Gained**	**Δy**
1	1	
		3
2	4	
		5
3	9	
		7
4	16	
		9
5	25	
		11
6	36	

The first differences in Option 2 are not constant, so this relation is nonlinear.

Mario should choose Option 2.

Mario gets 30 lives with Option 1 and 36 lives with Option 2.

You can also decide if a relation is linear or not from the degree of its equation.

Louisa's Solution: Thinking about the equations

Let p represent the number of pots of gold.

Let L represent the number of lives gained.

> I chose pots of gold as the independent variable and lives gained as the dependent variable.

Option 1:   lives = 5 × pots of gold

$$L = 5p$$
$$L = 5(6)$$
$$= 30$$

> Option 1 gives five lives for each pot.

> I created an equation for Option 1. It is of degree 1, so the relation is linear.

> I solved for L when $p = 6$. With Option 1, Mario gets 30 lives.

Option 2:   lives = (pots of gold)^2

$$L = p^2$$
$$L = 6^2$$
$$= 36$$

> I created an equation for Option 2. It is of degree 2, so the relation is nonlinear.

> I solved for $p = 6$. With Option 2, Mario gets 36 lives.

Mario should choose Option 2, because it gives more lives.

Reflecting

A.   Why would you expect the first differences to be constant for a linear relation but not constant for a nonlinear relation?

B.   How can you tell from a table, a graph, and an equation if a relation is linear or nonlinear?

APPLY the Math

EXAMPLE 2 | Using an algebraic strategy to identify a linear relation

The circumference of a circle is the diameter multiplied by π. Identify the relation between circumference and diameter as linear or nonlinear.

Kee's Solution

Let d represent the diameter and
C represent the circumference.
Then, $C = \pi d$. ⟵ | I created an equation for the relation.
The equation is of degree 1, so the
relation is linear.

EXAMPLE 3 | Using an algebraic strategy to identify a nonlinear relation

The volume of a cube is the length of one side cubed. Identify the relation between volume and side length as linear or nonlinear.

Joe's Solution

Let s represent the side length of a
cube and V represent the volume.
Then, $V = s^3$. ⟵ | I created an equation for the relation.
The equation is of degree 3, so the
relation is nonlinear.

EXAMPLE 4   Evaluating a relation

The number of bacteria, y, in a dish double every hour. An equation for this is $y = 2^x$, where x is time in hours. There is one bacterium at time 0. Predict the number of bacteria at 7 h.

Eva's Solution: Using a strategy involving graphing technology

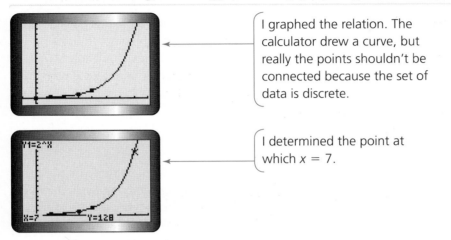

I graphed the relation. The calculator drew a curve, but really the points shouldn't be connected because the set of data is discrete.

I determined the point at which $x = 7$.

Tech | **Support**

For help determining the value of a relation on a graphing calculator, see Appendix B-4.

There should be 128 bacteria at 7 h.

Wes's Solution: Using a substitution strategy

$y = 2^x$
$y = 2^7$
$y = 128$

I substituted 7 for x in the equation, since this was the number of hours that had gone by.

Time (h)	Number of Bacteria
0	1
1	2
2	4
3	8
4	16
5	32
6	64
7	128

I used a table of values to see if my answer was reasonable.

I doubled the number of bacteria each hour.

I extended the table to 7 h.

At 7 h, there will be 128 bacteria.

EXAMPLE **5**	Thinking about slopes of nonlinear relations

Calculate the slopes of some line segments joining points on the graph of $y = 2x^2 + 1$. How do these compare to the slopes of segments joining points on the graph of a line?

David's Solution

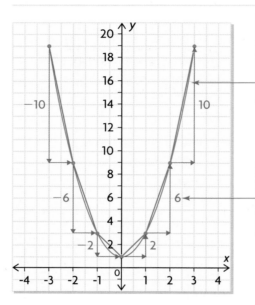

I drew line segments joining points on the graph that had *x*-coordinates 1-unit apart. That meant that for each segment, the run was 1.

Then I calculated the rise for each line segment. Since the run is 1 in each case, the rise is equal to the slope of each segment.

The slopes are not constant and that is different from the slopes of segments joining points on a linear relation.

I knew that the slopes of any line segment on a linear graph would be constant.

For this relation, the farther pairs of points are from 0, the steeper the slope becomes.

In Summary

Key Ideas

- Some relations are nonlinear.
- If a relation is nonlinear, then the following are true:
  - The graph is not a straight line.
  - The first differences are not constant.
  - The degree of its equation is not 1.

Need to Know

- In a nonlinear relation, the slope between pairs of points is not constant.

178 Chapter 3

CHECK *Your Understanding*

1. Identify each relation as linear or nonlinear. Explain how you know.

a)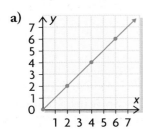

b)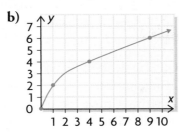

2. The area of a circle of radius r is $A = \pi r^2$. Identify this relation as linear or nonlinear. Explain.

PRACTISING

3. Identify each relation as linear or nonlinear.

a)

x	y
−3	9
−2	4
−1	1
0	0

b)

x	y
5	1
6	2
7	3
8	4

c)

x	y
1	0.25
2	0.50
3	0.75
4	1.00

4. Josie ran these distances while training for a marathon.

Time (min)	Distance Run (km)
0	0
10	2
20	4
30	6

a) Would you choose time or distance as the independent variable? Explain.

b) Identify the relation between distance and time as linear or nonlinear. Explain how you know.

5. This pattern is made from squares with sides of 1 cm.

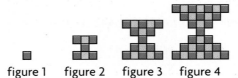

figure 1   figure 2   figure 3   figure 4

a) Use a table to show the perimeter of each figure in terms of its figure number.
b) Determine the perimeter of figure 12. Explain your reasoning.
c) Identify the relation in part a) as linear or nonlinear. Explain how you know.
d) Use a table of values to show the number of blue squares in terms of the figure number.
e) Determine the number of blue squares in figure 12. Explain your reasoning.
f) Identify the relation in part d) as linear or nonlinear. Explain how you know.

6. Identify each relation as linear or nonlinear. Explain your reasoning.

a) the relation between the number of circles in each figure and the figure number

b) the relation between the number of stars in each figure and the figure number

figure 1   figure 2   figure 3   figure 1   figure 2   figure 3   figure 4

7. The relation between kilometres driven, k, and the amount of gasoline, G, (in litres) in the tank of a hybrid car is $G = 80 - 0.2k$.
a) Identify this relation as linear or nonlinear. Explain how you know.
b) Use either a graph or a table to confirm your answer in part a).

8. The amount of cucumbers you can grow in a season depends on the amount of rainfall you get. This relation is represented by the equation $C = 0.006(R + 20)$, where R is the rainfall in millimetres and C is the cucumber yield in kilograms per square metre.
a) Identify this relation as linear or nonlinear. Explain how you know.
b) Use either a graph or a table of values to confirm your answer in part a).

9. When a piece of paper is folded in half, one crease line and two
T sections of paper are created. The paper is then folded in half again and again, each time increasing the number of crease lines by 1. Identify the relation between the number of creases and the number of sections of paper as linear or nonlinear. Justify your answer.

10. A large hailstone falls from a cloud 5000 m above the ground. This
A table shows its altitude at different times. About how many seconds
will it take for the hailstone to hit the ground? How do you know?

Time (s)	0	5	10	15	20
Altitude (m)	5000	4875	4500	3875	3000

11. Each pattern represents a relation between the figure number and the
C number of red triangles needed to make it.
   a) Which of these patterns are linear and which are nonlinear
   relations?
   b) Explain how you know.

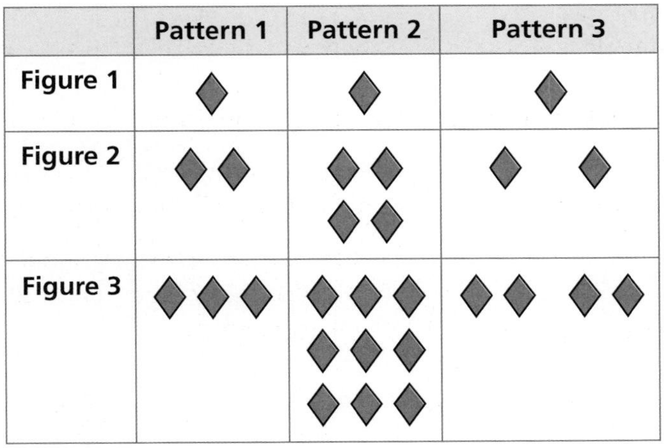

	Pattern 1	Pattern 2	Pattern 3
Figure 1	◆	◆	◆
Figure 2	◆◆	◆◆ ◆◆	◆ ◆
Figure 3	◆◆◆	◆◆◆ ◆◆◆ ◆◆◆	◆◆ ◆◆

Extending

12. Calculate the first, second, and third differences for each relation.
What is the connection between the degree of the equation and the
differences?

   a) $y = x^2$ **c)** $y = -2x^2$ **e)** $y = \dfrac{1}{3}x^2 + 2x - 1$

   b) $y = x^3$ **d)** $y = 4x^3$ **f)** $y = -2x^3 + x$

13. Identify each relation as linear or nonlinear. Use a graph or a table to
justify your answer.
   a) $y = (x + 1)(x - 2)$
   b) $y = 2(x - 1)(x + 3)$

   c) $y = x^{\frac{1}{2}}$

   d) $y = \sqrt{x}$

FREQUENTLY ASKED Questions

Study **Aid**

• See Lesson 3.4.
• Try Chapter Review
  Questions 5 and 6.

Q: How can you graph a linear relation in the form $Ax + By = C$?

A1: Plot and join x- and y-intercepts in a straight line, which are found by setting $y = 0$ and $x = 0$ in turn.

EXAMPLE

Graph $3x - 4y = 12$.

Solution

$$(y = 0)$$
$$3x - 4(0) = 12$$
$$3x = 12$$
$$x = 4$$
The x-intercept is 4.

$$(x = 0)$$
$$3(0) - 4y = 12$$
$$-4y = 12$$
$$y = -3$$
The y-intercept is -3.

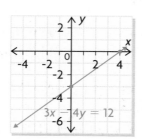

A2: Plot and join ordered pairs (x, y) from a table of values you create.

EXAMPLE

Graph $x + 2y = 8$.

Solution

Choose numbers for x and create a table of values.

$x + 2y = 8$				
x	-4	-2	0	2	4
y	6	5	4	3	2

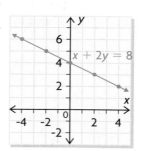

Q: How can you determine whether a relation is nonlinear?

A: A relation is nonlinear if its first differences are not constant, its graph is not a straight line, or the degree of its equation is a value other than 1.

Study **Aid**

• See Lesson 3.5.
• Try Chapter Review
  Questions 7 and 8.

EXAMPLE

Identify the relation $y = x^2$ as linear or nonlinear.

Solution

x	y	Δy
1	1	
		$4 - 1 = 3$
2	4	
		$9 - 4 = 5$
3	9	

nonlinear: first differences not constant

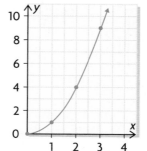

$y = x^2$

nonlinear: equation of degree 2

nonlinear: graph curved

PRACTICE Questions

Lesson 3.1

1. Represent each relation in another form.

a)

x	y
1	0
3	2
5	4

b)

x	y
−1	1
2	−2
5	−5

c) $y = 2x + 4$

d)
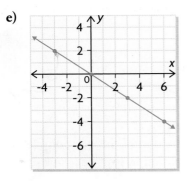

e)

f) $3x - 2y = 12$

Lesson 3.2

2. a) Identify each relation in question 1 as a direct or partial variation. Explain.

   b) Solve each relation in question 1 for $x = 7$.

Lesson 3.3

3. Calculate the slope of each line.

   a) The rise is 4 and the run is 5.

   b) $\Delta y = 8$ when $\Delta x = 2$.

   c) The change in x is 6 and the change in y is 10.

   d) The line passes through points $(2, 7)$ and $(6, -1)$

   e) The first differences are -5 when the change in x is 1.

4. Kristina is snowboarding down this hill.

   a) On which segment will she go fastest? Why?

   b) On which segment will she go slowest? Why?

   c) Prove your answers to parts a) and b) mathematically.

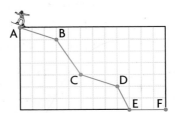

5. Determine two more ordered pairs that lie on each line.

   a) The rise is 3, the run is 4, and $(2, -5)$ is on the line.

   b) The slope is $\dfrac{2}{3}$ and the y-intercept is $(0, 5)$.

   c) The slope is $-\dfrac{3}{5}$ and the x-intercept is $(3, 0)$.

   d) $\Delta y = 5$, $\Delta x = 2$, and $(-1, -1)$ is on the line.

Lesson 3.4

6. a) Graph $y = \dfrac{2}{3}x - 4$

   b) Graph $3x - 6y = 12$

Linear Relations **183**

7. A rectangle has a perimeter of 210 cm.
  a) Explain why $2L + 2W = 210$ models the case. What are L and W?
  b) Graph $2L + 2W = 210$.
  c) Is the set of data discrete or continuous? Explain.
  d) Determine two combinations of length and width for this rectangle.

8. Is $x = 5$ the x-intercept of $2x - 3y = 10$? Explain how you know.

Lesson 3.5

9. Identify each relation as linear or nonlinear. Explain your reasoning.

  a)
  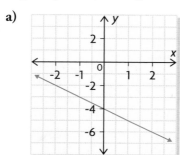

  b) $y = 0.25x - 3$

  c)

x	−3	−2	−1
y	2	3	4

  d)
  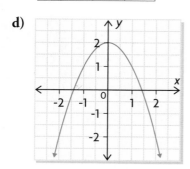

  e) $y^2 = 4 - x^2$

  f)

x	−3	−2	−1
y	27	8	1

10. A ball is hit straight up into the air. The table shows its height at various times.

Time (s)	Height (m)
0	1
1	26
2	41
3	46
4	41
5	26
6	1

  a) Identify the relation between height and time as linear or nonlinear.
  b) Graph the data.
  c) Estimate the height of the ball at 1.5 s.
  d) Estimate the time at which the height of the ball is 44 m.
  e) Determine the time at which the ball hits the ground.
  f) Determine the maximum height of the ball.

11. The table shows the value y, in dollars, of a rare coin that is x years old.

x	y
0	0.25
10	750.25
20	1500.25
30	2250.25

  a) Is this relationship linear or nonlinear?
  b) Graph the data.
  c) Find the equation of this relationship.
  d) Use the equation to find the value of the coin after 15 years.

1. A fruit stand sells apples for $0.25 each.
   a) Describe the relation between cost and number of apples bought using a graph, a table, or an equation.
   b) Which variable is independent and which is dependent?
   c) Is the set of data continuous or discrete?
   d) Determine the cost of 150 apples.

2. Gill rents a car for $45/day plus $0.15/km. Is the relation between distance and cost linear? Use a table to support your answer.

3. Which choice best describes the relation between distance and time?

Distance (m)	0	4	8	12	16	20	24
Time (s)	0	1	2	3	4	5	6

   A. a linear, direct variation
   B. a linear, partial variation
   C. a nonlinear, direct variation
   D. a nonlinear, partial variation

4. What is the slope of the line between points $(0, 4)$ and $(3, -1)$?

   A. $-\dfrac{3}{5}$ B. $\dfrac{3}{5}$ C. $-\dfrac{5}{3}$ D. $\dfrac{5}{3}$

5. What is the rate of change of the stretch of a spring with a weight attached?

Mass (g)	1	2	3	4
Stretch (cm)	5	10	15	20

   A. 5 cm/g   B. 1 g/5 s   C. 1 cm/5 g   D. 5 g/s

6. George is going 6 km on foot. He can run at 4 km/h and walk at 2 km/h.
   a) Explain why $4x + 2y = 6$ models the distance he will travel. What do x and y represent?
   b) How long would it take him to run all the way and to walk all the way?
   c) Graph the combinations of times that he could walk and run.
   d) Determine three combinations of times that George could walk and run.

7. Identify the relation between the figure number and the number of squares as linear or nonlinear. Use a table of values, a graph, and an equation to support your answer.

   a) □ □□ □□□
   figure 1   figure 2   figure 3

   b)
   figure 1   figure 2   figure 3

Choosing a Car

Atul is buying a new car. He is deciding between a four-cylinder car and a hybrid crossover car. He wants to choose the car with the better fuel economy.

The four-cylinder car holds 75 L and uses 14 L for every 100 km travelled.

The fuel consumption for the hybrid car is given by $y = 80 - 0.20x$, where y is the amount of fuel in the tank after x kilometres have been driven.

? Which car should Atul buy?

A. Make a table of values for each car.

B. Use the first differences to compare the rates of change in the fuel volume for each vehicle.

C. Graph the relation between the kilometres driven and the fuel remaining for each car.

D. What are the x- and y-intercepts and what do they mean?

E. What does the slope mean?

F. Use terms from this list to describe the relation between the fuel consumption of each car and the distance driven.
- partial variation
- direct variation
- discrete set of data
- continuous set of data
- linear relation
- nonlinear relation
- independent variable
- dependent variable
- rate of change

G. Write an equation relating the number of kilometres driven and the fuel remaining for the four-cylinder car.

H. Calculate the amount of fuel remaining after driving 250 km for each car.

I. Recommend to Atul which car he should buy. Justify your answer.

Multiple Choice

1. Which expression has the greatest value?
   A. $-5 - 2 + 4 \leq -3$
   B. $3 - 12 + 2$
   C. $-7 - (-2) + 1$
   D. $5 - (-3) - 10 - 7 - (-2) + 1$

2. Which expression has a positive value?
   A. $(-9.3)^2 = 9.2$ C. $(-9.3)^3$
   B. -9.3^2 D. -9.3^3

3. Which of these is not equal to $-5\frac{1}{5}$?

   A. $-\dfrac{26}{5}$ C. -5.2

   B. $-5 + \dfrac{1}{5}$ D. $-5 - \dfrac{1}{5}$

4. Which two numbers have a product of 7^8 and a quotient of 7^4?
   A. 7^6 and 7^1 C. 7^9 and 7^4
   B. 7^3 and 7^2 D. 7^6 and 7^2

5. Which expression is not equal to 2^9?
   A. 8^3 C. $(2^3)(2^3)$
   B. $\dfrac{(36^3)^3}{(18^3)^3}$ D. $(2^4)(2^3)(2)(2)$

6. Which expression do the tiles represent?

   A. $(x^2 + 2x + 4) - (3x^2 - 3x + 1)$
   B. $(x^2 + 2x + 4) - 3x^2 + 3x + 1$
   C. $(-3x^2 + 3x + 1) + (x^2 + 2x + 4)$
   D. $(-3x^2 - 3x - 1) + (x^2 + 2x + 4)$

7. Identify the simplification of
   $12 - 9(x - 5) - (3x + 4)$.
   A. $-12x - 37$ _   C. $-11x - 13$
   B. $-6x - 19$ D. $-12x + 53$

8. The area and length of a rectangle are shown. Determine the missing side.

   $A = 16x^2y$

   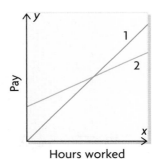

   $4x^2$

   A. $4y$ B. $4xy$ C. $12y$ D. $12xy$

9. Read these statements about the graph.
   i)   Line 1 is a direct variation.
   ii) Pay is the independent variable.
   iii) Line 2 represents a lower-paying job than line 1.

   Which choice best represents the statements?
   A. Only i) is true.
   B. Only ii) is true.
   C. Both i) and ii) are true.
   D. Both i) and iii) are true.

10. Which statement is false?
    A. A line with a negative slope rises to the right.
    B. A line with a positive slope rises to the right.
    C. The y-intercept of a line is the point where the x-coordinate is 0.
    D. If the rate of change of a relation is positive, then its graph goes up from left to right.

11. Identify the correct sum of $3\dfrac{3}{8} + \left(-2\dfrac{1}{6}\right)$.

A. $1\dfrac{5}{24}$ C. $1\dfrac{1}{14}$

B. $5\dfrac{13}{24}$ D. $-1\dfrac{5}{24}$

12. Identify the correct difference: $-\dfrac{3}{5} - 2\dfrac{1}{4}$

A. $-2\dfrac{4}{9}$ C. $-1\dfrac{11}{20}$

B. $-2\dfrac{17}{20}$ D. $-2\dfrac{7}{20}$

13. Which of the following is farthest to the right of zero on a number line?

A. $\left(\dfrac{5}{8}\right)^2$ C. $\left(-1\dfrac{2}{3}\right)^2$

B. $\left(\dfrac{-7}{8}\right)^2$ D. $\left(1\dfrac{1}{4}\right)^2$

14. Which of the following has a value of 1?

A. $1\dfrac{1}{2} \times \dfrac{1}{2}$ C. $\dfrac{3}{5} \div 1\dfrac{2}{3}$

B. $-\dfrac{3}{4} \times 1\dfrac{1}{3}$ D. $-2\dfrac{1}{4} \div \left(-2\dfrac{1}{4}\right)$

15. Which of the following are like terms?
   A. $2x$ and $3x^2$ C. $-6a^2$ and $-6a^3$
   B. $-5y$ and $4x$ D. $7c$ and $-9c$

16. What is the value of $4(2x - 3) + 6x^2$ when $x = -1$?
   A. -26 C. 14
   B. 26 D. -14

17. Which one of these ordered pairs is not on the graph of $y = -3x - 2$?
   A. $(4, -14)$ C. $(-1, 1)$
   B. $(-2, 3)$ D. $(0, -2)$

18. What is the slope of the line that passes through A(-4, 7) and B(3, -2)?

A. $\dfrac{9}{-7}$ C. $\dfrac{9}{7}$

B. $\dfrac{-7}{9}$ D. $\dfrac{7}{9}$

19. What are the x- and y-intercepts of $-2x - 5y = 20$?
   A. $x = 10$ and $y = -4$
   B. $x = -10$ and $y = -4$
   C. $x = -10$ and $y = 4$
   D. $x = 10$ and $y = 4$

20. Sara rents a car for a day. She is charged for $35 plus $0.20/km. Which one of the following statements is false?
   A. The initial cost value is $35.
   B. The rate of change is $0.20/km.
   C. The relation between cost and distance driven is a direct variation.
   D. It will cost Sara $55 to rent the car for one day and drive 100 km.

21. Which of the following statements are true?
   A. The first differences of a linear relation are constant.
   B. The equation of a linear relation has a degree of 1.
   C. The first differences of a nonlinear relation are not constant.
   D. All of the above.

22. A rectangle has a perimeter of 120 cm. Which of the following dimensions are not possible for this rectangle?
   A. length 55 cm and width 5 cm
   B. length 45 cm and width 15 cm
   C. length 26 cm and width 24 cm
   D. length 37 cm and width 23 cm

Investigation

Guessing the Second Number

Here is a number game for two people.
- Your partner tells you a number.
- Your partner multiplies this first number by 3.
- Your partner adds the product to a second number, so that the sum is 5.
- You guess what the second number is.

23. a) Why might you represent the relation in this game as shown?

b) Identify the relation between the first and second number as linear or nonlinear. Use as many different strategies as you can. Show what you did.

c) Use each number as the first number in the game. What is the second number?

    i) -2 **ii)** $\dfrac{3}{2}$ **iii)** $\dfrac{15}{8}$ **iv)** $-\dfrac{3}{5}$

d) Here is another number game for two people.
- Your partner tells you a number.
- Your partner multiplies this first number by $\dfrac{4}{9}$.
- Your partner adds the product to $\dfrac{1}{3}$ of a second number, so that the sum is $\dfrac{1}{2}$.
- You guess what the second number is.

    i) How are the equations for the two games alike? How are they different?

    ii) How are the graphs for the two games alike? How are they different?

e) Make up your own game, with both of these properties.
- If the first number is $\dfrac{1}{2}$, then the second number is $-\dfrac{4}{5}$;
- The graph is the same shape as that of the game in part d).

Linear Equations

▸ GOALS

You will be able to

- Solve linear equations using a variety of strategies
- Rearrange linear equations and formulas
- Find the point of intersection of two linear relations using a graph

> ❓ What variables could you use in an equation to model how long this diver can stay at the same depth with one tank of air?

WORDS YOU NEED to Know

1. Match each term with the highlighted example that best represents it.

   a) equation   **c)** variable   **e)** constant

   b) solution to an equation   **d)** algebraic expression   **f)** coefficient

   i) $3x + 4 = 10$ **iii)** $3x + 4$ **v)** $3x + 4$

   ii) $3x + 4$ **iv)** $3x + 4$ **vi)** $3x + 4 = 10$
                                                                  $x = 2$

Study | *Aid*

• For more help and practice, see Appendix A-13.

SKILLS AND CONCEPTS You Need

Equation Solving Strategies

You can use different strategies to solve an equation:

- systematic trial
- drawing a graph
- inspection and logical reasoning
- balancing

EXAMPLE

Solve: $2p + 10 = 30$.

Solution

Systematic Trial

p	$2p + 10$	Comparison to 30
8	$16 + 10 = 26$	too low
11	$22 + 10 = 32$	too high
10	$20 + 10 = 30$	correct

Drawing a Graph

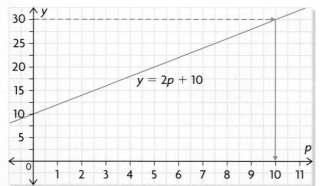

Inspection and Logical Reasoning

$2p + 10 = 30$

That means $2p$ must be 20.
If $2p = 20$, then p must be 10.

Balancing

$$2p + 10 = 30$$
$$2p + 10 - 10 = 30 - 10$$
$$2p = 20$$
$$2p \div 2 = 20 \div 2$$
$$p = 10$$

2. Use a graphing strategy to solve the following equations.
   a) $3n - 1 = 11$ **b)** $2x + 5 = 21$

3. Solve the following equations using the strategy of your choice.
   a) $6a + 12 = 18$ **b)** $10 = 4m + 2$ **c)** $3x - 5 = 10$

Solving an Equation to Solve a Problem

You can use equations to solve word problems. To do so, you need to define the variable for the unknown quantity, and then, create an equation using the variable and the information provided.

EXAMPLE

Rishi ordered 3 pizzas. What was the cost of each pizza if the delivery charge was $1.50 and the total bill was $27.00?

Solution

Let n represent the cost of each pizza.

$$3n + 1.50 = 27.00$$
$$3n + 1.50 - 1.50 = 27.00 - 1.50$$
$$3n = 25.50$$
$$3n \div 3 = 25.50 \div 3$$
$$n = 8.50$$

Check:
If each pizza cost $8.50, 3 pizzas would cost $3 \times \$8.50 = \$25.50$.
The $1.50 delivery charge would bring the total to $27.00.

Each pizza costs $8.50.

4. Use an equation to solve each of the following.
   a) Jillian bought 5 DVD's and the cost was $99.75. Determine the cost of each DVD.
   b) Bill's age 3 years ago was 18. How old is he now?
   c) Nazir has $14.50 in her pocket. Of this amount, $10 is in bills and the rest is quarters. How many quarters are in her pocket?
   d) Bart rented a truck for the day. His bill was $177. The rental company charged him a flat fee of $45 and a fee of $0.55/km for the distance he drove. How many kilometres did he drive?

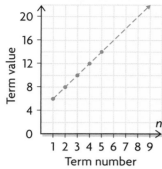

**Number Sequence
(Rule: 2n + 4)**

Term value (vertical axis): 0, 4, 8, 12, 16, 20
Term number (horizontal axis): 1 2 3 4 5 6 7 8 9

Study | **Aid**

• For help, see the Review of
Essential Skills and
Knowledge Appendix.

Question	Appendix
5, 6, 7, and 12	A-13
8	A-6
11	A-11

PRACTICE

5. Use the Number Sequence graph on the left to solve the equation
$2n + 4 = 20$.

6. Solve for x.

a) $\dfrac{x}{3} = \dfrac{6}{27}$ **3**

b) $\dfrac{2}{x} = \dfrac{10}{40}$

c) $\dfrac{3}{7} = \dfrac{x}{18}$

7. Solve each equation.

a) $78 = 6x$

b) $45 = 4m + 11$

c) $25n - 8.5 = 101.5$

8. Calculate.

a) $-8 + 1\dfrac{3}{5}$

b) $-3\dfrac{1}{5} - \left(-6\dfrac{3}{8}\right)$

9. Simplify.

a) $-3x - 2(4x + 7)$

b) $2x - 5.5 - 4.5x + 9$

10. a) Identify the initial value and the rate of change for $y = -3x + 13$.

b) How would you sketch the graph of $y = -3x + 13$?

11. Ethel is a junior programmer for EDUCAT Software. She is paid by
the hours worked. She is also paid a fixed amount for her expenses
every week. The table shows how much she will be paid for hours
worked in a week, including expenses.

Hours Worked	20	25	30	35	40
Earnings ($)	700	825	950	1075	1200

a) What fixed amount is Ethel paid for her expenses?

b) Write an equation for the relationship.

c) How much would Ethel be paid if she worked 32 h? 53 h?

12. Use what you know about equations to complete the vocabulary
organizer below. Add branches as needed.

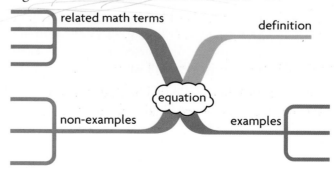

related math terms | definition

equation

non-examples | examples

APPLYING *What You Know*

YOU WILL NEED
- interlocking cubes
- grid paper

Painted Cubes

Toni made a large cube out of wooden blocks. She painted the outside of the large cube red. She let the paint dry, and then, took the cube apart. She noticed that

- some blocks had no paint on them
- some blocks had one face painted
- some blocks had two faces painted
- some blocks had three faces painted

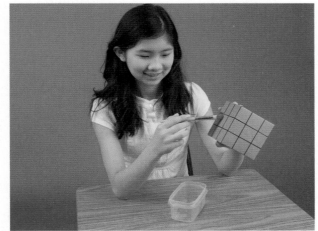

? For a 10 × 10 × 10 cube, how can you predict the number of blocks that have paint on 3, 2, 1, or 0 faces?

A. Build several different cubes from centimetre blocks.

B. Imagine painting each of your cubes.
Visualize how many faces of each centimetre block will be painted.

C. Complete a table of values showing the relationship between the number of centimetre blocks that are painted on 3 faces and the length of the side of the big cube.

D. Graph the relationship you found in part C.
Write a rule that describes the relationship.

E. Repeat parts C and D for the number of centimetre blocks that are painted on 2 faces, on 1 face, and on 0 faces.

F. Which rules from parts C to E represent linear relationships?

G. Predict the number of small blocks painted on 3, 2, 1, and 0 faces for a 10 × 10 × 10 cube. Explain how you made your prediction.

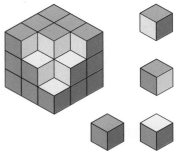

Interpreting the Solution of a Linear Equation

GOAL

Relate equations to tables of values and graphs.

LEARN ABOUT the Math

Mariane wants U-Host to host her website.

U-Host's Charges per Month
$19.00 monthly charge
$1.15/megabyte (MB) of storage used

? How many megabytes of storage can Mariane purchase for $60 per month?

EXAMPLE 1	**Solving a problem using different representations of the situation**

Determine the amount of storage Mariane can afford each month.

Jordan's Solution: Using a table of values to estimate a solution

MB	Total Cost ($)
0	19 + 1.15 × 0 = 19.00
10	19 + 1.15 × 10 = 30.50
20	19 + 1.15 × 20 = 42.00
30	19 + 1.15 × 30 = 53.50
40	19 + 1.15 × 40 = 65.00

I created a table of values to estimate the amount of storage that Mariane can purchase for $60. I used multiples of 10 for the numbers of megabytes to make the calculations easier.

I estimate that Mariane can afford about 35 MB of storage each month.

Since $60 is between $53.50 and $65.00, the answer must be between 30 MB and 40 MB of storage.

Check:
19 + 1.15 × 35 = 59.25
So, 35 MB will cost Mariane just under $60 per month.

I substituted my solution into the cost expression to see if my answer was reasonable.

Xavier's Solution: Using a graph to estimate the solution

total cost = monthly charge + cost per MB × number of MB

Total Monthly Cost

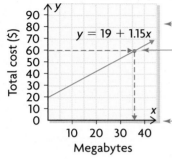

I graphed the relation $y = 19 + 1.15x$, where x represents the number of megabytes of storage, y represents the cost in dollars, 19 is the monthly charge, and 1.15 is the cost per MB.

I knew that the x-coordinate of the point that has a y-coordinate of 60 would be the solution.

From the graph, I saw that $60 would pay for about 36 MB.

Based on the graph, Mariane could purchase about 36 MB of storage for $60 per month.

Check:

$y = 19 + 1.15x$

$y = 19 + 1.15 \times 36$

$y = 60.40$

I substituted my solution into the cost expression to see if my answer was reasonable.

Jordan and Xavier's strategies provided estimates. You can use an equation to calculate an exact solution.

Eva's Solution: Using an equation to get an exact solution

total cost = monthly charge + cost per MB × number of MB

$60 = 19 + 1.15x$

$60 - 19 = 19 + 1.15x - 19$

$41 = 1.15x$

$\dfrac{41}{1.15} = \dfrac{1.15x}{1.15}$

$35.65 \doteq x$

I used x to represent the amount of storage (in MB) Mariane could purchase. I wrote a word equation and a **linear equation**.

I used a balancing strategy to solve the equation.

Mariane can purchase about 35.65 MB of storage for $60.

linear equation

an equation in the form $ax + b = 0$, or an equation that can be rewritten in this form; the algebraic expression involved is a polynomial of degree 1 (e.g., $2x + 3 = 6$ or $y = 3x - 5$)

Check:

$19 + 1.15x$
$= 19 + 1.15(35.65)$ ← I checked to see if 35.65 actually solved the equation.
$= 59.9975$

After rounding to the nearest cent, 35.65 MB will cost Mariane $60 per month.

Reflecting

A. Why does the algebraic solution from an equation provide the most accurate answer for Mariane?

B. Why can the table of values, the graph, and the equation all be used to find possible solutions to Mariane's problem?

APPLY the Math

EXAMPLE 2 | **Using a graphical representation of a relation to solve an equation**

Solve the equation $3.5x + 2.5 = 20$.

Kevin's Solution

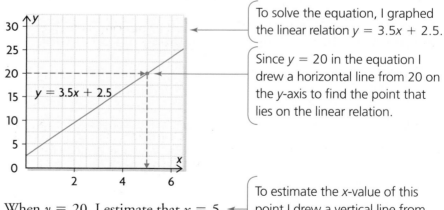

To solve the equation, I graphed the linear relation $y = 3.5x + 2.5$.

Since $y = 20$ in the equation I drew a horizontal line from 20 on the y-axis to find the point that lies on the linear relation.

When $y = 20$, I estimate that $x = 5$. ← To estimate the x-value of this point I drew a vertical line from this point to the x-axis.

Check:

$3.5x + 2.5$
$= 3.5(5) + 2.5$ ← I substituted my solution into the equation to see if it solved the equation.
$= 20$

So, $x = 5$ solves the equation.

| EXAMPLE **3** | Determining the *x*-intercept for a linear relation |

Tech | **Support**

For help using the **TRACE** function on your calculator, see Appendix B-4.

Determine the *x*-intercept of the graph of the relation $y = 3x + 2$.

Shayla's Solution: Using graphing technology

I graphed the linear relation on a graphing calculator. Since the *x*-intercept occurs when $y = 0$, I traced along the line until I found the point with a *y*-coordinate close to 0.

$x \doteq -0.66$
The *x*-intercept is approximately -0.66.

The line passes through $(-0.66, 0)$ on the *x*-axis.

Shayla's strategy provided an estimate of the location of the *x*-intercept. You can use algebra and the equation of the linear relation to determine its exact location.

Mike's Solution: Using algebra

$$y = 3x + 2$$

I substituted $y = 0$ because the *y*-coordinate of the *x*-intercept is 0.

$$0 = 3x + 2$$
$$0 - 2 = 3x + 2 - 2$$
$$-2 = 3x$$

I used a balancing strategy to solve the equation.

$$\frac{-2}{3} = \frac{3x}{3}$$
$$-\frac{2}{3} = x$$

So, the *x*-intercept is $-\frac{2}{3}$.

The line passes through $\left(-\frac{2}{3}, 0\right)$ on the *x*-axis.

EXAMPLE **4**

Solving a problem represented by a linear equation

A cell-phone company is offering this plan:
- $9.95 per month
- 50 minutes free
- $0.09 per minute after the first 50 minutes

Each month, after 50 minutes of air time, the company uses the exact air time to calculate the monthly bill.

About how many minutes can be purchased each month for $40?

Gail's Solution

Let x represent the number of minutes used each month and y the total cost for the month.

This equation shows how the monthly charge is calculated.

$$y = 9.95 + 0.09(x - 50)$$

I used a linear equation to represent the problem.

Since the first 50 minutes are free, I subtracted 50 from the number of minutes before I multiplied by the per-minute cost. I added the fixed cost of $9.95 to get the total cost.

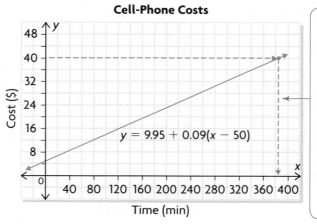

Cell-Phone Costs

To estimate the solution, I graphed the relation.

I located $y = 40$ on the graph of the relation, and then, drew horizontal and vertical lines to estimate the x-value for $y = 40$. The solution is about $x = 385$.

So, about 385 minutes can be purchased each month for $40.

In Summary

Key Ideas

- You can use a table or a graph to estimate the solution to an equation.
  For example, solve $3 = \frac{1}{5}x + 2$.

  $y = \frac{1}{5}x + 2$

x	y
0	2
5	3
10	4

  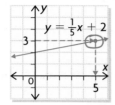

- The exact solution to an equation can be determined using a balancing strategy and algebra.
  For example,

  $$3 = \frac{1}{5}x + 2$$

  $$3 - 2 = \frac{1}{5}x + 2 - 2$$

  $$1 = \frac{1}{5}x$$

  $$1 \times 5 = \frac{1}{5}x \times 5$$

  $$5 = x$$

Need to Know

- The solution to a linear equation is the x- or y-coordinate of a point on the graph of its corresponding linear relation. If you know one of the coordinates, you can read or estimate the other coordinate from the graph.
- To check a solution, substitute the value of the solution into the equation and calculate both sides. If both sides work out to the same number, the solution is correct.

CHECK Your Understanding

1. Estimate the solution to $4.25x - 3 = 9.5$ using a table of values. Verify your solution.

2. Estimate the solution to $-2 = 5 - \frac{1}{4}x$ using a graph. Verify your solution.

3. Solve the equations in questions 1 and 2 using algebra.

4. Justin is purchasing chain link fence for his yard. It costs $5.25 per linear foot of fencing. How many feet of fencing can he buy if his budget is $600?

   a) Estimate the amount of fencing using a table of values or a graph.
   b) Determine the exact amount of fencing using algebra.
   c) Verify your solution.

PRACTISING

5. Estimate the solutions to the following equations using a graph.

   a) $-3x - 11 = 7$ **b)** $2x + 9 = 4$ **c)** $35 - 2t = 13$

6. Solve the equations in question 5 using algebra.

7. Estimate the solutions to the following equations using a table of values of the corresponding linear relation.

   a) $2x - 8 = -9$ **b)** $7 - 3x = 16$ **c)** $2.75x + 3.8 = 3.8$

8. Solve the equations in question 7 using algebra.

9. A rocket is launched from a hill that is 700 m high. The rocket's altitude increases by 35 m every 2 s.

   a) Create the linear relation that models the rocket's upward path.
   b) Graph the linear relation.
   c) Write the equations you would solve to determine the height of the rocket at 50 s and 100 s. Estimate the solution to these equations using the graph.
   d) Write the equation you would use to determine when the rocket reaches a height of 1000 m. Use the graph to estimate the solution to this equation.

35 m /2 s

700 m

10. Party Planners is catering a party. Its services cost $25 per person with a minimum of 50 guests, but it does not charge for the first 10 people.

   a) Create the linear relation that models the catering costs in terms of the number of people attending the party.
   b) Graph the linear relation.
   c) Write the equations you would solve to determine the costs for 50 people and 75 people. Solve these equations using the graph.
   d) Write the equations you would use to determine how many people could attend for a total cost of $1500. Estimate the solution using the graph.

11. Estimate the solution to each equation using either a graph or a table
K of values. Verify your solutions.

   a) $2x + 3 = 11$ **b)** $-17 = 3 - 4n$ **c)** $-2 + \dfrac{1}{2}n = -5$

12. Solve the equations in question 11 using algebra. Verify your solution.

13. This graph shows Samantha's earnings against hours worked.

A **a)** Write the linear relation that models this graph.

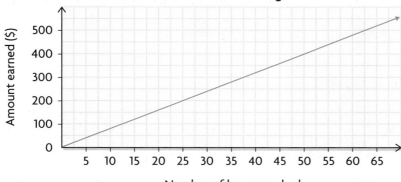

Samantha's Earnings

(y-axis: Amount earned ($), x-axis: Number of hours worked)

b) Write the equation you would solve to determine the number of hours worked if Samantha's earnings were $500.

c) Write the equation you would solve to determine her earnings for 40 hours worked.

d) How are the equations in parts b) and c) similar? How are they different?

e) Estimate the solution to each of the equations using the graph. Verify your solutions.

f) Solve the equations using algebra.

14. Use algebra to determine the *x*-intercept for each of the following:

a) $y = 4x + 8$ **b)** $y = \frac{1}{2}x - 5$ **c)** $y = x$ **d)** $y = -1$

15. A large water tank holds 100 L of water. It is leaking at a rate of 5 L/min.

a) Write the linear relation that models the amount of water remaining in the tank in terms of the number of minutes since the tank started leaking.

b) Write the equation you would solve to determine the amount of water remaining in the tank 13 minutes after the water started leaking.

c) Write the equation you would solve to determine when the tank would be half full.

d) How are the equations in parts b) and c) similar? How are they different?

e) Solve each equation using a graph.

f) Solve each equation using algebra. Verify your solution using the equation.

16. A rectangular field is 100 m long. It is fully enclosed by 500 m of fencing.
  a) Explain why the equation $500 = 2(100) - 2w$ can be used to determine w, the width of the field.
  b) Estimate the solution to the equation. Verify your solution.
  c) Solve the equation using algebra.
  d) How wide is the field?

17. a) Write an equation for the relationship between the figure number and number of counters in each figure.
  b) Use the equation to determine the figure that can be made with exactly 60 counters.
  c) Explain why there is no figure in this pattern that can be made with exactly 100 counters.

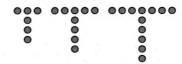

figure 1 figure 2   figure 3

18. Create a linear equation of the form $ax + b = c$. Draw a flow chart that shows the steps needed to estimate the solution using a graph.

Extending

19. Use a table of values or a graph to estimate solutions to the following equations. Verify your solution.

  a) $\dfrac{(x + 2)}{5} - 3x = 7$

  b) $\dfrac{1}{2}(x + 2) - \dfrac{1}{3}(x - 1) = 4$

  c) $x^2 + 7 = 16$

  d) $2x^2 - 3 = 11$

  e) $3x^3 - 9 = 72$

20. Determine an exact solution to each equation in question 19 using any method you can.

21. Given the linear relation $y = mx + b$, what equation would you solve to determine the x-intercept? Justify your answer.

Solving Linear Equations Using Inverse Operations

Solve equations by working backward.

LEARN ABOUT the Math

Michelle delivers paper waste to a recycling centre.
She had net earnings of $23.90 on her first trip.

Michelle's Costs	Michelle's Earnings
$8.00/trip for gas	$72.50/tonne of paper

> **Communication** | *Tip*
>
> Using inverse operations is the same as balancing.

? How much paper did Michelle deliver?

EXAMPLE 1   Using inverse operations as a strategy to solve an equation

Determine the amount of paper waste Michelle delivered on her first trip to the recycling centre.

Michelle's Solution

$72.50 \times (\text{\# of tonnes}) - \$8.00 = \$23.90$ ← I created a word equation to represent the situation.

Let p represent the number of tonnes of paper I delivered.

$72.50p - 8.00 = 23.90$ ← I wrote a linear equation that used a variable instead of words to represent the situation.

Try $p = 1$.   ← I used guess-and-check to get an idea of the amount of paper.
$72.50(1) - 8.00$
$= 72.50 - 8.00$

$= 64.50$ ← 64.50 is much greater than 23.90, so my guess was too high. There must have been less than 1 tonne of paper.

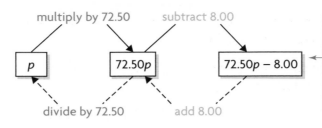

operations in the equation →

multiply by 72.50   subtract 8.00

p → $72.50p$ → $72.50p - 8.00$

divide by 72.50   add 8.00

←- - - - - - - - - inverse operations - - - - - - - - -

inverse operations

operations that undo, or reverse, each other, for example: addition is the inverse of subtraction; multiplication is the inverse of division

I used a diagram to show the operations in the equation and the **inverse operations** I needed to undo them.

isolating a term or a variable

performing math operations (e.g., addition, subtraction, multiplication, division) to get a term or a variable by itself on one side of an equation

$$72.50p - 8.00 + 8.00 = 23.90 + 8.00$$
$$72.50p = 31.90$$

I undid the last step by adding 8.00. This **isolated the term** 72.50p. Since I got the new equation by doing the same operation to both sides of the original, I knew they were **equivalent equations**.

equivalent equations

equations that have the same solution

$$72.50p \div 72.50 = 31.90 \div 72.50$$
$$p = 0.44$$

I isolated p by dividing both sides of the equation by 72.50 and solved the equation.

Check:

Left Side	Right Side
$72.50(0.44) - 8.00$	23.90
$= 23.90$	

I delivered 0.44 tonnes of paper.

When I checked my answer, it gave me the correct amount.

Reflecting

A. How did Michelle's estimate of 1 tonne help her determine the inverse operations needed to solve the equation?

B. Why is "isolating the term or variable" a good name for the process used to solve the equation?

C. How would doing the inverse operations in a different order affect Michelle's solution?

APPLY the Math

EXAMPLE 2	**Using an inverse operation strategy to solve an equation**

Solve $-2x + 4 = 14$.

Chelsea's Solution

The calculation steps are
- multiply by -2
- add 4

> I listed the operations on x in the equation following order of operations.

The reverse steps to solve are
- subtract 4
- divide by -2

> Then, I listed the inverse operations that would undo each operation in the equation.

$$-2x + 4 - 4 = 14 - 4$$
$$-2x = 10$$

> I isolated the term $-2x$ by subtracting 4 from each side to undo $+ 4$.

$$-2x \div (-2) = 10 \div (-2)$$
$$x = -5$$

> Then, I isolated the variable x by undoing multiplication by -2.

Check:

Left Side	Right Side
$-2(-5) + 4$	14
$= 10 + 4$	
$= 14$	

> I substituted my solution into the equation to make sure that it worked.

$x = -5$ is the correct solution.

EXAMPLE **3**

Using an inverse operations strategy to solve an equation with fractional coefficients

Solve $\dfrac{w}{3} - 13 = 7$.

Drake's Solution

$$\dfrac{w}{3} - 13 = 7$$

$$\dfrac{w}{3} - 13 + 13 = 7 + 13 \longleftarrow$$

I performed the inverse operations. The inverse operation of subtracting 13 is adding 13.

$$\dfrac{w}{3} = 20$$

$$3 \times \dfrac{w}{3} = 3 \times 20 \longleftarrow$$

$$w = 60$$

$\dfrac{w}{3} = w \div 3$

The inverse operation of dividing by 3 is multiplying by 3.

$w = 60$ is the correct solution. $\longleftarrow$

I used mental math to check that $\dfrac{60}{3} - 13$, or $20 - 3$, equals 7.

EXAMPLE 4   Solving a problem represented by linear equation

A photographer charges a sitting fee of \$100. The first four prints are free.
Each additional print costs \$5.25. How many prints can you buy with \$257.50?

Asad's Solution

$\$100 + \$5.25 \times (\text{\# of prints} - 4 \text{ free prints}) = \$257.50 \longleftarrow$
$$100 + 5.25(P - 4) = 257.50$$

I wrote a word equation, and then, an algebraic equation to describe the situation. I used P to represent the number of prints ordered.

$$100 - 100 + 5.25(P - 4) = 257.50 - 100 \longleftarrow$$
$$5.25(P - 4) = 157.50$$

I used inverse operations to isolate the term with the variable in it.

$$5.25(P - 4) \div 5.25 = 157.50 \div 5.25 \longleftarrow$$
$$1(P - 4) = 30$$

Then, I used other inverse operations to isolate the term in brackets.

$$P - 4 + 4 = 30 + 4 \longleftarrow$$
$$P = 34$$

I used inverse operations and added 4.

Check:
$100 + 5.25(34 - 4) \longleftarrow$
$= 100 + 157.50$
$= 257.50$
You can order 34 prints.

I checked to see if 34 prints would actually cost \$257.50.

In Summary

Key Ideas

- You can write an equation that is equivalent to a given equation by applying the same operation to both sides.
- You can use inverse operations to isolate individual terms or variables.

Need To Know

- You can substitute a value for the variable to get a sense of the inverse operations to use to solve an equation.

  For example, for the equation $3x - 17 = 34$, you might try $x = 10$. Since $3 \times 10 - 17 = 13$, is too low, you know the solution is greater than 10. You also know that the operations you have to undo are subtracting 17 and multiplying by 3.

- An equation in which the variable appears on only one side can be solved by
  - listing the operations that can be used to evaluate the expression in the order in which they would be used
  - performing the inverses of the operations one at a time, in their opposite order, until the variable is isolated

  For example:

  $$3x - 4 = 2$$
  $$3x - 4 + 4 = 2 + 4$$
  $$3x = 6$$
  $$\frac{3x}{3} = \frac{6}{3}$$
  $$x = 2$$

- You can check your solution by substituting it into the original equation. The solution is correct if both sides evaluate to the same number.
- There is sometimes more than one way to solve an equation using inverse operations. As long as you perform the same operations on both sides of the equation, the solution will be correct.

> **Communication | Tip**
>
> It's common practice to line up equal signs when solving equations. This makes it easier to check the results of each step. Only one equal sign appears in each line of a solution and it separates the left side from the right side.

CHECK Your Understanding

1. List the inverse operations and the order in which you would apply them to isolate the variable in each equation.
   a) $-3x + 2 = 15$
   b) $12.4x - 3.2 = 21.5$
   c) $\dfrac{x}{2} + 5 = 11$

2. Solve each equation in question 1. Show all steps.

3. An author is paid $5000. In addition, he receives a royalty of $1.25 for every book sold.
   a) Write an equation to represent the number of books that have to be sold for the author to earn $10 000.
   b) Solve the equation using inverse operations. Show all steps.
   c) Verify your solution.

PRACTISING

4. List the operations you would use to isolate the variable in each equation.
   a) $6b - 10 = -2$
   b) $2.5c + 1.0 = 1.5$
   c) $3f - 4 = 10$
   d) $6 - 2d = 4$
   e) $6 - 2e = 6$
   f) $-3 - h = -2$

5. Solve each equation in question 4. Show all steps and verify each solution.

6. The relation $C = 8.00 + 0.50T$ represents the cost of a pizza in dollars. T represents the number of toppings ordered.
   a) Write an equation that represents a $10 order.
   b) Solve the equation in a) to determine the number of toppings. Show all steps.

7. A submarine is currently submerged at a depth of 600 m. It rises at a rate of 4 m/s.
   a) Write a linear relation that shows the relationship between the depth of the submarine and the number of seconds it has been rising.
   b) Write the equation you must solve to determine when the submarine will reach a depth of 486 m.
   c) List the inverse operations you need to use to isolate the variable and solve the equation.
   d) Solve the equation. Show all the steps.
   e) Verify your solution.

8. Caroline told Marc that using balancing and solving linear equations was different from using inverse operations to isolate the variable. Was Caroline right? Explain.

9. A hot-air balloon is at a height of 500 m. It develops a steady leak and begins to descend at a rate of 60 m/min. Write and solve an equation to determine how long it takes for the balloon to reach a height of 20 m.

10. Solve each equation.

a) $\dfrac{x}{4} + 1 = 3$

b) $\dfrac{x}{2} - 10 = 3$

c) $5 - \dfrac{y}{3} = 3$

d) $10 + \dfrac{b}{5} = -1$

e) $\dfrac{w}{3} + 5 = 1$

f) $3 - \dfrac{d}{6} = -1$

11. Liz was testing Jane on solving with equations. She gave Jane the following problem:

"I am a number such that when you divide me by 7, and then, add 13 you get 32. What number am I?"

Write and solve an equation to determine Liz's number.

12. Solve each equation.

a) $3(x + 1) = 12$

b) $2(x - 4) = 4$

c) $\dfrac{(w + 3)}{4} = 2$

d) $\dfrac{(y - 5)}{3} = 6$

e) $\dfrac{(2a + 3)}{3} = 5$

f) $-2 = \dfrac{-2c}{5} + 1$

13. Jack's Restaurant charges $22.95 for brunch but allows one person per table to eat free. To figure out how many people attended the Sunday brunch, Jack collected the information in this table.

Table Number	Bill Total ($)
1	137.70
2	68.85
3	160.65
4	91.80
5	91.80

a) Why is it reasonable that Jack used the equation $22.95(x - 1) = T$ to determine the number of people at each table? What do the variables x and T represent?

b) Create and solve the equation for each table number.

c) How many people in total sat at the five tables?

14. The relationship between Celsius and Fahrenheit is represented by $C = \dfrac{5}{9}(F - 32)$.

    a) Determine the Celsius temperature that is equivalent to 58 °F.
    b) List the operations you used to calculate the Celsius temperature.
    c) List the inverse operations you would use to isolate F.
    d) Determine the Fahrenheit temperature that is equivalent to 25 °C.

15. When you use an inverse operation to isolate a variable, why can you say that the equation you get at each step is equivalent to the original one?

Extending

16. Solve each equation.

    a) $2x + 3 = 4(1 - x) + 5$ **b)** $\dfrac{1}{2}x - \dfrac{1}{4} = \dfrac{x}{3} + \dfrac{1}{6}$

17. The intercepts of a graph are the points at which the line crosses the x-axis and the y-axis. Consider the relation $3x + 5y = 15$.

    a) List the inverse operations you would use to express the relation in the form $y = mx + b$.
    b) Use your answer from part a) to solve the relation for y.
    c) List the inverse operations you would use to express and isolate the x-variable.
    d) Use your answer from part c) to solve the relation for x.
    e) Explain how you can use your answers to parts b) and d) to quickly graph this relation.

18. The members of a scout troop held a car wash for charity. They washed 49 vehicles. They charged $4 per car and $6 per truck and earned a total of $230. How many of each type of vehicle did they wash?

    a) Write an algebraic relation that models the number of vehicles washed.
    b) Write an algebraic relation that models the total money earned.
    c) Graph the relations and use the graphs to solve the problem.

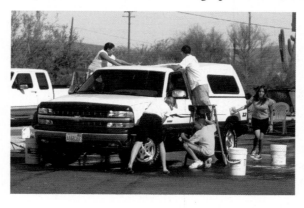

Solve equations where the variable appears on both sides of the equality.

LEARN ABOUT the Math

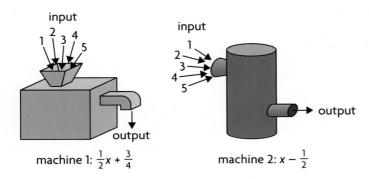

machine 1: $\frac{1}{2}x + \frac{3}{4}$ machine 2: $x - \frac{1}{2}$

Atish and Sara are playing a game on their computers. The goal of the game is to be the first to figure out which input will make the two machines generate the same output.

They have input several values. Here are their results:

Input	Machine 1 Output	Machine 2 Output
0	0.75	−0.5
2	1.75	1.5
4	2.75	3.5
6	3.75	5.5

?   What strategies can they use to win the game quickly?

EXAMPLE **1** — Selecting a strategy to solve an equation

Determine the input value that will result in the same output value for both machines.

Klint's Solution: Using a guess-and-test strategy

Input Value	Output Value		
x	Machine 1 $\frac{1}{2}x + \frac{3}{4}$	Machine 2 $x - \frac{1}{2}$	
0	0.75	−0.5	
2	1.75	1.5	
4	2.75	3.5	

> I noticed that when the input is 2, the output value of Machine 1 is greater than the output value of Machine 2. But, when the input is 4, the reverse is true.

$$x = 3$$

> I thought the answer must be between 2 and 4, so I tried 3.

Input Value	Output Value		
x	Machine 1 $\frac{1}{2}x + \frac{3}{4}$	Machine 2 $x - \frac{1}{2}$	
0	0.75	−0.5	
2	1.75	1.5	
3	2.25	2.5	

> The output value of Machine 1 is still greater when $x = 2$ and less when $x = 3$. The solution must be between 2 and 3.

$$x = 2\frac{1}{2}$$

> I chose an input value of $2\frac{1}{2}$, which is between 2 and 3. I tested this value in each machine.

$$x = \frac{5}{2}$$

> I rewrote the fraction as an improper fraction, and then, calculated the outputs.

Input Value	Output Value		
x	Machine 1 $\frac{1}{2}x + \frac{3}{4}$	Machine 2 $x - \frac{1}{2}$	
0	0.75	−0.5	
2	1.75	1.5	
2.5	2.00	2.0	

> When the input is $2\frac{1}{2}$, or 2.5, both machines have an output value of 2.

An input of $2\frac{1}{2}$ will produce equal outputs on both machines.

When an equation contains fractions, it is often easier to solve if you can rewrite it as an equivalent equation that does not contain fractions. This can be done using a common denominator. You can then use inverse operations to solve the resulting equation.

Dion's Solution: Using a common denominator and inverse operations to isolate the variable

$$\frac{1}{2}x + \frac{3}{4} = x - \frac{1}{2}$$

I created an equation to figure out what value of x would give the same output values

$$4\left(\frac{1}{2}x + \frac{3}{4}\right) = 4\left(x - \frac{1}{2}\right)$$

I tried to write an equivalent equation that didn't contain fractions. I knew that if I performed the same operation on both sides of the equation, the result is an equivalent equation. I decided to multiply both sides by 4, since both denominators will divide into this number, eliminating the fractions. This is also the lowest common denominator between 2 and 4.

$$4\left(\frac{1}{2}x\right) + 4\left(\frac{3}{4}\right) = 4(x) - 4\left(\frac{1}{2}\right)$$

I used the distributive property to expand, and then, simplified by multiplying.

$$\frac{4}{2}x + \frac{12}{4}x = 4x - \frac{4}{2}$$

$$2x + 3 = 4x - 2$$

$$2x + 3 - 3 = 4x - 2 - 3$$

I used inverse operations to solve the equation. I decided to undo $+ 3$ by subtracting 3 from both sides.

$$2x = 4x - 5$$

$$2x + 5 = 4x - 5 + 5$$

To undo $- 5$, I added 5 to both sides.

$$2x + 5 = 4x$$

$$2x + 5 - 2x = 4x - 2x$$

To isolate the variable term I had to undo $+ 2x$. I subtracted 2x from both sides

$$5 = 2x$$

$$\frac{5}{2} = \frac{2x}{2}$$

To solve for x, I used the inverse operation of multiply by 2 and divided both sides by 2.

$$\frac{5}{2} = x$$

$$2\frac{1}{2} = x$$

I rewrote the fraction as a mixed number.

The input that will produce the same output on both machines is $2\frac{1}{2}$.

Check:

When $x = \frac{5}{2}$,

Left Side

$\dfrac{1}{2}x + \dfrac{3}{4}$

$= \dfrac{1}{2}\left(\dfrac{5}{2}\right) + \dfrac{3}{4}$

$= \dfrac{5}{4} + \dfrac{3}{4}$

$= \dfrac{8}{4}$

$= 2$

Right Side

$x - \dfrac{1}{2}$

$= \dfrac{5}{2} - \dfrac{1}{2}$

$= \dfrac{4}{2}$

$= 2$

I checked the solution by entering the input value into the left hand and right hand sides separately.

Since the left side and right side both resulted in the same output, I knew my solution was correct.

Reflecting

A. How does solving the equation $\frac{1}{2}x + \frac{3}{4} = x - \frac{1}{2}$ show that there is only one value of x for which the machines have the same output?

B. Why does Klint's strategy only provide an estimate of the solution, while Dion's provides an exact solution?

C. How did Dion decide what number to multiply both sides of the equation by to eliminate the fractions?

D. How did Dion know which inverse operations to use in order to group the variables on one side of the equation and the constant terms on the other side?

APPLY *the Math*

EXAMPLE 2 | Using an inverse operations strategy to solve a problem represented by an equation

The square and equilateral triangle shown have the same perimeters. What are the dimensions of each figure?

$3k$ $2k + 1$

Kayla's Solution

$$4(3k) = 3(2k + 1)$$

> I used the expression $4 \times 3k$ to calculate the perimeter of the square and $3 \times (2k + 1)$ to calculate the perimeter of the triangle.
> I made these two expressions equal because the perimeters are the same.

$$12k = 6k + 3$$

> I used the distributive property on the right side of the equation to simplify it.

$$12k - 6k = 6k + 3 - 6k$$
$$6k = 3$$
$$\frac{6k}{6} = \frac{3}{6}$$
$$k = \frac{1}{2}$$

> I used inverse operations to group the variables on the left side of the equation. I chose the left because $12k$ is larger than $6k$ and my variable would have a positive coefficient.

When $k = \dfrac{1}{2}$,

Perimeter of the square:
$$4(3k)$$
$$= 4\left(3 \times \frac{1}{2}\right)$$
$$= 6$$

Perimeter of the triangle:
$$3(2k + 1)$$
$$= 3\left(2 \times \frac{1}{2} + 1\right)$$
$$= 6$$

> I checked my solution by finding the perimeter of the square and the triangle when $k = \dfrac{1}{2}$.

> Since the perimeters of both shapes are 6 units when $k = \dfrac{1}{2}$, I knew my solution was correct.

When $k = \dfrac{1}{2}$,

Dimensions of the square:

$3k$

$= \dfrac{3}{2}$

$= 1\dfrac{1}{2}$

To find the dimensions, I substituted $k = \dfrac{1}{2}$ into the expression for the side lengths of the triangle and of the square.

Dimensions of the triangle:

$2k + 1$

$= 2\left(\dfrac{1}{2}\right) + 1$

$= 1 + 1$

$= 2$

The perimeters are the same when the square has a side length of $1\dfrac{1}{2}$ and the triangle has a side length of 2.

EXAMPLE 3 | **Using an equation and an inverse operations strategy to solve a problem**

It takes Ryan 2 h to mow the lawn and water the garden. It takes Maria 3 h to do the same. How long would it take them if they worked together?

Abby's Solution

Let x represent the amount of time needed to complete the tasks if Ryan and Maria work together.

I used a variable to represent the time needed to complete the job if they worked together.

Fraction of work done by Ryan: $\dfrac{x}{2}$

I wrote an expression to represent the fraction of work done by each person:

Fraction of work done by Maria: $\dfrac{x}{3}$

$$\text{fraction of work done} = \dfrac{\text{time actually spent}}{\text{time to do the whole job alone}}$$

$$\dfrac{x}{2} + \dfrac{x}{3} = 1$$

Since both people are working together, the total of the fractions of work done must be 1. I used this to write an equation.

$$6\left(\frac{x}{2}\right) + 6\left(\frac{x}{3}\right) = 6(1)$$

I wanted to create an equivalent equation without fractions. I knew that if I multiplied both sides of the equation by 2, the $\frac{x}{2}$ would become $1x$, or just x. But I would still have the thirds on this side of the equation. So, I decided to multiply both sides by 2, and then, by 3. That's the same as multiplying by 6. I had to remember to multiply every term and not just the fraction terms or the new equation would not be equivalent.

$$\frac{6x}{2} + \frac{6x}{3} = 6$$
$$3x + 2x = 6$$
$$5x = 6$$

I multiplied, and then, simplified.

$$\frac{5x}{5} = \frac{6}{5}$$

I divided both sides by 5 to isolate the variable.

$$x = 1.2$$

It would take Ryan and Maria 1.2 h to mow the lawn and water the garden if they worked together.

Check:
Left Side

1.2/2+1.2/3
                    1

Right Side
1

I used my calculator to check my solution. Since the left side equals the right side when $x = 1.2$, I know my solution is correct.

In Summary

Key Ideas

- When you solve an equation in which the variable appears on both sides of the equal sign ($ax + b = cx + d$), you can use inverse operations to group the variable terms on one side of the equation.
- If an equation has fraction coefficients and constants, you can use a common denominator to write an equivalent equation with integer coefficients. To do this, multiply each term of the equation by the common denominator. Using the lowest common denominator keeps the numbers in the new equivalent equation as small as possible.

Need To Know

- Sometimes you have to use the distributive property to expand expressions involving brackets before you can collect like terms on each side of the equation before solving for the variable.
- You can check your solution to an equation of the form $ax + b = cx + d$ by substituting the value in each side of the equation and calculating the result. If you get the same value on both sides, then your result is correct.

CHECK Your Understanding

1. Use inverse operations to solve $2x + 4 = 4x - 2$.

2. To determine the dimensions of the rectangle with
   - perimeter 44 cm and
   - width 3 cm less than the length,

   Florence drew a diagram:

   a) Why is it reasonable for Florence to label the width "$L - 3$"?
   b) Create and solve the equation to determine the length of one side.
   c) What are the dimensions of the rectangle?

PRACTISING

3. Given each solved equation below, explain the mathematical reasoning for each step.

   a)
   $$2x + 8 = 4x - 18$$
   $$2x + 8 - 2x = 4x - 18 - 2x \qquad \text{Step A}$$
   $$8 = 2x - 18$$
   $$8 + 18 = 2x - 18 + 18 \qquad \text{Step B}$$
   $$26 = 2x$$
   $$\frac{26}{2} = \frac{2x}{2} \qquad \text{Step C}$$
   $$13 = x$$

   b)
   $$\frac{1}{2}x + \frac{2}{3} = 5$$
   $$6 \times \left(\frac{1}{2}x + \frac{2}{3}\right) = 5 \times 6 \qquad \text{Step A}$$
   $$3x + 4 = 30 \qquad \text{Step B}$$
   $$3x + 4 - 4 = 30 - 4 \qquad \text{Step C}$$
   $$3x = 26$$
   $$\frac{3x}{3} = \frac{26}{3} \qquad \text{Step D}$$
   $$x = 8\frac{2}{3} \qquad \text{Step E}$$

4. Explain why the equations in each group are equivalent equations.

   a) $5x + 8 = 2(2x - 3)$, $5x + 8 = 4x - 6$, and $5x - 4x = -6 - 8$

   b) $\dfrac{x}{4} + 5 = \dfrac{1}{3}$, $\dfrac{3x}{12} + \dfrac{60}{12} = \dfrac{4}{12}$, and $3x + 60 = 4$

   c) $5x - 8 = 12$, $\dfrac{5x}{6} - \dfrac{4}{3} = 2$, and $\dfrac{5x}{6} - \dfrac{8}{6} = \dfrac{12}{6}$

5. Solve each equation. Verify each solution.

   [K] **a)** $5x + 24 = 2x$ **c)** $-4x - 1 = -3x + 5$ **e)** $3b - 4 - 5b = -3b - 2$

      b) $2k = 4k - 15$ **d)** $2x - 3x + 6 = 7 - x + 2$ **f)** $a + 2a + 3a - 6 = 7a - 6$

6. Solve $n + (n + 1) + (n + 2) = 54$.

7. Solve each equation. Verify each solution.

   a) $3(x - 5) = 6$ **c)** $-3(5 - 6m) = 39$ **e)** $3(c + 5) = 4(1 - 2c)$

   b) $-5 = 5(3 + 2d)$ **d)** $2(x - 2) = 3x - 14$ **f)** $4(x - 2) = -3(2x + 6)$

8. A number, n, decreased by 5, is equal to 3 times the number plus 1. Determine the number.

9. The perimeter of a rectangle is 36 cm. The width is 5 cm less than the length. Determine the dimensions of the rectangle.

10. George is three times as old as Sam. Five years from now, the sum of their ages will be 46.

   a) Create an equation that represents the relationship between George's and Sam's ages five years from now.

   b) Use your equation to determine their current ages.

11. Fill in the missing column for each equation.

	Equation	Common Denominator of All Terms	Equation with Denominators Eliminated
a)	$\dfrac{3x}{4} + \dfrac{2}{3} = 2$		
b)	$\dfrac{1}{2} - \dfrac{x}{3} = \dfrac{1}{3}$		
c)	$\dfrac{2}{3} = 5 + x$		
d)	$\dfrac{x - 5}{4} + 1 = \dfrac{1}{2}$		
e)	$-16 = \dfrac{x}{5} + \dfrac{x}{3}$		
f)	$\dfrac{-2}{5}(x - 8) = 4$		
g)	$\dfrac{y + 2}{3} = \dfrac{1}{5}(2y + 3)$		

12. Solve each equation. Verify each solution.

a) $\dfrac{x}{3} = 2$

b) $\dfrac{d}{4} + 3 = 2$

c) $\dfrac{x}{2} + \dfrac{x}{3} = 10$

d) $\dfrac{c}{3} - \dfrac{c}{4} = 3$

e) $\dfrac{3k}{5} - 6 = \dfrac{k}{3}$

f) $\dfrac{2x + 1}{3} = 5$

13. The sum of one-half of a number, q, and three-fifths is two-thirds the number q. Determine the number.

14. For each of the following, create and solve an equation.

A   **a)** It takes Eli 4 hours to paint a room. It takes Mia 3 hours to paint a room. How long would it take them to paint the room together?

b) Amir can put together a puzzle in 30 minutes. Bob takes double the amount of time. How long will it take them to do it together?

c) A jet left Toronto for Vancouver, travelling at a speed of 600 km/h. At the same time, a jet left Vancouver for Toronto, travelling at a speed of 800 km/h. If the distance between Toronto and Vancouver is 3500 km, when will the jets pass each other?

15. A square has sides of length $2k - 1$ units. An equilateral triangle has sides of length $k + 2$ units. The square and the triangle have the same perimeter. What is the value of k?

16. Show that the equation $2x - 3 = 4 + 2x$ has no solution. Why do
T you think this happens?

17. Show that the equation $\dfrac{10 - 6x}{2} = 5 - 3x$ has an infinite number of solutions. Why do you think this happens?

18. Jennifer solved the equation $\dfrac{4x - 1}{4} + \dfrac{2x - 1}{5} = 2$ below. Explain
C the mathematical operation she used in each step.

$$\dfrac{4x - 1}{4} + \dfrac{2x - 1}{5} = 2$$

$$20\left(\dfrac{4x - 1}{4}\right) + 20\left(\dfrac{2x - 1}{5}\right) = 20(2) \qquad \text{Step A}$$

$$5(4x - 1) + 4(2x - 1) = 40 \qquad \text{Step B}$$

$$20x - 5 + 8x - 4 = 40 \qquad \text{Step C}$$

$$28x - 9 = 40 \qquad \text{Step D}$$

$$28x - 9 + 9 = 40 + 9 \qquad \text{Step E}$$

$$28x = 49 \qquad \text{Step F}$$

$$\dfrac{28x}{28} = \dfrac{49}{28} \qquad \text{Step G}$$

$$x = \dfrac{49}{28}$$

$$x = \dfrac{7}{4} \text{ or } 1\dfrac{3}{4} \qquad \text{Step H}$$

19. Samir thinks that solving an equation with x on both sides is like solving an equation where x is only on one side. Do you agree or disagree with Samir? Use an example to justify your answer.

Extending

20. David has 16 dimes and quarters. Colin has twice as many dimes and $\dfrac{1}{3}$ as many quarters as David.

They both have the same amount of money. What coins does each boy have?

	Number of Quarters	Number of Dimes	Value of Quarters (¢)	Value of Dimes (¢)
David	q	$16 - q$	$25q$	
Colin	$\dfrac{q}{3}$			

21. Determine the value of x in each diagram.

a)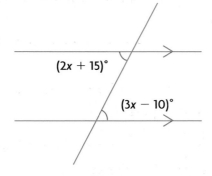
$(2x + 15)°$
$(3x - 10)°$

b)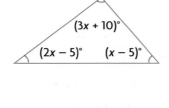
$(3x + 10)°$
$(2x - 5)°$ $(x - 5)°$

c)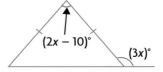
$(2x - 10)°$
$(3x)°$

22. Solve the equations:
a) $3x^2 - 2 = 25$
b) $2(x + 1)^2 - 1 = 71$

23. Chiaki is organizing a candy hunt for the children in her neighbourhood. She spent \$102 to buy 500 large candies and 400 small candies. The ratio of the price of a large candy to the price of a small candy is 7:4. Find the prices of one large and one small candy.

FREQUENTLY ASKED Questions

Q: What is the connection between the solution of a linear equation and the graph of a linear relation?

A: The solution to an equation is the x- or y-coordinate of a point on its graph.

EXAMPLE

Consider the graph of the linear relation represented by $y = 2x + 3$.

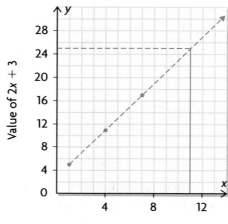

Graph of $y = 2x + 3$

Solving for y in $y = 2x + 3$
when $x = 11$ using the graph:
$y = 2(11) + 3$
• Locate 11 on the x-axis.
• Locate the point on the graph
  with that x-coordinate.
• Determine the y-coordinate of
  that point.
The solution is $y = 25$.

Solving for x in $y = 2x + 3$
when $y = 25$ using the graph:
$25 = 2x + 3$
• Locate 25 on the y-axis.
• Locate the point on the graph
  with that y-coordinate.
• Determine the x-coordinate of
  that point.
The solution is $x = 11$.

A2: You could also choose to keep the rational numbers, use inverse operations, and solve for the variable.

EXAMPLE

Solve $-\dfrac{1}{6}x + \dfrac{1}{2} = 7.$

Solution

$$-\frac{1}{6}x + \frac{1}{2} = 7$$

$$-\frac{1}{6}x + \frac{1}{2} - \frac{1}{2} = 7 - \frac{1}{2} \qquad \text{Subtract } \frac{1}{2} \text{ from both sides.}$$

$$-\frac{1}{6}x = 6\frac{1}{2}$$

$$-\frac{1}{6}x \div \left(-\frac{1}{6}\right) = 6\frac{1}{2} \div \left(-\frac{1}{6}\right) \qquad \text{Divide both sides by } -\frac{1}{6}.$$

$$x = \frac{13}{2} \times -\frac{6}{1}$$

$$x = -39$$

A3: You could write an equivalent equation by using the same denominator on both sides.

EXAMPLE

Solve $-\dfrac{1}{6}x + \dfrac{1}{2} = 7.$

Solution

$$-\frac{1}{6}x + \frac{1}{2} = 7 \qquad \text{Express both sides of the equation using an LCD of 6.}$$

$$-\frac{1}{6}x + \frac{1 \times 3}{2 \times 3} = \frac{7 \times 6}{1 \times 6}$$

$$-\frac{1}{6}x + \frac{3}{6} = \frac{42}{6} \qquad \text{Write the left side using a single denominator.}$$

$$\frac{-1x + 3}{6} = \frac{42}{6}$$

$$-1x + 3 = 42 \qquad \text{Equate the numerators.}$$

$$-1x + 3 - 3 = 42 - 3 \qquad \text{Solve for } x \text{ using inverse operations.}$$

$$-1x = 39$$

$$\frac{-1x}{-1} = \frac{39}{-1}$$

$$x = -39$$

PRACTICE Questions

Lesson 4.1

1. Use a graph to determine the solution to each equation.
   a) $x + 2 = 7$
   b) $4x - 4 = 8$
   c) $-2x - 9 = -5$
   d) $-7x - 14 = -14$

2. A submarine starts at sea level and descends 50 m every 5 min.
   a) Make a table of values of the submarine's depth. Use intervals of 5 min, up to 30 min.
   b) Graph the submarine's depth at 30 min.
   c) What patterns do you see in the table and the graph?
   d) If the submarine started at a depth of 219 m, what relation would model the submarine's location in relation to time?
   e) Create an equation to show how long it would take the submarine to reach a depth of 428 m. Use the graph to solve this equation.

Lesson 4.2

3. Solve using inverse operations.
   a) $2x - 5 = 7$
   b) $3x + 4 = 10$
   c) $-6 = 3 + 3x$
   d) $-2.1k + 5.6 = 20.2$
   e) $-8.75z + 12.5 = 12.5$
   f) $-a + 5 = 0$

4. Amit joins a book club. The first six books are free, but after that he pays $8.98 per book.
   a) Write an expression for the cost of b books.
   b) How much would he pay for eight books?
   c) Amit receives his first shipment of books with a bill for $53.88. Create and solve an equation to determine how many books he ordered.

Lesson 4.3

5. Solve. Verify your solution.
   a) $-x + 6 = 2x - 12$
   b) $\dfrac{2}{3}x - 2 = 4x + \dfrac{4}{3}$
   c) $4(x - 8) = -2(x - 5)$
   d) $\dfrac{2}{3}x - \dfrac{1}{2} = -\dfrac{1}{2} + \dfrac{1}{4}x$
   e) $\dfrac{1}{5}(a + 1) = \dfrac{1}{3}(2a - 3)$
   f) $\dfrac{(4a - 2)}{5} + \dfrac{1}{2} = \dfrac{(3a + 7)}{2} - 1$

6. For each equation, write an equivalent equation you could use to help solve it. Then, solve each equation.
   a) $\dfrac{k}{3} + 1 = 4$
   c) $-1\dfrac{2}{3}g + \dfrac{7}{9} = 0$
   b) $\dfrac{x}{2} - 3 = 1\dfrac{1}{6}$
   d) $\dfrac{2}{3}h + \dfrac{1}{4} = 3\dfrac{1}{2}$

7. Create and solve an equation to answer each problem below.
   a) The perimeter of a rectangle is 210 m. The length is 7 m longer than the width. Determine the dimensions of the rectangle.
   b) Recall that opposite angles are equal. Determine the value of each angle measure:

   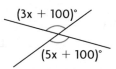

   c) Tom has 117 quarters and dimes worth a total of $15.75. How many of each coin does he have?
   d) Jim can paint a house in 10 h and Mario can paint the same house in 12 h. How long will it take if they work together?

Curious | Math

Crossing the T

Jeff told Erica that if she shaded a letter T on a number grid and told him the sum of all the numbers, he could tell her where the T is located.

Erica: "My sum is 320."
Jeff: "Your numbers are 57, 58, 59, 68, and 78!"

How did Jeff know what numbers Erica chose?

1	2	3	4	5	6	7	8	9	10
11	12	13	14	15	16	17	18	19	20
21	22	23	24	25	26	27	28	29	30
31	32	33	34	35	36	37	38	39	40
41	42	43	44	45	46	47	48	49	50
51	52	53	54	55	56	57	58	59	60
61	62	63	64	65	66	67	68	69	70
71	72	73	74	75	76	77	78	79	80
81	82	83	84	85	86	87	88	89	90
91	92	93	94	95	96	97	98	99	100

1. What expression can you use to describe the sum of the numbers in a T?

2. Try this trick with a partner.

3. Create another trick that would predict the numbers that form a letter E on the hundred chart if you know the sum.

Solving for a Variable in a Linear Relation

Use inverse operations to solve for a variable in a linear relation.

LEARN ABOUT the Math

Ralph and Bill work part time repairing bikes. They are paid $2 to install a tire and $5 to install gears. Their boss will pay a maximum of $100 per week.

? Which combinations of tire and gear installations will earn the boys exactly $100?

EXAMPLE 1	Strategies for determining ordered pairs in a linear relation

The boys developed the linear relation $2T + 5G = 100$ to represent the situation. T represents the number of tire installations and G represents the number of gear installations.

Determine the combinations of tire and gear installations that will earn them $100.

Ralph's Solution: Using guess-and-check to solve for one variable after substituting a value for the other

Let $T = 5$. ←——————————
So, $2T + 5G = 100$.

> I chose a value for T. I knew the value of G should depend on the value of T that I chose.

$$2(5) + 5G = 100$$
$$10 + 5G = 100$$
$$10 + 5G - 10 = 100 - 10$$
$$5G = 90$$
$$\frac{5G}{5} = \frac{90}{5}$$
$$G = 18$$

I substituted the value for T into the equation and solve for G.

Let $T = 6$:

I chose a different value for T.

$$2T + 5G = 100$$
$$2(6) + 5G = 100$$

I substituted the value into the equation.

$$12 + 5G - 12 = 100 - 12$$
$$5G = 88$$

I used inverse operations to solve for G.

$$\frac{5G}{5} = \frac{88}{5}$$
$$G = 17.6$$

It is impossible to do 17.6 gear installations, so $T = 6$ is not a reasonable value to choose.

Each time I chose a value, I ended up with an equation like $5G = \blacksquare$. I realized that whatever I subtract from 100 must be a multiple of 5 in order to divide and get a whole number. T must be a multiple of 5.

Let $T = 10$:

I tried $T = 10$ as a value.

$$2T + 5G = 100$$
$$2(10) + 5G = 100$$
$$20 + 5G - 20 = 100 - 20$$
$$5G = 80$$
$$\frac{5G}{5} = \frac{80}{5}$$
$$G = 16$$

5 tire installations and 18 gear installations will earn exactly $100. So will 10 tire installations and 16 gear installations.

Bill's Solution: Using algebra to rearrange the relation to solve for one variable in terms of the other

$$2T + 5G - 5G = 100 - 5G$$
$$2T = 100 - 5G$$

I thought I could save time if I wrote an equivalent relation that showed how to calculate one of the variables in terms of the other.

solve for a variable in terms of other variables

the process of using inverse operations to express one variable in terms of the other variable(s)

I decided to write an equation that **solved for T in terms of G.** That meant I first had to undo the $+ 5G$ on the left.

$$\frac{2T}{2} = \frac{100 - 5G}{2}$$
$$T = \frac{100 - 5G}{2}$$

I used inverse operations to isolate the variable T.

Let $G = 10$:
$$T = \frac{100 - 5G}{2}$$
$$T = \frac{100 - 5(10)}{2}$$
$$T = \frac{50}{2}$$
$$T = 25$$

I chose a value for G and substituted the value into the equation.

10 gear installations and 25 tire installations will earn exactly $100.

Let $G = 11$:
$$T = \frac{100 - 5G}{2}$$
$$T = \frac{100 - 5(11)}{2}$$
$$T = \frac{45}{2}$$
$$T = 22.5$$

I chose a different value for G and substituted the value into the equation.

It is impossible to do 22.5 tire installations, so $G = 11$ is not a reasonable value to choose.

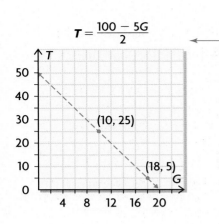

$$T = \frac{100 - 5G}{2}$$

I also found that 18 gear and 15 tire installations would work, so I plotted the points (10, 25) and (18, 5) and joined these with a dashed line since that data is discrete. This gave me the graph of the relation

$$T = \frac{100 - 5G}{2}.$$

Points outside the first quadrant are not possible because they would mean a negative number of tire or gear installations.

I can see from the graph that there are several combinations that would earn exactly $100. Some possible combinations are (0, 50), (2, 45), (4, 40), (6, 35), (8, 30).

I noticed that each increase of 2 tire installations resulted in a decrease of 5 gear installations.

Any point that lies on the line that has whole-number coordinates represents a combination that will earn $100.

Reflecting

A. How did Ralph and Bill know which inverse operations to use and in what order to apply them?

B. How would Bill's solution, equation, and graph be different if he chose to solve for G instead of T?

C. How is using inverse operations to solve a linear equation similar to using inverse operations to solve for one variable in terms of another? How is it different?

APPLY *the Math*

EXAMPLE 2 | Using an inverse operations strategy to solve a relation for one variable in terms of the other

Solve for y in terms of x for the line $\frac{2}{3}x + \frac{1}{5}y = 2$.

Agatha's Solution

$$\frac{2}{3}x + \frac{1}{5}y - \frac{2}{3}x = 2 - \frac{2}{3}x$$

I used an inverse operation to remove the $\frac{2}{3}x$ term and isolate the $\frac{1}{5}y$ term on the left.

$$\frac{1}{5}y = 2 - \frac{2}{3}x$$

$$5\left(\frac{1}{5}y\right) = 5\left(2 - \frac{2}{3}x\right)$$

Then, I multiplied both sides by 5 to solve for y. I added brackets to remind me to use the distributive property on the right side of the equation.

$$y = 10 - \frac{10}{3}x$$

I simplified the right side of the equation.

$$y = -\frac{10}{3}x + 10$$

I reordered the terms on the left.

The equation $\frac{2}{3}x + \frac{1}{5}y = 2$ is the same as $y = -\frac{10}{3}x + 10$.

EXAMPLE 3 | Rearranging an equation before solving it

Vicki puts $1500 in an investment account that earns 7.5% simple interest per year. If she wants to earn $200 in interest, how long must she leave the money in the investment?

Latifa's Solution

The simple interest formula is: $I = prt$.
- I represents the interest earned;
- p represents the principal amount invested (the initial amount put into the bank account);
- r represents the interest rate per year (expressed as a decimal);
- t represents the time (in years) that the money was invested.

$$I = prt$$

$$\frac{I}{pr} = \frac{prt}{pr}$$

Since I wanted to calculate the time needed for the investment, I decided to solve for T. I had to undo the multiplication by p and by r. The inverse of multiplying by p and r is to divide by p and r.

$$\frac{I}{pr} = t$$

$$I = \$200$$
$$r = 0.075$$
$$p = \$1500$$

$$\frac{200}{1500 \times 0.075} = t$$

$$1.8 = t$$

$$80\% \text{ of } 12 \text{ months}$$
$$= \frac{80}{100} \times 12$$
$$= 0.80 \times 12$$
$$\doteq 10 \text{ months}$$

> $r = 7.5\% = \dfrac{7.5}{100} = 0.075$
> I substituted the values for *I*, *p*, and *r* into the equation for *T*.

> 1.8 years is about 1 year and 80% of the second year.

> I calculated the number of months.

Vicki must leave her money in the investment for about 1 year and 10 months to earn $200 in interest.

In Summary

Key Idea

- You can use inverse operations to isolate any variable in a relation. This has the effect of solving for that variable in terms of the other variable(s) in the relation.

Need To Know

- The following strategy can be used to solve a relation for any variable:
  - Imagine that each of the other variables has been replaced by a number.
  - List the inverse operations needed to solve for the target variable.
  - Perform the inverse operations, one at a time, on the original relation, using the original variables until the target variable is isolated.

CHECK *Your Understanding*

1. Solve for the variable indicated.
   a) $3x + y = 5$; solve for x
   b) $2x + 5y = -10$; solve for y

2. Henri sharpens skates at a local arena. He charges $3.00 to sharpen a pair of figure skates and $2.50 for a pair of hockey skates. Last Saturday he earned a total of $240.

   a) To model this situation, John wrote: $3(number of pairs of figure skates) + $2.5(number of pairs of hockey skates) = $240. Write the relation using variables.

   b) Write the equation that expresses the number of hockey skates sharpened in terms of the number of figure skates.

   c) Write the equation that expresses the number of figure skates sharpened in terms of the number of hockey skates.

Practising

3. In each set of equations, identify the equation that is *not* equivalent to the others.

   a) $2a - b = 4$; $2a = b + 4$; $a = \dfrac{b}{2} + 2$; and $b = 2a + 4$

   b) $x + 2y = -6$; $y = \dfrac{x}{2} + 3$; $x = 2y - 6$; and $x - 2y + 6 = 0$

   c) $4m - 3n + 2 = 4$; $3n = 4m + 2$; $4m = 3n - 2$; and $3n - 4m = 2$

4. Solve for y in terms of x.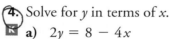

   a) $2y = 8 - 4x$

   b) $-2x - 3y = 12$

   c) $2.8x + 1.1y - 5.3 = 0$

   d) $\dfrac{7}{5}y + \dfrac{2}{3}x = \dfrac{11}{13}$

   e) $\dfrac{4}{5} = \dfrac{2}{3}x + 1\dfrac{1}{2}y$

   f) $3(y - 2) + 2x = 8$

5. A cell-phone company offers a plan of $25 per month and $0.10 per minute of talk. The cost, C, in dollars, is given by the relation $C = 25 + 0.10n$, where n is the number of minutes used per month. Each month the company uses the exact air time to calculate the monthly bill.

  a) Solve the relation for n in terms of C.

  b) Create a table of values for this new relation.

  c) Graph this relation.

  d) What is the independent variable? What is the dependent variable?

  e) Why might someone want to rearrange this relation and express it in terms of the cost?

6. Start with the relation $2x - 5y = 20$.

  a) Solve for y in terms of x.

  b) Graph this relation using x as the independent variable.

  c) State the slope and the intercepts of the graph.

  d) Solve for x in terms of y.

  e) Graph the relation using y as the independent variable.

  f) State the slope and intercepts of the graph.

  g) Compare the slope of the two graphs. Justify your comparison.

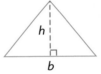

7. Solve the relation or formula for the variable indicated:

  a) $2a - 5b = 12$; solve for a

  b) $0.35m + 2.4n = 9$; solve for n

  c) $\frac{1}{2}p - \frac{2}{3}q = \frac{1}{4}$; solve for p

  d) $I = prt$; solve for r

  e) $P = 2L + 2W$; solve for L

  f) $C = 2\pi r$; solve for r

8. Look at the diagram.

  T a) Write a formula for h in terms of the base, b, and the area, A.

  b) Determine the height of the triangle if the area is 55 cm^2 and the base is 4 cm.

9. Ben has $42.50 in quarters and dimes.

  a) Write a linear relation expressing the total amount of money in terms of the number of quarters and dimes.

  b) Write an equation to express the number of quarters in terms of the number of dimes.

  c) Write an equation to express the number of dimes in terms of the number of quarters.

  d) Use one of your equations to determine the possible combinations of quarters and dimes Ben could have.

10. A candy store is making a mixture of chocolate-coated almonds and
Ⓐ chocolate-coated raisins. The almonds cost \$30/kg and the raisins
cost \$8/kg. The total cost of the mixture is to be \$150.
   a) Write a linear relation expressing the total cost in terms of the
   mass of almonds and the mass of raisins purchased.
   b) Write an equation to express the mass of almonds in terms of the
   mass of raisins.
   c) Write an equation to express the mass of raisins in terms of the
   mass of almonds.
   d) Which combinations of almonds and raisins will cost exactly \$150?

11. The Alltime Watch Company makes and sells two kinds of watches.
Ⓒ The profit on digital watches is \$15 per watch. The profit on analog
watches is \$20 per watch. The watch factory can only produce watches
in the ratio of 3 digital : 2 analog because of the machines it uses. Given
this ratio, how many watches of each type must be produced to meet
the company's profit target of at least \$20 000 per week?

12. When you multiply a number, x, by k, add n, and then divide by r, the
answer is w.
   a) Write the relation that models this situation.
   b) List the inverse operations that you would use, in the correct order,
   to isolate x.
   c) Solve the relation for x.
   d) How is rearranging a relation or formula for a particular variable
   similar to isolating a variable in a linear equation? How is it different?

Extending

13. Solve for x.
   a) $\dfrac{5}{x} + 2y = 9$
   b) $3x^2 + 50 = 197$
   c) $(x - 4)^2 - 12 = 24$
   d) $\dfrac{(3 + y)}{x} = -4$
   e) $\sqrt{x + 1} = 9$
   f) $2 - 8x^3 = 3$

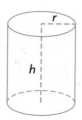

14. The formula for determining the surface area of a cylinder is
$SA = 2\pi r^2 + 2\pi rh$.
   a) Solve for h in terms of SA and r.
   b) Determine the height of a cylinder with radius 5 cm and surface
   area 300 cm².
   c) Solve for r in terms of the other variables.

Solving a Linear System Graphically

GOAL

Use a graph to solve a problem modelled by two linear relations.

YOU WILL NEED
- grid paper

Sari wants to join a website that allows its users to share music files. SHAREIT charges a $5 membership fee, plus $2.50 for each downloaded song. FILES 'R' US charges $3.00 per downloaded song.

? How can Sari determine which website she should join?

EXAMPLE 1   Solving a problem modelled by a system of linear equations

Determine the website that Sari should join.

Nick's Solution: Using a hand-drawn graph to solve a system of linear equations

I chose x to represent the number of music files downloaded and y to represent the costs for each company.

SHAREIT: $y = 5 + 2.5x$
FILES 'R' US: $y = 3x$

I created a **system of linear equations** to model this situation. The total cost, y, in each case depends on the number of music files, x, that are downloaded. I used each equation to create a table of values.

system of linear equations
a set of equations (at least two) that represent linear relations between the same two variables

Number of Songs, x	2	4	6	8	10	12
SHAREIT Cost, $y = 5 + 2.5x$	10	15	20	25	30	35
FILES'R'US Cost, $y = 3x$	6	12	18	24	30	36

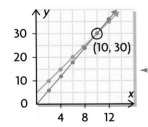

I drew both linear relations on the same graph.

Since the coordinate (10, 30) lies on both lines, this is the **point of intersection** and the **solution to the system of equations**.

If Sari plans to download exactly 10 songs, it doesn't matter which site she purchases from. They will both charge $30.

point of intersection
the point in common between two lines

solution to a system of linear equations
a point that satisfies both relations in a system of linear equations; the point of intersection represents an ordered pair that solves the system of linear equations

Check: ← I checked that the point (10, 30) works in both relations.

SHAREIT	FILES 'R' US
$y = 5 + 2.5x$	$y = 3x$
$y = 5 + 2.5(10)$	$y = 3(10)$
$y = 5 + 25$	$y = 30$
$y = 30$	

Sari should choose FILES 'R' US if she plans to download fewer than 10 songs. If she is going to download more than 10 songs, she should choose SHAREIT. ← From 1 to 9 songs downloaded, it costs less to purchase from FILES "R" US. I can tell because the graph is below the graph for SHAREIT. This switches when more than 10 songs are purchased.

Tech | **Support**

For help with using the graphing calculator to determine the point of intersection, see Appendix B-8.

Ben decided to use a graphing calculator to solve the problem.

Ben's Solution: Using technology to solve a system of linear equations

I chose x to represent the number of music files downloaded and y to represent the costs for each company.

SHAREIT: $y = 5 + 2.5x$ ← I created a **system of linear equations** to model this situation.

FILES 'R' US: $y = 3x$

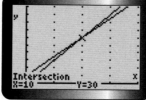

← I used my calculator to graph both relations and determine the point of intersection.

The point of intersection is (10, 30).

Sari should choose FILES 'R' US if she plans to download fewer than 10 songs. If she is going to download more than 10 songs, she should choose SHAREIT.

Reflecting

A. Why is it reasonable for the point of intersection to be called the solution to a system of linear equations?

B. Which student's strategy would you prefer to use? Why?

APPLY the Math

EXAMPLE 2 | **Determining the point of intersection of two lines**

What is the point of intersection of the graphs of

$3x + 2y = 12$ and $y = -\dfrac{3}{2}x + 2$?

Julie's Solution

$3x + 2y = 12$	
x	y
4	0
0	6

$y = \dfrac{-3}{2}x + 2$	
x	y
−2	5
0	2
2	−1
4	−4

To graph $3x + 2y = 12$, I calculated the intercepts and connected the points to see the relation.

To graph $y = -\dfrac{3}{2}x + 2$, I used a table of values. I chose numbers for x that were divisible by 2 because the coefficient of x has 2 in its denominator. I substituted these into the equation to find the values for y. I connected the points to see the relation. The lines are parallel, so they don't have a point in common.

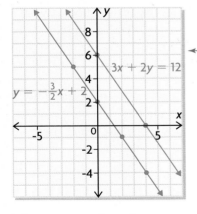

There is no point of intersection.

EXAMPLE 3   Using a graphing strategy to estimate a break-even point

Jean just opened a new company that makes MP3 players.
He uses two equations to compare cost and revenue. In order for the
company to break even, the cost must equal the revenue.

Cost equation:
- The company paid $5750 to set up the manufacturing line.
- The materials and labour cost for each machine is $50.
- The cost equation is $y = 50x + 5750$, where x is the number
  of MP3 players produced and y is the cost to produce x number
  of players.

Revenue equation:
- The company sells each player for $125.
- The revenue equation is $y = 125x$, where x is the number of MP3
  players sold and y is the revenue made for x number of MP3 players.

How many MP3 players must the company sell to break even?

Mason's Solution

Number of MP3 Players	Cost ($)	Revenue ($)
50	8 250	6 250
100	10 750	12 500
150	13 250	18 750

I created a table of values to find the break-even point.
This is the point where the cost and the revenue are
the same.
The cost is **more than** revenue when 50 MP3
players are sold.
The cost is **less than** the revenue when 100 MP3
players are sold.
This means that the break-even point must occur when
more than 50 but fewer than 100 players are sold.

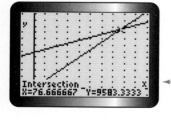

I used graphing technology to get a more accurate
solution. I entered the equation
$y = 50x + 5750$ in Y1 and $y = 125x$ in Y2. Then,
I determined the point of intersection.

Intersection at approximately (76.67, 9583.33).

The break-even point is at (76.67, 9583.33).

Since you cannot sell part of an MP3 player, the company
needs to sell about 77 MP3 players to break even.

If the company sells 77 MP3 players, its revenue and costs
will be about $9600.

| EXAMPLE **4** | Determining the number of solutions to a system of linear equations |

Determine the solution to each of the following:

a) $3x - y = 5$ and $y = 3x - 2$ **b)** $x - y = 2$ and $y = \dfrac{(2x - 4)}{2}$

Brent's Solution: Using graphing technology to solve the system of linear equations

a)

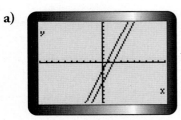

There is no solution to this system of linear equations because the lines are parallel.

I used graphing technology to graph each linear relation. I could not find the point of intersection. I rewrote $3x - y = 5$ in its equivalent $y = mx + b$ form: $y = 3x - 5$. It appears that the slopes of the two lines are the same because the lines look parallel. This means that they do not intersect at any point.

b)

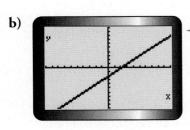

When I graphed both relations, the lines were identical.

$$x - y = 2$$
$$2 \times (x - y) = 2 \times 2$$
$$2x - 2y = 4$$

I realized that the equations were equivalent to each other. When I multiplied all the terms in the first equation by 2, I got the second equation.

There is an infinite number of solutions for this system of linear equations.

Since the equations are equivalent, all values that lie on one line also lie on the other line.

EXAMPLE **5**   Using technology to solve a system of linear equations

Find two numbers where:
- The sum of both numbers divided by 4 is 3.
- Two times the difference of the two numbers is –36.

Donna's Solution

Let x represent one number and y represent the other.

$$\frac{(x + y)}{4} = 3 \qquad\qquad 2(x - y) = -36$$

I created a system of linear equations to model the two statements.

$$4 \times \frac{(x + y)}{4} = 3 \times 4 \qquad\qquad \frac{2(x - y)}{2} = \frac{-36}{2}$$

$$(x + y) = 12 \qquad\qquad x - y = -18$$

$$x + y - x = 12 - x \qquad\qquad x - y + y = -18 + y$$

$$y = 12 - x \qquad\qquad x = -18 + y$$

$$y = -x + 12 \qquad\qquad x + 18 = -18 + y + 18$$

$$x + 18 = y$$

I used inverse operations to rearrange the relations into the form $y = mx + b$, so that I could graph both relations on a graphing calculator.

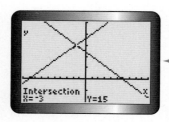

Intersection
X=-3   Y=15

I entered both relations into the equation editor and graphed the relations. I found the point of intersection using the graphing calculator. The point of intersection is $(-3, 15)$.

The numbers are -3 and 15.

Check:

Since the point of intersection satisfies both equations, the numbers are correct.

$$\frac{(x + y)}{4} = 3$$

Left Side   Right Side

$\dfrac{(-3 + 15)}{4}$ 3

$= \dfrac{12}{4}$

$= 3$

$$2(x - y) = -36$$

Left Side   Right Side

$2(-3 - 15)$ -36

$= 2(-18)$

$= -36$

In Summary

Key Ideas

- When solving a system of linear relations, the point of intersection of their graphs is the solution to that system of linear equations.

Need To Know

- The coordinates of the point of intersection can be estimated by graphing the relations by hand.
- Graphing technology helps determine the point of intersection with greater accuracy than is possible with a hand-drawn graph.
- A system of linear equations can have one point of intersection, zero points of intersection (if the graphs are parallel), or infinite points of intersection (if they are equivalent equations).

CHECK Your Understanding

1. Determine the point of intersection for each system of linear equations shown below.

a) $y = \dfrac{1}{2}x + 1$ and $y = -x + 4$

c) $y = 2x - 1$ and $y = -x + 3$

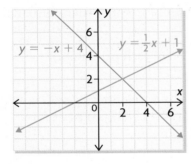

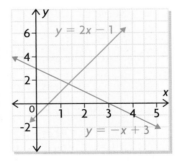

b) $y = x + 1$ and $y = 4x - 5$

d) $y = x$ and $y = -x$

2. Bill wants to earn extra money selling lemonade in front of his house. It costs $1.20 to start his business and each glass of lemonade costs $0.06 to make. He plans to sell the lemonade for $0.10 a glass.
   a) Write an equation that represents his cost.
   b) Write an equation that represents his revenue.
   c) Graph both equations on the same set of axes.
   d) What does the point of intersection mean in this case?
   e) Does Bill make a profit or lose money for
      i) 20 glasses sold?
      ii) 35 glasses sold?
      iii) 50 glasses sold?

Linear Equations **245**

PRACTISING

3. Determine the point of intersection of each pair of lines.
   a) $y = -3x - 2$ and $2x + 3y = 5$
   b) $2x + 4y = 7$ and $-x + 0.75y = 5$
   c) $0.25x - 0.5y = 1$ and $3.25x + 4y = 22.5$
   d) $y = 3x + 6$ and $1 = 3x - y$

4. The sum of two integers is 42. The difference of the two numbers is 17.
   a) Create a system of linear equations to model each statement above.
   b) Determine the integers using a graph.

5. Mike has $9.85 in dimes and quarters. If there are 58 coins altogether, how many dimes and how many quarters does Mike have?

6. Does each pair of lines intersect at the given point?
   a) $(2, 3)$: $y = x + 1$, $y = 4x - 5$
   b) $(1, -1)$: $y = 5x - 4$, $y = 2x - 3$
   c) $(0, 2)$: $y = 3x + 2$, $y = 5x - 1$
   d) $(-1, -3)$: $y = 4x + 1$, $y = x - 5$

7. Given the lines $y = 2$ and $y = 4x + 9$,
   a) Determine the point of intersection using a graph.
   b) Create the linear equation that you would solve to determine the x-value of the point of intersection.
   c) Solve the linear equation in part b) to verify your solution from part a).

8. Determine the point of intersection of each pair of lines:
   a) $y - x = 9$ and $x - \dfrac{1}{6}y = -\dfrac{2}{3}$
   b) $y = 2$ and $y = 5$
   c) $2x - y = 0$ and $y = 5 + 2x$
   d) $y = -4$ and $x = 1$

9. Marie charges $3 for every 4 bottles of water purchased from her store. She pays her supplier $0.25 per bottle, plus $250 for shelving and water delivery.
   a) Create a system of two linear equations to model this situation.
   b) How many bottles of water does she need to sell to break even?

10. Mr. Smith is trying to decide which Internet service provider (ISP) to use for his home computer. UPLINK offers a flat fee of $19 per month; BLUELINE offers a fee of $10 per month, but charges $0.59 per hour after the first 30 hours.
    a) Write the linear relation that models the cost in relation to the number of hours used for each plan.
    b) Estimate the point at which the costs for both companies would be the same.

c) What equation would you set up and solve to determine the exact point at which the costs would be the same? Why is this equation reasonable?

d) What advice would you give to Mr. Smith about which ISP to choose?

11. Mrs. Smith was trying to help her husband decide which ISP to use and she investigated two other companies on her own:

DOWNLINK offers a plan of $5 per month plus $1.15 per hour after the first 20 hours.

REDLINE offers a plan of $2.50 per month plus $1.80 per hour after the first 10 hours.

Should the Smiths consider either of these two companies in their decision? Why or why not?

12. Determine the point of intersection of each pair of lines:

a) $5x + 8y - 12 = 0$ and $-5x + 16y - 12 = 0$

b) $4x + y - 2 = 0$ and $8x + 2y - 4 = 0$

c) $\dfrac{1}{3}x - \dfrac{2}{5}y + \dfrac{1}{4} = 0$ and $2x - \dfrac{1}{7}y + \dfrac{1}{2} = 0$

d) $5x - 2.5y = 10$ and $3.1x + 4y = 6.2$

13. Given the relation $x + y = 5$, determine a second relation that:

T **a)** intersects $x + y = 5$ at $(2, 3)$

b) *does not* intersect $x + y = 5$

14. Movies to Go rents DVDs for $2.50 and has no membership fee. Films
C 'R' Us rents videos for $2 but has a $10 membership fee. What advice would you give to someone who is deciding which video store to use?

15. Why does a system of two linear equations usually have only one solution for each of the two variables?

Extending

16. To determine the point of intersection of $y = 2x + 5$ and $y = 4x - 3$, Elena wrote $2x + 5 = 4x - 3$ and solved the equation. Why is this a reasonable strategy for determining the point of intersection of the two lines?

17. Compare the strategies of solving $3x + 4 = 5x + 3$ by using inverse operations and by graphing the two relations.

18. a) Determine the point(s) of intersection of $y = 2x^2$ and $y = 8$ using a graph.

b) Create and solve the equation that you would use to determine where the point of intersection lies.

c) Are your solutions from parts a) and b) the same? Explain.

FREQUENTLY ASKED Questions

Study Aid

- See Lesson 4.4, Examples 2 and 3.
- Try Chapter Review Questions 5 and 6.

Q: How does solving a linear relation for a variable compare to solving a linear equation?

A: The processes are the same, but the solution for a linear equation is a number. When solving for a variable, you get an equation equivalent to the original one. To isolate the variable, you must undo each operation in the reverse order. The operation must be done to both sides of the equation to keep the equivalence of the relation or formula.

EXAMPLE

Rearrange the equation $90x + 45y = 360$ to solve for y in terms of x.

Solution

$$90x + 45y = 360$$
$$90x + 45y - 90x = 360 - 90x$$
$$45y = 360 - 90x$$
$$\frac{45y}{45} = \frac{360 - 90x}{45}$$
$$y = \frac{360 - 90x}{45}$$
$$y = 8 - 2x$$

Study Aid

- See Lesson 4.5, Example 1.
- Try Chapter Review Questions 7 and 8.

Q: How do you solve a problem that can be modelled by a system of linear relations?

A1: Use a hand-drawn graph to estimate the point of intersection.

EXAMPLE

The cost to make ice pops is $0.10 per ice pop, plus $9.00 in supplies. Each ice pop sells for $0.40. How many do you need to sell to break even?

Solution

Cost and Revenue of Ice Pops

Create a table of values for each equation, then graph both equations on the same axes. Find the point of intersection. Then, interpret the point of intersection.

The break-even point is located at (30, 12).

You need to sell 30 ice pops to break even.

A2: Use graphing technology to determine more accurate coordinates of the point of intersection.

EXAMPLE

Determine the point of intersection of the graphs of $2x + y = 8$ and $3x - 2y = 6$.

Solution

$$2x + y = 8 \qquad\qquad\qquad 3x - 2y = 6$$
$$2x + y - 2x = 8 - 2x \qquad 3x - 2y - 3x = 6 - 3x$$
$$y = -2x + 8 \qquad\qquad -2y = -3x + 6$$
$$\frac{-2y}{-2} = -3x + \frac{6}{-2}$$
$$y = \frac{3}{2}x - 3$$

> Solve for y in terms of x in both equations, so that they can be graphed on a graphing calculator.

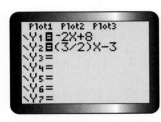
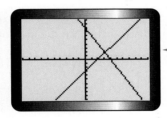

> Enter both equations into the equation editor of a graphing calculator and graph.

> Determine the point of intersection using the Intersect operation.

The point of intersection is about $(3.14, 1.71)$.

Q: In what ways can two lines intersect?

A: Two lines can intersect in one of three different ways.

The lines could be parallel resulting in 0 points of intersection.

The lines could intersect at exactly one point of intersection.

The lines could be identical resulting in an infinite number of points of intersection.

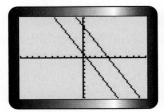
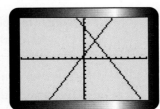

Linear Equations **249**

PRACTICE Questions

Lesson 4.1

1. Write the linear relation that corresponds to each equation. Estimate the solution graphically.
   a) $4x - 5 = 3$
   c) $-2(x - 3) = -4$
   b) $\dfrac{1}{2}x + 3 = 5$
   d) $\dfrac{1}{4}\left(x + \dfrac{2}{5}\right) = 0$

2. Solve each equation using algebra.
   a) $3x + 6 = 12$
   b) $5 - 2x = 11$
   c) $4x - 8 = 12$
   d) $-6x + 8 = -10$

3. Determine the x-intercept of each of the following.
   a) $y = -5x + 20$
   b) $2x + y = 10$

4. A promoter is holding a video dance. Tickets cost $15 per person, and he has given away 10 free tickets to radio stations.
   a) Create the linear relation that models the money the promoter will earn in ticket sales in terms of the number of people attending the dance.
   b) Graph the linear relation.
   c) Write the equation you would solve to determine the money from tickets sales if 100 people attend. Solve the equation using the graph.
   d) Write the equation you would use to determine how many people attended if ticket sales were only $600. Estimate the solution using the graph.

Lesson 4.2

5. Solve each equation in question 1 using inverse operations.

6. Erynn joins a CD club. The first 10 CDs are free, but after that she pays $15.95 for each CD she orders.
   a) Write an expression for the cost of x CDs.
   b) How much would she pay for 15 CDs?
   c) Erynn receives her first order of CDs with a bill for $31.90. Create and solve an equation to determine how many she ordered.

Lesson 4.3

7. Solve and verify each equation.
   a) $9x + 2 = 11x - 10$
   b) $-\dfrac{4}{5}x + \dfrac{2}{3} = 1\dfrac{3}{4}x + 2$
   c) $-3(x + 1) - 2 = 4x - 5(x - 3)$
   d) $\dfrac{(4 + x)}{3} + 4 = \dfrac{(x - 6)}{2} - 6$

8. To calculate the area of a trapezoid, you would use the expression: $\dfrac{h}{2}(b_1 + b_2)$. Determine the length of each base for the trapezoids below if they have the same area.

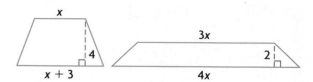

9. Is $x = 3$ the solution to $5(3x - 2) = 4 - 10(x + 1)$? Explain how you know.

Lesson 4.4

10. Solve each equation for the variable indicated.
    a) $P = 2l + 2w; l$
    c) $V = \pi r^2 h; h$
    b) $A = P + Prt; t$
    d) $Ax + By = C; y$

11. The formula $C = \dfrac{5}{9}(F - 32)$ is used to convert Fahrenheit temperatures to Celsius.
    a) Determine the Celsius temperature when $F = 90$.
    b) Solve for F in terms of C.
    c) Determine the Fahrenheit temperature when $C = 25$.

12. Solve for y in terms of x.

a) $8x - 4y = 12$

b) $5x = 10y - 20$

c) $3x - 3y - 9 = 0$

d) $\dfrac{x}{4} + \dfrac{y}{8} = 2$

13. Josh has $32.00 in loonies and toonies.

a) Write a linear relation expressing the total amount of money in terms of the number of loonies and toonies.

b) Write an equation to express the number of toonies in terms of the number of loonies.

c) Use your equation to determine the 4 different possible combinations of coins Josh could have.

d) Is it possible that Josh has 13 toonies and 5 loonies? Explain.

Lesson 4.5

14. John said, "To solve the equation $4 = -2x - 3$, I graphed $y = -2x - 3$ and $y = 4$. The x-value where the two lines intersect is the solution."

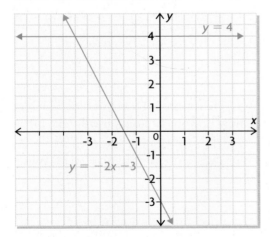

a) What is the solution to this equation based on the graph?

b) Verify the solution using algebra.

c) Why is John's strategy reasonable?

d) How could you use this strategy to solve $3x - 4 = 2x + 3$?

15. Solve each of the following systems of equations using a graph.

a) $y = 3x - 1$ and $y = -x + 5$

b) $y = -0.5x$ and $y = 6.5x + 3$

c) $3x - 4y = -12$ and $2x - 3y = 6$

16. Faster Fitness has a monthly membership fee of $90. Members pay $5 to take an aerobics class. At Drop-in Fitness, there is no membership fee, but clients pay $10 per class.

a) Write a linear relation for the yearly cost in terms of the number of aerobics classes.

b) Graph the equations on the same set of axes.

c) State the point of intersection.

d) What does the point of intersection mean in this case?

e) How would you advise someone who is trying to choose between the two fitness clubs?

17. The Video Vault rents DVDs for $3.00 each and has no membership fee. Videorenters rents DVDs for $2 each but has a $15 membership fee.

a) Write an equation for each situation.

b) Graph both equations on the same set of axes. Find the point of intersection.

c) What does the point of intersection mean in this case?

d) What advice would you give to someone who is deciding which video store to use?

1. **a)** Explain how each of the following illustrates a valid approach to solving the equation $3.50x + 2.70 = 6.55$.
   b) Which method leads to an exact solution?

Table of Values	Graph	Solve an Equation
x $3.50x + 2.70$ 0.0 2.70 0.2 3.40 0.4 4.10 0.6 4.80 0.8 5.50 1.0 6.20 1.2 6.90 1.4 7.60 1.6 8.30 1.8 9.00 2.0 9.70 The solution is between 1.0 and 1.2.	$y = 3.50x + 2.70$ The solution is $x \doteq 1.1$.	$3.50x + 2.70 = 6.55$ $3.50x + 2.70 - 2.70 = 6.55 - 2.70$ $3.5x = 3.85$ $3.5x \div 3.5 = 3.85x \div 3.5$ $x = 1.1$ The solution is $x = 1.1$.

2. Solve and verify each equation.

   a) $-2a + 5 = 3$

   b) $4 - 2x = 8$

   c) $\dfrac{5}{6}x - \dfrac{3}{4} = \dfrac{1}{4}$

   d) $3(x - 1) + 2(3x + 1) = 2$

3. Rearrange each equation to solve for the variable indicated.
   a) $-3x + 2y = 6$; solve for y.
   b) $y = 3x + 2$; solve for x.

4. David has two part-time jobs. He earns \$14/h at one and \$11/h at the other. David wants to know how many hours it will take him to earn \$1000.
   a) Find two combinations of the numbers of hours David could work at each job to earn \$1000.
   b) Graph the relation.

5. Determine the point of intersection for each system of linear equations.
   a) $y = 7x - 9$ and $y = -x - 1$
   b) $-x - 2y = -3$ and $3x + y = -2$

6. Justin charges \$21 per linear foot to install a wood fence. It costs him \$19 per linear foot plus \$4000 to purchase materials and hire installers each month. How many linear feet of fencing would he need to install each month to break even?

Planning the Burn

Carol enjoys high-impact aerobics and mountain biking. Steve prefers to swim and jog. Each of them works out for 45 minutes in a session.

Carol wants to burn 480 calories during her exercise sessions. Steve's target is 560 calories. The table shows the rate at which they burn calories in each type of activity.

Activity	Calories Burned per Hour	
	Carol	Steve
high-impact aerobics	444	620
jogging	636	880
mountain biking	540	752
swimming	508	708

? How should Carol and Steve plan their activities to meet their calorie targets?

A. Use algebraic expressions to represent each of Carol's and Steve's exercise plans.

B. Graph a relation for each.

C. Decide the amount of time Carol and Steve should spend on their preferred activities. Justify your choice.

D. Carol and Steve would like to choose two activities from the four to do together. Determine if they can do the same two activities for 45 minutes and meet their calorie targets.

Task | **Checklist**

✔ Did you draw and label your graphs?

✔ Did you explain your solutions?

✔ Did your solutions answer the questions?

✔ Did you use appropriate math language?

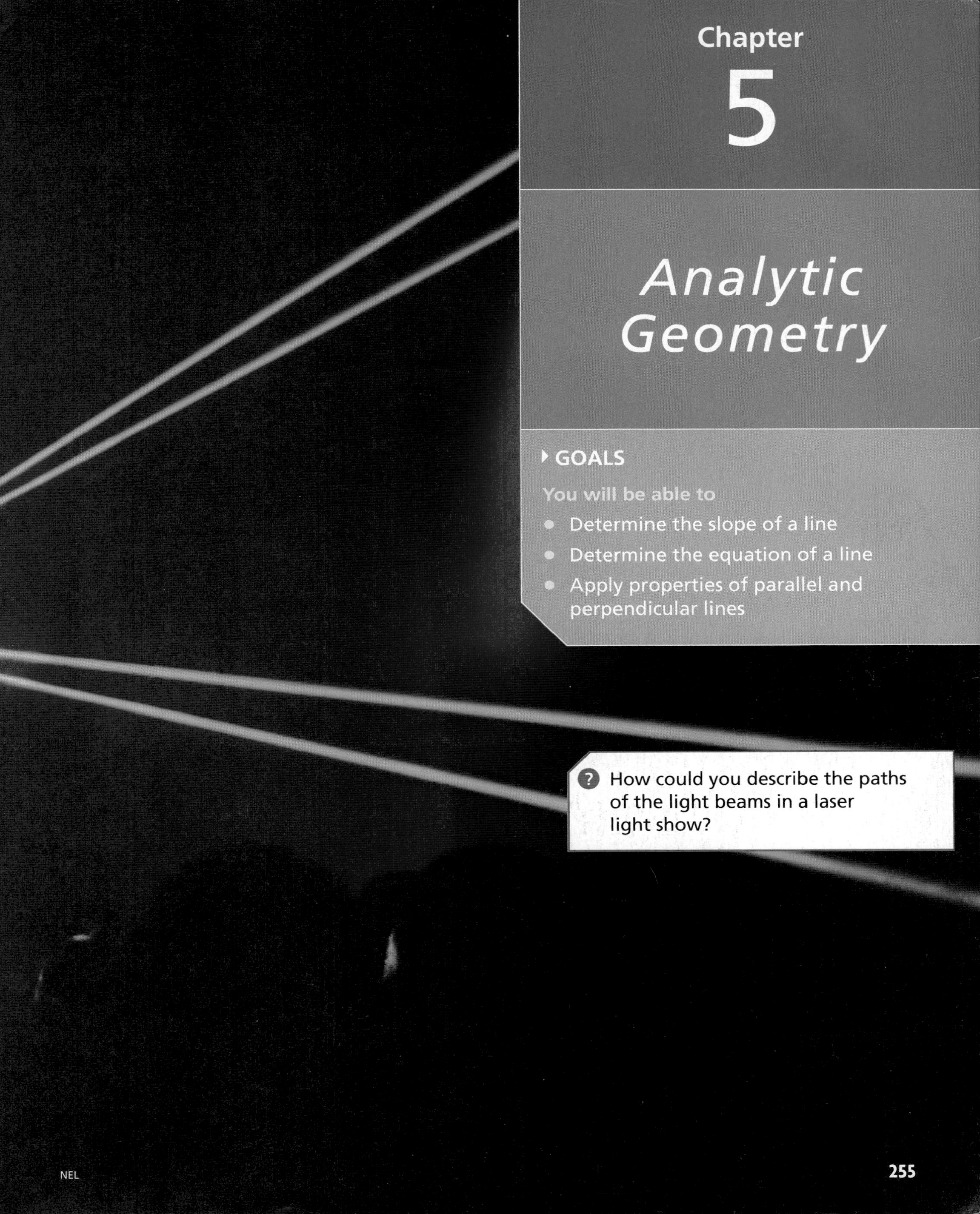

Chapter 5

Analytic Geometry

GOALS

You will be able to

- Determine the slope of a line
- Determine the equation of a line
- Apply properties of parallel and perpendicular lines

? How could you describe the paths of the light beams in a laser light show?

WORDS YOU NEED to Know

1. The graph shows the relationship between temperatures recorded using the Celsius scale and those recorded using the Fahrenheit scale. Match each word with the labelled part of the graph below that most closely represents it.

a) *x*-intercept
b) *y*-intercept
c) equation of a line
d) slope of a line
e) rise
f) run
g) independent variable
h) dependent variable

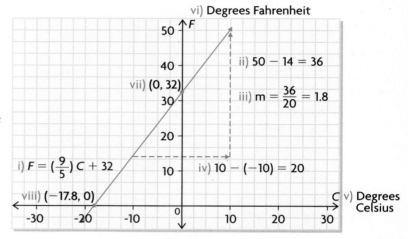

vi) **Degrees Fahrenheit**

ii) $50 - 14 = 36$

iii) $m = \dfrac{36}{20} = 1.8$

vii) $(0, 32)$

i) $F = \left(\dfrac{9}{5}\right) C + 32$

iv) $10 - (-10) = 20$

viii) $(-17.8, 0)$

v) **Degrees Celsius**

SKILLS AND CONCEPTS You Need

Determining the Reciprocal of a Rational Number

The product of a rational number and its reciprocal is 1.

The reciprocal of $\dfrac{a}{b}$ is $\dfrac{b}{a}$.

EXAMPLE

Determine the reciprocal of $-1\dfrac{1}{2}$.

Solution

$-1\dfrac{1}{2} = \dfrac{-3}{2}$

The reciprocal of $\dfrac{-3}{2}$ is $\dfrac{2}{-3} = \dfrac{-2}{3}$.

2. Determine the reciprocal of each rational number.

a) $\dfrac{-3}{5}$ b) $2\dfrac{3}{4}$ c) $-3\dfrac{1}{3}$ d) 1.5

Using Inverse Operations to Isolate a Variable

You can solve a relation or formula for one variable in terms of the other(s) by using inverse operations to isolate that variable.

EXAMPLE

Solve for m.

$$4m - 3n + 2 = 4$$

Solution

$$4m - 3n = 4 - 2$$
$$4m - 3n + 3n = 4 - 2 + 3n$$
$$4m = 2 + 3n$$
$$\frac{4m}{4} = \frac{2 + 3n}{4}$$
$$m = \frac{2 + 3n}{4}$$
$$m = \frac{3n}{4} + \frac{2}{4}$$
$$m = \frac{3n}{4} + \frac{1}{2}$$

3. Isolate or solve for the indicated variable.

a) $V = bh;\ b$ **c)** $P = 2l + 2w;\ w$ **e)** $I = Prt;\ r$

b) $3x + 5y = 15;\ y$ **d)** $v = \dfrac{d}{t};\ d$ **f)** $5x + 2y - 20 = 0;\ x$

Recognizing Parallel and Perpendicular Lines Geometrically

Parallel lines do not intersect and perpendicular lines intersect at 90°.

4. From the following graph, name pairs of lines that are parallel or perpendicular.

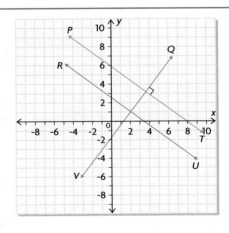

Study Aid

- For help, see the following examples.

Question	Examples
5	Lesson 4.2 Examples 1–3 and Lesson 4.3 Examples 1 and 3.
6	Lesson 3.5 Examples 1 and 2.
8 and 9	Lesson 3.4 Examples 2 and 3.

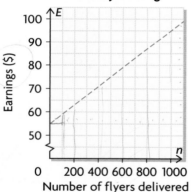

Terry's Flyer Delivery Earnings

PRACTICE

5. Solve each equation.

a) $4x - 15 = 13$ **c)** $12 - 5p = 3p + 8 - 7p$

b) $-4 = \frac{2}{3}m + 6$ **d)** $6t + 3(2t - 5) = 4 - 7t$

6. Tell why each of the following does or does not represent a linear relationship.

a) $y = 7.5x$ **b)** $y = 2x^2 - 8$ **c)** $4x + 2y - 14 = 0$

7. Create a table of values, then use it to graph each relation.

a) $y = 4x + 1$ **c)** $y = \frac{-1}{2}x - 3$

8. Determine the x- and y-intercepts for each of these linear equations.

a) $y = -5x + 4$ **b)** $2x + 7y + 14 = 0$

9. Terry delivers the local paper. He earns a fixed amount plus an additional amount based on the number of flyers he delivers with the paper as shown in the graph to the left.

a) What is the fixed amount Terry earns?

b) How much does Terry earn for each flyer delivered?

c) How does your answer in part b) relate to the slope of the line in the graph?

d) Express the slope of the graph as a rate of change value.

10. Keisha double-booked herself for babysitting Saturday night and now she must make a choice. The Herteises will pay her \$10 plus \$2/hour and the Farids will pay her \$6 plus \$4/hour.

a) Write an equation for each family to represent the relationship between the numbers of hours worked and Keisha's earnings.

b) Graph both equations.

c) For which family should Keisha choose to babysit? Explain.

11. Complete the following Anticipation Guide in your notes. Decide whether you agree or disagree with each statement. Justify your thinking.

	Statement	Agree	Disagree
a)	The slope of a line can only be found by graphing the line.		
b)	A line will always pass through at least two quadrants on a grid.		
c)	All points on a vertical line have the same x-coordinate.		
d)	When two lines on a Cartesian grid intersect at a 45° angle, one line has a slope greater than 1 and the other has a slope less than 1.		

APPLYING *What You Know*

Counting Coins

Meaghan has decided to cash in her piggy bank to buy her mom a birthday present. She has 59 coins, which are all quarters and dimes.

? How much money might Meaghan have?

A. If there were 10 quarters in Meaghan's piggy bank, how much money would she have?

Number of Quarters	Number of Dimes	Value of Quarters	Value of Dimes	Total Value
10				

B. Copy the table above and calculate at least five possible coin combinations using all 59 coins in her piggy bank.

C. What is the least amount of money that Meaghan could have in her piggy bank? How do you know?

D. What is the greatest amount of money that Meaghan could have in her piggy bank? How do you know?

E. Create a graph showing the total value versus number of quarters.

F. Is this a linear relationship? How do you know?

G. Use your graph to determine how many of each coin Meaghan has if the total value of her coins is $11.

Exploring the Equation of a Line

- dynamic geometry software

GOAL

Determine the significance of the values of m and b in the equation $y = mx + b$.

EXPLORE the Math

The graph on the left shows three lines and their equations.

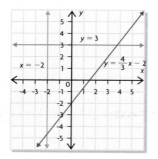

? How is the graph of a line related to its equation?

A. Use *The Geometer's Sketchpad* (GSP) to create a Cartesian grid with x- and y-axes.

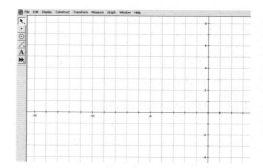

Tech | *Support*

For information on how to use *The Geometer's Sketchpad*, to plot points, and construct a line and determine its slope and equation, see Appendices B13 to B19.

B. Plot a point on the y-axis and label it A.

Use MEASURE to determine A's coordinates.

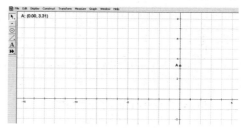

C. Plot a point *not* on the y-axis and label it B.

Construct a line to join A and B.

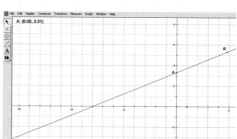

D. Use MEASURE to determine the slope of the line.

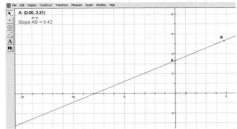

E. Use MEASURE to determine the equation of the line.

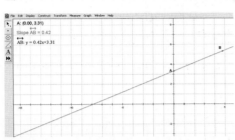

F. Move the line around the grid and observe what happens.

Copy and complete the table, then record five to ten different observations.

Slope	y-intercept	Linear Equation

G. Select point B and move the line around on the grid to create each of the types of lines shown below. Each time, observe the changes to the line's slope and equation.

Lines Rising to the Right

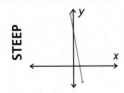 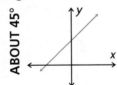 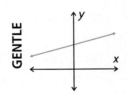

Horizontal Line

Lines Falling to the Right

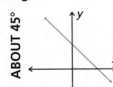 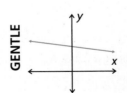 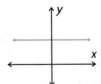

Vertical Line

Record your observations in a copy of the following table.

Description and Picture of Line	Possible Value(s) of Slope	Sample Equations

Analytic Geometry **261**

Reflecting

H. How does the slope value influence the steepness and direction of the line?

I. Given the equation of a line, how could you tell if the line was horizontal or vertical?

J. In the linear relation $y = mx + b$, how do the position and slope of the line change as m and b change?

K. Given the equation of the line in the form $y = mx + b$, how could you determine the line's slope and y-intercept? Use an example in your explanation.

In Summary

Key Idea

- $y = mx + b$ is the equation of a line where m represents the slope of the line and b represents the y-intercept of the line.

Need to Know

- The value of the slope determines the steepness and direction of the line. The greater the **magnitude** of the m-value, the steeper the line.
- The value of the y-intercept is a distance from the origin, where the graph crosses the y-axis.
- A line rising to the right has a positive slope.
- A line falling to the right has a negative slope.

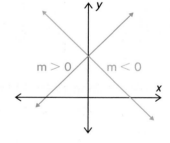

- A horizontal line has a slope of 0 and its equation has the form $y = b$, where b is the value of the y-intercept.
- A vertical line has an undefined slope and its equation has the form $x = a$, where a is the value of the x-intercept.

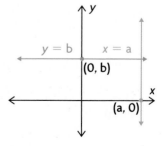

FURTHER Your Understanding

1. Match each linear equation with the graph that best represents it.

a) $y = -3x + 5$ **c)** $y = \dfrac{5}{8}x$ **e)** $x = 5$

b) $y = 7x - 4$ **d)** $y = -\dfrac{1}{4}x - 4$ **f)** $y = 3$

i)

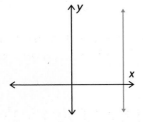

iv)

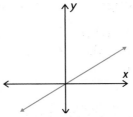

ii)

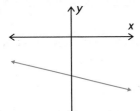

v)

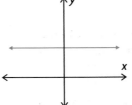

iii)

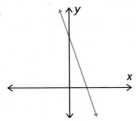

vi)

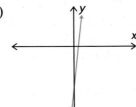

2. Consider the lines formed by each of the following equations.

a) $y = -2x + 8$ **b)** $y = \dfrac{1}{3}x + 1$

$y = -\dfrac{15}{2}x + 3$ $y = 3x - 9$

$y = -\dfrac{1}{2}x - 7$ $y = x + 5$

i) Identify the steepest and the least steep line in each of parts a) and b).

ii) Use the slope and y-intercept to sketch the graphs to verify your answers in i).

3. a) What linear equation represents the x-axis?

   b) What linear equation represents the y-axis?

Different Forms of the Equation of a Line

YOU WILL NEED

• graphing calculator

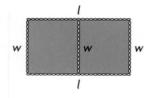

GOAL

Given an equation in the form $Ax + By + C = 0$ or $Ax + By = D$, express the equation in the form $y = mx + b$.

LEARN ABOUT the Math

David is a dog breeder and needs to construct two identical, adjacent rectangular pens to contain the male and female puppies. He has 24 m of fencing material available.

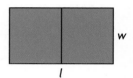

? What are some possible values for the length and width of the pens?

EXAMPLE 1   **Using an algebraic strategy**

Determine possible lengths and widths for the pens.

Pietr's Solution: Isolating *l* and using the slope and
                      y-intercept to sketch a graph

---

l represents the length of the pens and *w* represents the width.

$$2l + 3w = 24$$

> I chose variables to represent each value.
>
> I wrote an equation using two lengths and three widths to represent the total amount of fencing.

$$2l + 3w - 3w = 24 - 3w$$
$$2l = -3w + 24$$
$$\frac{2l}{2} = \frac{-3w + 24}{2}$$
$$\frac{2l}{2} = \frac{-3w}{2} + \frac{24}{2}$$
$$l = -\frac{3}{2}w + 12$$
$$y = -\frac{3}{2}x + 12$$

> I used inverse operations to isolate the length variable *l*, so that I could calculate a length to go with any width I chose.
>
> I replaced *l* with *y* since it is the dependent variable and *w* with *x* since it is the independent variable.

$$y = -\frac{3}{2}x + 12$$

The equation is in the form $y = mx + b$.

I know that m tells the slope and b tells the y-intercept.

$$\text{slope} = \frac{\text{rise}}{\text{run}} = -\frac{3}{2}$$

$$y\text{-intercept} = 12$$

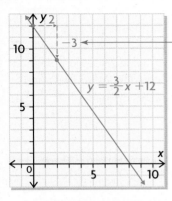

I plotted the y-intercept first.

Starting at the y-intercept, I used the run to move 2 units right and the rise to move 3 units down to determine a second point on the line.

Then, I drew the line joining the two points.

Some possible dimensions for the pens are:

$w = 2$ m and $l = 9$ m

$w = 3$ m and $l = 7.5$ m

$w = 4$ m and $l = 6$ m

$w = 6$ m and $l = 3$ m

I used the graph to locate other points that were on the line. Each ordered pair (x, y) or (w, l) represents the dimensions of a pen with a perimeter of 24 m.

Hanxiang's Solution: Isolating a variable to graph the relation with a graphing calculator

l represents the length of the pens and w represents the width.

I chose variables to represent each value.

$$2l + 3w = 24$$

$$2l + 3w - 2l = 24 - 2l$$

$$3w = -2l + 24$$

The diagram has 2 horizontal and 3 vertical sides, so I wrote a sum equal to the amount of fencing.

$$\frac{3w}{3} = \frac{-2l + 24}{3}$$

$$\frac{3w}{3} = \frac{-2l}{3} + \frac{24}{3}$$

$$w = -\frac{2}{3}l + 8$$

My graphing calculator requires linear relations to be entered in the form $y = mx + b$. I decided to isolate w so that l would be the independent variable.

Tech | **Support**

For help with graphing a linear
equation using a graphing
calculator, see Appendix B-3.

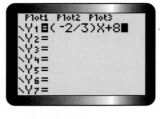

I entered the equation
into the graphing
calculator. I replaced the
independent variable *l*
with *x*, and the dependent
variable *w* with *y*.

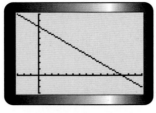

Since I knew that both the
width and the length had
to be positive, I changed
my window settings so that
I could focus on the graph's
values in quadrant 1.

Tech | **Support**

For help determining values of
a relation, see Appendix B-4.

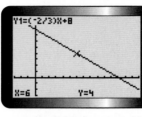

$l = 6$ and $w = 4$

I used the value operation
to get some possible
values for *l* and *w*.

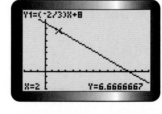

$l = 2$ and $w = 6.\overline{66}$

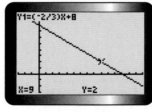

$l = 9$ and $w = 2$

Some possible dimensions are:
$l = 6$ m and $w = 4$ m
$l = 9$ m and $w = 2$ m
$l = 2$ m and $w \doteq 6.7$ m

This used a little more
than 24 m of fencing,
so I knew that the answer
wasn't exact.

Reflecting

A. Why do Pietr's and Hanxiang's forms of the equation give some of the same values for *l* and *w*?

B. How did isolating a variable help each student to solve the problem?

APPLY the Math

EXAMPLE 2 Using an algebraic strategy to determine the slope and the *y*-intercept

Determine the slope and the *y*-intercept of the line $3x + 4y + 8 = 0$.

Sara's Solution

$$3x + 4y + 8 = 0$$
$$3x - 3x + 4y + 8 - 8 = 0 - 3x - 8$$
$$4y = -3x - 8$$
$$\frac{4y}{4} = \frac{-3x - 8}{4}$$
$$y = \frac{-3}{4}x - \frac{8}{4}$$
$$y = \frac{-3}{4}x - 2$$

I wanted the equation in the form $y = mx + b$, to determine the values of m and b.

I used inverse operations to isolate y.

I knew that if the equation was in the form $y = mx + b$, m would give the slope, and b would give the y-intercept.

The slope is $-\frac{3}{4}$ and the *y*-intercept is -2.

EXAMPLE 3 Using an equation to represent and solve a problem

Sam has two part-time jobs. At the grocery store he earns $8/h and at the library he earns $10/h. Before going on vacation, he would like to save $280. Determine the fewest number of hours he needs to work to achieve his goal.

Aaron's Solution

G is the number of hours worked at the grocery store. *L* is the number of hours worked at the library.

I chose variables for the two unknowns.

$$8G + 10L = 280$$

$$8G - 8G + 10L = -8G + 280$$

$$10L = -8G + 280$$

$$\frac{10L}{10} = \frac{-8G + 280}{10}$$

$$\frac{10L}{10} = \frac{-8G}{10} + \frac{280}{10}$$

$$L = \frac{-4}{5}G + 28$$

I had to multiply each hourly rate by the number of hours to get the total earnings.

I used inverse operations to isolate L.

G	L	Total Hours Worked
0	$-\dfrac{4}{5}(0) + 28$ $= 28$	28
5	$-\dfrac{4}{5}(5) + 28$ $= 24$	29
7.5	$-\dfrac{4}{5}(7.5) + 28$ $= 22$	29.5
20	$-\dfrac{4}{5}(20) + 28$ $= 12$	32
45	$-\dfrac{4}{5}(45) + 28$ $= -8$	?

I calculated some possible solutions for the problem by choosing a value for G and substituting it into my equation.

My last choice meant that Sam worked a negative number of hours at the library, which is impossible. On the other hand, if Sam worked 45 hours at the grocery store he would earn $360, which is more than the $280 he wants to save.

If Sam worked 0 h at the grocery store and 28 h at the library, he would earn enough money for his vacation.

I chose the answer that showed the fewest total hours Sam had to work to earn $280.

I knew that this made sense because (28 h)($10/h) = $280.

In Summary

Key Idea

- You can take an equation that is in the form $Ax + By + C = 0$ or $Ax + By = D$ and rewrite it into the form $y = mx + b$ by using inverse operations to solve for y.
- You can locate two points on most lines by plotting the y-intercept and locating a second point using the rise and run of the slope. Joining these points with a straight line gives you a sketch of the relation.

Need to Know

- Equations in the form $Ax + By + C = 0$, $Ax + By = D$, and $y = mx + b$ represent linear relations.
- To enter equations into a graphing calculator, write linear equations in the form $y = mx + b$.

CHECK Your Understanding

1. Express the equation $5x + 6y + 15 = 0$ in the form $y = mx + b$.

2. A room contains three-legged stools and four-legged chairs. There are 48 legs altogether.
   a) Write an equation to represent the relationship between the number of stools, the number of chairs, and the total number of legs.
   b) How many stools could there be?

PRACTISING

3. Express each of the following equations in the form $y = mx + b$.
   K Then, state the slope and y-intercept of each line.
   a) $4x - 3y = 24$
   b) $2x + 5y = 15$
   c) $3x - 6y - 14 = 0$
   d) $8x + 5y = 0$
   e) $4x + 7y - 11 = 0$
   f) $2.4x + 1.5y = -3$

4. Use the slope and y-intercept to sketch the graphs of each of the linear relations in question 3.

5. a) Without graphing, predict whether each of the following lines will rise or fall to the right. How do you know?
   i) $2x + 3y = 5$
   ii) $x - 4y + 10 = 0$
   iii) $3x + 5y - 8 = 0$
   iv) $2x + 5y = 15$
   v) $2.5x - 15y = 20$
   vi) $\dfrac{x}{2} - 3y = 6$
   b) Check your predictions by graphing each line.

6. The dependent variable is d in each of the following equations. Isolate d to determine the d-intercept and the slope of each line.
   a) $4t + 3d = 9$
   b) $8d - 2h + 16 = 0$
   c) $15 + 5k - 6d = 0$

7. A farmer wants to build new enclosures for geese, ducks, and chickens.
   A He has 40 m of fencing to build the three identical, adjacent enclosures.

   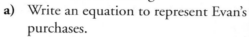

   a) Write an equation to represent the amount of fencing required.
   b) Rearrange your equation to isolate one of the variables.
   c) Graph the relationship.
   d) Suggest three possible sets of dimensions for the farmer's enclosures.

8. Evan spent a total of $18 on gourmet jellybeans and chocolate-covered almonds. The jellybeans cost $12/kg. The almonds cost $21/kg.
   a) Write an equation to represent Evan's purchases.
   b) Isolate the variable for the quantity of jellybeans in your equation.
   c) If Evan bought 250 g of almonds, how many grams of jellybeans did he buy?
   d) If Evan bought 100 g of almonds, how many grams of jellybeans did he buy?

9. Orenda has a total of 41 loonies and toonies in her piggy bank. Their
   T total value is $59.
   a) Write one equation for the total number of coins and a second equation for the total value.
   b) Graph both lines.
   c) Determine the coordinates of the point of intersection of the lines.
   d) How do you know that the coordinates of the point of intersection are the only possible combination of loonies and toonies that meets the conditions of this situation?

10. Amanda plans to make chocolate-chip cookies and oatmeal cookies for a bake sale. The chocolate-chip cookies use three eggs per batch. The oatmeal cookies use two eggs per batch. How many batches of each recipe can she make using two dozen eggs?

11. Textbooks have an average mass of 0.9 kg and notebooks have an average mass of 0.6 kg. To avoid straining his back, Stephen never puts more than 6 kg of books in his backpack.
    a) Write an equation to represent the relationship between the number of each type of book and the total maximum mass.
    b) Isolate one of the variables in your equation from part a).
    c) Determine all possible combinations of textbooks and notebooks that would have a total mass of 6 kg.

12. a) Show that $3x - 8y + 5 = 0$ and $y = \dfrac{3}{8}x + \dfrac{5}{8}$ represent the same line.

    b) Do $y = \dfrac{2}{3}x + \dfrac{1}{3}$ and $2x + 3y + 1 = 0$ represent the same line? How do you know?

13. Punitha really only understands how to graph a line if it is in the form
    C $y = mx + b$.
    a) As her tutor, how would you ensure that Punitha is able to graph lines expressed in any form?
    b) What can you tell Punitha about the similarities between all the linear equation forms?

Extending

14. Show that $y = \dfrac{2}{3}x + \dfrac{7}{3}$ and $x = \dfrac{3}{2}y - \dfrac{7}{2}$ represent the same line.

15. a) Determine the slope and y-intercept for each linear equation.
    i) $3x + 4y - 8 = 0$
    ii) $2x + 5y - 9 = 0$
    iii) $4x - 3y = -12$
    b) An equation is given in the form $Ax + By + C = 0$.
    i) What is the slope of this line?
    ii) What is the y-intercept of this line?

5.3 Slope of a Line

YOU WILL NEED
- grid paper
- ruler

GOAL

Determine the slope of a line.

INVESTIGATE the Math

Julien's parents are hiring a caterer for his brother's graduation party.

They found the advertisement to the right in the newspaper.

They wonder what the cost per person would be if they used Fred's catering service.

Fred's Fine Foods

Number of Guests	Total Cost ($)
10	250
30	650
45	950
80	1650

❓ How can Julien's parents determine the cost per person?

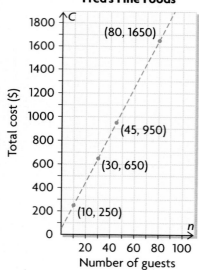

Fred's Fine Foods

(graph points: (10, 250), (30, 650), (45, 950), (80, 1650))

Total cost ($) vs Number of guests

A. Copy the graph into your notebook.

B. Select two of the four points given on the graph.

C. Draw a right triangle to illustrate the rise and run between the points.

D. Calculate the slope and express it in lowest terms.

E. Record your results in the following table.

First Point	Second Point	Rise	Run	Slope

F. Repeat parts B to E with a second and a third pair of points.

G. How could you have calculated the rise and run without drawing the graph?

H. What is the cost per person if Julien's parents hire Fred's Fine Foods?

Reflecting

I.   Why is the slope the same for any pair of points that you choose on the line?

J.   If (x_1, y_1) and (x_2, y_2) are points on a line, what formula could you write to calculate the slope of the line?

K.   Explain why it does not matter which point is (x_1, y_1) and which is (x_2, y_2) when calculating the slope of a line.

APPLY the Math

EXAMPLE 1   **Selecting a strategy to determine slope**

Calculate the slope of the line passing through points A(5, 3) and B(7, −4).

Rory's Solution: Reasoning by using a graph

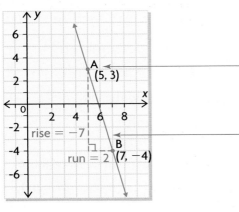

I plotted A and B on a grid and drew a line through them. Then, I drew a right triangle to determine the rise and run.

The line sloped down to the right, so I knew that the slope had to be negative.

The slope of the line is m $= -\dfrac{7}{2}$.

My answer seemed reasonable because the line was decreasing and steep.

Chong Sun's Solution: Calculating using a formula

$$m = \frac{y_2 - y_1}{x_2 - x_1}$$

I decided to use the slope formula.

$$A(\underset{\uparrow}{5}, \underset{\uparrow}{3}) \qquad B(\underset{\uparrow}{7}, \underset{\uparrow}{-4})$$
$$\quad x_1 \quad y_1 \qquad x_2 \quad y_2$$

I chose point A(5, 3) to be (x_1, y_1) and point B(7, −4) to be (x_2, y_2).

$$m_{AB} = \frac{(-4) - (3)}{(7) - (5)}$$

I substituted the values into the slope formula.

$$= \frac{-7}{2}$$

Since the y-value decreased a lot and the x-value increased only a little, I knew that my answer was reasonable.

The slope of the line is $m = -\dfrac{7}{2}$.

EXAMPLE 2 | **Selecting a strategy to determine an unknown coordinate**

Determine the value of k in point E using the graph to the left.

Galen's Solution: Reasoning by using a graph

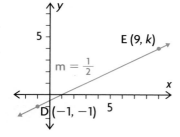

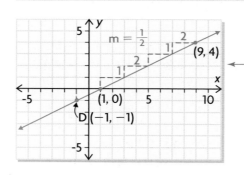

I started at point D. Since the slope was $\dfrac{1}{2}$, the rise was 1 and the run was 2.

I went up 1 unit from D and to the right 2 units and I got to (1, 0). I continued to go up 1 and right 2 until I got to point E where x was 9.

The point $(x, y) = (9, 4)$ was on the line with a slope of $\dfrac{1}{2}$ through points D and E.

The value of k is 4.

Pierce's Solution: Calculating using a formula

The slope of segment DE is

$$m = \frac{y_2 - y_1}{x_2 - x_1}$$

I substituted $\frac{1}{2}$ for m because it was given.

$$\frac{1}{2} = \frac{(k) - (-1)}{(9) - (-1)}$$

I chose point D as (x_1, y_1) and point E as (x_2, y_2).

I substituted the x- and y-values into the formula.

$$\frac{1}{2} = \frac{k + 1}{9 + 1}$$

$$\frac{1}{2} = \frac{k + 1}{10}$$

I simplified the equation.

$$10\left(\frac{1}{2}\right) = 10\left(\frac{k + 1}{10}\right)$$

I multiplied both sides of the equation by 10 so that I could work with integers instead of fractions.

$$5 = k + 1$$
$$5 - 1 = k + 1 - 1$$
$$4 = k$$

I solved the equation using inverse operations.

The value of k is 4.

Point E must have the coordinates (9, 4).

EXAMPLE 3 | **Using the slope formula to calculate a rate of change**

A bathtub is filling with water at a constant rate. After 3 min the water is 7.5 cm deep, and after 8 min the water is 15 cm deep. At what rate is the depth of water increasing?

Quinn's Solution

Time (min)	3	8
Depth (cm)	7.5	15

I organized the given information in table form.

$$m = \frac{15 - 7.5}{8 - 3}$$
$$= \frac{7.5}{5}$$
$$= 1.5$$

I knew that the slope of a line gave the rate of change of the relation, so I calculated the slope using the given values.

The water depth is increasing 1.5 cm/min.

EXAMPLE **4**   Using reasoning involving slope
to determine collinearity

collinear

three or more points are collinear if they lie on the same line

Determine if the points P(-6, 12), Q(3, 6), and R(12, 0) are **collinear**.

Angus's Solution

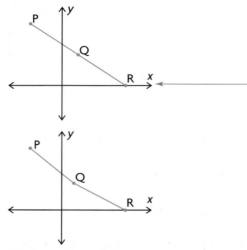

I started with a rough sketch of the three points, but I couldn't tell if they were on a straight line or not.

I knew that if the points were on a straight line then the graph would look like my first sketch. Otherwise, the graph would look like my second sketch.

Need to determine:
slope of $\overline{PQ}$ and slope of $\overline{QR}$

I noticed that in the second sketch, the slopes of $\overline{PQ}$ and $\overline{QR}$ were different. So, I wanted to calculate the slopes of those two line segments.

$$m_{PQ} = \frac{y_2 - y_1}{x_2 - x_1}$$

$$= \frac{12 - 6}{(-6) - 3}$$

$$= \frac{6}{-9}$$

I calculated the slope of line segment $\overline{PQ}$.

Q(3, 6)   P(-6, 12)

x_1 y_1 x_2 y_2

The slope of segment $\overline{PQ}$ is $-\frac{2}{3}$.

$$m_{QR} = \frac{y_2 - y_1}{x_2 - x_1}$$

$$= \frac{0 - 6}{12 - 3}$$

$$= \frac{-6}{9}$$

I calculated the slope of line segment $\overline{QR}$.

Q(3, 6)   R(12, 0)

x_1 y_1 x_2 y_2

The slope of segment $\overline{QR}$ is $-\frac{2}{3}$.

Since $m_{PQ} = m_{QR}$, P, Q, and R are collinear.

Since the slopes were the same for $\overline{PQ}$ and $\overline{QR}$, I knew that an accurate graph would look like my first rough sketch. My points had to be collinear.

In Summary

Key Idea

- You can use the formula $m = \dfrac{\text{rise}}{\text{run}} = \dfrac{y_2 - y_1}{x_2 - x_1}$ to calculate the slope of a line if you know the coordinates of two points on the line.

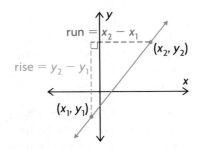

Need to Know

- When you use the coordinates of two points to calculate the slope of a line, either point can be (x_1, y_1).
- Points A, B, and C are collinear if the slopes of any pair of line segments (e.g., $\overline{AB}$, $\overline{BC}$, $\overline{AC}$) are equal.
- If you are given the slope and one point on a line, you can determine an unknown coordinate of another point on the line in two ways:

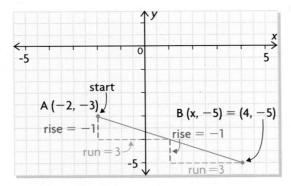

- Draw an accurate sketch by starting at the known point, and then use the rise and run repeatedly until you reach the required point. This method only works easily if the coordinates are all integers. For example: Determine the value of x if the slope of $\overline{AB}$ is $-\dfrac{1}{3}$ with $A(-2, -3)$ and $B(x, -5)$. The value of x is 4.
- Substitute both points and the given slope into the slope formula and use inverse operations to solve for the unknown coordinate.

CHECK Your Understanding

1. Calculate the slope of the line through each pair of points.
   a) A(3, 8) and B(10, 15)   b) C(9, −2) and D(8, 4)

2. The point (−2, −3) lies on a line with slope $\dfrac{2}{3}$. Determine the y-coordinate of the point on the line with x-coordinate 13.

PRACTISING

3. Calculate the slope of the line through each pair of points.
   K a) A(−2, 5) and B(4, −8)   d) G(−7, 8) and H(4, 8)
   b) C(0, 5) and D(−2, 3)   e) I(3.5, 4.8) and J(1.4, 6.2)
   c) E(5, 10) and F(5, −4)   f) K(32, 630) and L(58, 1020)

4. Write the coordinates of one other point that would be on the line passing through the point A(2, 5) with each of the following slopes.
   a) $-\dfrac{1}{4}$ b) $\dfrac{8}{3}$ c) −4   d) 0

5. For the points J, K, and L, the slope of segment $\overline{JK}$ is −4 and the slope of segment $\overline{KL}$ is −2. Explain how you know that J, K, and L are not collinear.

6. Determine whether the given points are collinear.
   a) A(−8, 0), B(−6, 1), and C(4, 6)
   b) D(−5, 17), E(−12, 40), and F(−42, 128)
   c) G(−30, −70), H(−15, −38), and I(17, 26)
   d) J(−9, 1), K(−12, 3), and L(6, −9)

7. a) Plot the points (−3, 8) and (5, 8) and draw the line that passes through them.
   b) Calculate the slope of the line using the slope formula.
   c) What can you conclude about the slope of a horizontal line?

8. a) Plot the points (4, 10) and (4, −1) and draw the line that passes through them.
   b) Calculate the slope of the line using the slope formula.
   c) What can you conclude about the slope of a vertical line?

9. a) Is the rise equal to zero for a vertical line or a horizontal line? Explain.
   b) Is the run equal to zero for a horizontal line or a vertical line? Explain.

10. How can you tell from the coordinates of two points if the line passing through them is horizontal, vertical, or slanted?

11. Estimate the slope of the red line in the "No cell phones" sign.
C (Assume the grid is square.) Explain how you determined your estimate.

12. Nolen was cycling toward his home. After 2 h of cycling he was 55 km
A from home, and after 4.5 h of cycling he was 17.5 km from home. Assuming he was cycling at a constant rate, how fast was he cycling?

13. Manpreet works for Vision Optical where she earns an hourly rate and receives a fixed amount each week to cover her expenses. This table shows her earnings for various hours worked.

Hours Worked	20	25	30	40	50
Weekly Earnings ($)	390	450	510	630	750

  a) Draw a graph of weekly earnings vs. hours worked.
  b) Calculate her rate of pay per hour.
  c) How long would Manpreet have to work in order to earn $900?
  d) Do you think it is likely that Manpreet will earn $900 in a single week? Explain.

14. A house worth $150 000 in 1999 increased by a constant rate to its value of $255 000 in 2007. Calculate the home's annual rate of increase in value.

15. A wheelchair ramp should have a slope of $\dfrac{1}{12}$ or less.
T
  a) Does this wheelchair ramp meet the requirements?
  b) If a second ramp is to be built with a rise of 90 cm, what is the shortest length that will still meet the building code?

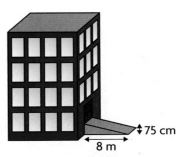

75 cm
8 m

16. Information about the three most popular runs at a ski resort is shown in the following table.

Name of Run	Vertical Drop (feet)	Length of Slope (feet)
Snowbowl	256	890
Bear Claw	480	4824
The Vortex	510	3438

  a) Use the Pythagorean theorem to determine the horizontal "run" for each ski slope. Assume each ski slope is perfectly straight (no dips or moguls).
  b) Use slopes to rank each ski run from easiest to most difficult.

17. If you hire Daminga's Delicious Dinners to cater a party, it will cost $450 for 20 guests and $675 for 35 guests. If the company charged a fixed rate per guest, calculate the cost per person.

18. Determine the value of k if the points X(3, 2), Y(k, 8), and Z($k + 7$, 29) are collinear.

19. Complete the following picture in your notebook to summarize what you know about slopes of lines.

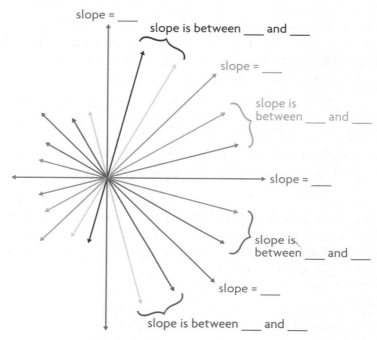

Extending

20. Consider the points A(7, k), B(11, 4), and C(13, 1 − 3k).
  a) If A, B, and C are collinear, determine the value of k.
  b) If A, B, and C are collinear, determine the coordinates of A and C.
  c) Determine a possible value for k for which the points would not be collinear.

21. For each situation, write an equation of the line in the form $y = mx + b$.
  a) The slope is 5 and the y-intercept is 2.
  b) The slope is −4 and the point (4, −3) is on the line.
  c) The slope is $\dfrac{2}{3}$ and the point (6, 4) is on the line.
  d) The line is vertical and passes through the point (2, 5).
  e) The line is horizontal and passes through (−1, −2).

FREQUENTLY ASKED Questions

Q: **In the equation $y = mx + b$, how are the values of m and b related to the graph of the line?**

A: The value of b identifies the y-intercept of the line. Changing the value of b will cause a change in where the line crosses the y-axis.

The value of m identifies the slope of the line, which indicates the steepness and direction of the line. The greater the **magnitude** of the m-value, the steeper the line. If m is negative, the line falls to the right; if m is positive, the line rises to the right.

The slope of a vertical line is undefined and its equation looks like $x = a$.

The slope of a horizontal line is 0 and its equation looks like $y = b$.

Q: **If the equation of a line is in the form $y = mx + b$, how can the values of m and b be used to graph the line?**

A: To graph a line in the form $y = mx + b$, start by plotting the y-intercept. From the y-intercept, follow the rise up if the slope is positive (or down, if the slope is negative), and then the run to the right. Plot this position as a new point. Draw the line through the y-intercept and the new point, and then label the line with its equation.

Study | Aid

• See Lesson 5.1.
• Try Mid-Chapter Review Questions 1 and 5.

Study | Aid

• See Lesson 5.1.
• Try Mid-Chapter Review Questions 1 and 5.

EXAMPLE

Graph the line $y = -\dfrac{1}{4}x + 4$.

Solution

1) Plot the y-intercept, which is 4.

2) Slope $= \dfrac{-1}{4}\left(= \dfrac{\text{rise}}{\text{run}}\right)$.

From the y-intercept, go down 1 unit and to the right 4 units and plot the position.

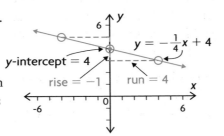

or

From the y-intercept, go up 1 unit and to the left 4 units and plot the position.

Study *Aid*

• See lesson 5.2,
  Example 2.
• Try Mid-Chapter Review
  Question 6.

Q: How can you convert an equation from the form $Ax + By + C = 0$ to the form $y = mx + b$?

A: You use inverse operations to isolate y.

EXAMPLE

Write the equation $4x - 3y + 10 = 0$ in the form $y = mx + b$.

Solution

$$4x - 3y + 10 = 0$$

$$4x - 4x - 3y + 10 - 10 = 0 - 4x - 10$$

$$-3y = -4x - 10$$

$$\frac{-3y}{-3} = \frac{-4x - 10}{-3}$$

$$y = \frac{-4x}{-3} - \frac{10}{-3}$$

$$y = \frac{4}{3}x + \frac{10}{3}$$

Study *Aid*

• See Lesson 5.3,
  Example 1.
• Try Mid-Chapter
  Review Questions
  9 and 10.

Q: How can you use the coordinates of points on a line to determine the slope of the line?

A: You can use the formula $m = \dfrac{y_2 - y_1}{x_2 - x_1}$ where (x_1, y_1) and (x_2, y_2) are any two points on the line.

EXAMPLE

Determine the slope of the line through the points $A(4, -3)$ and $B(-2, 5)$.

Solution

Let $A(4, -3) = (x_1, y_1)$ and $B(-2, 5) = (x_2, y_2)$.

$$m = \frac{y_2 - y_1}{x_2 - x_1}$$

$$= \frac{(5) - (-3)}{(-2) - (4)}$$

$$= \frac{8}{-6}$$

$$= -\frac{4}{3}$$

Let $A(4, -3) = (x_2, y_2)$ and $B(-2, 5) = (x_1, y_1)$.

$$m = \frac{y_2 - y_1}{x_2 - x_1}$$

$$= \frac{(-3) - (5)}{(4) - (-2)}$$

$$= \frac{-8}{6}$$

$$= -\frac{4}{3}$$

PRACTICE Questions

Lesson 5.1

1. Identify the slope and y-intercept of each line.
   a) $y = 4x - 5$
   b) $y = -2x + 3$
   c) $y = \dfrac{3}{7}x - \dfrac{2}{3}$

2. Describe each line using these words: *horizontal, vertical, rising to the right,* or *falling to the right.*
   a) $y = -3x + 5$ d) $x = 4.5$
   b) $y = -2$ e) $y = 4x - 1$
   c) $y = \dfrac{2}{3}$ f) $y = \dfrac{3}{4}x + \dfrac{1}{3}$

3. Order each of the following sets of lines based on slope, from closest to horizontal to closest to vertical.
   a) $y = x$
      $y = 7$
      $x = 2$
   b) $y = \dfrac{2}{3}x - 7$
      $y = 2.5x - 3.7$
      $y = \dfrac{9}{2}x + 4$
   c) $y = -\dfrac{1}{5}x + 8$
      $y = -6x - \dfrac{5}{8}$
      $y = -2x + 4$

4. Suppose each equation in question 3 represents a ski hill.
   a) Which two equations could not possibly represent ski hills? Why?
   b) Organize the rest of the equations in question 3 into three categories: Bunny Hills (most gentle), Intermediate Hills (moderately sloped), and Double Black Diamond Hills (steepest).

5. Sketch a graph of each of the following equations without using the slope and y-intercept.
   a) $y = 2x - 4$
   b) $y = -\dfrac{1}{4}x + 3$
   c) $y = -\dfrac{7}{6}x$

Lesson 5.2

6. Rewrite each of the following equations into the form $y = mx + b$.
   a) $6x - 3y - 15 = 0$
   b) $3x + 6y + 12 = 0$
   c) $2x - 8y = 10$
   d) $y - 10 = 0$
   e) $4x + y - 9 = 0$
   f) $2x - 3y = -1$

7. Movie tickets are $8 each and concert tickets are $12 each. Andrew spent a total of $100 on movie and concert tickets.
   a) Write an equation to represent the total cost for movie and concert tickets.
   b) Rewrite the equation in the form $y = mx + b$.
   c) Graph the relation.
   d) Determine possible combinations of movie and concert tickets that Andrew might have bought.

Analytic Geometry   **283**

8. Determine the slope of each of the following lines.

a)

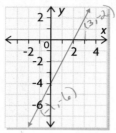

b)

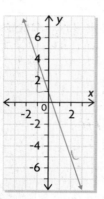

c)

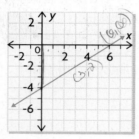

d)

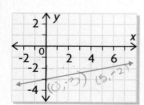

e)

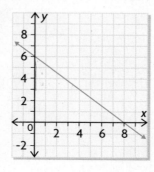

f)

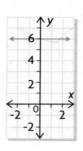

9. Calculate the slope of the line passing through each pair of points.

a) A(3, 8) and B(5, 7)

b) C(8, 9) and D(−2, −2)

c) E(−8, 4) and F(4, −8)

d) I(0, 0) and J(−3, −5)

e) M(0, 4) and N(−3, 4)

f) P(−2, −1) and Q(−2, −9)

10. Determine if the points in each part are collinear.

a) A(−3, −2), B(−2, 1), and C(2, 10)

b) D(7, −1), E(6, 5), and F(2, 1)

c) G(−7, −5), H(−2, 10), and I(−9, −11)

d) J(8, 9), K(−6, 7), and L(24, 11)

11. Point A has coordinates A(3, k), and the slope of $\overline{AB}$ is $\dfrac{2}{5}$. Determine the value of k for each point B.

a) B(7, −2)

b) B(13, 5)

c) B(−2, 2)

d) B(9, 10)

12. A catering company charges $550 for 20 guests and $775 for 35 guests. What is the cost per person?

13. At the end of July, the Robillard family headed home after a vacation. The Robillards were 750 km from home when they started out, but 4 h later they were only 394 km from home. They didn't stop and they maintained a constant speed. How fast were they driving?

Using Points to Determine the Equation of a Line

GOAL

Determine the equation of a line given information about related points.

LEARN ABOUT the Math

Ken's Kanine Kennel provides suites that dogs in the same family can share. Ken's charges a room fee for the family plus an additional amount for each dog. One day's stay costs $71 for 2 dogs and $113 for 5 dogs. Julie wants to know the daily cost to board her 3 dogs.

? How can you determine the equation of this relationship?

EXAMPLE 1 | Using a strategy involving the slope formula and equation solving

Determine the equation that describes the relationship between the number of dogs and the daily boarding cost.

Katerina's Solution

Let x represent the number of dogs and y represent the daily cost.

> I chose x to represent the number of dogs because it was the independent variable, and y to represent the cost because the cost depended on the number of dogs.

Cost per Day vs. Number of Dogs at Ken's Kanine Kennel

(5, 113)

(2, 71)

Cost per day ($)

Number of dogs

> I sketched the given information so that I could get an idea of what was happening.

$y = mx + b$

> I knew that the equation of a line can have the form $y = mx + b$. I needed to determine the slope (m) and the y-intercept (b).

Determine the slope:

$$m = \frac{y_2 - y_1}{x_2 - x_1}$$

$$= \frac{113 - 71}{5 - 2}$$

$$= \frac{42}{3}$$

$$= 14$$

$$y = 14x + b$$

> I used the slope formula and the coordinates of the two points.
>
> (2, 71)   (5, 113)
>

> I substituted the value of the slope into my equation.

Determine the y-intercept:

$$71 = 14(2) + b$$

$$71 = 28 + b$$

$$71 - 28 = 28 - 28 + b$$

$$43 = b$$

> From my sketch, I could tell the y-intercept was between 40 and 50. I also knew that the point (2, 71) was on the line, so if I substituted 2 for x in the equation, then the y-value had to be 71. That gave me enough information to solve for b.

$$y = 14x + 43$$

> Since I knew the values for both m and b, I could write the equation.

Check:

Left Side   Right Side

                  $14x + 43$

113            $= 14(5) + 43$

                  $= 70 + 43$

                  $= 113$

> I checked to see if boarding 5 dogs would cost $113 using my equation. Since both sides were equal, I knew that my equation was correct.

The relationship between the daily boarding cost and the number of dogs is $y = 14x + 43$. This means that Ken's charges a room fee of $43, plus an additional $14 per dog per day.

Reflecting

A. How was Katerina able to determine the slope and the exact value of the y-intercept of the line?

B. Explain why Katerina could have used the point (5, 113) to determine a value for b.

C. Katerina determined the value of m before she determined the value for b. Could she have determined b before m? Explain.

APPLY the Math

EXAMPLE 2 Using the slope and one point to determine the equation of a line

Determine the equation of the line that has a slope of 4 and passes through the point (2, 6).

Sherif's Solution

$$y = mx + b$$
$$y = 4x + b$$

I was given a value for the slope, so I substituted 4 for m.

Determine the *y*-intercept:

$$6 = 4(2) + b$$

(2, 6) was a point on the line, so I substituted its coordinates for *x* and *y*.

$$6 = 8 + b$$
$$6 - 8 = 8 - 8 + b$$
$$-2 = b$$

I solved the equation for b.

The equation of the line is $y = 4x - 2$.

X	Y1
-1	-6
0	-2
1	2
2	6
3	10
4	14
5	18

X=2

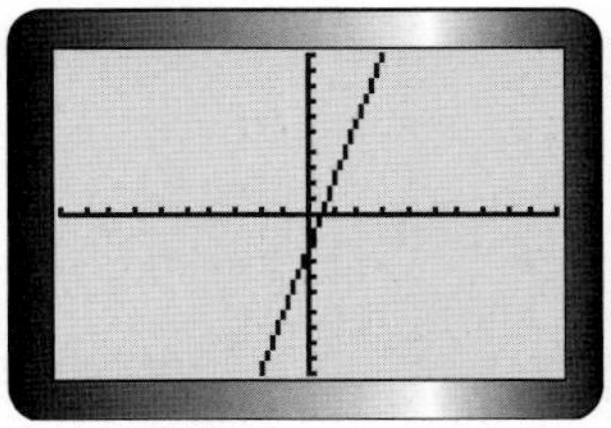

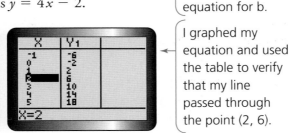

I graphed my equation and used the table to verify that my line passed through the point (2, 6).

EXAMPLE 3 Reasoning from properties of a line to determine its equation

Determine the equation of the line that has a slope of $-\frac{1}{3}$ and the same *y*-intercept as the line $2x - 4y + 7 = 0$.

Anayis's Solution

Determine the slope:

$$y = mx + b$$
$$y = -\frac{1}{3}x + b$$

I substituted the given value of $-\frac{1}{3}$ for the slope, m.

Determine the y-intercept:
$$2x - 4y + 7 = 0$$

> I needed to determine the y-intercept of $2x - 4y + 7 = 0$ because the lines had the same y-intercept.

$$2(0) - 4y + 7 = 0$$

> I knew that the x-coordinate was 0 for the point where the line crossed the y-axis.

$$-4y + 7 = 0$$
$$-4y + 7 - 7 = 0 - 7$$
$$-4y = -7$$
$$\frac{-4y}{-4} = \frac{-7}{-4}$$
$$y = \frac{7}{4}$$

> I used inverse operations to solve the equation for y.

$$b = \frac{7}{4}$$

> I knew that the b in the equation represented the y-intercept.

The equation of the line is
$$y = -\frac{1}{3}x + \frac{7}{4}.$$

EXAMPLE **4**	Using reasoning to determine the equation of a line through two points with the same x-coordinate

Determine the equation of the line that passes through the points $(-3, -3)$ and $(-3, 2)$.

Omar's Solution

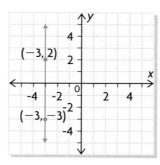

This line is vertical. The equation of the line is $x = -3$.

> From the sketch of the graph, I could see that the line was vertical and that every point on the line had -3 for its x-coordinate.

EXAMPLE 5	Using the equation of a line to solve a problem

The speed of sound in air can be calculated based on temperature using a linear relation. At 10 °C the speed of sound is 337.4 m/s, and at 21.5 °C the speed is 344.3 m/s. What is the speed of sound when the temperature is 32.3 °C?

Suhaila's Solution

Let T represent the temperature and S represent the speed of sound.

> I chose variables to represent each unknown quantity.

$$S = mT + b$$

> I wanted to find an equation for the relationship first. Using $y = mx + b$, I replaced y with S since sound is the dependent variable and x with T since temperature is the independent variable.

Determine the slope:

$$m = \frac{344.3 - 337.4}{21.5 - 10}$$

$$= \frac{6.9}{11.5}$$

$$= 0.6$$

> I substituted the points (10, 337.4) and (21.5, 344.3) into the slope formula.

This means the speed increases 0.6 m/s for each Celsius degree increase in temperature.

Determine the S-intercept:

$$S = 0.6T + b$$

> I substituted the slope value 0.6 into my equation.

$$337.4 = 0.6(10) + b$$
$$337.4 = 6 + b$$
$$337.4 - 6 = 6 - 6 + b$$
$$331.4 = b$$

> I used the point $(T, S) = (10, 337.4)$ in my equation to solve for b.

This means that when the temperature is 0 °C the speed of sound is 331.4 m/s. $S = 0.6T + 331.4$ represents the speed of sound S at temperature T.

$$S = 0.6(32.3) + 331.4$$
$$S \doteq 350.8$$

I substituted the given temperature 32.3 °C into my equation to solve the equation.

At 32.3 °C, the speed of sound is 350.8 m/s.

In Summary

Key Ideas

- You can determine the equation of a line in the form $y = mx + b$ if you know two points on the line or one point and the slope.

Need to Know

- You can determine the equation of a line as follows:
  - If the slope is not given, and you know two points on the line, use the coordinates of the points to calculate the slope.
  - Substitute the value of the slope for m and the coordinates (x, y) of a point on the line into $y = mx + b$ and solve for b.
  - Use the values of m and b to write the equation of the line.

CHECK Your Understanding

1. Complete the table on the right by determining the missing values.

	Slope	y-intercept	Equation
a)	3	5	
b)			$y = 5x + 1$

2. Match each equation to its corresponding graph.

   a) $x = -2$

   b) $x - 2y = 4$

   c) $y = -2$

   d) $y = -\dfrac{4}{3}x + 3$

   i)
   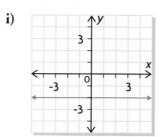

   iii)
   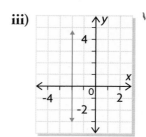

   ii)
   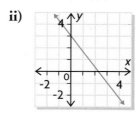

   iv)
   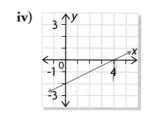

3. Determine the equation of the line with the following characteristics.
   a) has a slope of -2 and passes through the point A(5, 2)
   b) passes through the points B(4, 6) and C(1, −3)

$$x_1 y_1 \qquad x_2 y_2$$

PRACTISING

4. Complete the table shown below by determining the missing values.
   K

	Slope	y-intercept	Equation
a)	−5	3	
b)			$y = \dfrac{4}{3}x - 2$
c)	0	2	
d)			$y = \dfrac{1}{2}x$

5. Determine the equation of each line shown below.

a)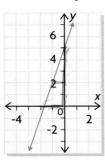

d)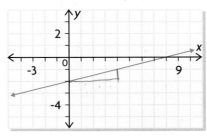

b)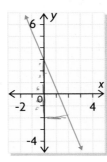

e)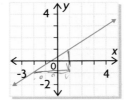

c)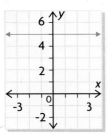

f)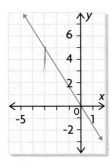

6. If the equation $y = 3x + b$ represents a line that passes through the given point, determine the value of the y-intercept, b.
  a) $(4, 1)$ **b)** $(-3, 2)$ **c)** $(1, -3)$

7. If the equation $y = mx + 3$ represents a line that passes through the given point, determine the slope value, m.
  a) $(2, 4)$ **b)** $(-3, 7)$ **c)** $(8, 2)$

8. Determine the equation of each line described below.
  a) passing through the point A$(0, 4)$, with a slope of $-\dfrac{8}{9}$

  b) passing through the point A$(3, -5)$, with a slope of $\dfrac{1}{5}$

  c) has an x-intercept of 4 and a y-intercept of -3
  d) has an x-intercept of 6 and passes through the point $(6, 4)$

9. Determine the equation of the line passing through each pair of points.
  a) A$(1, 9)$ and B$(1, -7)$ **d)** G$(6, 18)$ and H$(-12, 3)$
  b) C$(-8, -3)$ and D$(8, 27)$ **e)** I$(0, 5)$ and J$(0, 12)$
  c) E$(-12, 7)$ and F$(4, 7)$ **f)** K$(-5, -1)$ and L$(15, 1)$

10. Determine the equation of the line that has the same x-intercept as the line described by $x - 5y + 10 = 0$, and the same y-intercept as the line $3x + 2y - 6 = 0$.

11. The LeBlanc family is driving home. The LeBlancs are using cruise control so their speed is constant. After 3 h, they are 350 km from home. After 5 h, they are 130 km from home.
  a) Write an equation to represent this distance–time relationship.
  b) What do the slope and y-intercept of your equation mean in this situation?

12. A stress test evaluates the health of a patient's heart. While riding on a stationary bike or running on a treadmill, a patient has his or her heart rate measured by a technician and compared with a safe maximum heart rate. This safe heart rate is based on the patient's age as shown in the graph.

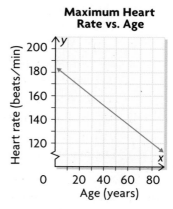

Maximum Heart Rate vs. Age

  a) What does the y-intercept represent in this situation?
  b) What does the slope of the graph represent?
  c) Determine the equation for the line.
  d) Ellen is 14 years old. Using your equation, determine her maximum safe heart rate.

13. The local fall fair charges a flat fee for admission plus an additional cost
T for ride tickets. Last year, Kelsey purchased 15 tickets and spent a total
of $19.50. His brother Quinn purchased 36 tickets and spent a total of
$30.00 at the fair.

a) Determine an equation to represent the relationship between the
total amount of money spent and the number of tickets purchased.

b) A ride pass, which gives a person entrance to the park and
unlimited use of the rides, costs $21. Write the equation for the
relationship between the total amount spent on a ride pass and the
number of rides it can be used for.

c) Last year, Erin used 25 tickets at the fall fair. Should Erin purchase
tickets again this year, or buy a ride pass? Explain.

d) Heather only likes the fun house, which requires one ticket. She
went on this ride 10 times last year. How much money would
Heather save by purchasing tickets instead of a ride pass?

14. Lori downloads music from the Music Genie site, which charges a
A monthly membership fee plus an amount for each song downloaded.
A three-month record of her activity on the site is shown.

Month	Number of Songs Downloaded	Monthly Bill ($)
January	54	26.90
February	38	25.30
March	21	23.60

a) Use two points from the table to determine the equation of the
relationship between numbers of downloads and her monthly bill.

b) Verify that the third point from the table also satisfies your
equation.

c) Lori's brother thinks she should change to Web Waves, which
doesn't have a membership fee and charges $0.95 per song. Based
on your calculations, do you think Lori should change music
companies? Explain.

d) Digital Beats charges $25 for a monthly membership, with
unlimited free downloads. Would you recommend Lori change to
Digital Beats? Explain.

15. Shawn says he can only figure out the equation of a line if he is given
C the y-intercept and the slope of the line. Barb says that she can figure
out the equation using the coordinates of any two points on the line.
With whom do you agree? Why?

Extending

16. Determine the equation of the **median** from Q to the midpoint of PR, in triangle PQR, with P(4, 8), Q(3, 2), and R(6, 4).

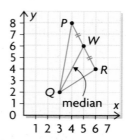

17. Given any two points on a line, the equation of the line can be determined from the point-slope form of the equation of the line: $y = m(x - p) + q$.

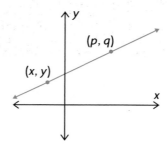

a) Show how the formula can be developed using the slope formula, $m = \dfrac{y_2 - y_1}{x_2 - x_1}$.

b) Use the point-slope form of the equation of a line to determine the equation of a line that has a slope of 3 and passes through the point (1, 2).

c) Determine the equation of the line in part b) using $y = mx + b$ to verify that the new formula works.

d) Use the point-slope form of the equation of a line to determine the equation for each of the following lines.
   i) passing through the points (4, −6) and (5, −1)
   ii) passing through the points (3, −1) and (9, 3)
   iii) passing through the points (4, 5) and (3, 9)

Parallel and Perpendicular Lines

YOU WILL NEED

- grid paper
- graphing calculator
- protractor (optional)

GOAL

Determine and apply properties and equations of parallel and perpendicular lines.

INVESTIGATE the Math

The graph below could represent the rows of vines in a Niagara vineyard.

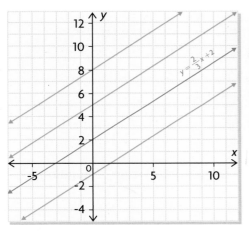 

This graph could represent two jet-plane trails that intersect at right angles.

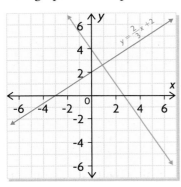 

? How can you tell from the equation of a line whether it is parallel or perpendicular to a given line?

A. Graph and label each of the following lines on separate grids.

$$y = \frac{2}{3}x - 4 \qquad y = -\frac{1}{5}x + 3$$

B. Carefully draw two lines parallel to each of the original lines, and then complete the following table.

	Rise	Run	Slope	y-intercept	Equation
First Original Line					$y = \dfrac{2}{3}x - 4$
Parallel line 1					
Parallel line 2					
Second Original Line					$y = -\dfrac{1}{5}x + 3$
Parallel line 1					
Parallel line 2					

C. For each of the lines in part A, write two linear equations that represent lines parallel to the original line.

D. Draw two lines that are perpendicular to each of the original lines, and then complete the following table.

	Rise	Run	Slope	y-intercept	Equation
First Original Line					$y = \dfrac{2}{3}x - 4$
Perpendicular line 1					
Perpendicular line 2					
Second Original Line					$y = -\dfrac{1}{5}x + 3$
Perpendicular line 1					
Perpendicular line 2					

E. For each of the lines in part A, write two more linear equations that represent lines perpendicular to the original line.

Reflecting

F. How were the equations of lines parallel to $y = \dfrac{2}{3}x - 4$ and $y = -\dfrac{1}{5}x + 3$ like the original equations? How were they different?

G. How were the equations of the lines perpendicular to $y = \dfrac{2}{3}x - 4$ and $y = -\dfrac{1}{5}x + 3$ related to the equations of the original lines?

APPLY *the Math*

| **EXAMPLE 1** | Reasoning about slope to determine whether lines are parallel or perpendicular |

Determine which of the following lines are parallel and which are perpendicular to the line defined by $x - 2y = 4$.

a) $y = -2x + 8$ **b)** $y = \dfrac{2}{4}x + 2$ **c)** $y = \dfrac{4}{5}x + 2$

Kimmy's Solution

Original line:

$x - 2y = 4$

$-2y = -x + 4$

$\dfrac{-2y}{-2} = \dfrac{-x + 4}{-2}$

$y = \dfrac{-x}{-2} + \dfrac{4}{-2}$

$y = \dfrac{1}{2}x - 2$ ◄——

> I rearranged the original line into the form $y = mx + b$ so that I could determine its slope.

So, m $= \dfrac{1}{2}$ ◄——

> I determined the slope of the line in part a).

a) $y = -2x + 8$ ◄——

$m = -2$

$y = -2x + 8$ is perpendicular to

$y = \dfrac{1}{2}x + 4$

> I knew that this line was perpendicular to the original line because their slopes were **negative reciprocals** of each other.

negative reciprocals

numbers that multiply to produce -1 are negative reciprocals of each other

(e.g., $\dfrac{3}{4}$ and $-\dfrac{4}{3}$; $-\dfrac{1}{2}$ and 2)

b) $y = \dfrac{2}{4}x + 2$ ◄——

> I determined the slope of the line in part b).

$m = \dfrac{2}{4}$

$= \dfrac{1}{2}$

$y = \dfrac{2}{4}x + 2$ is parallel to ◄——

$y = \dfrac{1}{2}x - 2$

> I knew that the two lines were parallel because their slopes were equal.

Analytic Geometry **297**

c) $y = \dfrac{4}{5}x + 2$

$m = \dfrac{4}{5}$

This line is neither parallel nor perpendicular to $y = \dfrac{1}{2}x - 2$.

> I determined the slope of the line in part c).
>
> Since the slope of this line was neither equal to nor the negative reciprocal of the slope of the original line, I knew that the lines could not be described as parallel or perpendicular.

EXAMPLE 2   Identifying perpendicularity by reasoning

Which line segments in the following diagram are perpendicular?

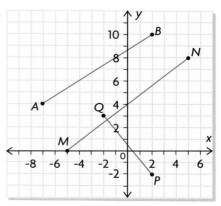

Liz's Solution

$A(-7, 4)$ $B(2, 10)$

   x_1 y_1 x_2 y_2

$m_{AB} = \dfrac{10 - 4}{2 - (-7)}$

$= \dfrac{6}{9}$

$= \dfrac{2}{3}$

> I calculated the slope of each line segment using the slope formula,
>
> $m = \dfrac{y_2 - y_1}{x_2 - x_1}.$

$M(-5, 0)$ $N(5, 8)$

   x_1 y_1 x_2 y_2

$m_{MN} = \dfrac{8 - 0}{5 - (-5)}$

$= \dfrac{8}{10}$

$= \dfrac{4}{5}$

$$P(2, -2) \qquad Q(-2, 3)$$

$\uparrow \quad \uparrow \qquad\qquad \uparrow \quad \uparrow$

$x_1 \quad y_1 \qquad\qquad x_2 \quad y_2$

$$m_{PQ} = \frac{3 - (-2)}{-2 - 2}$$

$$= \frac{5}{-4}$$

$$= -\frac{5}{4}$$

$$m_{AB} \times m_{MN} = \frac{2}{3} \times \frac{4}{5}$$

$$= \frac{8}{15}$$

$$m_{AB} \times m_{PQ} = \frac{2}{3} \times \left(-\frac{5}{4}\right)$$

$$= -\frac{10}{12}$$

$$= -\frac{5}{6}$$

$$m_{MN} \times m_{PQ} = \frac{4}{5} \times \left(-\frac{5}{4}\right)$$

$$= -\frac{20}{20}$$

$$= -1$$

> I multiplied the slopes to see if any were negative reciprocals.
>
> I knew that the line segments $\overline{MN}$ and $\overline{PQ}$ were perpendicular because the product of their slopes was -1.

The line segments $\overline{MN}$ and $\overline{PQ}$ are perpendicular.

EXAMPLE 3 **Reasoning about slope to determine the equation of a line that is parallel to another line**

Determine the equation of the line that is parallel to $y = -\frac{2}{7}x + 3$ and passes through the point $(14, 9)$.

Rahim's Solution

$$y = mx + b$$

> I started with the general equation of a line.

Determine the slope:

$$m = -\frac{2}{7}$$

> Since the new line is parallel to $y = -\frac{2}{7}x + 3$, I knew that it had the same slope.

Analytic Geometry **299**

$$y = -\frac{2}{7}x + b$$

Determine the y-intercept:

$$9 = -\frac{2}{7}(14) + b$$

$$9 = -4 + b$$

$$9 + 4 = -4 + 4 + b$$

$$13 = b$$

Therefore, $y = -\frac{2}{7}x + 13$.

I substituted the slope into my equation.

Since the line passed through the point (14, 9), I used $x = 14$ and $y = 9$ in the equation of the line to determine b.

I simplified, and then used inverse operations to solve for b.

I substituted my value for b to complete the equation.

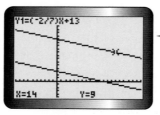

I used a graphing calculator to check that the equation I found was parallel to the original equation and passed through (14, 9).

EXAMPLE 4   **Selecting a strategy to determine the equation of a line that is perpendicular to another line**

Determine the equation of the line that is perpendicular to $y = 3x + 1$ and has the same y-intercept.

Priya's Solution: Using a strategy based on slope and y-intercept

$$y = mx + b$$

I knew that if I could determine the line's slope and y-intercept, I could write its equation in the form $y = mx + b$.

Determine the slope:

For $y = 3x + 1$:

$$m = 3$$

The slope of the given line was 3 because the line was in the form $y = mx + b$.

For the new perpendicular line:

$$m = \frac{-1}{3}$$

$$= -\frac{1}{3} \longleftarrow$$

The given line had a slope of 3, but I needed to find its negative reciprocal. I rewrote 3 as $\frac{3}{1}$. This made it easier for me to get the negative reciprocal.

Determine the *y*-intercept:

$$b = 1 \longleftarrow$$

I knew that the *y*-intercept of the new line had to be the same as the *y*-intercept of the line $y = 3x + 1$.

The equation is $y = -\dfrac{1}{3}x + 1$.

Jacob's Solution: Reasoning from a graph

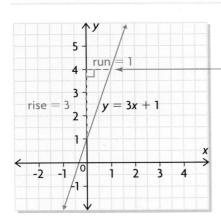

The slope was $\frac{3}{1}$ and the *y*-intercept was 1, so I used this to draw a graph of the original line.

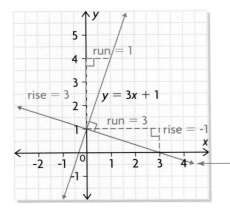

I rotated the original line 90° to get my new line.

Analytic Geometry **301**

$$\text{new slope} = \frac{1}{-3} = -\frac{1}{3}$$

$y\text{-intercept} = 1$

The equation of the new line is

$$y = -\frac{1}{3}x + 1.$$

I noticed that my rise and run also rotated, so the new rise was 1 and the new run was -3. I used those values to calculate the slope. The y-intercept was the same.

In Summary

Key Ideas

- The slopes of parallel lines are equal.
- The slopes of perpendicular lines are negative reciprocals.

Need to Know

- Two numbers are negative reciprocals if they have opposite signs and their denominators and numerators are exchanged.

  For example, $\frac{-2}{3}$ and $\frac{3}{2}$ are negative reciprocals.

  So are 3 and $\frac{-1}{3}$.

- The product of two negative reciprocals is always -1.

CHECK Your Understanding

1. a) State an equation of a line parallel to $y = -\frac{3}{2}x + 9$.

b) State an equation of a line perpendicular to $y = -\frac{3}{2}x + 9$.

2. Determine which of the following lines are parallel and which are perpendicular to each other.

a) $y = -\frac{1}{3}x + 2$ **e)** $y = \frac{1}{3}x + 1$

b) $y = -3x + 2$ **f)** $y = \frac{1}{-3}x - 8$

c) $y = \frac{7}{2}x - 4$ **g)** $y = \frac{-3}{9}x$

d) $y = \frac{2}{7}x - 3$ **h)** $y = \frac{-2}{7}x - 9$

PRACTISING

3. For each pair of equations, state whether the lines are parallel,
K perpendicular, or neither.

a) $y = 2x + 5$

$y = -\dfrac{1}{2}x - 4$

b) $y = \dfrac{2}{3}x - 2$

$y = -1.5x - 6$

c) $y = \dfrac{3}{7}x - 4$

$y = -\dfrac{3}{7}x - 4$

d) $x - 4y = 2$

$2x - 8y = 3$

e) $y = -0.2x - 1$

$y = -\dfrac{1}{5}x + 3$

f) $x - 5y + 8 = 0$

$5x - y = 0$

4. The following sets of points define the endpoints of line segments.
Determine which line segments are parallel and which line segments
are perpendicular.
A(6, 5) and B(12, 3)
P(−3, −4) and Q(5, 20)
G(0, −4) and H(6, −2)
U(−5, 9) and V(−6, 12)
K(2, 4) and L(6, 16)

5. Are the lines defined by the equations $y = 4$ and $x = 3$ parallel,
perpendicular, or neither? Explain.

6. a) Write the equation of a line parallel to the x-axis that passes
through the point (1, 4).

b) Write the equation of a line parallel to the x-axis that passes
through the point (3, −8).

c) In general, what is true about the equation of any line parallel to
the x-axis?

7. a) Write the equation of a line parallel to the y-axis that passes
through the point (−9, 3).

b) Write the equation of a line parallel to the y-axis that passes
through the point (6, 2).

c) In general, what is true about the equation of any line parallel to
the y-axis?

8. Use the given information to write the equation of each line.

   A **a)** a line parallel to the line defined by $y = 3x + 5$ and passing through the point $(3, -5)$

   b) a line perpendicular to the line defined by $y = 3x + 5$ and passing through the point $(3, -5)$

   c) a line parallel to the line defined by $3x + 2y = 7$ with y-intercept $= 3$

   d) a line perpendicular to the line defined by $2x - 3y + 18 = 0$ with the same y-intercept

9. Determine the equation of a line perpendicular to $4x - 3y - 2 = 0$ with the same y-intercept as the line defined by $3x + 4y = -12$.

10. Determine the equation of a line perpendicular to $2x - 5y = 6$ with the same x-intercept as the line defined by $3x + 8y - 15 = 0$.

11. For the given vertices, determine whether or not $\triangle ABC$ is a right triangle.

    a) $A(13, 3)$, $B(3, 5)$, and $C(-2, -20)$

    b) $A(5, 4)$, $B(-1, 2)$, and $C(2, -1)$

12. Show algebraically that the points $A(-4, 7)$, $B(6.5, 1)$, $C(-8, 0)$, and

    T $D(2.5, -6)$ form a rectangle.

13. Show algebraically that the points $E(-9, 4)$, $F(-5, -3)$, $G(1, -4)$, and $H(-3, 3)$ form a parallelogram, but not a rectangle.

14. Mr. Rite wants his roof to be $90°$ at its peak and have a slope of $-\dfrac{7}{2}$ on the sunny side of the house. If the height of his roof must be 210 cm, how wide is his house?

15. Determine the value of k in each graph.

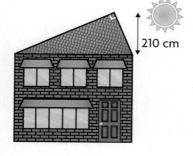

210 cm

a)

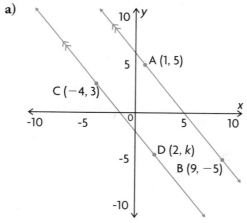

b)

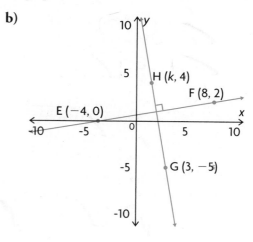

16. Explain why a line cannot be perpendicular to $y = \dfrac{3}{4}x + 2$ and also

C

be parallel to $y = \dfrac{4}{5}x - 8$.

Extending

17. A line segment has endpoints A(1, −5) and B(4, 1).
  a) Determine the coordinates of two points, C and D, that would make ABCD a parallelogram.
  b) Determine the coordinates of two points, C and D, that would make ABCD a rectangle.
  c) Determine the coordinates of two points, C and D, that would make ABCD a square.

18. $\overline{AM}$ is a median. Show that $\overline{AM}$ is perpendicular to $\overline{BC}$.

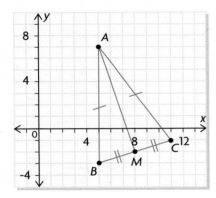

19. ABCD is a rhombus. Show that the diagonals of the rhombus are perpendicular to each other.

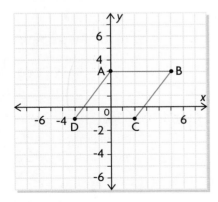

Curious | Math

Distance from a Point to a Line

Calculating the shortest distance from a point to a line can be quite complicated. However, if the equation of the line is written in the form $Ax + By + C = 0$, then finding the distance is as easy as substituting into a formula.

The shortest distance d from a point $P(x_0, y_0)$ to a line $Ax + By + C = 0$
is $d = \dfrac{|Ax_0 + By_0 + C|}{\sqrt{A^2 + B^2}}$

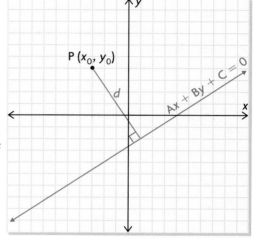

Note: The two lines surrounding the numerator are called absolute value bars. The **absolute value** of a number is its distance from zero, and distance is always positive. For example: $|-3| = 3$ and $|3| = 3$.

1. On grid paper, plot the point $A(-5, 4)$ and the line with equation $2x - 3y - 4 = 0$.

2. Determine the shortest distance from point $A(-5, 4)$ to the line in step 1, using the Pythagorean theorem.

3. Determine the shortest distance from point $A(-5, 4)$ to the line $2x - 3y - 4 = 0$ using the distance formula $d = \dfrac{|Ax_0 + By_0 + C|}{\sqrt{A^2 + B^2}}$.

4. Determine the distance from the given point to the given line for each of the following. Round to one decimal place as necessary.
   a) $A(5, -5)$ and $2x - 3y - 4 = 0$
   b) $A(1, 4)$ and $5x + 2y - 1 = 0$

5. Identify the coordinates of any point you wish. Create the equation of a line in the form $Ax + By + C = 0$. Use the distance formula above to determine the distance from your point to your line.

6. Determine the distance from the point $A(2, 1)$ to the line $4x - 9y + 1 = 0$. What does your answer tell you about the point and the line?

FREQUENTLY ASKED Questions

Q: **How can you determine the equation of a line?**

A1: If you know the slope and y-intercept of the line, you can write the equation in the form $y = mx + b$, where m is the slope and b is the y-intercept.

Study | **Aid**

• See Lesson 5.4, Example 1.
• Try Chapter Review Questions 10 and 11.

EXAMPLE

To determine the equation of the line that has a slope of $\dfrac{4}{3}$ and a y-intercept of -3, substitute the values directly into the formula.

Solution

$y = mx + b$

$m = \dfrac{4}{3}$

$b = -3$

The equation is $y = \dfrac{4}{3}x - 3$.

A2: If you know two points on the line, determine the slope and then use either point to calculate the y-intercept.

EXAMPLE

To determine the equation of the line that passes through points $A(-3, 17)$ and $B(4, -11)$, first determine the slope.

$$m = \frac{(-11) - 17}{4 - (-3)}$$

$$= \frac{-28}{7}$$

$$= -4$$

Next, substitute the slope into the equation.

$$y = -4x + b$$

Then, use this equation and substitute the coordinates of the point $(-3, 17)$ for x and y.

$$17 = -4(-3) + b$$

Then, solve for b.

$$17 = 12 + b$$

$$b = 5$$

Substitute the values for m and b to create the equation.

The equation is $y = -4x + 5$.

To verify your work, use a graphing calculator.

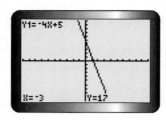 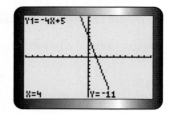

Study | **Aid**

- See Lesson 5.5,
  Example 1.
- Try Chapter Review
  Question 13.

Q: **How can you tell if two linear equations represent lines that are parallel or perpendicular without graphing them?**

A1: Two lines are parallel if they have the same slope.

EXAMPLE

Determine the slope of $3x + 2y + 24 = 0$.

Solution

$$3x + 2y + 24 = 0$$
$$3x - 3x + 2y + 24 - 24 = -3x - 24$$
$$2y = -3x - 24$$
$$\frac{2y}{2} = \frac{-3x - 24}{2}$$
$$y = \frac{-3x}{2} - \frac{24}{2}$$
$$y = -\frac{3}{2}x - 12$$

Slope $= -\dfrac{3}{2}$

Determine the slope of $y = -\dfrac{3}{2}x + 2$.

Slope $= -\dfrac{3}{2}$

The lines $3x + 2y + 24 = 0$ and $y = -\dfrac{3}{2}x + 2$ are parallel because their slopes are equal.

Study | **Aid**

- See Lesson 5.5,
  Example 2.
- Try Chapter Review
  Question 13.

A2: Two lines are perpendicular if the product of their slopes equals -1.

EXAMPLE

Given the lines $y = 2.5x - 3.2$ and $y = -0.4x + 8.1$.

$m_{line\ 1} = 2.5$ $m_{line\ 2} = -0.4$

These lines are perpendicular because $m_{line\ 1} \times m_{line\ 2} = 2.5 \times -0.4$
$$= -1$$

PRACTICE Questions

Lesson 5.1

1. Identify the slope and *y*-intercept for each line.
   a) $y = 3x + 4$
   c) $y = -1.11 + 9.7x$
   b) $y = -\dfrac{2}{5}x - 6.8$
   d) $y = 3$

2. Order each set of lines from closest to horizontal to closest to vertical.
   a) $y = 2x - 4$
      $y = x + 8$
      $y = \dfrac{1}{3}x - 2$
   b) $y = -\dfrac{1}{3}x + 5$
      $y = -8x - 2$
      $y = -\dfrac{5}{2}x + 3$

3. Copy and complete the table to identify whether the lines will rise or fall to the right.

	Equation	Rises to the Right	Falls to the Right
a)	$y = 4x + 5$		
b)	$y = -\dfrac{2}{3}x - 8$		
c)	$y = -2.8x + 4$		
d)	$y = \dfrac{21}{8}x$		
e)	$y = 1.5x + 4.5$		

Lesson 5.2

4. Determine the slope and *y*-intercept for each of these lines.
   a) $3x - 4y + 9 = 0$
   c) $2x + 6y = 32$
   b) $5x - y = 12$
   d) $8x + 2y - 4 = 0$

5. Evan and his sister Sarah shovel driveways during the winter. They charge $10 for a double driveway and $5 for a single driveway. This past winter, Evan earned $255 and Sarah earned $230.
   a) Write equations for both Evan and Sarah to represent the relationship between the amounts earned shovelling single and double driveways.

b) Isolate the variable used for single driveways in both equations.

c) If they both shovelled 10 double driveways, how many single driveways did each shovel?

Lesson 5.3

6. Calculate the slopes of the line segments shown below.

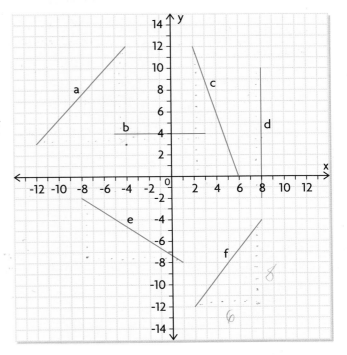

7. Calculate the slopes of the lines that pass through each of the following pairs of points.
   a) $A(8, 2)$ and $B(1, 9)$
   b) $E(-1, 5)$ and $F(3, 2)$
   c) $C(-1, 2)$ and $D(3, -8)$
   d) $G(-3, 2)$ and $H(-9, -11)$

8. The points $(-6, -3)$, $(k, 1)$, and $(8, 4)$ are collinear. Determine the value of *k*.

9. Three hours after beginning her long-distance bicycle trip, Cathy was 98 km from home. After seven hours, she was 182 km from home. Assuming she maintained the same speed throughout the trip, how fast was she cycling?

10. Determine the equation of each line.

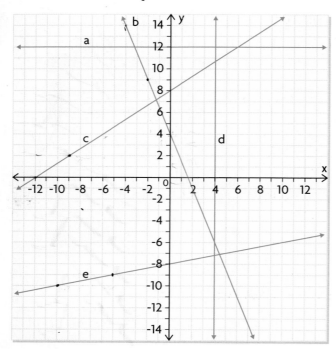

11. Determine the equations of the lines described below.

a) passing through the point M(6, 9) with slope $= -\dfrac{3}{4}$

b) passing through the points P(3, −11) and Q(0, 5)

c) passing through the points D(2, 9) and E(1, 13)

d) passing through the points A(5, 2) and B(5,−3)

e) passing through the points X(8, 5) and Y(2, 3)

12. Determine whether the points A(2, −6) and B(−3, 10) lie on the line $y = -4x + 2$.

13. For each pair of linear equations, determine if the lines are parallel, perpendicular, or neither. Justify your answers.

a) $y = 3x - 5$
$y = -3x - 5$

b) $y = 0.25x - 2$
$y = \dfrac{1}{4}x - 9$

c) $y = \dfrac{1}{2}x + 4$
$y = -2x - 8$

d) $2x - 4y = 9$
$x + 2y + 7 = 0$

e) $y = 0.625x - 2$
$y = -1.6x - 9$

f) $3x - 5y - 10 = 0$
$5x + 3y + 2 = 0$

14. Determine the equation for each line.

a) passing through the point W(2, 9) and parallel to $y = \dfrac{7}{2}x + 3$

b) passing through the point V(1, 6) and perpendicular to $y = -\dfrac{1}{4}x + 11$

c) passing through the y-intercept of the line defined by $2x + 3y - 18 = 0$ and perpendicular to $4x - 9y = 27$

15. a) Do you think that the diagonals of a square are perpendicular to each other?

b) Test your conjecture by plotting 4 points on grid paper that form a square. Draw the sides and diagonals of the square.

c) Calculate the slopes of the diagonals. Does this support your conjecture? Explain.

d) Repeat parts b) and c) using 4 different points. Is your result the same?

1. Which choice best describes the line defined by the equation $y = -4x + 27$?
   - **A.** rising to the right
   - **B.** falling to the right
   - **C.** horizontal
   - **D.** vertical

2. Which of the following statements is true about the line defined by the equation $y = \frac{1}{3}x + 2$?

   - **A.** It is steeper than the line defined by $y = \frac{1}{6}x - 4$.
   - **B.** It has the same y-intercept as the line defined by the equation $y = \frac{1}{5}x + 2$.
   - **C.** It is less steep than the line defined by $y = 5x - 6$.
   - **D.** all of the above

3. Which of the following equations represents the same line as described by $12x - 3y + 21 = 0$?
   - **A.** $y = \frac{1}{4}x - 7$
   - **B.** $y = -4x + 21$
   - **C.** $y = 4x + 7$
   - **D.** $y = \frac{1}{4}x + 63$

4. What can be said about the lines given by the equations $3x + 7y = 28$ and $y = \frac{7}{3}x - 2$?
   - **A.** they are perpendicular
   - **B.** they are parallel
   - **C.** they are the same
   - **D.** none of the above

5. A line passes through the point $(1, -4)$ and has a slope of $\frac{5}{2}$. Which of the following points would also be on this line?
   - **A.** $(6, -2)$
   - **B.** $(3, 1)$
   - **C.** $(-1, 1)$
   - **D.** $(3, -9)$

6. Sketch the graph of $y = \frac{-4}{5}x + 3$ using the slope and y-intercept.

7. Are the points $A(-10, -4)$, $B(-3, 7)$, and $C(2, 14)$ collinear? Explain how you know.

8. Points $M(14, 6)$ and $N(-7, k)$ lie on a line that has a slope of $\frac{3}{7}$. Determine the value of k.

9. Tickets for this year's major drama production cost $8 for adults and $6 for students. Last night's show earned $2200.

   a) Write an equation to represent the relationship between the number of adult tickets sold and the number of student tickets sold.

   b) Rearrange your relationship to isolate the variable representing the number of adult tickets.

   c) If no students purchased tickets, how many adult tickets were sold?

   d) If 148 students purchased tickets, how many adult tickets were sold?

10. Determine the equation of the line that passes through the points $(-5, 7)$ and $(5, 15)$.

11. Carrie-Lynn has just recorded her first CD and would like to create 400 CDs for her upcoming CD release party. The company CD-Clone charges $159 for 100 CDs and $297 for 250 CDs.

   a) Write the equation for the relationship between the numbers of CDs created and the total cost.

   b) Use your equation to calculate the cost for 400 CDs.

12. Determine the equation of the line that is perpendicular to the line $6x + 10y - 1 = 0$ and has the same y-intercept as $3x + y = 1$.

13. Create a mind map to organize what you know about determining the equation of a line. Include the following words in your mind map: *horizontal, vertical, slope, y-intercept, point(s), parallel,* and *perpendicular.* Start your mind map like this:

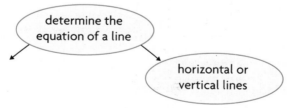

Urban Planning

YOU WILL NEED
• grid paper

Many downtown centres—such as Montreal and Ottawa—were laid out in a grid pattern by early urban planners. This image of Toronto illustrates the grid pattern. The coordinate axes have the origin at the CN Tower.

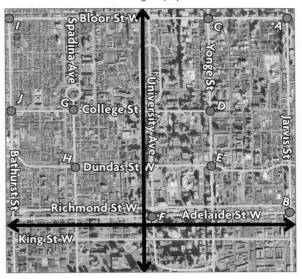

❓ Are the streets of downtown Toronto parallel and/or perpendicular to each other?

Using a scale of 1 unit = 100 m and dynamic graphing software, Macy determined the approximate coordinates of several major intersections and recorded them in a table.

Intersection	Label	Coordinates
Jarvis and Bloor	A	(13.9, 20.5)
Jarvis and Adelaide	B	(14.0, 1.1)
Yonge and Bloor	C	(6.3, 20.5)
Yonge and College	D	(6.4, 11.2)
Yonge and Dundas	E	(6.5, 5.7)
University and Adelaide	F	(0.6, 0.6)
Spadina and College	G	(−6.9, 11.4)
Spadina and Dundas	H	(−6.8, 5.7)
Bathurst and Bloor	I	(−13.1, 20.5)
Bathurst and College	J	(−12.9, 11.2)

A. Plot and label the given coordinates on a graph.

B. Assuming the streets are straight, determine equations to represent the following streets: Jarvis, Yonge, Spadina, Bathurst, Bloor, Adelaide, College, and Dundas. Express the slopes and y-intercepts to two decimal places.

C. Are any of the streets in part B parallel? Justify your answer.

D. Are any of the streets in part B perpendicular? Justify your answer.

E. Use the information you have to discuss whether the streets of downtown Toronto really do form a grid.

Task | *Checklist*

✔ Did you check to make sure that your equations match your graph?

✔ Did you remember to label your graph?

✔ Did you show all your work for your calculations?

✔ Did you check your calculations?

✔ Did you explain your thinking clearly?

✔ Did you justify your answers mathematically?

Population of African Elephants

Investigating Relationships

▸ **GOALS**

You will be able to

- Use a graph to describe and interpret experimental data

- Draw an appropriate line or curve of best fit

- Determine the equation of a line of best fit

- Identify a trend in a data set and formulate a conjecture

- Describe a situation that is explained by the events shown in a given graph

? The graph shows the population of African elephants for a few years. **If the pattern continues, approximately when might African elephants become extinct?**

WORDS YOU NEED to Know

1. The graph shows the amount of water that remains in a pool that is being drained at a constant rate.

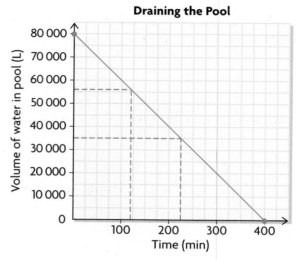

Draining the Pool

Match each phrase to the mathematical term that best represents it.

a) *x*-intercept

b) *y*-intercept

c) slope

d) partial variation

e) independent variable

f) dependent variable

i) The amount of water in the pool to start.

ii) The rate at which the volume of the water in the pool is changing.

iii) The time at which the water volume in the pool is recorded.

iv) The amount of water in the pool at a particular time.

v) The time at which the pool is empty.

vi) The kind of algebraic relation that describes how the amount of water in the pool changes with time.

SKILLS AND CONCEPTS *You Need*

Determine the equation of a line given the slope and *y*-intercept

The equation of a line can be determined by $y = mx + b$, where m represents the value of the slope and b represents the value of the *y*-intercept.

EXAMPLE

Determine the equation of the line with slope 5 and *y*-intercept 3.

Solution

$m = 5$ and $b = 3$, so the equation is $y = 5x + 3$.

Study | *Aid*

• For help, see Lesson 5.4, Examples 1 and 2.

2. Determine the equation of the line with the following slopes and *y*-intercepts.

 a) slope $= \dfrac{2}{3}$; *y*-intercept $= 4$

 b) slope $= -2$; *y*-intercept $= -2.5$

Determine the equation of a line given the slope and a point on the line

Substitute the value for the slope into m and the coordinates of the given point for x and y in the equation $y = mx + b$. Then, solve the equation for b.

EXAMPLE

Determine the equation of the line with slope 2 that passes through the point (3, 5).

Solution

Substitute $m = 2$, $x = 3$ and $y = 5$ into $y = mx + b$.

$5 = 2(3) + b$

$5 = 6 + b$

$-1 = b$

The equation of the line is $y = 2x - 1$.

3. Determine the equation of each line.

 a) slope $= -\dfrac{3}{5}$; passes through (5, 2)

 b) slope $= 1.8$; passes through (10, −1)

Determine the equation of a line through two given points

Use the coordinates of the points to determine the slope of the line. Then, use the slope and one of the points to determine the *y*-intercept (as shown in the previous example).

EXAMPLE

Determine the equation of the line that passes through the points $(-5, 5)$ and $(5, 7)$.

Solution

Calculate the slope.

$$m = \frac{7 - 5}{5 - (-5)}$$

$$= \frac{2}{10}$$

$$= \frac{1}{5}$$

Substitute $m = \frac{1}{5}$ and the coordinates of $(-5, 5)$ into $y = mx + b$.

$$5 = \left(\frac{1}{5}\right)(-5) + b$$

$$5 = -1 + b$$

$$6 = b$$

The equation of the line is $y = \frac{1}{5}x + 6$.

4. Determine the equation of each line.
   a) passes through $(1, 1)$ and $(-3, 4)$
   b) passes through $(5, 8)$ and $(6, 6)$

5. Determine the equation of each line.

a)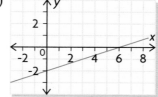

b)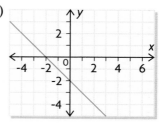

PRACTICE

6. Draw a graph of each equation.
    a) $y = 2x + 3$
    b) $y = -3x + 4$

7. A seed is placed 1 cm below the surface of the soil. The graph shows the height of the sprout as it grows.

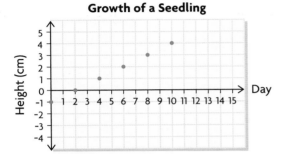

Growth of a Seedling

    a) Determine an equation for the graph.
    b) What does the y-intercept represent?
    c) Determine the rate at which the seedling is growing.
    d) What does the x-intercept represent?
    e) What do negative values of y represent? What do positive values of y represent?

8. The graphs below show how the values of certain cars change with time.
    a) For each graph, describe the changes in words.
    b) Use the graph to estimate the value of the newer car in 2008.
    c) Use the graph to estimate when the value of the vintage car was $9000.

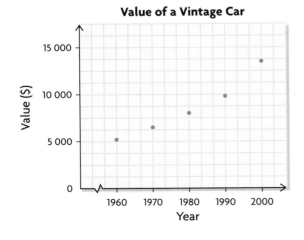

Value of a Vintage Car

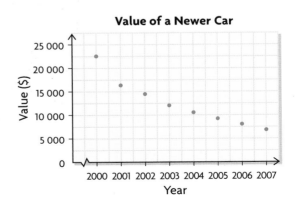

Value of a Newer Car

Question	Lesson
6	3.4 Examples 2 and 3
7	3.3 Examples 1 and 2
8	3.4 Example 2
9	3.5 Example 1

Study | Aid
• For help, see the following examples.

9. Consider the sequence of figures.

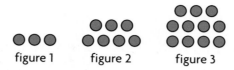

figure 1   figure 2   figure 3

a) State the pattern rule in words.

b) Construct a table of values for the number of circles in each figure. The first two rows are completed for you.

Figure Number	Number of Circles
1	3
2	7
3	
4	

c) Write a formula that you can use to predict the number of circles if you know the figure number.

d) Calculate the first differences and include them in another column of your table of values.

e) If you plotted a graph, would it be linear? How can you tell?

f) Plot the data on a scatter plot.

10. Several students collected this data for 12 triangles. Use it to determine what type of relationship exists between the hypotenuse of a right triangle and the size of one of the acute angles, when the base is fixed at 10 cm.

Angle (°)	5	10	15	20	25	30	35	40	45	50	55	60
Height (cm)	0.9	1.8	2.7	3.6	4.8	5.8	7.0	8.4	10	11.9	14.3	17.3

11. You are given the coordinates of two points on a line. Create a flowchart that summarizes the sequence of steps you would follow to determine the equation of this line.

APPLYING *What You Know*

Comparing Costs

The table shows how much a traveller paid for a hotel room and dinner in nine different cities.

City	Cost of Hotel Room ($)	Cost of Dinner ($)
1	48	20
2	50	21
3	69	19
4	67	11
5	91	39
6	72	45
7	57	30
8	125	19
9	63	33

? Is there a relationship between the cost of a hotel room and the cost of a dinner?

A. Draw a scatter plot of the data. Use "cost of hotel room" as the independent variable and "cost of dinner" as the dependent variable.

B. Look at the point for City 3. What do the coordinates of the point represent?

C. Describe any pattern that you observe in the data.

D. Identify any points that do not fit the pattern.

E. Suppose you use the graph to predict the cost of a dinner in a city where the hotel room cost is $80. How accurate do you expect your prediction to be?

F. Use the table of values and your scatter plot to help you describe the relationship between the cost of a hotel room and the cost of dinner for these nine cities.

Interpreting Data

YOU WILL NEED

- ruler and metre stick, or measuring tape
- grid paper

GOAL

Plot and interpret experimental data.

INVESTIGATE *the Math*

A character on a TV crime show predicted the height of a suspect based on hand span. Robin wants to find out what the relationship is.

? How is hand span related to height?

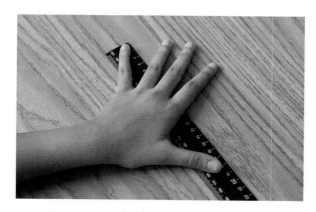

A. Measure your hand span.

B. Measure your height.

C. Gather the data for all members of your class and put it in a table.

D. Choose one variable as the independent variable and the other as the dependent variable.

Draw a scatter plot to represent the data.

E. Would you say the variables are **continuous** or **discrete**?

F. Are there any data points that don't fit the pattern? If so, explain.

G. How does the scatter plot suggest how hand span and height are related?

Reflecting

H. How did making a scatter plot from your data table help you to determine whether hand span and height are related?

I. Did your choice for the dependent variable in part D affect your conclusion about whether there is a relationship between hand span and height? Explain.

APPLY the Math

EXAMPLE 1	Representing and interpreting discrete data

The table below shows how many sit-ups Samantha did in gym class.

Time (min)	0.5	1	1.5	2	2.5	3	3.5	4
Sit-Ups Completed	17	33	48	62	72	80	86	91

Describe the relationship between completed sit-ups and time.

Hiro's Solution: Reasoning from a hand-drawn scatter plot

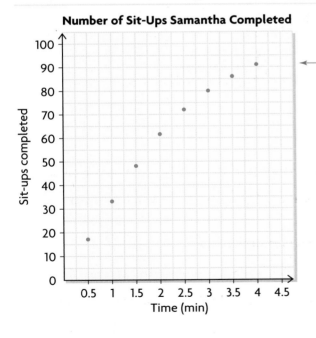

I plotted the data on a scatter plot. I chose "sit-ups completed" as the dependent variable, since the number of sit-ups that Samantha does depends on how much time she takes.

Number of Sit-Ups Samantha Completed

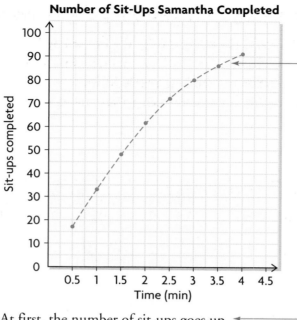

I joined the points with a dashed line. The "sit-ups completed" variable is discrete because you can only do a whole number of sit-ups.

At first, the number of sit-ups goes up by almost the same amount in each half minute.

The line is nearly straight at the beginning, but bends at the end.

Toward the end, she must be getting tired because she does fewer sit-ups every half minute.

Nadine's Solution: Reasoning from a graph drawn using technology

Tech | *Support*

- For help using your calculator to create a scatter plot, see Appendix B-9.

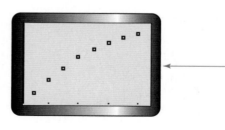

I plotted the data using the Lists in my graphing calculator. I entered "time" into L1 as the independent variable. I entered "sit-ups completed" into L2 as the dependent variable, since the number of sit-ups that Samantha does depends on how much time she takes.

The screen shows the same relationship that Hiro found plotting the data by hand.

EXAMPLE 2   Representing and interpreting continuous data

Students in Grade 9 and Grade 10 are trying out for the junior boys'
baseball team at their school. The speeds of their pitches were measured
with a hand-held radar gun and are shown in the table below.
Determine if there is a relationship between throwing speed and age.

Age (years)	14.1	14.6	14.9	15.3	15.5	15.6	15.7	15.8	15.9	16.3	16.4
Throwing Speed (km/h)	79.3	50.2	66.1	103.3	62.3	40.4	91.6	75.8	55.9	52.7	62.4

Jay's Solution

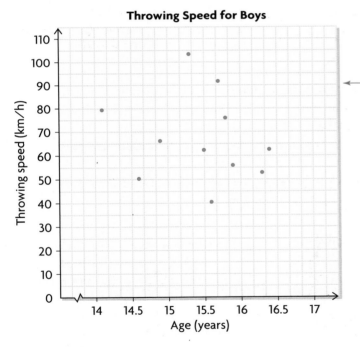

I didn't know which variable to choose as the
independent variable. I remembered that time
is usually on the horizontal axis, so I chose
"age" as the independent variable.

The data are continuous. I know because any
speed and any age between the ones in my
data set are valid.

I plotted the data.

There doesn't seem to be any relationship between
age and throwing speed for this set of data.

The data points are really scattered. I couldn't
see a simple pattern and didn't even try to
join data points.

Key Ideas

- You can use a table of values to organize numerical data collected from an experiment.
- If the data points on the scatter plot seem to follow a predictable pattern, you might suggest that there is a relationship between the variables.
- Often, the purpose of an experiment is to determine whether the values of the dependent variable actually do depend on the values of the independent variable.

Need to Know

- In some cases, either variable could be chosen as the independent variable, depending on your point of view.
- Sometimes, the points in a scatter plot are approximated by a line or smooth curve. The line or curve may help you see if there is a relationship between the variables.

CHECK *Your Understanding*

1. Suppose you were to survey your classmates to see if there is a relationship between math marks and the number of hours spent watching TV.
   a) What column headings would you use in a table of values designed to organize the data from your survey?
   b) Which variable would you choose as the independent variable? Explain.
   c) How would you interpret the ordered pair (2, 65) if it were to appear on a scatter plot of your data?

2. The scatter plot shows the sales of bottled water at a refreshment booth at the Canadian National Exhibition in Toronto for different days during a heat wave one summer.
   a) What information does point A represent? What does point B represent?
   b) What does the scatter plot show about the relationship between water sales and temperature?

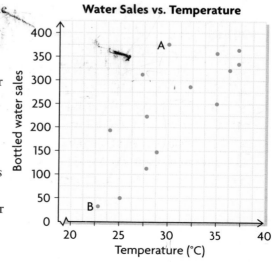

Water Sales vs. Temperature

PRACTISING

3. The scatter plot shows the ages of some tractors and their values.

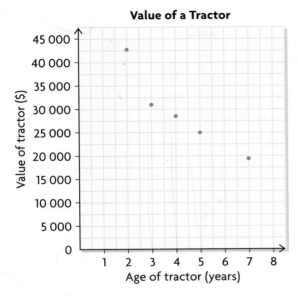

Value of a Tractor

a) Identify the independent variable and the dependent variable.
b) Would you consider the variables to be discrete or continuous? Would you use a dashed line or a solid line to join the points?
c) Does the scatter plot suggest a relationship between the age of a tractor and its value? Explain.

4. These data show the heights of some Grade 9 boys and their fathers.

Height of Grade 9 Boy (cm)	164	168	150	162	159	165	187	152	180	166	148	159
Height of Father (cm)	171	186	164	180	176	177	192	167	189	180	165	172

a) Identify the independent variable and the dependent variable.
b) Would you consider the variables to be discrete or continuous?
c) Would you use a dashed line or a solid line to join the points?
d) Construct a scatter plot for the data.
e) Does the scatter plot suggest a relationship between a boy's height and his father's height? Explain.
f) Is there is a relationship between the variables? Suggest reasons for this.

Use the data below for questions 5 and 6.

Countries and Films Represented at the Toronto International Film Festival

Year	2006	2005	2004	2003	2002	2001	2000
Countries	61	52	55	50	50	54	56
Films	352	335	336	339	345	326	329

5. a) Draw a scatter plot of the number of countries represented each year.
   b) Describe any patterns you see in the scatter plot of part a).
   c) Draw a scatter plot of the number of films shown each year.
   d) Describe any patterns you see in the scatter plot of part c).
   e) For each scatter plot, would you consider the variables to be discrete or continuous? Would you use a dashed line or a solid line for the graph?

6. a) Draw a scatter plot using the number of countries and the number of films.
   b) Explain how you chose the independent and dependent variables.
   c) Describe any patterns you see in the scatter plot.

7. The amount of fuel a hybrid car uses is measured at various speeds as
A shown in the table below.

Speed (km/h)	3	8	11	16	21	26	32	40	50	60	64	67	71	80	90	100	110
Fuel Consumption (L/100 km)	14.9	5.3	4.7	3.8	3.5	3.3	3.2	3.1	3.1	3.1	3.1	3.8	3.9	4.1	4.4	4.9	5.3

   a) Draw a scatter plot of the data.
   b) Describe any pattern you see.
   c) Does the pattern you described in part b) seem reasonable? Explain.
   d) Does the pattern you described in part b) suggest how you should drive in order to minimize fuel consumption?
   e) Who would want this information? Why?
   f) Are the variables discrete or continuous?
   g) Which variable did you choose for the independent variable? Explain.

8. This table shows the birth rates in four provinces over the last few years.

T **Number of Births per 1000 People**

Year	Alberta	British Columbia	Newfoundland and Labrador	Ontario
2001	12.4	9.8	8.8	10.9
2002	12.8	9.9	8.8	10.8
2003	12.9	9.7	8.9	10.9
2004	12.9	9.7	8.6	10.8
2005	12.7	9.6	8.6	10.6

a) Draw a scatter plot of the number of births for this five-year period for each province on a single grid.

b) Do any provincial data show a strong pattern?

9. Suppose that you have plotted some data on a scatter plot.

C **a)** How could you tell whether there is a relationship between the variables?

b) How could you decide whether to use a solid or dashed line?

Extending

10. The data on the right show the number of car accidents in a year for different age groups.

a) Choose an independent variable and a dependent variable. Explain how you chose.

b) Draw a scatter plot of the data. Use the median age for each age group.

c) Describe any trends you see in the scatter plot.

d) Is it appropriate to connect the plotted points with a line? If so, should the line be solid or broken? Explain.

e) Veera says that young people have more car accidents than old people. Are there sufficient data to support this claim? If not, what further information would be helpful? Explain.

Age Group	Number of Accidents
16–19	6 382
20–24	7 183
25–34	11 733
35–44	8 990
45–54	5 517
55–64	3 307
65–74	2 308

Lines of Best Fit

YOU WILL NEED

- ruler
- grid paper

GOAL

Sketch a line of best fit for a given set of data and determine the equation of the line.

LEARN ABOUT the Math

Over the past half century, the percentage of foreign-born players in the Black Horse Corners International Hockey League (BHCIHL) has increased. The data are summarized in the table and on the scatter plot.

Year	Percentage of Foreign-Born Players in the BHCIHL
1950	30
1955	33
1960	30
1965	37
1970	38
1975	39
1980	41
1985	45
1990	47
1995	49
2000	51
2005	52

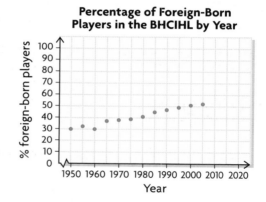

Percentage of Foreign-Born Players in the BHCIHL by Year

? How might the percentage of foreign-born players in BHCIHL in the year 2020 compare with the percentage in 1993?

EXAMPLE 1 | Representing a situation using a line of best fit

Use the scatter plot to estimate, and then, compare the number of foreign-born players in 2020 and in 1993.

Ryan's Solution: Using a graphing strategy

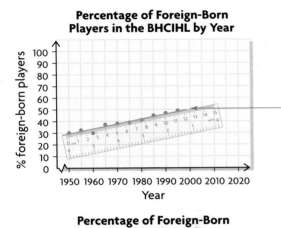

Percentage of Foreign-Born Players in the BHCIHL by Year

I drew a **line of best fit** to help me see the **trend**. I placed my transparent ruler over the plotted points so that most of them were close to the edge. I tried to "balance" the points on either side of the line.

I can see that the percentage of foreign-born players in the league is increasing as time passes.

Percentage of Foreign-Born Players in the BHCIHL by Year

I assumed that this increasing trend would continue and I extended the line of best fit until it went to 2020.

If the trend continues, the percentage of foreign-born players in the BHCIHL in 2020 will probably be about 59%.

I used the extended line of best fit to **extrapolate** the percentage for 2020.

The percentage of foreign-born players in the BHCIHL in 1993 was probably about 48%.

I used the line of best fit to **interpolate** the percentage for 1993.

Based on the trend I see, the number of foreign-born players in the BHCIHL will likely be quite a bit higher in 2020 than it was in 1993.

line of best fit
a line that best describes the relationship between two variables in a scatter plot

trend
a relationship between two variables for which the independent variable is time

Omar determined an equation to describe the relationship between the percentage of foreign-born players and time. He then used his equation to make a prediction for the year 2020.

Omar's Solution: Using an algebraic strategy

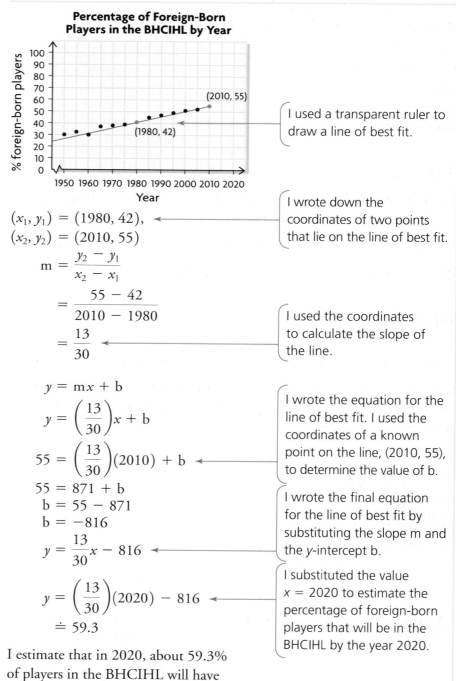

Percentage of Foreign-Born Players in the BHCIHL by Year

I used a transparent ruler to draw a line of best fit.

$(x_1, y_1) = (1980, 42),$
$(x_2, y_2) = (2010, 55)$

I wrote down the coordinates of two points that lie on the line of best fit.

$$m = \frac{y_2 - y_1}{x_2 - x_1}$$

$$= \frac{55 - 42}{2010 - 1980}$$

$$= \frac{13}{30}$$

I used the coordinates to calculate the slope of the line.

$$y = mx + b$$

$$y = \left(\frac{13}{30}\right)x + b$$

$$55 = \left(\frac{13}{30}\right)(2010) + b$$

I wrote the equation for the line of best fit. I used the coordinates of a known point on the line, (2010, 55), to determine the value of b.

$$55 = 871 + b$$
$$b = 55 - 871$$
$$b = -816$$

$$y = \frac{13}{30}x - 816$$

I wrote the final equation for the line of best fit by substituting the slope m and the y-intercept b.

$$y = \left(\frac{13}{30}\right)(2020) - 816$$

$$\doteq 59.3$$

I substituted the value x = 2020 to estimate the percentage of foreign-born players that will be in the BHCIHL by the year 2020.

I estimate that in 2020, about 59.3% of players in the BHCIHL will have been born outside of Canada.

$$y = \left(\frac{13}{30}\right)(1993) - 816$$

$$\doteq 47.6$$

> I substituted the value $x = 1993$ to estimate the percentage of foreign-born players that were in the BHCIHL in 1993.

I estimate that in 1993, about 47.6% of players in the BHCIHL had been born outside of Canada.

> These values are reasonable, since they are very close to the values that I could read off the graph of the line of best fit.

If the trend continues, in 2020 there will be almost 12% more foreign-born players in the league than there were in 1993.

Reflecting

A. Different students may use their rulers to draw different lines of best fit. How might that affect their estimates?

B. Do Ryan's and Omar's solutions seem to give similar results? Explain.

C. Which boy's strategy would you choose? Why?

APPLY the Math

EXAMPLE 2	Using a line of best fit to describe a trend

Kajsa and Erika make bead jewellery in their spare time. Their monthly income for 10 consecutive months is shown in the table. Describe the trend in their income.

Month	1	2	3	4	5	6	7	8	9	10
Income ($)	20	25	45	55	80	90	110	105	135	155

Kylie's Solution: Using a graphical representation

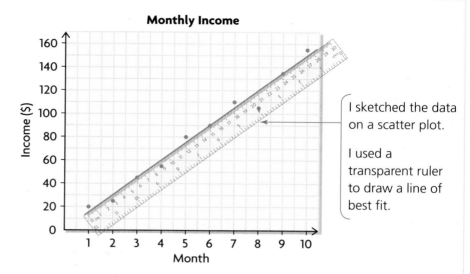

Monthly Income

I sketched the data on a scatter plot.

I used a transparent ruler to draw a line of best fit.

From the scatter plot and the line of best fit, the trend is that the monthly income increases steadily.

Jasper's Solution: Using an algebraic representation

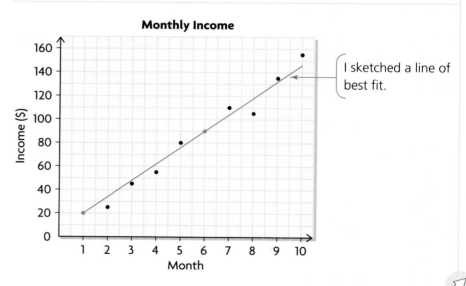

Monthly Income

I sketched a line of best fit.

$(x_1, y_1) = (1, 20),$
$(x_2, y_2) = (6, 90)$

$$m = \frac{y_2 - y_1}{x_2 - x_1}$$

$$= \frac{90 - 20}{6 - 1}$$

$$= 14$$

> I chose two points on the line and used their coordinates to calculate the slope of the line.

Their monthly income is increasing by $14 each month.

> The slope is the rate of change in their income each month.

$$y = mx + b$$
$$y = 14x + b$$
$$20 = 14(1) + b$$
$$20 = 14 + b$$
$$20 - 14 = b$$
$$6 = b$$
$$y = 14x + 6$$

> To determine b, I substituted 14 for m and the coordinates of the point (1, 20) into the equation for the line of best fit.

The equation of the line of best fit has a positive slope, so the trend for Kajsa and Erika's income is that their monthly income is increasing steadily.

EXAMPLE 4   Using a line of best fit to solve a problem

Using the data in Example 3, estimate when Kajsa and Erika's income will reach $200 for a month.

Mathieu's Solution: Using a graphing strategy

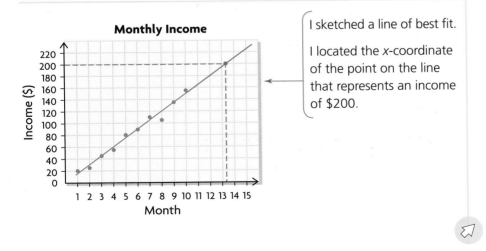

> I sketched a line of best fit.
>
> I located the x-coordinate of the point on the line that represents an income of $200.

Investigating Relationships   **335**

The *x*-value of this point is about $x = 13$. ⟵ I rounded the value of *x* because only whole numbers make sense for this situation.

Kajsa and Erika's income will reach $200 after about 13 months.

Cassandra's Solution: Using an algebraic strategy

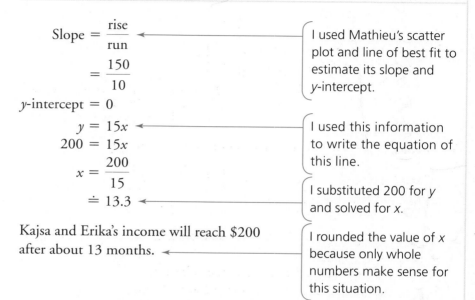

$$\text{Slope} = \frac{\text{rise}}{\text{run}}$$ ⟵ I used Mathieu's scatter plot and line of best fit to estimate its slope and *y*-intercept.

$$= \frac{150}{10}$$

y-intercept $= 0$

$$y = 15x$$ ⟵ I used this information to write the equation of this line.

$$200 = 15x$$

$$x = \frac{200}{15}$$

$$\doteq 13.3$$ ⟵ I substituted 200 for *y* and solved for *x*.

Kajsa and Erika's income will reach $200 after about 13 months. ⟵ I rounded the value of *x* because only whole numbers make sense for this situation.

In Summary

Key Ideas

- You can use a line of best fit to make predictions for values not actually recorded or plotted. This is done by interpolating or extrapolating.
- Predictions can be made by reading values off a graph, or by using an equation of the line of best fit.

Need to Know

- If the pattern of points on a scatter plot looks like it follows a straight line, a line of best fit can be used to represent the relationship between the variables.
- When you draw a line of best fit, the points on the scatter plot should be "balanced" on each side of the line.
- You can use the coordinates of two points on the line of best fit to determine its slope and its equation.

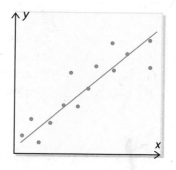

CHECK Your Understanding

1. This scatter plot shows the monthly profit for a car dealership when a certain number of cars are sold.

   a) Use the graph to estimate the monthly profit in a month where 23 cars are sold.

   b) Use the graph to estimate the number of cars sold in a month where the profit is $67 000.

Profit at a Car Dealership

2. The table shows temperatures at various times of the day.

Time (p.m.)	2	3	4	5	6	7
Temperature (°C)	−1	2	2.5	4	6.5	9

   a) Construct a scatter plot for the data in the table.
   b) Sketch a line of best fit.
   c) Determine an equation for the line of best fit.
   d) Predict the value of the temperature at 5:30 p.m.
   e) Predict the time when the temperature is 8 °C.

PRACTISING

3. In this table, x represents the number of people enrolled in various classes at a health club, and y represents the number in each class that are male.

x	19	10	6	16	15	9	12	21
y	10	4	2	5	7	3	8	8

   a) Construct a scatter plot for the data.
   b) Sketch a line of best fit.
   c) Use the line of best fit to estimate the value of y when $x = 14$.
   d) Use the line of best fit to estimate the value of y when $x = 27$.

Investigating Relationships **337**

4. The following data show the final marks for 10 students in a math class and the average number of hours they studied math per week.

Final Mark	75	81	68	62	88	83	90	77	89	60
Average Number of Study Hours Per Week	3	3	5	1	5	3	6	3	5	2

    a) Construct a scatter plot.
    b) Sketch a line of best fit.
    c) Determine an equation for the line of best fit.
    d) Use the equation to estimate the mark for a student who studies an average of 4 h per week.
    e) Use the graph to estimate the study time for a student whose final mark is 71.
    f) Is there a relationship between final mark and number of hours of study per week? If so, describe it.

5. A chair company has a contract to build all 1790 seats in a concert
K hall. The progress over the first week of work is shown in the table.

Number of Days	1	2	3	4	5	6	7
Total Number of Seats Completed	97	204	327	443	539	661	795

    a) Estimate the number of seats built after 9 days. How many are built by the middle of day 5?
    b) Estimate the number of days needed to build 1252 seats.
    c) The company gets a bonus if it is able to finish all of the seats in two weeks or less. If the workers continue to make chairs at about the same rate in the second week, will the company be able to collect the bonus?

6. Tomas is a member of the school track and field team. His times for
T running various distances are shown.

Distance (m)	50	100	150	200	250
Time (s)	6.1	12.0	18.3	25.2	31.7

    a) Determine an equation for the line of best fit if the data were plotted on a scatter plot.
    b) What is Tomas's time for a 175 m run likely to be?
    c) Is it reasonable to use the same line of best fit to determine the time needed to run 3000 m? Explain.
    d) What does the slope of the line of best fit tell you about how Tomas runs?

7. Kim is on her school basketball team. This table shows her statistics for
A the first 10 games of the season. (Each field goal made counts for two points, and each free throw made counts for one point.)

Game	Minutes Played	Field Goals		Free Throws		Points
		Made	Attempted	Made	Attempted	
1	32	5	13	4	6	14
2	30	4	10	3	3	11
3	24	2	6	1	1	5
4	29	1	3	2	4	4
5	36	3	6	0	1	6
6	19	5	11	2	2	12
7	12	0	3	0	4	0
8	21	1	5	1	2	3
9	18	3	5	1	5	7
10	19	3	7	2	6	8

a) Use a line of best fit to estimate the number of field goals Kim would make if nine were attempted.

b) Use a line of best fit to estimate the number of points Kim would score if she played for 40 min.

8. Suppose that you plotted some data on a scatter plot.
C a) How would you draw a line of best fit?
   b) How would you determine an equation for the line of best fit?
   c) How would you use the line of best fit to interpolate or extrapolate?

Extending

9. The tables at the right show how the world record times for the 100 m sprint have changed over the years for both men and women.
   a) Plot both sets of data on the same scatter plot.
   b) Describe the trend in each set of data.
   c) Sketch lines of best fit for each set of data.
   d) Do the lines of best fit in part c) suggest that the women's world record time will someday be less than the men's? If so, predict when this might occur if current trends continue.
   e) Do you expect current trends in each data set to continue forever? Explain.

Men:

Year	Time (s)
1960	10.0
1968	9.95
1983	9.93
1988	9.92
1991	9.86
1994	9.85
1996	9.84
1999	9.79
2005	9.77

Women:

Year	Time (s)
1960	11.3
1968	11.1
1976	11.01
1977	10.88
1983	10.81
1984	10.76
1988	10.49

Median-Median Line of Best Fit

You can determine a line of best fit without relying on judging by eye. Here's one way.

Use this set of data.

x	1	2	3	4	6	8	9	10	11
y	2	4	3	6	8	10	9	10	8

Step 1: Group the data into equal thirds in order from least to greatest x-value. The lowest third of the x-values go in the Left group, the highest third go in the Right group, and the middle third go in the Middle group.

	Left			Middle			Right		
x	1	2	3	4	6	8	9	10	11
y	2	4	3	6	8	10	9	10	8

(If there is one point left over, let the Middle group have an extra point. If there are two points left over, let the Left and Right groups each have one extra point.)

Step 2: Determine the **median** of the x-values for each group (x_L, x_M, and x_R), and the median of the y-values for each group (y_L, y_M, and y_R).

	Left (x_L, y_L)	Middle (x_M, y_M)	Right (x_R, y_R)
Median	(2, 3)	(6, 8)	(10, 9)

Step 3: Plot the median points (x_L, y_L) and (x_R, y_R). Lightly sketch a line through these two points.

Step 4: Plot the point (x_M, y_M). Move the line from Step 3 vertically one-third of the distance toward (x_M, y_M). The resulting line is called the median-median line of best fit.

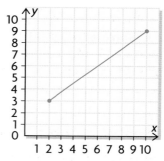

For the following data sets,

   i) Plot all of the points, then draw a line of best fit, as you have been doing throughout the chapter.

   ii) On the same grid, draw a median-median line of best fit.

   iii) Compare the two lines. Does either line seem to be a better approximation to the data? Explain.

   a) (5, 8), (6, 11), (11, 1), (3, 10), (9, 2), (10, 6), (12, 4), (7, 6), (4, 9), (5, 12)

   b) (1.3, 1), (2, 2.1), (3, 3), (3.5, 1.5), (5.2, 3), (6, 9), (9.1, 10.8), (10, 4.3), (11.6, 7.0), (12, 9.4)

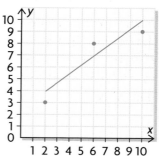

FREQUENTLY ASKED *Questions*

This scatter plot is used for all of the frequently asked questions:

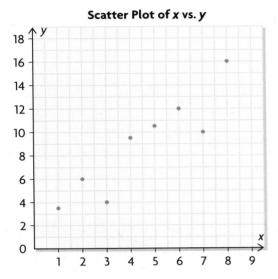

Scatter Plot of *x* vs. *y*

Q: How can you represent numeric data from an experiment involving two variables?

A: If any value between two plotted values of a variable is possible and meaningful, then the variable is continuous. You can organize the data into a table of values. Then, you can use the values to create a scatter plot. If the data points seem to follow a pattern, you can use a line or a curve to represent the pattern.

Use a solid line or curve if both variables are continuous. Use a dashed line or curve if one or both variables are discrete.

Study | Aid

- See Lesson 6.1, Examples 1 and 2.
- Try Mid-Chapter Review Question 1.

Q: How can you determine a line of best fit?

A: First, plot the data on a scatter plot. Then, position your ruler so that the slope of the line roughly follows the pattern of the plotted points. Also, try to position the ruler so that the plotted points are balanced on either side of the line of best fit. It helps if your ruler is transparent.

Study | Aid

- See Lesson 6.2, Example 1.
- Try Mid-Chapter Review Question 4.

EXAMPLE

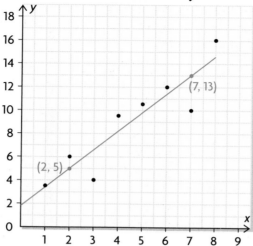

Scatter Plot of *x* vs. *y*

Study | *Aid*

• See Lesson 6.2, Example 2.
• Try Mid-Chapter Review
  Questions 4 and 5.

Q: How can you determine an equation for a line of best fit?

A: Choose two points on the line and read off their coordinates. Then, determine the slope and use it and the coordinates of one of the points to determine an equation.

EXAMPLE

The coordinates of two points on the line of best fit are (2, 5) and (7, 13). The slope of the line is

$$m = \frac{13 - 5}{7 - 2}$$
$$= 1.6$$

So, the equation of the line is $y = 1.6x + b$. To calculate the value of b, substitute the point (2, 5) into the equation to get

$$5 = 1.6(2) + b$$
$$5 - 3.2 = b$$
$$1.8 = b$$

The equation of the line of best fit is $y = 1.6x + 1.8$.

PRACTICE Questions

Lesson 6.1

1. Family doctors record the growth of their young patients. At each checkup, Jennifer's younger sister has her height and mass measured.

Height (cm)	58	60	64	68	73	74
Mass (kg)	5.0	6.3	7.3	8.1	8.8	8.2

a) Graph the data.
b) Should the graph consist of scattered points or can the points be connected by a line? If the points can be connected by a line, then should the line be solid or dashed? Explain.
c) Does the graph show a relationship between height and mass? If so, describe it.

2. The data show how many babies were born at Cook's Mills Hospital on the first 10 days of a month.

Day	1	2	3	4	5	6	7	8	9	10
Number of Births	8	2	5	5	1	9	1	8	7	1

a) Plot the data on a scatter plot.
b) Describe the pattern of the data.
c) Do you think that collecting more data (either including a longer time period or including more hospitals) might change your conclusion in part b)? Explain.

Lesson 6.2

3. The school rowing coach measures the maximum amount of weight that can be lifted by each member of the team.

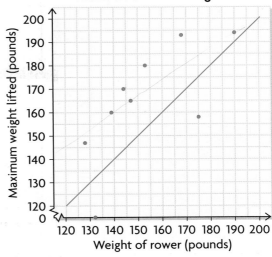

Maximum Weight Lifted by Members of the Rowing Team

(scatter plot: x-axis "Weight of rower (pounds)" from 120 to 200; y-axis "Maximum weight lifted (pounds)" from 120 to 200)

The results are shown in the above scatter plot. Is the line of best fit appropriate? If so, explain. If not, sketch an appropriate line of best fit.

4. Andrew took a hearing test.

The x-values represent times (in seconds) and the y-values represent loudness levels of a test sound.

x	0	1	2	3	4	5	6	8	10
y	0.0	1.0	1.7	2.1	2.4	2.6	2.8	3.1	3.3

a) Plot the data on a scatter plot.
b) Sketch a line of best fit.
c) Determine an equation for the line of best fit from part b).
d) Estimate the loudness after 3.7 s.
e) If the test followed the same pattern, when would the loudness reach a level of 4.2?

5. Markus and Joelle had the same set of data. Both students created a scatter plot and drew a line of best fit. They then determined the equations of their lines of best fit and compared their results. Should their answers be the same? Explain.

Curves of Best Fit

GOAL

Construct and interpret a curve of best fit for a given set of data.

LEARN ABOUT the Math

Sean and Parminder are studying the motion of a pendulum. Sean says that the pendulum will swing in the same way, no matter how long it is. Parminder is not so sure.

They did an experiment to see whether the length of a pendulum affects its period, which is how long it takes to go back and forth once.

Length, L(m)	0.1	0.2	0.3	0.4	0.5	0.6	0.7	0.8	0.9	1.0
Period, P(s)	0.64	0.90	1.10	1.27	1.53	1.55	1.70	1.75	1.90	2.01

? What is the period when the length is 0.38 m?

EXAMPLE 1 | Solving a problem using a curve of best fit

Estimate the period of a pendulum that has a length of 0.38 m.

Walid's Solution

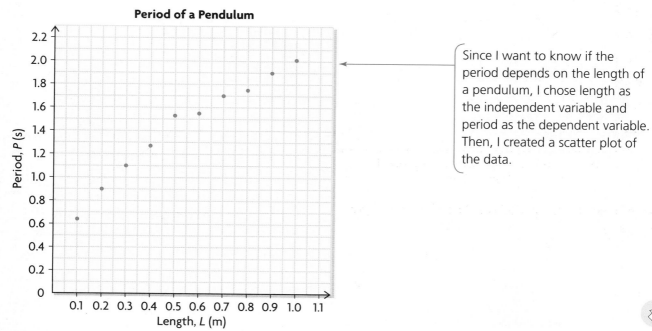

Since I want to know if the period depends on the length of a pendulum, I chose length as the independent variable and period as the dependent variable. Then, I created a scatter plot of the data.

PRACTICE Questions

Lesson 6.1

1. Family doctors record the growth of their young patients. At each checkup, Jennifer's younger sister has her height and mass measured.

Height (cm)	58	60	64	68	73	74
Mass (kg)	5.0	6.3	7.3	8.1	8.8	8.2

a) Graph the data.
b) Should the graph consist of scattered points or can the points be connected by a line? If the points can be connected by a line, then should the line be solid or dashed? Explain.
c) Does the graph show a relationship between height and mass? If so, describe it.

2. The data show how many babies were born at Cook's Mills Hospital on the first 10 days of a month.

Day	1	2	3	4	5	6	7	8	9	10
Number of Births	8	2	5	5	1	9	1	8	7	1

a) Plot the data on a scatter plot.
b) Describe the pattern of the data.
c) Do you think that collecting more data (either including a longer time period or including more hospitals) might change your conclusion in part b)? Explain.

Lesson 6.2

3. The school rowing coach measures the maximum amount of weight that can be lifted by each member of the team.

Maximum Weight Lifted by Members of the Rowing Team

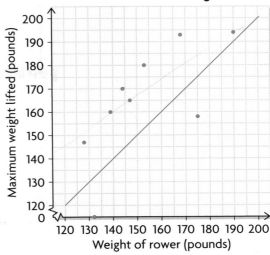

The results are shown in the above scatter plot. Is the line of best fit appropriate? If so, explain. If not, sketch an appropriate line of best fit.

4. Andrew took a hearing test.

The x-values represent times (in seconds) and the y-values represent loudness levels of a test sound.

x	0	1	2	3	4	5	6	8	10
y	0.0	1.0	1.7	2.1	2.4	2.6	2.8	3.1	3.3

a) Plot the data on a scatter plot.
b) Sketch a line of best fit.
c) Determine an equation for the line of best fit from part b).
d) Estimate the loudness after 3.7 s.
e) If the test followed the same pattern, when would the loudness reach a level of 4.2?

5. Markus and Joelle had the same set of data. Both students created a scatter plot and drew a line of best fit. They then determined the equations of their lines of best fit and compared their results. Should their answers be the same? Explain.

Curves of Best Fit

YOU WILL NEED

- grid paper
- ruler
- graphing calculator

Construct and interpret a curve of best fit for a given set of data.

LEARN ABOUT *the Math*

Sean and Parminder are studying the motion of a pendulum. Sean says that the pendulum will swing in the same way, no matter how long it is. Parminder is not so sure.

They did an experiment to see whether the length of a pendulum affects its period, which is how long it takes to go back and forth once.

Length, *L*(m)	0.1	0.2	0.3	0.4	0.5	0.6	0.7	0.8	0.9	1.0
Period, *P*(s)	0.64	0.90	1.10	1.27	1.53	1.55	1.70	1.75	1.90	2.01

? What is the period when the length is 0.38 m?

EXAMPLE 1   Solving a problem using a curve of best fit

Estimate the period of a pendulum that has a length of 0.38 m.

Walid's Solution

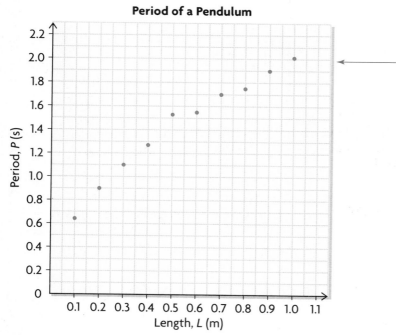

Since I want to know if the period depends on the length of a pendulum, I chose length as the independent variable and period as the dependent variable. Then, I created a scatter plot of the data.

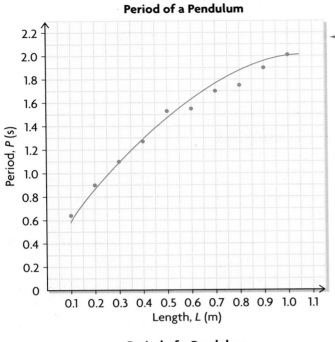

The plotted points seem to follow a curve, so I used a smooth curve of best fit instead of a line of best fit. I made the curve solid because the variables are continuous.

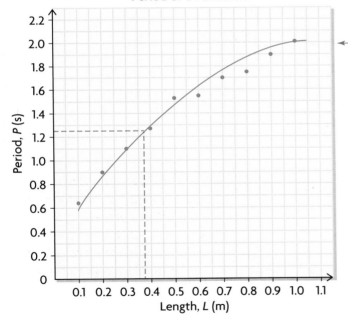

I used the curve to estimate the period for a pendulum 0.38 m long.

My estimate for the period is 1.24 s when the length is 0.38 m.

Investigating Relationships   **345**

Reflecting

A. How did Walid decide that a curve of best fit is a more appropriate representation than a line of best fit?

B. How did Walid use the curve of best fit to estimate the period when the length is 0.38 m?

C. If you were to draw a curve of best fit, would it be exactly the same as Walid's? If not, how would this change the estimate for the period when the length is 0.38 m?

APPLY the Math

EXAMPLE **2**	Using a curve of best fit to represent a trend

To help protect the environment, a steel factory is thinking about setting new standards for its carbon dioxide (CO_2) emissions. By 2012, the factory wants to emit less than 70 tonnes of CO_2 per year. If it does not change its practices, is the goal realistic?

CO_2 (tonnes)	165	145	130	117	107	100
Year	2001	2002	2003	2004	2005	2006

Shannon's Solution

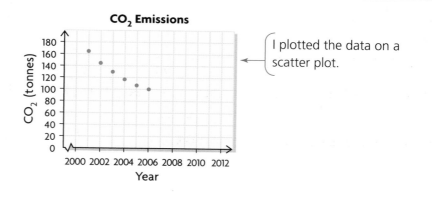

I plotted the data on a scatter plot.

CO₂ Emissions

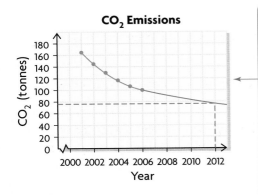

I sketched a curve of best fit. I could have used a line of best fit, but since the data seemed to follow a smooth curve, I thought using a curve of best fit would make my estimate more accurate. I used a solid curve because the variables are continuous.

I extended the curve out to the year 2012 assuming that this trend will continue.

I used the extrapolated graph to estimate the amount of CO_2 in 2012.

The emissions level for 2012 is estimated to be greater than 70 tonnes. This means the goal will probably not be met by 2012.

EXAMPLE 3   Using curves of best fit to reason about a trend

These tables show the population (in thousands) of two different bacterial colonies growing in separate Petri dishes.

Colony 1:

Time (h)	0	1	2	3	4	5	6	7	8	9	10	11
Population (thousands)	12	19	33	57	85	108	127	142	151	157	160	161

Colony 2:

Time (h)	0	1	2	3	4	5	6	7	8	9	10	11
Population (thousands)	3	6	11	20	36	65	110	190	250	380	590	980

Compare the growth patterns of the two colonies.

Alexis's Solution

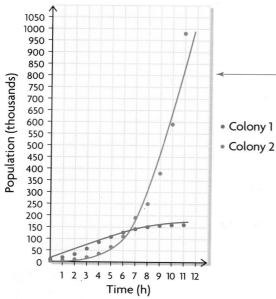

Populations of Bacterial Colonies

- Colony 1
- Colony 2

I plotted both sets of data on a single scatter plot so that I could compare them more easily. I sketched each curve so that it was close to most of the plotted points.

Colony 2 keeps growing more and more quickly, but Colony 1 is growing more and more slowly.

Both curves are always going up, so the populations of both colonies are increasing.

Colony 1 grows rapidly at first. But later the curve almost levels off. The colony still grows, but very slowly.

Colony 2 starts off with a lower population than Colony 1 but, because it grows more quickly, at about 6.5 h it catches up and passes Colony 2.

Where the curves are steep, it means that the population is increasing rapidly. Where the curves are less steep, the population is growing slower.

In Summary

Key Idea

- Sometimes a curve represents the trend or pattern in a scatter plot better than a line.

Need to Know

- You can use a curve of best fit to extrapolate and interpolate values.
- Extending a curve involves more guesswork than extending a line, so you can't be as sure of your predictions.
- Sometimes it's not clear whether a curve or line of best fit can be drawn. This could be because there is no relationship between the variables, or it could mean that more data need to be collected.

CHECK *Your Understanding*

1. Computers use code numbers that are made up of only the digits 0 and 1. The data in the chart represent the number of possible code numbers of each length. (For example, the code numbers of length 1 are 0 and 1, the code numbers of length 2 are 00, 01, 10, and 11, etc.)

Length of Code Number	1	2	3	4	5	6
Number of Possible Code Numbers	2	4	8	16	32	64

   a) Plot the data on a scatter plot.
   b) Sketch a line of best fit.
   c) Sketch a curve of best fit.
   d) Which approximates the data better: the line in part b) or the curve in part c)?
   e) Is it reasonable to use the line or curve of best fit to estimate the value of y when $x = 3.7$? Explain.

PRACTISING

2. Weekly earnings for the movie *Dude, Where's My Math Book?* in the weeks following its opening are listed in the table.

Earnings ($ millions)	9.2	21.4	34.0	25.7	19.6	14.1	13.3	11.2	6.6	3.1
Weeks Since Opening	1	2	3	4	5	6	7	8	9	10

   a) Plot the data on a scatter plot.
   b) Sketch a curve of best fit. Should you use a solid curve or a dashed curve? Explain.
   c) Does it make sense to use the curve of best fit to estimate the earnings after 3.5 weeks? Explain.
   d) Does it make sense to use the curve of best fit to estimate the earnings 20 weeks after opening? Explain.

3. A basketball is dropped from a height of 200 cm. The table shows how high it bounces on each bounce.

Maximum Height (cm)	200	120	72	44	26	16	10	6	4
Bounce Number	0	1	2	3	4	5	6	7	8

a) Plot the data on a scatter plot.
b) Sketch a curve of best fit. Should you use a solid curve or a dashed curve? Explain.
c) Does it make sense to use the curve of best fit for interpolation? Explain.
d) Does it make sense to use the curve of best fit for extrapolation? Explain.

4. In order to obtain a medical image of a patient's thyroid gland, a
C chemical is injected into the patient's bloodstream. The chemical's concentration in the blood gradually decreases with time.

Concentration (mg/L)	29.0	15.0	7.7	3.9	2.1	1.3	0.7	0.5	0.4
Time (h)	0	1	2	3	4	5	6	7	8

a) Plot the data on a scatter plot.
b) Sketch a curve of best fit. Did you use a solid curve or a dashed curve? Explain.
c) Describe the relationship between the variables.
d) Use your curve of best fit to estimate when the concentration of the chemical will be 6.1 mg/L.
e) Use your curve of best fit to estimate the concentration of the chemical after 12 h.

5. The ages and resting heart rates for some people are listed in the table.

Age (years)	21	24	26	29	31	35	39
Resting Heart Rate (beats per minute)	60	61	63	65	68	73	78

a) Plot the data on a scatter plot.
b) Sketch a curve of best fit. Did you use a solid curve or a dashed curve? Explain why.
c) Describe the relationship between the variables.
d) Does it make sense to use the curve of best fit for interpolation? Explain.
e) Does it make sense to use the curve of best fit to estimate the resting heart rate for an 85-year-old person? Explain.

6. In his experiments to study the Earth's gravity, Galileo rolled objects
A on inclined planes. In one such experiment, a ball is rolled up a plane,
and then, rolls back down. The data are in the following table.

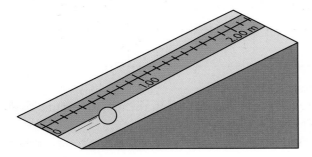

Time (s)	0	0.5	1.0	1.5	2.0	2.5	3.0	3.5
Position (m)	0	1.13	1.50	1.88	2.00	1.88	1.50	1.13

a) Use a graph to estimate the position of the ball after 0.3 s.
b) Use a graph to estimate when the ball will return to the bottom
of the inclined plane.

7. The table shows the population of a bacterial colony growing in a test
tube at various times.

Time (h)	0	1	2	3	4	5	6	7	8
Population (thousands)	1	1.4	2.0	2.7	3.8	5.4	7.5	10.5	14.8

a) Use a graph to describe the growth of the colony.
b) Use a graph to estimate the population of the colony after 7.5 h.

8. A herd of caribou is moved to a small, remote island
where they have no predators. Data on the population
of the herd were collected for 6 years.

Time (years)	0	1	2	3	4	5	6
Population	24	35	51	74	104	151	225

a) Sketch the data on a scatter plot.
b) Draw a line or curve of best fit through the
plotted points. Explain which is more appropriate.
c) Describe the growth of the herd.
d) Predict the population of the herd after
seven years.

9. In the Kingdom of Petrodalla, natural gas is the primary resource. The table shows the amount of natural gas produced each year.

Year	2008	2009	2010	2011	2012	2013	2014	2015	2016
Natural Gas Produced (millions of m³)	1.6	2.1	3.0	4.1	4.3	4.4	3.6	2.1	0.5

a) Sketch the data on a scatter plot.
b) Draw a line or curve of best fit through the plotted points. Explain which is more appropriate.
c) Describe how the production of natural gas changes over time.
d) Predict when natural gas production will decrease to zero.

10. Consider the carbon dioxide emission data from Example 2, which are
T repeated here:

CO_2 (tonnes)	165	145	130	117	107	100
Year	2001	2002	2003	2004	2005	2006

a) Instead of using a curve of best fit, as is done in the example, use a line of best fit to estimate carbon dioxide emissions in 2012.
b) Compare your estimate in part a) with the result of Example 2. Which result do you think is more reliable? Justify your choice.

11. a) How do you know when to use a curve of best fit, and when to use a line of best fit?
b) How can you use a curve of best fit for interpolation or extrapolation if you don't know the equation for the curve?
c) How do you know how far you can reasonably extrapolate?

Extending

12. Consider the carbon dioxide emission data in Example 2, which are repeated here.

CO_2 (tonnes)	165	145	130	117	107	100
Year	2001	2002	2003	2004	2005	2006

a) Suppose that the carbon dioxide emissions are reduced in each year after 2006 by a constant rate of 10% per year. Will the emission target of no more than 70 tonnes be reached by 2012?
b) Repeat part a) if the reduction is a constant 5% per year.
c) What is the minimum yearly percentage reduction after 2006 that will guarantee that the emission target will be reached by 2012?

13. The data given in Example 1 are shown in the following table.

Length, L (m)	0.1	0.2	0.3	0.4	0.5	0.6	0.7	0.8	0.9	1.0
Period, P (s)	0.64	0.90	1.10	1.27	1.42	1.55	1.70	1.80	1.90	2.01
Squared Period, P^2 (s²)	0.41	0.81	1.21							

a) Complete the new table, in which the periods are squared.
b) Plot the squared periods versus length.
c) Draw a line of best fit.
d) Calculate the slope of the line of best fit.
e) It's possible to show that the slope of the line of best fit should be equal to $\dfrac{4\pi^2}{g}$, where g is the acceleration due to the Earth's gravity. Use this formula and the results of part d) to calculate g.
f) Collect your own data on the period of a pendulum. Then, follow the steps in this exercise to obtain your own experimental value for the acceleration due to earth's gravity. How does your experimental value compare with values obtained in professional experiments?

14. Dorothy has 20 m of fencing to make a rectangular enclosure for her dog.
a) Draw all possible rectangular enclosures using whole numbers from 1 to 9 for the dimensions.
b) Organize the data in table of values with headings Length, Width, and Area.
c) Graph the relation area vs. length. Draw the line or curve of best fit.
d) What dimensions give the maximum area for a perimeter of 20 m.
e) Write an equation that relates the area of the enclosure to its length.

Reasoning About Data

GOAL

Determine whether a conjecture about the relationship between two variables is valid.

LEARN ABOUT the Math

Adrian and Maya are researching global climate change. Because of what they have heard in the news, they think that the concentration of carbon dioxide (CO_2) in the atmosphere is increasing. They read in a report that, by 2015, the atmospheric concentration of CO_2 will be above 385 parts per million (ppm).

They both found data for the atmospheric concentration of CO_2 in the Northern Hemisphere.

? Do Adrian's and Maya's data sets support the report's conjecture?

EXAMPLE 1 Verifying or rejecting a conjecture

Adrian found yearly data, but Maya found monthly data. Use their data to verify or reject the report's conjecture.

Adrian's Solution: Using a line of best fit to represent yearly data

Adrian finds these data.

Yearly Mean Atmospheric CO_2 Concentration (ppm)

Year	1995	1996	1997	1998	1999	2000	2001	2002	2003	2004
Atmospheric CO_2 Concentration (ppm)	361	363	364	367	368	369	371	373	376	377

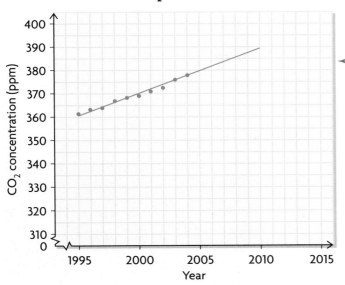

Northern Hemisphere CO₂ Concentration

> I plotted the data on a scatter plot.
>
> I saw that the data seem to lie almost perfectly on a line, so I sketched a line of best fit.

The line of best fit clearly shows the trend of the data: The carbon dioxide concentration steadily increases.

An equation for the line of best fit is

$$m = \frac{377 - 368}{2004 - 1999}$$

$$= 1.8$$

> I picked two points on the line of best fit. I read their coordinates off the graph. Then, I used the two points to calculate the slope of the line of best fit.

$$y = 1.8x + b$$
$$368 = 1.8(1999) + b$$
$$b = -3230.2$$

> I used the coordinates of one of the points on the line of best fit to calculate the value of b.

$$y = 1.8x - 3230.2$$
$$y = 1.8(2015) - 3230.2$$
$$= 3627 - 3230.2$$
$$= 396.8 \text{ ppm}$$

> I substituted 2015 for x so that I could estimate the CO₂ concentration in 2015.

If the pattern continues, the report that Maya read is correct: The atmospheric concentration of CO_2 in the Northern Hemisphere will be above 385 ppm by 2015.

Maya's Solution: Using a curve of best fit to represent monthly data

Maya obtains more detailed data. These data show the monthly variation for several years.

Monthly Mean Atmospheric CO_2 Concentration (ppm)

Year	Jan	Feb	Mar	Apr	May	Jun	Jul	Aug	Sept	Oct	Nov	Dec
1999	368.2	368.9	369.6	371.1	371.0	370.4	369.3	366.9	364.6	365.1	366.7	368.1
2000	369.1	369.5	370.5	371.7	371.8	371.7	370.1	368.1	366.6	366.7	368.3	369.5
2001	370.3	371.5	372.1	372.9	374.0	373.3	371.6	369.6	368.0	368.1	369.7	371.2
2002	372.4	373.1	373.5	374.9	375.6	375.4	374.0	371.5	370.7	370.2	372.1	373.8
2003	374.7	375.6	376.1	377.7	378.4	378.1	376.6	374.5	373.0	373.0	374.4	375.7
2004	376.7	377.4	378.4	380.5	380.6	379.6	377.8	375.9	374.1	374.2	375.9	377.5

Monthly Mean Atmospheric CO_2 Concentration

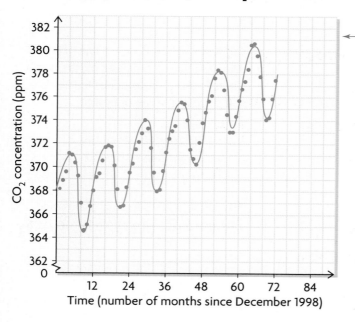

I plotted the data. I used $x = 1$ for January 1999, $x = 2$ for February 1999, and so on.

Looking at the graph, I didn't think a line of best fit would help me to approximate monthly data.

I drew a curve of best fit instead. It shows a general increasing trend, but there were short-term ups and downs in each year.

There are two trends here. ←
Year to year, atmospheric CO_2 concentration is
increasing.

These data also supported the
conjecture. But, since they are
more detailed, these data also
help show the short-term
changes in carbon dioxide
concentration.

Within each year, the CO_2 concentration decreases ←
each spring and summer, and then, increases each fall
and winter.

Looking at more detailed data
gave me new insights that I
wouldn't have had from the
yearly data alone.

I can't be certain that the report's conjecture is ←
correct.

There are 132 months
from December 2004 to
December 2015. Making a
prediction about that many
months in the future is not
reasonable.

Reflecting

A. Why do you think Adrian used a line of best fit instead of a curve of
best fit?

B. Why do you think Adrian calculated the slope of the line of best fit?

C. Could Maya have used a line of best fit instead of a curve of best fit to
show the trend in her data? Explain.

APPLY the Math

> **EXAMPLE 2**   **Reasoning about outliers**

Cristina thinks that people with higher incomes donate more money to
charities. She collects the following data.

Yearly Income ($ thousands)	21	33	40	41	46	55	68	87
Amount Donated to Charities ($)	310	450	225	240	265	180	170	120

Do the data support Cristina's conjecture?

Carla's Solution

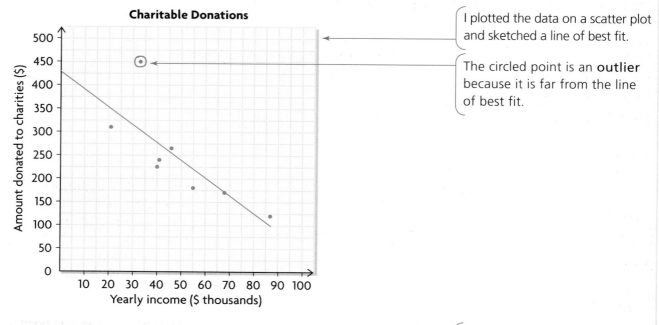

Charitable Donations

Yearly income ($ thousands)

Amount donated to charities ($)

I plotted the data on a scatter plot and sketched a line of best fit.

The circled point is an **outlier** because it is far from the line of best fit.

The line of best fit shows that the pattern of the data is decreasing. For this sample of people, the amount of money donated to charities generally decreases as income increases.

This conclusion is valid for this set of data, and does not support Cristina's conjecture.

Although there is an outlier, it does not contradict the pattern that the line of best fit shows. This means that the outlier does not support Cristina's conjecture either.

These data cannot be used to draw a conclusion about people in general, since the quantity of data is small. We have no way of knowing whether this small set of people is typical or unusual in some way.

So, in this case, it's not valid to use the line of best fit to make predictions about the general population. More data are needed.

EXAMPLE 3   Supporting a conjecture using a curve of best fit

Alison hypothesizes that adult mammals' resting heart rates, measured in beats per minute (bpm), are lower for larger species. Do the following data support Alison's conjecture?

Animal	Cow	Horse	Pig	Sheep	Sea Lion	Goat	Dog	Rabbit	Rat
Mean Resting Heart Rate (bpm)	58	52	70	75	116	79	83	257	250
Mean Mass (kg)	518	466	188	77.1	66.7	41.8	18.4	3.7	0.5

Chris's Solution

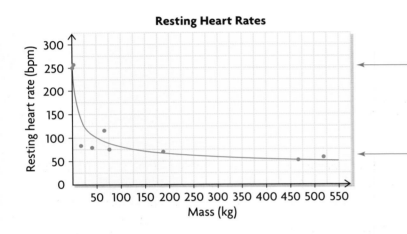

I plotted the data and drew a curve of best fit. I can see from the shape of the curve what the general trend in the data is. The curve is really steep for smaller masses and more gradual for larger masses.

If there were only one data point that showed a heart rate much higher than the rest, I might not have included it in my line or curve. But there are two points like that, so maybe they are part of a pattern and are not outliers.

The data supports Alison's conjecture.
Since there is a small quantity of data, more data would be helpful in deciding whether the conjecture is valid for a wider range of mammals. It's difficult to tell whether there is a strong pattern because there isn't a lot of data.

For small masses, as the mass of the species of animal increases, the heart rate decreases by quite a bit. Once the mass reaches a certain value (about 20 kg), as the mass increases, the decrease in heart rate is fairly small.

EXAMPLE 4   Using a scatter plot to reject a conjecture

Derek hypothesizes that a student's average mark in Grade 9 is related to his or her age. Analyze the sample of data to see if it supports his conjecture.

Age (years)	14.1	14.2	14.3	14.4	14.5	14.7	14.7	14.8	14.8
Mark (%)	61	82	73	88	64	91	65	87	68

Age (years)	14.1	14.2	14.3	14.4	14.4	14.6	14.6	14.8	14.9
Mark (%)	75	69	58	63	95	71	78	72	66

Age (years)	14.2	14.3	14.3	14.4	14.5	14.6	14.7	14.9	15.0
Mark (%)	55	57	70	82	78	60	73	80	92

Sonia's Solution

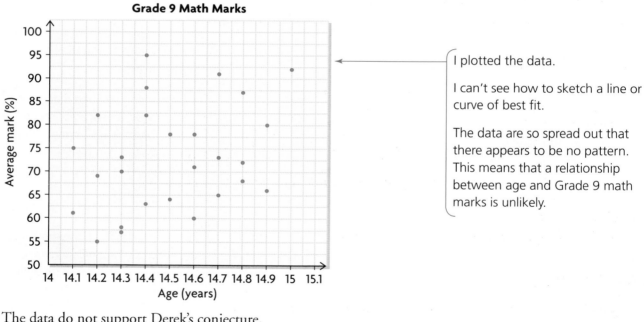

I plotted the data.

I can't see how to sketch a line or curve of best fit.

The data are so spread out that there appears to be no pattern. This means that a relationship between age and Grade 9 math marks is unlikely.

The data do not support Derek's conjecture.

In Summary

Key Ideas

- You can support or reject a conjecture about a relationship by examining trends or patterns in data.

Need to Know

- You may see a trend or pattern in plotted data; however, more detailed data might not support your original conjecture.
- If a trend or pattern in the data agrees with a conjecture, then the data support the conjecture.
- If there is no apparent trend or pattern in the data, or if there is a trend or pattern and it contradicts the conjecture, then the conjecture is not supported by the data.
- Conjectures made from data sets that contain a small number of observations may not be valid. The larger the number of observations made, the more likely the trend you see is valid.

CHECK Your Understanding

1. Consider the data for a sample of Grade 9 students.

Science Mark (%)	61	67	69	74	77	81	84	90	91	94
Math Mark (%)	62	63	60	75	70	78	89	95	84	82

   a) Make a conjecture about whether final marks in math and science are related.
   b) Plot the data on a scatter plot.
   c) Use a graph to support or reject your conjecture.

PRACTISING

2. Natalie collected this data for the heights of 14-year-old girls and their mothers.

Mother's Height (m)	1.62	1.53	1.51	1.58	1.76	1.59	1.53	1.49	1.51	1.71
Girl's Height (m)	1.55	1.55	1.57	1.61	1.68	1.75	1.62	1.56	1.54	1.61

   a) Plot the data on a scatter plot.
   b) If possible, sketch a line or curve of best fit.
   c) Is there a relationship between the variables? If so, describe it.

3. Research suggests that there is a relationship between age and
C vocabulary size for young children.

Explain how the following data can be used to support that statement.

Age (years)	1	2	2	3	3	4	4	5	5	6	6
Vocabulary Size (number of words)	10	450	500	1000	1150	1400	1600	2000	2150	2400	2750

4. Consider a car travelling on a dry asphalt road.
   a) Suppose the driver slams on the brakes. Make a conjecture about the relationship between the travelling speed and the braking distance.
   b) Consider the following data. Plot the data on a scatter plot.

Travelling Speed (km/h)	10	20	30	40	50	60	70	80	90	100
Braking Distance (m)	0.5	1.9	4.3	7.7	12.1	17.4	23.6	30.9	39.1	48.2

   c) Do the data support your conjecture? Explain.

5. Suppose you are analyzing a set of data to see if it supports your conjecture.
   a) Under what circumstances would you accept the conjecture?
   b) Under what circumstances would you reject the conjecture?
   c) Is it possible for two people to analyze the same scatter plot and reach different conclusions about the validity of a conjecture? Explain.

Extending

6. Suppose that you collected data on the total lengths of roads in Canada for the past 100 years, and the incidence of cancer for the past 100 years.
   a) If you plotted the data on a scatter plot, what would you expect a line or curve of best fit to look like?
   b) If two variables are related by a line or curve of best fit on a scatter plot, does that mean that one of the variables influences the other? Explain.

Describing Situations From Graphs

Use a given graph to describe the situation it represents.

Bill's mother sends him to the corner store for milk and tells him to be back in 30 min. The graph shown shows the relationship between his distance from home and time.

? How can the graph be used to describe Bill's trip?

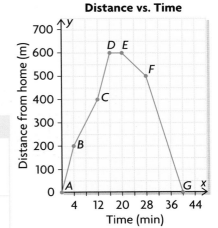

Distance vs. Time

EXAMPLE 1   **Connecting the situation to a given graph**

Use the graph to describe Bill's trip.

Marilyn's Solution

The line segments from points A to D represent his trip from his house to the store.

It took him 16 min to walk to the store.

The store is about 600 m from his home.

> The slopes of each of these lines are positive and represent the rate at which he can walk per minute. This means that as time increases his distance from home increases. This can only happen if he is walking away from home toward the store.

On his way to the store he walked at the same speed between 0 and 4 min and 12 and 16 min. He walked at a slower speed between 4 and 12 min.

> The line segments AB and CD are parallel. They have the same slope so he is walking at the same rate during these periods of time.
>
> The line segment BC is not as steep as AB and CD so its slope is less.

The line segment from D to E represents the time he spent at the store. He was at the store for about 4 min.

> DE is a horizontal line and its slope is 0. This means for this period of time between 16 and 20 minutes he wasn't walking from or to his home.

The line segments from points *E* to *G* represent his trip from the store to his house.

It took him 20 min to walk from the store to his house.

The slopes of each of these lines are negative and represent the rate at which he can walk per minute. This means that as time increases his distance from home decreases. This can only happen if he is walking away from the store toward his home.

On his trip back home he walked the fastest between 28 and 40 min. He walked at a slower rate between 20 and 28 min.

The line segment *FG* is steeper than *EF* which means between points *F* and *G* he is walking a greater distance each minute compared to the rate he walks between *E* and *F*.

Reflecting

A. In this graph, the slopes of each line segment represent a rate of change. What is another name for this rate of change?

B. Calculate the slopes of *AB*, *BC*, *DE*, *EF* and *FG*. Do these values correspond with Marilyn's analysis of the situation? Explain.

C. Did Bill make it home in 30 min? Justify your answer.

Apply the Math

EXAMPLE 2	Describing the situation from a graphical representation

A skydiver jumps from an airplane. The graph shows her height above the ground during the first 24 s of her free fall, prior to the parachute opening. Use the graph to describe her motion during this part of her jump.

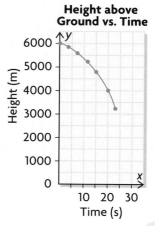

Height above Ground vs. Time

Daniel 's Solution

The graph is a curve so this is a nonlinear relationship. ← The points of the scatter plot do not lie along a straight line. The points of the scatter plot have been joined by a smooth curve since the data is continuous.

Since this is a nonlinear relationship the skydiver can't be falling at a constant rate or speed. I created a table of values by estimating the coordinates of the points on the graph and calculated the first differences. ← If the relationship was linear then the rate of change between each pair of points would be the same. This would indicate that the rate of change or speed would be constant.

Since height is on the vertical axis, it is the dependent variable and time, on the x-axis, is the independent variable. This makes sense since the skydiver's height above the ground depends on the length of time since she jumped.

Time (s)	Height (m)	First Differences
0	6000	
4	5920	−80
8	5680	−240
12	5280	−400
16	4720	−560
20	4000	−720
24	3120	−880

During the first 4 seconds she fell 80 m. Between 4 and 8 s she fell 240 m. Between 8 and 12 s she fell 400 m.

As time increases by 4 s intervals in the table, the change in height increases.

The first differences are not constant, which confirms my conjecture.

The skydiver is accelerating.

| EXAMPLE **3** | Using reasoning to connect a graph to its situation |

Suppose tap water, flowing from a faucet at a constant rate, is used to fill each of these containers.

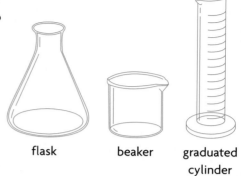

flask   beaker   graduated
                              cylinder

Match each of the following graphs with the appropriate container. Justify your choice.

A.

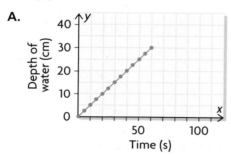

B.

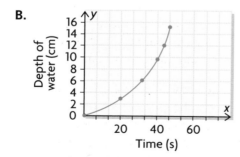

C.

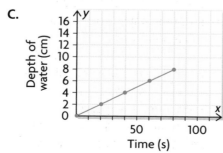

Jose's Solution

I think the flask matches with graph B.

I reasoned that as the water pours into the flask the depth of the water can't increase at a constant rate due to the flasks shape. This means the graph of water depth versus time must be nonlinear. Since the shape of the flask is wide at the bottom and narrow at the top, the water depth will increase slowly as the flask begins to fill. As the water level rises the water depth will start to increase faster as the water level gets closer to the top.

I think the graduated cylinder matches with graph A.

I reasoned that as the water pours into the graduated cylinder the depth of the water increases at a constant rate since its shape does not change. This means the graph of water depth versus time must be linear. I chose graph A over graph C because it has greater slope and it reaches a greater depth. The graph with the greater slope makes sense since the graduated cylinder is narrow the water depth will rise faster than the beaker. The graph that reaches the greater depth makes sense because the graduated cylinder is taller than the beaker.

I think the beaker matches with graph C.

I reasoned that as the water pours into the beaker the depth of the water increases at a constant rate since its shape does not change. This means the graph of water depth versus time must be linear. I chose graph C over graph A because it has less slope and it reaches a lesser depth. The graph with less slope makes sense since the beaker is wide the water depth will rise slower than the graduated cylinder. The graph that reaches the smaller depth makes sense because the beaker is not as tall as the graduated cylinder.

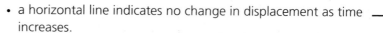
CHECK *Your Understanding*

1. Match each story to a graph on the next page that best describes the story.

a) Michael walks to school at a steady pace. He waits once for a stop light and continues to school at a faster pace. After being at school, he returns home without stopping or slowing down.

b) A log floating in a slow, steadily moving river goes through two sets of rapids before going over a waterfall into a lake.

c) A taxi driver charges a passenger to get in the cab plus a fixed amount for every 100 m.

d) A skydiver enters a plane that takes off and climbs at a steady rate. He jumps out and free-falls until the parachute opens. He descends the rest of the way at a constant speed.

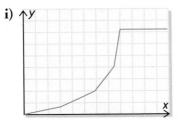

i)

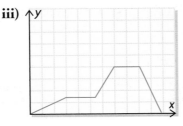

iii)

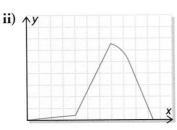

ii)

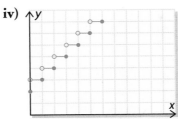

iv)

2. This graph shows how an all terrain vehicle (ATV) travels over time.

a) Over what interval of time is the ATV travelling the slowest? the fastest?

b) When does the ATV start to return to its starting point? When does it get there?

c) Determine the slope of the graph between 20 s and 26 s.

d) What does a zero slope mean in the context of this graph?

3. Describe a situation that could match this graph.

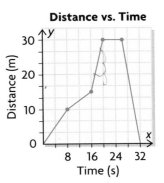

Distance vs. Time

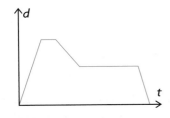

PRACTISING

4. A drag racer begins from a stopped position and drives the length of a race track. The graph shows the distance from his starting position after each second of his run.

a) Does the data represent a linear or nonlinear relationship?

b) Verify your answer to part a by creating a table of values and calculate the first differences.

c) Describe the motion of the drag racer as it moves down the drag strip to the finish line.

d) Once the drag racer crosses the finish line a parachute opens to slow it down. Redraw the graph to show what this might look like as the drag racer slows to a stop.

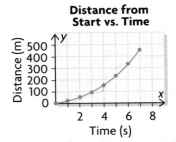

Distance from Start vs. Time

5. Write a story for each graph.

a)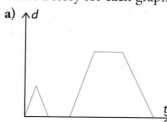

b)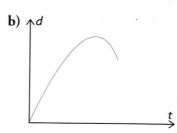

c)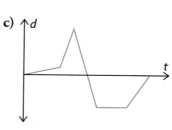

d)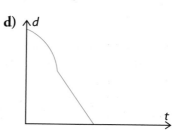

6. Water is poured into this container at a constant rate. Draw a graph that represents this situation where d is depth and t is time.

7. a) Plot each set of data, and then, determine if it represents a linear or nonlinear relationship. Justify your decision.

b) In each set of data, determine if the object is accelerating, decelerating, moving at a constant velocity, or a combination of all three.

i)

Time (s)	Distance (m)
7	19
8	22
9	25
10	28
11	31

ii)

Time (s)	Distance (m)
10	35
11	37
12	38
13	38.5
14	38.75

iii)

Time (s)	Distance (m)
0	0
1	7
2	16
3	29

8. A driver leaves at 8:00 a.m. and drives 120 km by 9:30 a.m. From then
A until 10:30 a.m., she travels another 50 km. She drives an additional
200 km by 12:30 p.m. She travels at a constant speed during each
period of time.
  a) Draw the distance-time graph that represents the trip.
  b) When is the car travelling the fastest? the slowest?
  c) What type of relationship is this?
  d) What is the average speed for the entire trip?

9. A baseball is hit straight up into the air. The table shows the height of
the ball after various time intervals.
  a) Does the data represent a linear or nonlinear relationship?
  b) Graph the data.
  c) What is the height of the ball after 1.5 s?
  d) When will the baseball be at 44 m?
  e) When is the ball accelerating? Decelerating?
  f) When is the ball stopped?
  g) What is the maximum height the ball reaches?
  h) What effect does gravity have on the velocity of the ball?

Time (s)	Height (m)
0	1
1	26
2	41
3	46
4	41
5	26
6	1

10. The table shows the length of time needed to drive 100 km at
various speeds.
  a) Copy and complete the table by determining the missing times.

$$\left(time = \frac{distance}{speed} \right)$$

  b) Graph the data. What is the dependent variable? the independent
  variable?
  c) Select three points on the graph that are separated by equal
  intervals of speed. Calculate the rate triangles between the first and
  second points and between the second and third points. Are the
  values the same or different?
  d) Is the relationship linear or nonlinear?

Speed (km/h)	Time (h)
100	1
75	
50	
25	
12.5	
10	
1	

11. A race car travels around a race track. The
graph of speed vs. time for the first lap by the
car is shown.
  a) What do the increasing parts of the graph
  represent? the decreasing parts?
  b) What do the horizontal parts of the graph
  represent?
  c) Using the graph, tell a story about the car
  as it makes its first lap around the track.

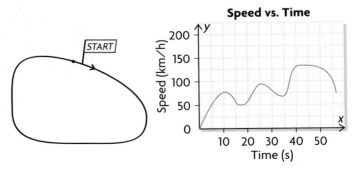

Speed vs. Time

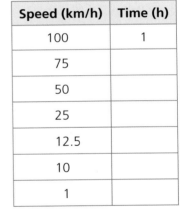

12. Draw the side profile of two different shaped containers that you could
T fill with water. For each shape you drew, draw the graph that shows the
relationship between water depth and time as the container fills with
water. Explain why you drew the graphs you did.

13. Draw a graph of speed versus time as a car makes one circuit of each
C track. The arrow shows the direction the car is moving.

a)

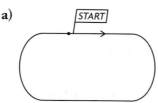

c)

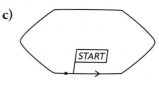

b)

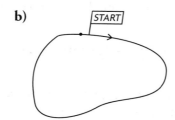

d)

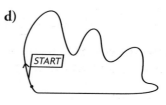

Extending

14. Sheila takes a driver education course
before applying for her driver's licence. One
of the topics studied is the relationship
between speed and stopping distance.
The instructor gives Sheila the table
on the right.

a) Graph the data using stopping
distance as the dependent variable.

b) Determine the rate triangle from
60 km/h to 70 km/h and from
70 km/h to 80 km/h.

c) What do you notice about the rate of
change in stopping distance as the
speed increases by 10 km/h in part b)?

d) Sheila says, "If I drive twice as fast,
I just need to leave twice as much
distance between my car and the car
in front of me." Explain whether this
is accurate.

Speed (km/h)	Stopping Distance (m)
10	3.7
20	7.6
30	12.0
40	17.1
50	22.9
60	29.8
70	37.9
80	47.5
90	58.6
100	71.6
110	86.5
120	103.5
130	122.8
140	144.7

FREQUENTLY ASKED *Questions*

Q: How can you determine a curve of best fit?

A: Plot the data on a scatter plot. If you notice that the plotted points do not seem to lie on a line, but seem to lie close to a fairly simple curve, then draw a curve of best fit to approximate the points.

Q: How can you use a curve of best fit to predict values not recorded in the data?

A: Use the curve of best fit to estimate the coordinates between recorded data points. Extend the curve of best fit to estimate the coordinates of points beyond the recorded data points.

Q: How can you test a conjecture about a pattern in data or a relationship between variables?

A: Plot the data on a scatter plot. Then, examine the pattern of the data points and the line or curve of best fit (if one exists) to see if it matches the conjecture.

> **Study | Aid**
> - See Lesson 6.3, Example 1.
> - Try Chapter Review Questions 5 and 6.

> **Study | Aid**
> - See Lesson 6.3, Examples 1, 2, and 3.
> - Try Chapter Review Question 7.

> **Study | Aid**
> - See Lesson 6.4, Examples 1 and 2.
> - Try Chapter Review Questions 12, 13, and 14.

EXAMPLE

Consider the conjecture that the period of a pendulum increases if its length increases. The scatter plot supports this conjecture, since the curve of best fit matches the conjecture.

Q: How can you interpret and describe a situation from a displacement or distance vs. time graph?

A: If the graph contains a series of different line segments, then use your knowledge of slope and constant rates of change to interpret what the graph represents. Line segments that rise indicate that displacement increases as time increases. Line segments that fall indicate that displacement decreases as time increases. Horizontal line segments indicate that there is no change in displacement as time increases.

If the graph is nonlinear and curved, then discuss how the rates of change differ between consecutive points on the graph. This will help you decide if an object is speeding up or slowing down.

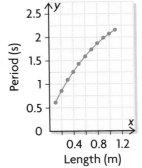

Period of a Pendulum vs. Length

> **Study | Aid**
> - See Lesson 6.5, Examples 1, 2, and 3.
> - Try Chapter Review Question 10.

PRACTICE Questions

Lesson 6.1

1. What might a scatter plot look like, if it shows a relationship between allergies and the cleanliness of the air we breathe? Explain the expected relationship.

2. Suppose you are studying the possible relationship between the variables "Available Money" and "Number of Days After Payday."
   a) When plotting the data, which variable would you choose for the independent variable? Which would be the dependent variable? Explain.
   b) Draw a possible scatter plot.
   c) Describe the relationship in your scatter plot.

Lesson 6.2

3. The scatter plot below shows the graphics quality (on a scale of 1 to 10) for a video game when it is played on various computers.
   a) Is the line of best fit appropriate? If so, explain why. If not, sketch a more appropriate one.
   b) Determine the equation of the most appropriate line of best fit.

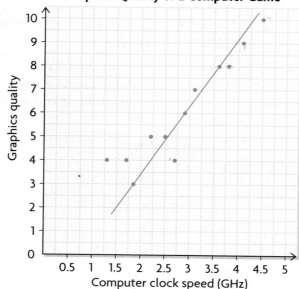

Graphics Quality of a Computer Game

4. Students in Ryan's social science class collected data to study whether marks scored on a test were related to the number of hours of TV watched the night before the test. Data were collected for 10 students.

Test Mark (%)	Hours of TV Watched
82	2
64	4
84	0
70	3
74	2
76	2
85	1
73	3
94	1
90	2

   a) Draw a scatter plot of the data.
   b) Do the data show a pattern? If so, describe it.
   c) Draw a line of best fit for the data.
   d) Determine an equation for your line of best fit.
   e) Using your line of best fit, predict the test score for a student who watched 2.5 h of TV.
   f) Do you expect your prediction to be the same as all of your classmates' predictions? Explain.

5. Sometimes a solid line is used to draw a line of best fit, while at other times a dashed line is used.
   a) Explain why these two different types of lines of best fit are used on scatter plots that show linear relationships.
   b) Provide an example of two variables whose scatter plot of data could result in a solid line of best fit.
   c) Provide an example of two variables whose scatter plot of data could result in a dashed line of best fit.

Lesson 6.3

6. The scatter plot shows the population of a colony of wolves in a wilderness region of Northern Ontario.

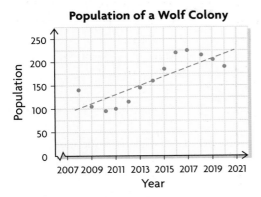

Population of a Wolf Colony

a) Explain whether the line of best fit is appropriate.
b) Would a curve of best fit be more appropriate? If so, sketch one. If not, explain why not.
c) Might both a line of best fit and a curve of best fit be appropriate? Explain.

7. Is it necessary for a line or curve of best fit to pass through any of the plotted points? Explain.

8. Data are collected on shoe sizes and heights for men.

Shoe Size	8.5	9.0	9.0	10.0	10.5
Height (cm)	166	174	169	178	175

Shoe Size	10.5	11.0	11.5	12.0	12.5
Height (cm)	183	187	182	190	184

a) Draw a scatter plot of the data.
b) Do the data show a pattern? If so, describe it.
c) Draw a line or curve of best fit for the data.
d) If you have drawn a line of best fit, determine an equation for it.
e) Using your line or curve of best fit, predict the shoe size of a man who is 180 cm tall.
f) Using your line or curve of best fit, predict the height of a man whose shoe size is 17.5.

Lesson 6.4

9. Do you think that the number of chess grandmasters in a country is related to the size of its population?
a) Formulate a conjecture about the relationship.
b) Consider the data for a sample of countries. Plot the data on a scatter plot.

Country	Population (millions)	Number of Grandmasters
Canada	33	6
U.S.A.	300	61
Russia	142	159
Ukraine	46	58
Iceland	0.3	10
China	1317	19
Netherlands	16	21
Hungary	10	37
Serbia	10	49
Germany	82	61

c) If possible, sketch a line or curve of best fit.
d) Is there a relationship between the variables? If so, describe it.
e) Suggest other influences on the number of grandmasters in a country.

10. A hotel courtesy bus takes David from the airport to his hotel. Use the Distance versus Time graph to create a story that traces the route of the bus.

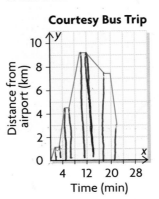

Courtesy Bus Trip

Investigating Relationships **375**

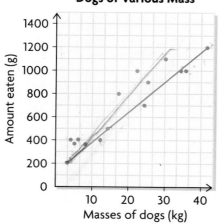

Amount Eaten by Dogs of Various Mass

1. The scatter plot at the left shows the amount of food eaten in a day by dogs of various masses. If the line of best fit is appropriate, explain why. If it is not appropriate, explain how you would draw an appropriate line.

2. The table shows the lengths of a sample of lake trout at various ages.

Age (years)	3	4	5	6	7	3	4	5	3	4	5	6
Length (cm)	28	34	40	42	48	30	34	40	28	34	36	37

   a) Which variable would you choose as the independent variable? Explain.
   b) Are the data continuous or discrete? Explain.
   c) Predict the relationship between the two variables.
   d) Plot the data on a scatter plot.
   e) Does the graph support your prediction? Explain.

3. Choose the statement that is true.
   A. A line of best fit must pass through at least one or two plotted points.
   B. If a line of best fit does not pass through at least two plotted points, then it is not possible to determine its slope.
   C. It is sometimes possible to draw both a line of best fit and a curve of best fit to approximate plotted points.
   D. A curve of best fit is more accurate than a line of best fit, since it can curve closer to the plotted points.

4. Grant leads a team of high school students who speak to elementary school students about the health problems that result from smoking cigarettes. Each high school student is responsible for one elementary school. Data on the number of hours spent by each high school student (in a year) and the corresponding number of smokers in each elementary school are summarized in the table.

Speaking Time (h)	24	31	40	41	50	29	38	62	47
Number of Smokers	36	27	16	10	3	23	20	1	19

   a) Plot the data on a scatter plot.
   b) Describe the pattern in the data.
   c) Sketch a line or curve of best fit, whichever is more appropriate.
   d) Can you conclude that the program of speaking to elementary school students has been effective in reducing smoking? Explain.

5. Choose the best ending for the sentence. "For a scatter plot,
  A. it is always possible to draw a line of best fit."
  B. it is always possible to draw a curve of best fit."
  C. it is always possible to draw either a line of best fit or a curve of best fit."
  D. none of the choices in A., B., or C. are true."

6. In the Kingdom of Petrodalla, the total length of all roads has increased over the past few decades, as has the percentage of the population that suffers from asthma. The data are summarized in the table:

Year	1980	1985	1990	1995	2000	2005	2010
Total Road Length (km)	105	123	147	161	201	240	310
Incidence of Asthma (%)	5	8	12	16	22	25	29

  a) Plot the data on a scatter plot. Use Road Length as the independent variable and the Incidence of Asthma as the dependent variable.
  b) Sketch a line of best fit.
  c) Determine the equation of your line of best fit.
  d) Use your equation to predict the percentage incidence of asthma when the total road length is 400 km.
  e) Since the percentage of asthma sufferers increases as the total length of the roads increases, Marianne concludes that roads cause asthma. Is this a valid conclusion? Explain.

7. Shasta runs one kilometre each day as part of her daily exercise. The graph shows her distance from home as she runs her route.

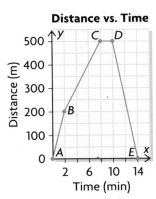

Distance vs. Time

  a) Between what two points does Shasta run the fastest?
  b) Describe what is happening between points C and D.
  c) When does Shasta begin to travel toward home?
  d) How long does it take her to get home?
  e) How fast was she running back home?

Up In Arms

Ananda and Justin watched a TV program on how archaeologists estimate the height of people who lived long ago. If scientists are able to find certain bones from a skeleton, they can use these to estimate the height of that person. One of these bones is the humerus, the upper arm bone that connects the shoulder to the elbow. The students wonder whether the relationship between the length of the humerus and a person's height is also valid for their classmates.

❓ **Is the height of a person related to the length of his or her humerus?**

A. Measure the height and length of humerus for 15 people in your class. Organize the data into a table.

B. Use your table from part A to create a scatter plot of the data.

C. Is there a relationship between the two variables? If so, describe it.

D. Sketch a line or curve of best fit, if appropriate.

E. Measure the humerus length of your teacher, or some other person not already in your data set. Use your line or curve of best fit to predict the height of the person. Then, measure the height of the person and comment on how accurate your prediction was.

F. Repeat part E, but this time measure the height and predict the humerus length.

G. Summarize your findings.

Task | Checklist

✔ Did you construct the table of values accurately?

✔ Did you plot the data correctly?

✔ Did you select the dependent and independent variables appropriately?

✔ Did you use the appropriate type of line or curve of best fit (solid or dashed)?

✔ Did you discuss whether it is appropriate to use your line or curve of best fit to extrapolate?

Multiple Choice

1. Andrew has two jobs in sales. He earns a commission of 4% on sales at a clothing store and 5% commission on sales at a shoe store. Last week Andrew earned $700. What equation describes this situation?
  A. $4c + 0.5s = 700$
  B. $40c + 50s = 700$
  C. $0.04c + 0.05s = 700$
  D. $5s + 4c = 700$

2. The solution to $-2x - 4 = 2$ is:
  A. $x = 0$
  B. $x = -3$
  C. $x = 2$
  D. $x = 4$

3. The next step in the solution of $-x - 28 = 3x$ could be:
  A. $2x - 28 = 0$
  B. $-28 = 2x$
  C. $-x - 28 = 0$
  D. $-28 = 4x$

4. Daniel builds rocking chairs and tables in his shop. It takes him 4 h to build a rocking chair and 7 h to build a table. Last week he worked 50 h. What equation expresses the number of tables he made in terms of the number of rocking chairs?
  A. $t = \dfrac{50 - 4r}{7}$
  B. $r = \dfrac{50 - 7t}{4}$
  C. $50 - 4r = 7t$
  D. $4r + 7t = 50$

5. Which of the following is true for the graph of $3x + 4y = 24$?
  A. The slope is -3.
  B. The x-intercept is 8.
  C. The y-intercept is 8.
  D. $(3, 2)$ is a point on the graph.

6. Which equation will let you solve $12 - 3y = 5x$ for y?
  A. $-3y = 5x - 12$
  B. $y = \dfrac{12 - 5x}{-3}$
  C. $y = 5x + 4$
  D. $y = \dfrac{12 - 5x}{3}$

7. Which equation represents a line with slope -4 and a y-intercept of 3?
  A. $x = -4y + 3$
  B. $y = -4x + 3$
  C. $x - 4y + 3 = 0$
  D. $-4x + y + 3 = 0$

8. The slope m and y-intercept b of the line $4x + 3y + 1 = 0$ are:
  A. $m = -4, b = 1$
  B. $m = -\dfrac{4}{3}, b = -\dfrac{1}{3}$
  C. $m = \dfrac{4}{3}, b = \dfrac{1}{3}$
  D. $m = \dfrac{3}{4}, b = -1$

9. The slope of the line that passes through $(5, -3)$ and $(-2, -1)$ is:
  A. $\dfrac{2}{7}$
  B. $-\dfrac{2}{7}$
  C. $\dfrac{7}{2}$
  D. $-\dfrac{7}{2}$

10. Which ordered pair is a solution to the pair of equations $3m + 2n = 13$ and $4m - 10 = n$?
A. $(3, 2)$
B. $(4, 6)$
C. $(5, -1)$
D. $(0, 5)$

11. The point $(5, 3)$ is the intersection of a pair of lines. If one line is represented by the equation $y = 2x - 7$, the equation of the other line is:
A. $y = 3x + 8$
B. $y = -x + 8$
C. $y = 2x - 4$
D. $y = x + 2$

12. Select the line that best represents the line of best fit for this scatter plot.

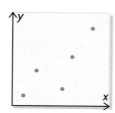

A.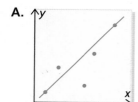

C.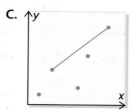

B.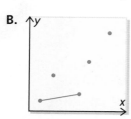

D.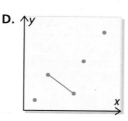

13. Which of the following pair of lines are perpendicular?
A. line 1: $m = \frac{2}{3}$ and line 2: $m = \frac{3}{2}$
B. line 1: $m = -\frac{3}{5}$ and line 2: $m = -\frac{3}{5}$
C. line 1: $m = -\frac{4}{3}$ and line 2: $m = \frac{3}{4}$
D. line 1: $m = \frac{7}{3}$ and line 2: $m = -\frac{7}{3}$

14. Which of these statements is true?
A. The line of best fit is drawn before the scatter plot is prepared.
B. The scatter plot is not required to draw the line of best fit.
C. The scatter plot is prepared before the line of best fit is drawn.
D. All the points of the scatter plot must lie on the line of best fit.

15. Use the line of best fit to predict the amount of rainfall for the ninth month of the year.

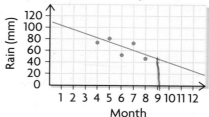

A. 50 mm
B. 40 mm
C. 30 mm
D. 20 mm

16. Suppose the pattern of the points in a scatter plot sloped up to the right. How can the relationship between the variables be described?
A. As the independent variable increases, the dependent variable decreases.
B. No relationship exists between the variables.
C. As the independent variable increases, the dependent variable increases.
D. As the independent variable increases, the dependent variable stays the same.

17. Which of the following pairs of lines are parallel and rise from left to right?
A. line 1: $m = -5$ and line 2: $m = -5$
B. line 1: $m = \frac{2}{3}$ and line 2: $m = -\frac{2}{3}$
C. line 1: $m = -\frac{4}{5}$ and line 2: $m = -0.8$
D. line 1: $m = \frac{5}{8}$ and line 2: $m = 0.625$

Investigation

When will women run faster than men?

For many years, the winning times for 100 m sprint at the Olympics have been dropping for both men and women. Some people claim that the female sprinters' times have been improving more quickly than the men's. They say that eventually, the fastest human on earth will be a woman.

Year	Women's 100 m Sprint		Time (s)	Men's 100 m Sprint		Time (s)
	Sprinter			Sprinter		
1936	Helen Stephens	USA	11.5	Jesse Owens	USA	10.3
1948	Fanny Blankers-Koen	NED	11.9	Harrison Dillard	USA	10.3
1952	Marjorie Jackson	AUS	11.5	Lindy Remigino	USA	10.4
1956	Betty Cuthbert	AUS	11.5	Bobby Morrow	USA	10.5
1960	Wilma Rudolph	USA	11.0	Armin Hary	FRG	10.2
1964	Wyomia Tyus	USA	11.4	Robert Hayes	USA	10.0
1968	Wyomia Tyus	USA	11.0	Jim Hines	USA	9.9
1972	Renate Stecher	GDR	11.07	Valeriy Borzov	URS	10.14
1976	Annegret Richter	FRG	11.08	Hassely Crawford	URS	10.08
1980	Lyudmila Kondratyeva	URS	11.06	Allan Wells	GBR	10.25
1984	Evelyn Ashford	USA	10.97	Carl Lewis	USA	9.99
1988	Florence Griffith-Joyner	USA	10.54	Carl Lewis	USA	9.92
1992	Gail Devers	USA	10.82	Linford Christie	GBR	9.96
1996	Gail Devers	USA	10.94	Donovan Bailey	CAN	9.84
2000	Marion Jones	USA	10.75	Maurice Greene	USA	9.87
2004	Yuliya Nesterenko	BLR	10.93	Justin Gatlin	USA	9.85

18. a) Use the data above to create a scatter plot for the 100 m winning times for women.
  b) Draw a line of best fit for the data.
  c) Repeat parts a) and b) for the men's times using the same grid.
  d) Use the graphs to predict if and when the women's winning time will be faster than the men's.
  e) Use the equations of the lines of best fit to validate your answer.

Properties of 2-D Figures

▸ **GOALS**

You will be able to

- Determine and apply properties of exterior and interior angles of polygons

- Determine and apply properties of the diagonals and the shapes formed by joining the midpoints of polygons

- Make and test conjectures based on investigations of geometric properties

? Examine the quadrilaterals in the picture.
What is the least number of angles you would have to measure to determine all the angles in each quadrilateral?

7 Getting Started

WORDS YOU NEED to Know

1. Match each word with the picture that best represents it.

a) parallelogram
b) rhombus
c) trapezoid
d) rectangle
e) diagonal
f) midpoint
g) isosceles triangle
h) equilateral triangle

i)

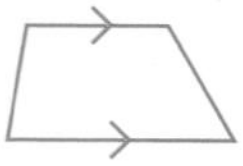

iii)

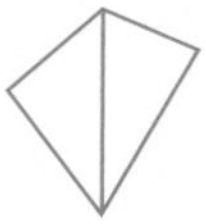

v)

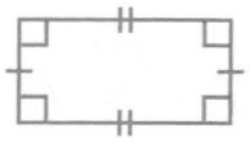

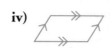

vii)

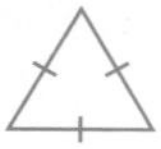

ii)

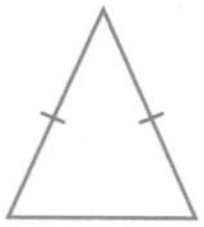

iv)

vi)

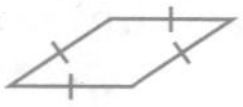

viii)

SKILLS AND CONCEPTS You Need

Straight Angles

The sum of angles that form a straight angle is 180°.
$\angle a + \angle b = 180°$

Study | *Aid*

- For more help and practice, see Appendix A-16.

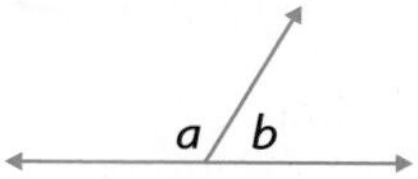

EXAMPLE

Determine the value of the unknown angle.

Solution

Since $\angle x$ and 77° form a straight angle, their sum is 180°.

$$77° + \angle x = 180°$$
$$\angle x = 180° - 77°$$
$$\angle x = 103°$$

2. Determine each unknown angle.

a)

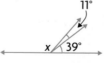

b)

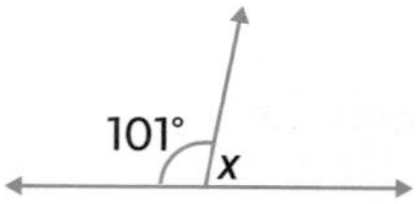

Interior and Exterior Angles of a Triangle

The sum of the interior angles in a triangle is 180°.
$\angle a + \angle b + \angle c = 180°$
Each exterior angle equals the sum of the two interior angles opposite it.

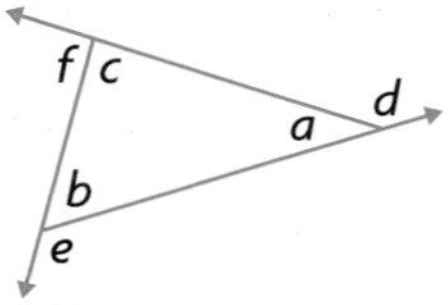

$\angle d = \angle b + \angle c$	$\angle e = \angle a + \angle c$	$\angle f = \angle a + \angle b$

EXAMPLE

Determine the value for the unknown angle.

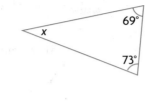

Solution

The sum of the interior angles in a triangle is $180°$.

$$\angle x + 73° + 69° = 180°$$
$$\angle x = 180° - 69° - 73°$$
$$\angle x = 38°$$

3. Determine the value of each unknown angle.

a)

b)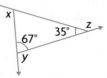

Angle Properties of Parallel Lines

When a transversal crosses 2 parallel lines:

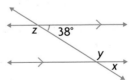

- Corresponding angles are equal.

  $\angle a = \angle e$ $\angle c = \angle g$

  $\angle b = \angle f$ $\angle d = \angle h$

- Alternate angles are equal.

  $\angle b = \angle h$ $\angle c = \angle e$

- The sum of the interior angles on the same side of the transversal is $180°$.

  $\angle b + \angle e = 180°$ $\angle c + \angle h = 180°$

EXAMPLE

Determine the values of the unknown angles.
Explain your solution.

Solution

- $\angle x = 38°$ since the angles are
  corresponding angles.
- The sum of the interior angles on the same side of the transversal is $180°$.
  This means that $\angle y = 180° - 38° = 142°$.
- $\angle z = \angle y = 142°$ since the two angles are alternate angles.

4. Determine the values of the unknown angles. Explain your solution.

a)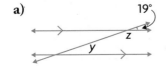

b)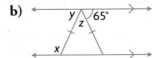

Study | *Aid*

• For help, see the Review of Essential Skills and Knowledge Appendix.

Question	Appendix
5 and 7	A-16
6, 8, and 9	A-17

PRACTICE

5. Match each property to its corresponding word.
  a) two lines at right angles to each other
  b) two angles or sides next to each other
  c) two straight lines that do not intersect
  d) identical in size and shape
  e) two angles whose sum is 180°
  f) a line that intersects two or more other lines
  g) an angle of 180°
  h) a polygon with equal sides and angles

  i) parallel
  ii) regular
  iii) transversal
  iv) perpendicular
  v) congruent
  vi) adjacent
  vii) straight angle
  viii) supplementary

6. Describe a difference and a similarity for each pair of shapes.
  a) a square and a rhombus
  b) a rectangle and a parallelogram
  c) a rhombus and a parallelogram
  d) an equilateral triangle and an isosceles triangle

7. Find each missing value.

  a)

  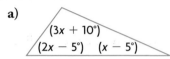

  b)

  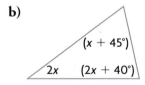

  c)

  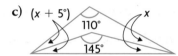

  d)

  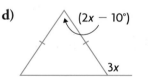

8. This web diagram classifies quadrilaterals.
  a) Copy the diagram into your notebook and draw any missing lines.
  b) Explain why these lines are needed.

  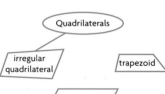

9. Name a quadrilateral with each property using the web diagram from question 8.
  a) four congruent sides
  b) four different angles
  c) two pairs of congruent sides
  d) two pairs of congruent angles
  e) only two right angles
  f) two acute angles and two obtuse angles

  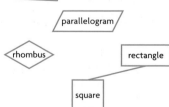

APPLYING *What You Know*

Triangle Tearing

Alyssa tore the corners off a triangular card. She noticed that when she put the three corners together, they seemed to form a straight line.

? Will the three corners of every triangle form a straight line?

A. Draw two copies of a large **equilateral** triangle.

Colour the corners and label them *A*, *B*, and *C*.

B. Cut out one copy.

C. Tear off the corners *A*, *B*, and *C*.

D. Fit the three corners together. Do they form a form a straight line?

E. Repeat parts A to D for triangles like these.

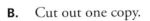

| right triangle | isosceles triangle | obtuse triangle | scalene triangle |

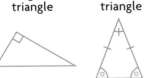

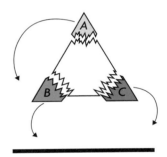

F. Go back to the uncut copy of each triangle.
Extend one side at each vertex. You have formed three new angles.

What do you think the sum of these angles is for each triangle?

G. For each triangle, cut out and then fit the three new angles together and measure their sum.

What do you notice?

H. You formed straight lines with the three corners of each triangle. What does this tell you about the sum of the angles of a triangle?

You formed circles with the outside angles of each triangle. What does this tell you about the sum of the outside angles of a triangle?

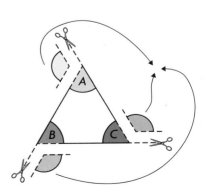

Exploring Interior Angles of Polygons

YOU WILL NEED
- grid paper
- protractor
- dynamic geometry software (optional)

interior angle

the angle formed inside each vertex of a polygon (e.g., $\triangle ABC$ has three interior angles: $\angle ABC$, $\angle BCA$, and $\angle CAB$)

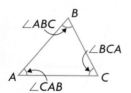

Communication | Tip

An *n*-sided polygon is often called an *n*-gon. So, a 20-sided polygon is called a 20-gon.

GOAL

Investigate the sum of the interior angles of polygons.

EXPLORE the Math

Denise created a triangle on the computer.

She began a pattern of polygons by adding non-overlapping right triangles.

Denise thought, "I know the sum of the **interior angles** of a triangle is 180°. I wonder if I can determine the sum of the angles of any polygon using non-overlapping triangles."

? How can you determine the sum of the interior angles of a 20-gon?

A. Draw a quadrilateral.

B. Estimate the sum of the interior angles and confirm it by measuring.

C. Draw as many non-overlapping diagonals as you can inside the figure.

D. Calculate the sum of the angles of all the triangles.

Compare to your answer from part A.

E. Repeat parts A to D for each polygon in the table on the next page.

Polygon	Number of Sides	Number of Triangles	Sum of Interior Angles	Sketch of Polygon
triangle	3	1	180° (180° × 1)	
quadrilateral	4	2	360° (180° × 2)	
pentagon	5	3	540° (180° × 3)	
hexagon	6	4	720	
heptagon	7	5	900	
octagon	8	6	1080	
n-gon	*n*	7	1260	

Tech | *Support*

For help on constructing a line segment, a triangle, or a polygon; measuring interior angles; or performing a calculation in *The Geometer's Sketchpad*, see Appendix B-16, B-20, B-21, and B-23.

F. Complete the table on the right.

Graph the ordered pairs in it.

x: Sides	*y*: Sum of Interior Angles
3	180°
4	360°
5	540°

G. What relationship do you see in your graph?

Explain whether you would join the points.

H. Write the equation of the line.

What is the slope?

What is the *y*-intercept for the linear relationship?

I. Determine the sum of the interior angles of any 20-gon using your equation from part H.

Reflecting

J. Why must the triangles in parts C and D not overlap?

K. What is the formula for the sum of the interior angles of any polygon? Write the formula two ways.

In Summary

Key Ideas

- You can draw non-intersecting diagonals to divide the interior of an *n*-gon into *n* − 2 non-overlapping triangles.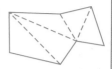
- The sum of the interior angles of an *n*-gon is (*n* − 2) × 180°.

Need to Know

- The sum of the interior angles of a triangle is 180°.
- The sum of the interior angles of a quadrilateral is 360°.

FURTHER *Your Understanding*

1. Copy the following polygons. Draw as many non-intersecting diagonals as possible to create non-overlapping triangles. What is the sum of the interior angles in each case?

    a)    **b)** 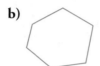   **c)**    **d)**

2. Calculate the sum of the interior angles of each polygon.

    a) 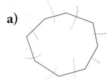   **b)**    **c)** 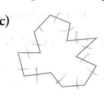   **d)**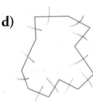

Communication | *Tip*

Regular polygons have equal sides and equal interior angles. Irregular polygons do not.

3. Polygon A is a regular 10-gon and polygon B is an irregular 10-gon. Are the sums of their interior angles equal? Explain.

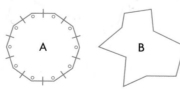

4. What is the measure of each interior angle of a regular 14-gon?

5. The sum of the interior angles in a polygon is 1440°. How many sides does the polygon have?

GOAL

Apply the exterior and interior angle properties of polygons.

INVESTIGATE *the Math*

Regan set up an orienteering trail around the lake at summer camp. Her trail formed a **convex polygon,** instead of a **concave polygon.** She measured the turn angles, or **exterior angles,** on her trail.

Regan's Trail

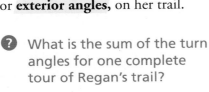

turn angle   turn angle   turn angle   turn angle   start

? What is the sum of the turn angles for one complete tour of Regan's trail?

A. Draw a rectangle.

B. Measure its interior and exterior angles.

Determine the sum of the exterior angles.

C. Repeat parts A and B for several different convex quadrilaterals.

D. Repeat parts A and B for several different convex polygons with five sides or more.

E. Cut out the exterior angles of each polygon.

Place the angles together so the vertices all touch.

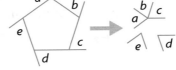

F. What do you notice?

What does this tell you about the sum of the turn angles on Regan's trail?

Reflecting

G. How are the exterior and interior angles at each vertex of a convex polygon related?

H. What conclusions can you draw about the sum of the exterior angles of any convex polygon?

YOU WILL NEED

- protractor
- scissors
- dynamic geometry software (optional)

convex polygon

a polygon with every interior angle less than 180°; any straight line through it crosses, at most, two sides

concave polygon

a polygon with at least one interior angle greater than 180°; a straight line through it may cross more than two sides

exterior angle

the angle formed by extending a side of a convex polygon; the angle between any extended side and its adjacent side

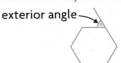

exterior angle

Tech | *Support*

For help on constructing and measuring exterior angles in *The Geometer's Sketchpad*, see Appendix B-22.

APPLY the Math

EXAMPLE **1**	Connecting exterior angle sums to interior angles

What is the sum of the exterior angles in a regular octagon?

Jordan's Solution

$$\text{sum of interior angles} = 180° \times (n - 2)$$
$$= 180° \times (8 - 2)$$
$$= 180° \times 6$$
$$= 1080°$$

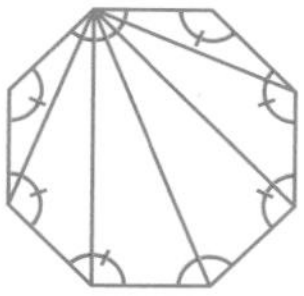

The sum was 1080°. ◄——————

> There were 8 sides, so there were $8 - 2 = 6$ triangles.
>
> I calculated the sum of the interior angles using the formula $180° \times (n - 2)$ where n is the number of sides.

$$\text{measure of one angle} = \frac{1080°}{8}$$
$$= 135°$$

> The interior angles are equal. So, I divided by 8 to determine their measure.

$$\text{exterior angle} + \text{interior angle} = 180°$$
$$\text{Therefore, one exterior angle} = 180° - \text{interior angle}$$
$$= 180° - 135°$$
$$= 45° \blacktriangleleft$$

> Each exterior angle and adjacent interior angle add to 180°. So, the measure of each exterior angle was 45°.

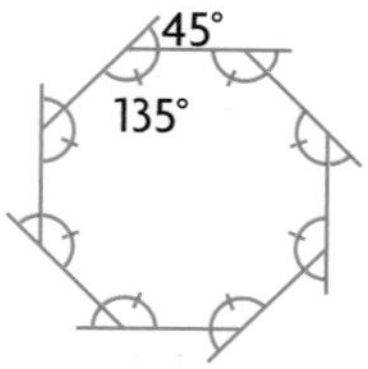

$$\text{sum of exterior angles} = 8 \times 45°$$
$$= 360°$$
The sum of the exterior angles was 360°.

> There were 8 exterior angles, so I multiplied by 8.

In any regular *n*-gon the exterior angles are equal. This helps you determine their measure if you know the value of *n*.

EXAMPLE 2 | **Determining exterior angles using reasoning**

Determine the measure of each exterior angle in a regular 11-gon.

Lakmini's Solution

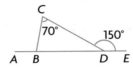

$$e = \frac{360°}{n}$$
$$= \frac{360°}{11}$$
$$\doteq 33°$$

> I knew the exterior angles are equal and add to 360° in any regular convex polygon.
>
> I divided 360° by the number of exterior angles.

Each exterior angle is about 33°.

EXAMPLE 3 | **Solving a problem using angle properties**

Determine the measure of $\angle CBA$.

Regan's Solution

$$\angle CDB = 180° - \angle CDE$$
$$= 180° - 150°$$
$$= 30°$$

> I saw that $\angle CDB$ and $\angle CDE$ were the interior and exterior angles at vertex D. So, they add to 180°.

$$\angle CBD + \angle CDB + \angle BCD = 180°$$
$$\angle CBD + 30° + 70° = 180°$$
$$\angle CBD + 100° = 180°$$
$$\angle CBD = 80°$$

> I knew the sum of the interior angles in a triangle is 180°.

$$\angle CBA = 180° - \angle CBD$$
$$= 180° - 80°$$
$$= 100°$$

> $\angle CBA$ and $\angle CBD$ add to 180°. This is because they were the interior and exterior angles at vertex B.

Properties of 2-D Figures **393**

In Summary

Key Ideas

- You can determine unknown angles in polygons using angle properties.
- The sum of the exterior angles of a convex polygon is 360°.

Need to Know

- You can form an exterior angle for a convex polygon by extending a side past its endpoint.
- An exterior angle and its adjacent interior angle are supplementary; they add to 180°.

CHECK *Your Understanding*

1. What is the relationship between the interior angle and the exterior angle at each vertex of a polygon?

2. Determine the measure of each missing angle.

   a)

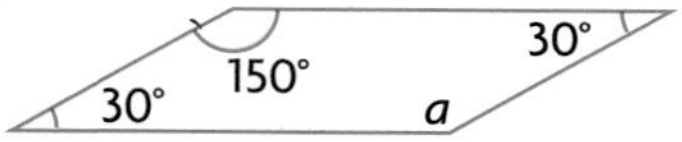

   b)

   c)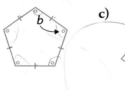

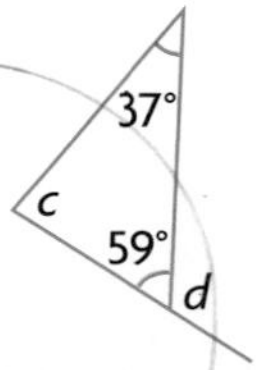

   d)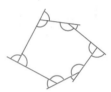

PRACTISING

3. Determine the measure of each missing angle.

   a)

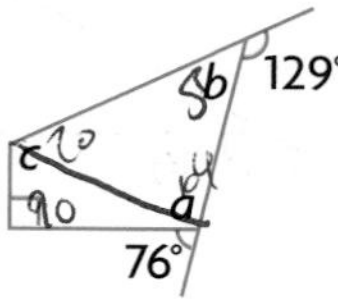

   b)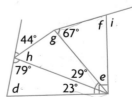

4. In this diagram, $\angle E$ in $\triangle BEC$ is a right angle. What is the sum of angles a and d?

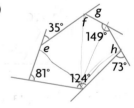

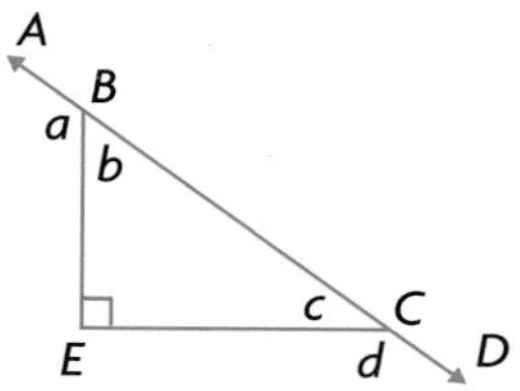

5. What is the measure of ∠CAB in this diagram?

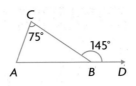

6. In the diagram, *AB* is parallel to *FG* and *BC* is parallel to *DE*.

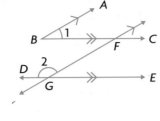

   a) What is the relationship between ∠1 and ∠2?

   b) Use *The Geometer's Sketchpad* or several examples to support your answer in part a).

   c) Write an expression for your answer.

7. Determine the measure of each missing angle.

   a)

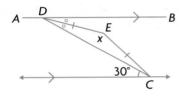

   c)

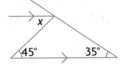

   b)

   d)

8. For each diagram, state the equation that expresses the relationship needed to solve the problem. Then, determine the measure of each variable. Show the steps in the solution.

   a)

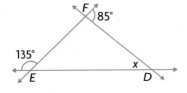

   c)

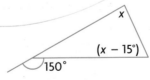

   b)

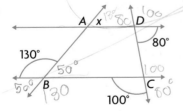

   d)

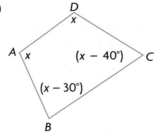

9. An interior angle of a parallelogram is the measure of the exterior angle adjacent to it multiplied by 4. Determine the measure of each interior angle. Draw the parallelogram.

10. In $\triangle ABC$, the measure of $\angle B$ is 21° less than the measure of $\angle A$
A multiplied by 4. The measure of $\angle C$ is 1° more than the measure of $\angle A$ multiplied by 5. Determine the measure of each interior angle and each exterior angle of $\triangle ABC$.

11. In a regular polygon, the ratio of the measure of the exterior angle to
T the measure of its adjacent interior angle is 1 to 4. How many sides does the polygon have?

12. For any regular n-gon, develop a formula for calculating the measure of each interior angle.

13. Why is the sum of the interior angles of a convex polygon usually greater than the sum of its exterior angles? Explain with an example.

Extending

14. When pattern blocks are used to tile a surface, they have to fit together to join along sides and vertices.

square   rhombus   rhombus

Pentagons were not included in the set of pattern blocks. Explain why pentagons cannot be used to tile a surface.

trapezoid   triangle   hexagon

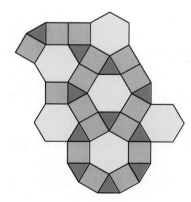

15. a) Suppose you are going to tile a floor with tiles shaped like an octagon and one other shape. What other shape can you use?
   b) Determine two other tile shapes you can use to tile a floor.

FREQUENTLY ASKED Questions

Q: **What is the formula for the sum of the interior angles of a polygon?**

A: The sum of the interior angles of a polygon with n sides is $(n - 2) \times 180°$. This is because the polygon can be divided into $n - 2$ non-overlapping triangles, and the sum of the interior angles of each triangle is 180°.

> **Study | Aid**
> - See Lesson 7.1.
> - Try Mid-Chapter Review Questions 1 and 2.

EXAMPLE

Determine the sum of the interior angles of this heptagon.

Solution

A heptagon has 7 sides and can be divided into 5 triangles. So, the sum of its interior angles is $(7 - 2) \times 180° = 900°$.

Q: **What is the relationship between the interior and exterior angles of a convex polygon?**

A: The interior and exterior angles at any vertex of a convex polygon form a straight angle, or 180°. That means that the measure of any exterior angle equals 180° minus the measure of its adjacent interior angle. They are supplementary angles.

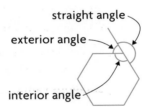

straight angle

exterior angle

interior angle

> **Study | Aid**
> - See Lesson 7.2, Example 2.
> - Try Mid-Chapter Review Questions 4, 5, and 6.

EXAMPLE

Calculate the measure of each interior angle in a regular hexagon.

Solution

In a regular hexagon, each exterior angle is 360° divided by 6 angles, or 60°. So, each interior angle is $180° - 60° = 120°$.

Q: **How can you calculate the sum of the exterior angles of a convex polygon?**

A: The sum of the exterior angles of any convex polygon is 360°. You can calculate this by measuring, by determining each exterior angle from its adjacent interior angle, or by using reasoning if the polygon is regular.

> **Study | Aid**
> - See Lesson 7.2, Examples 1, 2, and 3.
> - Try Mid-Chapter Review Questions 4, 5, and 6.

PRACTICE Questions

Lesson 7.1

1. Determine the measure of each missing interior angle.

a)
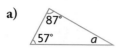

b)
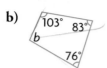

c)
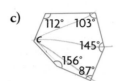

d)
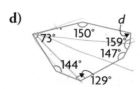

e)
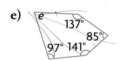

f)
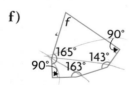

2. Determine the measure of the interior angles of each figure.
a) a regular 12-gon
b) a regular 15-gon
c) a regular 20-gon

Lesson 7.2

3. Each interior angle a in a regular n-gon has a measure of $a = 20n$. How many sides does the polygon have?

4. Determine the measure of each missing angle. Support your answer with mathematical reasoning.

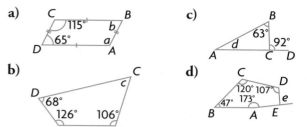

5. In a regular polygon, the ratio of the measure of the exterior angle to the measure of the adjacent interior angle is 2 to 3. How many sides does the polygon have?

6. Complete the table for each regular polygon.

Figure	Measure of Each Interior Angle	Measure of Each Exterior Angle	Sum of Interior Angles	Sum of Exterior Angles
C				
D				
E				
B				

7.3 Exploring Quadrilateral Diagonal Properties

Create and test conjectures about properties of quadrilaterals.

EXPLORE the Math

Santos was making flying **kites** of different shapes with two cross pieces. He made a **conjecture** that the shape of each kite depended on how he arranged the diagonals. He started with perpendicular diagonals.

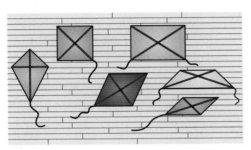

? How can Santos predict the shape of a quadrilateral by using line and angle properties of the diagonals?

A. Draw two intersecting perpendicular line segments of any length. An example is shown to the right.

B. Create a shape using the endpoints of the segments as vertices and the segments as diagonals. An example is shown to the right.

C. Describe the quadrilateral you created.

D. Form a conjecture about what types of quadrilaterals you can construct with perpendicular diagonals.

E. Sketch and label an example of each type of quadrilateral.

F. Draw two intersecting non-perpendicular line segments of any length.

G. Create a quadrilateral using the segments as diagonals.

H. What types of quadrilaterals can you construct?

I. Sketch and label an example of each type.

YOU WILL NEED
- grid paper
- dynamic geometry software (optional)

kite
a quadrilateral that has two pairs of equal sides with no sides parallel

conjecture
a guess or prediction based on limited evidence

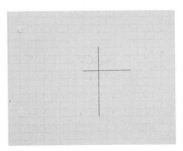

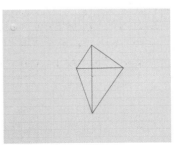

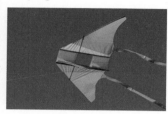

J. What is the arrangement of the diagonals for each shape?

parallelogram   rectangle   rhombus   square

irregular
quadrilateral   trapezoid   isosceles trapezoid   kite

Reflecting

K. Could you form a square, a rectangle, a rhombus, and a parallelogram using these diagonals? Explain how you know.

L. Explain why a square is always a rhombus but a rhombus is not always a square. Refer to diagonals in your answer.

M. How do the relationships between the diagonals help you predict the shape of a quadrilateral?

In Summary

Key Idea

- The diagonals of certain quadrilaterals have special properties:

Type of Quadrilateral	The diagonals...	The diagonals form angles that are...	Diagram
square	are equal and bisect each other.	all 90°.	
rhombus (not a square)	are not equal and bisect each other.	all 90°.	
rectangle (not a square)	are equal and bisect each other.	equal when opposite and supplementary when adjacent.	
parallelogram (not a rectangle or rhombus)	are not equal and bisect each other.	equal when opposite and supplementary when adjacent.	
isosceles trapezoid (not a rectangle or rhombus)	are equal and intersect to form two pairs of equal line segments.	equal when opposite and supplementary when adjacent.	
kite	may or may not be equal and only one is bisected by the other.	all 90°.	

Need to Know

- You can identify the type of quadrilateral by using its diagonal properties.

FURTHER *Your Understanding*

1. Each quadrilateral ABCD below has these three vertices: $A(0, 0)$, $B(3, 4)$, and $C(8, 4)$. Use diagonal properties to identify the coordinates of the fourth vertex D in each case. Explain your method.
   a) rhombus
   b) isosceles trapezoid
   c) kite

2. Match each pair of diagonals with its quadrilateral. Explain your reasoning.

   a)   c)   e)

   b)   d)    f)

   i)   iii)   v)

   ii)    iv)   vi)

3. Explain why the quadrilaterals are in different parts of the Venn diagram. Refer to the properties of sides, angles, and diagonals of quadrilaterals.

4. The diagonals and the sides of a quadrilateral form four triangles. Complete the table for the triangles formed by these quadrilaterals. Draw diagrams to support your answers.

Quadrilateral	Number of Congruent Triangles
square	
rhombus	
rectangle	
parallelogram	
isosceles trapezoid	
kite	

Properties of 2-D Figures   **401**

Reasoning About Triangle and Quadrilateral Properties

YOU WILL NEED

- protractor
- dynamic geometry software (optional)

> **GOAL**
>
> Form and test conjectures about properties of quadrilaterals.

LEARN ABOUT the Math

Jafar created square and parallelogram display boards for an art gallery. He made a border for the text area of each board by joining the **midpoints** with string to create the **midsegments.**

The shape inside the square board looked like a square and the shape inside the parallelogram looked like a parallelogram.

midsegment

a line segment connecting the midpoints of two adjacent sides of a polygon

❓ What figure is formed by the midsegments of a quadrilateral?

| EXAMPLE **1** | Forming and testing a conjecture |

Jafar, Maria, and Elani had different conjectures. They tested them in different ways.

Jafar's Solution: Rejecting a conjecture

Reasoning | *Checklist*

- ✔ Did you explain your reasoning clearly?
- ✔ Are your conclusions reasonable?
- ✔ Did you justify your conclusions?

Conjecture: The shape formed by the midsegments of a quadrilateral has the same shape as the original quadrilateral.

> I tried an isosceles trapezoid. I thought I would get a trapezoid. I joined the midpoints of the first two sides.

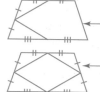

> I joined the midpoints of the last two sides. The shape in the middle was a rhombus, not a trapezoid.

counterexample

an example that proves that a hypothesis or conjecture is false

> I found a **counterexample** to my conjecture. So, I would have to test other quadrilaterals, and then form a new conjecture.

My conjecture was incorrect.

Maria's Solution: Revising a conjecture

I will test some quadrilaterals to revise Jafar's conjecture.

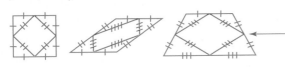

I joined the midpoints of some quadrilaterals. I always got a parallelogram. I thought this might happen for any quadrilateral.

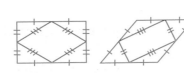

I checked more quadrilaterals. The shape in the middle was always a parallelogram.

Conjecture: All the interior shapes formed by the midsegments are parallelograms.

I still had to determine if this held for any quadrilateral. I could create more examples, but I could not be fully sure.

Elani's Solution: Supporting a conjecture

Conjecture: The shape formed by the midsegments of a quadrilateral is a parallelogram.

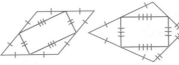

I joined the midpoints of these quadrilaterals. They confirmed my conjecture.

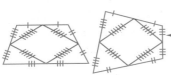

I checked more quadrilaterals. Each time, the shape in the middle was a parallelogram.

I joined the midpoints of another quadrilateral. The new shape was a parallelogram.

My examples support my conjecture.

Each interior shape formed by the midsegments is a parallelogram.

I reasoned my conjecture was very likely true. However, I could not be fully sure. There might be a counterexample.

Reflecting

A. Explain how Jafar determined that his conjecture was incorrect.

B. Should Maria have tested other quadrilaterals? Explain.

C. Explain how Elani's examples supported the conjecture she tested but did not prove it.

APPLY the Math

EXAMPLE 2   Confirming or denying a conjecture

Sven's sister saw him doing geometry homework on isosceles triangles. All isosceles triangles have two equal angles and a third angle. She told him that the **median** through the third angle is never perpendicular to the base. Sven decided to test her conjecture.

median

the line drawn from a vertex of a triangle to the midpoint of the opposite side

median

Sven's Solution

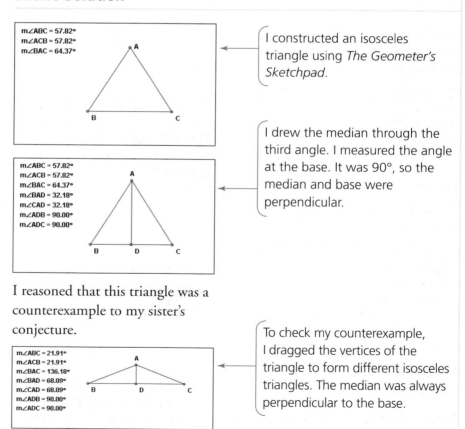

I constructed an isosceles triangle using *The Geometer's Sketchpad.*

I drew the median through the third angle. I measured the angle at the base. It was 90°, so the median and base were perpendicular.

I reasoned that this triangle was a counterexample to my sister's conjecture.

To check my counterexample, I dragged the vertices of the triangle to form different isosceles triangles. The median was always perpendicular to the base.

My sister's conjecture was incorrect.

Tech | Support

For help on constructing and labelling a triangle, measuring an angle, or constructing a midpoint in *The Geometer's Sketchpad*, see Appendix B-20, B-21, and B-25.

EXAMPLE 3 Testing and revising a conjecture

Make a conjecture about the relationship between the exterior angle of a triangle and the two interior angles opposite it. Then test your conjecture.

exterior angle   interior angles

Aisha's Solution

Conjecture: The sum of an exterior angle of a triangle and the two interior angles opposite it is 180°.

> I noticed that the sum of the exterior angle of a triangle and the two interior angles opposite it was sometimes 180°.

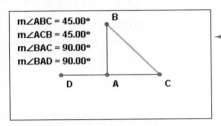

m∠ABC = 45.00°
m∠ACB = 45.00°
m∠BAC = 90.00°
m∠BAD = 90.00°

> I tested my conjecture with an exterior angle for a right isosceles triangle using *The Geometer's Sketchpad*.

The example confirmed my conjecture.

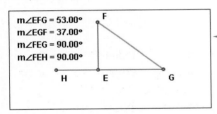

m∠EFG = 53.00°
m∠EGF = 37.00°
m∠FEG = 90.00°
m∠FEH = 90.00°

> I tested an exterior angle for a triangle with interior angles of 90°, 37°, and 53°. The sum of ∠FEH, ∠EFG, and ∠EGF was 180°.

The example confirmed my conjecture.

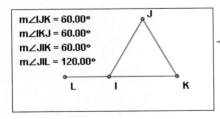

m∠IJK = 60.00°
m∠IKJ = 60.00°
m∠JIK = 60.00°
m∠JIL = 120.00°

> I tested an equilateral triangle. The sum of ∠JIL, ∠IJK, and ∠IKJ was 240°.

My conjecture was false. This was a counterexample to my conjecture.

New conjecture: The exterior angle of a triangle is equal to the sum of the two interior angles opposite to it.

> In each example, the exterior angle was equal to the sum of the two interior angles opposite it. I revised my conjecture. The new conjecture needed testing.

Tech | **Support**

For help on measuring an exterior angle in *The Geometer's Sketchpad*, see Appendix B-22.

EXAMPLE 4   Testing then confirming a conjecture

Jeff was making designs. He drew triangles and then formed the midsegments. He thought he saw a relationship between each midsegment and its opposite side.

Jeff's Solution

Conjecture: A midsegment of a triangle is half as long as its opposite side. ←

> I made a conjecture. I tested it by constructing examples.

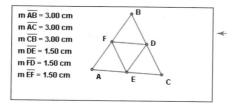

> I tested an equilateral triangle. I determined the lengths of the sides and midsegments using *The Geometer's Sketchpad*.

The lengths in the example supported my conjecture.

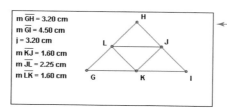

> I tested an isosceles triangle.

The lengths in the example supported my conjecture.

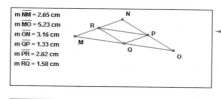

> I tested two scalene triangles.
>
> The lengths in the examples supported my conjecture.

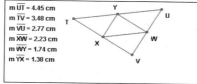

My examples confirm my conjecture. The length of the midsegment is half the length of the opposite side. ←

> I reasoned my conjecture was very likely correct. I could not be fully sure; a counterexample might still exist.

In Summary

Key Ideas

- Examples can support a conjecture about a geometric relationship, but do not prove it.
- You only need one counterexample to disprove a conjecture about a geometric relationship.

Need to Know

- The midsegments of any quadrilateral form a parallelogram:

Midsegments Form a Parallelogram	Midsegments Form a Rhombus	Midsegments Form a Rectangle	Midsegments Form a Square
• parallelogram	• rectangle	• rhombus	• square
• trapezoid	• isosceles trapezoid	• kite	
• irregular quadrilateral			

- The median through the angle formed by the two equal sides of an isosceles triangle is perpendicular to the third side.
- The exterior angle at a vertex of a triangle equals the sum of the two interior angles opposite it.
- The length of a midsegment in a triangle equals half the length of the side opposite it.

CHECK Your Understanding

1. Test this conjecture: "Midsegments in a triangle are always parallel to the side opposite to them." Support your reasoning with examples.

2. Test this conjecture: "If a quadrilateral has perpendicular diagonals, then it is a square." Support your reasoning with examples.

PRACTISING

3. Predict whether a polygon's sides are all equal if its interior angles are all equal. Support your conjecture with examples or disprove it with a counterexample.

4. Predict whether a polygon's interior angles are all equal if its sides are all equal. Support your conjecture with examples or disprove it with a counterexample.

5. Create a conjecture to predict the number of diagonals from any one vertex of a convex polygon with n sides. Support your conjecture with examples or disprove it with a counterexample.

6. Test this conjecture: "If the midsegments of a quadrilateral form a **T** square, then the quadrilateral is itself a square."

7. Test this conjecture: "The medians of a triangle always intersect at exactly one point."

8. Create a conjecture to predict the ratio of the area of a triangle to the area of the shape formed by its midsegments. Support your conjecture with examples or disprove it with a counterexample.

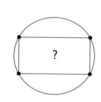

9. Test this conjecture: "It is always possible to draw a circle through all four vertices in a rectangle."

10. Geometric relationships and properties are often discovered using conjectures and counterexamples. Describe the process you use to solve geometric problems using words or diagrams, such as a flow chart.

Extending

11. Create a conjecture to predict when the midsegments of a pentagon form a regular pentagon. Support your conjecture with examples or disprove it with a counterexample.

12. Draw the inner quadrilateral of a square using its midsegments. Then, draw a new inner quadrilateral inside that one, and then another inside the second. Do the same for a rectangle, a rhombus, a parallelogram, a kite, and a trapezoid. Do you notice any patterns? Begin with a conjecture, then either support it with examples or disprove it with a counterexample.

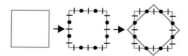

13. To trisect a line segment, divide it into three equal parts. Musim trisected each side of the red square. Then he drew lines to create the blue quadrilateral. What do you notice about it? Form a conjecture about the quadrilateral that is created when you trisect the sides of other quadrilaterals. Support your conjecture with examples or disprove it with a counterexample.

Curious | Math

Meeting of Midpoints

The area of the triangle formed by the midsegments of a triangle is always 25% of the area of the original triangle. Do you think the same relationship is true for other polygons?

Tech | **Support**

For help on measuring the area of a polygon in *The Geometer's Sketchpad*, see Appendix B-28.

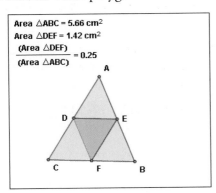

Area △ABC = 5.66 cm²
Area △DEF = 1.42 cm²
$\dfrac{\text{(Area △DEF)}}{\text{(Area △ABC)}} = 0.25$

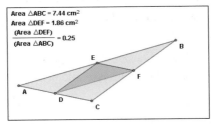

Area △ABC = 7.44 cm²
Area △DEF = 1.86 cm²
$\dfrac{\text{(Area △DEF)}}{\text{(Area △ABC)}} = 0.25$

1. Draw several quadrilaterals either on grid paper or using dynamic geometry software.

   Calculate or estimate their areas.

2. Mark midpoints on each side.

   Then draw the midsegments.

3. Calculate the areas of the shapes formed by the midsegments.

4. What are the ratios of the inner quadrilateral areas to the outer quadrilateral areas?

5. Predict the result if you were to change the number of sides from 4 to 5.

   Repeat parts 1 and 2 for pentagons to test your conjecture.

6. Do you think there is a relationship between the area of a polygon and the area of the shape formed by its midsegments?

   Form a conjecture, and then test it with hexagons, heptagons, and octagons.

Reasoning About Properties of Polygons

YOU WILL NEED
- construction paper
- ruler
- protractor
- scissors
- dynamic geometry software (optional)

GOAL

Apply properties of triangles and quadrilaterals.

INVESTIGATE the Math

In art class, Daniel created a mobile using shapes with three and four sides. He wanted to attach each shape to the string so that it would not hang crookedly. Daniel knew that every 2-D shape has a **centroid,** or centre of gravity.

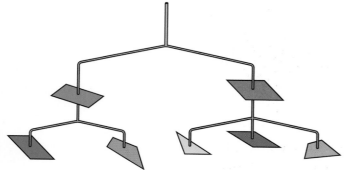

? How can Daniel determine the centroid of each shape using triangle and quadrilateral properties?

centroid

the centre of an object's mass; the point at which it balances; also known as the centre of gravity

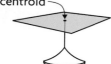

centroid

A. Cut a triangle out of construction paper.

How might you find its centre of gravity?

B. State a conjecture about the triangle's centroid based on the intersection of lines such as angle bisectors, perpendicular bisectors, or medians.

C. Construct the centroid using your conjecture.

Describe your construction method. What lines did you draw?

D. Test by placing the centroid on the eraser end of a pencil.

Does the triangle balance? Move the pencil until it does, if needed.

E. Cut out a square, a parallelogram, a trapezoid, and a kite.

F. State a conjecture about the centroid in each shape. Base your conjecture on the intersection of lines, such as diagonals, angle bisectors, perpendicular bisectors, or **bimedians.**

Then repeat parts B through D.

G. Draw medians for the triangle and bimedians for the square, parallelogram, trapezoid, and kite.

Try balancing each. What do you notice?

bimedian

the line joining the midpoints of two opposite sides in a quadrilateral

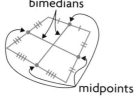

bimedians

midpoints

Reflecting

H. Where is the centroid located in a quadrilateral? in a triangle?

I. Describe how to determine the centroid of a quadrilateral using its midsegments.

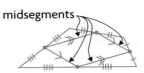

midsegments

APPLY the Math

EXAMPLE **1**	**Forming and testing a conjecture about the centroid of a triangle**

Daniel wanted to make a wind chime using geometric shapes. He needed to find the centroid of each shape to drill the hole it would hang from.

Daniel's Solution

I drew the triangle on cardboard. I cut it out and tried to balance it on a pencil eraser.

It seemed the centroid was on the median through vertex *A*. I thought each half of the triangle might balance the other that way.

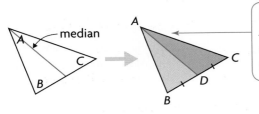

I drew the median through vertex *A*. I placed the median on the edge of a ruler. Each half of the triangle balanced out the other.

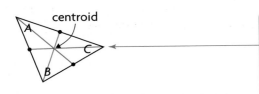

I drew the other medians. I verified that the centroid was on each by balancing on the edge of a ruler.

I realized that the centroid must be the intersection of the medians. I tested by hanging the triangle with string through it.

EXAMPLE **2**

Forming and testing a conjecture about bimedians

Mingmei drew the bimedian connecting the two non-base sides of a trapezoid. She noticed that it seemed parallel to the base sides. She decided to investigate the properties of the bimedian.

Mingmei's Solution

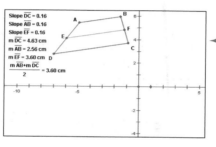

> I drew a trapezoid in *The Geometer's Sketchpad* to determine its centroid.
>
> I plotted the midpoints *E* and *F* of the non-base sides. Then I joined them to form the bimedian.

Tech | ***Support***

For help measuring the length of a segment in *The Geometer's Sketchpad*, see Appendix B-24.

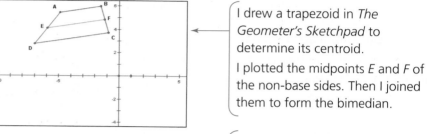

> I calculated the slopes of the bimedian and the base sides. The three lines were parallel.
>
> I determined the lengths of the bimedian and the base sides. The length of the bimedian was half the sum of the lengths of the base sides.

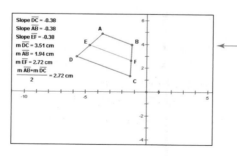

> I tested other trapezoids by dragging vertices. Each time, the bimedian was parallel to the base sides. Its length was always the mean of their lengths.
>
> I reasoned that these properties made sense. Triangle midsegments are parallel to the opposite side and half its length. Trapezoids are triangles with the top cut off parallel to the bottom side. So, the bimedian is like a triangle midsegment.

The bimedian between the non-base sides of each trapezoid I tested is half the length of the base sides and parallel to them.

In Summary

Key Ideas

- The centroid of a triangle is located at the intersection of its medians. Medians are lines from each vertex of a triangle to the midpoint of the opposite side.

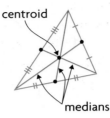

- The centroid of a quadrilateral is located at the intersection of its bimedians. Bimedians are lines joining the midpoints of opposite sides. They are the diagonals of the parallelogram formed by the midsegments of the quadrilateral.

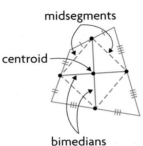

Need to Know

- You can determine the centroid of some quadrilaterals by locating the point of intersection of their diagonals. This works for squares, rectangles, rhombuses, and parallelograms, but not for trapezoids and kites.
- The bimedian of the non-base sides of a trapezoid is parallel to its bases. Its length is the mean of their lengths.

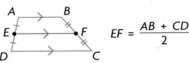

$$EF = \frac{AB + CD}{2}$$

CHECK Your Understanding

1. Choose three figures from this list: triangle, square, rhombus, rectangle, parallelogram, kite, isosceles trapezoid, non-isosceles trapezoid, irregular quadrilateral. Determine the centroid of each figure you chose.

2. Answer each question using mathematical terminology.
   a) What quadrilateral is formed by the midsegments of a rectangle?
   b) Where is the centroid of a parallelogram located?
   c) What quadrilateral is formed by the midsegments of a trapezoid?
   d) The bimedians of any quadrilateral form the diagonals of a smaller quadrilateral. What are the sides of this smaller quadrilateral called?

PRACTISING

3. Complete the table.

K

Quadrilateral	Centroid Construction Method	Bimedian Geometric Properties
square	intersection of bimedians or diagonals	• bisect each other • equal length • intersect at right angles • split square into four smaller congruent squares
rhombus		
rectangle		
parallelogram		
kite		
isosceles trapezoid		
non-isosceles trapezoid		
irregular quadrilateral		

4. Remi is building a triangular wooden
A shelving unit. The base measures 30 cm
and the slant sides measure 18 cm and
24 cm. He wants a horizontal shelf halfway
between the base and the top. What length
of wood should he cut for the shelf?

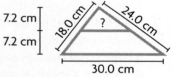

5. A trapezoid has parallel sides of length
51 cm and 144 cm. Its other sides
measure 34 cm and 65 cm.

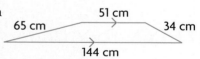

    a) Determine the length of the
bimedian joining the two non-parallel sides.

    b) The distance between the parallel sides is 8 cm. How far is the
bimedian from each?

6. Martin is making a stencil in the shape of an isosceles triangle. The
median to the base side is 12 cm long. The midsegment parallel to the
base is 5 cm long.

    a) What is the length of the base?

    b) What is the length of the slant sides?

7. Jerry is making a kite in the shape of an isosceles triangle. Two sides are
T 41 cm and the other side is 18 cm. Jerry wants to attach a plastic
support along the median meeting the midpoint of the shortest side.
   a) Determine the length of plastic Jerry must cut for the support.
   b) Jerry wants to place another plastic support along the midsegment
   opposite the 18 cm side. Determine the length of this plastic
   support.

8. Serwa constructed a quadrilateral for an art project. She located its
C centroid by drawing the bimedians. Then she decided to cut the
quadrilateral into two pieces along one bimedian. Explain how to
determine the centroids for her new quadrilaterals using only the
remaining bimedian.

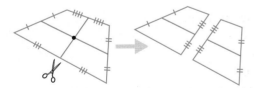

9. Explain how diagonal properties help determine the centroid in
different quadrilaterals.

Extending

10. Draw any irregular quadrilateral, then connect its diagonals. Locate
the midpoints of both diagonals, then join them.
   a) Determine the midpoint of the segment you just found. What
   special point have you constructed?
   b) Explain how you determined your answer.
11. Describe how to divide any quadrilateral into four equal regions
without using the midpoints of its sides.

FREQUENTLY ASKED Questions

Q: **How can you identify a quadrilateral using its diagonal properties and reasoning?**

A: Each type of quadrilateral has special properties associated with the diagonals.

- The diagonals of a square are equal and bisect each other at right angles.

- The diagonals of a rhombus bisect each other at right angles.

- The diagonals of a rectangle are equal and bisect each other.

- The diagonals of a parallelogram bisect each other.

- The diagonals of a non-isosceles trapezoid have no special properties. The diagonals of an isosceles trapezoid are equal and intersect to form two different pairs of equal line segments.

- The diagonals of a kite are perpendicular to each other, and one of the diagonals is bisected by the other.

Q: **How can you use reasoning to make conjectures about angle or line properties?**

A: First, start with information that you know. For example, to determine how to find the sum of the interior angles of any n-gon, start with what you know:

- every polygon with n sides can be divided into $n - 2$ non-overlapping triangles and
- the sum of the interior angles of each triangle is $180°$.

$$a + b + c = 180°$$
$$d + e + f = 180°$$
$$g + h + i = 180°$$

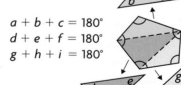

EXAMPLE

Determine the sum of the interior angles in a pentagon.

Solution

A pentagon has five sides, so it is made up of $5 - 2 = 3$ triangles.

Therefore, the sum of the interior angles of a pentagon is $3 \times 180° = 540°$.

EXAMPLE

Form your conjecture based on the facts you know. It seems as if the sum of the angles of a polygon is always the sum of the angles in each triangle. There are always $n - 2$ triangles in each n-gon, so the sum will always be $(n - 2) \times 180°$.

Q: **What properties do the midpoints of a quadrilateral have?**

A: • The midsegments of a square form a square.

Study | *Aid*

• See Lesson 7.4, Example 1.
• Try Chapter Review Question 13.

• The midsegments of a rhombus form a rectangle.

• The midsegments of a rectangle form a rhombus.

• The midsegments of a parallelogram form a parallelogram.

• The midsegments of an isosceles trapezoid form a rhombus.

• The midsegments of a kite form a rectangle.

Q: **How can you solve problems involving polygons?**

A: Look for a property of the polygon that seems related to the problem. Then, try to apply to the problem.

Study | *Aid*

• See Lesson 7.5, Examples 1 and 2.
• Try Chapter Review Questions 13, 14, and 15.

EXAMPLE

To locate the centroid of a triangle, draw the medians. These are lines from each vertex to the midpoint of the opposite side. The triangle balances on each median. So, the centroid lies on their intersection.

centroid

medians

To locate the centroid of a quadrilateral, draw the bimedians. These are lines between midpoints of opposite sides. The quadrilateral balances on each bimedian. So, the centroid lies at their intersection.

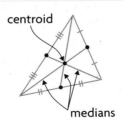

midsegments

centroid

bimedians

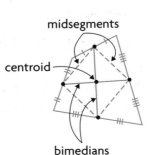

PRACTICE Questions

1. Calculate the missing angle in each case.

   a)

   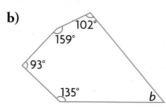

   b)

   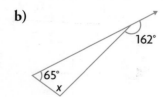

2. Bob claims that the sum of the interior angles of a regular octagon is 900°. Is he correct? Justify your decision.

3. The formula for calculating the sum of the interior angles of any n-gon is $(n - 2) \times 180°$.
   a) Explain why 2 is subtracted from n.
   b) Explain why $(n - 2)$ is multiplied by 180°.

Lesson 7.2

4. a) Calculate the measure of each interior angle of a regular 25-gon.
   b) What is the measure of each exterior angle?

5. Find the value of each unknown. 4140

   a)

   85°

   120°

   x

   c)

   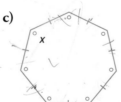

   x

   b)

   162°

   65°
   x

   d)

   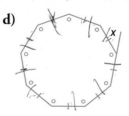

   x

6. Calculate the value of x in each case.

   a)

   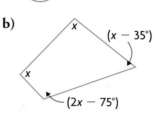

   35   (x − 25°)

   145°

   b)

   x   (x − 35°)

   x

   (2x − 75°)

Lesson 7.3

7. Complete each sentence using "always," "never," or "sometimes."
   a) A square is ■ a rhombus.
   b) The diagonals of a parallelogram ■ bisect its angles.
   c) A quadrilateral with one pair of congruent sides and one pair of parallel sides is ■ a parallelogram.
   d) The diagonals of a rhombus are ■ congruent.
   e) The consecutive sides of a rectangle are ■ congruent.
   f) The diagonals of a rectangle are ■ perpendicular to each other.
   g) The diagonals of a rhombus ■ bisect each other.
   h) The diagonals of a parallelogram are ■ perpendicular bisectors of each other.

8. Describe the possible type(s) of quadrilateral that could be made with each set of diagonals. Justify your answers.

a)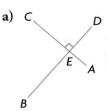

b)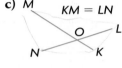

c)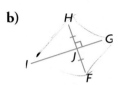

KM = LN

d)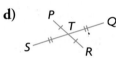

Lesson 7.4

9. Karim wanted to determine all the types of quadrilaterals whose midsegments form either a square or a rectangle. Create a conjecture for Karim's problem, then either support it with examples or disprove it with a counterexample.

10. Test this conjecture: "At least one median in every triangle is the angle bisector at the vertex it intersects."

11. Test this conjecture. "The median from the vertex joining the two equal sides of an isosceles triangle always bisects the angle formed by the two equal sides." Support your reasoning with examples.

12. Test this conjecture. "A median of a triangle always divides the area of the triangle in half." Support your reasoning with examples.

Lesson 7.5

13. What kind of figure is formed by joining the midpoints of the sides of a polygon? Explain your answer.

14. Draw a circle and plot four points on it. Join adjacent points to form a quadrilateral. Extend a side at each vertex.

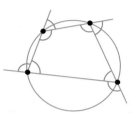

a) Compare each interior angle with the exterior angle at the opposite vertex. What do you notice?

b) Repeat your angle measurements for a quadrilateral whose vertices cannot all be plotted on one circle.

c) Form a conjecture from your observations, and explain how to test it.

15. A trapezoid has parallel sides 6 cm and 46 cm. The other sides measure 37 cm and 13 cm.

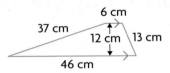

a) Determine the length of the bimedian joining the two non-parallel sides.

b) The distance between the parallel sides is 12 cm. How far is the bimedian from each?

1. What is the relationship between the number of sides of a polygon and the number of diagonals that can be drawn from one vertex?

2. Asad designed a tabletop in the shape of a regular pentagon. His teacher suggested he redesign it as a regular hexagon. By how much would each interior angle change?

   A. 12°   **B.** 30°   **C.** 36°   **D.** 180°

3. Determine the missing angles in each case.

   a)

   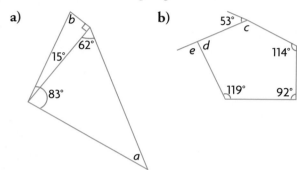

   b)

4. Use words or pictures to explain why the sum of the exterior angles of a convex pentagon is 360°.

5. Hannah cut a quadrilateral from a piece of cardboard. The diagonals were congruent, perpendicular, and bisected each other. Which type of quadrilateral did Hannah cut out?

   A. kite   **B.** rectangle   **C.** rhombus   **D.** square

6. Match the quadrilateral to the picture of its diagonals.
   a) rectangle

   b) isosceles trapezoid

   c) square

   d) rhombus

   i)

   ii)

   iii)

   iv)

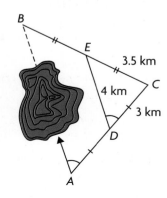

7. A straight train tunnel is being built through a mountain, as shown. The construction company needs to know the length of track needed from point A to point B. Determine the distance using the diagram. Explain your method.

8. Every median in a triangle can be divided into two parts: the length from the vertex to the centroid, and the length from the centroid to the midpoint of the opposite side. Test the conjecture that the longer segment is twice the length of the shorter segment, for the medians in any triangle.

Pentagonal Properties

Denise is putting together a poster presentation for the regional Math Fair. She decides to research geometric properties of pentagons.

1. She draws a large circle and marks five points on its circumference.

2. She draws a pentagon using the points on the circle as vertices.

3. She divides the pentagon by drawing diagonals from one vertex to the two opposite it.

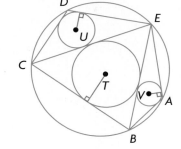

4. She draws an inscribed circle in each triangle. To do this, she determines the centre of the circle by locating the intersection of the lines that bisect the interior angles of the triangle. Then she calculates the radius by drawing a line from the centre of the circle perpendicular to any side of the triangle.

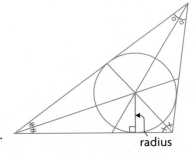

Denise divides the pentagon into triangles a different way. Then she measures the radii for the new set of inscribed circles. She discovers that the sums of the radii were equal. She thinks this must be true for all pentagons drawn on a circle.

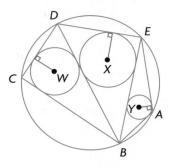

? How can you confirm or deny Denise's conjecture?

A. Construct a pentagon using Denise's method.

B. Does the sum of the radii of the inscribed circles depend on how you divide the pentagon into triangles?

C. Will Denise's conjecture work for any pentagon? Support your answer with examples.

D. Determine whether a result similar to that in part B is true for all polygons inscribed in a circle.

   Record your results in a table.

> Task | *Checklist*
> ✔ Did you check your geometric constructions for accuracy?
>
> ✔ Did you test the conjecture with several examples?
>
> ✔ Did you use a table to organize your results?
>
> ✔ Did you use appropriate math language?

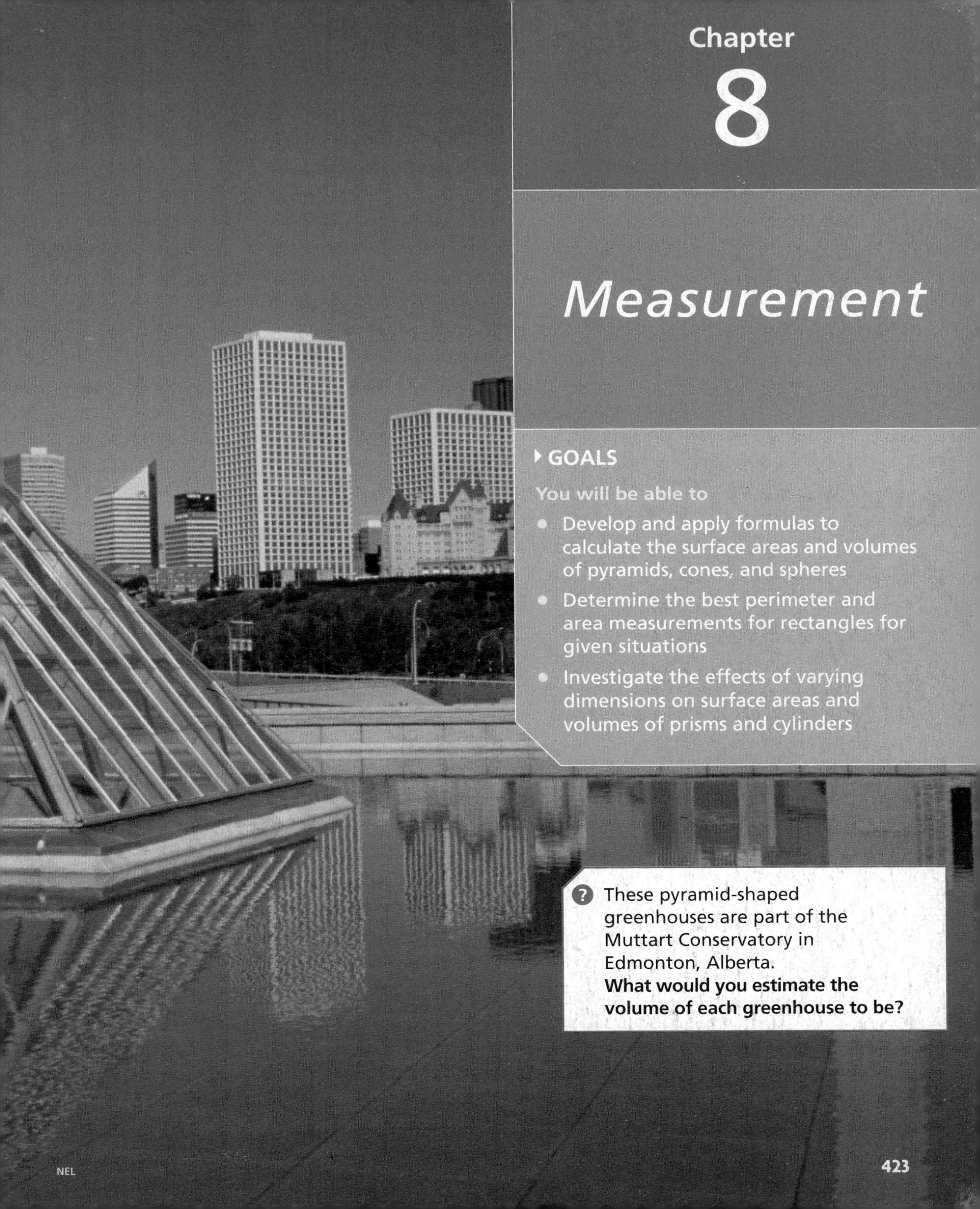

Measurement

▸ GOALS

You will be able to

- Develop and apply formulas to calculate the surface areas and volumes of pyramids, cones, and spheres

- Determine the best perimeter and area measurements for rectangles for given situations

- Investigate the effects of varying dimensions on surface areas and volumes of prisms and cylinders

❓ These pyramid-shaped greenhouses are part of the Muttart Conservatory in Edmonton, Alberta.
What would you estimate the volume of each greenhouse to be?

WORDS YOU NEED to Know

1. Match each term with the most appropriate picture.

a) hypotenuse   c) net   e) surface area   g) volume   i) composite shape

b) prism   d) pyramid   f) cylinder   h) sphere   j) cone

i)

iii)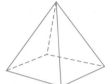

v)

vii)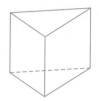

ix)

ii)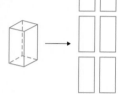

iv)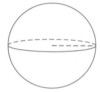

vi)

viii)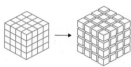

x)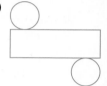

SKILLS AND CONCEPTS You Need

Calculating Volume and Surface Area

Study | Aid

• For more help and practice, see Appendix A-20.

EXAMPLE

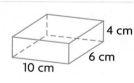

Area of base

B = area of top

   = 6 × 10

   = 60 cm²

Volume

$V = Bh$

   = 60 × 4

   = 240 cm³

Surface area

SA = surface area of faces

SA = 2(area of top) + 2(area of front) + 2(area of side)

   = 2(10 × 6) + 2(10 × 4) + 2(4 × 6)

   = 248 cm²

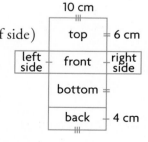

2. Determine the surface area of each figure.

  a) a cube with a side length of 10 cm

  b) a rectangular prism that is 3 cm by 5 cm by 8 cm

  c) a rectangular prism that is 10 cm by 20 cm by 5 cm

EXAMPLE

Area of base
B = area of top
$= \pi r^2$
$= \pi(4.0)^2$
$= 16\pi$ cm^2

Volume
$V = Bh$
$= 16\pi \times 12.0$
$\doteq 603.2$ cm^3

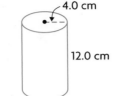

4.0 cm

12.0 cm

> **Communication** | **Tip**
>
> When calculating volume and surface area of 3-D figures, it is common practice to round off your answers to the same number of decimal places present in the given measurements.

Length of curved surface
$=$ circumference of base
$= \pi d$
$= \pi (8.0)$
$= 8\pi$ cm

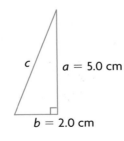

top ⟋ 4.0 cm

curved surface   12.0 cm

πd

base

Surface area
$SA = 2(\text{area of base}) + \text{area of curved surface}$
$\quad = 2\pi r^2 + \pi dh$
$\quad = 2\pi(4.0)^2 + \pi(8.0)(12.0)$
$\quad \doteq 402.1$ cm^2

3. Determine the surface area of each cylinder.
   a) a cylinder with a height of 10 cm and a radius of 5 cm
   b) a cylinder with a height of 8 cm and a diameter of 8 cm
   c) a cylinder with a diameter of 12 cm and a height of 9 cm

Calculating the Hypotenuse Using the Pythagorean Theorem

EXAMPLE

By the Pythagorean theorem, $c^2 = a^2 + b^2$.
$c^2 = 5.0^2 + 2.0^2$
$c^2 = 25.0 + 4.0$
$c^2 = 29.0$
$\ c = \sqrt{29.0}$
$\quad \doteq 5.4$ cm

> **Study** | **Aid**
>
> • For more help and practice, see Appendix A-19.

c ⟋ $a = 5.0$ cm

$b = 2.0$ cm

4. Determine the hypotenuse of each right triangle.
   a) a right triangle with legs of 4 cm and 8 cm
   b) a right triangle with both legs of 10 cm
   c) a right triangle with legs of 12 cm and 5 cm

PRACTICE

Study | **Aid**

- For help, see the Review of Essential Skills and Knowledge Appendix.

Question	Appendix
5	A-17 and A-18
6, 7, and 10	A-20
8	A-19

5. Calculate the area of each shape.

a) 33 cm

b) Bermuda, Miami, 1350 km, 1600 km, Puerto Rico

c) 90 cm, 66 cm

6. Calculate the total surface area and volume of each figure.

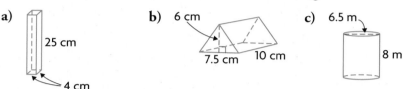

a) 25 cm, 4 cm

b) 6 cm, 7.5 cm, 10 cm

c) 6.5 m, 8 m

7. A company sells mints in three types of boxes: a cube, a triangular prism, and a cylinder. Each box has a capacity of 64 mL and they all have the same height.
   a) Draw a sketch that shows possible dimensions to the nearest tenth, for each type of box.
   b) Calculate the surface area of each box you sketched.

8. Calculate the length of the missing side.

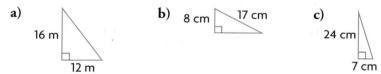

a) 16 m, 12 m

b) 8 cm, 17 cm

c) 24 cm, 7 cm

9. Do you agree or disagree?
   a) Rectangles with different side lengths can have the same area.
   b) The number of square units in the surface area of a cube is usually less than the number of cubic units in its volume.
   c) The longest that a rectangle with a perimeter of 50 cm can be is 24 cm.
   d) The area of a circle with diameter d is always less than d^2.

10. Copy and complete the table.

	Prism	Pyramid	Cone
Definition			
Properties			
Diagram			

APPLYING *What You Know*

Judging Jars

The student council is holding a jellybean guessing contest for a fundraiser.
They must use one of these jars. They know the following:

- Each jar is 12 cm high.
- Each jar holds 2400 jellybeans.
- Each jellybean has a volume of about 1 cm^3.
- 1 cm^3 = 1 mL

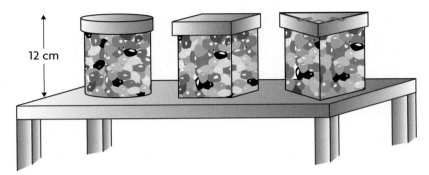

? What are possible dimensions for the base of each jar?

A. Copy the table.

Jar	Capacity Estimate (mL)	Base Area Estimate (cm²)	Shape of Base	Base Dimensions (Estimates in cm)
cylinder				diameter = ■
rectangular prism				side length = ■
triangular prism				base = ■, height = ■

B. Estimate the capacity of each jar.
C. Estimate the area of each base. Use the formula
$V_{\text{prism or cylinder}} = A_{\text{base}} \times$ height to help you.
D. Estimate the measurements of the base of each jar.

Determining Optimum Area and Perimeter

YOU WILL NEED

- 1 cm grid paper
- 24 cm piece of string
- geoboard and elastic band

6 cm

6 cm

Julie's Note Card

optimum

the most desirable of a number of possible choices

GOAL

Solve problems involving the dimensions of rectangles.

INVESTIGATE *the Math*

Julie showed Wyatt and Nick a rectangular note card she had made.
- Wyatt wanted to make a card with the greatest possible area and the same perimeter as Julie's.
- Nick wanted to make a card with the same area as Julie's and the least possible perimeter.

	Julie's Card	Wyatt's Card	Nick's Card
Area	36 cm²	greatest possible	36 cm²
Perimeter	24 cm	24 cm	least possible

❓ What are the dimensions for Wyatt's and Nick's cards?

A. Outline rectangles on 1 cm grid paper using a 24 cm piece of string. Include some rectangles with sides that are not whole numbers.

B. Draw each rectangle on the grid paper.

C. Determine the area of each rectangle.

D. What are the dimensions of the rectangle with the greatest area?

E. Form rectangles with an area of 36 cm² on a geoboard using an elastic band.

F. Draw each rectangle on grid paper.

G. Determine the perimeter of each rectangle.

H. What are the dimensions of the rectangle with the least perimeter?

I. Describe how you know that the dimensions you discovered are **optimum** measures.

Reflecting

J. What was special about the rectangle with the greatest area for a given perimeter?

K. What was special about the rectangle with the least perimeter for a given area?

APPLY *the Math*

EXAMPLE 1 Using a graphing strategy to determine minimum perimeter

At the local craft fair, the rectangular displays must have an area of 16 m². Marek wants to use the least amount of border for his entry. What dimensions can he use?

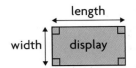

Marek's Solution

Factors of 16					
Length (m)	1	2	4	8	16
Width (m)	16	8	4	2	1
Perimeter (m)	34	20	16	20	34

Since the area must be 16 m², I compared rectangles with lengths and widths whose products were 16.

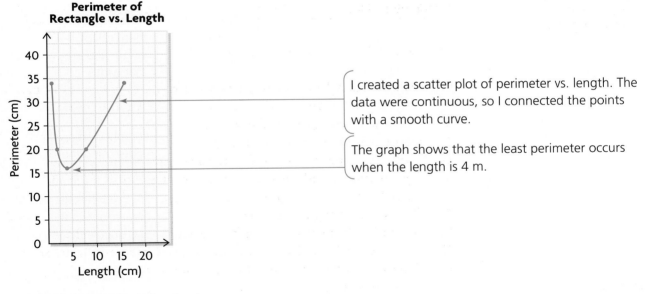

I created a scatter plot of perimeter vs. length. The data were continuous, so I connected the points with a smooth curve.

The graph shows that the least perimeter occurs when the length is 4 m.

The display has to be a 4 m by 4 m square.

EXAMPLE 2 — Using graphing technology to determine maximum area

Sunia's horticulture club is exhibiting at the city garden show. Each garden must be bordered by 18.0 m of wood against a brick display wall. What dimensions will maximize the area of the garden?

Sunia's Solution

The total length of the three sides is 18.0 m.

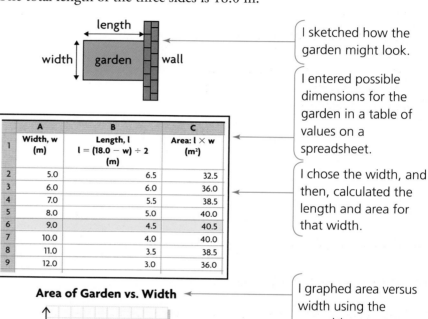

I sketched how the garden might look.

I entered possible dimensions for the garden in a table of values on a spreadsheet.

	A	B	C
	Width, w (m)	Length, l $l = (18.0 - w) \div 2$ (m)	Area: $l \times w$ (m²)
1			
2	5.0	6.5	32.5
3	6.0	6.0	36.0
4	7.0	5.5	38.5
5	8.0	5.0	40.0
6	9.0	4.5	40.5
7	10.0	4.0	40.0
8	11.0	3.5	38.5
9	12.0	3.0	36.0

I chose the width, and then, calculated the length and area for that width.

Area of Garden vs. Width

I graphed area versus width using the spreadsheet program.

I noticed the area was greatest when the width was double the length: 9.0 m and 4.5 m.

This makes sense. If the border was on all four sides, a square with dimensions 4.5 m by 4.5 m would give the greatest area.

I think the club should plan for a 9.0 m by 4.5 m garden exhibit.

Tech Support

For information on selecting columns from a table of values to form a scatter plot using a spreadsheet, see Appendix B-30.

In Summary

Key Ideas

- Rectangles with the same perimeter can have different areas, and the rectangle with a maximum area for a given perimeter is a square.
- Rectangles with different areas can have the same perimeter, and the rectangle with a minimum perimeter for a given area is a square.
- Collecting and plotting possible solution data helps to estimate optimal values.

Need to Know

- A rectangle with a border on three sides has a maximum area and a minimum border length when the side without a border and its opposite side are twice the length of the other two sides.

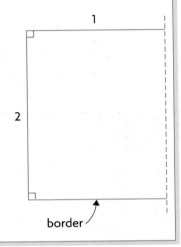

border

CHECK Your Understanding

1. Each rectangle has a perimeter of 64 units. Which one has the greatest area?

A.

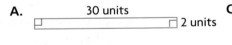

30 units

2 units

C.

20 units

12 units

B.

16 units

16 units

D.

8 units

24 units

2. Draw rectangles with areas of 36 square units on grid paper. Which one has the least perimeter?

PRACTISING

3. a) Determine the maximum area of a rectangle with each perimeter, to one decimal place.

     i) 100 cm   **ii)** 72 m   **iii)** 169 km   **iv)** 143 mm

b) Determine the minimum length of wood needed to build a rectangular frame for an art sketch of each area, to one decimal place.

     i) 1 m^2 **ii)** 70 cm^2 **iii)** 15.4 cm^2 **iv)** 28 cm^2

4. Sarah is fencing a vegetable garden to keep rabbits out. The hardware store sells fencing for \$25.50/m. Her family has \$165 to spend. What dimensions should Sarah use to build a garden with the greatest area?

5. An outdoor rectangular skating rink with an area of 126 m^2 will be built with one of its side lengths next to the community centre. To enclose the rink, 3 sides of fencing are needed.

a) Create a table of values that compares width, length, and perimeter of the rink for various widths of fencing shown.

Width (m)	1	2	3	4	6	9	12	14	21	42
Length (m)										
Perimeter (m)										

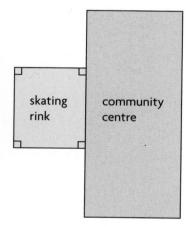

skating rink   community centre

b) Create a scatter plot of perimeter versus width.

c) Use your scatter plot to estimate the dimensions of the rink that will use the least amount of fencing needed to enclose the 3 sides.

6. The same piece of string was used to create these three rectangles. Which one has the maximum area? Explain your thinking.

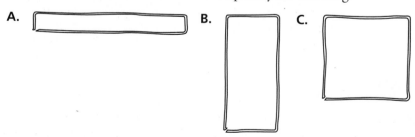

A.   B.   C.

7. A rectangular, indoor fish pond is being added to the lobby of a hotel. The budget allows for a stone border of 36 m around the pond. What dimensions will create a pond with the greatest area? How do you know?

8. Determine the dimensions of a rectangle with a perimeter of 40 cm and the greatest possible area.

9. What is the largest rectangular area that can be built with a 20 m fence in the corner of a building?

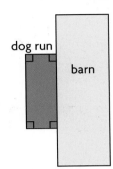

   a) Create a table of values showing possible perimeters, widths, lengths, and areas.
   b) Construct a scatter plot of the area versus the width.
   c) Explain your solution.

10. Randy is building a rectangular, fenced dog run beside his barn. He has 120 m of fencing and plans to use the side of the barn as one side of the fenced area. What are the dimensions of a dog run that maximizes the area Randy can enclose?

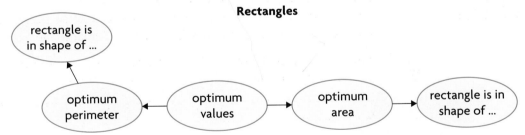

11. A farmer has $3600 to spend on fencing for three adjoining rectangular pastures, as shown. The pastures all have the same dimensions. A local contracting company charges $6.25/m for fencing. What is the largest area that the farmer can enclose?

12. Complete and extend the mind map for rectangles.

Rectangles

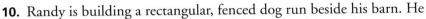

rectangle is in shape of ...

optimum perimeter

optimum values

optimum area

rectangle is in shape of ...

Extending

13. A 60 cm length of rope is to be cut into two pieces to form the perimeters of two separate squares. The total area of the two squares is to be a maximum. Calculate the dimensions of the squares to the nearest hundredth.

14. Diane is building a kennel with two stalls. She has 80 m of wood panelling for the outer walls and an inside wall to separate the two stalls. What dimensions would give each stall the maximum equal area?

Problems Involving Composite Shapes

YOU WILL NEED
- grid paper
- spreadsheet software (optional)

GOAL

Solve problems involving the area and perimeter of composite 2-D shapes.

LEARN ABOUT the Math

The town of Maple Beach is accepting proposals to create a new beach play area. All proposals must give the area and perimeter of each part of the design, the total area and perimeter, and the cost of the materials. Students from the local high school are submitting a proposal.

Beach Play Area Measurements Table

Area	Material	Area (m²)	Perimeter (m)
volleyball courts	sand and chalk trim		
food court	tinted cement and stone trim		
wading pool	pool tiles and fencing		
family beach area	lawn sod and plastic lawn trim		
Total Beach Play Area Measurements:			

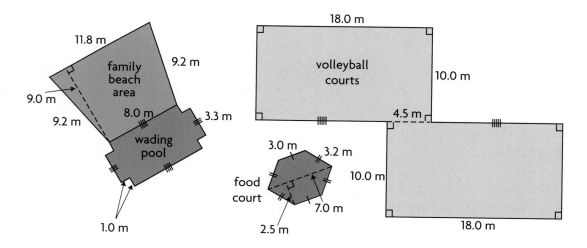

? How can the students determine the areas and perimeters of the figures to complete their proposal?

EXAMPLE 1   Decomposing shapes to solve an area and perimeter problem

Jamie's Solution

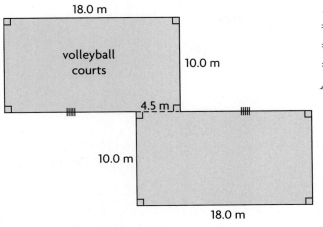

$A_{\text{rectangle}}$
$= l \times w$
$= 10.0 \times 18.0$
$= 180.0 \text{ m}^2$

$A_{\text{volleyball courts}} = 2 \times 180.0$
$= 360.0 \text{ m}^2$

> I started with the two volleyball courts. I calculated the area of one court, and then, doubled it.

Missing side length
$= 18.0 - 4.5$
$= 13.5 \text{ m}$

$P_{\text{volleyball courts}} = 2 \times 18.0 + 4 \times 10.0 + 2 \times 13.5$
$= 103.0 \text{ m}$

> The perimeter was the sum of the side lengths. Two sides were 18.0 m long and four sides were 10.0 m long. To determine the length of the last two sides, I subtracted the 4.5 m section from 18.0 m to get 13.5 m.

$$A_{\text{trapezoid}} = \frac{(b_1 + b_2) \times h}{2}$$

$$= \frac{(3.0 + 7.0) \times 2.5}{2}$$

$$= \frac{10.0 \times 2.5}{2}$$

$$= \frac{25.0}{2}$$

$$= 12.5 \text{ m}^2$$

$A_{\text{food court}} = 2 \times 12.5$
$= 25.0 \text{ m}^2$

> I divided the food court into two trapezoids. I calculated the area of one trapezoid and doubled it.

$P_{\text{food court}} = 2 \times 3.0 + 4 \times 3.2$
$= 6.0 + 12.8$
$= 18.8 \text{ m}$

> I calculated the perimeter of the food court.

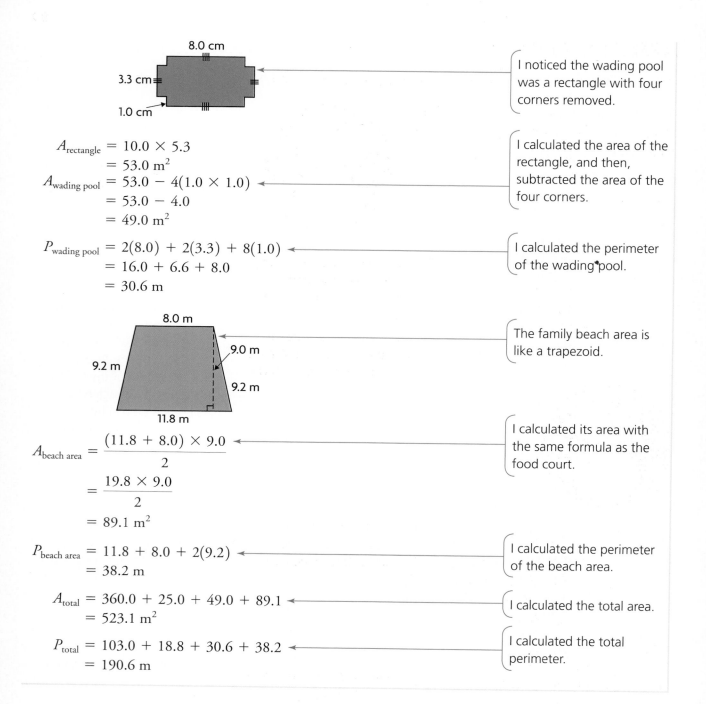

8.0 cm

3.3 cm

1.0 cm

> I noticed the wading pool was a rectangle with four corners removed.

$A_{rectangle} = 10.0 \times 5.3$
$= 53.0 \text{ m}^2$
$A_{wading\ pool} = 53.0 - 4(1.0 \times 1.0)$
$= 53.0 - 4.0$
$= 49.0 \text{ m}^2$

> I calculated the area of the rectangle, and then, subtracted the area of the four corners.

$P_{wading\ pool} = 2(8.0) + 2(3.3) + 8(1.0)$
$= 16.0 + 6.6 + 8.0$
$= 30.6 \text{ m}$

> I calculated the perimeter of the wading pool.

8.0 m

9.0 m

9.2 m

9.2 m

11.8 m

> The family beach area is like a trapezoid.

$A_{beach\ area} = \dfrac{(11.8 + 8.0) \times 9.0}{2}$
$= \dfrac{19.8 \times 9.0}{2}$
$= 89.1 \text{ m}^2$

> I calculated its area with the same formula as the food court.

$P_{beach\ area} = 11.8 + 8.0 + 2(9.2)$
$= 38.2 \text{ m}$

> I calculated the perimeter of the beach area.

$A_{total} = 360.0 + 25.0 + 49.0 + 89.1$
$= 523.1 \text{ m}^2$

> I calculated the total area.

$P_{total} = 103.0 + 18.8 + 30.6 + 38.2$
$= 190.6 \text{ m}$

> I calculated the total perimeter.

Reflecting

A. How did looking at simple shapes help Jamie determine the areas and perimeters of the composite shapes?

B. How else could Jamie have decomposed the shapes?

APPLY the Math

| EXAMPLE 2 | Using a subtraction strategy to calculate area |

Matti is designing a logo in his graphic arts class. How can Matti calculate the area of the blue section?

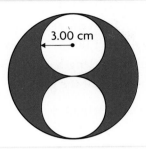

Matti's Solution

$A_{\text{blue circle}} = \pi r^2$
$\doteq 3.14 \times 6.00^2$
$= 3.14 \times 36.00$
$= 113.04 \text{ cm}^2$

I decided to calculate the area of the blue circle, and then, subtract the area of the white circles.

The radius of the blue circle was the same as the diameter of a white circle, or 6.00 cm.

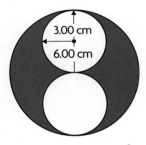

$A_{\text{white circle}} = \pi r^2$
$A_{\text{both white circles}} = 2 \times (\pi r^2)$
$\doteq 2 \times (3.14 \times 3.00^2)$
$= 2 \times (3.14 \times 9.00)$
$= 2 \times (28.26)$
$= 56.52 \text{ cm}^2$

Both white circles have a radius of 3 cm, so I calculated the area of one, and then, doubled it.

$A_{\text{blue circle}} \doteq 113.04 \text{ cm}^2$
$A_{\text{white circle}} \doteq 56.52 \text{ cm}^2$
$A_{\text{blue section}} \doteq 113.04 - 56.52$
$\doteq 56.52 \text{ cm}^2$

I subtracted to determine the area of the blue part.

The area of the blue section is about 56.52 cm^2.

I answered to two decimal places, because that is how the dimensions were given.

EXAMPLE 3 | Solving a problem using a right triangle

Rani is replacing a regular hexagonal window. The side length is 1.16 m and the distance from the centre to the middle of each side is 1.00 m. How can Rani calculate the length of the wooden framing and the area of the glass?

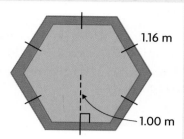

Rani's Solution

$$P_{\text{hexagon}} = n \times s$$
$$= 6 \times 1.16$$
$$= 6.96 \text{ m}$$

The perimeter of the hexagon is 6.96 m.

Each side of the frame is the same length, so I multiplied one side's length by 6 to get the perimeter.

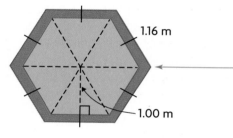

To determine the area, I divided the hexagon into 6 identical triangles.

$$A_{\text{triangle}} = \frac{1}{2}bh$$
$$= \frac{1}{2} \times 1.16 \times 1.00$$
$$= \frac{1}{2} \times 1.16$$
$$= 0.58 \text{ m}^2$$

I used the distance from the centre as the height and the side of the hexagon as the base.

$$A_{\text{hexagon}} = \text{number of sides} \times A_{\text{triangle}}$$
$$= 6 \times 0.58$$
$$= 3.48 \text{ m}^2$$

I calculated the area of the hexagon by multiplying the area of one triangle by 6.

The area of the hexagon is 3.48 m².

I realized my formula would work for any regular polygon because you can always divide it into identical triangles.

In Summary

Key Idea

- You can determine the area or perimeter of a geometric shape by decomposing it into simpler shapes whose formulas you know.

Need to Know

- The area of a shape created by joining smaller shapes is equal to the combined area of the smaller shapes. For example, the area of the yellow shape is equal to the sum of the areas of the blue and green shapes.

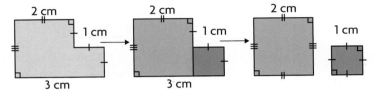

- When one shape is removed from another, the area of the remaining shape is equal to the area of the original shape minus the area of the shape that was removed.
- To calculate the perimeter of a new shape created from other shapes, determine whether some of the original shapes' sides are either duplicated or no longer part of the new perimeter. The perimeter of the yellow shape is not the same as the sum of the perimeters of the blue and green shapes.
- The formula for the perimeter of a regular polygon is $P = n \times s$, where n is the number of sides and s is the length of each side.
- To calculate the area of a regular polygon, divide it into triangles, and then, add their areas. Form the triangles by drawing a line from the centre to each vertex. The polygon side length is the base of each triangle, and the distance from the centre to the middle of each side is the height.

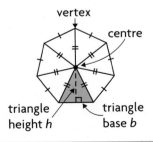

CHECK Your Understanding

Give your answers to the same number of decimal places as in the original measurements.

1. Calculate the shaded area of each figure.

   a)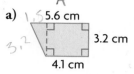
   5.6 cm
   3.2 cm
   4.1 cm

   b)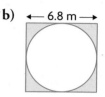
   ← 6.8 m →

   c)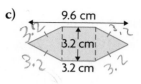
   9.6 cm
   3.2 cm
   3.2 cm

2. Calculate the perimeter and area of each shape.

   a)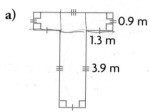
   0.9 m
   1.3 m
   3.9 m

   b)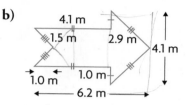
   4.1 m
   1.5 m   2.9 m
   4.1 m
   1.0 m   1.0 m
   6.2 m

PRACTISING

3. Calculate the shaded area of each figure.

   K

   a)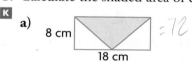
   8 cm
   18 cm

   c)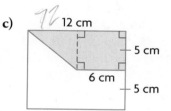
   12 cm
   5 cm
   6 cm
   5 cm

   b)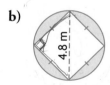
   4.8 m

   d)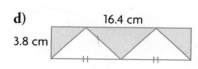
   16.4 cm
   3.8 cm

4. Calculate the area and perimeter of this shape.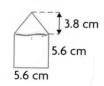
   3.8 cm
   5.6 cm
   5.6 cm

5. Calculate the area and perimeter of each regular polygon.

   a)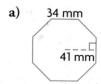
   34 mm
   41 mm

   b)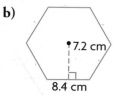
   7.2 cm
   8.4 cm

   c)
   20.4 cm
   14.4 cm

6. a) Copy this shape and [A] divide it into simpler polygons.

b) Calculate the area of the shape. Explain your thinking.

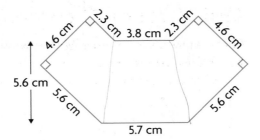

7. Calculate the length of one side of each regular polygon.

a)

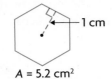

$A = 5.2 \text{ cm}^2$

b)

$A = 758 \text{ mm}^2$

8. a) Explain how you can calculate the area of this shape. Include what [T] measurements you would need to know to calculate the area.

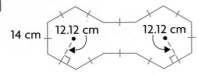

63 cm

b) Calculate the perimeter of the shape in part a).

9. Calculate the area and perimeter of this shape. Explain what you did.
[C]

 14 cm | 12.12 cm   12.12 cm

Extending

10. Determine an expression for the shaded area of each figure.

a)

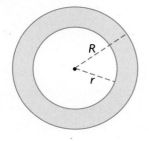

b)

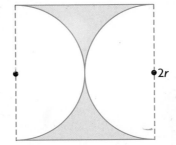

c)

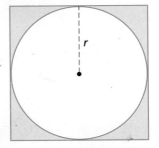

11. Show how to calculate the area of a regular polygon using only its perimeter and the distance from its centre to the midpoint of each side.

The Pythagorean Theorem

YOU WILL NEED
- grid paper
- scissors

Solve problems using the Pythagorean theorem.

LEARN ABOUT the Math

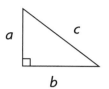

Julie is tutoring her friend, Annie, on using the Pythagorean theorem to solve problems. To help Annie understand, Julie creates a geometric representation of the theorem using a picture.

? What geometric model can Julie use to represent the Pythagorean theorem?

EXAMPLE 1   **Representing the Pythagorean theorem geometrically**

Julie's Solution

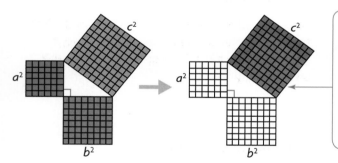

I used grid paper. I drew a right triangle with legs of 6 cm and 8 cm. I cut out a square to fit on each side of the triangle. I coloured the squares blue, red, and green.

I rearranged the blue and red squares on top of the green square on the long side or **hypotenuse**. The hypotenuse square had the same area as the sum of the two other squares.

$$\text{square of } a + \text{square of } b = \text{square of } c$$
$$a^2 + b^2 = c^2$$
$$6^2 + 8^2 = c^2 \text{ or } c^2 = 6^2 + 8^2$$
$$c^2 = 36 + 64$$
$$c^2 = 100$$
$$\sqrt{c^2} = \sqrt{100}$$
$$c = 10 \text{ cm}$$

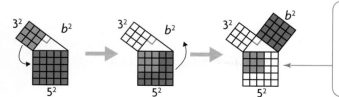

I tried another triangle. I discovered that the square on the side with a length of 3 had an area of 9 and the square on the side with a length of 5 had an area of 25. I subtracted 9 from 25 to get 16, which is 4 squared. I decided that side *b* had a length of 4.

Reflecting

A. How did a geometric model help to represent the Pythagorean theorem?

B. How can you use known sides of a right triangle to calculate an unknown side?

APPLY the Math

EXAMPLE 2 | Applying the Pythagorean theorem to calculate a length

Anil is constructing a 5.00 m tall windmill supported by wires. One wire must be 13.00 m long and the distance between the wires must be 16.75 m. Anil wanted to know what length to cut for the other wire.

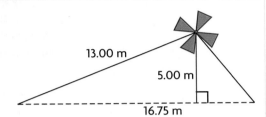

13.00 m
5.00 m
16.75 m

Anil's Solution

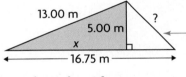

13.00 m
5.00 m
?
x
16.75 m

I divided the triangle into two right triangles. I started with the left-hand triangle since I knew two of its dimensions.

$$a^2 + b^2 = c^2$$
$$x^2 + 5.00^2 = 13.00^2$$
$$x^2 + 25.00 = 169.00$$
$$x^2 = 169.00 - 25.00$$
$$x^2 = 144.00$$
$$x = \sqrt{144.00}$$
$$x = 12.00 \text{ m}$$

I determined the distance, x, from the windmill to the base of the left-hand wire. I substituted the sides I knew into the Pythagorean theorem and solved for x.

The distance was 12.00 m.

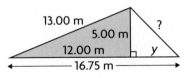

13.00 m
5.00 m
12.00 m
?
y
16.75 m

$$y = 16.75 - 12.00$$
$$= 4.75 \text{ m}$$

I calculated the distance, y, from the windmill to the right-hand wire's base.

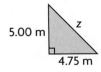

5.00 m
z
4.75 m

$$z^2 = 5.00^2 + 4.75^2$$
$$z^2 = 47.56$$
$$z = 6.90 \text{ m}$$

The other wire should be 6.90 m long.

The hypotenuse, z, is the length of wire needed. I calculated the hypotenuse using the legs.

EXAMPLE **3**

Solving a problem modelled by a right triangle

The Saamis Teepee in Medicine Hat, Alberta, is the tallest teepee in the world. In 2007, a windstorm damaged the teepee, reducing its height. Each beam originally was 81.7 m long and touched the ground 48.8 m from the centre of the base. What was the original height of the teepee?

Dave's Solution

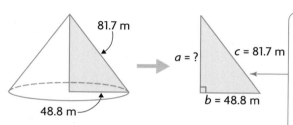

I assumed that the Teepee was a cone and I visualized a right triangle inside it.

The **slant height** of the cone is 81.7 m, and the radius of the base is 48.8 m.

I used the slant height, c, for the hypotenuse and the base radius for the horizontal leg, b.

slant height

the distance from the top to the base, at a right angle, along a slanted side of a **pyramid** or **cone**; it is measured to the midpoint of the base side for a pyramid

Height of cone:
$$a^2 + b^2 = c^2$$
So,
$$a^2 = c^2 - b^2$$
$$a^2 = 81.7^2 - 48.8^2$$
$$a^2 = 6674.89 - 2381.44$$
$$a^2 = 4293.45$$
$$a = \sqrt{4293.45}$$
$$a = 65.5 \text{ m}$$

I calculated the original height of the teepee, a, using the Pythagorean theorem. It is 65.5 m, to one decimal place.

In Summary

Key Idea

- The Pythagorean theorem describes both a numerical and a geometric relationship between the three sides of a right triangle.

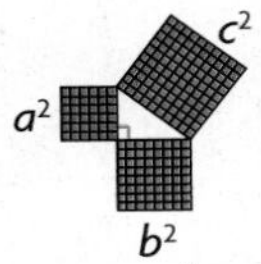

$$a^2 + b^2 = c^2$$

geometric relationship   numerical relationship

Need to Know

- The formula for the hypotenuse of a right triangle is $c = \sqrt{a^2 + b^2}$, where a and b are the lengths of the legs.

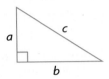

- The formula for the length of a leg of a right triangle is $a = \sqrt{c^2 - b^2}$, where c is the length of the hypotenuse and b is the length of the other leg.

CHECK *Your Understanding*

Give your answers to the same number of decimal places as in the original measurements.

1. Determine the missing length.

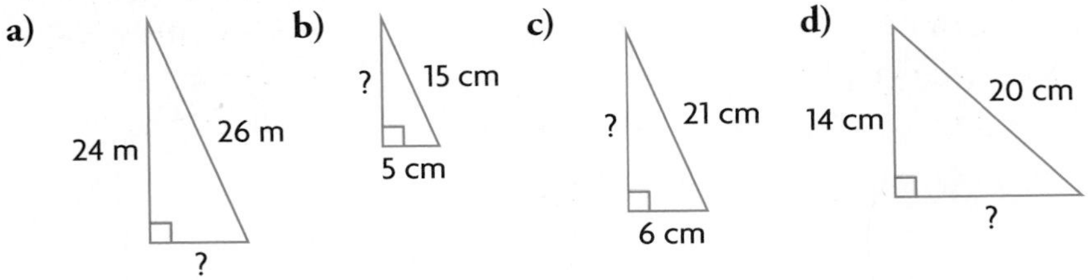

a)

24 m   26 m   ?

b)

?   15 cm
5 cm

c)

?   21 cm
6 cm

d)

14 cm   20 cm
?

2. What is the length of the direct flight path from Desaulniers to Callander?

Measurement   **445**

PRACTISING

3. Calculate the missing length.

a)

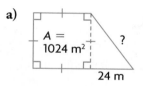

? 17 m
8 m
21 m

b)

40 cm
13 cm 12 cm
?

c)

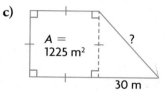

?
73 m
48 m
50 m

4. A path is being constructed between the
K corners of the school playground, as
shown. Determine the length of the path.

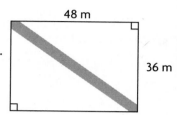

48 m
36 m

5. Determine the length of the hypotenuse.

a)

$A = 1024 \text{ m}^2$
?
24 m

b)

$A = 625 \text{ m}^2$
?
15 m

c)

$A = 1225 \text{ m}^2$
?
30 m

6. Determine the lengths of the boom
and the forestay to one decimal place.

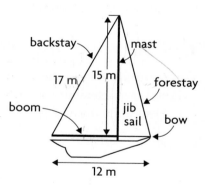

backstay   mast
17 m 15 m
forestay
boom
jib sail   bow
12 m

7. Determine the area of each square.

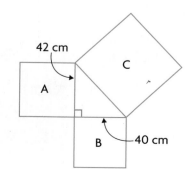

42 cm
C
A
B   40 cm

8. The outside play area of a daycare centre is shown. Show how you can
A use the Pythagorean theorem to ensure that the fence corners are at right angles.

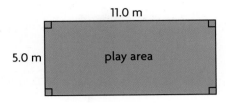

11.0 m

5.0 m   play area

9. A Pythagorean triple is a group of three whole numbers that can represent
T the lengths of the sides of a right triangle. The smallest Pythagorean triple is 3, 4, 5. Which of the following are Pythagorean triples?
a) 7, 24, 25   **b)** 3, 6, 8   **c)** 9, 21, 23   **d)** 31, 35, 38

10. Create a geometric problem that you would have to solve using the
C Pythagorean theorem. Write the problem and its solution, with diagrams.

Extending

11. A box is 12 cm long, 5 cm wide, and 12 cm high. A cardboard rectangle is inserted along the diagonal to divide the box vertically into two equal spaces. Determine the dimensions of the cardboard rectangle.

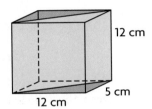

12 cm

5 cm

12 cm

12. A square-based pyramid has a slant height of 100 m. Determine two possible sets of dimensions for the height and side length of the pyramid.

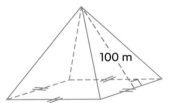

100 m

13. The red triangle shown is not right-angled. Explain how you know that the combined area of squares A and B does not equal the area of square C.

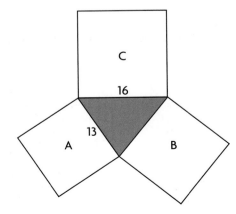

C

16

13

A

B

Surface Area of Right Pyramids and Cones

YOU WILL NEED

• grid paper

> **GOAL**
>
> Determine the surface area of a pyramid and a cone using a variety of strategies.

LEARN ABOUT the Math

right pyramid

a **pyramid** whose base is a regular polygon and whose top vertex is directly above the centre of the base

Yvonne is printing slogans on the side of this **right pyramid.** She wants to calculate its surface area.

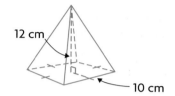

12 cm

10 cm

❓ How can Yvonne determine the area for slogans?

EXAMPLE 1   Calculating surface area using a net and slant height

Yvonne's Solution

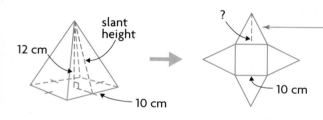

12 cm   slant height

10 cm

?   10 cm

> I visualized the box's net. It had four identical triangles for the sides and a square base.

$$c^2 = a^2 + b^2$$

> I calculated the slant height.

12 cm   12 cm   c

10 cm   5 cm

$$c^2 = 12^2 + 5^2$$
$$c^2 = 144 + 25$$
$$c^2 = 169$$
$$c = \sqrt{169}$$
$$c = 13$$

> The height of the pyramid, a, was 12 cm. The distance, b, from the centre of the base to the side was half of 10 cm, or 5 cm. I visualized the 12 cm and 5 cm lengths as legs of a right triangle. The slant height, c, was the hypotenuse.

$$A_{base} = s^2$$
$$= 10 \times 10$$
$$= 100 \text{ cm}^2$$

$$A_{triangle} = \frac{1}{2}bh$$
$$= \frac{1}{2} \times 10 \times 13$$
$$= 65 \text{ cm}^2$$

> I calculated the area of the square base and of each triangular face.

$$SA_{pyramid} = A_{4 \text{ triangles}} + A_{base}$$
$$= 4 \times 65 + 100$$
$$= 360 \text{ cm}^2$$

> I calculated the total surface area.

Reflecting

A. How did Yvonne use what she already knew about the area of 2-D shapes to determine the area for slogans on the box?

B. How would you explain to a friend how to calculate the surface area of a pyramid?

APPLY the Math

EXAMPLE 2	Solving a surface area problem using nets

Judy found a new box. It is a pyramid with six triangular faces on top of a hexagonal prism. What is its surface area?

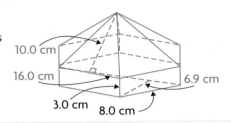

10.0 cm

16.0 cm

6.9 cm

3.0 cm   8.0 cm

Judy's Solution

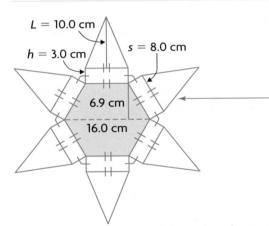

$L = 10.0$ cm

$h = 3.0$ cm $s = 8.0$ cm

6.9 cm

16.0 cm

> I used a net to see all the faces.
>
> There were six identical triangular faces and six identical rectangular faces. The base was a hexagon, so I divided it into two trapezoids.

$$A_{trapezoid} = \frac{1}{2}(base_1 + base_2) \times 6.9$$

$$= \frac{1}{2}(8.0 + 16.0) \times 6.9$$

$$= 82.8 \text{ cm}^2$$

> I calculated the area of one trapezoid.

$$A_{hexagon} = 2 \times A_{trapezoid}$$

$$= 2 \times 82.8$$

$$= 165.6 \text{ cm}^2$$

> I doubled that area to calculate the area of the base.

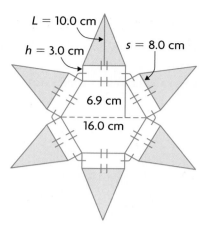

$$A_{6\text{ triangles}} = 6 \times \frac{sL}{2}$$

$$= 6 \times \frac{8.0 \times 10.0}{2}$$

$$= 240.0 \text{ cm}^2$$

I calculated the surface area of the six triangular faces using the base side length s and slant height L.

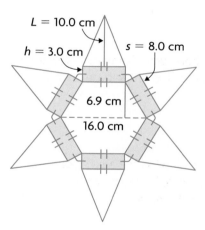

$$A_{6\text{ rectangles}} = 6 \times sh$$

$$= 6 \times 8.0 \times 3.0$$

$$= 144.0 \text{ cm}^2$$

I calculated the surface area of the six rectangular faces using the base side length s and rectangle height h.

$$SA = A_{\text{base}} + A_{\text{sides}}$$

$$= A_{\text{hexagon}} + A_{6\text{ triangles}} + A_{6\text{ rectangles}}$$

$$= 165.6 + 240.0 + 144.0$$

$$= 549.6 \text{ cm}^2$$

I calculated the total surface area of the box.

EXAMPLE 3	Using reasoning to develop a formula for surface area of a pyramid

Sarah wants to calculate the surface area of this pyramid. The perimeter of its base is 80 cm.

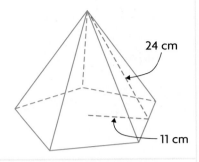

24 cm

11 cm

Sarah's Solution

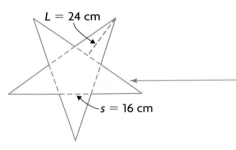

$L = 24$ cm

$s = 16$ cm

> I created a net. I labelled it with the dimensions that I needed. The base side length, s, was $\frac{1}{5}$ of 80 cm, or 16 cm, and the slant height, L, was 24 cm.

> There were five triangles, one for each side of the base.

$$A_{5\text{ triangular faces}} = 5 \times \frac{sL}{2}$$

> I multiplied the area of one triangle by the number of sides on the base.

$$= 5 \times \frac{16 \times 24}{2}$$

$$= 960 \text{ cm}^2$$

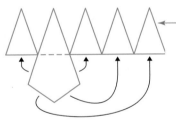

$h = 11$ cm

$b = 16$ cm

> I divided the base into five congruent triangles. Each triangle had a base length of 16 cm and a height of 11 cm.

$$A_{\text{triangle}} = \frac{bh}{2}$$

$$= \frac{11 \times 16}{2}$$

$$= 88 \text{ cm}^2$$

> I calculated the area of one triangle.

$$A_{\text{base}} = 5 \times 88$$ ← There were five triangles, so I multiplied the area by 5.

$$= 440 \text{ cm}^2$$ ← The area of the base was 440 cm².

$$SA = A_{\text{triangular sides}} + A_{\text{base}}$$
$$= 960 + 440$$
$$= 1400 \text{ cm}^2$$ ← I calculated the total surface area.

The pyramid has a surface area of 1400 cm².

EXAMPLE 4   Using reasoning to develop surface area of a cone

a) Develop a formula for calculating the surface area of any cone with radius r, height h, and slant height L.

b) Use the formula to calculate the surface area of a cone with a radius of 3 cm and a height of 7 cm.

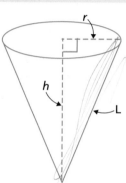

Melinda's Solution

a)

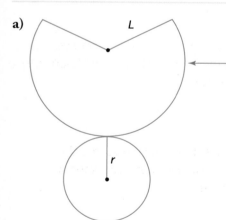

I drew a net for any cone. It is made up of two shapes. The base is a circle with a radius of r. The curved surface opens up to form a sector of the circle with a radius of L, the slant height of the cone.

The surface area of a cone is the sum of the areas of these two shapes.

$$A_{\text{base}} = \pi r^2$$ ← I used the formula for area of a circle to represent the area of the base of the cone.

$$\frac{Area\ of\ curved\ surface}{Area\ of\ circle\,(radius\ =\ L)} = \frac{Circumference\ of\ cone}{Circumference\ of\ circle\,(radius\ =\ L)}$$

$$\frac{Area\ of\ curved\ surface}{\pi L^2} = \frac{2\pi r}{2\pi L}$$

> For the curved surface, I reasoned that its arc length must be equal to the circumference of the circular base. I used proportional reasoning to write two equal ratios that compare areas to circumferences.

$$\pi L^2 \times \frac{Area\ of\ curved\ surface}{\pi L^2} = \pi L^2 \times \frac{2\pi r}{2\pi L}$$

$$\frac{1}{\cancel{\pi L^2}} \times \frac{Area\ of\ curved\ surface}{\underset{1}{\cancel{\pi L^2}}} = \overset{1}{\cancel{\pi L^2}}\overset{L}{} \times \frac{\overset{1}{\cancel{2\pi r}}}{\underset{1\ 1\ 1}{\cancel{2\pi L}}}$$

$$Area\ of\ curved\ surface = \pi rL$$

> I want to find the *Area of curved surface*, so I multiplied both sides of the equation by πL^2. Then, I simplified.

$$Surface\ area\ of\ a\ cone = area\ base + area\ of\ curved\ surface$$
$$= \pi r^2 + \pi rL$$

> I added the two areas that make up the surfaces. This gave me the formula where r = radius of the circular base and L = the slant height of the cone.

b) $r = 3$ cm
$h = 7$ cm
$L = ?$

> I know the radius of the cone and its height but I need to find the slant height L to calculate the surface area.

$$r^2 + h^2 = L^2$$
$$3^2 + 7^2 = L^2$$
$$9 + 49 = L^2$$
$$58 = L^2$$
$$\sqrt{58} = L$$

> r, h, and L are sides in a right triangle, so I used the Pythagorean Theorem to calculate L.

$$Surface\ area\ of\ a\ cone = \pi r^2 + \pi rL$$
$$= (3.14)(3)^2 + (3.14)(3)(\sqrt{58})$$
$$= 28.26 + 9.42(\sqrt{58})$$
$$\doteq 100\ cm^2$$

> I substituted the values into the formula, and then, calculated the answer.

Key Idea

- To calculate the surface area of a right pyramid, add the area of the base and the area of the faces.
- To calculate the surface area of a cone, add the area of the circular base and the area of the curved surface.

Need to Know

- The slant height of a right pyramid is the height of the triangular faces.
- To calculate the slant height of a right pyramid, use its height, the side length of the base, and the Pythagorean theorem.
- To calculate the area of the base of a right pyramid, divide it into isosceles triangles by drawing lines from the centre of the base to each vertex.
- The surface area of a 3-D figure is the combined area of the 2-D shapes in its net.
- The formula for the surface area of a square-based prism is $SA = A_{4triangles} + A_{base}$ or $2bL + b^2$, where b is the base side length and L is the slant height.
- The height of a cone is the distance from the top of the cone to the centre of its circular base.
- To calculate the slant height of a cone, use its radius and height and the Pythagorean theorem.
- The formula for the surface area of a cone is $SA = \pi r^2 + \pi rL$, where r is the radius of the circular base and L is the slant height.

CHECK *Your Understanding*

Give your answers to the same number of decimal places as in the original measurements.

1. Calculate the surface area of each type of candle.

   a)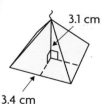
   3.1 cm

   3.4 cm

   b)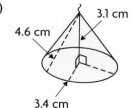
   4.6 cm
   3.1 cm

   3.4 cm

2. Calculate the surface area of each shape.

a)

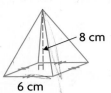

8 cm

6 cm

b)

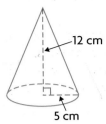

12 cm

5 cm

PRACTISING

3. Calculate the surface area.

K a)

19 m

6 m

b)

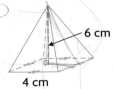

6 cm

4 cm

c)

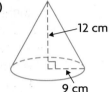

12 cm

9 cm

4. Determine the surface area of a square pyramid with a height of 11.0 cm and a base area of 36.0 cm^2.

5. a) Determine the slant height of a cone with a height of 8 cm and a radius of 4 cm.

b) Calculate the cone's surface area.

6. There are two shapes of snow-cone cups at the Fall Fair. Which cup uses less material? Assume that the bases are regular polygons.

cup A

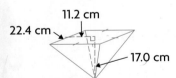

11.2 cm

22.4 cm

17.0 cm

cup B

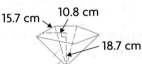

15.7 cm   10.8 cm

18.7 cm

7. Calculate the surface area of each regular pyramid.

a)

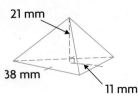

21 mm

38 mm

11 mm

b)

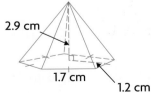

2.9 cm

1.7 cm

1.2 cm

c)

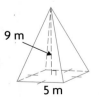

9 m

5 m

8. Calculate the surface area of each cone.

a)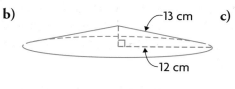
6 cm
8 cm

b) 13 cm
12 cm

c)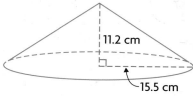
11.2 cm
15.5 cm

9. The local party store sells pyramid-shaped gift boxes. They have either a
A square base with a side length of 10 cm or a regular octagon base with a
distance of 6 cm from the centre of the base to the midpoint of each side.
Both boxes have a base perimeter of 40 cm. Each box has a height of
8 cm. Which box requires more wrapping paper? Explain your solution.

10. Calculate the surface area of this pyramid.

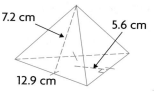
7.2 cm   5.6 cm
12.9 cm

11. Dennis bought a paperweight shaped like a regular hexagonal pyramid
for his sister's birthday. It has a measure of 2.6 cm from the centre of
its base to the midpoint of each side, a base perimeter of 18 cm, and a
height of 4 cm. He wants to know if he has enough wrapping paper
for it. Determine the pyramid's surface area.

12. Salt is stored in a bin shaped like an inverted square-based pyramid. The
sides of the base are 2.8 m long. The bin is 1.8 m high. Determine the
surface area of the bin, including the square base.

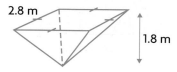
2.8 m
1.8 m

13. Determine the surface area of the tent.
Include the floor in your calculation.

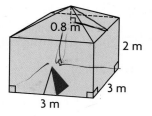
0.8 m
2 m
3 m
3 m

14. The Great Pyramid of Cheops was originally 147 m high. Its square
base had a side length of 230.4 m.
a) Calculate the surface area of the Great Pyramid, including its base.
b) The outside surface of each block in the Great Pyramid is 2.3 m
by 1.8 m. Estimate the number of blocks that make up the outside
facing of the Great Pyramid.

15. Two regular octagonal pyramids are 8 cm high. Pyramid A has a
 T surface area of 318.08 cm² and a measure of 6 cm from the centre
of its base to the midpoint of each side. Pyramid B has a measure of
15 cm from the centre of the base to the midpoint of each side. What
is the surface area of pyramid B?

16. Sketch a pyramid and label its dimensions. Show how to calculate its
 C surface area in at least two different ways.

Extending

17. Each of these regular pyramids is 10 cm high and measures 4 cm from
the centre of the base to the midpoint of each side. Which pyramid do
you think has the greatest surface area? Explain.

A.

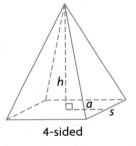

4-sided

C.

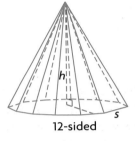

12-sided

B.

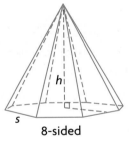

8-sided

D.

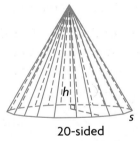

20-sided

18. a) This shape is composed of two
identical regular pyramids. They
each have a height of 5 cm and a
base side length of 7 cm. Determine
the surface area.

b) Another identical pyramid is joined
to the shape on one of its triangular
faces, as shown. Determine the new
surface area.

c) Write a formula for the surface area
of a shape with n pyramids joined in this way.

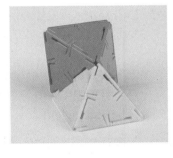

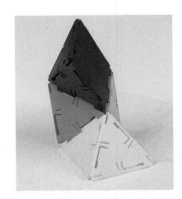

FREQUENTLY ASKED Questions

Study | Aid

- See Lesson 8.1, Example 1.
- Try Mid-Chapter Review Questions 1 and 3.

Q: **If many rectangles have the same perimeter, how can you determine which one has the greatest area?**

A1: The rectangle that is most like a square will have the greatest area.

> **EXAMPLE**

These rectangles all have a perimeter of 80 m, but C has the greatest area.

	30 m			32 m			20 m			36 m	
10 m	A		8 m	B		20 m	C		9 m	D
	$A = 300$ m^2			$A = 256$ m^2			$A = 400$ m^2			$A = 324$ m^2

A2: You can use a table of values and a graph.

> **EXAMPLE**

Here is a table of values for rectangles with perimeters of 80 m. The graph shows that the rectangle with the greatest area is a square.

Length (m)	Width (m)	Area (m²)
5	35	175
10	30	300
15	25	375
20	20	400
25	15	375
30	10	300
35	5	175

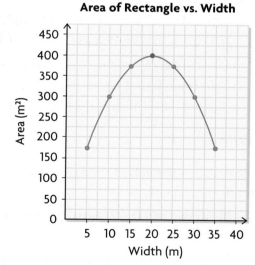

Study | Aid

- See Lesson 8.1, Example 2.
- Try Mid-Chapter Review Questions 2 and 4.

Q: **If several rectangles have the same area, how can you determine which one has the least perimeter?**

A: The rectangle that is most like a square will have the least perimeter.

> **EXAMPLE**

These rectangles all have an area of 100 m², but G has the least perimeter.

	50 m			25 m			10 m	
2 m			4 m				10 m	
	$P = 104$ m			$P = 58$ m			$P = 40$ m	
	E			F			G	

Q: **How can you determine the area or perimeter of a composite 2-D shape?**

Study Aid
- See Lesson 8.2, Examples 1, 2, and 3.
- Try Mid-Chapter Review Question 5.

A1: Separate the shape into simpler shapes and calculate their areas. Then, add the areas. To calculate its perimeter, add the length of each side.

A2: Subtract the area of a smaller shape from a larger shape to calculate the area left over. Add the length of each side on the border to calculate the perimeter.

EXAMPLE

The area of this square is 144 m² and the area of the circle is πr^2 or about 79 cm², so the blue area is about $144 - 79 = 65$ cm².

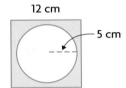

12 cm

5 cm

Q: **When is the geometric relationship of the Pythagorean theorem useful as a part of a problem-solving strategy?**

Study Aid
- See Lesson 8.3, Examples 1, 2, and 3.
- Try Mid-Chapter Review Questions 6 and 7.

A: You can use the Pythagorean theorem to determine the third side of a right triangle or the area of a square on the third side. The hypotenuse is $c = \sqrt{a^2 + b^2}$ and the length of a leg is $a = \sqrt{c^2 - b^2}$.

EXAMPLE

The length of one side of the green square is $\sqrt{3^2 + 4^2} = 5$ cm and its area is 5^2 or 25 cm².

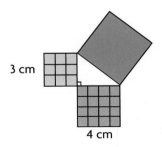

3 cm

4 cm

Q: **How can you calculate the surface area of a right pyramid or cone?**

A: For a right pyramid, you can use the formula $SA = A_{\text{base}} + A_{\text{triangular faces}}$

For a cone, use the formula $SA = \pi r^2 + \pi r L$, where r is the radius of the circular base and L is the slant height.

Study Aid
- See Lesson 8.4, Examples 1, 2, and 4.
- Try Mid-Chapter Review Questions 8 and 9.

PRACTICE Questions

Lesson 8.1

1. Each rectangle has a perimeter of 48 units. Predict which has the greatest area. Explain.

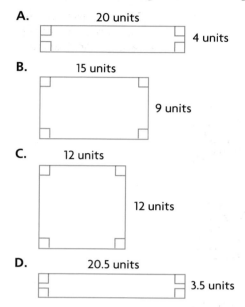

A. 20 units / 4 units

B. 15 units / 9 units

C. 12 units / 12 units

D. 20.5 units / 3.5 units

2. Draw rectangles with areas of 72 square units on grid paper. Determine which rectangle has the least perimeter, and then, calculate its perimeter.

3. Calculate the maximum area for a rectangle with each perimeter.
a) 100 cm   **b)** 20 m   **c)** 24 km

4. Josie is building a rectangular garden centre with an area of 98 m² attached to the side of her store. Determine the minimum length of wood needed for a fence on the three open sides.

Lesson 8.2

5. Sketch the deck plan. Divide the deck into polygons to show how to determine the area of the wooden section. List the dimensions you need to calculate the perimeter and area of the deck.

DECK

PATIO

DECK PLAN

Lesson 8.3

6. Arshad is creating this tile pattern. He wants to use a right triangle tile and several square tiles around it. What is the area of each tile?

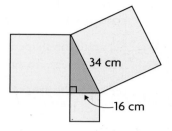

34 cm

16 cm

7. A new covered walkway is being constructed to connect two malls. The rectangular space between the two malls is 8.0 m by 7.0 m. The walkway will connect the malls' opposite corners. How long is the reference chalk line drawn between the corners?

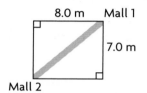

8.0 m   Mall 1

7.0 m

Mall 2

Lesson 8.4

8. Determine the surface area of each shape.

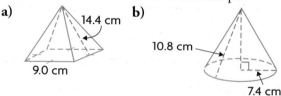

a) 14.4 cm / 9.0 cm

b) 10.8 cm / 7.4 cm

9. Janice needs to re-shingle the roof of her house. One bundle of shingles costs $35.99 and covers 2.25 m².
a) How many bundles of shingles does she need for the roof?
b) What is the total cost of re-shingling the roof?

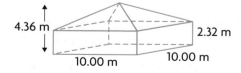

4.36 m   2.32 m

10.00 m   10.00 m

Volumes of Pyramids and Cones

GOAL

Investigate formulas for the volume of pyramids and cones.

INVESTIGATE the Math

The student art club recycles used candles. The students store yellow wax in cylinders, and red wax in prisms, as shown. They will pour the red wax into pyramids and the yellow wax into cones. Then, they will sell them with wicks as candle kits to raise money for field trips. The pyramids and prisms have the same height and base area. Likewise, the cylinders and cones have the same height and base area.

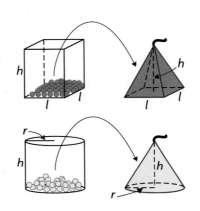

? How many pyramidal candles can be made from one prism, and how many conical candles can be made from one cylinder?

A. Estimate the pyramid's volume as a fraction of the prism's volume.

B. Fill the prism with sand.

C. How many times can you fill the pyramid with sand from the prism?

D. Estimate the cone's volume as a fraction of the cylinder's volume.

E. Fill the cylinder with sand.

F. How many times can you fill the cone with sand from the cylinder?

Reflecting

G. How is calculating the volume of the pyramid, from the volume of its corresponding prism, like calculating the volume of the cone from the volume of its corresponding cylinder?

H. What formula describes how to calculate the volume of a square-based pyramid with base length l and height h?

I. What formula describes how to calculate the volume of a cone with radius r and height h?

APPLY the Math

EXAMPLE **1**   Calculating the volume of a pyramid

John and Lisa bought an oil lamp with a reservoir in the shape of a pyramid with a regular pentagonal base. A diagram of the base is shown. The reservoir has a height of 8.1 cm. The oil comes in 750 mL bottles. How many times can they fill the lamp completely with one bottle of oil?

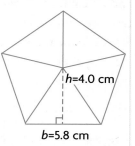

h=4.0 cm

b=5.8 cm

Henri's Solution

$$A_{\text{pentagon}} = 5 \times \frac{bh}{2}$$

$$= 5 \times \frac{5.8 \times 4.0}{2}$$

$$= 5 \times \frac{23.2}{2}$$

$$= 5 \times 11.6$$

$$= 58.0 \text{ cm}^2$$

The area of the base was 58.0 cm².

> I divided the base into five triangles.
>
> I multiplied by 5 to determine the total area.

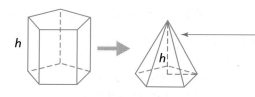

h

h

> I drew the prism that corresponds to the pyramid. Its volume is Ah. The volume of the pyramid is $\frac{1}{3}$ that of the prism.

$$V_{\text{pyramid}} = \frac{1}{3} Ah$$

$$= \frac{1}{3} \times 58 \times 8.1$$

$$= \frac{1}{3} \times 469.8$$

$$= 156.6 \text{ cm}^3$$

> I calculated the volume of the pyramid.

The volume was 156.6 cm³.
The capacity was 156.6 mL.

$750 \div 156.6 = 4.8$
You can fill the lamp completely four times with one bottle of oil.

> I determined how many times you can fill the lamp.

EXAMPLE 2   Selecting a strategy to calculate volume

A conical paper cup has a radius of 4 cm and a height of 10 cm. A cylindrical glass has a radius of 4 cm and a height of 20 cm. How many times do you need to fill the paper cup and pour it into the glass to fill the glass?

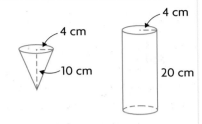

Marcy's Solution: Determining volume using a formula

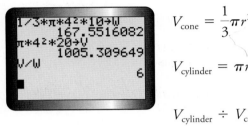

$V_{\text{cone}} = \dfrac{1}{3}\pi r^2 h$ ◄── I calculated the volume of the paper cup.

$V_{\text{cylinder}} = \pi r^2 h$ ◄── I calculated the volume of the glass.

$V_{\text{cylinder}} \div V_{\text{cone}}$ ◄── I divided the volume of the glass by the volume of the cup.

You have to fill the paper cup 6 times to fill the glass.

Wyatt decided he could solve the problem without any calculations.

Wyatt's Solution: volume using reasoning

If the glass were the same height as the paper cup, I would need to fill the paper cup 3 times. But, the glass is 20 cm high, so 2 cylinders with a height of 10 cm each will fit inside it. This means that I need to fill the paper cup 2 × 3 or 6 times.

◄── The glass has the same radius as the cup, and twice the height of the cup.

In Summary

Key Ideas

- The volume of a pyramid is $\frac{1}{3}$ the volume of a prism with an identical base and height.

- The volume of a cone is $\frac{1}{3}$ the volume of a cylinder with an identical base and height.

Need to Know

- The formula for the volume of a pyramid is $V = \frac{1}{3}Ah$ where A is the area of its base and h is its height.

- The formula for the volume of a cone is $V = \frac{1}{3}\pi r^2 h$ where r is the radius of its base and h is its height.

CHECK Your Understanding

Give your answers to the same number of decimal places as in the original measurements.

1. Calculate the volume of the gift box.

   7 cm

   8 cm

2. Calculate the volume of the cone.

   h = 4.2 m

   r = 3.2 m

PRACTISING

3. Determine the volume of sand that would fill a cone with a base radius of 6.5 cm and a height of 12.0 cm.

4. Sammy has a regular octagonal-based pyramidal paperweight filled with coloured liquid. It has a distance of 4.2 cm from the centre of its base to the midpoint of each side, a base perimeter of 19.0 cm, and a height of 6.0 cm. Determine the volume of the pyramid.

5. Calculate the volume of the cone.
   K

   l = 4.2 m

   r = 1.6 m

6. Sand for icy roads is stored in a conical pile 14.2 m high with a base diameter of 34.4 m.
   a) Calculate the volume of the pile.
   b) One sander can take 6.9 m³ of sand. How many sanders can be filled from the pile?

7. A square-based pyramid has a volume of 100 cm³ and a base area of 40 cm². What is its height?

8. Candles in the shape of square-based pyramids are sold in three volumes: 75 cm³, 150 cm³, and 175 cm³. The base side length of each candle is 5 cm. What are the heights of the candles?

9. **T** A pyramid and a prism with the same height both have a base area of 64 cm². How do their volumes compare?

10. **A** Each conical paper cup for a water fountain has a height of 9 cm and a radius of 3 cm. An average of 45 cups of water is drunk each day. What volume of water is drunk each week?

11. **C** Describe the problem-solving process you would use to compare the volume of a square-based pyramid and a cone with the same height.

Extending

12. For each right pyramid, the base is a regular polygon with $a = 4$ cm and $h = 10$ cm.

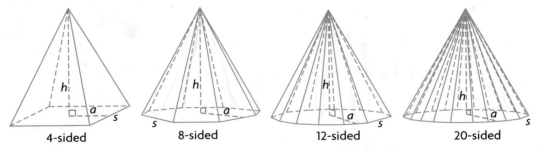

4-sided   8-sided   12-sided   20-sided

   a) Develop a formula to compute the volume of each pyramid in terms of a and h.
   b) Use your result to state a formula for the volume of a cone with a height of 10 cm and a radius of a.

Volume and Surface Area of a Sphere

- orange
- scissors and tape
- paper
- sand
- paper plates

GOAL

Develop formulas for the volume and surface area of a sphere.

INVESTIGATE the Math

Exercise balls are **spheres** filled with liquid for weight training. They are sold in cylindrical packages. The manufacturer wants to calculate how much water will fill an exercise ball with a radius of 18 cm, and how much material is needed to make the ball.

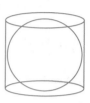

> **?** How can you determine the volume and surface area of a spherical shape like the exercise ball?

A. Use an orange to represent the exercise ball.
Construct a paper tube to represent the cylindrical package.
It should be the same height as the orange and have the same circumference as the equator of the orange.

B. Calculate the volume of the paper tube in millilitres using the formula $V = \pi r^2 h$ (1 mL = 1 cm^3).

C. Place the tube on a paper plate.
Put the orange in the tube.
Pour the sand into the tube, filling the regions above and below the orange.

D. Remove the tube, leaving the sand and orange on the plate.
Pour the same sand back into the tube again, using a second plate.

E. Compare the volume of the sand left in the tube with the volume of the tube.

F. Trace the base of the paper tube several times on paper.

G. Calculate the area of the circles, using the formula $A = \pi r^2$.

H. Peel the orange and place the pieces of peel over the circles that you traced using the base of the paper tube.

I. Estimate the area of the orange.

J. Compare the surface area of the peel (sphere) to the area of the base of the tube.

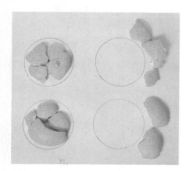

Reflecting

K. About what fraction of the cylinder did the orange fill?
The cylinder's height was twice its radius.
Use this fact and your result to create a formula to describe the volume of a sphere in terms of its radius.

L. About how many copies of the base of the cylinder did you cover with the orange peel?
How might you use your results to create a formula for the surface area of a sphere?

APPLY the Math

EXAMPLE 1   Using a formula to calculate volume

Dylan must buy 100 spherical balloons for $0.08 each and enough helium to inflate them. Helium costs $0.024/L. Each balloon will inflate to a surface area of 900.00 cm². How much will it cost to buy and inflate them?

Dylan's Solution

$$SA_{sphere} = 4\pi r^2$$
$$4(3.14 \times r^2) \doteq 900.00$$

> I used the surface area to determine the radius.

$$3.14 \times r^2 = \frac{900.00}{4}$$

$$3.14 \times r^2 = 225.00$$

$$r^2 = \frac{225.00}{3.14}$$

$$r^2 \doteq 71.66$$

> I took the square root of 71.66 to calculate r.

$$r \doteq 8.47 \text{ cm}$$

$$V = \frac{4}{3}\pi r^3$$

$$\doteq \frac{4}{3}(3.14) \times (8.47)^3$$

> I calculated the volume of one balloon.

$$\doteq 2544 \text{ mL or } 2.544 \text{ L}$$

Cost of helium for one balloon
= cost of helium × volume of balloon
= 0.024 × 2.544
= $0.061

Cost of 100 balloons with helium
100 × (0.08 + 0.061)
= 100 × 0.141
= $14.10
The total cost will be $14.10.

Zuri wanted to make a bowl in shop class. She decided to hollow out
a half-sphere from a cube. She needed to know the surface area to
varnish the bowl. She also wanted to know the final volume of wood used.

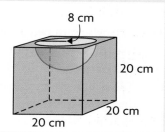

8 cm

20 cm

20 cm

20 cm

Zuri's Solution

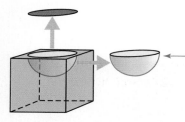

I visualized the surface area as a half-sphere plus a cube. But the cube was missing the area of the circle where the half-sphere was cut.

$$SA_{\text{bowl}} = SA_{1 \text{ half-sphere}} + SA_{6 \text{ squares}} - SA_{1 \text{ circle}}$$

$$SA_{\text{sphere}} = 4\pi r^2$$

I counted the half-sphere and six square sides minus the circle.

$$SA_{\text{half-sphere}} = \frac{1}{2} \times 4\pi r^2$$

$$\doteq \frac{1}{2} \times 4 \times 3.14 \times 8^2$$

$$= 2 \times 3.14 \times 64$$

$$= 2 \times 200.96$$

$$\doteq 402 \text{ cm}^2$$

The surface area of the half-sphere is about 402 cm².   I calculated the surface area of the half-sphere.

$$SA_{\text{square}} = s^2$$

$$SA_{\text{circle}} = \pi r^2$$

$$SA_{6 \text{ squares}} - SA_{1 \text{ circle}} = 6 \times s^2 - \pi r^2$$

$$\doteq 6 \times 20^2 - 3.14 \times 8^2$$

$$= 6 \times 400 - 3.14 \times 64$$

$$= 2400 - 200.96$$

$$= 2199.04$$

$$\doteq 2199 \text{ cm}^3$$

The surface area is about 2199 cm³.

I calculated the surface area of the square sides minus the circle.

$SA_{bowl} = 402 + 2199$

$\quad\quad = 2601 \text{ cm}^3$

The surface area of the bowl is 2601 cm³. ← I calculated the total surface area of the bowl.

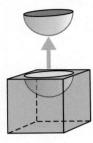

$V_{wood} = V_{cube} - V_{half\text{-}sphere}$ ← I determined the volume of wood. I visualized the volume as a cube minus a half-sphere.

$V_{sphere} = \dfrac{4}{3}\pi r^3$

$V_{half\text{-}sphere} = \dfrac{1}{2} \times \dfrac{4}{3}\pi r^3$

$\quad\quad \doteq \dfrac{1}{2} \times \dfrac{4}{3} \times 3.14 \times 8^3$

$\quad\quad = \dfrac{2}{3} \times 3.14 \times 512$

$\quad\quad = \dfrac{2}{3} \times 1607.68$

$\quad\quad \doteq 1071.79 \text{ cm}^3$

The volume of the half-sphere is about 1071.79 cm³. ← I calculated the volume of the half-sphere.

$V_{cube} = s^3$

$\quad\quad = 20^3$

$\quad\quad = 8000 \text{ cm}^3$

The volume of the cube is 8000 cm³. ← I calculated the volume of the cube.

$V_{wood} = 8000 - 1071.79$

$\quad\quad = 6928.21 \text{ cm}^3$

The volume of wood used for the bowl is ← I calculated the total volume of the wood used.
6928.21 cm³.

In Summary

Key Ideas

- The surface area of a sphere is four times the area of the circular cross-section that goes through its diameter.

- The volume of a sphere is $\frac{2}{3}$ the volume of a cylinder with the same radius and height.

Need to Know

- The formula for the surface area of a sphere with radius r is $SA = 4\pi r^2$.
- The formula for the volume of a sphere with radius r is $V = \frac{4}{3}\pi r^3$.
- The surface area of a 3-D figure composed of other 3-D figures is the sum of the exposed surface areas of the other figures.
- The volume of a 3-D figure composed of other figures is the combined volume of the other figures.
- When one 3-D figure is removed from another, the volume of the remaining figure is the volume of the original figure minus the volume of the figure that was removed.

CHECK Your Understanding

Give your answers to the same number of decimal places as in the original measurements.

1. Calculate the surface area of a tennis ball with a radius of 3.0 cm.

2. Calculate the volume of the beach ball.

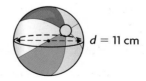

$d = 11$ cm

PRACTISING

3. Calculate the surface area of a soccer ball with a radius of 12 cm. Explain what you did.

4. Calculate how much water you would need to fill a round water balloon with a radius of 5 cm.

5. Jim runs a company that makes ball bearings. The bearings are shipped in boxes that are then loaded onto trucks. Each bearing has a diameter of 0.96 cm.
   a) Each box can hold 8000 cm³ of ball bearings. How many ball bearings can a box hold?
   b) Each ball bearing has a mass of 0.95 g. Determine the mass of each box.
   c) The maximum mass a truck can carry is 11 000 kg. What is the maximum number of boxes that can be loaded into a truck?
   d) Besides the ball bearings' mass, what else must Jim consider when loading a truck?

6. Ice cream is sold to stores in cylindrical containers as shown. Each scoop of ice cream in a cone is a sphere with a diameter of 4.2 cm.
   a) How many scoops of ice cream are in each container?
   b) An ice cream cone with one scoop sells for 86¢. How much money will the ice cream store charge for each full cylinder of ice cream that it sells in cones?

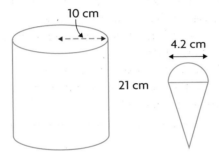

7. a) Earth has a circumference of about 40 000 km. Estimate its radius to the nearest tenth of a kilometre and use the radius to calculate the surface area to the nearest hundred square kilometres.
   b) Mars has a surface area of about 144 800 000 km². Determine the circumference of Mars to the nearest hundred kilometres.

8. a) Frederic has a sphere of clay with a radius of 10 cm. What additional volume of clay does he need to enlarge his sphere to one with a radius of 20 cm?
   b) How much foil would be needed to wrap the larger sphere?

9. a) A tennis ball has a radius of 3.4 cm. What volume of this cylinder is empty?
   b) This pattern is used to create the surface of one tennis ball. How much material will be left over?

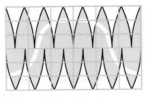

Measurement **471**

10. A baseball has an inner core covered with string. The ball's circumference is between 23 cm and 23.5 cm. Between what values must the surface area fall?

11. A cylinder just fits inside a 10 cm by 10 cm by 10 cm cubic box. Which shape has the smaller surface area? Verify your answer by determining the surface area of each shape.

12. a) Complete the table.

Shape	Surface Area (cm²)	Dimensions (cm)	Volume (cm³)
square-based prism	1000	$s = 10, h = $ ■	
cylinder	1000	$r = 10, h = $ ■	
sphere	1000	$r \doteq $ ■	

b) Which shape has the greatest volume?

13. Determine the surface area of a ball bearing with a volume of 6.75 cm³.

14. A pharmaceutical company creates a capsule for medication in the
A shape of a cylinder with hemispherical ends as shown. How much medication will the capsule hold?

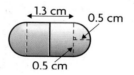

15. How can you calculate the volume and surface area of a sphere if you
C know its radius? Create a diagram and dimensions for a sphere from your experience to support your explanation.

Extending

16. Which has a larger volume: a sphere with a radius of r or a cube with a side length of $2r$? Which has a larger surface area?

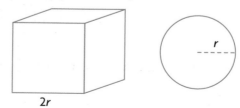

17. A balloon is inflated to a radius of 10 cm. By how much will the radius increase if you add 1 L of air to the balloon?

Curious | Math

Surprising Surface Area

The greater an object's surface area, the faster it will give off heat. That is why radiators have a large surface area.

Radiators are coiled, so that they do not take up much space. This way, they give off a large amount of heat without taking up much room.

The same principle applies to living things. For instance, a penguin's body has the smallest possible surface area. This way, it will not lose much body heat in cold weather.

1. Compare the ears of the jackrabbit and the Arctic hare. Why do you think they are so different in size?

jackrabbit in desert

Arctic hare

2. Investigate how surface area plays a role in the bodies of other animals, such as in the ears of an African elephant.

3. Investigate whether your lungs or your classroom floor covers a greater area.

Exploring Optimum Volume and Surface Area

GOAL

Explore to determine optimum measures.

EXPLORE the Math

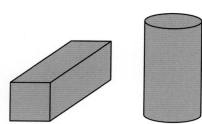

Diane showed Michael and Katie two packages, one a square-based prism and one a cylinder. Each package had a volume of 1331 cm^3 and a surface area of 728 cm^2.

- Michael wanted one of each type with the same volume and least possible surface area.
- Katie wanted one of each type with the same surface area and greatest possible volume.

	Diane's Packages		Michael's Packages		Katie's Packages	
	Cylinder	**Square-Based Prism**	**Cylinder**	**Square-Based Prism**	**Cylinder**	**Square-Based Prism**
Volume	1331 cm^3	1331 cm^3	1331 cm^3	1331 cm^3	greatest volume	greatest volume
Surface Area	728 cm^2	728 cm^2	least surface area	least surface area	728 cm^2	728 cm^2

? How can Michael and Katie determine the optimum dimensions for their packages?

A. Complete the table, showing possible dimensions for five to ten square-based prisms with a volume of 1331 cm^3.

Prism	Volume (cm^3)	Base Side Length (cm)	Height (cm)	Surface Area (cm^2)
1	1331			
2	1331			

B. Graph the relationship between base side length and surface area. Use the base side length as the independent variable.

C. Repeat parts A and B for cylinders. This time, graph the relationship between the surface area and radius of the base using the radius as an independant variable.

D. Use strategies like those in parts A and C to investigate what happens when the surface area remains at 728 cm² and the volume changes.

Reflecting

E. What were the dimensions of the figures with the optimum surface area? What were the dimensions of the figures with the optimum volume?

F. How did using a graph help you to determine the optimum surface area and the optimum volume?

In Summary

Key Idea

- When the volume or surface area of a square-based prism or cylinder is given, you can determine the shape with the least surface area or greatest volume in these ways:
  - List possible dimensions for various figures.
  - Locate the corresponding points on the graph of surface area or volume versus one of the dimensions.

Need to Know

- Graphing a table of values will often help you to recognize relationships, patterns, and/or trends.
- Changing one of the dimensions of a 3-D figure will affect the surface area and volume of the figure.

FURTHER *Your Understanding*

1. What strategy did you use to select dimensions to investigate?

2. **a)** Create a problem requiring the minimum surface area for a fixed volume.
   b) Graph possible dimensions to determine the dimensions that best solve the problem.

8.8 Optimum Volume and Surface Area

YOU WILL NEED

- grid paper
- graphing calculator or spreadsheet software

GOAL

Determine and apply optimum measures to solve problems.

LEARN ABOUT the Math

The student council sells popcorn in square-based prisms and cylinders. Both packages are made from 600.0 cm² of card stock. Meredith wants to ensure it is priced fairly.

? How can Meredith determine the maximum volume of each package?

EXAMPLE 1   Using a graphing strategy to determine maximum volume

Meredith's Solution

Side Length (cm) s	Height (cm) $h = (600 - 2s^2) \div 4s$	Volume (cm³) $V = s^2h$
6.0	22.0	792.0
8.0	14.8	947.2
10.0	10.0	1000.0
12.0	6.5	936.0
14.0	3.7	725.2

I created a table for square-based prisms with a surface area of 600.0 cm². I chose a side length, s, and then, determined the height and volume for that length.

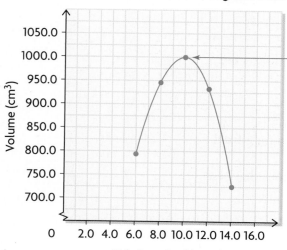

Volume of Prism vs. Side Length of Base

I graphed the relation between volume and side length.

The highest point was at a volume of 1000.0 cm³.

The maximum volume of a square-based prism with a surface area of 600 cm² is 1000.0 cm³.

Radius (cm) r	Height (cm) $h = \dfrac{(600 - 2\pi r^2)}{2\pi r}$	Volume (cm³) $V = \pi r^2 h$
3.6	22.9	932.0
4.6	16.2	1077.0
5.6	11.4	1123.0
6.6	7.9	1081.0
7.6	5.0	907.0

I created a table for cylinders with a surface area of 600.0 cm². I chose a radius, r, and then, determined the height and volume for that radius.

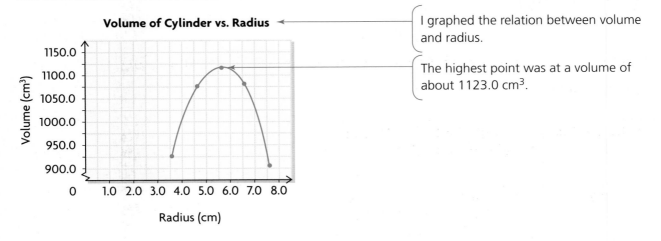

Volume of Cylinder vs. Radius

I graphed the relation between volume and radius.

The highest point was at a volume of about 1123.0 cm³.

The maximum volume of a cylinder with a surface area of 600.0 cm² is about 1123.0 cm³.

Reflecting

A. When either the volume or surface area was kept the same, how did changing the value of one dimension affect the values of the other dimensions of the shapes?

B. For the prism and the cylinder that hold the optimum volume of popcorn, what is the relation between the height and the base dimensions?

APPLY *the Math*

EXAMPLE 2   Using graphing technology to solve a problem

Sasha will use 6400.0 cm³ of ice to make an ice sculpture. It will
be either a prism with a square base or a cylinder. The less surface
area the sculpture has, the more slowly it will melt. Which shape
should Sasha make and what dimensions should it have?

Sasha's Solution

	A	B	C
1	**Side Length (cm)** s	**Height (cm)** $h = 6400 \div s^2$	**Surface Area (cm²)** $SA = 2s^2 + 4sh$
2	16.0	25.0	2112.0
3	17.0	22.1	2080.8
4	18.0	19.8	2073.6
5	19.0	17.8	2067.2
6	20.0	16.0	2080.0

I created a table using a spreadsheet for square-based prisms with a volume of 6400.0 cm³. I chose a side length, s, and then, determined the height and surface area for that side length.

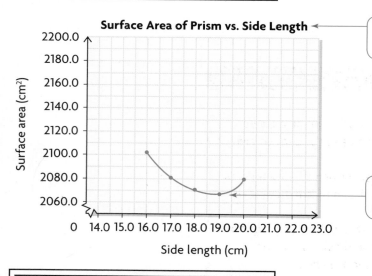

Surface Area of Prism vs. Side Length

I graphed the relation between surface area and side length.

The lowest point was for a prism with a side length of 19 cm and a surface area of 2067.2 cm².

	A	B	C
1	**Radius (cm)** r	**Height (cm)** $h = 6400 \div r^2$	**Surface Area (cm²)** $SA = 2\pi r^2 + 2\pi rh$
2	4.0	127.4	3300.5
3	6.5	48.2	2234.6
4	9.0	25.2	1930.9
5	11.0	16.8	1923.5
6	14.5	9.7	2203.1

I created a table using a spreadsheet for cylinders with a volume of 6400.0 cm³. I chose a radius, r, and then, determined the height and volume for that radius.

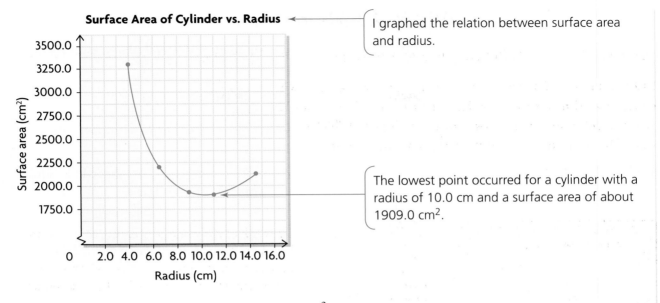

Surface Area of Cylinder vs. Radius ← I graphed the relation between surface area and radius.

The lowest point occurred for a cylinder with a radius of 10.0 cm and a surface area of about 1909.0 cm^2.

The cylinder has less surface area because 1909.0 cm^2 are less than 2067.2 cm^2. I should create a cylinder with a radius of 10.0 cm and a height of 20.4 cm.

In Summary

Key Ideas

- If you multiply one dimension of a prism or cylinder, you must divide another dimension by a proportional amount to keep the surface area or volume constant.
- A cube is the square-based prism with the least surface area for a given volume, and a cylinder with equal height and diameter is the cylinder with the least surface area for a given volume.
- A cube is the square-based prism with the greatest volume for a given surface area, and a cylinder with equal height and diameter is the cylinder with the greatest volume for a given surface area.

Need to Know

- You can use tables, graphs, graphing calculators, or spreadsheets to determine the effect of varying a dimension on the volume or surface area of a prism or cylinder.
- When you graph a changing dimension of a prism or cylinder versus surface area or volume, the graph has one of these shapes: ∪ or ∩. The optimum value for the dimension is at either the lowest or the highest point.

CHECK Your Understanding

Give your answers to the same number of decimal places as in the original measurements.

1. **a)** Determine the maximum possible volume of a square-based prism with a surface area of 325 cm².
   b) Determine the maximum possible volume of a cylinder with a surface area of 325 cm².

2. In a bulk food store, rice is kept in cardboard boxes shaped like square-based prisms. Each box has a volume of 28 000 cm³.
   a) Determine the dimensions of the box that will use the least amount of cardboard.
   b) Customers use scoops to take the rice from a container. Each scoop holds 1275 cm³ of rice. How many scoopfuls are in a full box of rice?

PRACTISING

3. Determine the dimensions of the square-based prism with the least
   K possible surface area for each volume.
   a) 125 m²
   b) 3375 cm³
   c) 21.952 cm³
   d) 3112.136 cm³

4. Sugar is sometimes packaged as cubes. Each cube of sugar must have a volume of 3.376 cm³. Determine the following.
   a) the dimensions of a cube, to one decimal place
   b) the volume of 64 cubes of sugar, to the nearest cubic centimetre
   c) the dimensions of a box in the shape of a square-based prism, made from the least possible amount of material, that will hold 64 cubes

5. The student council is testing new shapes for popcorn boxes. One box will be a cylinder and one will be a square-based prism. They will be made from 900.0 cm² of card stock.
   a) What is the maximum volume the cylinder can be?
   b) What is the maximum volume the prism can be?

6. Parnehoi is making an ice sculpture with 8200 cm³ of ice. It will either be a prism with a square base or a cylinder. Which shape will have the least surface area and what dimensions will it have?

7. Each area below is the surface area of a square-based prism with the greatest possible volume. Determine the height, the side length of the base, and the volume of each prism.
   a) 150 m²   **b)** 864 cm²   **c)** 541.5 cm²   **d)** 4873.5 cm²

8. Complete this table for cylinders that hold 1000 mL. Which cylinder uses the least amount of material?

Radius (cm)	Height (cm)	Surface Area (cm²)
1		
2		
3		
4		
5		
6		
7		
8		
9		
10		

9. Determine the dimensions of a square-based, open-topped prism with a volume of 24 cm³ and a minimum surface area.

10. An office supply company is producing an open-topped cylindrical
 Ⓐ pen-holder with a volume of 314.0 cm³. Determine the base radius and height that will use the minimum amount of material. What is the optimal surface area?

11. A cylinder has a radius of 12 cm and a height of 29 cm. What are the dimensions of a square-based prism with the same volume as the cylinder?

12. What is the greatest volume for an open-topped cylinder with a surface
 Ⓣ area of 25 cm²?

13. Create a set of cue cards that a newscaster could read to explain to an
 Ⓒ audience how to calculate optimum surface area and volume of a cylinder and square-based pyramid. Include any visuals that might appear behind the newscaster as the cue cards were read.

Extending

14. A rectangular cardboard box must be designed to package 12 cans of peas. Each can has a radius of 5 cm and a height of 10 cm.
   a) Determine the dimensions of the box that would require the least amount of cardboard.
   b) If you had to ship 144 cans, would packaging 12 cans per box be the most economical use of cardboard? Explain.

FREQUENTLY ASKED *Questions*

Q: How can you calculate the volume of a pyramid?

A1: Determine the volume of the prism with the same base and height as the pyramid. Multiply the area of the base by the height. Then, multiply by $\frac{1}{3}$.

A2: Use the formula $V = \frac{1}{3}Ah$ where A is the area of the base and h is the height of the pyramid.

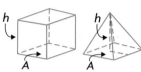

EXAMPLE

Calculate the volume of this pyramid.

Solution

The base is a square with side length 6 cm.
The height of the pyramid is 15 cm.

$$V = \frac{1}{3}Ah$$

$$= \frac{1}{3}(6^2)(15)$$

$$= \frac{1}{3}(36)(15)$$

$$= 180 \text{ cm}^3$$

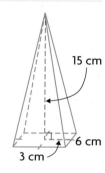

15 cm

6 cm

3 cm

Q: How can you calculate the volume of a cone?

A1: Determine the volume of the cylinder with the same base and height as the cone. Multiply the area of the base, A, by the height, h. Then, multiply by $\frac{1}{3}$.

A2: Use the formula $V = \frac{1}{3}\pi r^2 h$ where r is the radius of the base and h is the height of the cone.

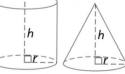

EXAMPLE

Calculate the volume of this cone.

Solution

The radius of the base is 15.5 cm.
The height of the cone is 11.2 cm.

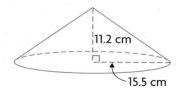

11.2 cm

15.5 cm

$$V = \frac{1}{3}\pi r^2 h$$

$$\doteq \frac{1}{3} \times 3.14 \times 15.5^2 \times 11.2$$

$$= \frac{1}{3} \times 3.14 \times 240.25 \times 11.2$$

$$\doteq 2816.4 \text{ cm}^3$$

Q: How can you calculate the surface area and volume of a sphere?

A1: Use the formula $SA = 4\pi r^2$ where r is the radius.

A2: Use the formula $V = \frac{4}{3}\pi r^3$ where r is the radius.

Study Aid

• See Lesson 8.6, Examples 1 and 2.
• Try Chapter Review Questions 11 and 12.

EXAMPLE

Calculate the volume and surface area of this sphere.

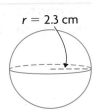

$r = 2.3$ cm

Solution
The radius is 2.3 cm.

$SA = 4\pi r^2$
$\quad = 4\pi(2.3)^2$
$\quad = 4 \times 3.14 \times 5.29$
$\quad \doteq 66.4 \text{ cm}^2$

$V = \frac{4}{3}\pi r^3$
$\quad \doteq \frac{4}{3} \times 3.14 \times 2.3^3$
$\quad = \frac{4}{3} \times 3.14 \times 12.167$
$\quad \doteq 50.1 \text{ cm}^3$

Q: Which square-based prisms and cylinders optimize volume and surface area?

A: This table shows the square-based prisms and cylinders that optimize volume and surface area:

Study Aid

• See Lesson 8.8, Examples 1 and 2.
• Try Chapter Review Question 14.

Figure	Optimizes Surface Area	Optimizes Volume
Square-Based Prism	A cube has the minimum surface area for a given volume.	A cube has the greatest volume for a given surface area.
Cylinder	The cylinder whose height equals its diameter has the minimum surface area for a given volume.	The cylinder whose height equals its diameter has the maximum volume for a given surface area.

PRACTICE Questions

Lesson 8.1

1. Arianna is creating a rectangular outdoor space for her pet rabbit. Fencing material costs $15.25/m. She has $145. What dimensions give the greatest area, to the nearest tenth of a metre?

2. What is the minimum perimeter possible for a rectangle with an area of 500 cm^2?

3. Sarah has 20 m of garden edging. What are the dimensions of the rectangular garden with the greatest area can she enclose with the edging?

4. Denzel wants to rope off a 800 m^2 rectangular swimming area using the beach as one of the sides. What should the dimensions of the rectangle be in order to use the minimum amount of rope?

Lesson 8.2

5. Calculate the area of the figure.

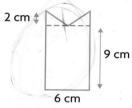

6. Michelle created an octagonal quilt piece for a quilt-making class project. It was cut from a square with a side length of 10.0 cm. To make the piece, Michelle cut off the four corners of the square, by measuring 2.9 cm from each corner, and then, cutting the diagonal. What are the area and perimeter of the octagonal quilt piece?

7. A school field has the dimensions shown.

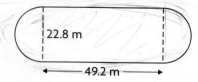

   a) Calculate the length of one lap of the track.
   b) If Amanda ran 625 m, how many laps did she run?
   c) Calculate the area of the field.

8. Calculate the area and perimeter of each regular polygon.

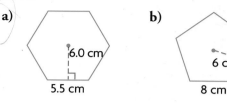

Lesson 8.3

9. A baseball diamond is a square. The distance between the bases is 27.4 m. Calculate the direct distance from first base to third base.

10. Find the length of x accurate to the nearest tenth.

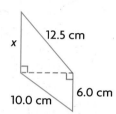

11. Determine the length of the fence around the playground.

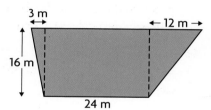

12. A right triangle's legs are 20 cm and 48 cm. What is the area of the square whose side length is equal to the hypotenuse?

Lesson 8.4

13. Calculate the surface area of the regular pyramid.

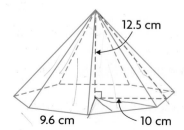

14. Janice and Wilson have bought a new house. They decide to paint the exterior of the house, including the door, and re-shingle the roof. One 4-L can of paint covers 35 m². One bundle of shingles covers 2.25 m².

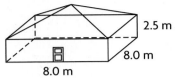

2.5 m

8.0 m

8.0 m

height from ground to peak = 5.0 m

a) How many bundles of shingles do they need for the roof? (Hint: Find the slant height of the roof first.)

b) How many cans of paint do they need?

c) One can of paint is $29.95 and one bundle of shingles is $35.99. Find the total cost of the job.

15. Determine the surface area of a square-based pyramidal candle with a base side length of 8 cm and a slant height of 10 cm.

16. Determine the height of a square-based pyramid with a base side length of 8.0 cm and a surface area of 440.0 cm².

Lesson 8.5

17. Calculate the volume and surface area of each figure.

a)

12 cm

9 cm

b)

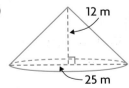

12 m

25 m

18. Gum is packaged in a square-based pyramid-shaped box with a distance of 6 cm from the centre of the base to the sides and a height of 12 cm.

a) How much material was used to create the box?

b) What is the volume of the box?

19. A solid figure is said to be truncated when a portion of the bottom is cut and removed. The cut line must be parallel to the base. Many paper cups, such as the one shown here, are truncated cones. Calculate the volume of this paper cup.

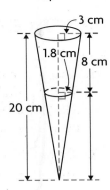

3 cm

1.8 cm

8 cm

20 cm

Lesson 8.6

20. Calculate the volume and surface area of this sphere.

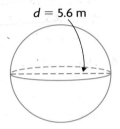

d = 5.6 m

21. A spherical bar of soap just fits inside its package, which is a cube with a side length of 8 cm.

a) What is the volume of the bar of soap?

b) Calculate the amount of empty space in the box.

22. A toy company makes rubber balls with a diameter of 20 cm. How much rubber would be saved per ball if the balls had a diameter of 15 cm?

Lesson 8.7

23. A square-based pyramid has a base side length of 13 cm and a height of 16 cm. What are the dimensions for a cylinder having the same volume as the pyramid?

Lesson 8.8

24. Determine, to one decimal place, the dimensions of the rectangular square-based prism that would have the greatest volume for each surface area. Show your solution.

a) 210 cm²

b) 490 cm²

25. What is the greatest volume for an open-topped rectangular prism with a surface area of 101.25 cm²?

1. Jamal wants to install a rectangular 2025 cm² window in his garden shed. That area of window comes in several length/width combinations, and he wants to minimize the perimeter to prevent drafts. What is the least perimeter possible for the window?

2. Calculate the area and perimeter of each shape.

a)
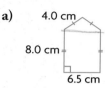

4.0 cm
8.0 cm
6.5 cm

b)
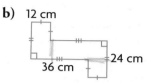

12 cm
36 cm
24 cm

3. Determine the volume of a square-based pyramid with base length 8.0 cm and slant height 10.0 cm. Sketch and label the pyramid in your solution. Explain your thinking.

4. Choose the surface area of the square-based pyramid.
   A. 85.5 cm²
   B. 100.0 cm²
   C. 297.2 cm²
   D. not possible to calculate

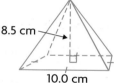

8.5 cm
10.0 cm

5. Calculate the volume and surface area of each figure.

a)

4.5 cm
5.0 cm

b)

8.5 cm
9.0 cm

6. The diameter of an inflatable dog toy is 6.5 cm.
   a) What amount of material was required to produce it?
   b) What is the volume of air inside it?

7. A cylinder is being designed to hold rice pudding. It will hold 1078.0 mL of pudding. Which radius minimizes the surface area?
   A. 5.6 cm   C. 8.5 cm
   B. 7 cm   D. 10 cm

8. Suppliers sell centimetre cubes to schools in packages shaped like square-based prisms. Determine the dimensions of the package that would require the least material to hold 1200 cubes.

Storage Capacity of a Silo

Tony is building a new silo to store corn as animal feed. It will be a cylinder topped with a half-sphere, and must store 21 000 t of corn. The entire silo can be filled with corn. Tony wants to minimize the surface area of the silo to reduce materials and paint costs. He has the following information:

- 1 m³ of corn has a mass of 700 kg.
- Building costs are \$8/m², taxes included.
- Paint comes in 3.8 L cans. Each can covers 40 m² and costs \$35, taxes included.
- Corn costs \$140 per tonne (\$140/t), taxes included. Recall that 1 t = 1000 kg.

? **What is the total cost to build, paint, and fill a silo with the least surface area?**

A. Sketch the silo. Label any measurements you will need.

B. Calculate the volume of the silo using the mass of feed it must hold.

C. Create a table listing possible dimensions for the silo.

D. Graph the surface area versus base radius.

E. Determine the minimum surface area.

F. Calculate the silo's building cost (before painting).

G. Calculate the silo's paint cost.

H. Calculate the cost to fill the silo with corn.

I. Determine the total cost.

J. Prepare a written report that shows your calculations and explains your thinking.

Task | *Checklist*

✔ Did you label all your table values and calculate entries correctly?

✔ Did you draw your sketch and label your graph accurately?

✔ Did you support your choice of surface area?

✔ Did you explain your thinking clearly?

Multiple Choice

1. Melissa cut two vertices off a triangle. What is the maximum amount the sum of the interior angles of the resulting shape will increase by?
- **A.** 180°
- **C.** 360°
- **B.** 540°
- **D.** 90°

2. In which diagram is $x = 150°$?

A.

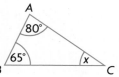

B.

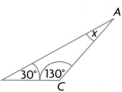

C.

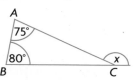

D.

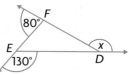

3. Which statement is not always true?
- **A.** If the two pairs of opposite sides of a quadrilateral are congruent, the figure must be a parallelogram.
- **B.** The diagonals of a rhombus are perpendicular.
- **C.** The diagonals of a square are perpendicular bisectors.
- **D.** The diagonals of a parallelogram are always congruent.

4. Which statement is not always true?
- **A.** The midsegments of a rhombus form a rectangle.
- **B.** The midsegments of a square form a square.
- **C.** The midsegments of a parallelogram form a parallelogram.
- **D.** The midsegments of a rectangle form a rectangle.

5. Determine the length of the red line segment.
- **A.** 60 cm
- **C.** 30 cm
- **B.** 35 cm
- **D.** 16 cm

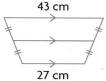

6. The police seal off accident scenes with yellow tape. Determine the dimensions of the maximum rectangular area that can be surrounded with 300 m of tape.
- **A.** 100 m by 50 m
- **C.** 75 m by 75 m
- **B.** 150 m by 2 m
- **D.** 125 m by 25 m

7. A stop sign shaped like a regular octagon is 120 cm from side to side and each side is 50 cm long. Estimate the area of the sign.
- **A.** 24 000 cm^2
- **C.** 6000 cm^2
- **B.** 12 000 cm^2
- **D.** 3000 cm^2

8. Determine the radius of a sphere with a volume of 117.00 cm^3.
- **A.** 3.03 cm
- **C.** 6.04 cm
- **B.** 1.02 cm
- **D.** 58.50 cm

9. A sugar sculpture is a triangular pyramid 18.0 cm high. The base is an equilateral triangle with 3.0 m sides. Determine the volume of the sculpture.
- **A.** 23.4 cm^3
- **C.** 54.0 cm^3
- **B.** 27.0 cm^3
- **D.** 70.1 cm^3

10. The sum of the interior angles in a polygon is 1800°. How many sides does it have?
- **A.** 9
- **C.** 11
- **B.** 10
- **D.** 12

11. Which of the following is not a convex polygon?

A.

C.

B.

D.

12. What is the measure of each exterior angle in a regular 12-gon?
- **A.** 30°
- **C.** 20°
- **B.** 45°
- **D.** 35°

13. In any polygon what is the sum of any interior angle and its corresponding exterior angle?
- **A.** 360°
- **C.** 90°
- **B.** 180°
- **D.** 270°

14. If the diagonals of a quadrilateral are perpendicular, equal in length, and bisect each other, then the shape is a:
- **A.** rectangle
- **C.** kite
- **B.** rhombus
- **D.** square

15. How many counterexamples are needed to disprove a conjecture?
- **A.** 1
- **C.** 5
- **B.** 2
- **D.** 10

16. In which of the following quadrilaterals do the midsegments form a parallelogram?
- **A.** rhombus
- **C.** rectangle
- **B.** trapezoid
- **D.** all of the above

17. What lines can be used to locate the centroid of any quadrilateral?
- **A.** diagonals
- **C.** midsegments
- **B.** bimedians
- **D.** medians

18. What is the greatest rectangular area that can be enclosed with a 100 m roll of fencing?
- **A.** 100 m^2
- **C.** 625 m^2
- **B.** 250 m^2
- **D.** 825 m^2

19. Determine the area of the shaded region.

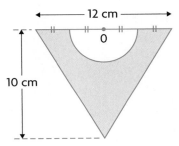

- **A.** 60 cm^2
- **C.** 106 cm^2
- **B.** 46 cm^2
- **D.** 75 cm^2

20. A sphere has a diameter of 10 cm. Both the diameter and the height of a cone are 10 cm. A cube has a side length of 10 cm. Both the side length and the height of a square-based pyramid are 10 cm. Which shape has the least volume?
- **A.** sphere
- **C.** cone
- **B.** cube
- **D.** pyramid

21. For a given volume, the cylinder with the least surface area occurs when:
- **A.** radius = height
- **B.** radius = height ÷ 2
- **C.** diameter = height
- **D.** 2(diameter) = height

Investigation

Mystery of the Pyramids

22. Jeremy is creating a piece of art for an exhibit. He starts with a square-based right pyramid, as shown. He makes a cut parallel to the base through the midpoints of the lateral edges. Then, he removes the top of the pyramid.

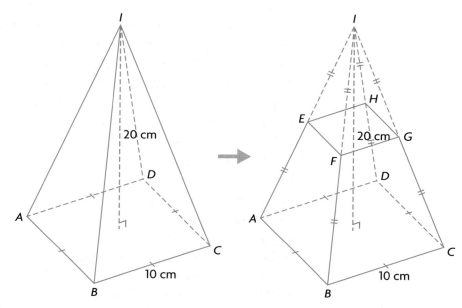

a) Determine the volume of the original pyramid.

b) Determine what volume of the pyramid was removed.

c) In terms of volume, what fraction of the original pyramid was removed?

d) Investigate whether this fraction would be the same if the original pyramid had a rectangular base.

Review of Essential Skills and Knowledge

A–1 Powers

A power is an expression that shows repeated multiplication.

EXAMPLE

Evaluate the power 2^4.

Solution

$$2^4 = 2 \times 2 \times 2 \times 2$$
$$= 16$$

2 is the base of the power and 4 is the exponent.

Practice

1. Write the product represented by each power. Then, evaluate the expression.

   a) 2^2 **c)** 2^4 **e)** 10^3 **g)** 4^2 **i)** 5^3

   b) 2^3 **d)** 3^2 **f)** 10^4 **h)** 4^3 **j)** 5^5

A–2 Order of Operations

You can remember the order of operations by using the memory aid "BEDMAS."

Brackets
Exponents
Divide and **M**ultiply from left to right
Add and **S**ubtract from left to right

EXAMPLE

Evaluate the integer expression $(2 \times 3 - 2^2) + 4(6 - 1)$.

Solution

$$(2 \times 3 - 2^2) + 4(6 - 1) = (6 - 4) + 4(5)$$
$$= 2 + 20$$
$$= 22$$

Practice

1. Evaluate using the rules for order of operations.

   a) $(3 + 6 \div 3)^2$

   b) $4(2^3 - 3 \times 2)$

   c) $[(8 + 6 \div 3) - 5]^2$

   d) $2(3^2 + 1) \div 5$

   e) $(9 + 1)^3 \div (3^2 + 1)$

   f) $4[(32 - 5^2) - (2^3 - 1)]$

A–3 Adding and Subtracting Integers

The Zero Principle states that when you add opposite integers, the result is 0.
The + sign is often not used for positive integers.

EXAMPLE 1

Add $(-24) + (+39)$ using integer counters.

Solution

$(-24) + (+39) = 15$

24 counters   39 counters

$(\bullet\ldots\bullet) + (\bullet\ldots\bullet)$

24 blue/red counters 15 counters

$= ((\bullet\bullet)\ldots(\bullet\bullet)) + (\bullet\ldots\bullet)$
      0   0

15 counters

$= (\bullet\ldots\bullet)$

EXAMPLE 2

Add $-24 + 39$ using a number line.

Solution

$-24 + 39 = 15$

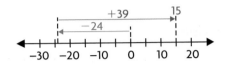

EXAMPLE 3

Add $-24 + 39$ using the Zero Principle.

Solution

$$-24 + 39 = (-24 + 24) + 15$$
$$= 0 + 15$$
$$= 15$$

EXAMPLE 4

Subtract $-2 - (-5)$ using integer counters.

Solution

$-2 - (-5) = 3$

$(\bullet\bullet) - (\bullet\bullet\bullet\bullet\bullet)$

$= (\bullet\bullet\boxed{\bullet\bullet}\boxed{\bullet\bullet}\boxed{\bullet\bullet}) - (\bullet\bullet\bullet\bullet\bullet)$

$= (\otimes\otimes\boxed{\otimes\bullet}\boxed{\otimes\bullet}\boxed{\otimes\bullet}) - (\otimes\otimes\otimes\otimes\otimes)$

$= (\bullet\bullet\bullet)$

EXAMPLE 5

Subtract $-15 - (-20)$ using a number line.

Solution

$-15 - (-20) = 5$

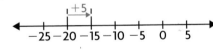

EXAMPLE 6

Subtract $-15 - (-20)$ using the Zero Principle.

Solution

$$-15 - (-20) = -15 + 20$$
$$+ (-20)$$
$$- (-20)$$
$$= -15 + 20$$
$$= 5$$

Practice

1. Represent each operation using integer counters or a number line.
   a) $-6 + (-3)$
   b) $5 + (-2)$
   c) $-23 + 8$
   d) $5 - (-4)$
   e) $-20 - 16$
   f) $-9 - 6$

2. Determine each sum.
   a) $-3 + (-2)$
   b) $2 + (-3)$
   c) $-18 + 8$
   d) $-6 + 4$
   e) $-40 + (-15)$
   f) $32 + (-46)$

3. Determine each difference.
   a) $4 - (-3)$
   b) $-5 - (-2)$
   c) $5 - (-13)$
   d) $-14 - (-7)$
   e) $6 - (-6)$
   f) $-43 - 4$

4. Calculate.
   a) $3 - (-4) + 10$
   b) $-7 + 2 - (-1)$
   c) $-5 - (-3) + 4$
   d) $-41 + (-32) + 15$

A–4 Multiplying and Dividing Integers

The following patterns describe the results of multiplying or dividing two integers:

$$(+) \times (+) = + \qquad (-) \times (+) = - \qquad (+) \times (-) = - \qquad (-) \times (-) = +$$
$$(+) \div (+) = + \qquad (-) \div (+) = - \qquad (+) \div (-) = - \qquad (-) \div (-) = +$$

EXAMPLE 1

Multiply 4×3, $4 \times (-3)$, -4×3, and $-4 \times (-3)$ using integer counters.

Solution

$4 \times 3 = 12$

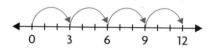

$4 \times (-3) = -12$

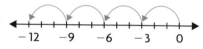

$-4 \times 3 = -12$

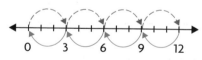

$-4 \times (-3) = 12$

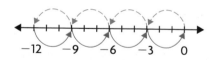

EXAMPLE 2

Multiply 4×3, $4 \times (-3)$, -4×3, and $-4 \times (-3)$ using a number line.

Solution

$4 \times 3 = 12$

$4 \times (-3) = -12$

$-4 \times 3 = -12$

$-4 \times (-3) = 12$

EXAMPLE 3

Divide $12 \div 3$, $-12 \div 3$, $12 \div (-3)$, and $-12 \div (-3)$ by solving the related multiplication equations.

Solution

$12 \div 3 = 4$
because
$3 \times 4 = 12$

$-12 \div 3 = -4$
because
$3 \times (-4) = -12$

$12 \div (-3) = -4$
because
$-3 \times (-4) = 12$

$-12 \div (-3) = 4$
because
$-3 \times 4 = -12$

Practice

1. Represent each operation using integer counters or a number line.
  a) -2×5
  b) $-5 \times (-4)$
  c) $3 \times (-6)$
  d) $-6 \times (-9)$

2. Calculate each product.
  a) $(-3)(2)$
  b) $(-4)(-9)$
  c) $(4)(-3)$
  d) $(-7)(-3)$
  e) $(5)(4)$
  f) $(-2)(7)$

3. Calculate each quotient.
  a) $-18 \div (-6)$
  b) $-24 \div 6$
  c) $51 \div (-17)$
  d) $-42 \div (-14)$
  e) $60 \div (-12)$
  f) $-30 \div (-15)$

4. Evaluate.
  a) $(-5)(-5)$
  b) $-56 \div 8$
  c) $(-2)(5)(-4)$
  d) $(8)(4) \div (-2)$
  e) $(4)(81) \div (-27)(-2)$
  f) $64 \div [(-4)(-4)(-4)]$

A–5 Evaluating Integer Expressions with Several Operations

Expressions involving many integer operations are evaluated using the same order of operations as for whole numbers.

EXAMPLE 1

Evaluate the expression
$-4(-3-6) + (-2 + (-1))$.

Solution

$$-4(-3-6) + (-2 + (-1)) = -4(-9) + (-3)$$
$$= 36 + (-3)$$
$$= 33$$

EXAMPLE 2

Evaluate the expression $(-2)(4) + (-3)^2$.

Solution

$$(-2)(4) + (-3)^2 = (-2)(4) + 9$$
$$= -8 + 9$$
$$= 1$$

Practice

1. Evaluate using the order of operations.
   a) $5 - (3 - 4)$
   b) $(5 - 7) - (3 - 4)$
   c) $-3(-4) - (5 - 7)$
   d) $(3)(2) - (3 + 5)$
   e) $-(5 - 9) - (-2)(2)$
   f) $(4 - 3) - 2(3 - 4)$

2. Evaluate.
   a) $2(-3)^2 - 4(-2)$
   b) $-4(-2)^3 - 3(-4)^2$
   c) $(-3 - 2)^2 - (2 + 4)^2$
   d) $3(-2 + 4)^3 - 2(-4 + 1)^2$
   e) $2(-1 - 3)^2 - (1 + 3)^2$
   f) $5(-2)^2 - 3(-1 - 2)^3$

A–6 Adding and Subtracting Fractions

EXAMPLE 1

Add $\dfrac{3}{5} + \dfrac{1}{2}$ using fraction strips.

Solution

$$\frac{3}{5} + \frac{1}{2} = \frac{6}{10} + \frac{5}{10}$$
$$= \frac{11}{10} \text{ or } 1\frac{1}{10}$$

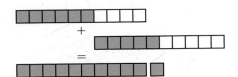

EXAMPLE 2

Subtract $\dfrac{3}{5} - \dfrac{1}{2}$ using fraction strips.

Solution

$$\frac{3}{5} - \frac{1}{2} = \frac{6}{10} - \frac{5}{10}$$
$$= \frac{1}{10}$$

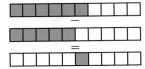

EXAMPLE **3**

Add $\frac{3}{4} + \frac{1}{7}$ using a grid.

Solution

$$\frac{3}{4} + \frac{1}{7} = \frac{21}{28} + \frac{4}{28}$$

$$= \frac{25}{28}$$

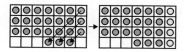

EXAMPLE **4**

Subtract $\frac{3}{4} - \frac{1}{7}$ using a grid.

Solution

$$\frac{3}{4} - \frac{1}{7} = \frac{21}{28} - \frac{4}{28}$$

$$= \frac{17}{28}$$

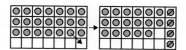

EXAMPLE **5**

Add $\frac{1}{3} + \frac{1}{4}$ using a number line.

Solution

$$\frac{1}{3} + \frac{1}{4} = \frac{4}{12} + \frac{3}{12}$$

$$= \frac{7}{12}$$

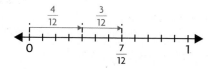

EXAMPLE **6**

Subtract $\frac{1}{3} - \frac{1}{4}$ using a number line.

Solution

$$\frac{1}{3} - \frac{1}{4} = \frac{4}{12} - \frac{3}{12}$$

$$= \frac{1}{12}$$

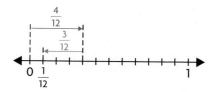

EXAMPLE **7**

Add $\frac{2}{3} + \frac{1}{6}$ using the least common denominator.

Solution

$$\frac{2}{3} + \frac{1}{6} = \frac{4}{6} + \frac{1}{6}$$

$$= \frac{5}{6}$$

EXAMPLE **8**

Subtract $\frac{2}{3} - \frac{1}{6}$ using the least common denominator.

Solution

$$\frac{2}{3} - \frac{1}{6} = \frac{4}{6} - \frac{1}{6}$$

$$= \frac{3}{6} \text{ or } \frac{1}{2}$$

Practice

1. Represent each operation using a grid, fraction strips, or a number line.

   a) $\dfrac{3}{4} + \dfrac{1}{5}$ **c)** $\dfrac{4}{5} - \dfrac{1}{3}$

   b) $\dfrac{3}{4} + \dfrac{5}{6}$ **d)** $\dfrac{1}{6} - \dfrac{1}{9}$

2. Add.

   a) $\dfrac{1}{7} + \dfrac{3}{7}$ **c)** $\dfrac{3}{8} + \dfrac{1}{8}$ **e)** $\dfrac{1}{3} + \dfrac{1}{6}$

   b) $\dfrac{2}{9} + \dfrac{5}{9}$ **d)** $\dfrac{1}{3} + \dfrac{1}{9}$ **f)** $\dfrac{1}{3} + \dfrac{5}{12}$

3. Subtract.

   a) $\dfrac{5}{9} - \dfrac{1}{9}$ **c)** $\dfrac{7}{15} - \dfrac{2}{5}$ **e)** $\dfrac{3}{4} - \dfrac{1}{6}$

   b) $\dfrac{14}{15} - \dfrac{7}{15}$ **d)** $\dfrac{5}{6} - \dfrac{3}{8}$ **f)** $\dfrac{1}{3} - \dfrac{1}{6}$

4. Evaluate.

   a) $\dfrac{3}{4} + \dfrac{3}{10}$ **c)** $\dfrac{2}{5} + \dfrac{6}{7}$ **e)** $\dfrac{7}{2} + \dfrac{3}{5}$

   b) $\dfrac{4}{3} - \dfrac{2}{11}$ **d)** $\dfrac{8}{15} - \dfrac{1}{16}$ **f)** $\dfrac{14}{5} - \dfrac{5}{7}$

A–7 Multiplying and Dividing Fractions

EXAMPLE 1

Multiply $\dfrac{2}{5} \times \dfrac{1}{10}$ using an area model.

Solution

The product of the denominators indicates the length and width of the rectangle to create. The product of the numerators indicates the length and width of the rectangle to be shaded.

$$\dfrac{2}{5} \times \dfrac{1}{10} = \dfrac{2}{50}$$

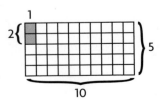

EXAMPLE 2

Multiply $\dfrac{2}{5} \times \dfrac{1}{10}$ using fraction strips.

Solution

$\dfrac{2}{5} \times \dfrac{1}{10}$ is the same as $\dfrac{2}{5}$ of $\dfrac{1}{10}$.

Each box representing $\dfrac{1}{10}$ must be divided into 5 equal parts. Two of these parts must be shaded.

This is $\dfrac{2}{50}$ or $\dfrac{1}{25}$ in lowest terms.

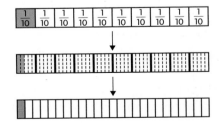

EXAMPLE 3

Multiply $\dfrac{2}{5} \times \dfrac{1}{10}$ by multiplying numerators and denominators.

Solution

$$\dfrac{2}{5} \times \dfrac{1}{10} = \dfrac{2 \times 1}{5 \times 10}$$

$$= \dfrac{2}{50} \text{ or } \dfrac{1}{25} \text{ in lowest terms}$$

EXAMPLE **4**

Divide $\dfrac{4}{5} \div \dfrac{1}{3}$ using fraction strips.

Solution

$$\dfrac{4}{5} \div \dfrac{1}{3} = \dfrac{12}{5} \text{ or } 2\dfrac{2}{5}$$

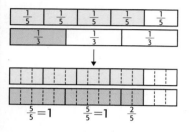

$\dfrac{5}{5} = 1 \qquad \dfrac{5}{5} = 1 \qquad \dfrac{2}{5}$

EXAMPLE **5**

Divide $\dfrac{4}{5} \div \dfrac{1}{3}$ using the least common denominator.

Solution

$$\dfrac{4}{5} \div \dfrac{1}{3} = \dfrac{12}{15} \div \dfrac{5}{15}$$
$$= 12 \div 5$$
$$= \dfrac{12}{5} \text{ or } 2\dfrac{2}{5}$$

EXAMPLE **6**

Divide $\dfrac{4}{5} \div \dfrac{1}{3}$ using a reciprocal.

Solution

$$\dfrac{4}{5} \div \dfrac{1}{3} = \dfrac{4}{5} \times \dfrac{3}{1}$$
$$= \dfrac{12}{5} \text{ or } 2\dfrac{2}{5}$$

Practice

1. Represent each operation using an area model or fraction strips.

a) $\dfrac{1}{3} \times \dfrac{1}{5}$

c) $\dfrac{2}{5} \div \dfrac{1}{2}$

b) $\dfrac{3}{4} \times \dfrac{2}{5}$

d) $\dfrac{3}{4} \div \dfrac{2}{3}$

2. Multiply.

a) $\dfrac{1}{2} \times \dfrac{3}{5}$

c) $\dfrac{3}{4} \times \dfrac{8}{15}$

b) $\dfrac{3}{4} \times \dfrac{7}{10}$

d) $\dfrac{2}{3} \times \dfrac{9}{11}$

3. Divide.

a) $\dfrac{3}{7} \div \dfrac{4}{5}$

c) $\dfrac{3}{4} \div \dfrac{7}{8}$

b) $\dfrac{2}{11} \div \dfrac{3}{5}$

d) $\dfrac{5}{8} \div \dfrac{13}{16}$

4. Evaluate.

a) $\dfrac{2}{3} \times \dfrac{8}{13}$

c) $\dfrac{5}{8} \div \dfrac{1}{4}$

b) $\dfrac{3}{5} \times \dfrac{3}{5}$

d) $\dfrac{8}{9} \times \dfrac{3}{8}$

A–8 Evaluating Fraction Expressions with Several Operations

Expressions involving many fraction operations are evaluated using the same order of operations as for whole numbers.

EXAMPLE

Evaluate the fraction expression $\dfrac{3}{2} - \dfrac{2}{5} \div \dfrac{1}{5} \times \left(\dfrac{3}{8} + \dfrac{1}{8} \right)^2 + \dfrac{2}{3}$.

Solution

$$\dfrac{3}{2} - \dfrac{2}{5} \div \dfrac{1}{5} \times \left(\dfrac{3}{8} + \dfrac{1}{8} \right)^2 + \dfrac{2}{3} = \dfrac{3}{2} - \dfrac{2}{5} \div \dfrac{1}{5} \times \left(\dfrac{1}{2} \right)^2 + \dfrac{2}{3}$$

$$= \dfrac{3}{2} - \dfrac{2}{5} \div \dfrac{1}{5} \times \dfrac{1}{4} + \dfrac{2}{3}$$

$$= \dfrac{3}{2} - 2 \times \dfrac{1}{4} + \dfrac{2}{3}$$

$$= \dfrac{3}{2} - \dfrac{1}{2} + \dfrac{2}{3}$$

$$= 1\dfrac{2}{3}$$

Practice

1. Calculate using the order of operations.

a) $\dfrac{1}{2} - \dfrac{1}{3} \times \dfrac{1}{4} + \dfrac{1}{5} \div \dfrac{1}{6}$

b) $\left(\dfrac{1}{2} - \dfrac{1}{3} \right) \times \left(\dfrac{1}{4} + \dfrac{1}{5} \div \dfrac{1}{6} \right)$

c) $\left(\dfrac{1}{2} - \dfrac{1}{3} \times \dfrac{1}{4} + \dfrac{1}{5} \right) \div \dfrac{1}{6}$

d) $\left(\dfrac{1}{2} + \dfrac{1}{3} - \dfrac{1}{6} \right)^3 + \dfrac{2}{3} \times \dfrac{4}{5}$

e) $\dfrac{5}{4} \times \dfrac{1}{2} - \dfrac{2}{3} \div 2 + \dfrac{1}{2}$

f) $\left(\dfrac{2}{3} + \dfrac{1}{6} \right)^2$

A–9 Multiplying and Dividing Decimals

Estimate the answer before solving a decimal problem. Then, compare your result to your prediction.

EXAMPLE 1

Estimate the product 0.6×0.5.

Solution

0.6 is a little more than $\dfrac{1}{2}$ and 0.5 is $\dfrac{1}{2}$, so the product will be a little more than $\dfrac{1}{2} \times \dfrac{1}{2} = \dfrac{1}{4}$ or 0.25

EXAMPLE 2

Multiply 0.6×0.5 using a grid model.

Solution

$0.6 \times 0.5 = \dfrac{30}{100}$

$\qquad\qquad = 0.30$

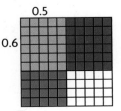

EXAMPLE 3

Multiply 0.6 × 0.5 using equivalent whole numbers.

Solution

$$0.6 = 6 \div 10 \text{ and } 6 \times 0.5 = 3.0.$$

So, $0.6 \times 0.5 = 3.0 \div 10$

$$= 0.3$$

EXAMPLE 4

Multiply 0.6 × 0.5 using an algorithm.

Solution

```
    0.6
  × 0.5
   3 0
  0 0
  0.3 0
```

EXAMPLE 5

Estimate the quotient 2.5 ÷ 0.45.

Solution

0.45 is close to 0.5, which is $\frac{1}{2}$.

Dividing by $\frac{1}{2}$ is the same as

multiplying by 2. So, 2.5 ÷ 0.45
is about 2.5 × 2 = 5.0.

EXAMPLE 6

Divide 2.5 ÷ 0.45 using equivalent whole numbers.

Solution

$2.5 \div 0.45$ is the same as $\frac{2.5}{0.45}$.

So, $\frac{2.5}{0.45} = \frac{2.5 \times 100}{0.45 \times 100}$

$$= \frac{250}{45}$$

```
       5.5
  45)250
     225
     25.0
     22.5
      2.5
      ...
```

The remainder repeats, so the answer is $5.\overline{5}$.

Practice

1. Determine each product. Round to the nearest hundredth if necessary.
   a) 1.4 × 2.5
   b) 0.75 × 2.0
   c) 3.25 × 1.4
   d) 4.5 × 2.5
   e) 3.73 × 2.17
   f) 5.81 × 1.01

2. Determine each quotient. Round to the nearest hundredth if necessary.
   a) 8.37 ÷ 3.1
   b) 15.84 ÷ 3.2
   c) 10.25 ÷ 4.1
   d) 7.14 ÷ 4.76
   e) 24.375 ÷ 8.125
   f) 20.265 ÷ 2.1

A–10 Expanded Form and Scientific Notation

Expanded form is a way of writing a number that shows the value of each digit using a power of 10.

Scientific notation is a way of writing a number as a decimal between 1 and 10, multiplied by a power of 10.

EXAMPLE 1

Write the number 70 120 in expanded form.

Solution

$70\,120 = 7 \times 10\,000 + 1 \times 100 + 2 \times 10$
$\qquad\quad = 7 \times 10^4 + 1 \times 10^2 + 2 \times 10$

EXAMPLE 2

Write the number 70 120 using scientific notation.

Solution

The answer is $7.012 \times 10^4 = 70\,120$. This is because 7.012 is between 1 and 10 and 10^4 is a power of 10.

Practice

1. Express each number in expanded form.
a) 1234   c) 10 005
b) 11 125   d) 1 045 301

2. Express each number using scientific notation.
a) 1234   c) 10 005
b) 11 125   d) 1 045 301

3. Copy and complete the table.

Standard Form	Expanded Form	Scientific Notation
451	$4 \times 10^2 + 5 \times 10 + 1 \times 10^0$	4.51×10^2
1026		
	$2 \times 10^3 + 5 \times 10$	
		4.72×10^5

A–11 Patterns and Relationships

A geometric pattern is a sequence of figures made up of several pieces. There is often a relationship between the number of a figure in a pattern and the number of pieces required to build it. The pattern can be described in various ways.

A geometric pattern:

figure 1   figure 2   figure 3

EXAMPLE 1

Draw figure 4 in the pattern.

Solution

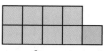
figure 4

EXAMPLE 2

Determine the number of squares in figure 4 in the pattern using a table of values.

Solution

The table of values shows the number of squares in the first four figures of the pattern. Figure 4 has 9 squares.

Figure Number	Number of Squares
1	3
2	3 + 2 = 5
3	5 + 2 = 7
4	7 + 2 = 9

EXAMPLE 3

Determine the number of squares in figure 4 in the pattern using words or an algebraic expression.

Solution

The number of squares seems to be 1 more than twice the figure number. The pattern is $s = 2n + 1$ where s is the number of squares and n is the figure number. So, figure 4 has $s = 2(4) + 1 = 9$ squares.

EXAMPLE 4

Determine the number of squares in figure 4 in the pattern using a scatter plot.

Solution

The scatter plot shows the relationship between the figure number and the number of squares in the figure. Figure 4 has 9 squares.

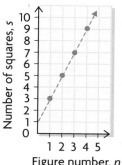

Number of Squares vs. Figure Number

Practice

1. a) Copy and complete the table of values.

Figure Number	Figure	Number of Counters
1		
2		
3		
4		
5		

b) Construct a scatter plot that represents the pattern.

2. a) Describe the pattern rule using an algebraic expression. Represent the figure number as n. Represent the number of toothpicks in the figure as t.

figure 1   figure 2   figure 3

b) Construct a table of values that shows the toothpicks required to build the first five figures in the pattern.

c) Construct a scatter plot that represents the pattern.

A–12 The Cartesian Coordinate System

A Cartesian coordinate system uses a horizontal number line (the *x*-axis) and
a vertical number line (the *y*-axis) to determine the coordinates of points.

EXAMPLE

Determine the location and the signs
of the coordinates of each point.

Solution

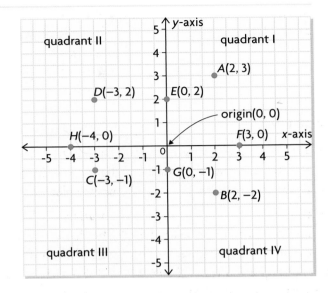

Point	Location	Signs of Coordinates (x, y)
A	quadrant I	$(+, +)$
B	quadrant IV	$(+, -)$
C	quadrant III	$(-, -)$
D	quadrant II	$(-, +)$
E and G	*y*-axis	$(0, y)$
F and H	*x*-axis	$(x, 0)$

Practice

1. Write the coordinates of each point shown in
the graph.

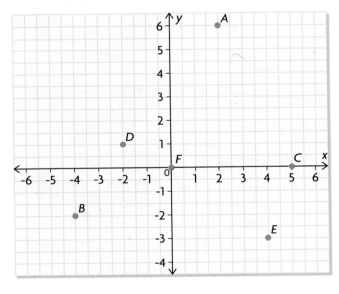

2. Plot each point on a Cartesian coordinate system.
   a) $(2, 3)$ **d)** $(5, 0)$
   b) $(0, 0)$ **e)** $(-4, -6)$
   c) $(0, -3)$ **f)** $(-7, 2)$

3. Answer the following questions about the points
in the previous question.
   a) Which points are on an axis? Which axis?
   b) In which quadrant is each point not on an
   axis located?

4. State the coordinates of a point that satisfies
each set of conditions.
   a) The point is in quadrant I. The *x*-coordinate
   is greater than the *y*-coordinate.
   b) The point is on the *x*-axis between
   quadrants II and III.
   c) The point is in quadrant III. The *x*- and
   y-coordinates have the same value.
   d) The point is in quadrant II. The *y*-coordinate
   is the square of the *x*-coordinate.

A–13 Equations

An equation is a statement that two mathematical quantities or expressions have the same value.

A solution to an equation is a value for which the equation is true. Solutions to equations can be found in different ways.

EXAMPLE 1

Solve the equation $3n + 2 = 17$ using inspection and logical reasoning.

Solution

$3n + 2 = 17$
That means $3n = 15$.
So, n must be 5.

EXAMPLE 2

Solve the equation $3n + 2 = 17$ using systematic trial.

Solution

n	$3n + 2$	Comparison to 17
10	$3(10) + 2 = 32$	too big
4	$3(4) + 2 = 14$	too small
5	$3(5) + 2 = 17$	correct

The answer is $n = 5$.

EXAMPLE 3

Estimate the solution to the equation $3n + 2 = 17$ by using a graph.

Solution

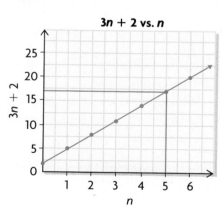

$3n + 2$ vs. n

From the graph, n is about 5.

EXAMPLE 4

Solve the equation $3n + 2 = 17$ using a balancing strategy.

Solution

$$3n + 2 = 17$$
$$3n + 2 - 2 = 17 - 2$$

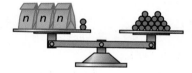

$$3n = 15$$
$$3n \div 3 = 15 \div 3$$

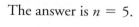

The answer is $n = 5$.

Practice

1. Solve.

a) $n + 3 = 7$

b) $f + 5 = 2$

c) $9 = 3 + x$

d) $9 + g = 3$

e) $n - 4 = 7$

f) $z - 2 = 13$

2. Solve.

a) $2x = 6$

b) $3n = 18$

c) $4c = -16$

d) $-4m = 20$

e) $-30 = 6h$

f) $-25 = -5a$

3. Solve.

a) $2k + 1 = 7$

b) $6 + 3k = 27$

c) $18 = 4a - 2$

d) $11 = 2 - 3y$

e) $4p - 3 = 9$

f) $-6 = 8 - 7v$

g) $3h - 4 = -4$

h) $4y - 2 = 2$

4. Solve.

a) $\dfrac{1}{3}m = 4$

b) $\dfrac{3}{4}e = 15$

c) $-6 = \dfrac{3}{4}h$

d) $20 = \dfrac{-5}{8}a$

e) $\dfrac{-5}{8}y = -30$

f) $\dfrac{-3}{11}c = 0$

A–14 Ratios and Rates

Ratios compare quantities measured with the same units or no units at all.
Rates show how one quantity changes with respect to the other.
Both ratios and rates can be written using ":" to separate the terms, or as fractions.
A proportion is an equation that states that two ratios or two rates are equivalent.

EXAMPLE 1

Provide examples of a ratio and a rate.

Solution

A ratio example: Suppose a bag contains 40 green and 60 red jelly beans. The ratio of green to red is 40 : 60. This simplifies to 4 : 6 or 2 : 3 in lowest terms.

A rate example: Suppose a car travels 40 km in 60 min. The rate at which the distance is covered in terms of time is the speed and it is $\dfrac{40}{60}$ km/min. This simplifies to a unit rate of $\dfrac{2}{3}$ km/min.

EXAMPLE 2

Determine the missing value in the proportion $\dfrac{2}{23} = \dfrac{\blacksquare}{92}$.

Solution

$$\frac{2}{23} = \frac{\blacksquare}{92}$$

$$\frac{2}{23} = \frac{2 \times 4}{23 \times 4}$$

$$= \frac{8}{92}$$

The missing value is 8.

Practice

1. Write each ratio in lowest terms.
   a) $4:8$
   b) $6:18$
   c) $8:20$
   d) $12:42$
   e) $\dfrac{15}{25}$
   f) $\dfrac{30}{42}$

2. Write each comparison as a ratio.
   a) 7 mm to 3 cm
   b) 17 s to 1 min
   c) 25 m to 5 cm
   d) 15 s to 1 min

3. Calculate each missing term.
   a) $2:5 = \blacksquare : 10$
   b) $3:7 = \blacksquare : 21$
   c) $\dfrac{4}{7} = \dfrac{8}{\blacksquare}$
   d) $\dfrac{5}{8} = \dfrac{15}{\blacksquare}$

4. Express each comparison as a rate.
   a) 4 tins for \$2
   b) \$75 for 8 h work
   c) \$4 for 3 novels
   d) 79 km in 4 h
   e) 3 goals for 4 shots
   f) 17 min to deliver 23 papers

A–15 Percent

A percent is a ratio of the form $\dfrac{\text{percent}}{100} = \dfrac{\text{part}}{\text{whole amount}}$.

EXAMPLE 1

Write a ratio or a fraction as a percent.

Solution

For example,

$$\dfrac{3}{5} = \dfrac{3 \times 20}{5 \times 20}$$
$$= \dfrac{60}{100}$$
$$= 60\%$$

EXAMPLE 2

Calculate 6% of 120 using a proportion.

Solution

$6 : 100 = \blacksquare : 120$

Multiply 6 by 1.2 since $100 \times 1.2 = 120$.

$$\dfrac{6}{100} = \dfrac{6 \times 1.2}{120}$$
$$= \dfrac{7.2}{120} \qquad \text{So, 6\% of 120 is 7.2.}$$

Practice

1. Write each percent as a fraction or ratio in lowest terms.
   a) 49%
   b) 75%
   c) 1%
   d) $\dfrac{1}{2}\%$
   e) $33\dfrac{1}{3}\%$
   f) $7\dfrac{1}{2}\%$

2. Write each fraction as a percent.
   a) $\dfrac{73}{100}$
   b) $\dfrac{3}{10}$
   c) $\dfrac{7}{50}$
   d) $\dfrac{1}{4}$
   e) $\dfrac{5}{8}$
   f) 1

3. Calculate each percent to one decimal place.
   a) 15% of 75
   b) 75% of 68
   c) 150% of 60
   d) $\dfrac{1}{2}\%$ of 244
   e) $2\dfrac{3}{4}\%$ of 748

A–16 Angle Properties

Here is a review of special angle relationships.

Complementary angles $a + b = 90°$ 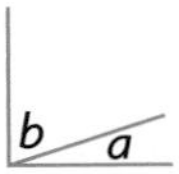	Isosceles triangle $a = b$ 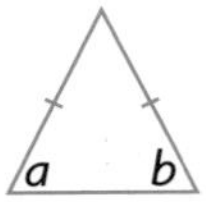	Alternate interior angles $c = f, d = g$ 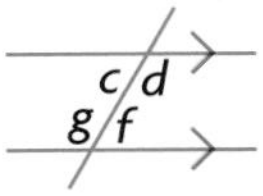	Supplementary angles $a + b = 180°$
Sum of the angles of a triangle $a + b + c = 180°$ 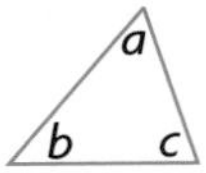	Corresponding angles $a = e, b = f, c = g, d = h$ 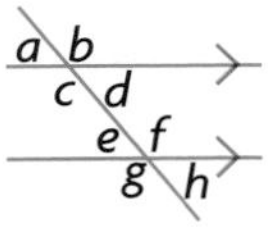	Vertically opposite angles $a = b, c = d$ 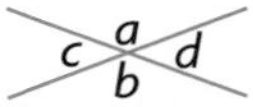	Exterior angle of a triangle $a + b = c$ 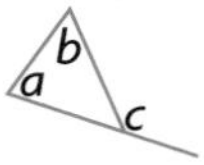

EXAMPLE 1

Determine the angles formed by the parallel lines.

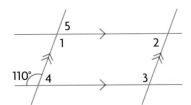

Solution

$\angle 4 = 180° - 110°$
$\quad = 70°$

$\angle 5 = \angle 4$
$\quad = 70°$

$\angle 1 = 180° - \angle 5$
$\quad = 180° - 70°$
$\quad = 110°$

$\angle 2 = \angle 5$
$\quad = 70°$

$\angle 3 = 180° - \angle 4$
$\quad = 180° - 70°$
$\quad = 110°$

EXAMPLE 2

Determine the angles in the triangles.

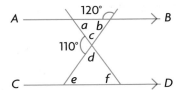

Solution

$\angle b = 180° - 120°$
$\quad = 60°$

$\angle e = \angle b$
$\quad = 60°$

$\angle a = \angle f$
$\quad = 50°$

$\angle c = 180° - 110°$
$\quad = 70°$

$\angle d = \angle c$
$\quad = 70°$

$\angle f = 180° - \angle d - \angle e$
$\quad = 180° - 70° - 60°$
$\quad = 50°$

Appendix A: Review of Essential Skills and Knowledge

Practice

1. Find the measure of each unknown angle.

a)

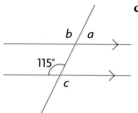

c)

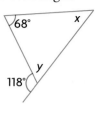

e)

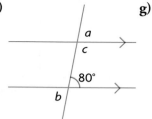

g)

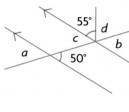

b)

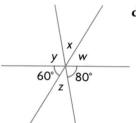

d)

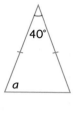

f)

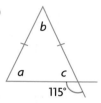

h)

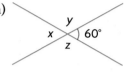

2. Find each missing measure.

a)

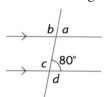

b)

c)

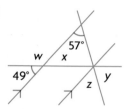

d)

A–17 Area and Perimeter of Polygons

Perimeter measures the distance around the outside of a closed figure.

Area measures the number of square units needed to cover a surface.

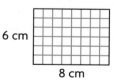

The perimeter of the triangle is
$$P = 7 + 4 + 5$$
$$= 16 \text{ cm}$$

The area of the rectangle is
$$A = 6 \times 8$$
$$= 48 \text{ cm}^2$$

Shape	Perimeter	Area
triangle 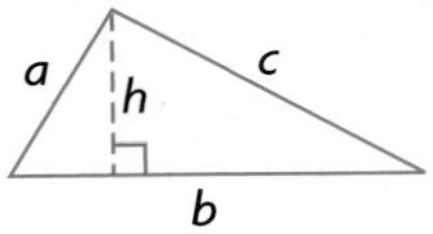	$P = a + b + c$	$A = \frac{1}{2}(b \times h)$
square 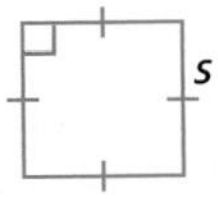	$P = 4s$	$A = s^2$
rectangle 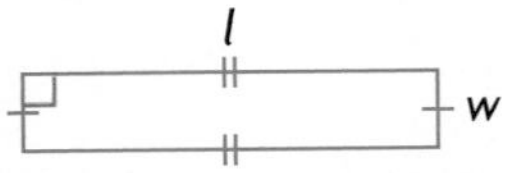	$P = 2(l + w)$	$A = lw$
parallelogram 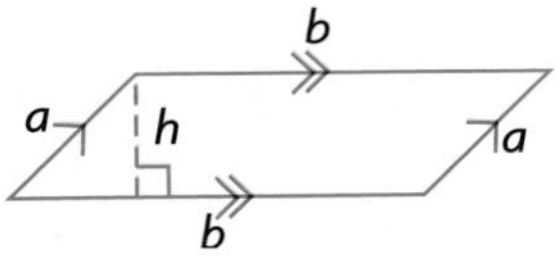	$P = 2(a + b)$	$A = bh$
trapezoid 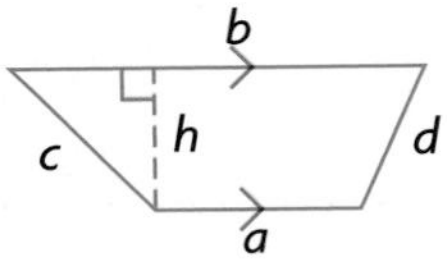	$P = a + b + c + d$	$A = \frac{1}{2}(a + b)h$

EXAMPLE 1

Calculate the area of
the parallelogram.

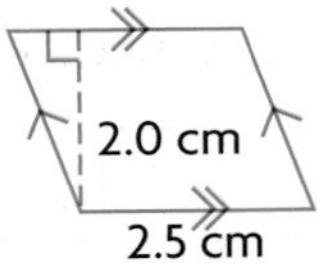

Solution

$A = bh$

$\quad = 2.5 \times 2.0$

$\quad = 5.0 \text{ cm}^2$

EXAMPLE 2

Calculate the area of
the triangle.

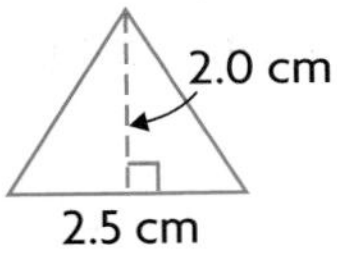

Solution

$A = \frac{1}{2}(b \times h)$

$\quad = \frac{1}{2}(2.5 \times 2.0)$

$\quad = 2.5 \text{ cm}^2$

EXAMPLE 3

Calculate the area of the trapezoid.

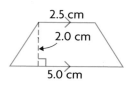

Solution

$$A = \frac{1}{2}(a + b)h$$

$$= \frac{1}{2}(5.0 + 2.5) \times 2.0$$

$$= 7.5 \text{ cm}^2$$

EXAMPLE 4

Determine the area of the orange region.

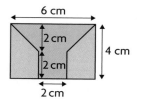

Solution

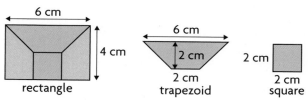

$$A_{\text{orange region}} = A_{\text{rectangle}} - A_{\text{trapezoid}} - A_{\text{square}}$$

$$= 6 \times 4 - \frac{1}{2}(6 + 2) \times 2 - 2 \times 2$$

$$= 24 - 8 - 4$$

$$= 12 \text{ cm}^2$$

Practice

1. Calculate the perimeter of each figure.

a)

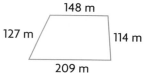

b)

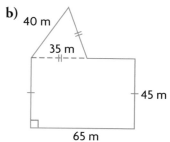

c)

d)

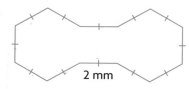

2. Calculate the area of each figure.

a)
8.8 cm
8.0 cm

d)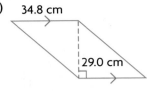
34.8 cm
29.0 cm

b)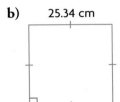
25.34 cm

e)
10 cm
4 cm   12 cm

c)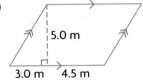
2.3 m
3.1 m
5.9 m

f)
5.0 m
3.0 m   4.5 m

3. Calculate the area of each figure.

a)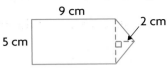
9 cm
5 cm
2 cm

b)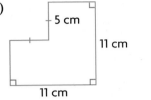
5 cm
11 cm
11 cm

c)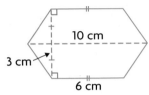
10 cm
3 cm
6 cm

d)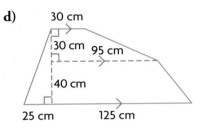
30 cm
30 cm   95 cm
40 cm
25 cm   125 cm

A–18 Circumference and Area of a Circle

Circle	Perimeter	Area
diameter (d), radius (r), arc, chord, arc circumference	In a circle, the distance around the outside is called the circumference. $C = 2\pi r$ or $C = \pi d$	$A = \pi r^2$

EXAMPLE

Calculate the circumference and
area of the circle.

10.00 m

Solution

$C = \pi d$

$\quad = \pi \times 10.00$

$\quad \doteq 31.42$ m

$A = \pi r^2$

$\quad = \pi \times 5.00^2$

$\quad = \pi \times 25.00$

$\quad \doteq 78.54$ m^2

Practice

Record your answers to two decimal places.

1. Calculate the area and circumference of a circle
with each measurement.

a) 2 cm radius   **c)** 20 cm radius

b) 2 cm diameter   **d)** 20 cm diameter

2. The circle is divided into three identical
sections.

a) Determine the area of
each section.

b) Determine the length
of the arc for each
section.

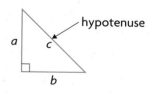

4.1 cm

3. Determine the area of each shaded region.

a)

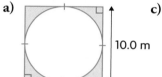

10.0 m

c)

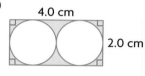

4.0 cm

2.0 cm

b)

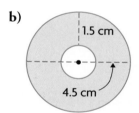

1.5 cm

4.5 cm

d)

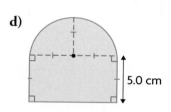

5.0 cm

A–19 The Pythagorean Theorem

The Pythagorean theorem states that $c^2 = a^2 + b^2$ when c is the
hypotenuse of a right triangle and a and b are its other sides.

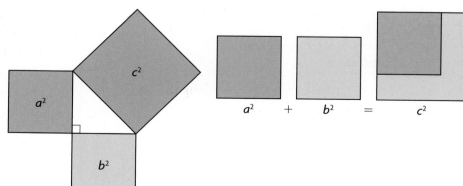

EXAMPLE

Erik and Calvin are flying a kite as shown in the diagram. How high is the kite above Calvin?

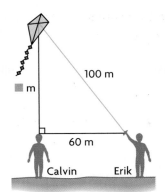

Solution

H stands for the height of the kite in metres above Calvin.

$$H^2 + 60^2 = 100^2$$
$$H^2 + 3600 = 10\ 000$$
$$H^2 = 10\ 000 - 3600$$
$$= 6400$$
$$H = \sqrt{6400}$$
$$= 80 \text{ m}$$

The kite is 80 m above Calvin.

Practice

1. For each right triangle, write the equation for the Pythagorean theorem.

a)

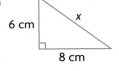
6 cm, x, 8 cm

b)

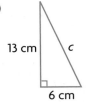
13 cm, c, 6 cm

c)

9 m, y, 5 m

d)

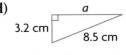
3.2 cm, a, 8.5 cm

2. Calculate the length of the unknown side of each triangle in the previous question. Record each answer to one decimal place.

3. Calculate the distance saved if Jim hops the fence and takes a shortcut by walking along the diagonal of a rectangular lot that measures 150 m by 200 m.

4. Determine the length of the diagonals of each rectangle to the nearest tenth.

a)

5 m, 10 m

b)

6 cm, 3 cm

c)

5.2 cm, 5.2 cm

d) 1.2 m, 4.8 m

5. An apartment building casts a shadow. From the tip of the shadow to the top of the building is 100 m. The tip of the shadow is 72 m from the base of the building. How tall is the building?

6. A communications tower is supported by four guy wires. The tower is 155 m tall, and each guy wire is staked into the ground at a distance of 30 m from the base of the tower. What is the total length of wire used to support the tower?

A–20 Surface Area and Volume of Prisms and Cylinders

The surface area of a prism or cylinder is the sum of the areas of its faces. This is the area of the object's net.

The volume of a prism or cylinder is the product of the area of the base and the height.

EXAMPLE 1

Determine the volume of the gift and the area of paper that covers it.

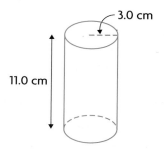

Solution

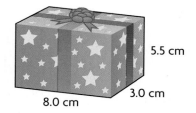

$$SA = 2 \times A_{top} + 2 \times A_{side} + 2 \times A_{front}$$
$$= 2 \times (8.0 \times 3.0) + 2 \times (3.0 \times 5.5)$$
$$+ 2 \times (8.0 \times 5.5)$$
$$= 48.0 + 33.0 + 88.0$$
$$= 169.0 \text{ cm}^2$$

$$V = A_{base} \times h$$
$$= (3.0 \times 8.0) \times 5.5$$
$$= 132.0 \text{ cm}^3$$

EXAMPLE 2

Determine the surface area and volume of the cylinder.

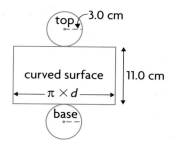

Solution

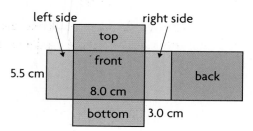

$$SA = 2 \times A_{base} + A_{curved \ surface}$$
$$= 2 \times \pi r^2 + \pi dh$$
$$= 2\pi \times 3.0^2 + \pi \times 6.0 \times 11.0$$
$$\doteq 263.9 \text{ cm}^2$$

$$V = A_{base} \times h$$
$$= \pi r^2 h$$
$$= \pi \times 3.0^2 \times 11.0$$
$$\doteq 311.0 \text{ cm}^3$$

Practice

Round all answers to the nearest tenth of a unit.

1. Calculate the surface area and volume for each shape.

a)

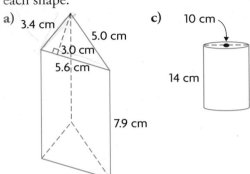
3.4 cm
5.0 cm
3.0 cm
5.6 cm
7.9 cm

c)
10 cm
14 cm

b)

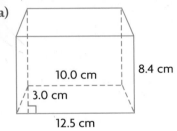
9.8 cm
10.7 cm
4.6 cm

d)
14 cm
10 cm

2. Determine the total volume of each figure.

a)

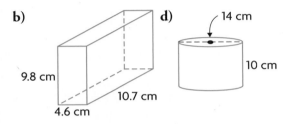
10.0 cm
8.4 cm
3.0 cm
12.5 cm

b)

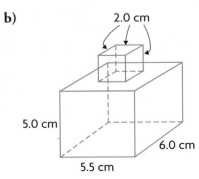
2.0 cm
5.0 cm
6.0 cm
5.5 cm

3. Determine the total volume of these figures.

a)

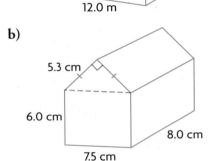
2.5 m
8.0 m
6.5 m
4.0 m
12.0 m

b)

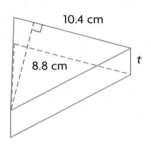
5.3 cm
6.0 cm
8.0 cm
7.5 cm

4. A triangular piece of cheese has a volume of 146.4 cm³. Find the thickness, *t*, of the cheese.

10.4 cm
8.8 cm
t

5. The dimensions of a room are shown.

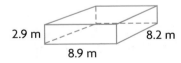
2.9 m
8.2 m
8.9 m

a) Calculate the volume of the room.
b) Calculate the total surface area of the room.
c) The walls and ceiling are to be painted. A 4 L can of paint covers an area of 52.2 m². How many cans of paint are needed?

Review of Technical Skills

PART 1 USING THE TI-83 PLUS/TI-84 PLUS GRAPHING CALCULATOR

B–1 Evaluating Powers and Roots

1. **Evaluate the power $(5.3)^2$.**
   Press [5] [.] [3] [x²] [ENTER].

2. **Evaluate the power $(7.5)^5$.**
   Press [7] [.] [5] [^] [5] [ENTER].

3. **Evaluate the power $8^{\frac{-2}{3}}$.**
   Press [8] [^] [(] [(-)] [2] [÷] [3] [)] [ENTER].

4. **Evaluate the square root of 46.1.**
   Press [2nd] [x²] [4] [6] [.] [1] [)] [ENTER].

5. **Evaluate $\sqrt[4]{256}$.**
   Press [4] [MATH] [5] [2] [5] [6] [ENTER].

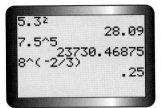

B–2 Preparing the Calculator for Graphing

Before you graph any function, be sure to clear any information left on the calculator from the last time it was used. You should always do the following:

1. **Clear all data in the lists.**
   Press [2nd] [+] [4] [ENTER].

2. **Turn off all stat plots.**
   Press [2nd] [Y=] [4] [ENTER].

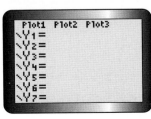

3. **Clear all equations in the equation editor.**
   Press [Y=], then press [CLEAR] for each equation.

4. Set the window so that the axes range from -10 to 10.

Press ⌜ZOOM⌝ ⌜6⌝. Press ⌜WINDOW⌝ to verify.

Note: It is possible to completely reset the calculator's memory and settings. This procedure removes all data and programs stored in the calculator, so be cautious.

Press ⌜2nd⌝ ⌜+⌝ ⌜7⌝ ⌜1⌝ ⌜2⌝.

B–3 Entering and Graphing Relations

Enter the equation of the function into the equation editor. The calculator will display the graph.

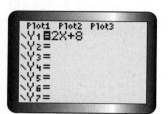

1. Enter an equation.

To enter $y = 2x + 8$, press ⌜Y=⌝ ⌜2⌝ ⌜X,T,θ,n⌝ ⌜+⌝ ⌜8⌝. The equation will be displayed as shown.

2. Enter all linear equations in the form $y = mx + b$.

For example, enter $-2x + y = 8$ in the form $y = 2x + 8$, as shown. If m or b is a fraction, enter it between brackets.

3. Press ⌜GRAPH⌝ to view the graph.

4. Resize the window using ZoomFit.

If the graph does not fit the window or is not visible in the window, the **ZoomFit** operation will automatically resize the window to show the graph. Press ⌜ZOOM⌝ ⌜0⌝.

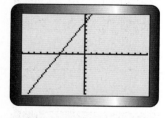

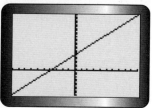

B–4   Evaluating a Relation

Sometimes you want the calculator to determine the value of a relation for a given value of the x-variable. For example, suppose you want it to determine the value of y in the relation $y = 2x + 8$ when $x = -1$.

1. **Enter the relation into the equation editor.**
   To enter $y = 2x + 8$, press [Y=] [2] [X,T,θ,n] [+] [8]. The equation will be displayed as shown.

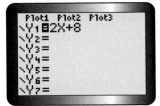

2. **Press the [TRACE] key.**
   [TRACE] shows you the coordinates of points on the graph of the relation. Use the left and right arrow keys to move the point along the graph.
   [TRACE] can only provide an approximate value based on the scale of the graph.

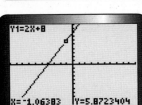

3. **Obtain exact values using the value operation.**
   Press [2nd] [TRACE] [1].

   Then press [(-)] [1].

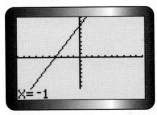

   Press [ENTER]. The calculator displays the graph with the value of y that corresponds to $x = -1$.

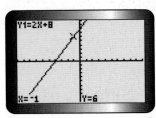

B–5   Changing Window Settings

The window settings can be changed to show a graph for a given range of values for x and y.

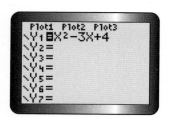

1. **Enter the relation $y = x^2 - 3x + 4$ in the equation editor.**

   To enter $y = x^2 - 3x + 4$, press [Y=] [X,T,θ,n] [x²] [−] [3] [X,T,θ,n] [+] [4]. The equation will be displayed as shown.

2. **Use the [WINDOW] function to set the graph window limits for x and y.**

   To display the graph for x between -2 and 5 and y between 0 and 14, press [WINDOW] [(-)] [2] [ENTER], then [5] [ENTER] [ENTER], then [0] [ENTER], then [1] [4] [ENTER].

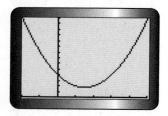

3. **Press [GRAPH] to show the relation with these settings.**

B–6   Showing a Table of Values for a Relation

The calculator can display a table of values for a relation such as $y = 2x + 8$.

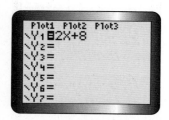

1. **Enter the relation into the equation editor.**

2. **Set the start point and step size for the table.**

   Press [2nd] [WINDOW]. The cursor is at **TblStart=**. To start at $x = -5$, press [(-)] [5] [ENTER]. The cursor is now at **ΔTbl=** (Δ, the Greek capital letter delta, stands for "change in"). To increase the x-value in steps of 1, Press [1] [ENTER].

3. **To view the table, press** 2nd GRAPH.

Use ▲ and ▼ to move up and down the table. Notice that you can look at higher or lower x-values than the original range.

B–7 Making a Difference Table for a Relation

To create a table with the first and second differences for a relation, use the STAT lists.

1. **Press** STAT 1 **and enter the x-values into L1.**

For the relation $y = 2x + 8$, use x-values from -5 to 5. Enter -5 by pressing (-) 5 ENTER. Then enter $-4, -3, -2, \ldots, 4, 5$ in the same way.

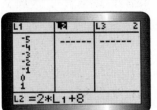

2. **Enter the relation.**

Scroll right and up to select **L2**. Enter the relation using **L1** to represent the variable x.

Press 2 × 2nd 1 + 8 .

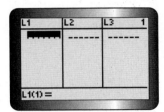

3. **Press** ENTER **to display the values of the relation in L2.**

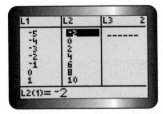

4. **Find the first differences.**

Scroll right and up to select **L3**. Then press 2nd STAT. Scroll right to **OPS** and press 7 to choose **ΔList(**.

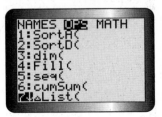

Enter **L2** by pressing 2nd 2) .

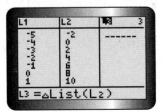

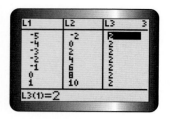

Press <kbd>ENTER</kbd> to see the first differences displayed in **L3**.

B–8 Determining the Points of Intersection of Two Relations

1. Enter two relations into the equation editor.

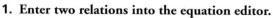

This example uses $y = 5x + 4$ and $y = -2x + 18$.

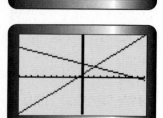

2. Graph both relations.

Press <kbd>GRAPH</kbd>. Adjust the window settings until the point(s) of intersection are displayed.

3. Use the intersect operation.

Press <kbd>2nd</kbd> <kbd>TRACE</kbd> <kbd>5</kbd>.

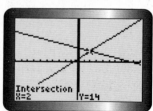

4. Determine a point of intersection.

You will be asked to verify the two curves and enter an optional estimate for the intersection point. Press <kbd>ENTER</kbd> after each screen appears.

The point of intersection is exactly (2, 14).

B–9 Creating a Scatter Plot from Data

This table gives the height of a baseball above ground level, from the time it was hit to the time it touched the ground.

Time (s)	0	1	2	3	4	5	6
Height (m)	2	27	42	48	43	29	5

Create a scatter plot of the data.

1. **Enter the data into STAT lists.**
   To start, press STAT ENTER. Move the cursor to the first position in **L1** and enter the time values. Press ENTER after each value. Repeat this for the heights in **L2**.

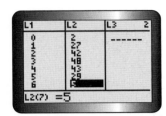

2. **Create a scatter plot.**
   Press 2nd Y= and 1. Turn on **Plot 1** by making sure that the cursor is over **On**, the **Type** is set to the scatter plot graph type, and **L1** and **L2** appear after **Xlist** and **Ylist**, respectively.

3. **Display the graph.**
   Press ZOOM 9 to activate **ZoomStat**.
   This displays the scatter plot.

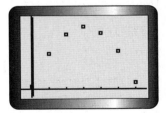

PART 2 USING THE GEOMETER'S SKETCHPAD

B–10 Defining the Tool Buttons and Sketchpad Terminology

Sketches and Dynamic Geometry

Your ability to change objects dynamically is the most important feature of *The Geometer's Sketchpad*. Once you have created an object, you can move it, rotate it, dilate it, reflect it, hide it, and change its label, colour, shade, or line thickness. No matter what changes you make, *The Geometer's Sketchpad* maintains the mathematical relationships between the object and the other objects to which it is related. This is the principle of dynamic geometry. It is the basis of the power and usefulness of *The Geometer's Sketchpad*.

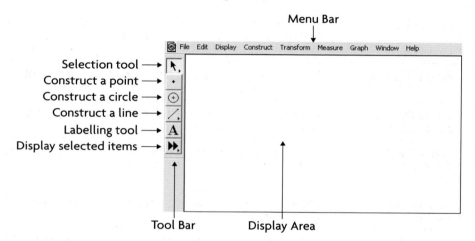

Selection tool
Construct a point
Construct a circle
Construct a line
Labelling tool
Display selected items

Menu Bar

Tool Bar   Display Area

Sketchpad Terminology

Selecting means to move the mouse pointer to the desired location and click the mouse button (left-click for Windows users).

Deselecting means to select the selection tool and click anywhere in the display area away from any figures you have drawn.

Dragging means to move the mouse pointer to the point or figure you would like to move. Click on the point or figure and, while holding down the mouse button, move it to a new location. Release the mouse button when the point or figure is in the desired position.

B–11 Selections on the Construct Menu

Command	What it constructs:	What you must select:
Point On Object	A point on the selected object(s)	One or more segments, rays, lines, or circles
Point At Intersection	A point where two objects intersect	Two straight objects, two circles, or a straight object and a circle
Point At Midpoint	The midpoint of the segment(s)	One or more segments
Segment/Ray/Line	The segment(s), ray(s), or line(s) defined by the points	Two or more points
Perpendicular Line	The line(s) through the selected point(s) and perpendicular to the selected straight object(s)	One point and one or more straight objects, or one straight object and one or more points
Parallel Line	The line(s) through the selected point(s) and parallel to the selected straight object(s)	One point and one or more straight objects, or one straight object and one or more points
Angle Bisector	The ray that bisects the angle defined by three points	Three points (select the vertex second)
Circle By Centre And Point	The circle with the given centre and passing through the given point	Two points (select the centre first)
Circle By Centre And Radius	The circle with the given centre and with a radius equal to the length of the given segment	A point and a segment
Arc By Three Points	The arc passing through the three given points	Three points
Arc On Circle	The arc on a circle extending counterclockwise from the first point to the second	A circle and two points on the circle's circumference
Polygon Interior	The polygon interior defined by using the given points as its vertices	Three or more points
Circle Interior	The interior of a circle	One or more circles
Sector Interior	The interior of an arc sector	One or more arcs
Arc Segment Interior	The interior of an arc segment	One or more arcs
Locus	The locus of an object	One geometric object and one point constructed to lie on a path

B–12 Graphing a Relation on a Cartesian Coordinate System

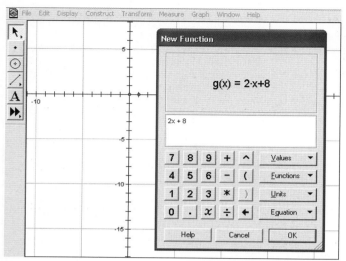

You can graph relations on a Cartesian coordinate system in *The Geometer's Sketchpad*. For example, use the following steps to graph the relation $y = 2x + 8$.

1. **Turn on the grid.**
   From the **Graph** menu, choose **Show Grid**.

2. **Enter the relation.**
   From the **Graph** menu, choose **Plot New Function**. The **New Function** calculator should appear. Use either the calculator keypad or the keyboard to enter "2 * x + 8".

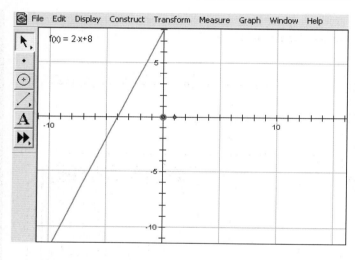

3. **Graph the relation $y = 2x + 8$.**
   Press **OK** on the calculator keypad. The graph of $y = 2x + 8$ should appear on the grid.

4. Adjust the origin and/or scale.

To adjust the origin, click on the point at the origin to select it. Then click and drag the origin as desired. To adjust the scale, click in blank space to deselect, then click on the point at (1, 0) to select it. Click and drag this point to change the scale.

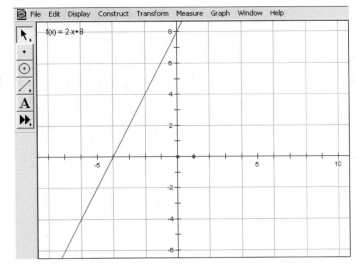

B–13 Placing Points on a Cartesian Coordinate System: Plot Points

Sometimes, you want to plot points without graphing a relation. For example, suppose you want to plot (2, 1), (3, 5), and (–2, 0).

1. Turn on the grid.

2. Enter the coordinates of a point.

From the **Graph** menu, select **Plot Points ….** For each point you want to plot, enter the *x*-coordinate followed by the *y*-coordinate. Use the Tab key to move from one coordinate entry space to the next. Press the Enter key when you have entered both coordinates of a point. *The Geometer's Sketchpad* allows you to continue entering point coordinates until you click **Done**.

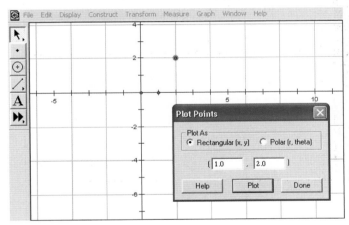

B–14 Placing Points on a Cartesian Coordinate System: The Point Tool

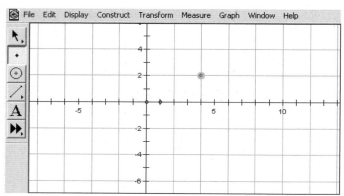

Sometimes, you want to plot points without graphing a relation. For example, suppose you want to plot (4, 2).

1. **Turn on the grid.**

2. **Select the Point Tool.**
   The selection arrow will now look like a dot to indicate that when you click on the grid, a point will be placed at the location you clicked.

B–15 Determining the Coordinates of a Point

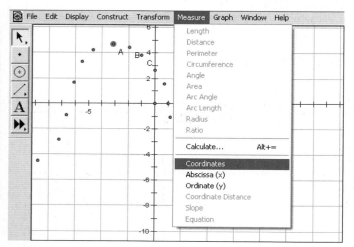

1. **Turn on the grid.**

2. **Plot some points on the grid.**

3. **Use the Selection Tool to select a point.**

4. **From the Measure menu, select Coordinates.**

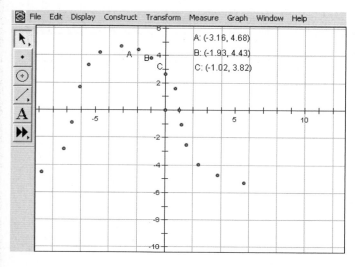

The coordinates of the selected point(s) will be displayed.

B–16 Constructing a Line, Segment, or Ray Through a Given Point

1. **Turn the grid on.**

2. **Plot the point you want the line to pass through.**

3. **Plot a second point anywhere on the grid.**

4. **Shift-click to make sure both points are selected.**

   If you are constructing a ray, make sure the point from which the ray begins is selected first.

5. **From the Construct menu, select Line (or Segment or Ray).**

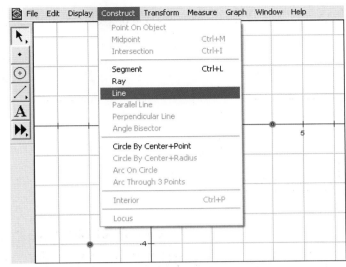

B–17 Constructing and Labelling a Point on a Line, Segment, or Ray

1. **Turn the grid on.**

2. **Draw a line (or segment or ray).**

3. **Select the line by clicking on it.**

4. **From the Construct menu, select Point On Line.**

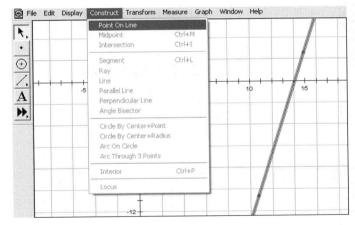

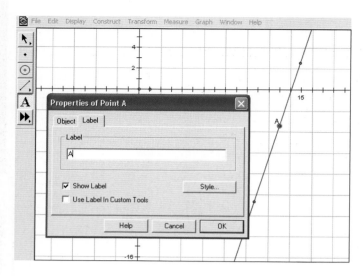

5. **Select the Label Tool. Use it to double click on the point you constructed.**

   A label will appear beside the point, as well as a Properties box for the point. You can change the label of the point by changing the contents of the label entry in the Properties box.

B–18 Determining the Slope and Equation of a Line

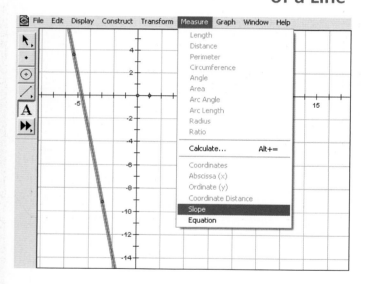

1. **Turn the grid on.**

2. **Draw a line.**

3. **Use the Selection Tool to select the line.**

4. **From the Measure menu, select Slope or Equation.**

B–19 Moving a Line

1. **Turn the grid on.**

2. **Draw a line.**

3. **Copy the line by clicking Copy and then Paste from the Edit menu.**

4. **To keep the new line parallel to the original line:**
   Use the Selection Tool to click and hold only the line. Hold the mouse button down while you move the mouse. The line will move parallel to the original.

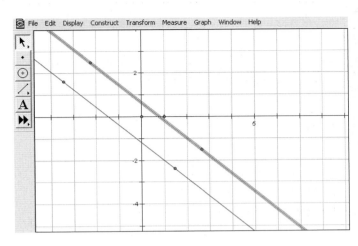

5. **To move the new line so that one point stays in the same position:**
   Use the Selection Tool to select a point on the line other than the one that is to stay in the same position. Hold the mouse button down while you move the mouse. The line will move as the mouse moves, but the original point will stay fixed.

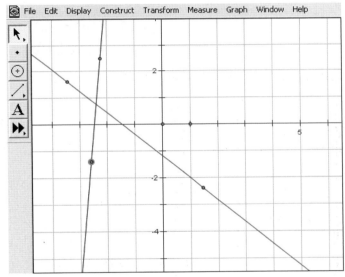

B–20 Constructing a Triangle and Labelling Vertices

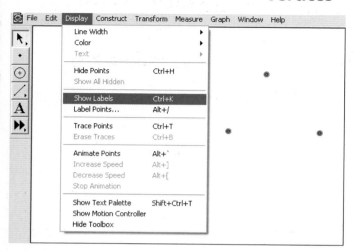

1. **Open a new sketch.**

2. **Use the Point Tool to place three points.**
   If you hold the Shift key down while you place the points, all of the points will remain selected as you place them.

3. **From the Display menu, select Show Labels.**

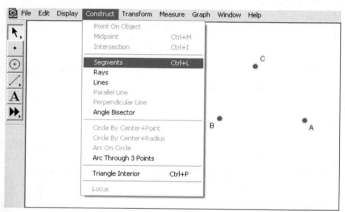

4. **From the Construct menu, select Segments.**

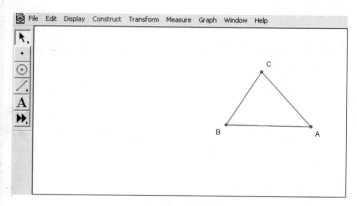

5. **The three triangle sides will be displayed.**

B–21 Measuring Interior Angles in a Triangle

1. **Open a new sketch and draw a triangle with vertex labels displayed.**

2. **Shift-click to select the vertices that form an angle.**

   To measure $\angle ABC$, select vertex A, then vertex B, and then vertex C.

3. **From the Measure menu, select Angle.**

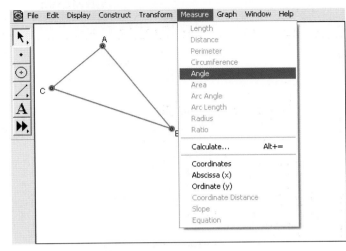

4. **Repeat for each angle.**

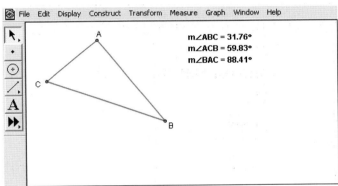

B–22 Constructing and Measuring an Exterior Angle of a Triangle

1. **Open a new sketch and draw a triangle with vertex labels displayed.**

2. **Select two vertices. From the Construct menu, select Ray.**

   This extends one side of the triangle to form an exterior angle.

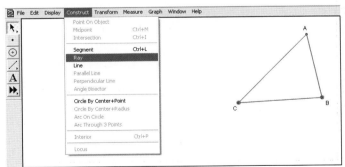

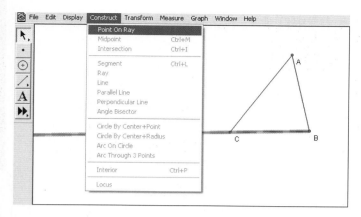

3. While the ray is selected, from the Construct menu, select Point On Ray.

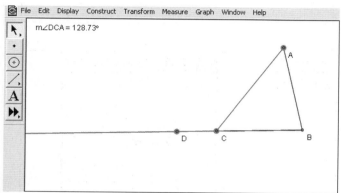

4. Drag the point so that it is outside the triangle. Display the label for the point.

5. Select the point, then the vertex for the angle, and then the final vertex. From the Measure menu, select Angle.

B–23 Determining the Sum of the Interior Angles of a Triangle

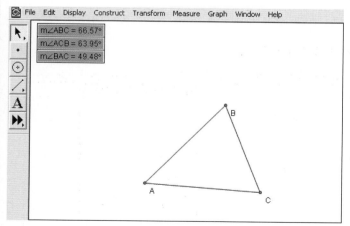

1. Open a new sketch and draw a labelled triangle.
   Measure all three interior angles.
   Shift-click to select all three angle measures.

2. **From the Measure menu, select Calculate.**
   A New Calculation window will appear.

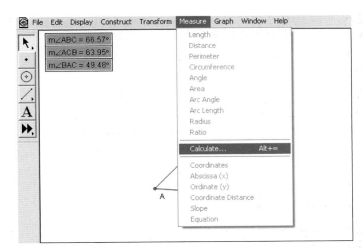

3. **Use the Values pop-up menu to create the formula for the sum of the selected angles.**
   Choose an angle from the Values pop-up, then enter "+" and continue entering addends until the formula is complete.
   Click **OK** when you are finished.

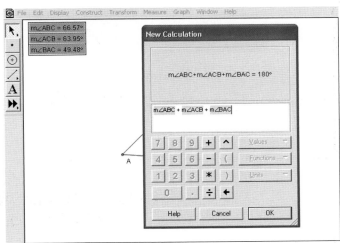

B–24 Measuring the Length of a Line Segment

1. **Open a new sketch and draw a line segment.**

2. **While the line segment is selected, choose Length from the Measure menu.**

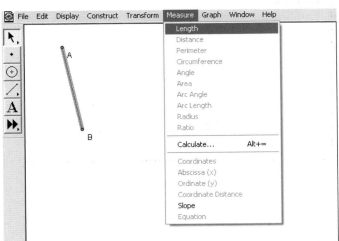

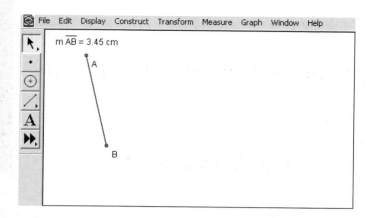

3. The length will be displayed.

B–25 Constructing the Midpoint of a Line Segment

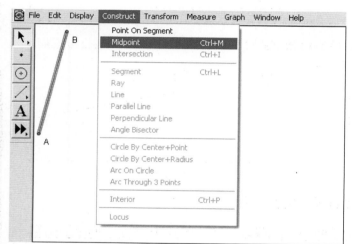

1. Open a new sketch and draw a line segment.

2. With the line segment selected, choose Midpoint from the Construct menu.

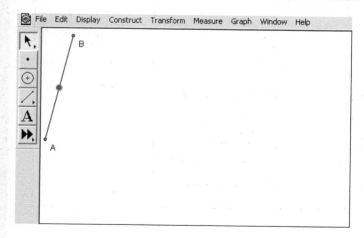

3. The midpoint will be displayed.

B–26 Constructing the Perpendicular Bisector of a Line Segment

1. Open a new sketch and draw a line segment.

2. With the line segment selected, choose Midpoint from the Construct menu.

3. Select the segment and the midpoint.

4. From the Construct menu, choose Perpendicular Line.

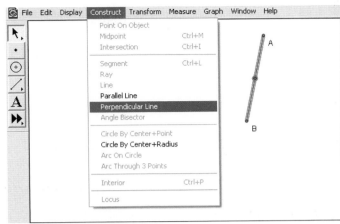

5. The perpendicular bisector will be displayed as a line through the selected point.

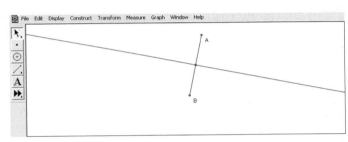

B–27 Constructing the Bisector of an Angle

1. Open a new sketch and place three points to form an angle.

2. Use the Ray Tool or the Segment Tool to draw the angle.

3. Select the vertices that form the angle.

4. From the Construct menu, choose Angle Bisector.

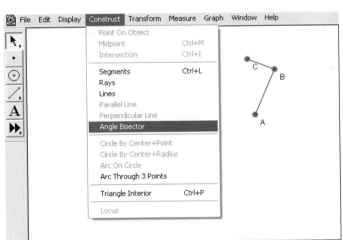

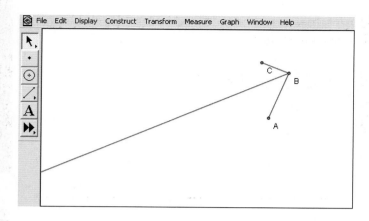

5. The angle bisector will be displayed as a ray going out from the angle.

B–28   Measuring the Area of a Polygon

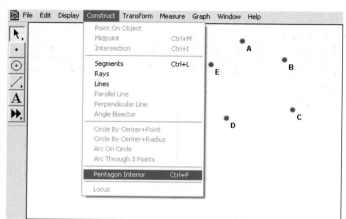

1. Open a new sketch and place points to form the vertices of a polygon and their labels.

2. While the points are selected, use the Construct Polygon Interior operation in the Construct menu to form a polygon.
The Geometer's Sketchpad will name the polygon depending on the number of vertices you have selected.

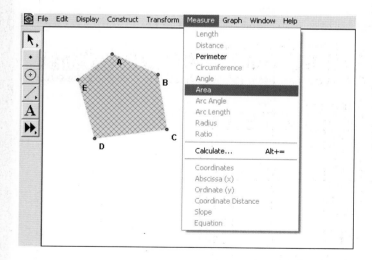

3. While the interior is highlighted, select Area from the Measure menu.

4. The area will be displayed.

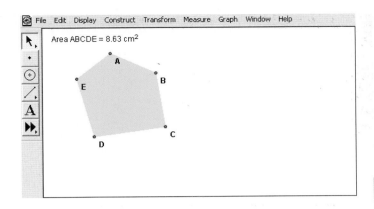

PART 3 USING FATHOM

B–29 Creating a Scatter Plot from Data

1. Create a case table.

Drag a case table from the object shelf, and drop it in the document.

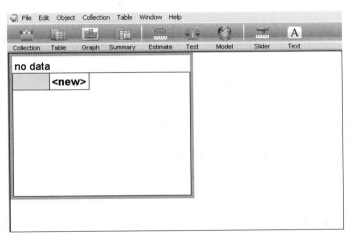

2. Enter the Variables and Data.

Click the **<new>** button, and then type a name for the new variable or attribute. Press the Enter key. (If necessary, repeat this step to add more attributes; pressing the Tab key instead of the Enter key moves you to the next column.)

When you name your first attribute, *Fathom* creates an empty collection to hold your data (a small empty box). The collection is where your data are actually stored. Deleting the collection deletes your data. When you add cases by typing values, the collection icon fills with gold balls. To enter the data, click in the blank cell under the attribute name and begin typing values. (Press the Tab key to move from cell to cell.)

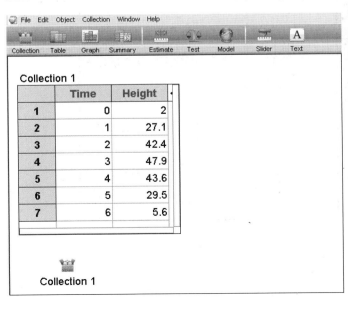

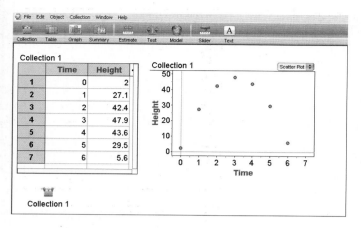

3. Graph the data.

Drag a new graph from the object shelf at the top of the *Fathom* window, and drop it in a blank space in your document. Drag attributes from the case table, and drop them on the prompts below and to the left of the axes in the graph.

PART 4 USING A SPREADSHEET

B–30 Introduction to a Spreadsheet

A spreadsheet is a computer program that can be used to create a table of values and then graph the values. It is made up of cells that are identified by column letter and row number, such as **A2** or **B5**. A cell can hold a label, a number, or a formula.

Creating a Table

Use spreadsheets to solve problems like this: How much interest will you pay if you borrow $3000 and pay it back at an interest rate of 5% per year over 8 years using the Add-On charge method?

	A	B
1	**Time (years)**	**Amount ($)**
2	0	0
3	=A2+1	=A3*3000*0.05
4		
5		
6		
7		
8		
9		
10		
11		
12		

To create a spreadsheet, label cell **A1** as "Time (years)" and cell **B1** as "Amount ($)". Enter the initial values "0" in **A2** and "0" in **B2**. Enter the formulas "=A2+1" in **A3** and "=A3*3000*0.05" in **B3** to generate the next values in the table.

	A	B
1	**Time (years)**	**Amount ($)**
2	0	0
3	1	150
4		
5		
6		
7		
8		
9		
10		
11		
12		

Notice that an equal sign is in front of each formula and an asterisk (*) is used for multiplication. Next, use the cursor to select cells **A3** to **B3** and several rows of cells below them. Use the **Fill Down** command. This command inserts the appropriate formula into each selected cell.

When the **Fill Down** command is used, the computer automatically calculates and enters the values in each cell, as shown.

	A Time (years)	B Amount ($)
1	Time (years)	Amount ($)
2	0	0
3	1	150
4	2	300
5	3	450
6	4	600
7	5	750
8	6	900
9	7	1050
10	8	1200
11	9	1350
12	10	1500

Creating a Graph

Use the spreadsheet's graphing command to graph the results. Use the cursor to highlight the portion of the table you would like to graph. In this case, select columns **A** and **B** to graph Amount vs. Time.

	A Time (years)	B Amount ($)
1	Time (years)	Amount ($)
2	0	0
3	1	150
4	2	300
5	3	450
6	4	600
7	5	750
8	6	900
9	7	1050
10	8	1200
11	9	1350
12	10	1500

Different spreadsheets have different graphing commands. Check your spreadsheet's instructions to find the proper command. A graph like this will appear.

You will pay $1200 in interest over 8 years.

Amount of Interest vs. Time

Glossary

Instructional Words

C

calculate: Figure out the number that answers a question. Compute.

clarify: Make a statement easier to understand. Provide an example.

classify: Put things into groups according to a rule and label the groups. Organize into categories.

compare: Look at two or more objects or numbers and identify how they are the same and how they are different (e.g., compare the numbers 6.5 and 5.6; compare the size of the students' feet; compare two shapes).

conclude: Judge or decide after reflection or after considering data.

construct: Make or build a model. Draw an accurate geometric shape (e.g., use a ruler and a protractor to construct an angle).

create: Make your own example.

D

describe: Tell, draw, or write about what something is or what something looks like. Tell about a process in a step-by-step way.

determine: Decide with certainty as a result of calculation, experiment, or exploration.

draw: 1. Show something in picture form (e.g., draw a diagram).
2. Pull or select an object (e.g., draw a card from the deck; draw a tile from the bag).

E

estimate: Use your knowledge to make a sensible decision about an amount. Make a reasonable guess (e.g., estimate how long it takes to cycle from your home to school; estimate how many leaves are on a tree; what is your estimate of 3210 + 789?).

evaluate: 1. Determine if something makes sense. Judge.
2. Calculate the value as a number.

explain: Tell what you did. Show your mathematical thinking at every stage. Show how you know.

explore: Investigate a problem by questioning, brainstorming, and trying new ideas.

extend: 1. In patterning, continue the pattern.
2. In problem solving, create a new problem that takes the idea of the original problem further.

J

justify: Give convincing reasons for a prediction, an estimate, or a solution. Tell why you think your answer is correct.

M

measure: Use a tool to describe an object or determine an amount (e.g., use a ruler to measure the height or distance around something; use a protractor to measure an angle; use balance scales to measure mass; use a measuring cup to measure capacity; use a stopwatch to measure the time in seconds or minutes).

model: Show or demonstrate an idea using objects and/or pictures (e.g., model addition of integers using red and blue counters).

P

predict: Use what you know to work out what is going to happen (e.g., predict the next number in the pattern 1, 2, 4, 7, …).

R

reason: Develop ideas and relate them to the purpose of the task and to each other. Analyze relevant information to show understanding.

relate: Describe how two or more objects, drawings, ideas, or numbers are similar.

represent: Show information or an idea in a different way that makes it easier to understand (e.g., draw a graph; make a model).

S

show (your work): Record all calculations, drawings, numbers, words, or symbols that make up the solution.

sketch: Make a rough drawing (e.g., sketch a picture of the field with dimensions).

solve: Develop and carry out a process for finding a solution to a problem.

sort: Separate a set of objects, drawings, ideas, or numbers according to an attribute (e.g., sort 2-D shapes by the number of sides).

V

validate: Check an idea by showing that it works.

verify: Work out an answer or solution again, usually in another way. Show evidence.

visualize: Form a picture in your head of what something is like. Imagine.

Mathematical Words

A

absolute value: Written as $|x|$; describes the distance of x from 0; equals x when $x \geq 0$ or $-x$ when $x < 0$. For example, $|3| = 3$ and $|-3| = -(-3) = 3$.

algebraic expression: A collection of symbols, including one or more variables and possibly numbers and operation symbols. For example, $3x + 6$, x, $5x$, and $21 - 2w$ are all algebraic expressions.

algebraic term: Part of an algebraic expression; often separated from the rest of the expression by an addition or subtraction symbol. For example, the expression $2x^2 + 3x + 4$ has three terms: $2x^2$, $3x$, and 4.

B

base: 1. The face that determines the name and the number of edges of a prism or pyramid
2. In a 2-D shape, the line segment that is perpendicular to the height
3. The number that is used as a factor in a power. For example, in the power 5^3, 5 is the base.

BEDMAS: A made-up word used to recall the order of operations, standing for **B**rackets, **E**xponents, **D**ivision, **M**ultiplication, **A**ddition, **S**ubtraction

bimedian: The line joining the midpoints of two opposite sides in a quadrilateral

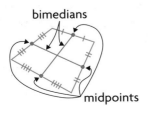
bimedians
midpoints

binomial: An algebraic expression containing two terms (e.g., $3x + 2$)

C

centroid: The centre of an object's mass; the point at which it balances; also known as the centre of gravity

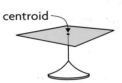
centroid

circle: The set of all the points in a plane that are the same distance, called the radius (r), from a fixed point called the centre. The formula for the area of a circle is $A = \pi r^2$.

circumference: The boundary of a circle; the length of this boundary. The formula to calculate the length is $C = 2\pi r$, where r is the radius, or $C = \pi d$, where d is the diameter.

coefficient: The factor by which a variable is multiplied. For example, in the term $5x$, the coefficient is 5.

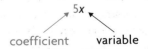
$5x$
coefficient   variable

collinear: Three or more points are collinear if they lie on the same line.

composite shape: A shape that can be divided into more than one of the basic shapes

concave polygon: A polygon with at least one interior angle greater than 180°. A straight line through it may cross more than two sides.

cone: A solid figure with a flat base and a curved side that meets at a point

conjecture: A guess or prediction based on limited evidence

constant: A value in a mathematical expression or formula that does not change. For example, in the expression $3x + 2$, 2 is a constant.

continuous: A set of data that can be broken down into smaller and smaller parts and still have meaning

convex polygon: A polygon with every interior angle less than 180°. Any straight line through it crosses at most two sides.

counterexample: An example that proves that a hypothesis or conjecture is false

cylinder: A 3-D figure with two congruent, parallel, circular faces and one curved surface

D

data point: An item of factual information derived from measurement or research. On a graph created on a Cartesian plane, each data point is represented as a dot at the location denoted by coordinates of an ordered pair where (x, y) = (value of the independent variable, value of the dependent variable).

degree: For a power with one variable, the degree is the variable's exponent. When there is more than one variable, the degree is the sum of the exponents of the powers of the variables. For example, x^4, x^3y, and x^2y^2 all have degree 4.

denominator: The number in a fraction that represents the number of parts in the whole set, or the number of parts the whole set has been divided into. For example, in $\frac{4}{5}$, the fractional unit is fifths.

dependent variable: In a relation, the variable whose values you calculate; usually placed in the left column in a table of values and on the vertical axis in a graph

diagonal: In a polygon, a line segment joining two vertices that are not next to each other (i.e., not joined by one side)

diameter: A line segment that joins two points on a circle and passes through the centre; the length of this line segment

direct variation: A relation in which one variable is a multiple of the other

discrete: A set of data that cannot be broken into smaller parts

displacement: How far out of place an object is; the object's overall change in position in reference to its starting point (origin)

distributive property or law: The property that states that when a sum is multiplied by a number, each value in the sum is multiplied by the number separately, and the products are then added. For example, $4 \times (7 + 8) = (4 \times 7) + (4 \times 8)$.

dividend: A number being divided. For example, in $18 \div 3 = 6$, 18 is the dividend, 3 is the divisor, and 6 is the quotient.

divisor: A number by which another is divided. For example, in $18 \div 3 = 6$, 3 is the divisor, 18 is the dividend, and 6 is the quotient.

E

equation: A mathematical statement in which the value on the left side of the equal sign is the same as the value on the right side of the equal sign. For example, the equation $5n + 4 = 39$ means that 4 more than the product of 5 and a number equals 39.

equation of a line: An equation of degree 1 that gives a straight line when graphed on the Cartesian plane. The equation can be expressed in several forms: $Ax + By = C$, $Ax + By + C = 0$, or $y = mx + b$ are the most common. For example, the equations $4x + 2y = 8$, $4x + 2y - 8 = 0$, and $y = -2x + 4$ all represent the same straight line when graphed.

equilateral: In a triangle, having all sides equal in length

equivalent equations: Equations that have the same solution

exponent: The number that tells how many equal factors are in a power

exterior angle: The angle formed by extending a side of a convex polygon; the angle between any extended side and its adjacent side

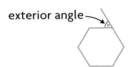

exterior angle

extrapolate: To predict a value by following a pattern beyond known values

F

first difference: The difference between two consecutive y-values in a table in which the difference between the x-values is constant

G

geometric pattern: Any pattern created with straight lines. These patterns are created primarily with right angles, triangles, squares, and other geometric shapes.

H

hypotenuse: The longest side of a right triangle; the side that is opposite the right angle

I

improper fraction: A fraction in which the numerator is greater than the denominator (e.g., $\frac{5}{4}$)

independent variable: In a relation, the variable whose values you choose; usually placed in the right column in a table of values and on the horizontal axis in a graph

integers (I): All positive and negative whole numbers, including zero: ... $-3, -2, -1, 0, 1, 2, 3, ...$

interior angle: The angle formed inside each vertex of a polygon. For example, ΔABC has three interior angles: $\angle ABC$, $\angle BCA$, and $\angle CAB$.

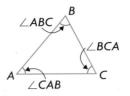

interpolate: To estimate a value between two known values

inverse operations: Operations that undo, or reverse, each other. For example, addition is the inverse of subtraction; multiplication is the inverse of division.

isolating a term or a variable: Performing math operations (e.g., addition, subtraction, multiplication, division) to get a term or a variable by itself on one side of an equation

isosceles: In a triangle, having two sides equal in length

K

kite: A quadrilateral that has two pairs of equal sides with no sides parallel

L

least common multiple (LCM): The least whole number that has all given numbers as factors. For example, 12 is the least common multiple of 4 and 6.

like terms: Algebraic terms that have the same variables and exponents apart from their numerical coefficients (e.g., $2x^2$ and $-3x$)

linear equation: An equation in the form $ax + b = 0$, or an equation that can be rewritten in this form. The algebraic expression involved is a polynomial of degree 1 (e.g., $2x + 3 = 6$ or $y = 3x - 5$).

linear relation: A relation in which the graph forms a straight line

line of best fit: A line that best describes the relationship between two variables in a scatter plot

lowest common denominator (LCD): The smallest common multiple of the denominators of two or more fractions. For example, the LCD of $\frac{3}{4}$ and $\frac{1}{6}$ is 12.

M

magnitude: The size of a quantity, measured in units of that quantity. For example, the magnitude of each angle of a regular hexagon is 120°.

median: 1. The middle value in a set of ordered data. For example, when there is an odd number of numbers, the median is the middle number; when there is an even number of numbers, the median is the mean of the two middle numbers.
2. The line drawn from a vertex of a triangle to the midpoint of the opposite side

3. The middle number in a set, such that half the numbers in the set are less and half are greater when the numbers are arranged in order

midpoint: The point that divides a line segment into two equal parts

midsegment: A line segment connecting the midpoints of two adjacent sides of a polygon

mixed number: A number made up of a whole number and a fraction (e.g., $5\frac{1}{7}$)

monomial: An algebraic expression with one term (e.g., $5x^2$, $4xy$)

N

natural number (N): One of the counting numbers (e.g., 1, 2, 3, 4). A natural number is used as a cardinal number when it describes how many things there are in a set (e.g., ten runners in a race), and as an ordinal number when it marks the position of something in a sequence (e.g., the runner in place number ten).

negative reciprocals: Numbers that multiply to produce -1 are negative reciprocals of each other (e.g., $\frac{3}{4}$ and $-\frac{4}{3}$, $-\frac{1}{2}$ and 2).

net: A 2-D pattern you can fold to create a 3-D shape

nonlinear relation: A relation whose graph is not a straight line

numerator: The number in a fraction that shows the number of parts of a given size the fraction represents

O

opposites: Two numbers with opposite signs that are the same distance from zero. For example, $+6$ and -6 are opposites.

optimum: The most desirable of a number of possible choices

order of operations: Rules describing what sequence to use when evaluating an expression:
1. Evaluate within brackets.
2. Calculate exponents and square roots.
3. Divide or multiply from left to right.
4. Add or subtract from left to right.

outlier: A data point that is separated from the rest of the points on a graph

P

parallelogram: A quadrilateral with equal and parallel opposite sides. For example, a rhombus, rectangle, and square are all types of parallelograms.

partial variation: A relation in which one variable is a multiple of the other plus a constant amount

pattern rule: A description of how a pattern starts and how it continues

point of intersection: The point in common between two lines

polynomial: An expression that comprises a sum and/or difference of monomials

power: A numerical expression that shows repeated multiplication. For example, the power 5^3 is a shorter way of writing $5 \times 5 \times 5$. A power has a base and an exponent: the exponent tells the number of equal factors there are in a power.

principle: A basic truth or rule about the way something works

prism: A 3-D figure with two parallel, congruent polygonal bases. A prism is named by the shape of its bases (e.g., rectangular prism, triangular prism).

pyramid: A 3-D shape with a polygon for a base. The other faces are triangles that meet at a single vertex.

Q

quotient: The result of dividing one number by another. For example, if 12 is divided by 5, the quotient is 2.4.

R

radius (plural **radii**): A line segment that goes from the centre of a circle to its circumference; the length of this line segment

rate of change: The change in one variable relative to the change in another

rational numbers (Q): Numbers that can be expressed as the quotient of two integers where the divisor is not 0

rectangle: A parallelogram with four square corners

relation: A description of how two variables are connected

repeating decimal: A decimal in which a block of one or more digits eventually repeats in a pattern

$$\left(\text{e.g., } \frac{25}{99} = 0.252\,525\,252\,\ldots; \right.$$
$$\left. \frac{1}{7} = 0.142\,857\,142\,857\,\ldots \right)$$

rhombus: A parallelogram with four equal sides

right pyramid: A pyramid whose base is a regular polygon and whose top vertex is directly above the centre of the base

rise: The vertical distance between two points

run: The horizontal distance between two points

S

scatter plot: A graph that attempts to show a relationship between two variables by means of points plotted on a coordinate grid. It is also called a scatter diagram.

slant height: The distance from the top to the base, at a right angle, along a slanted side of a pyramid or cone. It is measured to the midpoint of the base side for a pyramid.

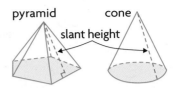

slope: A measure, often represented by m, of the steepness of a line; the ratio comparing the vertical and horizontal distances (called the rise and run) between two points; $m = \dfrac{\text{rise}}{\text{run}} = \dfrac{\Delta y}{\Delta x}$

solution to an equation: The value of a variable that makes the equation true. For example, in the equation $5n + 4 = 39$, the value of n is 7 because $5(7) + 4 = 39$.

solution to a system of linear equations: A point that satisfies both relations in a system of linear equations. The point of intersection represents an ordered pair that solves a system of linear equations.

solve for a variable in terms of other variables: The process of using inverse operations to express one variable in terms of the other variable(s)

sphere: The set of points in three dimensions in which the points are all the same distance, r, from a fixed point, called the centre; r is the radius of the sphere.

surface area: The total area of all the faces of any 3-D shape

system of linear equations: A set of equations (at least two) that represent linear relations between the same two variables

T

table of values: An orderly arrangement of facts set out for easy reference (e.g., an arrangement of numerical values in vertical and horizontal columns)

trapezoid: A quadrilateral with one pair of parallel sides

trend: A relationship between two variables for which the independent variable is time

trinomial: An algebraic expression containing three terms (e.g., $2x^2 - 6xy + 7$)

V

variable: A symbol used to represent an unspecified number. For example, x and y are variables in the expression $x + 2y$.

velocity: The rate of change of displacement or the rate of displacement. It includes an object's speed in a specified direction. $v = \dfrac{\Delta d}{\Delta t}$ where v is velocity, d is displacement, and t is time.

volume: The amount of space occupied by an object

W

whole numbers (W): The counting numbers that begin at 0 and continue forever: 0, 1, 2, 3, …

X

x-intercept: The value at which a graph meets the x-axis. The value of y is 0 for all x-intercepts.

Y

y-intercept: The value at which a graph meets the y-axis. The value of x is 0 for all y-intercepts.

Z

zero principle: Two opposite integers that, when added, give a sum of zero. For example, $(-1) + (+1) = 0$.

Answers

Chapter 1

Getting Started, page 4

1. **a)** iv)   **d)** vii)   **g)** viii)
   b) ix)   **e)** ii)   **h)** v)
   c) vi)   **f)** i)   **i)** iii)

2. **a)** $\frac{5}{6}$ **b)** $\frac{7}{8}$ **c)** $\frac{9}{10}$ **d)** $1\frac{1}{15}$

3. **a)** $\frac{1}{6}$ **b)** $\frac{5}{8}$ **c)** $\frac{3}{10}$ **d)** $\frac{5}{14}$

4. **a)** $\frac{1}{8}$ **b)** $\frac{1}{2}$ **c)** $\frac{3}{25}$ **d)** $\frac{2}{15}$

5. $5\frac{7}{4} = 6\frac{3}{4}$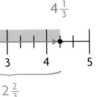

6. $\frac{8}{12} + \frac{9}{12} = \frac{17}{12} = 1\frac{5}{12}$

7. **a)**

$1\frac{2}{3}$ $4\frac{1}{3}$

$2\frac{2}{3}$

  b) $4\frac{1}{3} - 1\frac{2}{3} = 2\frac{2}{3}$

8. **a)** $\frac{9}{20}$ **b)** $\frac{5}{6}$

9. **a)** 4   **b)** -7 **c)** 15   **d)** 5

10. 7 shots

11. **a)** -24 **b)** 15   **c)** -20 **d)** 2

12. **a)** 4.22   **b)** 11.49   **c)** 0.66   **d)** 20

13. **a)** $8 \times 8 = 64$ **b)** $5.2 \times 5.2 \times 5.2 = 140.608$

14. **a)** -1 **b)** 65

15. Answers may vary, e.g.,

Definition	What do you know about them?
A number made up of a whole number and a fraction.	• the whole number cannot be zero • the fraction is a proper fraction • mixed numbers can be renamed as improper fractions and vice versa (e.g., $5\frac{1}{2} = \frac{11}{2}$) • mixed numbers can be renamed as decimals greater than 1 and vice versa (e.g., $5\frac{1}{2} = 5.5$)
Examples values such as: $2\frac{2}{3}$ $1\frac{5}{8}$ $10\frac{10}{19}$	**Non-examples** values such as: $\frac{3}{7}$ $\frac{15}{2}$ 4 $\frac{7}{8}$

(center: **Mixed Numbers**)

Lesson 1.1, page 16

1. **a)** 4   **b)** $4\frac{1}{3}$

2. **a)** First, I would model each of the mixed numbers using whole strips and the appropriate fraction strips. Since the $\frac{1}{6}$ strips are not the same length as the $\frac{1}{2}$ strip, I would replace the $\frac{1}{2}$ strip with 3 of the $\frac{1}{6}$ strips since $\frac{1}{2} = \frac{3}{6}$. Then, I would have 10 whole strips and $8\frac{1}{6}$ strips. Since 6 of the $\frac{1}{6}$ strips make a whole, I would replace them with 1 whole strip to make 11 whole strips and $2\frac{1}{6}$ strips. But $2\frac{1}{6}$ strips are the same length as $1\frac{1}{3}$ strip. The value of the expression is $11\frac{1}{3}$.

  b) First, I would model $9\frac{1}{8}$ using 9 whole strips and $1\frac{1}{8}$ strip. Since I have to subtract $6\frac{3}{4}$, I would remove 6 whole strips. Then, I would have $3\frac{1}{8}$ left, but I still need to subtract $\frac{3}{4}$. If I take $\frac{3}{4}$ away from one of the whole strips, then that strip would still have $\frac{1}{4}$ left and I would also have 2 whole strips and the $\frac{1}{8}$ strip. I could replace the $\frac{1}{4}$ strip with $2\frac{1}{8}$ strips so my fraction parts are all the same length. The value of the expression is $2\frac{3}{8}$.

3. **a)** $11\frac{1}{2}$

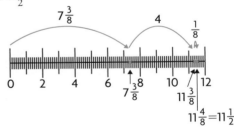

  b) $3\frac{1}{4}$

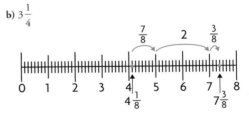

  c) $12\frac{1}{3}$

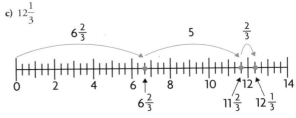

d) $1\frac{3}{5}$

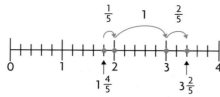

4. a) 12 and 13   **c)** 16 and 17   **e)** 51 and 52
   b) 9 and 10   **d)** 8 and 9   **f)** 53 and 54

5. a) $12\frac{2}{3}$ **c)** $16\frac{23}{24}$ **e)** $51\frac{9}{20}$
   b) $9\frac{19}{20}$ **d)** $8\frac{7}{15}$ **f)** $53\frac{1}{10}$

6. a) between 2 and 3   **d)** between 0 and 1
   b) between 1 and 2   **e)** between 6 and 7
   c) between 5 and 6   **f)** between 25 and 26

7. a) $2\frac{3}{10}$ **c)** $5\frac{3}{4}$ **e)** $6\frac{3}{16}$
   b) $1\frac{5}{12}$ **d)** $\frac{71}{72}$ **f)** $25\frac{5}{6}$

8. $6\frac{2}{15}$ h

9. a) $2\frac{3}{4}$ h   **b)** $1\frac{1}{4}$ h

10. $7\frac{11}{12}$ cups

11. a) Answers may vary, e.g., $2\frac{3}{10} + 1\frac{1}{2} = 3\frac{4}{5}$. I chose $1\frac{1}{2}$ because it had a different denominator than $3\frac{4}{5}$. Since addition and subtraction are inverse operations, I subtracted $1\frac{1}{2}$ from $3\frac{4}{5}$. Since $2\frac{3}{10}$ did not have 2 as a denominator, I knew I had a valid answer.

OR

Answers may vary, e.g., $1\frac{3}{5} + 2\frac{2}{10}$. I selected whole numbers that add to 3, then split the fraction into two fractions with a sum of $\frac{4}{5}$. I chose $\frac{3}{5}$ and $\frac{1}{5}$. But the denominators had to be different, so I changed $\frac{1}{5}$ to $\frac{2}{10}$.

b) Answers may vary, e.g., $5\frac{3}{10} - 1\frac{1}{2} = 3\frac{4}{5}$. Once again I chose $1\frac{1}{2}$ because it had a different denominator than $3\frac{4}{5}$. This time I added $1\frac{1}{2}$ to $3\frac{4}{5}$ to get a valid answer of $5\frac{3}{10}$.

OR

Answers may vary, e.g, $5\frac{1}{20} - 1\frac{1}{4}$. I decided to start with a different denominator than 5. I chose $5\frac{1}{20}$, then subtracted $3\frac{4}{5}$ from $5\frac{1}{20}$ to get $1\frac{1}{4}$.

12. a) Substitute $1\frac{2}{5} + 2$ for $3\frac{2}{5}$. Since $2 - 1\frac{4}{7} = \frac{3}{7}$, the question now becomes $1\frac{2}{5} + \frac{3}{7}$ or $\frac{3}{7} + 1\frac{2}{5}$.

b) Subtracting 2 is like subtracting $1\frac{5}{6}$ and then subtracting another $\frac{1}{6}$.
So, $3\frac{5}{6} - 2 = 3\frac{5}{6} - 1\frac{5}{6} - \frac{1}{6}$. By regrouping, the question is $3\frac{5}{6} - \frac{1}{6} - 1\frac{5}{6}$. This is equivalent to $3\frac{4}{6} - 1\frac{5}{6}$ or $3\frac{2}{3} - 1\frac{5}{6}$.

13. a) $13\frac{43}{60}$ laps   **c)** $10\frac{19}{30}$ laps
   b) $3\frac{1}{12}$ laps   **d)** 6720 m

14. 20' $5\frac{3}{8}$ "

15. a) Answers may vary, e.g., $63\frac{8}{13} + 27\frac{4}{7}$.

b) I think most people would calculate the answer to my question by creating equivalent fractions for the fraction parts. This method would be easier than renaming the mixed numbers as equivalent improper fractions because the numbers used in the calculation would be a lot smaller.

16. a) $1\frac{3}{4}$

b) i) 2;   **ii)** $\frac{1}{2} - \frac{1}{4} = \frac{2}{4} - \frac{1}{4} = \frac{1}{4}$;   **iii)** $2 - \frac{1}{4} = 1\frac{3}{4}$

c) $3\frac{7}{12}$; **i)** 4;   **ii)** $\frac{3}{4} - \frac{1}{3} = \frac{9}{12} - \frac{4}{12} = \frac{5}{12}$;   **iii)** $4 - \frac{5}{12} = 3\frac{7}{12}$

d) $1\frac{11}{15}$; **i)** 2;   **ii)** $\frac{2}{3} - \frac{2}{5} = \frac{10}{15} - \frac{6}{15} = \frac{4}{15}$;   **iii)** $2 - \frac{4}{15} = 1\frac{11}{15}$

e) The whole part for the second mixed number was always less than the whole part for the first mixed number. So, the difference can be found between the whole parts to see how many whole parts remain. The second mixed number's fraction part was always greater than the first mixed number's fraction part. So, you would have to subtract the fraction part in the first mixed number and then take a little more away. Finding the difference in part ii) meant finding how much greater the second fraction part was. This is what would still have to be taken away. Since there weren't enough fraction parts to take it away from, the remaining fraction is taken away from the whole parts. Looking at the process algebraically:

$$3\frac{1}{4} - 1\frac{1}{2} = 3 + \frac{1}{4} - \left(1 + \frac{1}{2}\right)$$
$$= 3 + \frac{1}{4} - 1 - \frac{1}{2}$$
$$= 3 - 1 - \frac{1}{2} + \frac{1}{4}$$
$$= 3 - 1 - \left(\frac{1}{2} - \frac{1}{4}\right)$$
$$= 2 - \frac{1}{4}$$
$$= 1\frac{3}{4}.$$

17. The smaller number is $1\frac{1}{4}$ and the larger number can be any mixed number.

Lesson 1.2, page 28

1. a) $6\frac{3}{4} \times 4\frac{2}{3}$ b) $31\frac{1}{2}$

2. $\frac{15}{2} \times \frac{12}{5} = 18$

3. $4\frac{1}{2} \div 1\frac{1}{4} = 3\frac{3}{5}$

4. $\frac{22}{15} \times \frac{25}{36} = 1\frac{1}{54}$

5. a) i) $3\frac{2}{5} \times 1\frac{1}{3}$ ii) $5\frac{1}{2} \times 2\frac{3}{4}$

   b) i) $5\frac{2}{3}$ ii) $15\frac{1}{8}$

6. a) about 6   c) about $5\frac{1}{2}$

   b) about 42   d) about 6

7. a) $10\frac{1}{9}$ c) $5\frac{3}{16}$ e) 22

   b) $4\frac{2}{3}$ d) $19\frac{1}{6}$ f) $6\frac{4}{7}$

8. a) 7   b) 4   c) 19

9. a) $\frac{27}{64}$ b) $\frac{125}{8}$ c) $\frac{4096}{125}$

10. a) 3   c) $3\frac{5}{8}$ e) $\frac{52}{63}$

   b) $\frac{25}{76}$ d) $\frac{3}{4}$ f) $1\frac{67}{108}$

11. a) i) $\frac{2}{3}$ ii) $2\frac{1}{3}$ iii) $1\frac{3}{4}$

   b) $\frac{2}{3} = \frac{2 \times 4}{3 \times 4} = \frac{8}{12}$

   $\frac{2}{3} \div \frac{1}{4} = \frac{8}{12} \div \frac{1}{4} = \frac{8 \div 1}{12 \div 4} = \frac{8}{3} = 2\frac{2}{3}$

12. a) $\frac{57}{2} = 28\frac{1}{2}$ b) $\frac{2}{7}$

13. a) 26 m   b) $42\frac{1}{4}$ m^2

14. a) 9 feet   b) 78 blocks

15. $5\frac{1}{2} = \frac{11}{2}$ and its reciprocal is $\frac{2}{11}$. Dividing by $\frac{11}{2}$ is the same as multiplying by its reciprocal, $\frac{2}{11}$.

16. Any whole number 8 or greater.

17. a) i) $19\frac{5}{6}$; $3\frac{1}{2}$ ii) $4\frac{1}{14}$; $4\frac{3}{4}$ iii) $15\frac{3}{10}$; $6\frac{4}{5}$

   b) The triangles' values equal the first values in the first statements. The second statements deal with the inverse operation of the first statements. Multiplication and division are inverse operations.

   c) Answers may vary, e.g., $2\frac{2}{5} \div 3\frac{1}{8} = 7\frac{1}{2}$; $7\frac{1}{2} \div 3\frac{1}{8} = 2\frac{2}{5}$.

18. 6 large bottles

19. $14.82

20. $5 \div 10 = \frac{1}{2}$, so a value *less than* 5 divided by 10 is less than $\frac{1}{2}$.

21. The first step is an extra step. This adds another chance of making a mistake. With this method, most of the numbers will get a lot bigger, making the multiplication step more difficult. It is easier to multiply smaller numbers than to multiply large numbers.

22. Answers may vary, e.g., $30\frac{1}{4}$, $35\frac{3}{4}$.

23. $\frac{3}{4}$ units by $\frac{3}{4}$ units

Lesson 1.3, page 35

1. a) negative   c) positive   e) negative
   b) negative   d) negative   f) positive

2. a) -8 c) 8   e) -16
   b) -8 d) -16 f) 16

3. a) $-49 - 2(-27) = -49 - (-54) = -49 + 54 = 5$
   b) $-16 - (16) - 16 = -32 - 16 = -48$

4. a) 6   b) -2 c) -10

5. a) 3   c) 5   e) 2
   b) 3   d) 3   f) (-2) or -2

6. a) -125 c) -64 e) -81
   b) 36   d) -64 f) 27

7. 8, (-8)

8. a) -40 c) 64   e) 2
   b) 47   d) -23 f) -8

9. a) error in second line; in the square brackets, must multiply before subtract

   $-4[5 - 2(-3)]$
   $= -4[5 - (-6)]$
   $= -4(5 + 6)$
   $= -4(11)$
   $= -44$

   b) error in second line; evaluate the power before multiply
   $-2(3)^2$
   $= -2(9)$
   $= -18$

10. Robin reasoned that 5 groups of -2 tiles subtract 3 groups of -2 tiles makes 2 groups of -2 tiles, which is -4.

11. a) 3   c) -27 e) -2
   b) 80   d) -8 f) -1

12. 23

13. a) Negative. If n is odd, then both $-b^n$ and $(-b)^n$ would have negative values. When you add two negative values, the answer would be negative.

   b) Zero. If n is even, then $-b^n$ would be negative and $(-b)^n$ would be positive. The magnitudes of the numbers would be equal, so the values would be opposites. The sum of two opposite numbers is zero.

14. a) i) -128 ii) 256   iii) 64
   b) i) $(-2)^7$ ii) $(-2)^8$ iii) $(-2)^6$
   c) Keep the common base -2 and add the exponents.

15. a) i) 9   ii) 81   iii) 81
   b) i) $(-3)^2$ ii) $(-3)^4$ iii) $(-3)^4$
   c) Keep the common base -3 and subtract the exponents.

16. a) When the same value of n is substituted into both expressions, the expressions will always give the same answer.
   b) $3(2^n) - 2^n$ is the same as $(3 - 1)(2^n) = 2(2^n)$. This is 2^{n+1}.

Mid-Chapter Review, page 40

1. a) $9\frac{5}{6}$ b) $6\frac{3}{20}$ c) $\frac{1}{12}$ d) $4\frac{12}{35}$

2. a) Answers may vary, e.g., whole numbers add to 9 and the sum of the fraction parts are a little less than one whole. The answer is between 9 and 10, but closer to 10.

b) Answers may vary, e.g., $\frac{2}{5}$ is $\frac{1}{4}$ + a bit. So, the fraction parts add to 1 + a bit. The whole numbers add to 5. The answer is a bit more than 6.

c) Answers may vary, e.g., whole numbers subtract to zero. $\frac{3}{4} - \frac{2}{4} = \frac{1}{4}$. Since $\frac{2}{3}$ is larger than $\frac{2}{4}$, $\frac{3}{4} - \frac{2}{3}$ would be less than $\frac{1}{4}$. The answer is between 0 and $\frac{1}{4}$.

d) Answers may vary, e.g., $9 - 4 = 5$. Since $\frac{4}{5}$ is larger than $\frac{1}{7}$, the answer would have to be less than 5. The answer is between 4 and 5.

3. $9\frac{3}{4}$ h

4. $3\frac{1}{5} = 3 + \frac{1}{5}$. Now subtract $2\frac{1}{4}$ from 3. 3 is $2 + \frac{4}{4} - 2\frac{1}{4} = \frac{3}{4}$. Now you have $\frac{3}{4} + \frac{1}{5}$.

5. **a)** $\frac{21}{22}$ **b)** $2\frac{2}{35}$ **c)** $8\frac{2}{3}$ **d)** $34\frac{4}{5}$

6. **a)** $11\frac{1}{2}$ **b)** $\frac{2}{23}$ **c)** $3\frac{1}{13}$ **d)** $1\frac{127}{128}$

7. **a)** $2\frac{5}{6}$ **b)** $\frac{1}{2}$ **c)** $24\frac{8}{9}$ **d)** $1\frac{1}{2}$

8. $9\frac{5}{12}$"

9. $1\frac{3}{8} \div \frac{11}{64} = 8$ rows and $2 \div \frac{1}{8} = 16$ characters per row. $8 \times 16 = 128$ characters.

10. **a)** 121   **b)** -64 **c)** -49 **d)** -216

11. Answers may vary, e.g., $(-8)^2$, 2^6, $(-2)^6$, 4^3.

12. 253

13. **a)** 14   **b)** -28 **c)** 5   **d)** 1

Lesson 1.4, page 45

1. **a)** $\frac{-9}{4}$ **b)** $\frac{-41}{7}$

2. **a)** 0.2   **b)** $-0.\overline{571428}$ **c)** -0.75 **d)** $-7.8\overline{3}$

3. **a)** $-\frac{7}{20}$ **b)** $\frac{37}{8}$ **c)** $-\frac{573}{50}$

4. **a)** -2.25 **c)** -0.75 **e)** 1.75
   b) -1.5 **d)** 0.5

5. **a)** $-\frac{11}{3}$ **c)** $-\frac{2}{3}$ **e)** $\frac{8}{3}$
   b) $\frac{7}{3}$ **d)** $\frac{4}{3}$

6. Tammy is correct. Jasmine's error is when she added in this step: $\frac{(-2 \times 2 + 1)}{2}$. She should subtract $\frac{(-2 \times 2 - 1)}{2}$.

7. **a)** $>$; zero is greater than every negative value.
b) $<$; -4.3 is to the left of -3.4.
c) $<$; all negative values are less than positive values.
d) $=$; decimal values are equal.
e) $=$; decimal values are equal.
f) $>$; $-2\frac{3}{10}$ is further to the right on the number line.

8. $-3\frac{1}{4} = -1 \times 3\frac{1}{4} = -\left(3 + \frac{1}{4}\right) = -3 - \frac{1}{4}$, whereas $-3 + \frac{1}{4} = -2\frac{3}{4}$.

9. **a)** Answers may vary, e.g., $\frac{5}{16}$, $\frac{7}{24}$, $\frac{8}{24}$ or $\frac{1}{3}$.
b) Use the opposites, e.g., $-\frac{5}{16}$, $-\frac{7}{24}$, $-\frac{1}{3}$.
c) Yes, since they are fractions. Any number that can be expressed as a fraction, without a denominator of zero, is a rational number.

10. **a)** True. Write the whole number followed by the decimal part, which is the numerator of the fraction part divided by the denominator. Put a bar over the digits that repeat.
b) False. Zero is an integer but cannot be a denominator.
c) False. They must also be the same distance from zero.
d) True. Any positive number is greater than any negative number.

11. **a)** $\frac{13}{30}$ **b)** $\frac{1}{6}$ **c)** $\frac{19}{75}$

12.

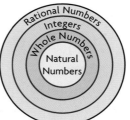

13. $-a > -b$; Suggestion: plot a, b, and their opposites on a number line to help explain.

Lesson 1.5, page 53

1. **a)** -5.0 **b)** -19.0 **c)** -7.0 **d)** -16.0

2. **a)** -1 **b)** $-\frac{1}{2}$ **c)** $\frac{24}{35}$ **d)** $-\frac{16}{25}$

3. all

4. **a)** 76 and 77   **c)** -16 and -15
   b) 65 and 66   **d)** -1 and 0

5. **a)** 76.54   **c)** -15.3
   b) 65.65   **d)** -0.3046

6. **a)** $\$53.87$ **b)** $-\$0.87$

7. $-18.9\overline{6}$ °C

8. **a)** $1\frac{3}{8}$ **c)** $-15\frac{17}{20}$ **e)** $-9\frac{2}{15}$
   b) $-2\frac{5}{6}$ **d)** $-\frac{3}{10}$ **f)** $1\frac{1}{4}$

9. **a)** $\frac{2}{9}$ **c)** $-32\frac{1}{7}$ **e)** -8
   b) 4   **d)** $-\frac{9}{10}$ **f)** $2\frac{8}{13}$

10. $\frac{7}{12}$ h, or 35 min

11. **a)** $2\frac{3}{4}$ **c)** $-\frac{4}{7}$
   b) $-2\frac{3}{4}$ **d)** $-1\frac{3}{4}$

12. **a) i)** $2\frac{1}{6}$; $-3\frac{1}{2}$ **ii)** $15\frac{3}{10}$; $-6\frac{4}{5}$

b) The triangles' values are the same as the first values in the first statements. The second statements deal with the inverse operation of the first statements.

c) Answers may vary, e.g., $4\frac{2}{7} \div -1\frac{7}{8} = -2\frac{2}{7}$; $-2\frac{2}{7} \times -1\frac{7}{8} = 4\frac{2}{7}$.

13. a) $+; 18.56$ **c)** $-; -44.05$ **e)** $-; -1.91\overline{6}$
b) $-; -70.3$ **d)** $-; -123.008$ **f)** $-; -4.5$

14. a) $-3\frac{49}{60}$ **b)** $1\frac{4}{5}$ **c)** $-\frac{23}{24}$ **d)** $8\frac{7}{16}$

15. a) $36\frac{2}{3}\,°C$ **b)** $-38\frac{8}{9}\,°C$ **c)** $32\,°F$

16. a) $212\,°F$ **b)** $98.6\,°F$

17. a) -16.18 **c)** $-3\frac{1}{8}$
b) -54.59 **d)** $-2\frac{1}{6}$

18. a) $2\frac{9}{10}$ or -2.9 **b)** $16.781\,25$ or $16\frac{25}{32}$

19. $1{:}31{:}57.7$ h; almost 1 h 32 min longer

20. a) $-1\frac{7}{20}$
b) $-1\frac{17}{42}$
c) $-1.35; -1.\overline{4047619}$
d) Answers may vary, e.g., for part a), I would prefer decimal form because the values were not so large to calculate and each was a terminating decimal. For part b), I would prefer fraction form because the fractions were easier to calculate than the repeating decimals.

21. a) -1.6875 or $-1\frac{11}{16}$ **b)** $-5\frac{7}{27}$ or $-5.\overline{259}$

22. a) $1 + \cfrac{1}{1 + \cfrac{1}{\left(\frac{3}{2}\right)}} = 1 + \cfrac{1}{\left(1 + \frac{2}{3}\right)} = 1 + \left(\cfrac{1}{\frac{5}{3}}\right)$
$= 1 + \frac{3}{5} = \frac{8}{5}$
b) $1\frac{4}{5} = 1 + \frac{4}{5} = 1 + \left(\cfrac{1}{\frac{5}{4}}\right) = 1 + \cfrac{1}{1 + \frac{1}{4}}$

23. length $\times$ width: $21\frac{1}{3}$ m $\times$ $5\frac{1}{3}$ m

Lesson 1.6, page 62

1. a) 20.25 **c)** -91.125
b) -20.25 **d)** -91.125
2. a) positive **c)** negative **e)** negative
b) negative **d)** positive **f)** positive
3. a) $\frac{4}{9}$ **c)** $-\frac{4}{9}$ **e)** $-\frac{8}{27}$
b) $-\frac{4}{9}$ **d)** $\frac{8}{27}$ **f)** $\frac{32}{243}$
4. a) subtract in the brackets, square the answer, multiply answer by 2, add result to -4.5
b) 85.28
5. a) -1.34 **c)** 0 **e)** 19.567
b) 59.582 **d)** 3.96 **f)** $-0.751\overline{8}$

6. a) $\frac{2}{9}$ **c)** $\frac{369}{400}$ **e)** $\frac{13}{56}$
b) $-2\frac{1}{27}$ **d)** $689\frac{1}{16}$ **f)** $\frac{625}{16}$ or $39\frac{1}{16}$
7. a) 2; answers may vary, e.g., I multiplied 2.4 by itself until the answer was 5.76.
b) 2; answers may vary, e.g., I used the result from part a) to get the answer.
c) 3; answers may vary, e.g., I multiplied 3.5 by itself until the answer was 42.875.
d) -3.5; answers may vary, e.g., looking at part c), I knew the base would have to be the same but negative.
8. a) Rob earned more interest because the money he invested had more time to earn interest.
b) Rob: $162.89; Sharon: $161.05
9. a) Diego's investment earns interest twice a year, every year for 5 years. So, interest would be earned 10 times at the end of 5 years.
b) $2687.83
10. a) Tanjay: $148.02; Eda: $148.59
b) Eda's investment earned interest more often.
11. a) 500 g; 250 g; $\frac{125}{128}$ g
b) 0; nothing of the sample remains after 1 year.
12. a) 19.25 **c)** -2.375
b) -12.75 **d)** -225.792
13. a) $-\frac{3}{16}$ **c)** $39\frac{4}{5}$
b) $\frac{17}{27}$ **d)** $19\frac{3}{4}$
14. Both sides of first equality yield $-\frac{27}{8}$ or $-3\frac{3}{8}$. The odd exponent keeps positive signs positive and negative signs negative. For $-\left(1\frac{1}{2}\right)^4$, the answer is negative but when the negative is in the brackets and raised to an even exponent, the answer is positive.
15. The sign of the numbers.
16. about $530.83
17. $x = 2$ or $x = -2$

Chapter Review, page 66

1. a) $11\frac{1}{6}$ **b)** $\frac{1}{2}$ **c)** $6\frac{5}{8}$ **d)** $2\frac{1}{12}$
2. $36\frac{9}{16}$ in.
3. $-2\frac{5}{8}$
4. a) $6\frac{1}{8}$ **b)** 39 **c)** $\frac{10}{29}$ **d)** $\frac{1}{2}$
5. $5\frac{19}{25}$
6. $5\frac{23}{64}$ m^3
7. a) $14\frac{5}{6}$ in. **b)** $12\frac{2}{3}$ in.^{2}
8. For -8^2: multiply 8 by itself to get 64; then multiply 64 by -1 to get -64.
For $(-8)^2$: multiply -8 by itself to get 64.
9. a) 9 **b)** -2 **c)** 19 **d)** 3
10. a) 21 **b)** 60 **c)** 2 **d)** -1

11. **a)** Since $-2.6 = -2 - 0.6$, the number would be 2 units to the left of zero and then another 0.6 further to the left.

b) Since $-\dfrac{24}{5} = -4\dfrac{4}{5} = -4 - \dfrac{4}{5}$, the number would be 4 units to the left of zero and then another $\dfrac{4}{5}$ further to the left.

12. **a)** $-\dfrac{29}{3} = -9\dfrac{2}{3}$, because $-\dfrac{31}{3}$ is greater than -10.

13. Callander. $-4\dfrac{5}{6} = -4.8\overline{3}$, which is further to the left of zero along a number line than -4.8. So, it is a lower (colder) value.

14. **a)** $-1\dfrac{1}{3}, \dfrac{-3}{5}, \dfrac{1}{-3}$ **c)** $-0.\overline{3}, -0.3, 0.7$

b) $-2\dfrac{1}{5}, -\dfrac{2}{5}, \dfrac{4}{5}$ **d)** $-2, -1.5, 0$

15. **a)** $>$; compare placement of decimal equivalents on number line
b) $>$; compare second decimal digits (hundredths)
c) $=$; compare decimal equivalents
d) $<$; all negative values are less than positive values

16. about $-\$2.26$

17. **a)** $-3\dfrac{1}{12}$ **c)** $-34\dfrac{1}{2}$

b) $-2\dfrac{13}{20}$ **d)** $-2\dfrac{103}{120}$

18. Answers may vary, e.g., $-3\dfrac{1}{3} - 6; -28\left(\dfrac{1}{3}\right)$.

19. **a)** 0.1 **c)** -1
b) -8.4 **d)** 1.184

20. **a)** $-1\dfrac{1}{3}$ or $-\dfrac{4}{3}$ **c)** $-\dfrac{1}{2}$

b) $-1\dfrac{1}{3}$ or $-\dfrac{4}{3}$ **d)** $-\dfrac{2}{5}$

21. **a)** -370.146232 **c)** $-2\dfrac{2997}{8000}$

b) 708.681 **d)** $7\dfrac{27}{40}$

22. about $\$136.86$
23. **a)** $<$; negative values are always less than positive values.
b) $>$; positive values are always greater than negative values.

c) $=$; each equals $\dfrac{1}{4}$.

d) $<$; compare decimal equivalents.

24. **a)** 84.9 cm² **c)** 248.7 m²

b) $21\dfrac{3}{5}$ in.² **d)** $68\dfrac{2}{5}$ in.²

25. **a)** $\dfrac{4}{9}$ **c)** $2\dfrac{1}{4}$

b) 1.44 **d)** -456.533

Chapter Self-Test, page 68

1. **D.** $\dfrac{4}{5}$

2. **C.** -10

3. **C.** $-2\dfrac{2}{5}, -\dfrac{11}{5}, \dfrac{-11}{-5}$

4. **a)** $9\dfrac{11}{14}$ **b)** $6\dfrac{1}{4}$

5. $19\dfrac{5}{12}$ in.

6. To calculate $(-2)^2$: multiply -2 by itself; answer $= 4$.
To calculate -2^4: multiply 2 by itself 4 times to get an answer of 16, and then multiply 16 by -1; answer $= -16$.

7. **a)** -56 **b)** -1.811

8. $-4\dfrac{1}{3} = -4.\overline{3}$ and its opposite, $4.\overline{3}$, would be farther to the right of zero along a number line than 4.3. Since $-4\dfrac{1}{3}$ is the same distance from zero as $4.\overline{3}$, $-4\dfrac{1}{3}$ is farther from zero than 4.3.

9. **a)** $1\dfrac{13}{14}$ **b)** $-3\dfrac{5}{9}$

10. $-3.58\,°C$

11. $-5\dfrac{31}{100}$

Chapter 2

Getting Started, page 72

1. **a)** i **c)** iii **e)** ii
b) v **d)** iv **f)** vi

2. **a)**

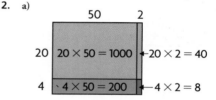

$24 \times 52 = (20 + 4) \times (50 + 2)$
$= 20 \times 50 + 20 \times 2 + 4 \times 50 + 4 \times 2$
$= 1000 + 40 + 200 + 8 = 1248$

b)

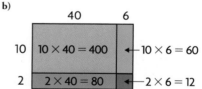

$12 \times 46 = (10 + 2) \times (40 + 6)$
$= 10 \times 40 + 10 \times 6 + 2 \times 40 + 2 \times 6$
$= 400 + 60 + 80 + 12 = 552$

c)

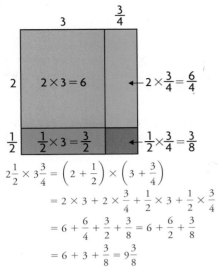

$$2\frac{1}{2} \times 3\frac{3}{4} = \left(2 + \frac{1}{2}\right) \times \left(3 + \frac{3}{4}\right)$$
$$= 2 \times 3 + 2 \times \frac{3}{4} + \frac{1}{2} \times 3 + \frac{1}{2} \times \frac{3}{4}$$
$$= 6 + \frac{6}{4} + \frac{3}{2} + \frac{3}{8} = 6 + \frac{6}{2} + \frac{3}{8}$$
$$= 6 + 3 + \frac{3}{8} = 9\frac{3}{8}$$

d)

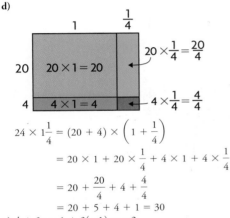

$$24 \times 1\frac{1}{4} = (20 + 4) \times \left(1 + \frac{1}{4}\right)$$
$$= 20 \times 1 + 20 \times \frac{1}{4} + 4 \times 1 + 4 \times \frac{1}{4}$$
$$= 20 + \frac{20}{4} + 4 + \frac{4}{4}$$
$$= 20 + 5 + 4 + 1 = 30$$

3. **a)** $b + 3c = 1 + 3(-1) = -2$
   b) $3b + 2c - d = 3(1) + 2(-1) - 2 = -1$
   c) $2a^2 + b - d = 2(0)^2 + 1 - 2 = -1$
   d) $3(2b - 3c) = 3[2(1) - 3(-1)] = 15$
   e) $-4(a + b + c) = -4(0 + 1 + -1) = 0$
   f) $(5c - 6b)^2 = [5(-1) - 6(1)]^2 = (-5 - 6)^2 = 121$

4. **a)** $P = 2(3 + 5) = 16$ cm
   b) $A = \dfrac{(5.5 \times 4)}{2} = 11$ m
   c) $V = 12^3 = 1728$ cm
   d) $c = \sqrt{a^2 + b^2} = \sqrt{5^2 + 12^2} = 13$ m

5. **a)** 13^4 **b)** $(-8)^6$ **c)** $7^2 \times 6^2$ or 42^2

6. **a)** $7 \times 7 \times 7 \times 7$ **b)** $(-7)(-7)(-7)(-7)$ **c)** $-7 \times 7 \times 7 \times 7$

7. 2×10^3 is 2×1000 or 2000.
   6×10^2 is 6×100 or 600.
   7×10^1 is 7×10 or 70.
   When I add $2000 + 600 + 70 + 3$, I get 2673.

8. $1 \times 10^3 + 2 \times 10^2 + 5 \times 10^1 + 4$

9. 16, 100, 25, 1; because 16 can be thought of as 4×4, 100 as 10×10, 25 as 5×5, and 1 as 1×1.

10. $T = 5A + 2.50C$, where T is the total cost.

11. $A = 4s^2 + 2\left(\dfrac{1}{2}\right)bh$ or $4s^2 + bh$, where A is the total area.

12. Answers may vary, e.g.,

Math term	Drawing or description
base of a power	4^3, x^2
My definition	**Reminds me of this**
A base of a power is the number that you multiply together, and the exponent tells you how many times to multiply it. For example, in the power x^2, x is the base.	This also reminds me of the numbers in scientific notation that we sometimes see in science class. In 2.1×10^{23}, for example, the number 10 is the base of the power 10^{23}.

Math term	Drawing or description
algebraic expression	$4x + 3y$
My definition	**Reminds me of this**
An algebraic expression has letters and numbers. Sometimes these are combined using addition, subtraction, multiplication and division, and exponents.	The formula for the perimeter of a rectangle $P = 2l + 2w$.

Math term	Drawing or description
variable	This square has side length s and area s^2.
My definition	**Reminds me of this**
A variable is a value that can change. I use a letter like x to represent an amount if I don't have a number value for it.	x and y labels on the axes when I draw a graph.

Lesson 2.1, page 80

1. **a)** c^3 **b)** c **c)** d^2 **d)** d^3
2. **a)** $\sqrt{49} = 7$; 7 cm
   b) 10 and 11, because $10 \times 10 = 100$ and $11 \times 11 = 121$

3. a)

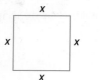

c) _____ y _____

b)

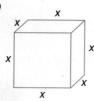

d)

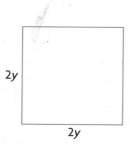

$2y$

$2y$

4. a) 12 km; 12 km $\times$ 12 km = 144 km^2
   b) Estimate 8.7 cm; 8.7 cm $\times$ 8.7 cm = 75.7 cm^2
   c) 0.1 m^2; (0.1 m)(0.1 m) = 0.01 m^2
5. a) $(3y)^3$ **c)** $\sqrt{(2x^2)}$
   b) $2x$ **d)** $(3y)^2$
6. The better estimate is 7.2 m, since 7 squared is 49 and 8 squared is
   64. Since 50 is closer to 49 than to 64, the better estimate is closer to
   7 than to 8. We need an area of 50 m^2, and 7.2 m gives an area closer
   to what is needed.
7. The area is 1000 cm^2. I can check by multiplying $\sqrt{1000}$ cm, which
   is about 31.62 cm, by itself to get the area. The result is 999.82 cm^2
   so my answer is correct.

8. a)

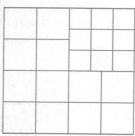

   b) and **c)** The side length is 12 cm because the tiles must be arranged
   either 2 + 2 + 2 + 3 + 3 or 3 + 3 + 3 + 3 on a side in order
   to make a square.
9. The term 4^2 can represent the area of a square with side lengths
   of 4, and the term 4^3 can represent the volume of a cube with side
   lengths of 4.

10. Answers may vary, e.g., the rectangle has area ab. The square has area
   a^2. They're the same because they're both models of two-dimensional
   area. They're different because the square has all sides the same length,
   and the rectangle has sides of different lengths. I can see the difference
   between them by looking at their shapes and the algebraic expressions
   for their areas.

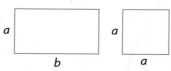

11. Both are models of the volume of rectangular prisms, but the one at
   left has 3 different dimensions and its volume is abc. The one at right
   has 2 dimensions the same, and its volume is ab^2.

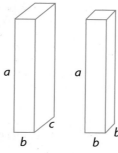

12. Answers may vary, e.g., the length of the side of a cube can be thought
   of as the cube root of its volume. If the volume of a cube is 64, the
   side of the cube is 4, and this is the cube root of 64. I can check by
   seeing if $4 \times 4 \times 4$ is 64. It is.

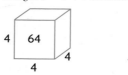

Lesson 2.2, page 89

1. a) 2^5 **b)** x^7
2. a) 2^3 **b)** y^3
3. a) $2^2 = 4$ **b)** $(5)(3^2) = 45$
4. a) $\dfrac{x^7}{x^6} = x = 2$ **b)** $y^3(x) = 250$
5. a) (5^{10}) **b)** (m^6) **c)** $(7^4)(x^6)$ **d)** $\left(\dfrac{2}{5}\right)^9$
6. a) $(n^8)(w^{13})$ **c)** $2^7(p^{13})$ **e)** $(x^9)(-2)^4$
   b) $(m^9)(r^{10})$ **d)** $3^6(b^{15})$ **f)** 3^3a^{10}
7. The bases in each problem are the same, and in each expression the
   exponents add to 11, so the results are all the same.
8. a) 5^5 **b)** m^2 **c)** $2x$ **d)** $(-5)^2y$
9. a) 7^5a^2 **b)** $10^2x^3y^4$ or $100x^3y^4$ **c)** xy^2 **d)** $\dfrac{y^3}{x}$
10. Answers may vary, e.g.,
   $(7^2)(7^2)(7^2)(7^2) = 7^8$
   $(7^3)(7)(7^4) = 7^8$
   $\dfrac{7^{12}}{7^4} = 7^8$
   $\dfrac{7^2 7^{12}}{7^6} = 7^8$

11. **a)** $2^3 = 8$ **c)** $(3^3)(7^2) = 1323$ **e)** $\left(\dfrac{2}{7}\right)^2 = \dfrac{4}{49}$

b) $4^4 = 256$ **d)** 4.2 **f)** $\left(\dfrac{4}{5}\right)^3 = \dfrac{64}{125}$

12. **a)** $x = 2$ **c)** $(x)(y^3) = 250$ **e)** $2(x)(y^3) = 500$

b) $y = 5$ **d)** $2y^3 = 250$ **f)** $\left(\dfrac{3}{4}\right)x^2y = 15$

13. Because the two numbers have the same base, I know that I add the powers to get 10. I also know that I subtract one power from the other to get 2. The powers could be 6 and 4. I can check by seeing that $7^6 \times 7^4 = 7^{10}$ and $\dfrac{7^6}{7^4} = 7^2$.

14. $(50 \times 10^{12})(6 \times 10^9) = 300 \times 10^{21}$ or 3×10^{23}

15. Answers may vary, e.g., exponents say how many times a base is to be multiplied by itself. If the bases are different, their exponents will say how many times to multiply different numbers. So, I won't be able to add or subtract these exponents and get correct results. For instance, when I work out $4^3 3^2$ I get $4 \times 4 \times 4 \times 3 \times 3 = 576$. However, if I add the exponents I get 4^5, 3^5, or 12^5. These are not the same and do not work out to 576. So to use the exponent principles the bases have to be the same.

16. **a)**

	Millimetres	Centimetres	Metres	Kilometres
Millimetres		10^{-1}	10^{-3}	10^{-6}
Centimetres	10^1		10^{-2}	10^{-5}
Metres	10^3	10^2		10^{-3}
Kilometres	10^6	10^5	10^3	

b) 500 000 cm **c)** 4000 mm

17. $40\,000 \text{ cm}^3 = 4 \times 10^4 = 4 \times 10\,000 = 40\,000 \text{ cm}^3$

18. 1.5×10^3 kg

19. **a)** $\dfrac{3^5}{3^5} = \dfrac{243}{243} = 1$

b) $\dfrac{3^5}{3^5} = 3^{5-5} = 3^0$

c) $\dfrac{3^5}{3^5} = \dfrac{3 \times 3 \times 3 \times 3 \times 3}{3 \times 3 \times 3 \times 3 \times 3}$ All of the 3's divide out to leave $\dfrac{1}{1}$, which is 1.

d) Answers may vary, e.g., based on my answers to a) and c), 3^0 must equal 1.

e) Answers may vary, e.g., the power a^0 should have a similar meaning for most values of a. As with a base of 3 above, the exponent 0 will make the expression equal to 1. The only exception would be if $a = 0$. In that case 0^0 is not 1. 0^0 is undefined.

Lesson 2.3, page 96

1. **a)** 7^{15} **b)** x^{24} **c)** c^6

2. **a)** 2^4 or 4^2 **b)** 2^6, 4^3, or 8^2 **c)** 3^8 or 81^2

3. **a)** 3^8 **c)** 2^{15} **e)** x^6

b) 9^{12} **d)** 10^{36} **f)** 5^8

4. **a)** 4^4 **b)** 2^8 **c)** 5^6 **d)** 3^9

5. Answers may vary, e.g.,

a) This principle shows that, to simplify a power of a power, you multiply the exponents. For example, $(2^3)^4 = 2^{12}$.

b) This principle shows that when a power applies to more than one factor, you multiply the exponent of each factor by the exponent outside the brackets. For example, $(2^3 3^4)^2 = (2^3)^2 (3^4)^2 = 2^6 3^8$.

c) This principle shows that when you have the power of a quotient, the outer exponent refers to each term inside the brackets. For example, $\left(\dfrac{5^2}{4^3}\right)^2 = \left(\dfrac{5^4}{4^6}\right) = \dfrac{625}{4096}$.

6. **a)** 3^{13} **c)** 2^5 or 32 **e)** 5^4 or 625

b) 5^{24} **d)** 10^2 or 100 **f)** 3^4 or 81

7. **a)** y^{12} **b)** m^6 **c)** c^9 **d)** n^{12}

8. **a)** v^5 **c)** k^{13} **e)** x^2

b) n^{18} **d)** j^6 **f)** y^6

9. **a)** $27a^6$ **c)** $16m^8$ **e)** $100a^4b^6$

b) $25x^{10}$ **d)** $4096p^8$ **f)** $27x^{12}y^6$

10. **a)** $4^{21}3^{10}$ **c)** $2^2 5^2$ or 100

b) $2^9 x^{22}$ **d)** $5^3 \dfrac{a^5}{b^4}$ or $125\dfrac{a^5}{b^4}$

11. **a)** $16y^{12}$ **c)** $6561a^{16}b^4$ or $3^8 a^{16}b^4$

b) $9x^{10}$ **d)** $5^7 a^{14}$

12. Answers may vary, e.g.,

a) The exponents 2×6 and 3×4 both equal 12, and $3^{12} - 3^{12}$ is zero.

b) The exponents 2×8 and 4×4 both equal 16, and $10^{16} - 10^{16}$ is zero.

c) The exponents are 2×3 and 3×2, which are equal. The numbers are equal. The first term has an even exponent, so it is positive. The second term has an odd exponent, so it is negative. Sum is 0.

13. $SA = 6(3^5)^2 = 6(3^{10})$; $V = (3^5)^3 = 3^{15}$

14. $25x^2$

15. **a)** 4 **c)** 12 **e)** $\dfrac{1}{25}$

b) 125 **d)** 35 **f)** 2^{12} or 4096

16. **a)** $a^3 = 8$ **b)** $b^6 = 1$ **c)** $c = 4$ **d)** $a^2b^2 = 4$

17. $3^{10} = 3^{2 \times 5} = (3^2)^5 = 9^5$

18. **a)** $x^7 = 128$

b) $m + n = 7$

c) Answers may vary, e.g., by using exponent principles, I simplified the expressions a lot. The numbers left were much smaller, and I could work out the answers quickly in my head.

19. **a)** 6 **b)** 3 **c)** 4 **d)** 12

20. **a)** 2^{10} **b)** 3^{12} **c)** 3^{12} **d)** $(-5)^{21}$

21. Answers may vary, e.g., I can write 2^{30} as $(2^3)^{10}$, and 3^{20} as $(3^2)^{10}$. Since 2^3 is less than 3^2, I know that $(2^3)^{10}$ must be less than $(3^2)^{10}$.

22. Answers may vary, e.g., the principle for multiplying powers having the same base is to add their exponents. The principle for dividing powers having the same base is to subtract the exponent of the denominator (divisor) from the exponent of the numerator (dividend). The power of a power principle says that any factors inside brackets are multiplied by the exponents outside the brackets. For example, $(2^4)^3 = 2^{12}$ because $(2^4)^3$ is the same as $(2^4)(2^4)(2^4)$. When I expand the expression like this I can check by adding the exponents: $4 + 4 + 4 = 12$.

23. **a)** She can input 25^4 as $(5^2)^4$ or 5^8.

b) She can input (16^2) as 4^4 or 2^8.

24. Answers may vary, e.g., you need an even number of 2's to group into pairs to get a new base of 4. You can not do this for 2^7 and have an integer as an exponent because you would have an extra 2 left over.

Mid-Chapter Review, page 101

1. Answers may vary, e.g., these are the models I created.

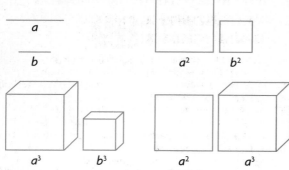

a) Models a and b are alike because they both have exponents of 1. This is why they are shown as lines. They are different because line a is twice as long as line b.

b) Models a^2 and b^2 are alike because they both have exponents of 2. This is why they are shown as squares. They are different because a^2 has twice the side length and four times the area of b^2.

c) Models a^3 and b^3 are alike because they both have exponents of 3. This is why they are shown as cubes. They are different because a^3 has twice the side length and eight times the volume of b^3.

d) These models are alike because their side lengths are the same. They are different because they have different dimensions, as a^2 is a square and a^3 is a cube.

2. a) ![3y square] b) ____ $3y$ c) cube y, y, y

3. **a)** $8 \times 8 = 64$ and $9 \times 9 = 81$, so the length of x is about half-way between these two numbers. My estimate is 8.5.

b) $\sqrt{72}$

c) 8.49

4. **a)** 5^9 **c)** 5^4 **e)** $(7^5)(2^{11})$

b) $(2)^{10}$ **d)** 7^8 **f)** 7×2 or 14

5. **a)** $\left(\dfrac{5}{7}\right)^9$ **b)** $\left(\dfrac{-2}{5}\right)^6$ **c)** $(3.1)^{10}$ **d)** $(0.012)^2$

6. **a)** x^8 **c)** m **e)** $a^4 b^{11}$

b) y^9 **d)** n^4 **f)** $x^2 y^5$

7. **a)** $2^5 x^7$ or $32x^7$ **c)** $64m^5$

b) $5^6 y^9$ **d)** $36q^3$

8. If the bases are different, their exponents will say how many times to multiply different numbers. For instance, $5^2 2^4$ is $5 \times 5 \times 2 \times 2 \times 2 \times 2 = 400$. If I add the exponents I get 6, but I'm not multiplying 6 of the same thing, so I can't write 5^6 or 2^6. To use the exponent principle when multiplying powers, the bases have to be the same.

9. about 108 Earths

10. **a)** 5^{15} **c)** $2^7 x^{21}$ or $128x^{21}$

b) x^{12} **d)** $\left(\dfrac{8}{5}\right)^{12}$ or $\dfrac{8^{12}}{5^{12}}$

11. **a)** 2^{15} **b)** 9^4 **c)** 3^8 **d)** 10^{30}

12. **a)** 5^{31} **c)** $2^7 m^{24} x^{42}$ or $128m^{24} x^{42}$

b) x^{32} **d)** $2^2 m^3 x^8$ or $4m^3 x^8$

13. In each case the base is the same and the exponents multiply to 36.

14. $SA = 6(2^5)^2 = 6(2^{10})$ cm; $V = (2^5)^3 = 2^{15}$ cm^3

Lesson 2.4, page 109

1. **a)** 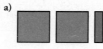   **c)**

b)

2. **a)** ③x and ⊖$2x$

b) ⑥m and ⊖$15m$

3. **a)** $3x^2 - 2x$ **b)** $-3y^2 + 2x + 4$

4. $5x^2 + 6x + 5$

5. **a)** $5x$ **c)** $7x - 2y$ **e)** $x + 1$

b) $5y^2$ **d)** $7x - 1$ **f)** $-2x$

6. **a)**

b)

c)

d)

7. **a)** ⊖$2g$ and ⊖$5g$ **c)** ⊖$21g^3$ and ⊖$0.8g^3$

b) ⊖$\dfrac{1}{2}y$ and ②$\dfrac{1}{2}y$ **d)** ⊖$3.75rs$ and ④$25rs$

8. **a)** $2x^2 + 3x$ **c)** $-2xy + 2x$ **e)** $2x^2 - 2x + 1$

b) $3x^2 - 2y^2$ **d)** $2x^2 + x - 3$

9. **a)** $5h + 6$ **b)** $3x^2 + 4y$ **c)** $-w^2$ **d)** $\dfrac{1}{2}a + \dfrac{1}{5}b$

10. **a)** $5x - 2y$ **b)** $-3y^2 + 2y + 1$ **c)** $9x^2 - 12xy + 3y^2$

11. **a)** $2x - 6y$ **b)** $8y^2 - 4y + 4$ **c)** $-3x^2 + 4xy + 9y^2$

12. **a)** $-y + 2x^2$

 is

b) $-2y^2 - 1$

Check by adding: Does $-2y^2 - 1 + (3y^2 - 2y + 3)$
$= y^2 - 2y + 2$? Yes, it does.

13.

	Initial Polynomial	Polynomial to Be Added	Final Polynomial
a)	$x^2 + 3x$	$-2x^2 + 2x$	$-x^2 + 5x$
b)	$2x^2y^2 - 4y^2$	$3x^2y^2 + y^2$	$5x^2y^2 - 3y^2$
c)	$-7xy + 4x$	$-x - 2$	$-7xy + 3x - 2$
d)	$2x^2 - 3x - 4$		$-2x^2 + 3x - 6$

14. The cost is $28(2x^2) + 2.25(6x)$ or $56x^2 + 13.5x$, where x is the width of the table in metres. When $x = 1.5$ m, the cost is \$146.25.

15. **a)** $43.5x + 35$ **b)** $38.75x + 41$ **c)** $82.25x + 76$ **d)** \$734.00

16. **a)** $220t - 160$ **c)** $380t - 285$
b) $160t - 125$ **d)** \$1615.00
e) Answers may vary, e.g., no, because t is the number of tables they each work, the polynomial in c) is valid only if they work the same number of tables.

17. **a)** $1000 + 125c - 250w$ **b)** \$3875

18. Answers may vary, e.g.,
a) $a + b + 1$ and $c + d + 1$ add to $a + b + c + d + 2$
b) $a + b + 1$ and $2a + 3b + 4$ add to $3a + 4b + 5$
c) $a + b + 1$ and $a - b - 1$ add to $2a$

19. Answers may vary, e.g., when simplifying polynomials, I have to combine the coefficients of like terms. This is done using the same principles as adding and subtracting integers. The zero principle means that I can combine any two equal values with opposite signs, like $+3$ and -3 or $+4.5$ and -4.5, and the result will be 0.

20. **a)** $-2x + 6y + 3z$ **b)** $-10abc - 7ab$ **c)** $-3xyz + 9xy + 5yz$

21. **a)** $9x - 2y$ **b)** $-8ab + 13a$ **c)** $3xy + 5y^2$

22. **a)** Answers may vary, e.g., this is never true. When I add two monomials, I can get a monomial, a binomial, or zero. Two monomials cannot be added to make a trinomial.
b) Answers may vary, e.g., this is sometimes true. One polynomial could include $+y$ and the other could include $-2y$, but it could also be that one polynomial has $-y$ and the other polynomial has no y term.
c) Answers may vary, e.g., this is always true. There is no x term in the sum, so if one polynomial has $+2x$, the other must have $-2x$ so they cancel out.
d) Answers may vary, e.g., this is sometimes true. They could both be binomials, like $3x^2 - 2y$ and $y + 4$. But they could also be a binomial and a monomial, like $3x^2 + 4$ and $-y$.

Lesson 2.5, page 116

1. **a)** $2x(x + 4) = 2x^2 + 8x$ **b)** $2x(2x + 3) = 4x^2 + 6x$
2. **a)** $8a^5 - 2a^4$ **b)** $-2y^2 + 2y + 2$
3. **a)** $6x + 8$ **b)** $3x^2 + 6x$
4. **a)** $2x^2 + x$; verifying using a diagram:

b) $20 + 4x$; verifying using algebra tiles:

is

c) $6x^2 + 10x$; verifying using the distributive property:
$(3x + 5)(2x) = (3x)(2x) + (5)(2x) = 6x^2 + 10x$

5. **a)** $2(3x + 1) = 6x + 2$ **c)** $x(4x + 2) = 4x^2 + 2x$
b) $3x(3 + 2x) = 9x + 6x^2$

6. **a)** $-2y^2 - 2y - 2$ **d)** $-x^2 + 3x - 7$
b) $2b^5 - 4b^3 + b^2$ **e)** $-4x^3 + 12x^2$
c) $15m^5 + 18m^4 - 12m^3$ **f)** $-6n^3 + 10n^2 - 8n^5$

7. **a)** $3(2x - 10) = 6x - 30$
b) $2x^2(x^3 - 5x - 4) = 2x^5 - 10x^3 - 8x^2$
c) $-4a^3(3a^4 - a + 2) = -12a^7 + 4a^4 - 8a^3$

8. **a)** 68
b) 15
c) 1150
d) 295
e) Answers may vary, e.g., I know the answer should be the same before and after I expand each statement because both forms are just different ways of writing the same expression.
f) Answers may vary, e.g., in some cases it was easier to evaluate before using the distributive property, as in b). At other times it was easier for me to expand first, as in a).

9. **a)** $P = 14x - 4$, $A = 12x^2 - 8x$
b) $P = 12x + 6$, $A = 6x^2 + 9x$
c) $P = 18y + 4$, $A = 16y^2 + 8y$
d) $P = 52$ cm, $A = 160$ cm^2

10. Answers may vary, e.g., when I use the distributive property to simplify $x(2x + 7)$, I multiply both terms inside the brackets by x. When I multiply 20×47, I can rewrite this as $20(40 + 7)$, and then multiply both terms inside the brackets by 20 to get $20 \times 40 + 20 \times 7$.

11. **a)** $2xy - 6xz$ **b)** $-3x^2y - 3xyz$
12. **a)** $5(4x + 3)$ **b)** $5x(x + 5)$ **c)** $2x^2(2x^3 + 4x - 1)$
d) Answers may vary, e.g., I could multiply them out using the distributive property.

13. **a)** Answers may vary, e.g., $6x(2x - 1)$.
b) Answers may vary, e.g., $7y(3y^2 + y - 2)$.
c) Answers may vary, e.g., $5x(x - 2y + 6)$.

Lesson 2.6, page 125

1. **a)** $7x + 1$ **b)** -4
2. **a)** $7x^5 + 4x^3 - 3x^2$ **b)** $-3y^5 - y^2$
3. $12(20 + 95h) + 8(25 + 120h)$ or $2100h + 440$
4. **a)** $2(x - 1) + 3(2x + 2) = 8x + 4$
b) $3(y^2 - 1) - 2(y^2 + 1) = y^2 - 5$
c) $(x^2 + 1) + 2(x^2 - 1) = 3x^2 - 1$

5. **a)** $26c + 88$ **d)** $5y^3 - 8y^2 + 14y$
b) $-2x - 39$ **e)** $11y$
c) $-4x^2 + 6x + 15$ **f)** $6x^5 + 11x^3 - 18x + 12$

6. **a)** $9a + 24$, 51 **c)** $-2a^2 - 10a - 14$, -62
b) $-2a + 25$, 19 **d)** $a^3 - a^2 - 2a$, 12

7. **a)** $4x^2 + 17x - 21$ **c)** $4y^2 + 17y - 21$
b) $7x + 7$ **d)** $5p^2 + 13p + 5$

8. **a)** $8x^5 - 4x^4$ **c)** $2m^5 - 23m^4 + 13m^3$
b) $-6y^7 + 5y^5 - 3y^2$ **d)** $-3x^4 + 8x^3$

9. a) $\frac{3}{10}a - 3\frac{1}{3}$

c) $-6.455m + 4.13$

b) $\frac{7}{10}a + \frac{1}{9}b - \frac{1}{6}$

10. a) $(40x + 8)$ cm

d) 2112 cm^2

b) 208 cm

e) $2000x^2 - 1600x + 240$ cm^2

c) $100x^2 - 80x + 12$ cm

11. a) $-38\,100x + 308\,700$

b)

	A	B	C	D
1	Number of Years	Value of One Sedan	Value of One Sport Utility	Total Value
2	0	$19 600	$24 500	$308 700
3	1	17 200	21 400	270 600
4	2	14 800	18 300	232 500
5	3	12 400	15 200	194 400
6	4	10 000	12 100	156 300
7	5	7600	9000	118 200
8	6	5200	5900	80 100

c) The company paid $73 500 for the SUVs and $235 200 for the sedans.

d) The sport utilities are depreciating at a faster rate.

12. a) $-13x + 52$

b) Answers may vary, e.g., order of operations must be considered when doing this problem. Multiplication must happen before addition or subtraction. The "10" in front of the brackets means each term inside the brackets must be multiplied by 10 before subtraction can be carried out.

13. a) sometimes true

b) Answers may vary, e.g., I can use algebra tiles to simplify algebraic expressions that require the distributive property as long as the degree is at most 3. This is because algebra tiles can only show up to 3 dimensions. The exponent of x is 1, for instance, so I can represent it using a long, narrow tile or line. For $-x$, I can use a tile or line of the same length but of a different colour or shade.

To represent x^2, I can use a square tile or draw a square of the same colour or shade of x. For $-x^2$, I can use a square tile or draw a square of the same area but with the same colour or shade as the $-x$ tile.

To represent x^3, I can use a cube of side x or draw a 3D cube having x side lengths. I can use the same size cube to represent $-x^3$ but change the colour or shade to that of the $-x$ tile. I cannot represent x^4 degree 4 or higher using algebra tiles.

14. a) $-2x - 39y$ **b)** $3x^2 - xy$ **c)** $-4x^2 + 6xy + 15y$

15. a) $2x^2 + 10x + 12$ **b)** $y^2 + 3y + 2$ **c)** $2x^2 + 3xy + y^2$

16. a) $4x^2 - 2x - 6$ **b)** $x^2 - xy - 2y^2$ **c)** $8x^2 + 5x - 15$

Chapter Review, page 131

1. a)

y
y

c)

x x

b)

y y
y

d)

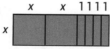
$2x$
$2x$

2. Answers may vary, e.g., the side length must be between 20 cm and 25 cm, because $20 \times 20 = 4007$ and $25 \times 25 = 625$. My estimate is 20.5 cm. Using my calculator, I found that the side length to two decimal places is 20.30 cm.

3. The bases are all the same in each problem and when I add the exponents in the numerator and subtract the exponent in the denominator, I get 3 in each case. So the answer is always 5^3.

4. a) $x = -2$ **b)** $x^2y^2 = 36$ **c)** $-2x^3 = 16$

5. The numbers are 9^4 (or 6561) and 9^2 (or 81), because

$$(9^4)(9^2) = 9^6 \text{ and } \frac{9^4}{9^2} = 9^2.$$

6. Answers may vary, e.g., I can round 9.5×10^{16} km to 10×10^{16} km. When I divide this value by 10×10^8 km/h, I get 1×10^8 h, or about 100 000 000 h. That is close to 11 500 years.

7. a) a^6 **b)** $256x^{12}$ **c)** $2y^6$

8. a) Answers may vary, e.g., the bases are the same and the exponents in both cases multiply to 15; $10^{15} - 10^{15} = 0$.

b) Answers may vary, e.g., I can also represent 9^2 as 3^4. If I substitute 3^4 in the expression it becomes $(3^4)^2 - (3^4)^2$, which is zero.

9. a) 2^9 **b)** 5^8 **c)** 3^6

10. $SA = 6(5^3)^2 = 6(5^6) = 93\,750$; $V = (5^3)^3 = 5^9 = 1\,953\,125$

11. a) y; checking, e.g., using algebra tiles:

 and is

b) $6xy^2$ **c)** $7x^2 - 6x$ **d)** $2y^2 + 4xy$

12. a) $\frac{3}{5}a$ **b)** $3a + \frac{1}{3}b$ **c)** $-4.00m + 5.0$

13. a) $10h + 25$ **b)** $9h + 8$ **c)** $19h + 33$ **d)** $128.00

14. a) $3y - 6$

b) $2x^2 + 4x$; checking, e.g., using a diagram:

x x 1 1 1 1
x

c) $15m^4 + 10mn$ **e)** $2y^6 + 6y^5 - 2y^4$

d) $-3x^3 + 3x^2$ **f)** $-4a^5 + 5a^4 - 2a^3$

15. a) $x + 4$ **b)** $\frac{1}{4}a + 4b$ **c)** $-4.2m^2 - 3.3m$

16. a) $P = 2[(x + 20) + x]$ **c)** 220 cm

b) $P = 4x + 40$ **d)** $P = 2x + 2(x + 20)$

e) The expression in d) is what I get when I remove the square brackets from the expression in a), so the results will be the same.

17. a) $5x$; checking, e.g., using algebra tiles:

and is

b) $2y^2 + y - 10$ **c)** $9x^2 - 4x + 6$ **d)** $13x^3 - 16x^2$

18. a) $26x^2 + 200x$ **b)** 14 400 cm^2 or 1.44 m^2

19. a) $9x - 6$ **b)** $19x - 19y$ **c)** $-13.4x^2 - 33.72x$

20. a) $22(3y + 15) + 18(2y + 12) = 102y + 546$

b) $1158.00

560   Answers

1. a)

b) $\dfrac{\cdot}{m}$

c)

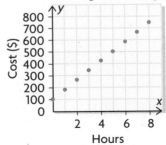

Answers may vary, e.g., my sketches are the same in that they are all geometric shapes: a square, a line, and a cube. However, the line has only one dimension, the square two, and the cube three. The cube has the same side length as the line, but the side length of the square is different.

2. a) $\sqrt{310}$

b) Answers may vary, e.g., I know that 15^2 is 225 and 20^2 is 400. 310 is slightly closer to 225 than to 400, so my guess is 17.4 cm.

c) 17.61 cm

3. 57.4 m

4. a) 3^{10} **b)** $\dfrac{4}{5}$ **c)** x^8 **d)** $(6.1^{12})(5^2)$

5. C.

6. Answers may vary, e.g., suppose I have the expression $(x^5)^3$. This means x gets multiplied by itself 5 times and that the result gets multiplied by itself another 3 times. All together that is the same as x multiplied by itself 15 times. Expanded, the expression would look like $(xxxxx)(xxxxx)(xxxxx)$, which is the same as x^{15}.

7. Simplify

a) 6^6 **c)** $5^5 x^{20}$ or $3125x^{20}$ **e)** y^{16}

b) x^{10} **d)** $\left(\dfrac{2}{5}\right)^{20}$ **f)** $\dfrac{25}{x^4}$

8. Answers may vary, e.g., "like terms" means that the variable and exponent parts of terms are the same. I can represent terms with exponents up to 3 using algebra tiles or diagrams. When I use algebra tiles, I know that tiles of the same shape and size are like terms. I can also represent like terms having one dimension as lines, with two dimensions as squares, and with three dimensions as cubes. The tiles or diagrams do not have to be the same colour, since positive and negative terms can still be alike. In this way I can quickly identify like terms.

9. a) $3x$; checking, e.g., using algebra tiles:

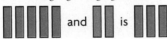

b) $9xy$

c) $7x^2 - 6a$

10. A.

11. a) $2x - 6$; checking, e.g., using algebra tiles:

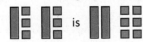

b) $12x^3 - 15x^2$

c) $5y^9 + 3y^8 - y^7$

12. a) $5x$; checking, e.g., using algebra tiles:

b) $2y^2 + y - 10$

c) $7.2x^2 - 4x + 0.6$

13. a) $114h + 430$ **b)** \$4078.00

14. Answers may vary, e.g., $x(2x + 1) + (x^2 - x)$.

Chapter 3

Getting Started, page 138

1. a) v) **c)** iv) **e)** iii)

b) ii) **d)** i) **f)** vi)

2.

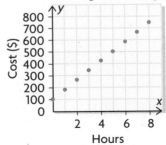

3.

Number of Hours	Charge ($)
0	100
1	180
2	260
3	340
4	420
5	500
6	580
7	660
8	740

Plumbing Elite Charges

4. a) 17 **b)** 7 **c)** $\dfrac{9}{4}$

5. a) $3x - 6$ **b)** $x - 3$ **c)** $4\dfrac{9x}{4}$

6. a) $t = 2n + 4$

b) The orange tiles are represented by $2n$. The blue tiles are represented by the constant 4.

c) 38

d)

Figure	Number of Squares
1	6
2	8
3	10
4	12
5	14

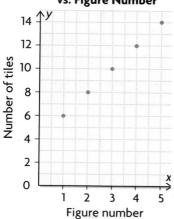

Number of Tiles vs. Figure Number

7. Answers may vary, e.g., the Cartesian coordinate system is made of the intersection of two axes. An ordered pair is plotted on the Cartesian coordinate system. A scatter plot is made by plotting the values in a table of values. A table of values is made of ordered pairs. The values of variables are used to make a table of values. An algebraic expression is made of variables and constants. An algebraic expression can be plotted on axes. The relation between two variables results in an ordered pair.

Lesson 3.1, page 146

1. $s = 2f + 3$

Figure	1	2	3
Number of Squares	5	7	9

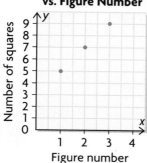

Number of Squares vs. Figure Number

2. **a)** Answers may vary, e.g., $p = 3s$.

b) Answers may vary, e.g., $c = 0.5k + 2.5$.

Distance (km)	2	3	4	5
Fare ($)	3.50	4.00	4.50	5.00

3. **a)**

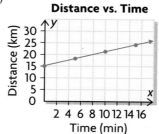

Distance vs. Time

b)

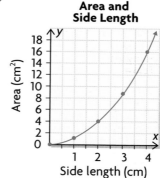

Area and Side Length

c)

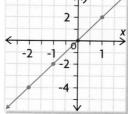

4. **a)** $d = \frac{3}{5}t + 15$ **b)** $a = s^2$ **c)** $y = 2x$

5. **a)** time is independent, distance is dependent
b) Answers may vary, e.g., 4.4 km.

c) and **d)**

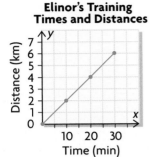

Elinor's Training Times and Distances

d) From the graph, if $x = 22$ km, then $y = 4.4$ min.

6. **a)** $y = x$ **b)** $y = 0.5x + 3$

7. **a)**

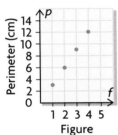

b) 30, because $p = 3f$

c)

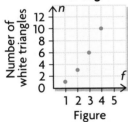

Number of White Triangles Per Figure

d) There are 55 white triangles. For example, the number goes up by one more than the figure number each time; 1, 3, 6, 10, 15, 21, 28, 36, 45, 55 or $n = \frac{1}{2}f(f + 1)$.

8. **a)** Answers may vary, e.g., F, because the equation is $C = $.

b)

Fahrenheit (°)	32	41	50	59	68
Celsius (°)	0	5	10	15	20

c)

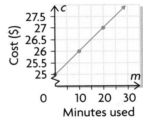

Celsius and Fahrenheit

d) continuous

e) Answers may vary, e.g., 38 °C.

f) $37.\overline{7}$ °C

g) Answers may vary, e.g., because a graph or table gives an estimate, while an equation gives a more exact value.

9. **a)** Answers may vary, e.g., cost depends on time. There is a $25 charge to start with, before any minutes are used.

b)

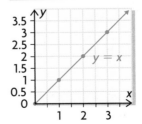

Cost and Time

c) continuous

d) $c = \dfrac{m}{10} + 25$

e) Answers may vary, e.g., an equation, since it will give exact value.

f) $35

10. **a)** Answers may vary, e.g., $e = 5h + 8$.

b) Antwan's earnings depend on time, so e is the dependent variable and t is the independent variable.

11. **a)** Answers may vary, e.g., $d = 75 - 0.125l$, $l = 75 - 0.125d$.

b) 600 km

12. **a)** A, B, D   **b)** A, B, C

13. **a)**

x	0	1	2	3
y	0	1	2	3

$y = x$

b)

x	0	1	2	3
y	3	5	7	9

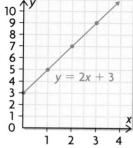

$y = 2x + 3$

c)

x	0	1	2	3
y	1	0	−1	−2

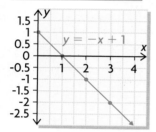

$y = -x + 1$

d)

x	0	1	2	3
y	−3.5	−3.25	−3.0	−2.75

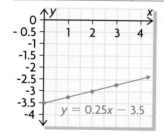

$y = 0.25x - 3.5$

e)

x	0	1	2	3
y	0	$-\dfrac{1}{2}$	−1	

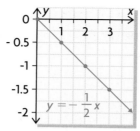

$y = -\dfrac{1}{2}x$

f)

x	0	1	2	3
y	$\dfrac{1}{6}$	$-\dfrac{3}{6}$	$-\dfrac{7}{6}$	$-\dfrac{11}{6}$

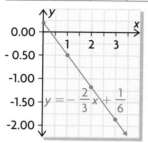

$y = -\dfrac{2}{3}x + \dfrac{1}{6}$

14. a) C, ii); values in table match the points on the graph and are solutions of the equation.
b) A, iii); values in table match the points on the graph and are solutions of the equation.
c) B, i); values in table match the points on the graph and are solutions of the equation.

15. $m = -2.50w + 50$

Week	Money in Bank ($)
0	50.00
1	47.50
2	45.00
3	42.50
4	40.00

Money vs. Time

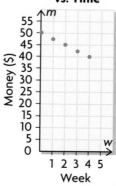

16. Group 2

17. **a)** One inch is the same length as 2.54 centimetres.

b) The Fahrenheit temperature is the same as 32 degrees more than $\frac{9}{5}$ of the temperature in Celsius.

c) One kilogram is the same weight as 2.2 pounds.

d) The temperature in Kelvin is 273 degrees more than the temperature in Celsius.

18. **a)**

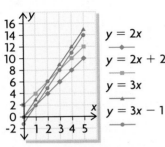

$y = 2x$
$y = 2x + 2$
$y = 3x$
$y = 3x - 1$

b) If there is no constant, the graph will pass through the origin. If there is a constant, it will not.

19. **a)**

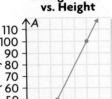

Triangle Area vs. Height

b) $A = 5h$

20.

t	0	0.25	0.50	0.75	1
h	2	2.44	2.25	1.44	0

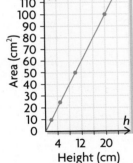

Rocket's Height vs. Time

Lesson 3.2, page 151

1. **a)** direct   **c)** partial   **e)** direct

    b) partial   **d)** partial   **f)** partial

2. **a)** $h = 35t + 1500$

b)

Time (s)	0	1	2	3	4
Height (m)	1500	1535	1570	1605	1640

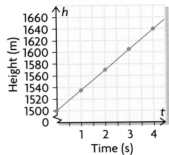

Rocket Launch

c) partial variation; graph does not go through (0, 0)

3. **a)** Plan A: $C = 0.75g$; Plan B: $C = 0.25g + 10.00$

b) Plan A, \$15; Plan B, \$15

c) Plan A, \$22.50; Plan B, \$17.50

d) For less than 20 glasses of milk choose Plan A, for more than 20 glasses choose Plan B, and for 20 glasses choose either.

e) Plan A is a direct variation, Plan B is a partial variation.

f) For example, in a partial variation there is a flat cost and a cost per glass, so you have to pay even if you do not buy any milk. In a direct variation, there is no flat cost.

Lesson 3.3, page 156

1. **a)** linear; first differences constant

b) linear; graph is straight line

c) nonlinear; first differences not constant

d) nonlinear; graph not a straight line

2. **a)** 3   **b)** -2

3. **a)** 3   **b)** -2 **c)** 8   **d)** -2

4. **a)** x-values are out of order

b)

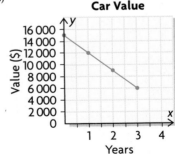

Car Value

c) -3000. This is the change in the value of the car each year.

d) $x = 5$. This does not seem realistic because usually many years must pass for a car to be worth \$0.

5. $\frac{3}{5}$

6. **a)** 18 cm   **b)** 100 cm   **c)** $\frac{18}{25}$

7. a) 1   **c)** −34   **e)** 3

    b) $\dfrac{1}{5}$ **d)** 9   **f)** −1

8. a) The *y*-intercept is the flat charge for a luncheon, $150, and the slope is the extra cost per person attending the luncheon, $8.

    b) The *y*-intercept is the value of the copier before any time has elapsed, $7000, and the slope is how much the value of the copier decreases for each passing year, −$1000.

9. a) Answers may vary, e.g., (−1, 3) if the run is −3 the rise is −2; (2 − 3, 5 − 2), (5, 7) if the run is 3 the rise is 2; (2 + 3, 5 + 2).

    b) Answers may vary, e.g., (−4, 1) if the run is −4 the rise is 3; (0 − 4, −2 + 3), (4, −5) if the run is 4 the rise is −3; (0 + 4, −2 − 3).

    c) Answers may vary, e.g., (0, −11) if the run is −1 the rise is −5; (1 − 1, −6 − 5), (2, −1) if the run is 1 the rise is 5; (1 + 1, −6 + 5).

    d) Answers may vary, e.g., (−3, −1) if the run is −1 the rise is 2; (−2 − 1, −3 + 2), (−1, −5) if the run is 1 the rise is −2; (−2 + 1, −3 − 2).

10. a)

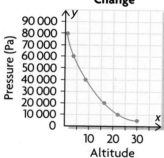

Air Pressure Change

    b) The graph shows that the air pressure has a large negative rate of change at low altitudes but changes as the altitude increases to become a small negative rate of change at high altitudes.

    c) approximately 12 500 Pa using the curved graph

11. a) slope is 3   **d)** slope is $-\dfrac{1}{5}$

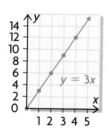 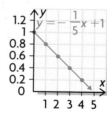

    b) slope is −2   **e)** slope is −1

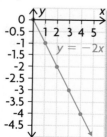 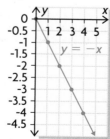

c) slope is $\dfrac{3}{4}$ **f)** slope is $\dfrac{2}{3}$

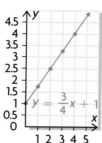 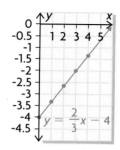

12. a) $125 000   **c)** $177 500

    b) $140 000   **d)** $7500 increase each year

13. a) *x*, the number of weeks is independent; *y*, the amount of money in account is dependent.

    b) Answers may vary, e.g., the amount he takes out each week does not change, or the degree of the equation is 1.

    c) −$70/week

    d) the amount of money taken out of account each week

    e) It is the same as the number in front of the *x* term the slope.

    f) 58 weeks

14. a) the maximum safe heart rate for a 20-year-old person

    b) the rate at which the maximum heart rate decreases per year of age of the person

    c) $b = -(a - 20) + 220$, where *b* is maximum beats per minute and *a* is age in years.

    d) 162 beats per minute

15. No, if he sold $1000 at 5 % commission, his earnings would be 0.05(1000) + 300 = $350. If he sold $1000 at 10 % commission, they would be 0.1(1000) + 300 = $400, which is not twice $350.

16. a)

x	y	First Differences
0	0	
		0.25
1	0.25	
		0.25
2	0.50	
		0.25
3	0.75	
		0.25
4	1.00	

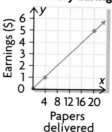

Paper Delivery Earings

    b) The first differences are the amount she earns per paper.

    c) $0.25/paper

    d) $y = 0.25x$, where *y* is her total earnings and *x* is the number of papers delivered, $68.75.

17. **a)** $y = \frac{3}{5}x + 2$ **c)** $y = \frac{1}{3}x + 5$ **e)** $y = -\frac{1}{2}x + 1.5$

b) $y = -4x$ **d)** $y = 2x - 7$ **f)** $y = \frac{4}{7}x - 2$

18. **a)** $2x + 5y = 10$

x	0	1	2	3	4
y	2	$\frac{8}{5}$	$\frac{6}{5}$	$\frac{4}{5}$	$\frac{2}{5}$

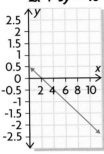
2x + 5y = 10

$4x - 2y = 7$

x	0	1	2	3	4
y	$-\frac{7}{2}$	$-\frac{3}{2}$	$-\frac{1}{2}$	$\frac{5}{2}$	$\frac{9}{2}$

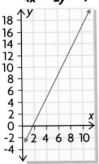
4x − 2y = 7

$x + y = -2$

x	0	1	2	3	4
y	−2	−3	−4	−5	−6

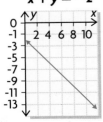
x + y = −2

b)

Equation	Slope	y-intercept	x-intercept
$2x + 5y = 10$	$-\frac{2}{5}$	2	5
$4x - 2y = 7$	2	$-\frac{7}{2}$	$\frac{7}{4}$
$x + y = -2$	−1	−2	−2

c) The equations are in the form $ax + by = c$. Notice that the slope is $-\frac{a}{b}$, the x-intercept is $\frac{c}{a}$, and the y-intercept is $\frac{c}{b}$.

Mid-Chapter Review, page 163

1. **a)**

Figure	Circles	Stars
1	3	5
2	6	5
3	9	5

$c = 3f$, where f is figure number and c is number of circles; $s = 5$, where s is number of stars; or $t = 3f + 5$, where f is the figure number and t is the total number of shapes

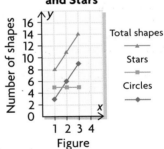
Circles and Stars

b) 225 **c)** 5

2. **a)** partial variation; does not pass through (0, 0)
   b) partial variation; does not pass through (0, 0)
   c) direct variation; passes through (0, 0)

3. **a)** $\frac{10}{3}$ **b)** 40 words/min **c)** 3

4. **a)** linear, graph is a straight line
   b) linear, degree of the equation is 1
   c) nonlinear, graph is not a straight line
   d) linear, when graphed all points lie on a straight line

5. **a)** −50, means that she withdraws $50 for each passing week
   b) y-intercept = 1250, this is her original amount of money
   c) after 25 weeks

Lesson 3.4, page 169

1. a)

$$-3x + 2y = 6$$

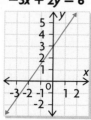

b)

$$\frac{1}{2}x + \frac{2}{3}y = \frac{1}{6}$$

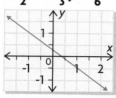

c)

$$x = -3$$

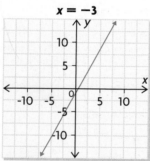

2. a) $x + y = 38$

b) The maximum amount she can work at each particular job.

3. Answers may vary, e.g., $(0, -18)$, $(1, -12)$, $(2, -6)$.

$$6x - y = 18$$

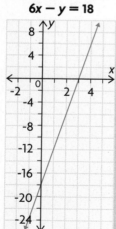

4. a)

$$2x - 5y = 10$$

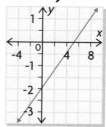

b)

$$4x + 5y = 20$$

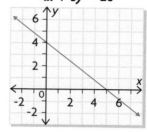

c)

$$x + y = 0$$

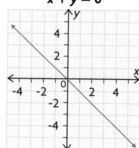

d)

$$2x + 3y = 0$$

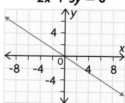

5. a) Answers may vary, e.g., x is the number of dimes and y is the number of quarters he has. They multiply by their respective worth and add to give $14.50.

b) yes, equation is of degree 1

c) x-intercept is 145; y-intercept is 58; they are the maximum values of dimes or quarters if he only has one or the other.

d) discrete, because he cannot have partial dimes or quarters

6. a) x is the hours worked at the coffee shop and y is the hours worked at the grocery store. They multiply by their respective wages and add to give his total earnings, $288.

b) yes, equation is of degree 1

c) 32; 25.6; They are the maximum amount of hours he could have worked at either job.

d) Answers may vary, e.g., 17 h at coffee shop and 12 h at grocery store.

7. **a)** x is the amount of time spent going downstream and y is the amount of time going upstream, they multiply by their respective speeds and add to give the total distance travelled, 60 km.

b) x-intercept, 20: the mooring point of the boat; y-intercept, 30: the starting point of boat

c)

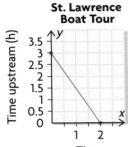

St. Lawrence Boat Tour

Time upstream (h) vs Time downstream (h)

8. **a)**

$$2x + \frac{4}{5}y = 11$$

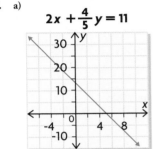

b)

$$\frac{1}{4}x + \frac{2}{3}y = 1$$

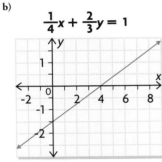

c)

$$-\frac{5}{6}x + y = -\frac{1}{3}$$

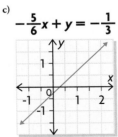

d)

$$-\frac{2}{7}x - \frac{1}{3}y = -\frac{5}{42}$$

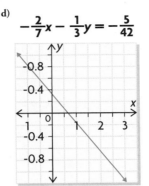

9. The paths do not cross.

10. **a)** Answers may vary, e.g., 40 figure skates and 48 hockey skates, or 20 figure skates and 72 hockey skates.

b) 10 figure skates and 84 hockey skates

11. **a)** x is the mass of raisins and y is the mass of peanuts. Multiply by their respective costs and add to give the total cost, $3.00.

b) x-intercept 3.4, y-intercept 3. These are the maximum amounts of each type of nuts and raisins she can include.

c)

$$0.88x - 1y = 3.00$$

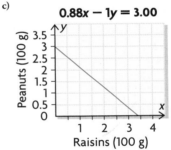

Peanuts (100 g) vs Raisins (100 g)

12. Answers may vary, e.g., 172 of the $3.50 shares and 104 of the $5.75 shares, or 80 of the $3.50 shares and 160 of the $5.75 shares.

13.

	x-intercept	y-intercept	Slope
a)	3	2	$-\frac{2}{3}$
b)	9	$\frac{9}{4}$	$-\frac{1}{4}$
c)	5	-2	$\frac{2}{5}$
d)	2	$-\frac{4}{3}$	$\frac{2}{3}$

14. The slope is equal to the negative of the y-intercept divided by the x-intercept, which for an equation in the form $Ax + By = C$ is the same as $-\dfrac{A}{B}$.

15. **a)** $y = -2x + 4$ **b)** $y = -x + 2$ **c)** $y = \frac{3}{4}x + \frac{1}{4}$

16. **a)** $x - 2y = 4$ **c)** $-3x + y = -3$
   b) $6x + 4y = 3$ **d)** $9x + 2y = 6$

Answers

17. a) 0   **b)** 2, −2   **c)** −8

d)

x	−2	−2	−1	0	1	2	3
y	10	0	−6	−8	−6	0	10

$$y = 2x^2 - 8$$

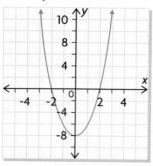

Lesson 3.5, page 179

1. a) linear; graph is straight line
    b) nonlinear; points lie on curve
2. nonlinear; equation is degree 2, not degree 1
3. a) nonlinear   **b)** linear   **c)** linear
4. a) time, since distance depends on time
    b) linear, first differences are constant
5. a)

Figure Number	1	2	3	4
Perimeter	4	16	28	40

    b) 136 units, because Perimeter = $4(3f - 2)$ where f is the figure number.
    c) linear, first differences are constant
    d)

Figure Number	1	2	3	4
Blue Squares	1	5	11	19

    e) The number of blue squares in the figure increases by a number two more than the last; e.g., the blue squares increase by 4, 6, 8... Figure 12 will have 155 blue squares.
    f) nonlinear; first differences not constant
6. a) linear, one shape is added for each new figure
    b) nonlinear; different number of shapes are added for each new figure
7. a) linear, equation is of degree 1
    b)

d	0	100	200	300	400
G	80	60	40	20	0

Hybrid Mileage

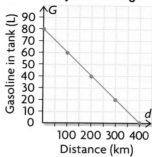

8. a) linear; equation is of degree 1
    b) using a table to show the first differences are constant

R	$C = 0.006(R + 20)$	First Differences
0	0.12	
		0.006
1	0.126	
		0.006
2	0.132	
		0.006
3	0.138	

Cucumber Yield

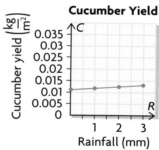

9. nonlinear; number of sections doubles for each paper fold
10. At approximately 30 s. The first differences decrease by −250 for each time.
11. a) The relation in Pattern 1 is linear, while the number of shapes in Pattern 2 and Pattern 3 are nonlinear.
    b) The differences between each figure in Pattern 1 is constant, and the ones in Pattern 2 and Pattern 3 are not.
12. a) 1st differences: 1, 3, 5, 7; 2nd differences: 2, 2, 2; 3rd differences: 0, 0
    b) 1st differences: 1, 7, 19, 37; 2nd differences: 6, 12, 18; 3rd differences: 6, 6
    c) 1st differences: −2, −6, −10, −14; 2nd differences: −4, −4, −4; 3rd differences: 0, 0
    d) 1st differences: 4, 28, 76, 148; 2nd differences: 24, 48, 72; 3rd differences: 24, 24
    e) 1st differences: $\frac{7}{3}, \frac{9}{3}, \frac{11}{3}, \frac{13}{3}$; 2nd differences: $\frac{2}{3}, \frac{2}{3}, \frac{2}{3}$; 3rd differences: 0, 0
    f) 1st differences: −1, −13, −37, −73, −121; 2nd differences: −12, −24, −36, −48; 3rd differences: −12, −12, −12
In an equation with degree 2, the 2nd differences are constant and the 3rd differences are zero. In an equation with degree 3, the 2nd differences are linear and the 3rd differences are constant.

13. **a)** nonlinear; first differences not constant

x	y = (x + 1)(x − 2)	First Differences
−1	0	
		−2
0	−2	
		0
1	−2	
		2
2	0	
		4
3	4	

b) nonlinear; first differences not constant

x	y = 2(x − 1)(x + 3)	First Differences
−1	−8	
		2
0	−6	
		6
1	0	
		10
2	10	
		14
3	24	

c) nonlinear

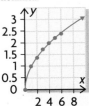

d) nonlinear

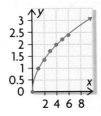

Chapter Review, page 183

1. **a)** Answers may vary, e.g., $y = x - 1$.
b) Answers may vary, e.g., $y = -x$.
c) Answers may vary, e.g.,

x	0	1	2	3
y	4	6	8	10

d) Answers may vary, e.g., $y = -x + 1$.
e) Answers may vary, e.g., $y = -\dfrac{2x}{3}$.

f)

x	0	1	2	3
y	−6	$-\dfrac{9}{2}$	−3	$-\dfrac{3}{2}$

2. **a)** a) partial variation; graph does not cross point (0, 0)
b) direct variation; graph crosses point (0, 0)
c) partial variation; (0, 0) is not a solution
d) partial variation; graph does not cross point (0, 0)
e) direct variation; graph crosses point (0, 0)
f) partial variation; (0, 0) is not a solution

b) a) $y = 6$ c) $y = 18$ e) $y = -\dfrac{14}{3}$

b) $y = -7$ d) $y = -6$ f) $y = \dfrac{9}{2}$

3. **a)** $\dfrac{4}{5}$ **c)** $\dfrac{5}{3}$ **e)** −5

b) 4   **d)** −2

4. **a)** section DE, since the slope is a larger negative number than the other sections' slopes
b) section EF, since the slope is flat
c) For part a), the slope is −2 since the rise is down 2 and the run is 1. For part b), the y values of the points E and F are equal, so Δy will be 0 regardless of their x values and so the slope is 0.

5. **a)** $(6, -2), (10, 1)$ **c)** $(-2, 3), (8, -3)$
b) $(-3, 3), (3, 7)$ **d)** $(1, 4), (3, 9)$

6. **a)**   **b)**

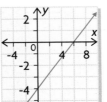 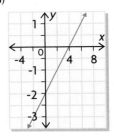

7. **a)** L is length and W is width, the equation is correct since the perimeter of the figure is the sum of the lengths of its sides. Using this definition and a perimeter of 210, we arrive at this equation.
b)

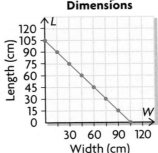

Rectangle Dimensions

Length (cm) vs Width (cm)

c) continuous, a side of a rectangle can have any length, one that is not necessarily a whole number
d) Answers may vary, e.g., $L = 50$ cm and $W = 55$ cm, or $L = 100$ cm and $W = 5$ cm.

8. Yes, as shown in the graph, when $x = 5$, $y = 0$.

$$2x - 3y = 10$$

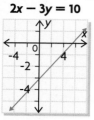

9. a) linear; graph is straight line
b) linear; equation is of degree 1
c) linear; first differences constant
d) nonlinear; graph not a straight line
e) nonlinear; equation is of degree 2
f) nonlinear; first differences not constant

10. a) nonlinear
b)

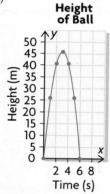

Height of Ball

c) approximately 35 m
d) at 2.4 s and 3.6 s
e) at 6.0 s
f) 46 m

11. a) linear
b)

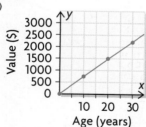

c) $y = 75x + 0.25$
d) $1125.25

Chapter Self-Test, page 185

1. a) $C = 0.25a$, where C is cost and a is number of apples
b) total cost is dependent, apples bought is independent
c) discrete
d) $37.50

2. linear; first differences constant

Distance (km)	Total Cost ($)
0	45.00
100	60.00
200	75.00
300	90.00
400	105.00

3. A.
4. C.
5. A.
6. a) x is the time spent running and y is the time spent walking. This makes sense because they multiply by their respective speeds and add to give the total distance travelled, 6 km.
b) 1.5 h, 3 h
c)

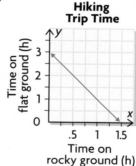

Hiking Trip Time

d) Answers may vary, e.g., $x = 1$ and $y = 1$, or $x = 0.5$ and $y = 2$, or $x = 0.25$ and $y = 2.5$.

7. a) linear; first differences are constant

Figure Number	1	2	3
Number of Squares	1	2	3

linear; graph is a straight line

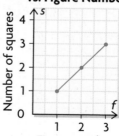

Number of Squares vs. Figure Number

linear; equation is of degree 1: $s = f$

b) nonlinear; first differences are not constant

Figure Number	1	2	3
Number of Squares	1	4	9

nonlinear; graph is not a straight line

**Number of Squares
vs. Figure Number**

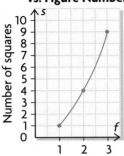

nonlinear; equation is of degree 2: $s = f^2$

Chapters 1–3 Cumulative Review, page 187

1. A.
2. A.
3. B.
4. D.
5. C.
6. D.
7. D.
8. A.
9. A.
10. A.
11. A.
12. B.
13. C.
14. D.
15. D.
16. D.
17. B.
18. A.
19. B.
20. C.
21. D.
22. C.
23. **a)** Answers may vary, e.g., representing the relation as a balance helps because you can see that if you remove a certain amount from one side of the balance, you must remove the same amount from the other side to keep the balance even.
   b) The relation is linear. e.g., make a table of values:

First Number	1	2	3	4	5
Second Number	2	−1	−4	−7	−10

The second number decreases by a constant, 3, each time, so the relation is linear.

Or write the equations out, where x is the first number and y is the second number:
$$3x + y = 5$$
$$y = -3x + 5$$
It is in the form $y = mx + b$, so the relation is linear.

c) i) 11   **ii)** $\frac{1}{2}$ **iii)** $-\frac{5}{8}$ **iv)** $6\frac{4}{5}$

d) i) Answers may vary, e.g., write out the equation for the new game, where x is the first number and y is the second number:
$$\frac{4}{9}x + \frac{1}{3}y = \frac{1}{2}, \; y = -\frac{4}{3}x + \frac{3}{2}$$
Both games' equations are in the form $y = mx + b$, m is negative in both games, and b is positive in both games. However, both m and b are fractions in this game while in the first game they were integers.
   ii) Both graphs have negative slopes, both graphs have positive y-intercepts, and both graphs are linear. However, the graph for the second game has a shallower slope than the graph in the first game, and the graph for the first game has a higher y-intercept.

e) Answers may vary, e.g.,
   • Your partner tells you a number.
   • Your partner multiplies this first number by 2.
   • Your partner adds the product to 5 times a second number, so that the sum is −3.
   • You guess what the second number is.

Chapter 4

Getting Started, page 192

1. **a)** i   **c)** ii   **e)** v
   b) vi   **d)** iii   **f)** iv
2. **a)** $n = 4$

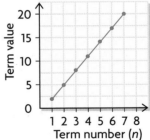

   b) $x = 8$

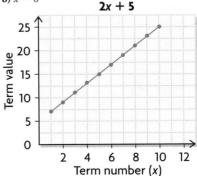

3. **a)** $a = 1$ **b)** $m = 2$ **c)** $x = 5$
4. **a)** \$19.95   **b)** 21   **c)** 18   **d)** 240 km
5. $n = 8$

6. a) $x = \dfrac{2}{3}$ **b)** $x = 8$ **c)** $n = \dfrac{54}{7}$

7. a) $x = 13$ **b)** $m = 8.5$ **c)** $n = 4.4$

8. a) $\dfrac{-32}{5}$, or $-6\dfrac{2}{5}$ **b)** $3\dfrac{7}{40}$

9. a) $-11x - 14$ **b)** $-2.5x + 3.5$

10. a) initial value: 13, rate of change: -3
   b) Plot one coordinate at (0,13). The rest of the points on the line go down 3, right 1.

11. a) $200   **c)** 32 h, $1000; 53 h, $1525
   b) $y = 200 + 25x$

12. Answers may vary, e.g., related math terms: solution, inverse operations, linear.
   Definition: a mathematical statement in which two expressions are equated

   Non-examples: $3x - 4; 2 + \dfrac{5}{6}; x(x - 4) < 8$

   Examples: $3x + 2 = 8; x = 4; 2x^2 + 7x - 8 = 0$

Lesson 4.1, page 201

1. $y = 4.25x - 3$

x	y = 4.25x − 3
1	1.25
2	5.5
3	9.75

From the table of values, the solution to the equation is between 2 and 3, but closer to 3. So, a reasonable estimate is about 2.8.
Check: $4.25(2.8) - 3 = 8.9$

2.

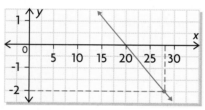

   Answers may vary, e.g., $x = 28$.

   Check: $5 - \dfrac{1}{4}(28) = -2$

3. question 1: $x = 2\dfrac{16}{17}$, question 2: $x = 28$

4. a) Answers may vary, e.g.,

Amount of Fencing (lin. ft)	50	100	150
Cost	262.5	525	787.5

   Justin can purchase between 100 and 150 linear feet of fencing for $600.

   b) $114\dfrac{2}{7}$ linear feet   **c)** $114\dfrac{2}{7} \times $5.25 = 600

5. a)

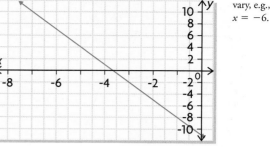

$y = -3x - 11$

Answers may vary, e.g., $x = -6$.

b)

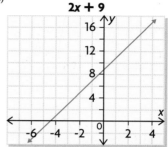

$2x + 9$

Answers may vary, e.g., $x = -2.5$.

c)

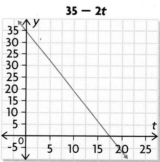

$35 - 2t$

Answers may vary, e.g., $t = 11$.

6. a) $x = -6$ **b)** $x = -2.5$ **c)** $t = 11$

7. a)

x	1	0	−1
2x − 8	−6	−8	−10

x is between 0 and -1

b)

x	−5	−4	−3
7 − 3x	22	19	16

$x = -3$

c)

x	−2	−1	0
2.75x + 3.8	−1.7	1.05	3.8

$x = 0$

8. a) $x = -\dfrac{1}{2}$ **b)** $x = -3$ **c)** $x = 0$

9. a) $y = 700 + \dfrac{35}{2}x$

b)–d)

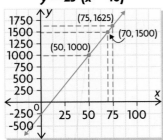

$y = 700 + \dfrac{35}{2}x$

(100, 2450)

(50, 1575)

c) $y = 700 + \left(\dfrac{35}{2}\right)(50)$, $y = 700 + \left(\dfrac{35}{2}\right)(100)$

At 50 s, the rocket would be about 1575 m high.
At 100 s, the rocket would be about 2450 m high.

d) $1000 = 700 + \left(\dfrac{35}{2}\right)x$

The rocket reaches a height of 1000 m at 17 s.

10. a) $y = 25(x - 10)$

b)–d)

$y = 25\,(x - 10)$

(75, 1625)

(70, 1500)

(50, 1000)

c) $y = 25(50 - 10)$; $y = 25(75 - 10)$
For 50 guests, the cost would be about \$1000.
For 75 guests, the cost would be about \$1625.

d) $1500 = 25(x - 10)$
For \$1500, you could invite 70 guests.

11. using tables and verifying

a)

x	0	1	2	3	4
2x + 3	3	5	7	9	11

b)

n	1	2	3	4	5	$n = 5$
3 − 4n	−1	−5	−9	−13	−17	

c)

n	−8	−6	−4	−2	0
$-2 + \dfrac{1}{2}n$	−6	−5	−4	−3	−2

11. using graphs

a)

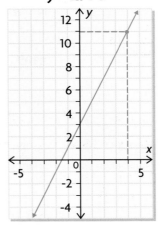

$y = 2x + 3$ $x = 4$

b)

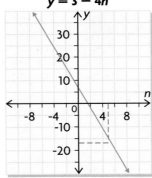

$y = 3 - 4n$ $n = 5$

c)

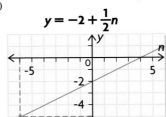

$y = -2 + \dfrac{1}{2}n$ $n = -6$

12. a) $x = 4$; $2(4) + 3 = 8 + 3 = 11$

b) $n = 5$; $3 - 4(5) = 3 - 20 = -17$

c) $n = -6$; $-2 + \dfrac{1}{2}(-6) = -2 + -3 = -5$

13. a) $y = 8x$ **b)** $500 = 8x$ **c)** $y = 8(40)$

d) The y-intercepts are the same. One solves for the independent variable while the other solves for the dependent variable.

e)

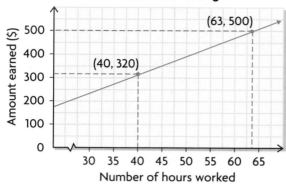

Samantha's Earnings

63 hours is the estimated solution to $500 = 8x$. $320 is the estimated solution to $y = 8(40)$.

f) $x = 62.5; y = 320$

14. a) $x = -2$ **c)** $x = 0$
   b) $x = 10$ **d)** $0 = -1$; no solution

15. a) $y = 100 - 5x$ **b)** $y = 100 - 5(13)$ **c)** $50 = 100 - 5x$
   d) Answers may vary, e.g., both are equations, but the relation in part b) is easier to calculate since the variable is already isolated.
   e)

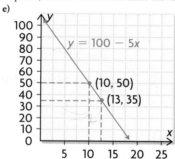

$y = 100 - 5x$

f) $y = 35, y = 5(13) = 35$
   $x = 10, 50 = 5(10)$

16. a) $2(100) + 2w = 500$ Perimeter is $2l + 2w = 500$ with $l = 100$
   b) $w \doteq 150$
   c) $w = 150$
   d) 150 m

17. a) $C = 3n + 3$; C represents the number of counters, n represents the figure number
   b) Figure 19 would have 60 counters.
   c) The solution to the equation $100 = 3n + 3$, is $n = 32.33333\ldots$ Since you cannot have a partial number of figures, there is no figure that has 100 counters.

18. Answers may vary, e.g.,

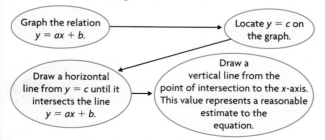

19. using tables and verifying
   a)

x	-3	-2	-1	0
$\dfrac{(x + 2)}{5} - 3x$	8.8	6	3.2	0.4

$x \doteq -2.5; \dfrac{(-2.5 + 2)}{5} - 3(-2.5) = 7.4$

   b)

x	$\dfrac{1}{2}(x + 2) - \dfrac{1}{3}(x - 1)$
0	1.333
5	2.167
10	3
15	3.833
20	4.667

$x \doteq 16; \dfrac{1}{2}(16 + 2) - \dfrac{1}{3}(16 - 1) = 4$

   c)

x	0	1	2	3	4
$x^2 + 7$	7	8	11	16	23

$x = 3; 3^2 + 7 = 16$

x	0	-1	-2	-3	-4
$x^2 + 7$	7	8	11	16	23

$x = -3; (-3)^2 + 7 = 16$

   d)

x	0	1	2	3	4
$2x^2 - 3$	-3	-1	5	15	29

$x \doteq 2.6 ; 2(2.6)^2 - 3 = 10.52$

x	0	-1	-2	-3	-4
$2x^2 - 3$	-3	-1	5	15	29

$x = -2.6; 2(-2.6)^2 - 3 = 10.52$

   e)

x	0	1	2	3	4
$3x^3 - 9$	-9	-6	15	72	183

$x = 3; 3(3^3) - 9 = 72$

19. using graphs
  a) $x = -2.3$
  Answers may vary, e.g.,

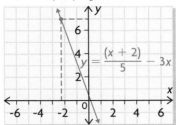

  b) $x = 16$
  Answers may vary, e.g.,

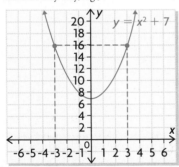

  c) $x = +3; x = -3$
  Answers may vary, e.g.,

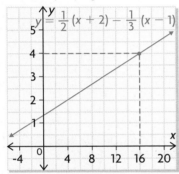

  d) $x = +2.6; x = -2.6$
  Answers may vary, e.g.,

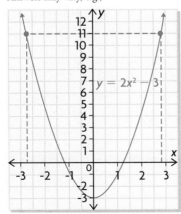

  e) $x = +3$
  Answers may vary, e.g.,

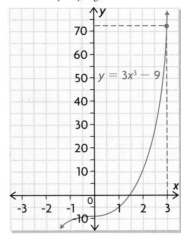

20. **a)** $x = -2\dfrac{5}{14}$ **d)** $x = \sqrt{7}, x = -\sqrt{7}$
  b) $x = 16$ **e)** $x = +3$
  c) $x = +3$ or $x = -3$

21. $0 = mx + b$. Since the y-value on the x-axis is zero, I would substitute this value in for y and solve the equation.

Lesson 4.2, page 210

1. **a)** subtract 2, divide by -3 **c)** subtract 5, multiply by 2
  b) add 3.2, divide by 12.4

2. **a)** $x = -\dfrac{13}{3}$ **b)** $x \doteq 2$ **c)** $x = 12$

3. **a)** $10\ 000 = 1.25x + 5000$
  b) $x = 4000$
  c) $1.25(4000) + 5000 = 10\ 000$

4. **a)** add 10, divide by 6   **d)** subtract 6, divide by -2
  b) subtract 1, divide by 2.5   **e)** subtract 6, divide by -2
  c) add 4, divide by 3   **f)** add 3, divide by -1

5. **a)** $6b = -2 + 10, 6b = 8, b = \dfrac{4}{3}; 6\left(\dfrac{4}{3}\right) - 10 = -2$

  b) $2.5c = 1.5 - 1.0, 2.5c = 0.5, c = \dfrac{1}{5}; 2.5\left(\dfrac{1}{5}\right) + 1.0 = 1.5$

  c) $3f = 10 + 4, 3f = 14, f = \dfrac{14}{3}; 3\left(\dfrac{14}{3}\right) - 4 = 10$

  d) $2d = 4 - 6, -2d = -2, d = 1; 6 - 2(1) = 4$
  e) $-2e = 6 - 6, -2e = 0, e = 0; 6 - 2(0) = 6$
  f) $-h = -2 + 3, -h = -1, h = -1; -3 - (-1) = -2$

6. **a)** $10 = 8.00 + 0.50T$
  b) $20 = 16 + T, 20 - 16 = T, 4 = T$

7. **a)** $D = -600 + 4t$ **d)** $t = 28.5$
  b) $-486 = -600 + 4t$ **e)** $-600 + 4(28.5) = -486$
  c) add 600, divide by 4

8. No. The process of balancing and using inverse operations is the same. Balancing is performing the same operation to each side of an equation with the goal of isolating the variable. Using inverse operations means using operations that are the reverse of those operating on the variable to isolate it and solve the equation.

9. $H = 500 - 60t$
   $20 = 500 - 60t$
   $t = 8$
10. **a)** $x = 8$ **c)** $y = 6$ **e)** $w = -12$
    b) $x = 26$ **d)** $b = -55$ **f)** $d = 24$
11. $\dfrac{x}{7} + 13 = 32; x = 133$
12. **a)** $x = 3$ **c)** $w = 5$ **e)** $a = 6$
    b) $x = 6$ **d)** $y = 23$ **f)** $c = \dfrac{15}{2}$
13. **a)** The number of people at each table is represented by x.
    $22.95(x - 1)$ represents the charge of 22.95 multiplied by the number of people at a table, subtract the one free person. T represents the total cost; $x =$ the number of people per table; $T =$ bill total
    b) Table 1: $22.95(x - 1) = 137.70, x = 7$
    Table 2: $22.95(x - 1) = 68.85, x = 4$
    Table 3: $22.95(x - 1) = 160.65, x = 8$
    Table 4: $22.95(x - 1) = 91.80, x = 5$
    Table 5: $22.95(x - 1) = 91.80, x = 5$
    c) 29 people
14. **a)** $14\dfrac{4}{9}\,°C$ or about $14.4\,°C$
    b) subtract 32, multiply by 5, divide by 9
    c) multiply by 9, divide by 5, add 32
    d) $77\,°F$
15. Balancing: You do the same inverse operations to both sides.
16. **a)** $x = 1$ **b)** $x = \dfrac{5}{2}$
17. **a)** subtract $3x$, divide by 5
    b) $y = -\dfrac{3}{5}x + 3$
    c) subtract $5y$, divide by 3
    d) $x = -\dfrac{5}{3}y + 5$
    e) You can plot the x- and y-intercepts and that will allow you to draw a straight line.
18. **a)** $x + y = 49$; x represents the number of cars and y represents the number of trucks
    b) $4x + 6y = 230$
    c)
    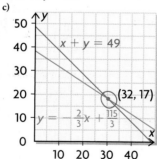
    32 cars and 17 trucks were washed.

Lesson 4.3, page 220

1. $x = 3$
2. **a)** The width is 3 less than the length L
   b) $44 = 2(L + L - 3); L = 12.5$
   c) 12.5 cm by 9.5 cm
3. **a)** A: subtract $2x$ to isolate the variable term
   B: add 18 to isolate the variable term
   C: divide by 2 to isolate the variable
   b) A: multiply both sides by 6 (LCD of 3 and 2) to remove the fractions
   B: distribute the 6 through the bracket on the left; multiply 5×6 to simplify
   C: subtract 4 from both sides to isolate the variable term
   D: divide both sides by 3 to isolate the variable
   E. simplify $\dfrac{26}{3}$ and express as a mixed number
4. **a)** Each equation is the same because if you use the distributive property on the right side of the first equation, it simplifies to the second equation; if you collect the like terms from the second equation so that the variables are on the left and the numbers on the right, you arrive at the third equation. Each equation has the same solution, $x = -14$.
   b) Each equation is the same because if you multiply the equations containing fractions by the lowest common denominator and simplify, you will arrive at the equation without any fractions. Each equation has the same solution, $x = -\dfrac{56}{3}$.
   c) Each equation is the same because if you multiply the equations containing fractions by the lowest common denominator and simplify, you will arrive at the equation without any fractions. Each equation has the same solution, $x = 4$.
5. **a)** $x = -8; 5(-8) + 24 = 2(-8)$
   b) $k = \dfrac{15}{2}; 2\left(\dfrac{15}{2}\right) = 4\left(\dfrac{15}{2}\right) - 15$
   c) $x = -6; -4(-6) - 1 = -3(-6) + 5$
   d) no solution
   e) $b = 2; 3(2) - 4 - 5(2) = -3(2) - 2$
   f) $a = 0; 0 + 2(0) + 3(0) - 6 = 7(0) - 6$
6. $n = 17$
7. **a)** $x = 7; 3(7 - 5) = 6$
   b) $d = -2; -5 = 5(3 + 2(-2))$
   c) $m = 3; -3(5 - 6(3)) = 39$
   d) $x = 10; 2(10 - 2) = 3(10) - 14$
   e) $c = -1; 3(-1 + 5) = 4(1 - 2(-1))$
   f) $x = -1; 4(-1 - 2) = -3(2(-1) + 6)$
8. $n - 5 = 3n + 1; n = -3$
9. 11.5 cm by 6.5 cm
10. **a)** $(x + 5) + (3x + 5) = 46$
    b) George is 27 years old; Sam is 9 years old.

11.

	Equation	Common Denominator of All Terms	Equation with Denominators Eliminated
a)	$\dfrac{3x}{4} + \dfrac{2}{3} = 2$	12	$9x + 8 = 24$
b)	$\dfrac{1}{2} - \dfrac{x}{3} = \dfrac{1}{3}$	6	$3 - 2x = 2$
c)	$\dfrac{2}{3} = 5 + x$	3	$2 = 15 + 3x$
d)	$\dfrac{x-5}{4} + 1 = \dfrac{1}{2}$	4	$(x-5) + 4 = 2$
e)	$-16 = \dfrac{x}{5} + \dfrac{x}{3}$	15	$-240 = 3x + 5x$
f)	$\dfrac{-2}{5}(x - 8) = 4$	5	$-2(x - 8) = 20$
g)	$\dfrac{y+2}{3} = \dfrac{1}{5}(2y + 3)$	15	$5(y + 2) = 3(2y + 3)$

12. a) $x = 6; \dfrac{6}{3} = 2$ **d)** $c = 36; \dfrac{36}{3} - \dfrac{36}{4} = 3$

   b) $d = -4; \dfrac{-4}{4} + 3 = 2$ **e)** $k = 22.5; \dfrac{3}{5}(22.5) - 6 = \dfrac{22.5}{3}$

   c) $x = 12; \dfrac{12}{2} + \dfrac{12}{3} = 10$ **f)** $x = 7; \dfrac{2(7) + 1}{3} = 5$

13. $\dfrac{1}{2}q + \dfrac{3}{5} = \dfrac{2}{3}q; q = \dfrac{18}{5}$, or $3\dfrac{3}{5}$

14. a) $\dfrac{1}{4}x + \dfrac{1}{3}x = 1, x = \dfrac{12}{7}$ or $1\dfrac{5}{7}$

   b) $\dfrac{1}{30}x + \dfrac{1}{60}x = 1, x = 20$ min

   c) x represents the number of hours time the jets have been in the air; $600x = 3500 - 800x; x = 2.5$.

15. $k = 2$

16. The equation simplifies to $0x = 7$. Since no value of x will multiply by zero and make 7, there is no solution to the equation.

17. The equation simplifies to $0x = 0$. Any value of x will make this equation true. Therefore, there is an infinite number of solutions. This happens because the expressions on the left and right hand of the equation are equivalent.

18. Step A: The LCD of 4 and 5 is 20. She multiplied by 20 to remove the fractions.
Step B: Jennifer eliminated the fractions by dividing 20 by 4 to get 5 and 20 by 5 to get 4. She multiplied the 20 and 2 on the right side of the equation.
Step C: Jennifer used the distributive property to simplify the left side of the equation.
Step D: Jennifer combined like terms.
Step E: Jennifer used inverse operations to group the numbers on the right side of the equation.
Step F: Jennifer added the numbers on the both sides of the equation.
Step G: Jennifer divided both sides of the equation by 28 because the operation between 28 and x is multiplication. Division is the inverse operation of multiplication.
Step H: Jennifer expressed the solution as an improper fraction in lowest terms and as a mixed number.

19. Agree: Solving an equation with variables on both sides of the equation involves using inverse operations to collect the variables on one side.
$$3x + 2 = 5x - 8$$
$$3x + 2 - 3x = 5x - 8 - 3x$$
$$2 = 2x - 8$$
$$2 + 8 = 2x - 8 + 8$$
$$10 = 2x$$
$$5 = x$$

20.

	David	Colin
Number of Quarters	q	$\dfrac{q}{3}$
Number of Dimes	$16 - q$	$2(16 - q)$
Value of Quarters (¢)	$25q$	$25\left(\dfrac{q}{3}\right)$
Value of Dimes (¢)	$10(16 - q)$	$10 \times 2(16 - q)$

David has 6 quarters and 10 dimes; Colin has 2 quarters and 20 dimes. They each have $2.50.

21. a) $x = 25$ **b)** $x = 30$ **c)** $x = 42.5$

22. a) $x = +3, x = -3$ **c)** no solution
   b) $x = 5$ or $x = -7$

23. One large candy costs $0.14 or 14 cents and one small candy costs $0.08 or 8 cents.

Mid-Chapter Review, page 228

1. a)

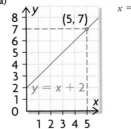

$x = 5$
$(5, 7)$
$y = x + 2$

b)

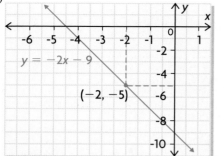

$x = -2$

$y = -2x - 9$

$(-2, -5)$

c)

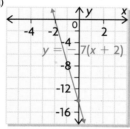

$x = 3$

$(3, 8)$

$y = 4x - 4$

d)

$x = 0$

$y = -7(x + 2)$

2. a)

Time (min)	5	10	15	20	25	30
Depth (m)	50	100	150	200	250	300

b) Answers may vary, e.g.,

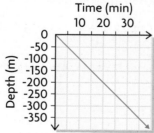

Depth of a Submarine

c) For every 5 min increase in time, there is a 50 m decrease in depth.
d) Answers may vary, e.g., $y = -219 - 10x$

e)

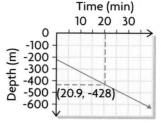

Depth of a Submarine

$-428 = -219 - 10x,$
$x = 20.9$

$(20.9, -428)$

3. a) $x = 6$ **c)** $x = -3$ **e)** $z = 0$
b) $x = 2$ **d)** $k \doteq -6.95$ **f)** $a = 5$

4. a) $8.98(b - 6)$ **c)** $53.88 = 8.98(b - 6); b = 12$
b) $17.96

5. a) $x = 6; -(6) + 6 = 0$ and $2(6) - 12 = 12 - 12 = 0$

b) $x = -1; \dfrac{2}{3}(-1) - 2 = -\dfrac{2}{3} - 2 = -2\dfrac{2}{3}$ and

$4(-1) + \dfrac{4}{3} = -4 + \dfrac{4}{3} = -\dfrac{12}{3} + \dfrac{4}{3} = -\dfrac{8}{3} = -2\dfrac{2}{3}$

c) $x = 7; 4[(7) - 8] = 4(-1) = -4$ and
$-2[(7) - 5] = -2(2) = -4$

d) $x = 0; \dfrac{2}{3}(0) - \dfrac{1}{2} = -\dfrac{1}{2}$ and $-\dfrac{1}{2} + \dfrac{1}{4}(0) = -\dfrac{1}{2}$

e) $a = \dfrac{18}{7}$ or $2\dfrac{4}{7}; \dfrac{1}{5}\left[\left(\dfrac{18}{7}\right) + 1\right] = \dfrac{1}{5} \times \dfrac{25}{7} = \dfrac{5}{7}$ and

$\dfrac{1}{3}\left[2\left(\dfrac{18}{7}\right) - 3\right] = \dfrac{1}{3}\left(\dfrac{36}{7} - 3\right) = \dfrac{1}{3} \times \dfrac{15}{7} = \dfrac{5}{7}$

f) $a = -\dfrac{24}{7}$ or $-3\dfrac{3}{7};$

$\dfrac{4\left(-\dfrac{24}{7}\right) - 2}{5} + \dfrac{1}{2} = \dfrac{-\dfrac{96}{7} - 2}{5} + \dfrac{1}{2} =$

$\dfrac{-\dfrac{110}{7}}{5} + \dfrac{1}{2} - \dfrac{22}{7} + \dfrac{1}{2} = -\dfrac{37}{14}$ and

$\dfrac{3\left(-\dfrac{24}{7}\right) + 7}{2} - 1 = \dfrac{-\dfrac{72}{7} + 7}{2} - 1 =$

$\dfrac{-\dfrac{23}{7}}{2} - 1 = -\dfrac{23}{14} - 1 = -\dfrac{37}{14}$

6. a) $k + 3 = 12, k = 9$

b) $3x - 18 = 7, x = \dfrac{25}{3}$ or $8\dfrac{1}{3}$

c) $-15g + 7 = 0, g = \dfrac{7}{15}$

d) $8h + 3 = 42, h = \dfrac{39}{8}$ or $4\dfrac{7}{8}$

7. a) $2(2x + 7) = 210$; the dimensions are 49 m by 56 m.
b) $3x + 100 = 5x + 100, x = 0$; the angles are each 100 degrees.
c) $0.25q + 0.10(117 - q) = 15.75$; 27 quarters and 90 dimes
d) $\dfrac{1}{10}t + \dfrac{1}{12}t = 1, t = 5\dfrac{5}{11}$ h or about 5.45 h

Lesson 4.4, page 235

1. a) $x = \dfrac{(5 - y)}{3}$ **b)** $y = \dfrac{(-10 - 2x)}{5}$

2. a) $3x + 2.5y = 240$, where x is the number of pairs of figure skates and y is the number of pairs of hockey skates

b) $y = -\dfrac{3}{2.5}x + 96$ or $-\dfrac{6}{5}x + 96$

c) $x = -\dfrac{2.5}{3}y + 80$ or $-\dfrac{5}{6}y + 80$

3. a) $b = 2a + 4$ **c)** $4m - 3n + 2 = 4$
b) $x + 2y = -6$

4. a) $y = 4 - 2x$

b) $y = -4 - \dfrac{2}{3}x$

c) $y = \dfrac{(5.3 - 2.8x)}{1.1}$

d) $y = \dfrac{-10}{21}x + \dfrac{55}{91}$

e) $y = \dfrac{-4}{9}x + \dfrac{8}{15}$

f) $y = -\dfrac{2}{3}x + \dfrac{14}{3}$

5. a) $n = \dfrac{(C - 25)}{0.10}$ or $n = 10C - 250$

b)

Cost C	25	50	100
Number of Minutes (n)	0	250	750

c)

$$n = \frac{(C - 5)}{0.10}$$

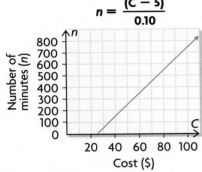

d) The independent variable in this relation is the number of minutes and the dependent variable is the cost.

e) Answers may vary, e.g., someone might want to use the cost as the independent variable if they are trying to determine how many minutes they could afford each month.

6. a) $y = -4 + \dfrac{2}{5}x$

b)

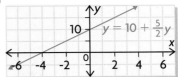

c) slope $= \dfrac{2}{5}$; x-intercept $= 10$; y-intercept $= -4$

d) $x = 10 + \dfrac{5}{2}y$

e)

$$y = 10 + \frac{5}{2}y$$

f) slope $= \dfrac{5}{2}$; x-intercept $= -4$; y-intercept $= 10$

g) The slopes are the inverse of each other. $\dfrac{5}{2}$ is the inverse of $\dfrac{2}{5}$.

7. a) $a = \dfrac{(12 + 5b)}{2}$ or $a = 6 + \dfrac{5}{2}b$

b) $n = \dfrac{(9 - 0.35m)}{2.4}$ or $n = \dfrac{15}{4} - \dfrac{7}{48}m$

c) $p = \left(\dfrac{1}{4} + \dfrac{2}{3}q\right) \div \left(\dfrac{1}{2}\right)$ or $p = \dfrac{1}{2} + \dfrac{4}{3}x$

d) $r = \dfrac{I}{pt}$

e) $L = (P - 2W) \div 2$ or $L = \dfrac{1}{2}P - W$

f) $r = \dfrac{C}{2\pi}$

8. a) $\dfrac{2A}{b} = h$ **b)** 27.5 cm

9. a) $0.10x + 0.25y = 42.50$

b) $y = \dfrac{42.50 - 0.10x}{0.25} = 170 - 0.4x$

c) $x = \dfrac{42.50 - 0.25y}{0.10} = 425 - 2.5y$

d) Answers may vary, e.g., (0, 170), (5, 168), (10, 166).

10. a) $30a + 8r = 150$

b) $a = 5 - \dfrac{4}{15}r$

c) $r = \dfrac{75 - 15a}{4} = 18.75 - 3.75a$

d) Answers may vary, e.g.,

Mass of Almonds (kg)	0.5	1	1.5	2
Mass of Raisins (kg)	16.875	15	13.125	11.25

11. Answers may vary, e.g., at least 708 digital watches and 472 analog watches should be produced.

12. a) $\dfrac{(xk + n)}{r} = w$

b) operations acting on x: multiply by k, add n, divide by r
inverse operations to isolate x: multiply by r, subtract n, divide by k

c) $x = \dfrac{(wr - n)}{k}$

d) The process is the same since rearranging an equation or formula or linear relation provides an equivalent version. But, the end result is quite different. When solving a linear equation, the result is a number. The result when rearranging for a variable is an equivalent equation, relationship or rule.

13. a) $x = \dfrac{5}{(9 - 2y)}$

b) $x = 7$ or $x = -7$

c) $x = 10$ or $x = -2$

d) $x = \dfrac{(3 + y)}{-4}$ or $x = \dfrac{-3 - y}{4}$

e) $x = 80$

f) $x = -\dfrac{1}{2}$

14. a) $h = \dfrac{SA}{2\pi r} - r$

b) 4.55 cm

c) The radius has two different exponents in the original equation, so it cannot be isolated.

Lesson 4.5, page 245

1. a) $(2, 2)$ c) $\left(\dfrac{4}{3}, \dfrac{5}{3}\right)$

b) $(2, 3)$ d) $(0, 0)$

2. a) $y = 1.20 + 0.06x$

b) $y = 0.10x$

c)

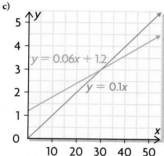

d) the break-even point

e) i) loss   ii) profit   iii) profit

3. a) $x = -\dfrac{11}{7}; y = \dfrac{19}{7}$ c) $x = \dfrac{122}{21}; y = \dfrac{19}{21}$

b) $x = -\dfrac{59}{22}; y = \dfrac{34}{11}$ d) no solution; the lines are parallel

4. a) $x + y = 42; x - y = 17$

b) Answers may vary, e.g., because the answers are not integers there is no solution.

5. 31 dimes and 27 quarters

6. a) yes   b) no   c) no   d) no

7. a)

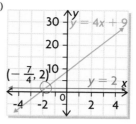

$\left(-\dfrac{7}{4}, 2\right)$

b) $2 = 4x + 9$

c) $\left(-1\dfrac{3}{4}, 2\right)$

8. a) $(1, 10)$

b) no point of intersection; the lines are parallel

c) no point of intersection; the lines are parallel

d) $(1, -4)$

9. a) $y = \dfrac{3}{4}x; y = 250 + 0.25x$; x represents the number of bottles of water purchased/sold; y represents the total amount of money either spent or made.

b) 500 bottles

10. a) Uplink: $y = 19$; Blueline:
$y = 10 + 0.59(x - 30) = 0.59x - 7.7$

b) Answers may vary, e.g., $(45, 19)$.

c) $19 = 10 + 0.59(x - 30)$. This equation is reasonable because both y values are the same at this point.

d) Answers may vary, e.g., I would tell Mr. Smith that if he plans to use less than 45 h per month, Blueline is cheaper. If he plans to use more than 45 h per month, Uplink is cheaper.

11. Answers may vary, e.g., while these companies might be initially cheaper, their cost per hour is very expensive. As the number of hours increases, the costs rise more quickly. Downlink exceeds the monthly cost of Uplink after about 12 hours of use and Redline after about 9 hours. Blueline also gives more free hours, which is a factor that should be considered.

12. a) $(0.8, 1)$ c) at about $(-0.22, 0.44)$

b) intersects everywhere on the line   d) $(2, 0)$

13. Answers may vary, e.g.,

a) $2x + y = 7$ or $y = -2x + 7$

b) $y = -x + 2$. These equations have the same slope, so they are parallel and therefore do not intersect.

14. The point of intersection is $(20, 50)$. If the customer intends to rent more than 20 movies, the customer should use Films 'R' Us. If the customer plans to rent fewer than 20 movies, the customer should use Movies to Go.

15. The solution is the point of intersection of the two lines. Two lines can intersect at most once unless they are the same line.

16. The points of intersection have the same y-value, which makes the $mx + b$ parts equal, too.

17. When solving using inverse operations, you are able to determine the exact value of the point of intersection. Graphing sometimes can only give an approximation.

18. a) $(2, 8)$ and $(-2, 8)$

b) $2x^2 = 8; x = 2, x = -2$

c) Yes. There are two points of intersection on the graph and so there must be two values that solve the equation.

Chapter Review, page 250

1. a) $y = 4x - 5$

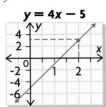

Answers may vary, e.g., $x = 2$.

b) $y = \dfrac{1}{2}x + 3$

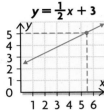

Answers may vary, e.g., $x = 4$.

c) $y = -2(x - 3)$

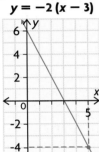

Answers may vary, e.g., $x = 5$.

d) $y = \dfrac{1}{4}\left(x + \dfrac{2}{5}\right)$

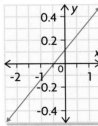

Answers may vary, e.g., $x = -\dfrac{2}{5}$.

2. a) $x = 2$ **b)** $x = -3$ **c)** $x = 5$ **d)** $x = 3$

3. a) $x = 4$ **b)** $x = 5$

4. a) $y = 15(x - 10)$

b)

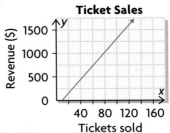

c) $y = 15(100 - 10)$; $y \doteq 1350$

d) $600 = 15(x - 10)$; $x \doteq 50$

5. a) $x = 2$ **b)** $x = 4$ **c)** $x = 5$ **d)** $x = -\dfrac{2}{5}$

6. a) $y = 15.95(x - 10)$

b) \$79.75

c) $\dfrac{y}{15.95} + 10 = x$; $x = 12$; Erynn ordered 12 CDs

7. a) $x = 6$ **b)** $x = -\dfrac{80}{153}$ **c)** $x = -10$ **d)** $x = 86$

8. $x = 2$; 2 units and 5 units, 6 units and 8 units

9. No. I substituted $x = 3$ into both sides of the equation and got different values.

10. a) $l = \dfrac{(P - 2w)}{2}$ **c)** $\dfrac{V}{\pi r^2} = h$

b) $\dfrac{(A - P)}{(Pr)} = t$ **d)** $y = \dfrac{(C - Ax)}{B}$

11. a) $32\dfrac{2}{9}\,°C$ or about $32.2\,°C$ **c)** $77\,°F$

b) $F = \dfrac{9C}{5} + 32$

12. a) $y = -3 + 2x$ **c)** $x - 3 = y$

b) $\dfrac{1}{2}x + 2 = y$ **d)** $y = 16 - 2x$

13. a) $x + 2y = 32$; x represents the number loonies, y represents the number of toonies

b) $y = \dfrac{32 - x}{2}$

c) Answers may vary. e.g., 0 loonies and 16 toonies, 2 loonies and 15 toonies, 16 loonies and 8 toonies, 10 loonies and 11 toonies

d) No. Answers may vary, e.g., the total value of the toonies is always an even number, so the number of loonies has to be an even number.

14. a) -3.5

b) $-2(-3.5) - 3 = 4$; the solution is correct.

c) $y = 4$ is a straight horizontal line, so it will have to intersect the other relation at some point. There can only be one point of intersection.

d) You could graph the lines $y = 3x - 4$ and $y = 2x + 3$. They will intersect because their slopes are not equal. Then use the graph to determine the point of intersection.

15. a)

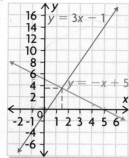

$(1.5, 3.5)$

b)

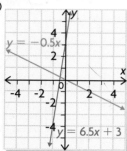

$\left(-\dfrac{3}{7}, \dfrac{3}{14}\right)$

c)

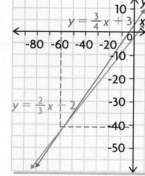

$(-60, -41)$

16. a) $y = 90 + 5x; y = 10x$

b)

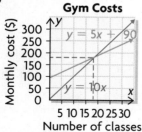

Gym Costs

c) The point of intersection is $(18, 180)$.

d) The cost for 18 classes is $180 regardless of which gym you join.

e) If you are going to take more than 18 classes a month, you should choose Faster Fitness. Any less and Drop-in Fitness is cheaper.

17. a) Video Vault: $C = 3v$

Videorenters: $C = 15 + 2v$

b) $(15, 45)$

c) In this case, the point of intersection represents the number of DVDs that have to be rented (15) to yield the same price ($45) at both video stores.

d) If a customer is going to rent more than 15 DVDs in a year, then the customer should use Videorenters. If the customer is going to rent less than 15 DVDs in a year, then the customer should use Video Vault.

Chapter Self-Test, page 252

1. a) • The table of values is valid because it shows the exact value of the expression for various values of the variable.

• The graph is valid because it shows the exact value of the expression for all values of the variable.

• The algebraic model is valid because each equation is equivalent.

b) algebraic model

2. a) $a = 1$ **b)** $x = -2$ **c)** $x = \dfrac{6}{5}$ **d)** $x = \dfrac{1}{3}$

3. a) $y = \dfrac{(6 + 3x)}{2}$ or $y = \dfrac{3}{2}x + 3$

b) $\dfrac{(y - 2)}{3} = x$

4. a) Answers may vary. e.g., 7 h at the $14/h job and 82 h at the $11/h job; 18 h at the $14/h job and 68 h at the $11/h job.

b)

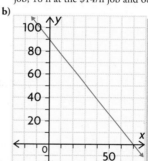

5. a) $(1, -2)$ **b)** $(-1.4, 2.2)$

6. 2000 linear feet

Chapter 5

Getting Started, page 256

1. a) viii   **c)** i   **e)** ii   **g)** v

b) vii   **d)** iii   **f)** iv   **h)** vi

2. a) $\dfrac{5}{-3} = \dfrac{-5}{3}$ **b)** $\dfrac{4}{11}$ **c)** $\dfrac{-3}{10}$ **d)** $\dfrac{2}{3}$

3. a) $b = \dfrac{V}{h}$ **c)** $w = \dfrac{P}{2} - l$ **e)** $r = \dfrac{I}{Pt}$

b) $y = \dfrac{-3}{5}x + 3$ **d)** $d = vt$ **f)** $x = \dfrac{-2}{5}y + 4$

4. Line PT is parallel to line RU $(PT \parallel RU)$.

Line QV is perpendicular to line PT $(QV \perp PT)$.

Line QV is perpendicular to line RU $(QV \perp RU)$.

5. a) $x = 7$ **b)** $m = -15$ **c)** $p = 4$ **d)** $t = 1$

6. a) linear; for each unit increase in x, there is an increase of 7.5 in y or the degree of the variables is 1

b) nonlinear; first differences in table of values are not constant or the degree of the variables is not 1

c) linear; first difference in table of values are constant $(= -2)$ or the degree of the variables is 1

7. a)

x	y
−2	−7
−1	−3
0	1
1	5
2	9

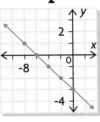

$y = 4x + 1$

b)

x	y
−8	1
−6	0
−4	−1
−2	−2
0	−3

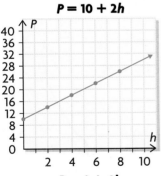

$y = -\dfrac{1}{2}x - 3$

8. a) $x = \dfrac{4}{5}$; $y = 4$ **b)** $x = -7$; $y = -2$

9. a) \$55   **b)** \$0.04   **c)** equal   **d)** \$0.04/flyer

10. a) Herteises: $P = 10 + 2h$; Farids: $P = 6 + 4h$

b)

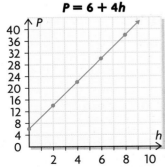

$P = 10 + 2h$

$P = 6 + 4h$

c) earns more money if babysits for Farids longer than 2 hours, else select Herteises

11. a) disagree; could look for first differences in a table of values without graphing

b) agree, the line is extended to both ends so it passes through 2 or more quadrants

c) agree, vertical lines have an equation $x = a$, where a is a number. Therefore all points (x, y) have $x = a$.

d) disagree, consider two lines passing through the origin. One line can have a large negative slope and the other can have a small negative slope and be 45° apart.

Lesson 5.1, page 263

1. a) iii   **c)** iv   **e)** i
    b) vi   **d)** ii   **f)** v

2. i) a) steepest: $y = -\dfrac{15}{2}x + 3$ **b)** steepest: $y = 3x - 9$

least steep: $y = -\dfrac{1}{2}x - 7$ least steep: $y = \dfrac{1}{3}x + 1$

ii) a)

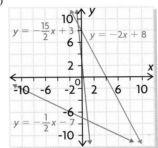

b)

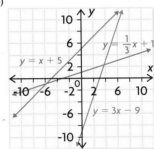

3. a) $y = 0$ **b)** $x = 0$

Lesson 5.2, page 269

1. $y = -\dfrac{5}{6}x - \dfrac{5}{2}$

2. a) $3s + 4c = 48$ **b)** 16, 12, 8, 4, or 0 stools.

3. a) $y = \dfrac{4}{3}x - 8$; slope $= \dfrac{4}{3}$; y-intercept $= -8$

b) $y = -\dfrac{2}{5}x + 3$; slope $= -\dfrac{2}{5}$; y-intercept $= 3$

c) $y = \dfrac{1}{2}x - \dfrac{7}{3}$; slope $= \dfrac{1}{2}$; y-intercept $= -\dfrac{7}{3}$

d) $y = -\dfrac{8}{5}x$; slope $= -\dfrac{8}{5}$; y-intercept $= 0$

e) $y = -\dfrac{4}{7}x + \dfrac{11}{7}$; slope $= -\dfrac{4}{7}$; y-intercept $= \dfrac{11}{7}$

f) $y = -\dfrac{8}{5}x - 2$; slope $= -\dfrac{8}{5}$; y-intercept $= -2$

4. a)

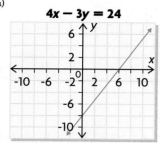

4x − 3y = 24

b)

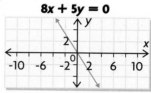

2x + 5y = 15

c)

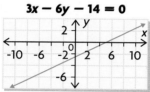

3x − 6y − 14 = 0

d)

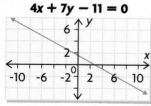

8x + 5y = 0

e)

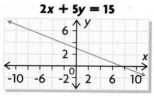

4x + 7y − 11 = 0

f)

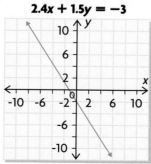

2.4x + 1.5y = −3

5. a) i) fall (slope is negative) **iv)** fall (slope is negative)
 ii) rise (slope is positive) **v)** rise (slope is positive)
 iii) fall (slope is negative) **vi)** rise (slope is positive)

b) i)

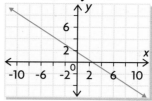

2x + 3y = 5

ii)

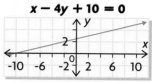

x − 4y + 10 = 0

iii)

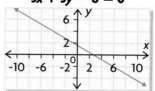

3x + 5y − 8 = 0

iv)

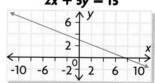

2x + 5y = 15

v)

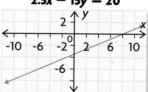

2.5x − 15y = 20

vi)

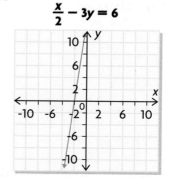

$$\dfrac{x}{2} - 3y = 6$$

6. a) $d = \dfrac{-4}{3}t + 3$; d-intercept $= 3$; slope $= \dfrac{-4}{3}$

b) $d = \dfrac{1}{4}h - 2$; d-intercept $= -2$; slope $= \dfrac{1}{4}$

c) $d = \dfrac{5}{6}k + \dfrac{5}{2}$; d-intercept $= \dfrac{5}{2}$; slope $= \dfrac{5}{6}$

7. a) $2l + 4w = 40$

b) Answers may vary, e.g., $l = -2w + 20$ or $w = 10 - \dfrac{1}{2}l$.

c)

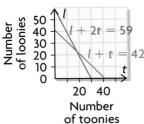

$l = -2w + 20$

d) Answers may vary, e.g.,

w	2	4	5
l	16	12	10

8. a) $12j + 21a = 18$ **c)** 1062.5 g

b) $j = \dfrac{-7a + 6}{4} = \dfrac{-7a}{4} + \dfrac{3}{2}$ **d)** 1325 g

9. a) total number of coins: $l + t = 41$; total value: $l + 2t = 59$

b)

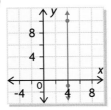

c) $(t, l) = (18, 23)$

d) The intersection is the one point that satisfies both equations.

10.

Chocolate Chip Batches	Oatmeal Batches
0	12
2	9
4	6
6	3
8	0

11. a) $0.9t + 0.6n = 6$, where t is the number of textbooks and n is the number of notebooks.

b) $t = \dfrac{-2}{3}n + \dfrac{20}{3}$ or $n = \dfrac{-3}{2}t + 10$

c)

Textbooks (t)	0	2	4	6
Notebooks (n)	10	7	4	1

12. a) $3x - 8y + 5 = 0$ can be solved for y and gives $y = \dfrac{3}{8}x + \dfrac{5}{8}$, so they must be the same line.

b) No. $2x + 3y + 1 = 0$ equals $y = \dfrac{-2}{3}x - \dfrac{1}{3}$.

13. a) Answers may vary, e.g., as Punitha's tutor, I would ensure Punitha was comfortable manipulating an equation (isolating variables and knowing what each component of the equation represented).

b) You can find all characteristics of a line from any linear equation form; the intercepts, the slope, and so on.

14. both are equivalent to $2x - 3y + 7 = 0$

15. a) i) slope $= \dfrac{-3}{4}$ **ii)** slope $= \dfrac{-2}{5}$ **iii)** slope $= \dfrac{4}{3}$

y-intercept $= 2$ y-intercept $= \dfrac{9}{5}$ y-intercept $= 4$

b) i) $-\dfrac{A}{B}$ **ii)** $-\dfrac{C}{B}$

Lesson 5.3, page 278

1. a) 1   **b)** -6

2. $y = 7$

3. a) $-\dfrac{13}{6}$ **c)** undefined   **e)** $-\dfrac{2}{3}$

b) 1   **d)** 0   **f)** 15

4. a) Answers may vary, e.g., $(6, 4)$.

b) Answers may vary, e.g., $(5, 13)$.

c) Answers may vary, e.g., $(3, 1)$.

d) Answers may vary, e.g., $(10, 5)$.

5. Slopes are not equal.

6. a) yes   **b)** no   **c)** no   **d)** yes

7. a)

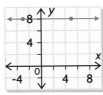

b) $m = 0$ **c)** The slope of a horizontal line is 0.

8. a)

b) slope is undefined

c) The slope of a vertical line is undefined.

9. a) horizontal; a horizontal line does not "rise"

b) vertical; a vertical line does not "run"

10. If the x-coordinates are the same, the line is vertical. If the y-coordinates are the same, the line is horizontal. If no coordinates are the same, the line is slanted.

11. Answer may vary, e.g., slopes close to -1 are reasonable.

12. 15 km/h

13. a)

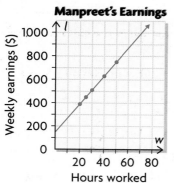

Manpreet's Earnings

b) \$12/h

c) 62.5 h without overtime. 55 h at time and one half above 40 h.

d) Answers may vary, e.g., unlikely since the average work week is 40 h.

14. \$13 125/year

15. a) No   **b)** 1080 cm or 10.8 m

16. a) Snowbowl: 852 ft; Bear Claw: 4800 ft; The Vortex: 3400 ft

    b) Bear Claw, The Vortex, Snowbowl

17. \$15/person

18. $k = 5$

19. From the top, clockwise: undefined; between 1 and positive infinity, 1; between 0 and 1; 0; between 0 and -1; -1; between -1 and negative infinity

20. a) $k = -2$

    b) A(7, -2); C(13, 7)

    c) Any other value of k will make the three points non-collinear. Answers may vary, e.g., $k = 0$

21. a) $y = 5x + 2$ **c)** $y = \frac{2}{3}x$ **e)** $y = -2$

    b) $y = -4x + 13$ **d)** $x = 2$

Mid-Chapter Review, page 283

1.

	Slope	y-intercept
a)	4	-5
b)	-2	3
c)	$\frac{3}{7}$	$-\frac{2}{3}$

2. a) falling to the right   **c)** horizontal   **e)** rising to the right

    b) horizontal   **d)** vertical   **f)** rising to the right

3. a) $y = 7$ **b)** $y = \frac{2}{3}x - 7$ **c)** $y = -\frac{1}{5}x + 8$

    $y = x$ $y = 2.5x - 3.7$ $y = -2x + 4$

    $x = 2$ $y = \frac{9}{2}x + 4$ $y = -6x - \frac{5}{8}$

4. a) $y = 7$ is horizontal, which is flat; $x = 2$ is vertical, which represents a cliff.

b) Bunny Hills

$y = \frac{2}{3}x - 7$

$y = -\frac{1}{5}x + 8$

Intermediate Hills

$y = x$

Double Black Diamond Hills

$y = -2x + 4$

$y = 2.5x - 3.7$

$y = \frac{9}{2}x + 4$

$y = -6x - \frac{5}{8}$

5. a)

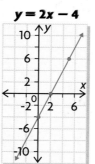

$y = 2x - 4$

c)

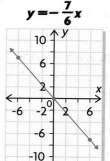

$y = -\frac{7}{6}x$

b)

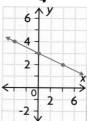

$y = \frac{1}{4}x + 3$

6. a) $y = 2x - 5$ **c)** $y = \frac{1}{4}x - \frac{5}{4}$ **e)** $y = -4x + 9$

    b) $y = \frac{-1}{2}x - 2$ **d)** $y = 0x + 10$ **f)** $y = \frac{2}{3}x + \frac{1}{3}$

7. a) $8x + 12y = 100$, where x is the number of movie tickets and y is the number of concert tickets.

    b) $y = \frac{-2}{3}x + \frac{25}{3}$

    c)

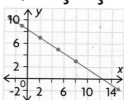

$y = -\frac{2}{3}x + \frac{25}{3}$

    d)

Movie	2	5	8	11
Concert	7	5	3	1

8. a) 2   **c)** $\frac{2}{3}$ **e)** $-\frac{3}{4}$

    b) -3 **d)** $\frac{1}{5}$ **f)** 0

9. a) $-\dfrac{1}{2}$ **c)** -1 **e)** 0

   b) $\dfrac{11}{10}$ **d)** $\dfrac{5}{3}$ **f)** undefined

10. a) no   **b)** no   **c)** yes   **d)** no

11. a) $k = -\dfrac{18}{5}$ or -3.6 **c)** $k = 4$

   b) $k = 1$ **d)** $k = \dfrac{38}{5}$ or 7.6

12. $15 per person
13. 89 km/h

Lesson 5.4, page 290

1. a) $y = 3x + 5$ **b)** $5; 1$
2. a) iii   **b)** iv   **c)** i   **d)** ii
3. a) $y = -2x + 12$ **b)** $y = 3x - 6$
4. a) $y = -5x + 3$ **b)** $\dfrac{4}{3}; -2$ **c)** $y = 2$ **d)** $\dfrac{1}{2}; 0$

5. a) $y = 3x + 5$ **c)** $y = -\dfrac{5}{3}x$ **e)** $y = \dfrac{1}{4}x - 2$

   b) $y = 5$ **d)** $y = -\dfrac{5}{2}x + 3$ **f)** $y = \dfrac{2}{3}x + \dfrac{1}{3}$

6. a) -11 **b)** 11 **c)** -6
7. a) $\dfrac{1}{2}$ **b)** $\dfrac{-4}{3}$ **c)** $\dfrac{-1}{8}$

8. a) $y = \dfrac{-8}{9}x + 4$ **c)** $y = \dfrac{3}{4}x - 3$

   b) $y = \dfrac{1}{5}x - \dfrac{28}{5}$ **d)** $x = 6$

9. a) $x = 1$ **c)** $y = 7$ **e)** $x = 0$

   b) $y = \dfrac{15}{8}x + 12$ **d)** $y = \dfrac{5}{6}x + 13$ **f)** $y = \dfrac{1}{10}x - \dfrac{1}{2}$

10. $y = \dfrac{3}{10}x + 3$

11. a) $y = -110x + 680$, where x is the time in hours and y is the distance from home in kilometres.

   b) The slope of -110 means that the distance is decreasing at a rate of 110 km/h. The y-intercept of 680 means they began their trip 680 km from home.

12. a) maximum heart rate in a stress test for a newborn baby

   b) the rate of decline of maximum heart rate in a stress test over the years

   c) $y = \dfrac{-4}{5}x + 184$

   d) about 173 beats/min

13. a) $C = 0.50t + 12$, where C is the total cost, in dollars, and t is the number of ride tickets purchased.

   b) $C = 21$, where C is the total cost, in dollars.

   c) Answers may vary, e.g., since 25 tickets cost $24.50, she should buy the ride pass.

   d) $4

14. a) $B = 0.1d + 21.50$, where B is the total bill and d is the number of songs downloaded.

   b) $B = 0.1(21) + 21.50 = 23.60$, so the third point also satisfies the equation.

   c) Answers may vary, e.g., if she downloads more than 25 songs per month on average she should not change companies.

   d) Answers may vary, e.g., if she averages 35 downloads or more per month then she should consider changing to Digital Beats.

15. Barb is correct. The slope and y-intercept can be determined from any two pieces of information, such as two points, or the x- and y-intercepts.

16. $y = 2x - 4$

17. a) Substitute the coordinates into the slope formula $\dfrac{y - q}{x - p} = m$ then isolate y.

   b) $y = 3(x - 1) + 2$, which simplifies to $y = 3x - 1$

   c) $y = 3x - 1$

   d) i) $y = 5(x - 4) - 6$ or $y = 5(x - 5) - 1$; both simplify to $y = 5x - 26$

     ii) $y = \dfrac{2}{3}(x - 3) - 1$ or $y = \dfrac{2}{3}(x - 9) + 3$; both simplify to $y = \dfrac{2}{3}x - 3$

     iii) $y = -4(x - 4) + 5$ or $y = -4(x - 3) + 9$; both simplify to $y = -4x + 21$

Lesson 5.5, page 302

1. a) Answers may vary, e.g., $y = -\dfrac{3}{2}x - 9$.

   b) Answers may vary, e.g., $y = \dfrac{2}{3}x + 9$.

2. a, g, and f are parallel; perpendicular pairs: b and e, c and h

3. a) perpendicular   **c)** neither   **e)** parallel

   b) perpendicular   **d)** parallel   **f)** neither

4. PQ is parallel to KL; AB $\perp$ PQ; AB $\perp$ KL; GH $\perp$ UV.

5. Perpendicular; one line is horizontal and one line is vertical, so they are perpendicular lines.

6. a) $y = 4$

   b) $y = -8$

   c) horizontal line equation has the form: $y = y$-coordinate of point through which it passes

7. a) $x = -9$

   b) $x = 6$

   c) vertical line equation has the form: $x = x$-coordinate of point through which it passes

8. a) $y = 3x - 14$ **c)** $y = \dfrac{-3}{2}x + 3$

   b) $y = \dfrac{-1}{3}x - 4$ **d)** $y = \dfrac{-3}{2}x + 6$

9. $y = \dfrac{-3}{4}x - 3$

10. $y = \dfrac{-5}{2}x + \dfrac{25}{2}$

11. a) yes   **b)** no

12. $m_{AB} = -\dfrac{4}{7}$ $m_{AC} = \dfrac{7}{4}$ $m_{CD} = -\dfrac{4}{7}$ $m_{DB} = \dfrac{7}{4}$

AB is perpendicular to AC and to DB.
CD is perpendicular to AC and to DB.
The quadrilateral ABDC has four right angles, so it must be a rectangle.

13. $m_{EF} = -\dfrac{7}{4}$ $m_{FG} = -\dfrac{1}{6}$ $m_{GH} = -\dfrac{7}{4}$ $m_{HE} = -\dfrac{1}{6}$

EF and GH are parallel.
FG and HE are parallel.
No sides are perpendicular.
The quadrilateral EFGH is a parallelogram but not a rectangle.

14. 795 cm
15. a) -4.5 **b)** 1.5

16. A line perpendicular to $y = \dfrac{3}{4}x + 2$ has a slope of $\dfrac{-4}{3}$ and a line parallel to $y = \dfrac{4}{5}x - 8$ has a slope of $\dfrac{4}{5}$. A single line cannot have both of these slopes.

17. **a)** Answers may vary, e.g., C(2, 5) and D(−1, −1).
    b) Answers may vary, e.g., C(6, 0) and D(3, −6).
    c) Answers may vary, e.g., C(−2, 4) and D(−5, −2).

18. $m_{AM} = -3$ and $m_{BC} = \dfrac{1}{3}$ and $m_{AM} \times m_{BC} = -1$

19. $m_{AC} = -2$ and $m_{BC} = \dfrac{1}{2}$ and $m_{AC} \times m_{BC} = -1$

Chapter Review, page 309

1. **a)** 3; 4   **b)** $\dfrac{-2}{5}$; −6.8   **c)** 9.7; −1.11   **d)** 0; 3

2. **a)** $y = \dfrac{1}{3}x - 2$; $y = x + 8$; $y = 2x - 4$

    b) $y = -\dfrac{1}{3}x + 5$; $y = -\dfrac{5}{2}x + 3$; $y = -8x - 2$

3.

	Equation	Rises to the Right	Falls to the Right
a)	$y = 4x + 5$	✓	
b)	$y = -\dfrac{2}{3}x - 8$		✓
c)	$y = -2.8x + 4$		✓
d)	$y = \dfrac{21}{8}x$	✓	
e)	$y = 1.5x + 4.5$	✓	

4. **a)** $\dfrac{3}{4}$; $\dfrac{9}{4}$ **b)** 5; −12   **c)** $\dfrac{-1}{3}$; $\dfrac{16}{3}$ **d)** −4; 2

5. **a)** Evan: $10d + 5s = 255$; Sara: $10d + 5s = 230$, where d is the number of double driveways and s is the number of single driveways.
    b) Evan: $s = -2d + 51$; Sara: $s = -2d + 46$
    c) Evan: 31; Sara: 26

6. **a)** $\dfrac{9}{8}$ **c)** −3   **e)** $-\dfrac{2}{3}$
    b) 0   **d)** undefined   **f)** $\dfrac{4}{3}$

7. **a)** −1   **b)** $-\dfrac{3}{4}$ **c)** $-\dfrac{5}{2}$ **d)** $\dfrac{13}{6}$

8. 2

9. 21 km/h

10. **a)** $y = 12$ **c)** $y = \dfrac{2}{3}x + 8$ **e)** $y = \dfrac{1}{5}x - 8$
    b) $y = \dfrac{-5}{2}x + 4$ **d)** $x = 4$

11. **a)** $y = \dfrac{-3}{4}x + \dfrac{27}{2}$ **c)** $y = -4x + 17$ **e)** $y = \dfrac{1}{3}x + \dfrac{7}{3}$
    b) $y = \dfrac{-16}{3}x + 5$ **d)** $x = 5$

12. A is on the line, B is not on the line.

13. **a)** neither   **c)** perpendicular   **e)** perpendicular
    b) parallel   **d)** neither   **f)** perpendicular

14. **a)** $y = \dfrac{7}{2}x + 2$ **b)** $y = 4x + 2$ **c)** $y = \dfrac{-9}{4}x + 6$

15. **a)** yes
    b) Answers may vary, e.g.,

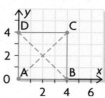

    c) $m_{AC} = 1$, $m_{BD} = -1$. $1 \times -1 = -1$, so the diagonals are perpendicular.
    d) Using A(1, 0), B(0, 1), C(−1, 0), and D(0, −1), one diagonal is horizontal and one is vertical, so they are perpendicular. The diagonals of a square are perpendicular.

Chapter Self-Test, page 311

1. B.
2. D.
3. C.
4. A.
5. B.
6.

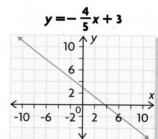

$$y = -\dfrac{4}{5}x + 3$$

7. No, since $m_{AB} \neq m_{BC}$

8. −3

9. **a)** $8a + 6s = 2200$, where a is the number of adult tickets and s is the number of student tickets.
    b) $a = \dfrac{-3}{4}s + 275$ **c)** 275   **d)** 164

10. $y = \dfrac{4}{5}x + 11$

11. **a)** $C = 0.92d + 67$, where C is the total cost and d is the number of CDs produced.
    b) \$435

12. $y = \dfrac{5}{3}x + 1$

13. Answers may vary, e.g.,

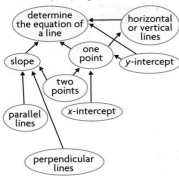

Chapter 6

Getting Started, page 316

1. a) v **c)** ii **e)** iii
b) i **d)** vi **f)** iv

2. a) $y = \frac{2}{3}x + 4$ **b)** $y = -2x - 2.5$

3. a) $y = -\frac{3}{5}x + 5$ **b)** $y = 1.8x - 19$

4. a) $y = -\frac{3}{4}x + \frac{7}{4}$
b) $y = -2x + 18$

5. a) $y = \frac{1}{3}x - 2$ **b)** $y = -x - 2$

6. a)

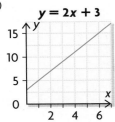

b)

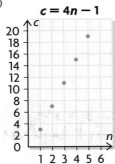

7. a) $y = \frac{1}{2}x - 1$
b) the depth or height of the seed at time $t = 0$
c) 1 cm every 2 days
d) the time when the seedling reaches the surface of the ground
e) depths below ground level; heights above ground level

8. a) Vintage car: The value increases with age. Newer car: The value decreases with age.
b) about $5000
c) around 1985

9. a) Each figure has four more shapes than the previous figure.
b)

Figure Number (n)	1	2	3	4	5
Number of Circles (c)	3	7	11	15	19

c) $c = 4n - 1$
d) 4
e) Yes. The number of shapes increases by the same amount for each figure and the first difference is a constant 4.
f)

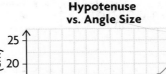

10. Calculating the length of the hypotenuse for each case produces a set of data in which first differences are not constant. The resulting graph is nonlinear.

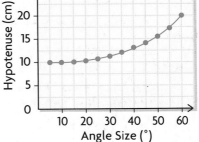

Angle (°)	Height (cm)	Hypotenuse (cm)
5	0.9	10.0
10	1.8	10.2
15	2.7	10.4
20	3.6	10.6
25	4.8	11.1
30	5.8	11.6
35	7.0	12.2
40	8.4	13.1
45	10	14.1
50	11.9	15.5
55	14.3	17.4
60	17.3	20.0

11. Answers may vary, e.g.,

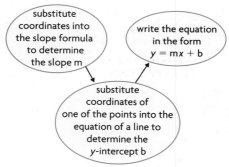

Lesson 6.1, page 326

1. **a)** Hours Spent Watching TV; Math Mark
   b) Time, e.g., time is usually the independent variable.
   c) A student watches TV for 2 hours and has a mark of 65.
2. **a)** A: On a day when the temperature was 30 °C, 376 bottles of water were sold. B: On a day when the temperature was 23 °C, 32 bottles of water were sold.
   b) Sales of bottled water tend to increase when the temperature increases.
3. **a)** independent variable: age of tractor; dependent variable: value of tractor
   b) continuous; solid line
   c) Yes. Newer tractors tend to be worth more than older tractors.
4. **a)** independent variable: Height of Father; dependent variable: Height of Grade 9 Boy
   b) continuous
   c) solid line

d)

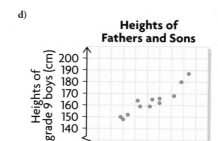

e) Yes. Taller fathers tend to have taller sons.
f) Yes. Answers may vary, e.g., maybe the tendency to be taller or shorter is inherited.

5. **a)**

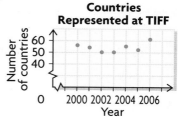

b) Answers may vary, e.g., the number of countries represented has been fairly constant.
c)

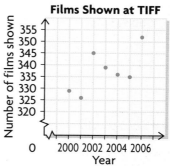

d) Answers may vary, e.g., overall there has been an increase in the number of films screened, although there have been years when the number has decreased.
e) discrete; dashed

6. **a)**

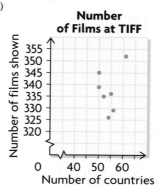

b) Answers may vary, e.g., I couldn't decide which to choose but I remembered that *x* was usually in the left-hand column of a data table, so I chose Number of countries as the independent variable and Number of films shown as the dependent variable.

c) There are no clear trends in the scatter plot.

7. a)

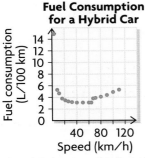

Fuel Consumption for a Hybrid Car

Fuel consumption (L/100 km) vs *Speed (km/h)*

b) The car's fuel consumption decreases rapidly until about 20 km/h, is fairly constant until about 70 km/h, then increases steadily as speed increases.

c) Yes. Answers may vary, e.g., it makes sense that a car uses more fuel at higher speeds.

d) Yes. Drive at moderate speeds to save fuel.

e) Answers may vary, e.g., people who own a hybrid car could determine what speed consumes less fuel.

f) continuous

g) Speed. Answers may vary, e.g., I thought that the amount of fuel used would depend on the speed at which you were driving.

8. a)

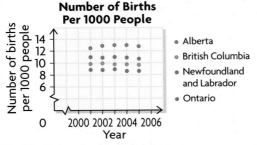

Number of Births Per 1000 People

Number of births per 1000 people vs *Year*

- Alberta
- British Columbia
- Newfoundland and Labrador
- Ontario

b) Yes. The birthrate is approximately constant.

9. a) The data generally go in one direction or another.

b) Use a solid line for continuous variables; use a dashed line for discrete variables.

10. a) I chose Age group to be the independent variable because times and ages aren't affected by other variables.

b)

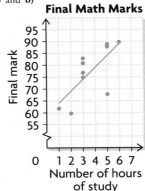

Car Accidents by Age Group

Number of car accidents vs *Age group*

c) Answers may vary, e.g., the number of accidents peaks in the 25–34 age group.

d) Yes. A dashed line because the data is discrete.

e) No. Answers may vary, e.g., we don't know the total number of younger drivers and the total number of older drivers. It is possible that there are more younger drivers than older drivers. If we knew the total numbers, we could calculate the percentage of younger drivers and the percentage of older people who have had accidents.

Lesson 6.2, page 337

1. a) about $56 000
  b) about 28

2. a) and **b)**

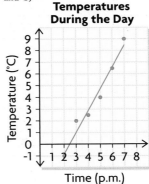

Temperatures During the Day

Temperature (°C) vs *Time (p.m.)*

  c) $y = 1.9x - 4.5$
  d) about 6 °C
  e) about 6:45 p.m.

3. a) and **b)**

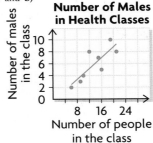

Number of Males in Health Classes

Number of males in the class vs *Number of people in the class*

  c) about 6
  d) about 12

4. a) and **b)**

Final Math Marks

Final mark vs *Number of hours of study*

c) $y = 5x + 59$

d) about 79

e) about 2.4 h

f) Yes. Students who study more tend to achieve higher marks.

5. a) 1013; 610

b) about 11 days

c) no

6. a) $y = 0.13x - 0.66$ with distance as the independent variable

b) about 22 s

c) No. For such a long race, a runner cannot keep the same pace as in the shorter races for which we have data.

d) Answers may vary, e.g., the slope of the line of best fit is related to Tomas's average speed.

7. a) 4

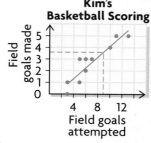

Kim's Basketball Scoring

b) 11

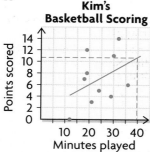

Kim's Basketball Scoring

8. a) Use a transparent ruler. Choose the slope of the ruler so that it follows the pattern of the data. Balance the plotted points on each side of the ruler.

b) Choose two points on the line, read off the coordinates, find the slope and the y-intercept.

c) Answers may vary, e.g., I could extend the line (if necessary) and then construct vertical and horizontal lines in the right places in order to read the value at the point of intersection.

9. a) and **c)**

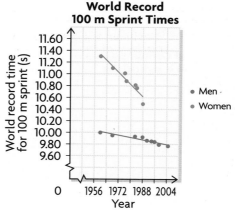

World Record 100 m Sprint Times

b) For both sets of data, the world record time is decreasing. However, the record time for women seems to be decreasing slightly more rapidly.

d) Yes. Maybe around the year 2025.

e) No. First, the women's world record has not changed for many years, so future changes may not follow the same line of best fit. Second, it could be that changes for both men and women will become much more gradual because of human limitations. If the trends continued forever, the record times would eventually be negative, which is impossible.

Mid-Chapter Review, page 343

1. a)

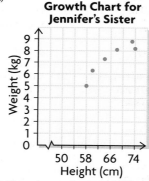

Growth Chart for Jennifer's Sister

b) The points can be connected by a solid line because Jennifer's sister always has a height and a weight.

c) Yes. The general trend is that as the height increases, so does the weight.

2. a)

Births at Cook's Mills Hospital

b) There is no clear pattern.

c) Possibly. This data set is probably too small to draw any solid conclusions from.

3. No. The points are not balanced on either side of the line.

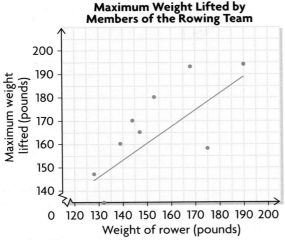

Maximum Weight Lifted by Members of the Rowing Team

4. **a)** and **b)**

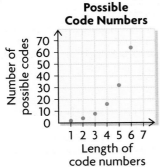

Loudness Levels

c) $y = 0.3x + 0.8$

d) 1.9 using the line of best fit

e) 11 s

5. No. If they drew their lines by eye, they most likely ended up with different lines. The equations of the different lines would be different, but they would be close in value.

Lesson 6.3, page 349

1. **a)**

Possible Code Numbers

b)

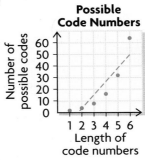

Possible Code Numbers

c)

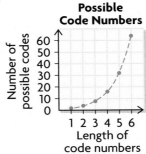

Possible Code Numbers

d) curve

e) Neither, since code numbers have a whole number of digits.

2. **a)** and **b)** Answers may vary, e.g.,

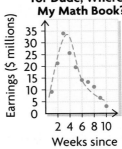

Weekly Earnings for Dude, Where's My Math Book?

A dashed curve, because the data is discrete.

c) No. The figures are only released on a weekly basis.

d) No. Answers may vary, e.g., there's a good chance that the movie will not be playing after 20 weeks.

3. **a)** and **b)**

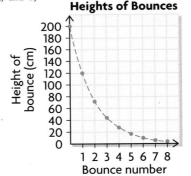

Heights of Bounces

Dashed curve. The data represents the peak height after each bounce, not any in-between heights.

c) No. The data are discrete.
d) Yes. You could extrapolate up to a certain point. But eventually, the ball will stop moving.

4. a) and b)

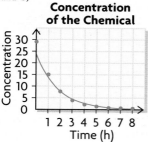

Concentration of the Chemical

Solid, since you could measure the concentration at any moment.

c) The concentration decreases quickly at first, then decreases more gradually.
d) about 2.3 h
e) about 0.2 mg/L

5. a) and b)

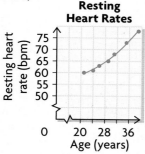

Resting Heart Rates

Solid, because the variables are continuous.

c) Resting heart rate increases as age increases.
d) Yes. The variables are continuous.
e) No. It's not wise to extrapolate far outside the range of the data.

6.

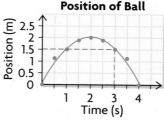

Position of Ball

a) about 0.6 m
b) about 4 s

7.

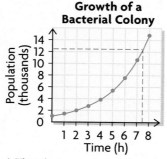

Growth of a Bacterial Colony

a) The colony grows more and more rapidly as time passes.
b) about 12 600

8. a) and b)

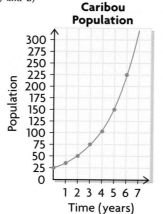

Caribou Population

The data points seem to follow a curve.

c) The herd's population grew gradually at first, then at an increasing pace.
d) about 325

9. a) and b)

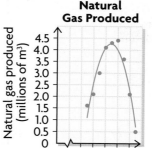

Natural Gas Produced

The plotted points seem to fall on a curve.

c) Production increases for the first 5 years or so, reaches a peak for a couple of years, then falls to near zero.
d) around 2017

10. a)

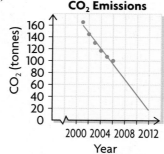

CO$_2$ Emissions

About 18 tonnes

b) The estimate using a line is much lower. The curve seems more reliable, since the plotted points seem to lie on a curve rather than on a line.

11. a) If the plotted points seem to lie on a simple curve, then a curve of best fit may be more appropriate. Otherwise, a line of best fit may be better.
b) Use horizontal and vertical guidelines to help you read values off the axes.
c) Use your judgement. It's not wise to extrapolate too far outside the range of the data.

12. a) yes   **b)** no   **c)** about 5.8%

13. a)

Length, L (m)	Squared Period, P^2 (s)
0.1	0.41
0.2	0.81
0.3	1.21
0.4	1.61
0.5	2.02
0.6	2.40
0.7	2.89
0.8	3.24
0.9	3.61
1.0	4.04

b) and c)

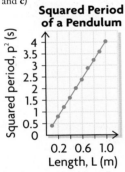

Squared Period of a Pendulum

d) m = 4
e) about 9.87
f) Answers may vary, e.g.,

Length, L (m)	Period, P (s)	Squared Period, P^2 (s^2)
0.1	0.60	0.36
0.2	0.93	0.86
0.3	1.14	1.30
0.4	1.20	1.44
0.5	1.35	1.82
0.6	1.45	2.10
0.7	1.74	3.03
0.8	1.80	3.24
0.9	1.87	3.50
1.0	2.06	4.24

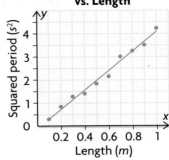

Squared Period vs. Length

Slope = 4.13

Since slope = $\dfrac{4\pi^2}{g}$, $g = \dfrac{4\pi^2}{slope}$

$g \doteq \dfrac{4(3.14)^2}{4.13} \doteq 9.6 m/s^2$

14. a)

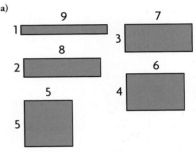

b)

Length (m)	1	2	3	4	5
Width (m)	9	8	7	6	5
Area (m^2)	9	16	21	24	25

c)

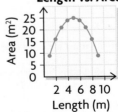

Length vs. Area

d) 5 m by 5 m
e) $A = l(10 - w)$

Lesson 6.4, page 361

1. a) People who tend to do well in math also do well in science, so math marks increase as science marks increase.

b) and c)

Math Marks and Science Marks

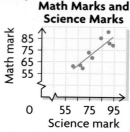

On my scatter plot, science marks increase as math marks increase, so the graph supports my conjecture.

2. a) and b)

Heights of Mothers and Their Children

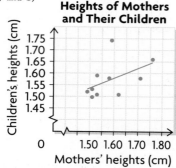

c) Yes. Although there are a few outliers, it seems that there is a slight increase in daughter height as mother height increases.

3. If the data were plotted, the line of best fit would have a positive slope. The positive slope means that as age increases, so vocabulary size increases.

4. a) Answers may vary, e.g., the greater the initial speed, the longer the stopping distance.

b)

Stopping Distances

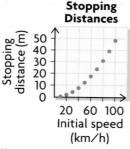

c) Yes. My scatter plot shows that the greater the initial speed of the car, the greater the stopping distance.

5. a) If it is possible to draw a line of best fit, and the interpretation of the line of best fit matches the hypothesis, then the data supports the hypothesis.

b) If it is not possible to draw a line of best fit, or if the line of best fit contradicts the hypothesis, then the data does not support the hypothesis.

c) Yes. They may draw different lines of best fit, or one person may judge that it is not possible to draw a line of best fit.

6. a) upward sloping
b) Not necessarily. It is possible that one variable influences the other. It's also possible that neither influences the other.

Lesson 6.5, page 368

1. a) iii   **b)** i   **c)** iv   **d)** ii

2. a) The ATV is stopped from 20 s–26 s. Its slowest speed while actually moving is from 8 s–16 s. Its fastest speed is from 26 s–32 s.
b) The ATV begins to return to its starting point at the 26 s mark, and reaches its starting point at the 32 s mark.
c) The slope of the graph between 20 s and 26 s is 0 m/s.
d) A zero slope (0 m/s) means that the object is not moving during a particular time interval.

3. Answers may vary, e.g., Jim ran to the library to return some overdue books. He then started to walk home. On his way home he called on his friend and he stayed at his house for a while playing video games. He left and ran home so he wouldn't be late for dinner.

4. a) nonlinear relationship
b) Answers may vary, e.g.,

Time (s)	Distance (m)	First Differences
0	0	
1	9	9
2	37	28
3	84	47
4	150	66
5	235	85
6	335	100
7	455	120

c) Since the first differences are increasing, the dragster is speeding up or accelerating down the track.
d) Assuming that the parachute slows the drag racer to a complete stop.

Distance from Start vs. Time

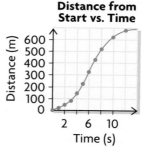

5. a) Answers may vary, e.g., Martina started to walk to school from home. She turned around and went back to her home because she felt ill. She rested at home while her mom called the doctor. She went to the doctor's office, was examined, and then returned home.
b) Answers may vary, e.g., Joe kicks his soccer ball. Its height increases and then it begins to fall. The ball comes to rest in a tree.
c) Answers may vary, e.g., Sarit walks to Amy's house. They are then driven to Jane's house by Amy's mom. Jane's dad drives all three girls to the library so they can get some books for their science project. They remain at the library for a while. Jane's dad then drives all three girls to Sarit's house so they can work on their project.
d) Answers may vary, e.g., a sky diver jumps out of a plane and free falls for some time, opens the parachute, and descends to the ground at a constant rate.

6.

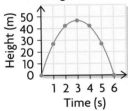

7. i) **a)** linear, **b)** constant velocity
ii) **a)** nonlinear, **b)** decelerating
iii) **a)** nonlinear, **b)** accelerating

8. a)

Distance vs. Time

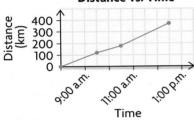

b) The car travels fastest from 10:30 a.m. to 12:30 p.m. The car travels slowest from 9:30 a.m. to 10:30 a.m.
c) nonlinear
d) about 82 km/h

9. a) nonlinear
b)

Height vs. Time

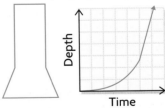

c) 34.75 m
d) at the 2.37 s mark or the 3.63 s mark
e) in the time interval from 3 s to 6 s; in the time interval from 0 s to 3 s
f) at 3 s
g) 46 m
h) Gravity accelerates the ball downward.

10. a)

Speed (km/h)	100	75	50	25	12.5	10	1
Time (h)	1	$1\frac{1}{3}$	2	4	8	10	100

b)

Time vs. Speed

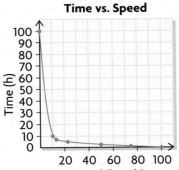

Speed is the independent variable, while time is the dependent variable.

c) Answers may vary, e.g., (25, 4), (50, 2), and $\left(75, 1\frac{1}{3}\right)$.

Rate triangle 1: Slope $= \dfrac{2 - 4}{50 - 25} = -\dfrac{2}{25}$

Rate triangle 2: Slope $= \dfrac{1\frac{1}{3} - 2}{75 - 50} = \dfrac{-\frac{2}{3}}{25} = -\dfrac{2}{75}$

The values are different.

d) The relationship is nonlinear.

11. a) The increasing parts represent time intervals when the race car is accelerating.
The decreasing parts represent time intervals when the race car is decelerating.
b) The horizontal parts of the graph represent time intervals when the race car is at a constant speed.
c) Answers may vary, e.g., the car starts from rest and accelerates until it approaches the first corner, then it decelerates as it travels through this corner. As it leaves the corner, it accelerates then decelerates as it travels through the second corner. It accelerates again and reaches a constant speed before it decelerates through the final corner.

12. Answers may vary, e.g.,

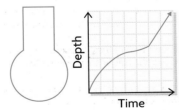

13. Answers may vary, e.g.,

a)

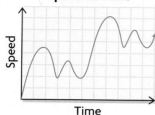

Speed vs. Time

b)

Speed vs. Time

c)

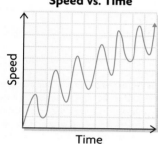

Speed vs. Time

d)

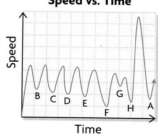

Speed vs. Time

14. **a)**

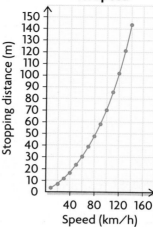

Stopping Distance vs. Speed

b) rate triangle 1: slope $= \dfrac{37.9 - 29.8}{70 - 6} = \dfrac{8.1}{10} = 0.81$

rate triangle 2: slope $= \dfrac{47.5 - 37.9}{70 - 60} = \dfrac{9.6}{10} = 0.96$

c) The rate of change in stopping distance also increases as the speed increases.

d) This is not an accurate observation on Sheila's part, as the relationship is nonlinear. She will need to leave more than twice the distance if she drives twice as fast.

Chapter Review, page 374

1. Answers may vary, e.g., we might expect the number of people with allergies to increase when the air becomes dirtier.
2. **a)** I would choose Number of days after payday for the independent variable, since I have no control over that, and Available money as the dependent variable.

   b) Answers may vary, e.g.,

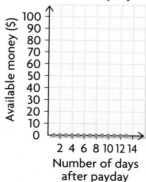

Money Available After Payday

   c) Answers may vary, e.g., the person seems to have spent all of his or her money on payday, and has none left for the next two weeks.

3. a) no

Graphics Quality of a Computer Game

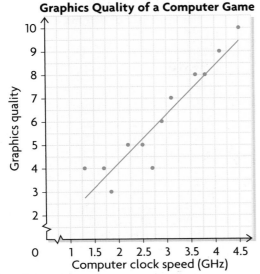

b) $y = 2.1x$

4. a) and **c)**

Test Marks in Ryan's Class

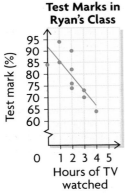

b) Yes. Marks tend to decrease as the amount of TV watched increases.

d) $y = -6.3x + 91.9$

e) about 75

f) No. Each of us may use a different line of best fit, but our answers will be close in value.

5. a) A solid line indicates that the data is continuous. Every point on the line of best fit represents an ordered pair that belongs to the linear relationship. A dashed line indicates the data is discrete. Only points with whole number coordinates that lie on the line of best fit belong to the linear relationship.

b) Answers may vary, e.g., independent variable: time, dependent variable: student's height

c) Answers may vary, e.g., independent variable: day number of the month, dependent variable: number of students in class that day.

6. a) Answers may vary, e.g., yes, it might give a good estimate for a long-term trend.

b) Answers may vary, e.g., yes, it might give a good estimate for short-term variation.

Population of a Wolf Colony

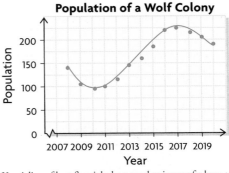

c) Yes. A line of best fit might be a good estimate of a long-term trend and a curve of best fit might be a good estimate of a short-term trend.

7. No. The plotted points just need to be "balanced" on either side of the line or curve of best fit.

8. a) and **c)**

Shoes Sizes and Heights of Men

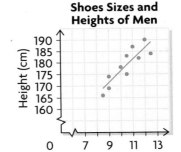

b) Yes. Height tends to increase as shoe size increases.

d) $y = 5.1x + 125.7$

e) 10.5 or 11

f) about 215 cm

9. a) Answers may vary, e.g., the bigger the population of a country, the more chess grandmasters there are in the country.

b)

Chess Grandmasters in Various Countries

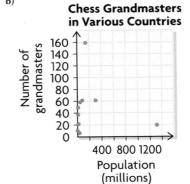

c) No line or curve of best fit is helpful.

d) no

e) Answers may vary, e.g., culture, history, leadership.

10. It took the bus 22 minutes to get to David's hotel from the airport. The bus travelled for 1 minute then made a stop for over a minute to probably pick up passengers at a different pickup location. It travelled for about 2 minutes before it made another pickup. It traveled for over 4 minutes and stopped again. At this stop the bus was at its furthest distance from the airport. The bus then started to travel back toward the airport for 6 minutes and made one final 2 minute stop. The bus then travelled at its greatest speed for 2 minutes before stopping at David's hotel.

Chapter Self-Test, page 376

1. The slope of the line of best fit is about right, but the line needs to be shifted. As drawn, too many points are above the line. The points should be "balanced" on both sides of the line.

2. **a)** Age, since we have no control over it.
b) continuous
c) Older fish tend to be longer.
d)

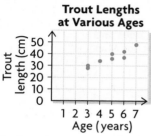

Trout Lengths at Various Ages

e) Yes. As age increases, so does length.

3. C.

4. **a)** and **c)**

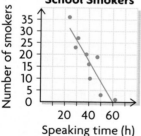

Influence of Speakers on the Number of Elementary School Smokers

b) Elementary schools at which peer leaders speak for longer times have fewer smokers.
d) Not necessarily. Answers may vary, e.g., we don't know how many students smoked before the speaking program, and we don't know how many students go to each school.

5. D.

6. **a)** and **b)**

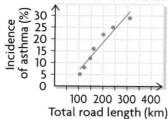

Total Road Length and the Incidence of Asthma

c) $y = 0.12x - 5.4$
d) 42.6 %
e) No. The two variables may not be related, or their increase may be influenced by a third variable.

7. **a)** between D and E
b) Shasta is resting.
c) after 10 min
d) 4 min
e) Shasta ran 125 m/min on her way home.

Chapters 4–6 Cumulative Review, page 379

1. C.
2. B.
3. D.
4. A.
5. B.
6. D.
7. B.
8. B.
9. B.
10. A.
11. B.
12. A.
13. C.
14. C.
15. B.
16. C.
17. D.
18. **a)** Answers may vary, e.g.,

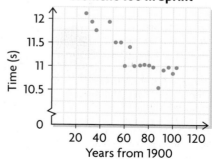

Women's 100 m Sprint

b)

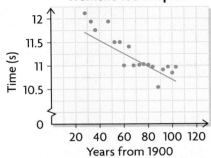

Women's 100 m Sprint

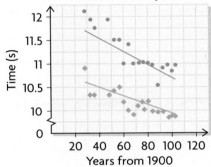

Men's 100 m Sprint

d) Answers may vary, e.g., 2150.
e) Answers may vary, e.g., 2151.

Chapter 7

Getting Started, page 384

1. **a)** iv)   **c)** i)   **e)** iii)   **g)** ii)
   b) vi)   **d)** v)   **f)** vii)   **h)** viii)
2. **a)** $x = 130°$ **b)** $x = 79°$
3. **a)** $x = 62°$ **b)** $x = 102°$, $y = 113°$, $z = 145°$
4. **a)** $y = 19°$, $z = 161°$
   b) $x = 115°$, $y = 65°$, $z = 50°$
5. **a)** iv) perpendicular   **e)** viii) supplementary
   b) vi) adjacent   **f)** iii) transversal
   c) i) parallel   **g)** vii) straight angle
   d) v) congruent   **h)** ii) regular
6. **a)** similarity: Answers may vary, e.g., both have 4 equal sides.
      difference: Answers may vary, e.g., square's sides meet at 90°, rhombus's sides meet at varying angles.
   b) similarity: Answers may vary, e.g., both have 2 pairs of equal sides.
      difference: Answers may vary, e.g., rectangle's sides meet at 90°, parallelogram's sides meet at varying angles.
   c) similarity: Answers may vary, e.g., both have opposite sides that are parallel.
      difference: Answers may vary, e.g., rhombus has 4 equal sides, parallelogram has 2 pairs of equal sides, which are not always equal to each other.
   d) similarity: Answers may vary, e.g., both have interior angles that sum to 180°.
      difference: Answers may vary, e.g., equilateral triangle has 3 equal sides and 3 equal angles, isosceles triangle has 2 equal sides and the 2 equal angles, the third angle and side can be different.

7. **a)** $x = 30°$ **c)** $x = 15°$
   b) $x = 19°$ **d)** $x = 42.5°$
8. **a)**

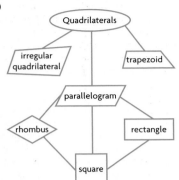

b) Answers may vary, e.g., a trapezoid and a parallelogram are quadrilaterals because they have four sides. A rectangle, square, and rhombus are parallelograms because they have two pairs of parallel opposite sides. A square is a rhombus because it has four congruent sides.
9. **a)** Answers may vary, e.g., square or rhombus.
   b) Answers may vary, e.g., irregular quadrilateral.
   c) Answers may vary, e.g., rectangle or parallelogram.
   d) Answers may vary, e.g., rhombus or parallelogram.
   e) Answers may vary, e.g., trapezoid.
   f) Answers may vary, e.g., parallelogram or rhombus.

Lesson 7.1, page 390

1. **a)** 360°   **b)** 720°   **c)** 540°   **d)** 1260°
2. **a)** 1080°   **b)** 540°   **c)** 1980°   **d)** 1620°
3. Yes. Answers may vary, e.g., because polygons with the same number of sides will always divide into the same number of non-overlapping triangles.
4. 154.3°, to one decimal place
5. 10

Lesson 7.2, page 394

1. They are supplementary angles.
2. **a)** $a = 150°$
   b) $b = 108°$
   c) $c = 84°$; $d = 121°$
   d) $e = 145°$; $f = 114°$; $g = 66°$; $h = 107°$
3. **a)** $a = 104°$; $b = 51°$; $c = 115°$
   b) $d = 78°$; $e = 38°$; $f = 75°$; $g = 94°$, $h = 57°$, $i = 105°$
4. 270°
5. 70°
6. **a)** They are supplementary angles.
   b) The angles are always supplementary.
   c) $\angle 1 + \angle 2 = 180°$
7. **a)** $x = 150°$ **c)** $x = 45°$
   b) $x = 20°$ **d)** $x = 135°$; $y = 45°$
8. **a)** $360° = x + 80° + 100° + 130°$; $x = 50°$
   b) $180° = x + (180° - 135°) + (180° - 85°)$; $x = 40°$
   c) $180° = x + (x - 15)° + (180° - 150°)$; $x = 82.5°$
   d) $360° = x + x + (x - 30)° + (x - 40)°$; $x = 107.5°$

9. Interior angle measures are 36°, 144°, 36°, and 144°.

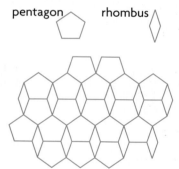

10. Vertex A interior angle: 20°, exterior angle: 160°;
Vertex B interior angle: 59°, exterior angle: 121°;
Vertex C interior angle: 101°, exterior angle: 79°

11. 10

12. 180° $\times (n - 2) \div n$

13. Answers may vary, e.g., the sum of the exterior angles is always 360°, but the sum of the interior angles for a polygon with more than four sides is greater than 360°. An example is the hexagon. Its interior angles add to 720°. Its exterior angles add to 360°.

14. Answers may vary, e.g., the set of pattern blocks include equilateral triangles, squares and regular hexagons. The blocks fit together because the interior angles of the shapes add easily to 360°. The interior angles are 60° for the triangle, 90° for the square, and 120° for the hexagon. You can tile a floor with these shapes because their interior angles all divide into 360° evenly. The interior angle of a regular pentagon is 108°. This does not divide evenly into 360°. So, it cannot tile a floor. Also, it does not add well with the angles of the other three shapes.

15. **a)** You can tile a floor using octagons with a square at each side.
b) Answers may vary, e.g., you can tile a floor with a regular pentagon and a rhombus:

pentagon   rhombus

Mid-Chapter Review, page 398

1. **a)** 36°   **c)** 117°   **e)** 80°
b) 98°   **d)** 98°   **f)** 69°

2. **a)** 150°   **b)** 156°   **c)** 162°

3. 3 or 6 sides

4. **a)** $a = 115°, b = 65°$ **c)** $d = 29°$
b) $c = 60°$ **d)** $e = 87°$

5. 5 sides

6.

Figure	Measure of each Interior Angle	Measure of each Exterior Angle	Sum of Interior Angles	Sum of Exterior Angles
square	90°	90°	360°	360°
pentagon	108°	72°	540°	360°
hexagon	120°	60°	720°	360°
octagon	135°	45°	1080°	360°

Lesson 7.3, page 401

1. **a)** (5, 0): The diagonals had to be perpendicular and bisecting.
b) (11, 0): The diagonals had to be congruent and intersect to form two pairs of equal line segments.
c) Answers may vary, e.g., (6, −2); the diagonals had to be perpendicular and one had to bisect the other.

2. **a)** iii); perpendicular, congruent, bisecting
b) v); perpendicular, bisecting
c) i); congruent, divided congruently
d) ii); bisecting
e) vi); perpendicular, one bisects the other
f) iv); congruent, bisecting

3. Answers may vary, e.g., a quadrilateral has 2 diagonals; a kite has perpendicular diagonals; a parallelogram has diagonals that bisect each other; a rhombus has perpendicular diagonals that bisect each other; a rectangle has congruent diagonals that bisect each other; a square has congruent, perpendicular diagonals that bisect each other; a trapezoid has one pair of opposite parallel sides; an isosceles trapezoid has one pair of opposite parallel sides and equal length diagonals that intersect to form two pairs of equal line segments (not the midpoint).

4.

Quadrilateral	Number of Congruent Triangles
square	4 congruent triangles
rhombus	4 congruent triangles
rectangle	4 congruent triangles
parallelogram	2 pairs of congruent triangles
isosceles trapezoid	1 pair of congruent triangles
kite	2 pairs of congruent triangles

Lesson 7.4, page 407

1. The conjecture is most likely true. I tested an equilateral triangle, two isosceles triangles, a right triangle, and two scalene triangles. The midsegments were parallel to the opposite side in each one.

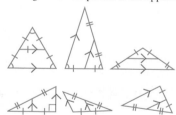

2. The conjecture is false. A rhombus is a counterexample.

3. Answers may vary, e.g., I predict it will not always have all sides equal. A counterexample is a rectangle. All the angles are 90°, but the sides are not all equal.

4. Answers may vary, e.g., I predict it will not always have all angles equal. A counterexample is a rhombus. All the sides are equal length, but the angles are not all equal.

5. Answers may vary, e.g., I predict there are $n - 3$ diagonals from each vertex in an n-sided polygon. I think my conjecture is true. All my examples support it. A triangle has 0 diagonals, a square has 1 diagonal, a pentagon has 2 diagonals, and a hexagon has 3 diagonals.

6. The conjecture is false. For a counterexample, I constructed an isosceles trapezoid with bimedians forming a square.

7. The conjecture is true. Answers may vary, e.g., I drew several triangles using *The Geometer's Sketchpad* and then drew their medians. The medians for each triangle always intersected in one point. All my examples—an equilateral triangle, an isosceles triangle, a right triangle, and two scalene triangles—supported the conjecture.

8. Answers may vary, e.g., I predict the area of the shape formed by a triangle's midsegments is $\frac{1}{4}$ the area of the triangle's area. I drew several triangles using *The Geometer's Sketchpad* and then drew their midsegments. For each one, I calculated the area of shape formed by the midsegments. It was always $\frac{1}{4}$ of the area of the triangle. The conjecture is true.

9. The conjecture is true. Answers may vary, e.g., I drew different rectangles using *The Geometer's Sketchpad*. Then I looked for possible circles. The centre of the circle was always at the intersection of the diagonals of the rectangle. I intersected the diagonals of every rectangle and then drew a circle with a centre at the intersection point. I always found one that intersected each vertex.

10. Answers may vary, e.g.,

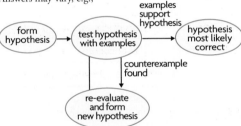

11. I predict that only regular pentagons have midsegments that form regular pentagons. All my examples support my conjecture.

These midsegments of this regular pentagon form a regular pentagon.

The midsegments of this irregular pentagon do not form a regular pentagon.

12. Answers may vary, e.g., I predict that the inner quadrilaterals will alternate back and forth between two types of quadrilaterals. I tested with several examples. My conjecture was wrong. Only some quadrilaterals alternate. My results are:

Initial Quadrilateral	Quadrilateral Formed by Midsegments of Initial Quadrilateral
square	square
rhombus	rectangle
rectangle	rhombus
parallelogram	parallelogram
kite	rectangle
trapezoid	parallelogram
isosceles trapezoid	rhombus

13. Answers may vary, e.g., I predict that each new quadrilateral formed will be a parallelogram. I drew several different quadrilaterals using *The Geometer's Sketchpad*. Each one supported my conjecture. However, I cannot be fully sure. There might be a counterexample that I have not found.

Lesson 7.5, page 413

1.

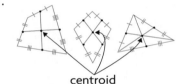

centroid

2. **a)** a rhombus
   b) the intersection of the diagonals
   c) a parallelogram
   d) the midsegments

3.

Quadrilateral	Centroid Construction Method	Bimedian Geometric Properties
square	intersection of bimedians or diagonals	bisect each other, equal length, intersect at right angles, split square into 4 smaller congruent squares
rhombus	intersection of bimedians or diagonals	bisect each other, intersect at right angles, split rhombus into 4 smaller congruent rhombuses
rectangle	intersection of bimedians or diagonals	bisect each other, equal length, split rectangle into 4 smaller congruent rectangles
parallelogram	intersection of bimedians or diagonals	bisect each other, split parallelogram into 4 smaller congruent parallelograms
kite	intersection of bimedians	bisect each other, equal length, split kite into 4 quadrilaterals, 2 of which are smaller kites
isosceles trapezoid	intersection of bimedians	bisect each other, intersect at right angles, split isosceles trapezoid into 2 pairs of smaller congruent trapezoids, bimedian between 2 non-base sides parallel to base sides
non-isosceles trapezoid	intersection of bimedians	bisect each other, bimedian between 2 non-base sides parallel to base sides
irregular quadrilateral	intersection of bimedians	bisect each other

4. 15 cm

5. a) 97.5 cm   **b)** the bimedian is 4 cm from each side

6. a) 10 cm   **b)** 13 cm

7. a) 40 cm   **b)** 9 cm

8. Answers may vary, e.g., construct the bimedians in the new quadrilaterals. One is already drawn so you just need one. The bimedians intersect at the centroid.

9. Answers may vary, e.g., the intersection of the diagonals determines the centroid for squares, rhombuses, rectangles, and parallelograms. It does not determine the centroid for any other quadrilateral.

10. a) the centroid of the quadrilateral

b) Answers may vary, e.g., I determined the midpoint of the segment joining the diagonal midpoints. Then I drew the bimedians. They intersected at the point. I realized the point I had constructed was the centroid of the quadrilateral.

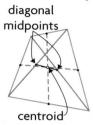

diagonal midpoints

centroid

11. Answers may vary, e.g., draw one of the diagonals and then divide it into 4 equal sections by drawing three points on it. Draw lines from the points on the diagonal to the other two vertices and then erase the diagonal. There quadrilateral is now divided into 4 equal parts.

Chapter Review, page 418

1. a) 132°   **b)** 51°

2. He is incorrect. Answers may vary, e.g., I know the sum of the interior angles of an n-gon is $180 \times (n - 2)$ degrees. This works out to 1080° for an octagon.

3. a) 2 is subtracted from n to give the number of triangles that are formed by the diagonals of the n-gon.

b) $(n - 2)$ is multiplied by 180°, because there are 180° in each of the triangles that are formed by the diagonals of the n-gon.

4. a) Interior angle: 165.6°

b) Exterior angle: 14.4°

5. a) $x = 155°$ **c)** $x = 128.6°$ to one decimal place

b) $x = 97°$ **d)** $x = 40°$

6. a) $x = 85°$ **b)** $x = 94°$

7. a) always   **d)** sometimes   **g)** always

b) sometimes   **e)** sometimes   **h)** sometimes

c) never   **f)** sometimes

8. a) irregular quadrilateral. One of the diagonals has to be bisected for the quadrilateral to be a kite.

b) kite. The diagonals have to bisect each other for the quadrilateral to be a parallelogram.

c) irregular quadrilateral. The diagonals have to intersect so that they have equal distances on either side for the quadrilateral to be an isosceles trapezoid.

d) parallelogram. Bisecting diagonals means two pairs of congruent sides.

9. Answers may vary, e.g., I predicted that only squares, kites, and rhombuses have midsegments forming a square or a rectangle. I tested my conjecture with several examples. Each one supported it. However, I could not be fully sure, as there still might be a counterexample.

10. The conjecture is false. Answers may vary, e.g., a scalene triangle with interior angles of 76°, 53°, and 51° is a counterexample.

11. The conjecture is true. Answers may vary, e.g., I tested several isosceles triangles by drawing the median from the vertex joining the two equal sides in *The Geometer's Sketchpad*. The median bisected the angle between the two equal sides each time.

12. The conjecture is true. Answers may vary, e.g., I tested several triangles by drawing a median. I calculated the area on either side of the median using *The Geometer's Sketchpad*. Each time, the areas were equal.

13. If a polygon with n sides is used, then the new shape formed by the midsegments is another polygon with n sides. This is because there are n midpoints, which are the n vertices for the new polygon. The polygon might be regular or it might be irregular.

14. **a)** They are equal.
b) They are not equal.
c) Answers may vary, e.g., Conjecture: Every quadrilateral whose vertices lie on a circle has supplementary opposite angles, and these are the only quadrilaterals that do. I could test this conjecture by drawing many quadrilaterals. I would divide them into 2 groups. One group would have quadrilaterals whose vertices lie on a circle. The other group would have all the other quadrilaterals. Then I could measure the angles for each quadrilateral.

15. **a)** 26 cm **b)** 6 cm

Chapter Self-Test, page 420

1. Answers may vary, e.g., if n is the number of sides, the number of diagonals drawn from one vertex is $n - 3$.
2. **A.**
3. **a)** $a = 35°$, $b = 75°$
b) $c = 127°$, $d = 88°$, $e = 92°$
4. Answers may vary, e.g., each pair of opposite interior and exterior angles adds to 180°, so in total, the sum of both the exterior and interior angles of the pentagon is $5 \times 180°$, or 900°. The sum of the interior angles of a pentagon is 540°. I know this from the formula for the sum of the interior angles of a polygon. $900° - 540° = 360°$, so the sum of the exterior angles must be 360°.

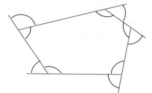

5. **D.**
6. **a)** iii) **b)** i) **c)** ii) **d)** iv)
7. 8 km, everything in $\triangle ABC$ is twice that of $\triangle DEC$.
8. I tested the conjecture for several triangles and it was true each time. It is true.

Chapter 8

Note: Answers are given to the same number of decimal points as the numbers in each question.

Getting Started, page 424

1. **a)** v **e)** ii **h)** iv
b) vii **f)** ix **i)** vi
c) x **g)** viii **j)** i
d) iii
2. **a)** 600 cm² **b)** 158 cm² **c)** 700 cm²
3. **a)** about 471 cm² **b)** about 302 cm² **c)** about 565 cm²
4. **a)** about 9 cm **b)** about 14 cm **c)** 13 cm
5. **a)** about 3421 cm² **b)** 1 080 000 km² **c)** 5940 cm²
6. **a)** surface area 432 cm², volume 400 cm³
b) about surface area 262 cm², about volume 225 cm³
c) about surface area 230 m², about volume 265 m³
7. **a)** Answers may vary, e.g.,

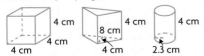

b) Answers may vary, e.g., cube 96 cm², triangular prism 109 cm², cylinder 91 cm².
8. **a)** 20 m **b)** 15 cm **c)** 25 cm
9. **a)** agree **c)** disagree
b) agree **d)** agree
10. Answers may vary, e.g.,
Prism:

Definition	Properties	Diagram
a shape with two opposite faces that are the same and with the sides joining them all rectangles	The two opposite faces have the same shape and area and are parallel. The sides joining the two equal opposite faces might be different rectangles.	

Pyramid:

Definition	Properties	Diagram
a shape with a base in the form of a regular polygon, and with triangles connecting the sides of the base to a common vertex	The triangular faces have the same shape and area. A pyramid is like a prism but with one end face shrunk to a point.	

Cone:

Definition	Properties	Diagram
a shape with a circle for a base, and one curved surface that goes from the circumference of the circle to a single vertex	The single vertex should be directly above the centre of the base when the cone is placed upright. A cone is like a prism with circles as the opposite faces but with one circle shrunk to a point.	

Lesson 8.1, page 431

1. **B.**
2. a square 6-by-6 units
3. **a)** **i)** 625.0 cm² **b)** **i)** 4.0 m
ii) 324.0 m² **ii)** 33.5 cm
iii) 1785.1 km² **iii)** 15.7 cm
iv) 1278.1 mm² **iv)** 21.2 cm
4. 1.62 m by 1.62 m
5. **a)** Answers may vary, e.g.,

W	1	2	3	4	6	9	12	14	21
L	126	63	42	31.5	21	12	10.5	9	6
P	128	67	48	39.5	33	30	34.5	37	48

b)

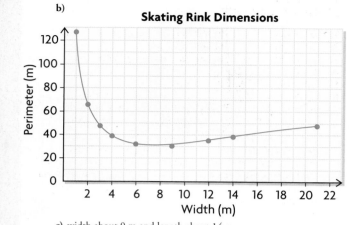

Skating Rink Dimensions

c) width about 9 m and length about 14 m
6. C, since it is a square.
7. 9 m by 9 m, e.g., this is a square.
8. 10 cm by 10 cm
9. a)

Length (m)	Width (m)	Perimeter (m)	Area (m²)
19	1	20	19
18	2	20	36
17	3	20	51
16	4	20	64
15	5	20	75
14	6	20	84
13	7	20	91
12	8	20	96
11	9	20	99
10	10	20	100
9	11	20	99
8	12	20	96
7	13	20	91
6	14	20	84
5	15	20	75
4	16	20	64
3	17	20	51
2	18	20	36
1	19	20	19

b)

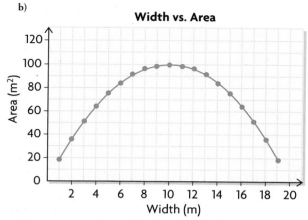

Width vs. Area

c) Answers may vary, e.g., the largest rectangular area is when the length and width are both 10 m. This is because this forms a square, which is the optimum rectangle for maximising area for a given perimeter.
10. 30 m by 60 m, with the 60 m section parallel to the barn wall
11. 10 368 m²
12. Answers may vary, e.g., a rectangle in the shape of a square has the least perimeter, which is often the optimum perimeter. A rectangle in the shape of a square has the greatest area, which is often the optimum area.
13. 14.99 cm by 14.99 cm and 0.01 cm by 0.01 cm
14. 10.0 m by 13.3 m uses 79.9 m of wood.

Lesson 8.2, page 440

1. a) 15.5 cm²   **b)** 9.9 m²   **c)** 20.5 cm²
2. a) perimeter 17.4 m, area 8.6 m²
    b) perimeter 19.0 m, area 11.9 m²
3. a) 72 cm²   **c)** 45 cm²
    b) 6.6 m²   **d)** 31.2 cm²
4. perimeter 26.2 cm, area 42.0 cm
5. a) perimeter 272 mm, area 5576 mm²
    b) perimeter 50.4 cm, area 181.4 cm²
    c) perimeter 102.0 cm, area 734.4 cm²
6. a) Answers may vary, e.g.,

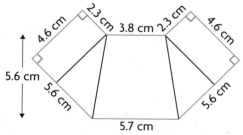

b) The area of each rectangle is 10.6 cm², the area of each triangle is 7.6 cm², and the area of the trapezoid is 26.6 cm². E.g., I multiplied the area of the rectangles by 2 and I multiplied the area of the triangles by 2, then I added the new numbers to the area of the trapezoid. That's because there are 2 each of the triangles and rectangles. The total area is about 63.0 cm.
7. a) about 1.7 cm   **b)** about 17 mm

8. a) Answers may vary, e.g., I would divide the shape into a square, a pentagon, and a hexagon. I would then divide the hexagon and pentagon into six and five triangles, respectively, so I would need height measurements to determine the areas of the triangles.
    b) 693 cm
9. Answers may vary, e.g., I created the following shape:

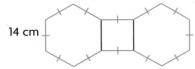

14 cm

- Divide the compound shape into smaller shapes with areas that are easier to determine.
- Add the areas of the smaller shapes together.
- Determine the length of each section of the perimeter and add them together. The perimeter of the shape is 168 cm and the area is about 1214 cm^2.
10. a) $A = \pi R^2 - \pi r^2$ b) $A = 4r^2 - \pi r^2$ c) $A = 4r^2 - \pi r^2$
11. $A_{\text{regular polygon}} = \dfrac{Pa}{2}$, where P is the perimeter and a is the distance from the centre to the midpoint of each side.

Lesson 8.3, page 445

1. a) 10 m   c) about 20 cm
    b) about 14 cm   d) about 14 cm
2. about 91 km
3. a) 10 m   b) 37 cm   c) 69 m
4. 60 m
5. a) 40 m   b) about 29 m   c) about 46 m
6. boom 8.0 m, forestay 15.5 m
7. A: 1764 cm^2; B: 1600 cm^2; C: 3364 cm^2
8. If the corners meet at a right angle, the diagonal will measure about 12.1 m.
9. a) yes   c) no
    b) no   d) no
10. Answers may vary, e.g., determine the perimeter of the square on the hypotenuse in the diagram.

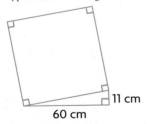

11 cm

60 cm

Solution: 244 cm
11. 13 cm long by 12 cm high
12. Answers may vary, e.g., height of 80 cm and side length of 120 cm. Or height of 60 cm and side length of 160 cm.
13. Answers may vary, e.g., because the triangle is not a right triangle. I know this because if the triangle were right angled, squares A and B would be smaller and the Pythagorean theorem would work and give an answer for the area of C. Since A and B are bigger than they would be in a right triangle, the Pythagorean theorem could not work, because it would give a different answer for the area of C.

Lesson 8.4, page 454

1. a) 35.6 cm^2 b) 85.4 cm^2
2. a) 139 cm   b) 283 cm^2
3. a) 600 m^2 b) 66.6 cm^2 c) 678.2 cm^2
4. 172.8 cm^2
5. a) 8.9 cm   b) 162.0 cm^2
6. cup B
7. a) 1977 mm^2 b) 18.4 cm^2 c) 118 m^2
8. a) 452.2 cm^2 b) 942 cm^2 c) 1685.1 cm^2
9. The pyramid with the octagon base. I calculated the surface area of each pyramid and the one with the octagon base has a greater surface area. The surface area of the pyramid with the square base is 289 cm^2, and the surface area of the pyramid with the octagon base is 320 cm^2.
10. 211.4 cm^2
11. 66.3 cm^2
12. 20.6 m^2
13. 43.2 m^2
14. a) 139 144.1 m^2 b) about 20 788 blocks
15. about 1590 cm^2
16. Answers may vary, e.g.,

8 cm

2 cm

To determine the surface area, I can find the area of the square base by doubling and squaring the distance from the centre to the middle of a side, and then calculate the area of one of the triangular sides by multiplying the slant height by the base side length and dividing by two. I would then multiply the area of one triangle by four and add the area of the base to determine the surface area. Or, I could use the formula for the surface area of a pyramid.
17. Answers may vary, e.g., I think the 20-sided container has the greatest surface area. I looked at the equation for the surface area of a pyramid. The variables in the equation are P for perimeter, a for the distance between the centre of the base and the midpoint of each side, and L for slant height. Since the distance between the centre of the base and the midpoint of each side and height are given to be the same, then I can determine the slant height for each pyramid and it will be the same, too. I know that the distance between the centre of the base and the midpoint of each side and slant height are the same for each pyramid. So the equation tells me that the pyramid with the greatest perimeter will have the greatest surface area. The perimeters seem to get bigger as the number of sides increases, so the 20-sided container should have the greatest surface area.
18. a) 226 cm^2
    b) 318 cm^2
    c) $49n + (7n + 7) \times \sqrt{37.25}$

Mid-Chapter Review, page 460

1. C; Answers may vary, e.g., C is a square and I know that a square will maximize the area for a given perimeter.

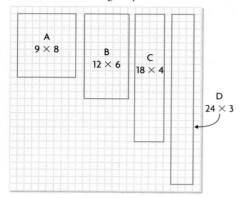

2. Rectangle A has the least perimeter. It has a perimeter of 34 units.
3. **a)** 625 cm²   **b)** 25 m²   **c)** 36 km²
4. 28 m
5. Answers may vary, e.g.,

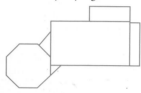

I would need the length of one side of the hexagon, the side lengths of the two triangles, and the length and width of the three rectangles.
6. The square on the left edge is 900 cm², the square on the bottom edge is 256 cm², the square on the hypotenuse is 1156 cm², and the triangle is 240 cm².
7. 10.6 m
8. **a)** 340.2 cm²   **b)** 422.9 cm²
9. **a)** 48 bundles of shingles   **b)** $1727.52

Lesson 8.5, page 464

1. 149 cm³
2. 45.0 m³
3. 530.9 cm³
4. 79.8 cm³
5. 11.3 m³
6. **a)** 4399.2 m³
   b) 637 sanders, leaving some sand left over
7. 7.5 cm
8. 9 cm, 18 cm, 21 cm
9. The volume of the pyramid is $\frac{1}{3}$ the volume of the prism.
10. 26 719 mL
11. Answers may vary, e.g., I would measure the base side length of the pyramid and the base radius of the cone. Then, I would calculate the base area for each figure. I would use the formula s^2 for the base of the pyramid, where s is the base side length. I would use the formula πr^2 for the base of the cone, where r is the base radius. Then, I would multiply the base area of each figure by the height and divide by three. I would compare the volumes to determine which was greater.

12. **a)** $V = \frac{1}{6} nhsa$, where V is the volume of an n-sided pyramid, s is its side length, and a is the distance from the centre of the base to the midpoint of an edge.
    b) $V = \frac{10}{3} \pi a^2$

Lesson 8.6, page 470

1. 113.1 cm²
2. 697 cm³
3. Answers may vary, e.g., $4\pi \times 12$ cm $\times 12$ cm $= 1810$ cm².
4. 524 mL
5. **a)** 17 269 ball bearings
   b) 16 405.55 g
   c) 670 boxes
   d) Answers may vary, e.g., the shape, size, and mass of each box.
6. **a)** 170 scoops   **b)** $146.20
7. **a)** radius 6366.2 km, surface area 509 296 200 km²
   b) 21 300 km
8. **a)** 29 322 cm³ of modelling clay   **b)** 5027 cm² of foil
9. **a)** 247.0 cm³   **b)** 82.9 cm²
10. between 168.4 cm² and 175.8 cm²
11. the cylinder: Its surface area is 471 cm², while the cube's is 600 cm².
12. **a)**

Shape	Surface Area (cm²)	Dimensions (cm)	Volume (cm³)
square-based prism	1000	$s = 10$, $h = 20$	2000
cylinder	1000	$r = 10$, $h \doteq 5.92$	1858.88
sphere	1000	$r \doteq 9$	2974

    b) sphere
13. 17.27 cm²
14. 1.5 cm³
15. Answers may vary, e.g., the formula for the volume of a sphere with radius r is $\frac{4}{3}\pi r^3$. The volume is a fraction of the volume of the cylinder with base radius r and height $2r$. You can see this by placing an orange in a cylindrical glass of the same height full of water, then measuring how much water spills when you put the orange inside. The formula for the surface area of a sphere with radius r is $4\pi r^2$. The surface area is equal to the area of 4 circles with radius r. You can see this by taking the peel of an orange and placing it on 4 circles that have radius equal to the orange's radius.

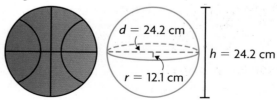

One sphere from my experience is a basketball, which has a radius of 12.1 cm:
volume of basketball 7420.7 cm³
surface area of basketball 1839.8 cm²

16. The cube has a greater volume and surface area.

17. by 0.7 cm

Lesson 8.7, page 475

1. Answers may vary, e.g., I chose a square-based prism with a fixed volume of 1000 cm³.

2. **a)** Answers may vary, e.g., what is the minimum amount of cellophane packaging needed to wrap a piece of chocolate in the shape of a prism if its volume is 1000 cm³?

b)

Volume (cm³)	Length of Square Base (cm)	Height (cm)	Surface Area (cm²)
1000	10	30.00	632.46
1000	11	24.79	596.73
1000	12	20.83	577.01
1000	13	17.75	572.07
1000	14	15.31	580.81
1000	15	13.33	602.08
1000	16	11.72	634.64
1000	17	10.38	677.24
1000	18	9.26	728.71
1000	19	8.31	788.04
1000	20	7.50	854.40

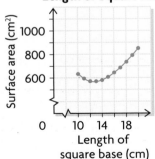

Surface Area vs. Length of Square Base

The minimum amount of cellophane needed is about 572 square centimetres when the base of the piece of chocolate is a 13 cm × 13 cm square.

Lesson 8.8, page 480

1. **a)** about 7 cm by 7 cm by 8 cm
b) radius of about 4 cm and height about 9 cm

2. **a)** 30 cm by 30 cm by 30 cm
b) 22 scoopfuls

3. **a)** 5 m by 5 m by 5 m
b) 15 cm by 15 cm by 15 cm

c) 2.800 cm by 2.800 cm by 2.800 cm
d) 14.600 cm by 14.600 cm by 14.600 cm

4. **a)** 1.5 cm by 1.5 cm by 1.5 cm
b) 216 cm³
c) 6 cm by 6 cm by 6 cm

5. **a)** 3217.0 cm² with radius 8.0 cm and height 16.0 cm
b) 1837.1 cm² as a cube with side length 12.2 cm

6. A cylinder with radius 10.9 cm and height 21.9 cm. It would have a surface area of 2251.1 cm².

7. **a)** 5 m by 5 m by 5 m, volume 125 m³
b) 12 cm by 12 cm by 12 cm, volume 1728 cm³
c) 9.5 cm by 9.5 cm by 9.5 cm, volume 857.4 cm³
d) 28.5 cm by 28.5 cm by 28.5 cm, volume 23 149.1 cm³

8. The cylinder with radius of 5 cm and height of 13 cm uses the least material, 556 cm².

Radius (cm)	Height (cm)	Surface Area (cm²)
1	318	2006
2	80	1025
3	35	724
4	20	601
5	13	556
6	9	558
7	7	594
8	5	653
9	4	729
10	3	829

9. side length 3.6 cm, height 1.8 cm

10. radius 4.6 cm, height 4.7 cm, surface area 203 cm²

11. Answers may vary, e.g., a cube with side length 24 cm.

12. 13 cm³

13. Answers may vary, e.g., the cue cards read:
- "Case 1: You know the surface area or volume."
- "For cylinders, create a chart of different heights and radii satisfying the surface area or volume, then determine the dimensions that minimize surface area *and* maximize volume."
- "The height should be twice the radius." With visual of cylinder with height twice the radius.
- "For prisms, create a chart of different heights and base lengths satisfying the surface area or volume, then determine the dimensions that minimize surface area *and* maximize volume."
- "The height should equal the base length, so the prism should be a cube." With visual of a cube.
- "Case 2: You know one dimension of the cylinder or prism."
- "For cylinders, if you know the radius, set the height equal to twice the radius."
- "If you know the height, set the radius to half the height."
- "For prisms, if you know the base side length, set the height equal to it. The prism is a cube."
- "If you know the height, set the base side length equal to it. The prism is a cube."

14. a) 20 cm by 20 cm by 30 cm
b) No, packaging them 8 cans per box would be more economical because it would create a perfect cube.

Chapter Review, page 484

1. 2.4 m by 2.4 m
2. 89 cm
3. 5 m × 5 m
4. 20 m × 40 m with longer side parallel to the beach
5. 60 cm^2
6. area 83.2 cm^2, perimeter 33.2 cm
7. a) 170 m   **b)** 3.7 laps   **c)** 1530 m^2
8. a) area: 99 cm^2, perimeter 33 cm
b) area 120 cm^2, perimeter 40 cm
9. 38.7 m
10. 9.6 cm
11. 99 m
12. 2704 cm^2
13. 874 cm^2
14. a) 34 bundles   **b)** 3 cans of paint   **c)** $1313.51
15. 224 cm^2
16. 23.2 cm
17. a) V = 324 cm^3, SA = 312 cm^2
b) V = 1963 cm^3, SA = 1171 cm^2
18. a) 466 cm^2 **b)** 576 cm^3
19. 148 cm^3
20. Volume: 92 cm^3
Surface Area: 99 m^2
21. a) 268 cm^3 **b)** 244 cm^3
22. 2422 cm^3 of rubber
23. Answers may vary, e.g., radius of 6 cm and height of 8 cm.
24. a) The square-based prism with the greatest volume for a given surface area is a cube. 210 cm^2 ÷ 6 = 35 cm^2, so each side has an area of 35 cm^2. That means that the side length of one side is $\sqrt{35}$, which is about 6. So the square-based prism with the greatest volume and a surface area of 210 cm^2 is a cube with side length 6 cm.
b) Using the same process as part a), the answer is a cube of side length 8 cm.
25. 98 cm^3

Chapter Self-Test, page 486

1. 180 cm
2. a) area 59.6 cm^2, perimeter 30.5 cm
b) area 864 cm^2, perimeter 168 cm
3. The volume is 195.5 cm^3. To determine the volume, I needed to know the area of the base and the height. I knew the side length was 8.0 cm, so the area of the base is 64.0 cm^2. To determine the height, I used the Pythagorean theorem with the distance from the centre of the base to the midpoint of an edge and slant height. The distance from the centre of the base to the midpoint of an edge is half of the side length, so 4.0 cm. I had one leg and the hypotenuse of the right triangle. I used the Pythagorean theorem to solve for the height. I solved $h^2 + 4.0^2 = 10.0^2$ to get 9.165 cm for the height. I didn't round off yet so that the answer would be accurate.

The volume is $\frac{1}{3}$ multiplied by the height multiplied by the area of the base, which is $\frac{1}{3} \times 9.165 \times 64.0 = 195.5$ cm^3.

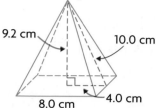

4. C
5. a) V = 353.3 cm^3, SA = 184.1 cm^2
b) V = 229.5 cm^3, SA = 254.1 cm^2
6. a) 132.7 cm^2 **b)** 143.8 cm^3
7. A
8. 11 cm by 11 cm by 10 cm

Chapters 7–8 Cumulative Review, page 488

1. C.
2. D.
3. D.
4. D.
5. B.
6. C.
7. B.
8. A.
9. A.
10. D.
11. C.
12. A.
13. B.
14. D.
15. A.
16. D.
17. B.
18. C.
19. B.
20. C.
21. B. and **C**.
22. a) $\frac{2000}{3}$ cm^3 **c)** $\frac{1}{8}$
b) $\frac{250}{3}$ cm^3 **d)** yes

Appendix A

A–1, page 492

1. a) 4   **d)** 9   **g)** 16   **j)** 3125
b) 8   **e)** 1000   **h)** 64
c) 16   **f)** 10 000   **i)** 125

A–2, page 492

1. a) 25   **c)** 25   **e)** 100
b) 8   **d)** 4   **f)** 0

A–3, page 493

1. a)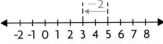

   b)

   c)

   d)

   e)

   f)

2. a) -5 c) -10 e) -55
   b) -1 d) -2 f) -14
3. a) 7 c) 18 e) 12
   b) -3 d) -7 f) -47
4. a) 17 b) -4 c) 2 d) -58

A–4, page 494

1. a)

   b)

   c)

   d)

2. a) -6 c) -12 e) 20
   b) 36 d) 21 f) -14
3. a) 3 c) -3 f) 2
   b) -4 d) 3 e) -5
4. a) 25 c) 40 e) 24
   b) -7 d) -16 f) -1

A–5, page 495

1. a) 6 c) 14 e) 8
   b) -1 d) -2 f) 3
2. a) 26 c) -11 e) 16
   b) -16 d) 6 f) 101

A–6, page 497

1. a)

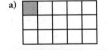

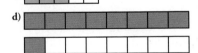

2. a) $\frac{4}{7}$ c) $\frac{1}{2}$ e) $\frac{1}{2}$
   b) $\frac{7}{9}$ d) $\frac{4}{9}$ f) $\frac{3}{4}$
3. a) $\frac{4}{9}$ c) $\frac{1}{15}$ e) $\frac{7}{12}$
   b) $\frac{7}{15}$ d) $\frac{11}{24}$ f) $\frac{1}{6}$
4. a) $\frac{21}{20}$ or $1\frac{1}{20}$ d) $\frac{113}{240}$
   b) $\frac{38}{33}$ or $1\frac{5}{33}$ e) $\frac{41}{10}$ or $1\frac{1}{10}$
   c) $\frac{44}{35}$ or $1\frac{9}{35}$ f) $\frac{73}{35}$ or $2\frac{3}{35}$

A–7, page 498

1. a)

   b)

   c)

   d)

2. a) $\frac{3}{10}$ b) $\frac{21}{40}$ c) $\frac{2}{5}$ d) $\frac{6}{11}$
3. a) $\frac{15}{28}$ b) $\frac{10}{33}$ c) $\frac{6}{7}$ d) $\frac{10}{13}$
4. a) $\frac{16}{39}$ b) $\frac{9}{25}$ c) $\frac{5}{2}$ or $2\frac{1}{2}$ d) $\frac{1}{3}$

A–8, page 499

1. a) $\frac{97}{60}$ or $1\frac{37}{60}$ d) $\frac{1471}{1080}$ or $1\frac{391}{1080}$
   b) $\frac{29}{120}$ e) $\frac{19}{24}$
   c) $\frac{37}{10}$ or $3\frac{7}{10}$ f) $\frac{25}{36}$

A–9, page 500

1. a) 3.5
    b) 1.5
    c) 4.55
    d) 11.25
    e) 8.09
    f) 5.87
2. a) 2.7
    b) 4.95
    c) 2.5
    d) 1.5
    e) 3
    f) 9.65

A–10, page 501

1. a) $1 \times 10^3 + 2 \times 10^2 + 3 \times 10 + 4 \times 10^0$
    b) $1 \times 10^4 + 1 \times 10^3 + 1 \times 10^2 + 2 \times 10 + 5 \times 10^0$
    c) $1 \times 10^4 + 5 \times 10^0$
    d) $1 \times 10^6 + 4 \times 10^4 + 5 \times 10^3 + 3 \times 10^2 + 1 \times 10^0$
2. a) 1.234×10^3 c) 1.0005×10^4
    b) 1.1125×10^4 d) $1.045\,301 \times 10^6$

Standard Form	Expanded Form	Scientific Notation
451	$4 \times 10^2 + 5 \times 10 + 1 \times 10^0$	4.51×10^2
1026	$1 \times 10^3 + 2 \times 10 + 6 \times 10^0$	1.026×10^3
2050	$2 \times 10^3 + 5 \times 10$	2.050×10^3
472 000	$4 \times 10^5 + 7 \times 10^4 + 2 \times 10^3$	4.72×10^5

A–11, page 502

1. a)

Figure Number	Figure	Number of Counters
1		3
2		5
3		7
4		9
5		11

b)

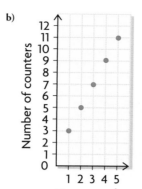

2. a) $t = 3n + 3$
    b)

Figure Number, n	Number of Toothpicks, t
1	6
2	9
3	12
4	15
5	18

c)

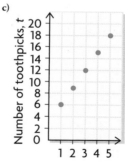

A–12, page 503

1. A: $(2, 6)$
    B: $(-4, -2)$
    C: $(5, 0)$
    D: $(-2, 1)$
    E: $(4, -3)$
    F: $(0, 0)$

2.

3. **a)** b) and d) on the *x*-axis, b) and c) on the *y*-axis
b) a) I, e) III, f) II
4. **a)** Answers may vary, e.g., (3, 2).
b) Answers may vary, e.g., (−4, 0).
c) Answers may vary, e.g., (−1, −1).
d) Answers may vary, e.g., (−2, 4).

A–13, page 505

1. **a)** $n = 4$ **c)** $x = 6$ **e)** $n = 11$
b) $f = -3$ **d)** $g = -6$ **f)** $z = 15$
2. **a)** $x = 3$ **c)** $c = -4$ **e)** $h = -5$
b) $n = 6$ **d)** $m = -5$ **f)** $a = 5$
3. **a)** $k = 3$ **c)** $a = 5$ **e)** $p = 3$ **g)** $h = 0$
b) $k = 7$ **d)** $y = -3$ **f)** $v = 2$ **h)** $y = 1$
4. **a)** $m = 12$ **c)** $h = -8$ **e)** $y = 48$
b) $e = 20$ **d)** $a = -32$ **f)** $c = 0$

A–14, page 506

1. **a)** $1 : 2$ **c)** $2 : 5$ **e)** $\dfrac{3}{5}$

b) $1 : 3$ **d)** $2 : 7$ **f)** $\dfrac{5}{7}$

2. **a)** $7 : 30$ **c)** $25 : 0.05$ or $2500 : 5$ or $500 : 1$
b) $17 : 60$ **d)** $15 : 60$ or $1 : 4$
3. **a)** 4   **b)** 9   **c)** 14   **d)** 24

4. **a)** 2 tins/dollar   **d)** $\dfrac{79}{4}$ km/h

b) $\dfrac{75}{87}$ dollars/h   **e)** $\dfrac{3}{4}$ goals/shot

c) $\dfrac{4}{3}$ dollars/novel   **f)** $\dfrac{17}{23}$ min/paper

A–15, page 506

1. **a)** $\dfrac{49}{100}$ **c)** $\dfrac{1}{100}$ **e)** $\dfrac{1}{3}$

b) $\dfrac{3}{4}$ **d)** $\dfrac{1}{200}$ **f)** $\dfrac{3}{40}$

2. **a)** 73%   **c)** 14%   **e)** 62.5%
b) 30%   **d)** 25%   **f)** 100%
3. **a)** 11.3   **c)** 90   **e)** 20.6
b) 51   **d)** 1.2

A–16, page 508

1. **a)** $a = 65°$, $b = 115°$, $c = 115°$
b) $w = 60°$, $x = 40°$, $y = 80°$, $z = 40°$
c) $x = 50°$, $y = 62°$
d) $a = 70°$
e) $a = 80°$, $b = 80°$, $c = 100°$
f) $a = 65°$, $b = 50°$, $c = 65°$
g) $a = 50°$, $b = 50°$, $c = 50°$, $d = 75°$
h) $x = 60°$, $y = 120°$, $z = 120°$
2. **a)** $a = 80°$, $b = 100°$, $c = 100°$, $d = 100°$
b) $x = 37°$, $y = 71°$, $z = 71°$
c) $w = 131°$, $x = 49°$, $y = 74°$, $z = 57°$
d) $a = 48°$, $b = 106°$, $c = 26°$, $d = 106°$

A–17, page 510

1. **a)** 598 m   **b)** 260 m   **c)** 24 cm   **d)** 24 mm
2. **a)** 70.4 cm²   **c)** 12.7 m²   **e)** 80 cm²
b) 642.1 cm²   **d)** 1009.2 cm²   **f)** 37.5 m²
3. **a)** 50 cm²   **c)** 48 cm²
b) 96 cm²   **d)** 6775 cm²

A–18, page 512

1. **a)** $A = 12.57$ cm², $C = 12.57$ cm
b) $A = 3.14$ cm², $C = 6.28$ cm
c) $A = 1256.64$ cm², $C = 125.66$ cm
d) $A = 314.16$ cm², $C = 62.83$ cm
2. **a)** 17.59 cm²   **b)** 8.59 cm
3. **a)** 21.46 m²   **c)** 1.72 cm²
b) 14.13 cm²   **d)** 89.27 cm²

A–19, page 513

1. **a)** $6^2 + 8^2 = x^2$ **c)** $5^2 + y^2 = 9^2$
b) $13^2 + 6^2 = c^2$ **d)** $3.2^2 + a^2 = 8.5^2$
2. **a)** $x = 10$ cm   **c)** $y = 7.5$ cm
b) $c = 14.3$ cm   **d)** $a = 7.9$ cm
3. 100 m
4. **a)** 11.2 m   **b)** 6.7 cm   **c)** 7.4 cm   **d)** 4.9 m
5. 69.4 m
6. 631.5 m

A–20, page 515

1. **a)** $SA = 127.4$ cm², $V = 66.4$ cm³
b) $SA = 398.3$ cm², $V = 482.4$ cm³
c) $SA = 596.9$ cm², $V = 1099.6$ cm³
d) $SA = 747.7$ cm², $V = 1539.4$ cm³
2. **a)** 283.5 cm³   **b)** 173 cm³
3. **a)** 469.1 m³   **b)** 472.4 cm³
4. 3.2 cm
5. **a)** 211.6 m³   **b)** 245.1 m²   **c)** 4 cans

Answers

Index

A

Absolute value, 306
Addition
 of fractions, 4
 of mixed numbers, 8–10, 13–14, 16–18, 37
 of polynomials, 102–12, 130
 of rational numbers, 50–51
Algebraic expressions
 binomials, 105
 evaluation of, 33–34, 73–74, 86–88
 finding missing terms, 106–7, 116
 in fraction form, 34
 modeling, 76–80, 113–14
 monomials, 105, 113–18
 polynomials, 102–12
  multiplication of, 113–18
  simplifying, 119–27
 representing relations with, 143
 simplifying, 86, 105–6, 107, 119–27, 128
 trinomials, 105
 with two variables, 86–88
 writing, 76–77, 105–6
Algebraic reasoning, 107, 120
Algebraic terms, 77, 78
Algebra tiles, 102–7, 113, 121, 128
Analytic geometry
 equation of a line, 260–71, 285–94
 parallel lines, 295–305
 perpendicular lines, 295–305
 slope of a line, 272–80
Angle properties
 of parallel lines, 385
 of polygons, 391–96
Angles
 concave, 391
 convex, 391
 exterior, 384–85, 391, 397
 interior, 384–85, 388–90, 397, 416
 straight, 384
Area
 See also Surface area
 of composite shapes, 434–41, 459
 of rectangles, 428–33, 458
 of squares, 78–79
Area models, 5, 23–24, 28, 38
 calculating products with, 72
 of polynomials, 113–14, 129

B

Balancing equations, 192, 199
Base, 424
BEDMAS (memory aid), 33
Bimedians, 410, 412–13
Binomials, 105
Brackets (), 24, 33–34, 78
Break-even point, 242

C

Calculators
 fractional operations on, 14
 graphing, 145, 199, 240, 243–44, 265–66, 324, 430, 478–79
 order of operations with, 33
 rational number operations on, 50, 59
Cartesian coordinate system, 138–39
Celsius, conversion to Fahrenheit, 48
Centroid, 410–11
Chapter reviews, 65–67, 128–32, 182–84, 248–51, 307–10, 373–75, 416–19, 482–85
Chapter self-tests, 68, 133–34, 185, 252, 311–12, 376–77, 420, 486
Chapter tasks, 69, 135, 186, 253, 312, 378, 421, 487
Coefficients, 77
Collinear points, 276
Common denominators, 4, 5, 9
 division of mixed numbers using, 22
 solving equations with, 215–16
Composite shapes, 434–41, 459
Computer spreadsheets, 120
Concave polygons, 391
Cones
 slant height of, 444
 surface area of, 452–54, 459
 volume of, 461–65, 482
Conjectures
 about polygons, 411–13
 about quadrilaterals, 399, 402–8
 based on numeric examples, 84–85
 confirming, 404, 406
 counterexamples and, 402, 404, 407
 forming and testing, 402, 411–12
 rejecting, 354–57, 360, 404
 revising, 403, 405
 supporting, 357–59, 403
 testing, 373, 402, 405, 406, 411–12
 verifying, 354–57
Continuous data, 144, 165, 322, 325, 341
Convex polygons, 391, 397
Coordinate system, Cartesian, 138–39
Counterexamples, 402, 404, 407
Cubes
 surface area, 424
 volume of, 78, 144, 424
Cumulative review, 187–89, 379–81, 488–90
Curves of best fit, 344–53, 356–57, 359, 373
Cylinders
 optimum measures of, 474–81, 483
 surface area of, 425
 volume of, 73, 425

D

Data
 conjectures about, 354–60, 373
 continuous, 144, 165, 322, 325, 341
 curves of best fit for, 344–53
 discrete, 143, 322, 323–24, 341
 interpretation of, 322–29
 outliers, 357–58
 reasoning about, 354–62
 representing, with lines of best fit, 330–39
 in scatter plots. *See* Scatter plots
 trends, 331, 333–35, 346–48
Decimals
 with exponents, 88
 rational numbers as, 43, 59–60
Degree of a term, 77
Delta, 153
Denominators
 common, 4, 5, 9, 22, 215–16
 lowest common, 13
Dependent variables, 142
Diagonal properties, 399–401, 416
Diagrams, representing products using, 114
Direct variations, 150–51, 161
Discrete data, 143, 322, 323–24, 341
Displacement, 368, 373
Distance, from point to a line, 306
Distance problems, 88–89, 363–64
Distributive property, 114–16, 121–24, 129, 130
Division
 of mixed numbers, 20–30, 38–39
 of powers, 83–91

E

Equations
 See also Linear equations
 equivalent, 206, 215–16, 226–27
 of lines, 260–63, 281–82
  determining, 307–8, 317–18
  forms of, 264–71
  graphing, 165–69
  parallel, 295–96
  perpendicular, 295–96
  problem-solving using, 289–90
  using points to determine, 285–94
 for lines of best fit, 342
 of nonlinear relations, 175
 problem-solving strategies for, 192–93, 213–23
 problem-solving using, 193, 267–68, 332–33
 rearranging, 234–35
 with variables on both sides, 213–19, 225–26
 writing, 145, 332–33
Equilateral triangles, 387
Equivalent equations, 206, 215–16, 226–27
Equivalent fractions
 addition of mixed numbers using, 8–9
 subtraction of mixed numbers using, 11, 14
Expanded form, 83–84
Exponent principles, 85–89, 94–95, 100, 123